THE *Spiritual* FRANCISCANS

Library of Congress Cataloging-in-Publication Data

Burr, David, 1934–
    The spiritual Franciscans : from protest to persecution in the century
    after Saint Francis / David Burr.
        p.   cm.
    Includes bibliographical references and index.
    ISBN 0-271-02128-4 (alk. paper)
    1. Franciscans—History.   I. Title.

BX3606.2 .B87 2001
271'.3—dc21   2001041171

CONTENTS

PREFACE

DURING THE LAST FEW DECADES, scholars have shown substantial interest in the spiritual Franciscans. The result has been a number of books and articles, most of them on specific problems or figures. A single volume covering the entire movement now seems desirable.

A topic like the spiritual Franciscans presents its own difficulties when it comes to deciding how narrowly the limits should be set. It is not easy to decide precisely what one means by the term and whether it can be applied to a single identifiable group. I will spend some time agonizing over these matters in the course of the book and see no reason why I should do so at length in the preface as well, but some introductory remarks seem necessary. It should be noted at the outset that the term "spiritual Franciscans" as normally employed today is largely a construct of modern historians. Inquisitors in the 1320s could speak of "the spirituals" as a well-defined group in southern France who had just been put in their place by John XXII.[1] The label hardly came into existence at that point. A 1316 document accused zealots in the order of insisting that they be called *fratres spirituales*, although the zealots themselves denied the charge in their response.[2] Whatever they thought they were denying, it would have been inaccurate for them to claim that they never used such terms to describe themselves. In late 1310 or early 1311, during the round of accusations and counteraccusations leading up to the Council of Vienne, Ubertino da Casale could protest that strictures in the Franciscan rule against wearing shoes were being ignored by all "except a few who are called *spirituales*."[3] Called such by whom, though—themselves or their detractors? Shortly thereafter Ubertino provided an answer. Leaders of the order, he said, required brothers to wear more luxurious clothing than the rule allowed and subjected them to persecution if they protested, "nor can such spiritual men [*viri spirituales*] find peace among the brothers."[4] In response, Franciscan leaders insisted that the truly spiritual were honored, but not "some who pretend to be spiritual" yet "under the guise of the spirit act insolently."[5]

Obviously, by this point, the term had become a party label applied to a group of rigorists in the order, and that label was used not only by those who opposed the group but also by those within it. Yet it is hard to go further back and still find the term used in quite this fashion. Even in the mass of polemical literature generated in 1310–12, the term was used only sporadically. Ubertino da Casale, in his defense of the zealots, was more likely to describe his faction simply as those who were trying to observe the Franciscan vow. Others—referring to the group that Ubertino was defending—were likely to call them "Ubertino and his associates from the province of Provence" or simply "Ubertino and his adherents."[6]

The term "spiritual" was certainly used before the first decade of the fourteenth century. As we will see, it had roots in the Franciscan rule as well as Joachite apocalyptic thought and was employed throughout the thirteenth century. Toward the end of the century, Petrus Iohannis Olivi tied it to an existing faction when he suggested that he and his contemporaries stood at the beginning of a contest pitting a small group of *viri spirituales* against the forces of carnality—and he was not the first to use the term in that way. The problem comes when we try to relate that theoretical faction described by Olivi to a concrete group that labeled itself (and was labeled by others) as "spirituals," as was the case with those rigorists of 1310–12. We find thirteenth-century rigorists, and we find some of them described as pretending to be more spiritual than others, but we will see that such evidence is rendered problematic by the fact that it is found in substantially later documents that may reflect later terminology.[7]

In short, we can speak of the "spiritual Franciscans" from the early fourteenth century on and enjoy at least some degree of confidence that we are using a category that would have made sense to those in the order at that time, but we should have remarkably less confidence that this would have been the case in the thirteenth century. Why use the term "spiritual Franciscans" at all, then, much less write a book about them? Because, problematic as the name might be, we see the reality it describes taking shape before our eyes from the 1270s on. What we find is not a single group but several of them, each with its own history and peculiarities. But by the late 1270s, these groups were already meeting and discovering mutual interests. By the Council of Vienne, they would be seen as having enough in common to be considered a single problem in search of a single solution. The spiritual Franciscans were on their way to becoming a movement well before contemporaries found a name for it. (It would never be a completely homogeneous movement, but few movements ever are.) One can circumvent the term entirely, speaking instead of "zealots" or "rigorists," and at one point I attempted to do just that, yet such terms have their own difficulties. They, too, obscure the varieties of opinion and behavior encountered by anyone who examines the subject closely. In the end, one might just as well use the term "spiritual Franciscans" accompanied by the necessary warnings.

One could express similar reservations about terms normally used for the spirituals' opponents. "The conventuals" is particularly anachronistic. "The community" is less anachronistic than confusing. What does it mean? Does it imply that the entire rest of the order was united against the spirituals? In what sense? Those who opposed them certainly preferred to see matters in this way—but should we? We could avoid this problem by speaking of the spirituals' opponents as those who preferred to settle for a lower standard of poverty than the spirituals desired, and that would be partly accurate, but, as we will see, not entirely so. At Vienne the spirituals were opposed by those currently running the order (not by "the community" in any inclusive sense), and it might be better, then, to speak of "the leaders."

Nevertheless, by that point in the narrative, I too will speak of "the community" and will feel that I am uttering something more than nonsense. Here, as in the case of the spirituals, we have a group in the process of defining itself. By the time the inquisitors were at work in the 1320s, the leadership group had won its battle, and the order had taken a general shape that excluded the spirituals and their aims. Here, again, the result was not entirely homogeneous, and before the century was over an element espousing many of the same ideals the spirituals had held would gain permission to realize them within the order. When dealing with words like "spirituals" and "community," I suppose that the important thing is not to define precisely what the terms mean but to recognize that they cannot be used all that precisely.

All events have both causes and effects and thus are part of a continuous thread of historical development spun out over a much longer period. Writing a book about anything at all means cutting out a section of that thread and presenting it as if it had some integrity, as if it constituted a story with something resembling a beginning and an end. In the following pages, I will present my bit of thread in the full knowledge that it could be substantially longer. I depict the spiritual Franciscan movement as beginning to take some recognizable form in the 1270s and 1280s, but I do so knowing that the fathers of the movement had fathers themselves—not all of them Franciscan. While I devote limited attention to that family tree in the first two chapters, I nonetheless feel that there is some virtue beyond brevity in commencing my detailed account in the 1270s. At this point we see factions forming—groups whose fortunes we can trace over the next few decades—and we see leaders emerging who would play important roles during those decades.

Likewise, I am painfully aware that the spirituals, particularly the Italian spirituals, did not mysteriously disappear around the third decade of the fourteenth century, much as the dinosaurs had done earlier. In Italy, the *fraticelli*— in some ways a more suitable term than "spirituals" for the Italian zealots, since it was the term more likely to be used in Italy[8]—continued to play a significant role well into the fifteenth century, and a less important one even beyond that. In fact, it is no accident that some of the good modern work on the spirituals has been done by Capuchins, who represent, in certain ways, a continuation of the spiritual Franciscan legacy. Nevertheless, the Capuchins will go unmentioned in this book, for I choose to end close examination in the 1330s. Extending the narrative that far allows me to round off the biographies of the major characters and to make it clear that, whatever the defeat of the spirituals meant, it did not mean the end of reform in the Franciscan order.

The question of limits has another dimension. When I began research on this book many years ago, I thought of it as largely a book about the first order of Saint Francis. In the intervening years, I have become aware of the extent to which scholars like Mario Sensi, Giovanna Casagrande, and Anna Benvenuti Papi are rewriting the history of lay piety in medieval Italy and, in the process, emphasizing the complex relationship between the first and third orders—or, for that matter, between the first order and the penitential movement in general. I also have spent some time reading through those volumes of the Collection Doat that contain inquisitorial processes aimed at the southern French beguins, an exercise that reinforced the same lesson. As a result, this book pays attention to more groups than the first-order Franciscans. This wider interest is shown particularly in the two chapters that deal heavily with the beguins and in the appendix (which concentrates on female Italian mystics), but it appears elsewhere as well.

There are a number of people to whom I owe a great deal, too many to name here. Of those who deserve special thanks, there are the scholars whom I was already reading as a graduate student many years ago and who made a strong enough impression on me to impel me in this direction. I am especially indebted to Raoul Manselli, Edith Pásztor, Rosalind Brooke, and Malcolm Lambert, who taught me to appreciate the importance and the sheer excitement of the subject addressed in this work. Among those more or less my age, I particularly thank Robert Lerner, who has been, over the years, a model of how scholars ought to proceed in their dealings with one another. I also thank Paul Lachance for his help and very good advice.

One normally assumes that older scholars should help younger ones, but in my case the roles have been reversed. I am deeply indebted to Kevin Madigan, Sylvain Piron, and Louisa Burnham, among others, for their willingness to share their ideas with me. While I have no serious intention of leaving the world in the near future, I have every confidence that if I did so, the field would be in good hands. I regret that the dissertations recently completed by Sylvain and Louisa arrived too late to be incorporated into this book.

Finally, there are my good friends, including Ray and Jerry, Ben and Tatiana, and most of all, my wife, Annette, who has thought better of me than I ever thought of myself.

THE FRANCISCAN DILEMMA

IN THE SPRING OF 1317, the Franciscans at Narbonne received a letter from Pope John XXII. It was not the sort of message that they would have wanted to read. John ordered them to appear at the papal court in Avignon within ten days and explain why they had violently seized control of their house, ejecting their superiors in the process. The friars at Béziers, who had done the same thing, received the same letter.

When the erring friars arrived at Avignon, what they faced was not so much a hearing as an ultimatum. John told them to obey; most did, and those who did not were burned at the stake. The first executions took place on May 7, 1318. Victims and inquisitor alike were Franciscans. It was very much a family affair.

How did Saint Francis's order manage to work itself into this situation? That is a very complex story and will take a long time to tell. It is essentially the story of a movement that grew up within the order. We think of them as the "spirituals," and by John's time they were actually called such, yet the problem they addressed was much older than the name itself.

Francis and His Order

It was, in fact, as old as the order. Around 1210, when Francis of Assisi sought approval for his nascent group, what he hoped to achieve with it included poverty, but only as one aspect of a more complex, more evanescent quality of life. The word "humility" brings us closer. Poverty was important as a manifestation of humility, just as obedience was. But in the final analysis, even "humility" is insufficient as a description. Francis's basic goal was the sort of self-emptying he saw in Christ, a behavior that involved not only humility but also love. Thus, in Franciscan legend, the final stamp of approval on Francis's project was given not by the pope but by Christ himself on Mount Alverna when, toward the end of Francis's life, he was granted Christ's stigmata.

All of this sounds straightforward enough, and it can be at least relatively so if one manages to follow Christ into sacrificial death. That was at times Francis's intention. Twice he attempted to seek martyrdom at the hands of the Moslems, and when five Franciscans actually achieved it in 1220, Francis was reported to have exclaimed, "Now I can truly say I have five brothers!"[1] The problem comes when one tries to translate the ideal into an administrative structure. The difficulty was less obvious at the beginning, because there were, after all, only twelve Franciscans. It was a like-minded group that could submit directly to Francis's charismatic leadership. Its original rule could be a short document consisting mainly of quotations from the gospels.[2]

Unfortunately, that situation changed rapidly. As the order grew numerically and spread geographically, Francis was forced to produce something more substantial. He attempted to do so with the rule of 1221, which never received papal approval, and then with the rule of 1223, which did. The difference between the two rules says a great deal about what was happening. In 1221 Francis admonished the brothers to study their superior's conduct carefully and, if they found it unedifying, to denounce him at the next general chapter meeting. They were to withhold obedience if told to act in violation of the rule or their own souls.[3]

That may seem an odd way to show humility, but it has a certain logic. Francis was concerned about leaders as well as followers. In the 1221 rule and elsewhere he emphasized that, like the Son of Man, they should want to serve rather than be served.[4] He explicitly rejected the word *prior* as a title, despite the fact that it was traditionally used in monasticism and would soon be adopted by the Dominicans.[5] Instead, he chose words such as "minister," "guardian," and "custodian," all of which implied not superiority but commitment to caring for others. Francis's call for fraternal surveillance was consistent with this perspective. It decreased the distance between leaders and followers.

There is still a problem, of course. There is little point in preventing arrogant, domineering leaders if the price is encouraging fractious, contentious followers. Francis's solution, insofar as he offered one, was to observe that those who refused to obey orders they considered harmful to their souls should humbly submit to any resultant persecution rather than separate themselves from their brothers. In other words, their resistance should assume the least self-assertive form possible. Nevertheless, it is hard to ignore the extent to which Francis's emphasis on the *duty* of refusal highlighted individual responsibility.[6]

Even by 1221, the order had grown to the point where such surveillance activities seemed disruptive and therefore dangerous. The rule of 1223 eliminated them, although even there, obedience was limited to "those things which [the brothers] have promised the Lord to observe and which are not against their souls or our rule."[7] Nevertheless, the rule of 1221, though not the official one, remained available for consultation. So did the example of Francis himself, who embodied some of the resulting tensions in an intensified form once he stepped down as head of the order.

In Francis's *Testament*, dictated shortly before his death in 1226, these tensions were presented for the consideration of later generations. The document reveals a man who, in his final days, was anxious about the future of his order and wanted to state his position one more time as forcefully as possible. Since he was now, administratively speaking, simply one more Franciscan, his *Testament* highlighted the tension between juridical and charismatic authority within the order, between the power that stemmed from holding the job of minister general and that which flowed from being the divinely inspired archetype of Franciscanism. Francis punctuated his instructions with the observation that he wanted to obey those who had been given the former sort of power; that observation, however, did not erase the fact that he was giving instructions and expected them to be followed, not because he held a high administrative position, but because he was Francis, the man who knew what God wanted the order to become. "And when God gave me brothers, no one showed me what I should do, but the Most High revealed to me that I should live according to the form of the holy gospel."[8] Francis insisted that his *Testament* should not be taken as another rule, but he then announced that "the general minister and all other ministers and custodians are bound by obedience not to add or subtract from these words. And they must always have this writing with them in addition to the rule. And in all chapter meetings held by them, when they read the rule, they must also read these words."

Francis's *Testament* created a problem for the order because a number of his instructions accorded ill with what was already beginning to happen. He told them not to seek papal intervention on their behalf and, if the clergy in some town prevented them from preaching or even settling there, to move on to some other town.[9] He forbade them "to place glosses on the rule or say, 'This is what it means.'" These were serious limitations. In a world where many clergy did try to keep them out, how could Franciscans carry out their preaching and teaching mission without papal protection? In a world of bewildering complexity, how could they interpret the rule to an army of new recruits unless learned theologians were allowed to determine how it applied to the varied situations in which they found themselves? In 1230, leaders of the order asked Pope Gregory IX whether the *Testament* was binding and were told that it was not, since Francis had not consulted the ministers and since he had no power to bind future leaders, his equals.[10]

New Responsibilities

However much or little sense Gregory's decision made, it avoided what would have emerged as a major crisis had the *Testament* been recognized alongside the rule as a basic document. The order was evolving. It was growing rapidly—the number of Franciscans by midcentury has been estimated at as many as thirty thousand—and it was taking on a series of new functions. As educated men joined the order, they were tapped to fill roles that would have been unsuitable for Francis and his original colleagues. Some brought the roles with them. Alexander of Hales was already a master at the University of Paris when he became a Franciscan and needed only to stay where he was to become the first Franciscan master at the university. In other cases, the roles slowly developed out of a coalescence of societal need and Franciscan ability. For example, the cities were growing rapidly, but the urban parish system was not, so when Franciscans entered the cities to preach, they encountered a substantial population in need not only of preaching but also of pastoral care.

Of course, it is one thing for the need to exist and another for those in authority to recognize it. That is where the pope came in. Franciscans—and Dominicans, who arrived concurrently—soon discovered that the university masters were not entirely happy to see them, and bishops were often hesitant to allow them a foothold in the cities. Thus they needed papal support, and the popes were normally willing to give it. They recognized that the mendicant orders were a positive influence in both contexts and that, being directly loyal to the pope, the friars offered a way of exerting influence on university and diocese alike.

Once they recognized mendicant virtues, the popes could reward and utilize the new orders in a variety of ways. Friars became not only teachers, preachers, and pastors, but also inquisitors, bishops, and cardinals.[11] Secular leaders found them equally useful.[12] When, in 1247, King Louis IX of France decided to appoint investigators (enquêteurs) whose task it was to travel through the kingdom hearing and adjudicating complaints against royal administrators, he entrusted the task largely to Franciscans and Dominicans.[13] When, in 1260, the Florentine exile Farinata degli Uberti was conspiring with Siena to lure his native city into the military campaign that would result in Florentine defeat at Montaperti, he sent two Franciscans to bait the trap with false information; when the credulous Florentines began to prepare for war, Farinata sent two more friars—whether they were Franciscan or Dominican is unclear—to enlist Florentine Ghibellines in the plot.[14] On a more peaceful note, by that date we find the city of Perugia entrusting Franciscans with various governmental functions, and in 1266 we read of one being consulted as an expert on financial affairs! That same year saw the Perugians, who had decided to construct a series of new fountains, enlist the aid of "friars minor known for their skill in that task" and beg the pope to throw his considerable weight behind their attempt to bring one Brother Deodato, magister fontium, to town.[15] By the second half of the thirteenth century, then, well-placed friars were exerting power in many contexts all over Europe.

The Costs of Responsibility

This situation profoundly affected the order. It hastened the process of clericalization, taking the word clericus in its full medieval sense: not only in holy orders but also well educated. This was in itself an important change. Francis's order was originally open to priests and laity alike. The important thing was a willingness to live the Franciscan life, which was conceived in a way that made it equally accessible to cleric and non-cleric. Francis did not actually condemn education, but his early biographers suggest that he saw it as a danger, exposing the friar to pride and vainglory. When one of the earliest learned friars, Anthony of Padua, sought permission to teach the brothers theology, Francis sent a brief—one might call it terse—note giving permission as long as it did not destroy the spirit of holy prayer and devotion in them.[16] Nevertheless, by midcentury the order was doing things that called for education and ordination. Thus the number of unlettered laymen entering the order was subjected to restriction, and most new friars were channeled into a highly effective education program.[17]

These new activities and the internal changes they inspired had some effect on the sorts of people who might want to join the order. It was not a question of intelligent, educated men wanting for the first time to become Franciscans. They were already entering the order. Otherwise, it would not have seemed so useful to popes and rulers. The difference was that once the Franciscans became established in important positions throughout Europe, the order became more attractive to those who wanted to hold such positions. If a younger son became a friar, his parents could see his choice not merely as a way of fleeing the world, but also as a way of advancing in it—in fact, as a way of advancing the family's interests in it. Even if we ignore the rewards to be gained from having a son serve as *enquêteur* for Louis IX, or rule a great diocese, and ask instead what could be accomplished within the confines of a single town, we find that there were advantages to be gained. If the son of an ambitious family joined the order and eventually found his way back to his hometown, he could become their man in the monastery, their link to an important institution within that town. If his route took him through Paris or some other educational center and he returned to fill an important position, such as guardian or lector, within the local Franciscan house, so much the better.

It follows, then, that the new activities accepted by Franciscans did more than make the order attractive to those who might wish to fill such positions. It also gave Franciscans power and thus altered their relation to society. Here again the comparison with Francis's aims is instructive. He wanted to obey, not to command. He saw this desire as entailed in the *ordo fratrum minorum*, the order of lesser brothers. This much is clear from the *Testament*. Once his friars accepted worldly power, though, they were exposed to temptations Francis would have wished to spare them. The Florentine chronicler Dino Compagni offers an arresting cameo of Cardinal Matthew of Aquasparta, O.F.M., sent to Florence in 1300 on a political mission by Boniface VIII. Compagni, who was one of the Florentine priors at that time, says that he brought Matthew two thousand florins in a silver cup and told him that it was the most the priors could offer him without opening the decision to public scrutiny. "He replied that he appreciated the offer; and he gazed at them for a long time, but did not take them."[18] Matthew resisted temptation. Others did not. In 1302 the pope was so incensed by the corrupt practices of Franciscan inquisitors in Padua and Vicenza that he removed them from office and turned inquisitorial functions in those cities over to the Dominicans.[19]

That is hardly our only evidence that temptations presented by the new offices could occasionally prove overwhelming. Yet even the word "temptation" seems to understate the problem. The functions themselves often seemed to demand modes of behavior at variance with the original Franciscan ideal. A Franciscan bishop, for example, might ask himself whether he was in some sense *condemned* to accept the episcopal lifestyle, with all its pomp and circumstance, since that lifestyle represented not so much a perquisite as a symbolic reinforcement of episcopal authority. Even if that bishop decided to trim his own household down to a minimum, he still might not escape money problems. John Pecham, whom modern historians recognize as a strong advocate of poverty, was a Franciscan who took his vocation seriously; even so, when he became archbishop of Canterbury, the cost of going to Rome, getting mitred, and then traveling to England gave him debts that weighed him down for the rest of his life.[20]

Had Pecham eventually returned to the papal court as a cardinal, he would have seen, as Matthew of Aquasparta did, how much money changed hands there, and how much of it was pressed into the palms of cardinals. Matthew himself received two hundred florins per year from the Flemings in return for his advice and support in their battle with the French king. As one of the Flemings at Rome wrote to his prince, "the court of Rome is very desirous; it has many needs and one must give it many gifts." It is easy to say that Matthew should have rejected such gifts, but institutions are rather hard to defy once one accepts a place within them, and at least Matthew was not selling out to the highest bidder. The prince, Guy of Dampierre, himself observed that "if he who gives most gets most, the King of France has an advantage over us which we cannot regain, because he can outbid us by a hundred to one."[21]

The problem was hardly limited to those in more elevated ranks, such as bishop and cardinal. It repeated itself on a local level. A Franciscan confessor whose duties brought him to the homes of wealthy merchants might find himself dining well, since the rule instructed him to eat what was placed before him. A friar teaching at Paris might discover that his mission demanded a large, expensive library. Once Franciscans inserted themselves into the world, they found worldly comforts difficult to escape.

If new functions seemed to encourage and even demand relaxed standards of poverty, that compromise was only one aspect of a more general compromise with *minoritas*. What was at stake was the nature of the Franciscans' relationship with their fellow human beings. In assuming positions of power, Franciscans entered the power struggles that characterize worldly activity. If they were largely successful in these contests, it was not because they were powerful in themselves, but because they had powerful backers. In their battles with university masters, secular clergy, and purported heretics, they could rely on the pope. When performing inquests for Louis IX, they were backed by yet another powerful authority. One could go on.

Those who found themselves bullied into compliance by that power might have long memories. Secular masters who had unsuccessfully opposed the friars' establishment at the University of Paris certainly had excellent powers of recall. So did the secular clergy who had fruitlessly contested the friars' right to exercise pastoral duties. So, perhaps, did any number of French royal officials once Franciscan enquêteurs accepted complaints against them as valid, or any number of plaintiffs when the same enquêteurs rejected their complaints as spurious. Indeed, one can imagine that Florentines who knew of Franciscan involvement in the plotting that led to the 1260 slaughter at Montaperti emerged from the experience with a new caution about accepting Franciscans at their word. Here again it is worth citing Dino Compagni's description of Matthew of Aquasparta and his 1300 mission to Florence. He was ostensibly there to reconcile opposing factions. It was a very Franciscan thing to do. According to Thomas of Celano, Francis's first biographer, Francis had performed a similar task at Arezzo.[22] Unfortunately, it soon dawned on the priors that Matthew had been sent *not* to mediate even-handedly between the factions (as he claimed) but to work for the victory of one over the other. "His wishes were understood by many, and disliked thoroughly. And so someone who was not very bright picked up a crossbow and shot an arrow at the window of the bishop's palace [where the cardinal was staying]; it stuck in the shutter. The cardinal left there out of fear, and for greater security he went to stay across the Arno at the house of messer Tommaso dei Mozzi."[23] Matthew had been thrust into a political contest that involved the pope, and as the pope's agent, he could not easily extricate himself from it. He might have encountered the same problem as a bishop or even as an inquisitor. The Franciscans began to assume such duties at a moment when Italy was divided between Guelfs and Ghibellines, and the pope was very Guelf. Thus it was often hard to exercise ecclesiastical duties, including inquisitorial duties, without becoming a player in the Guelf-Ghibelline contest. Matthew's story shows that even at moments when the Guelfs dominated, the problem did not disappear.

The Franciscans' power affected the way in which they were regarded—not only by those on whom that power was exerted, but also by those who had given them that power in the first place. In a book on Louis IX, William Jordan notes that "as the traditional mendicant orders became more staid and sophisticated in the course of the thirteenth century, Louis sought out those offshoots of the great orders which seemed more effectively to be preserving the original fervor of the movements," groups like the Sack Friars and Crutched Friars.[24] The old question—"yes, but will you still respect me in the morning?"—was one the mendicants might well have considered.

The Difficulties of Disengagement

If accepting these functions wrought such dramatic changes, why did the Franciscans accept them at all? Why didn't they just say "no"? It is tempting to invoke such perennial human attributes as greed and the lust for power in answering this question. While explanations of that sort undoubtedly have some truth to them, it is also true that from the Franciscans' viewpoint, these changes could seem regrettable by-products of activities that were in themselves valuable, even necessary. A number of mendicants thought that their orders ought to engage in activities like preaching, pastoral work, and teaching because these activities needed to be performed by competent, holy men, and the friars were just that. They should be bishops and cardinals for the same reason. Hugh of Digne, regarded by his contemporaries and modern historians alike as a model Franciscan and by some as a spiritual *avant la lettre,* observed that no one was more fit to become a Parisian master and teach the gospel than the Franciscans, who professed and observed it. He cited the case of Alexander of Hales, already a master at Paris when he joined the order. "What sane person would suggest that while he was rich Brother Alexander of Hales had a right to preach and teach on the text 'blessed are the poor in spirit,' but the moment he became a poor friar he should have retired from that task?"[25] One of Hugh's associates, the chronicler Salimbene, addressed the matter of whether they should be cardinals in much the same way. "I absolutely believe—in fact, I'm firmly persuaded of it—that there are a thousand brothers minor in the Franciscan order . . . who, because of their learning and holy lives, are more suited to be cardinals than many who are currently promoted to that state by Roman pontiffs because of their family connections."[26] One senses something resembling *noblesse oblige* here. The Franciscans should perform the duties because they are so good at them. If that means assuming authority, so be it. Having assumed the duties, they must have the resources to do them well. If that means compromising poverty, so be it. Limiting *minoritas* was the price paid for other benefits gained by the church.

In certain areas the limitations were, in some sense, identical with the benefits. For example, voluntary poverty was a good thing, but so was charitable giving to the poor—and whatever else the friars represented to their world, they were one especially attractive variety of the poor. Thus the laity, for the sake of their immortal souls, wanted to give them things. Prosperous burghers gave their local Franciscan houses money for special meals. King Louis IX and others provided sumptuous banquets at provincial and general chapter meetings.[27]

These gifts brought a variety of spiritual benefits beyond the merit of having given to the poor. Testators eager to make restitution for ill-gotten gains but unable to identify all their victims often left money to the "poor of Christ," who served as proxies for those unidentified victims. Who among the "poor of Christ" made better recipients than the local friars? Those same testators needed a place for themselves and their families to be buried, and they wanted prayers to be said for their speedy exodus from purgatory. All these things could be accomplished by giving the local Franciscans money to cover the construction and long-term endowment of a chapel in their church. Such gifts were designed to aid both the giver and the receiver. If the Franciscans rejected them as destructive to Franciscan poverty, they would in the process frustrate the givers' efforts at spiritual self-improvement.

Thus concern for their fellow human beings made it hard for the Franciscans to reject their new roles. So did their commitment to obedience. Francis envisaged a *minoritas* that would involve not only poverty and humility but obedience as well. The paradox of such *minoritas* is that it can be maintained toward all only so long as those in authority allow one to do so. In the thirteenth century the pope, the supreme authority, decided otherwise. He decreed that friars should maintain it toward him and selectively practice *maioritas* over certain others. By making them bishops, cardinals, professors, and inquisitors, he put them in a situation where, in order to obey him, they had to stop obeying others and start ordering them about.

TWO

PROTOSPIRITUALS

Franciscan Response: The Basic Questions

IF FRANCISCAN LIFE WAS CHANGING, Franciscans had to decide how they should react to that change. Historians often paint the picture of an order torn between two alternatives. Most friars chose to embrace the changes and accept the inevitable compromise of Franciscan poverty necessitated by them, but a small group of brothers (whom scholars have labeled "spiritual Franciscans") protested against increasing laxity and insisted on observance of the rule as Francis intended that it be observed, even if that meant rejecting the worldly involvement wished on the order by secular and ecclesiastical leaders.

This view is hardly the invention of modern historians. It is more or less the one propounded by spiritual Franciscan leader Angelo Clareno in his *History of the Seven Tribulations of the Franciscan Order,* written around 1323–26.[1] Angelo presents the suffering of the spiritual Franciscans in his own day at the hands of their leaders as one more episode in a long series of persecutions stretching back to the beginning. For Angelo, the two opposing factions are as old as the order itself. It is understandable that Angelo might derive some comfort from adopting that perspective in the 1320s, but less clear why modern historians should be eager to accept it today.

There are two basic questions here. The first is whether there were two opposing factions in the order. The second is whether one of them was called the "spiritual Franciscans." We will take these questions in order. Certainly there were two groups at some point. During the deliberations of 1309–12 leading up to and concurrent with the Council of Vienne, the debate rested on that assumption. We will see, in Chapters 5 and 6, that even then the spirituals were not a coherent group with a single agenda, yet we will also note that those included under the rubric were similar enough to make common cause against leaders of the order. Certainly, too, we can follow the development of these groups through the period 1274–1309. We will do so in Chapters 3 and 4. The question for the moment is whether we are justified in tracing the two groups back even further, whether in fact we are justified in assuming that they existed throughout the entire thirteenth century.

We are not. There were indeed differences of opinion. There was dispute. This much seems so predictable that it is almost insulting to try to demonstrate it. Anyone who works in an organization of five people or more could predict as much. It seems equally pointless to try to prove that Franciscans differed from the beginning on the question of how much poverty was enough. That too is predictable. What we really need to know is whether those who engaged in the dispute saw themselves as belonging to factions and whether we can trace a continuous development of these factions.

Elias of Cortona and Francis's Companions

It is at least arguable that such factions existed during the tenure of the third Franciscan minister general, Elias of Cortona. Elias had been one of Francis's early and close associates. One might have expected him to be a strong spokesman for the apostolic life as Francis conceived it. Yet his generalate was a stormy one, and it ended so badly that of the Franciscan *legenda*[2] only I Celano, which was written before Elias's fall, speaks well of him. Indeed, II Celano and Bonaventure do not speak of him at all. Thirteenth-century Franciscan chroniclers such as Jordan of Giano, Salimbene, and Thomas of Eccleston are largely negative in their appraisal, and many succeeding writers follow suit. Angelo Clareno presents Francis and Elias as symbolizing (and to a great extent initiating) two basic factions within the order. Francis was supported by other early companions, such as Giles of Assisi and Leo, who would serve as witnesses to Francis's intention and the frustration of that intention. Elias would be backed by a leadership group that, like him, sought worldly success rather than the apostolic life.

Angelo's view has some basis in history. Francis seems to have spent his final years removed from the decision-making process, surrounded by a few companions who were equally remote from it. After his death, early companions like Leo continued to favor a more or less eremitical life free from administrative responsibilities. Perhaps that was the only reasonable course for them. The 1223 rule had marked one more stage in the process by which a relatively free-wheeling movement was becoming a disciplined order. The latter was what the papacy wanted and what some Franciscans wanted. Angelo describes Elias going to Pope Gregory IX after Francis's death and warning him that, "casting off the reins of holy obedience and ruling themselves by their own sense, certain brothers who are held in great reverence by laity and clergy because they were Saint Francis's companions are now traveling around here and there without a leader and saying things that will eventually cause scandal in the order."[3] That may not be what Elias said, but it was certainly what the thirteenth-century popes feared regarding not only the Franciscans but also a series of other movements. They were living in a period of remarkable religious creativity, and they were concerned about keeping it under control.[4]

The result was a double focus within the order: on the one hand, an eremitical group free to pursue its vision of the primitive Franciscan life; on the other, a group engaged in preaching, pastoral ministry, and education, one that was encouraged if not forced by its activities to temper that primitive Franciscanism. The first group had no great occasion to understand the problems faced by leaders of the order, but they were strategically placed to note and deplore what could only appear to them as a departure from primitive virtue. And they lived a very long time. (Giles died in 1261, Leo in 1271 or later.[5]) That gave them ample opportunity to reshape their memories of Francis into something that spoke to their own reading of subsequent events. It also gave them time to pass those memories on to another generation of Franciscans who would themselves adjust the memories to fit their own views.

Granting that the companions did so adjust their recollection of Francis, when do we get wind of it? One moment when we would not expect to hear their disappointed cries is in Thomas of Celano's first life of Francis, ordered by Pope Gregory IX in 1228 to justify Francis's canonization. It was, in that sense, a pendant to the building of a basilica to house his remains, and thus one would expect to find little evidence of dissent in it. Many historians have assumed that its shape was guided by Gregory and Elias. Elias was not minister general at the time—the 1227 general chapter had chosen Giovanni Parenti as Francis's successor—but several scholars have imagined that Gregory and Elias controlled events nonetheless, and that Parenti's election simply gave Elias a chance to concentrate on the basilica, which was begun in 1228 and ready for the translation of Francis's body by 1230.[6] They have pointed to the positive role played in I Celano by both Elias and Gregory IX, who previously, as Cardinal Hugolino, had been designated protector of the nascent order.

Recent historians are less sure that Parenti's election was blessed by Elias, and they are more willing to entertain the possibility that the good things said about the latter in I Celano represent a real choice on Celano's part.[7] Moreover, Jacques Dalarun argues that what we find in I Celano is not adulation of Elias and Gregory at the expense of those early companions who represented the eremitical wing, but a balancing of the two elements. Dalarun says, "It seems to me that his discourse in 1228 was as follows: There was among us, blessed by the saint, a good contract, a good equilibrium which transcended a latent opposition. This contract was cancelled and Elias was betrayed, and the founder along with him."[8] Celano feels that Elias was Francis's vicar, the man Francis trusted, and that he should have been elected minister general in 1227.

Thus we come to an ominous remark in I Celano: Thomas breaks off a description of Francis's physical maladies to announce that "he had found some who outwardly agreed with him but inwardly disagreed with him behind his back, who acquired credit for themselves but made the upright suspect to him. For wickedness often tries to blacken purity, and because of a lie that is familiar to many, the truth spoken by a few is not believed."[9] There was, then, a group of false brothers, but who were they? Obviously not Elias and his supporters, and equally obviously not the eremitical element. Dalarun suggests that they were those who engineered the election of Giovanni Parenti and broke the pre-1226 contract. That explanation makes as good sense as any other. The important thing for our purposes is that we have evidence in I Celano of tension within the order, but it is not tension along the lines Angelo Clareno seems to suggest.

Crescentius of Iesi and His Generalate

Once we move on to Celano's second *legenda*, commissioned in 1244 by a Franciscan general chapter and the new minister general, Crescentius of Iesi, the picture changes. A number of memorable events had occurred since Celano completed his first work. In 1230, the body of Saint Francis had been transferred to its new resting place in the basilica under conditions that caused scandal. Precisely what occurred remains unclear, although apparently the body was moved to the basilica before the prearranged day, thus robbing the minister general and others, who were to assemble in Assisi for a general chapter meeting, of their opportunity to participate. Many historians, following Thomas of Eccleston's lead,[10] have assumed that Elias must have been at the heart of it; the papal letter that followed, however, ordered the citizens of Assisi to come and explain their behavior but did not mention Elias.[11]

Shortly after the 1230 general chapter ended, a delegation of friars set another important event in motion by going to the pope and asking for his guidance on the meaning of their rule. The result was *Quo elongati*, the first official attempt to exposit the rule. It dealt with some important questions, such as how the friars could maintain their lack of possessions and still manage to survive. The 1223 rule had provided for recourse to "spiritual friends" who could use money to buy clothes and care for ailing brothers.[12] *Quo elongati* developed this idea, allowing the friars to have a *nuntius* who would represent the giver and be subject to his rather than the friars' control.[13] Historians sometimes see this arrangement as a major step toward the corruption of Francis's ideal.[14] If it was actually such, though, then the ideal had been corrupted one hundred times over by that point, including in the rule itself.

Quo elongati might seem to compromise Francis's express order in his *Testament*, "I firmly forbid my brothers, both clerics and laymen, to place glosses on the rule or say, 'This is what it means.'" That too was taken into account, as we have seen. Gregory's announcement that the *Testament* was not binding was a significant one, although future ministers would discover that the *Testament* was not that easy to neutralize. For the moment, however, the relevant question is whether there is any compelling evidence that in 1230 the pope was asked to rule on the *Testament* because a zealot group in the order was brandishing it. The answer is "no."

Another memorable choice was made when, in 1238, another group of Franciscans sought recourse to Rome—this time seeking aid against Elias, who had been elected minister general in 1232. The pope called for a general chapter to be held at Rome in 1239, and when it occurred, the brothers voted Elias out of office, accusing him of carnality and cruelty. A few months later Elias was in the court of Emperor Frederick II, a major adversary of the pope. He remained an excommunicated renegade almost until his death in 1253, thus causing substantial embarrassment to his order.

However Elias may have offended the order, it was not by playing the role later assigned him by Angelo Clareno. Opposition to him seems to have stemmed partly from an autocratic tendency that prevented him from acknowledging that a substantially larger order extending throughout Europe had to be organized in a way that allowed more decision making on a provincial level.[15] This may seem to have little import for the topic at hand, but in another sense, Elias's removal was very important indeed. While he had not expressed any opposition to education (and indeed had facilitated the rise of some educated brothers to positions of authority), he had retained Francis's ideal of an order that not only contained laymen but also considered them no less valuable than learned clerics. By the late 1230s, that degree of inclusion seemed not only wrong but even absurd to many educated friars like Salimbene, who saw the early position of laymen in the order as a temporary expedient justified by the lack of educated clerics. Salimbene thought it only logical that once the order could recruit the latter, it should largely deny entrance to the former. After all, clerics could perform the tasks now being assumed by the order, while the laymen were good at nothing except eating and sleeping.[16] Salimbene saw Elias's admission and promotion of laymen as one of his major flaws, and the chapter that removed Elias seems to have agreed. At any rate, Elias's fall marked the seizure of power by an educated clerical group that would gradually restrict leadership to itself and seriously limit the number of laymen allowed to become Franciscans.[17]

These events shaped Celano's work to some extent. First and most obviously, Elias had become The Name That Cannot Be Named. Nor would he be mentioned later in the final, officially commissioned *legenda*, the one demanded of Bonaventure in 1260 and approved in 1263.[18] Second (and more important for our purposes), when the project was undertaken, the order had issued a general call for material, and some of Francis's early companions had responded. One receives the impression that by the 1240s, they found the changes disturbing and were already projecting their discomfort back onto Francis himself.

Not all of them were disgruntled. We can begin with the document we know as *Anonymus perusinus*—a misnomer of sorts, because the "Perugian" refers not to the author's provenance but to the place where the manuscript was found, and because we have reason to believe that the author was one Giovanni, a former *socius* of Brother Giles, who probably produced it between March 1240 and August 1241.[19] Thus the document was not actually a response to the 1244 request, but it is worth considering here because it was one of the new sources used by II Celano.

The *Perugian Anonymous* acknowledges that the order has changed. The early group is presented as part of the penitential movement. "Some people asked them, 'Where are you from?' and others asked, 'To what order do you belong?' They replied simply, 'We are penitents and we were born in Assisi,' for at that point the *religio* of the brothers was not yet called an order."[20] At that stage, there were those who said that they seemed crazy or drunk, and some persecuted them because of their ascetic lives; still, they endured and grew in number. Francis saw that the Lord wanted to make them a large group (*magnam congregationem*) and decided that they should go to Rome. In time, they had a rule, were confirmed as an order, continued to grow, "and thus was fulfilled the prediction Francis had made to the brethren: 'In a short time many wise, prudent and noble men will come and live with us.'"[21] Dalarun summarizes the message of *Anonymus perusinus* as follows: "I who address you did not arrive in an order that was already established. I knew men's scorn, was considered crazy along with the rest of the brothers, and considered money to be like excrement. We should not vary on these points. But because I myself . . . [was part of that time] I am all the more authorized to tell you that the transition from *religio* to *ordo* was not a betrayal but the only way to defend the original ideal." The story is told, Dalarun says, with "no bitterness, no reproof, little nostalgia."[22]

We turn to another source, this time directly inspired by the request of 1244, the so-called *Legend of the Three Companions* [*Socii*], which partly depends on the *Perugian Anonymous*.[23] It begins with a letter to Crescentius, written from Greccio in 1246, in which the authors identify themselves as Leo, Rufino, and Angelo. They announce that what follows transmits some of the many events concerning which "we were either eyewitnesses or heard from holy friars," some of whom they name. One of these holy friars is Giovanni, Giles's *socius*. The call from Crescentius had expressed special interest in miracle stories, but the three *socii* say that they will not report miracles, "which are not the cause of sanctity, although they prove it." Instead, they will describe a few events from Francis's life that may help those who wish to follow in his footsteps. They will not present these stories "in the form of a legend," since other legends already have been written, but will instead "gather the most beautiful flowers blooming in a pleasant field" without following a historical sequence, omitting what can already be found in existing legends.

What follows is oddly at variance with that promise. It is, in fact, a chronologically ordered legend and it does depend on what has gone before, including I Celano and the *Perugian Anonymous*. Thus some historians have suggested that the letter and the legend do not belong together, and some have identified the letter with the next document we will examine, the *Legend of Perugia*, or at least part of it. That leaves the presently considered legend fatherless. Some have decided that it was written much later; others insist that it (or at least parts of it) served as one source for II Celano; still others suggest that what we actually see is a common dependence of II Celano and the so-called *Legend of the Three Companions* on another source, now lost. In any event, this work resembles the *Perugian Anonymous* in justifying what the order had become in 1240.[24]

So far, we have little to suggest discontent within the order, but we have one document left to examine, the *Legend of Perugia*, so called because it exists in MS Perugia 1046, which dates from around 1311. It contains, among other things, a section—now normally called the *Intentio regulae*—mirroring a long quotation in Ubertino da Casale's *Arbor vitae* in which Ubertino, a major spokesman for the spiritual Franciscan position, claims to be quoting Brother Leo. Another section—normally called the *Verba Sancti Francisci*—mirrors material that Angelo Clareno presents at length in his rule commentary as Leo's work.[25] MS Perugia 1046 is a compilation[26] and contains much that is not by Brother Leo, but clearly some of it is. Ubertino claimed in 1305 that the Leo materials had been in Santa Chiara at Assisi, but were now missing, or at least so he had heard.[27] By 1311 he had discovered that they were still in existence, and in a document from that year, he located them in the friars' bookcase at Assisi.[28] Perugia 1046 was probably copied there.

When did Leo produce this material? It need not all have been written by 1246, but some of it was, at any rate, available to Thomas of Celano when he did his second legend. Rosalind Brooke argues that the *Verba* was written after 1247, but probably before 1260, when Bonaventure began the *Legenda maior*, and Brooke tentatively suggests that it was produced by Leo in 1257 in reaction to John of Parma's fall, an event we will examine in a moment.[29]

Théophile Desbonnets describes the material as follows: "There is great disorder; there is no plan; the evocations are joined to each other without concern for chronology and arise from associations that are not always evident. Furthermore, a very definite tendency to digress is evident—a habitual fault with old people."[30] Others have suggested that what Desbonnets attributes to advancing senility might instead reflect the intention of presenting a bouquet rather than a chronologically coherent legend. This—or at least the part of it attributable to Leo and the other two companions, or even only some of that, if we assume that Brooke is correct in dating the *Verba* later—may be the material originally sent with the 1246 Greccio letter. That is, in fact, the conclusion reached by Brooke, who presents an edition joining the 1246 Greccio letter with both the material she sees as submitted by the three companions and what she sees as added later by Leo. That solution is supported by no manuscript evidence and leaves us with the question of why later authors like Ubertino, Angelo, and others should have spoken only of Leo, ignoring the other two companions, but these seem minor problems compared with that of trying to imagine why Leo, Rufino, and Angelo sent what we currently describe as the *Legend of the Three Companions* and prefaced it with a letter promising a different sort of document—or why, for that matter, Leo should have joined with Rufino and Angelo in presenting one picture of the order, and then, on his own, produced materials that described it in quite another way.

Much of the *Scripta Leonis* (to use, in abridged form, the title provided by Brooke) fits the promise of the Greccio letter. It is edifying material meant to inspire and it is not openly critical of the present situation. One might suspect that its heavy emphasis on the dire poverty of the early days and its portrayal of Francis as insisting that such poverty be strictly observed at the Portiuncula, the center of early Franciscan life, as an example to the rest of the order stems from the author's feeling that the order desperately needs such an example, but much of the time that opinion remains unstated.

In the *Intentio* and the *Verba*, though, the criticism is explicit and unremitting. Here we find Francis's original aim challenged by leaders in the order who want to mitigate the demands of poverty.[31] We find Francis comparing a proud group in the order, a group that pursues learning, with a humble, eremitical group. We find him acknowledging that the order has declined and predicting further decline. We find Christ himself weeping for the friars. We find Francis suggesting that he renounced leadership because the order was in decline. He says that he offered his illness as an excuse at the time, but in fact would still be willing to lead the order if the friars actually wished to follow him.[32]

The point made here and elsewhere is that Francis's authority is and always has been spiritual. He offers his example and hopes others will follow, but he seeks no power to coerce. He pursues a different way, and so should the order. When some complain that bishops sometimes forbid them to preach and ask Francis to seek a privilege from the pope, he replies,

> You do not comprehend the will of God and do not permit me to convert the whole world in the way God wills. For I wish to convert the prelates first through humility and reverence, and when they see our holy life and reverence for them, they will ask you to preach and convert the people, and this will serve you better than the privileges you want, which will lead you to pride. If you are free from all avarice and persuade the people to render their dues to the churches,

they will ask you to hear the confessions of their people; though you ought not to be concerned with this, as, if they have been converted, they can well find confessors. For myself, I wish to have this privilege from the Lord, that I have no privilege from man.[33]

The passage reflects Francis's admonition in his *Testament* and stands in stark contrast to the policies currently pursued by the order.

All of the various reports ended up on Celano's desk and he had to do something with them. He was surprisingly inclusive. Three episodes in II Celano are taken from I Celano; 5 seem to depend on the *Perugian Anonymous*; 34 reflect the so-called *Legend of the Three Companions*; 87 echo the *Scripta Leonis*; and 131 resemble no known source.[34] Parallels with the so-called *Legend of the Three Companions* are concentrated in the early, chronologically ordered section. Here, in a reflection of the emphasis on divine predestination characteristic of the latter, we find young Francis, a prisoner of war in Perugia, informing his fellow inmates that he is happy in captivity because he knows that he will eventually be venerated as a saint![35] We also find strong criticism of those who run off and fail to obey their superiors.[36]

Nevertheless, rather soon in II Celano we encounter a strong emphasis on poverty.[37] Moreover, although one passage affirms Francis's respect for doctors of theology, every other passage that mentions learning (and there are many of them) presents it as something of a problem. There is a notable tendency for mention of the word to inspire the use of other words, such as "vain" and "curious." In describing the ideal minister general, Francis suggests that even though he may be very learned, as a minister "he should not be a collector of books, nor given to much reading." He notes that on entering the order "a great cleric must in some way give up even his learning," for "learning takes from many people their docility and does not permit them to bend to humble practices." Francis's inspired understanding of the Bible is seen as superior to academic learning.

The point is not that Celano is against the sort of learning that represents little more than vain curiosity—of course he would be, and so would everyone else—but that it is practically the only sort of learning he wants to discuss. Nor is he worrying about a vague possibility. Francis, he says, sensed that in the future, "knowledge would be an occasion of ruin." He knew through visionary experience that his ideal would be opposed not only by some outside the order but also by some within it. He prophesied a time when those outside the order would speak ill of it because of the bad example being set by some friars, and he withdrew from the company of the brothers mainly because he could not bear to hear such criticism.[38] At one point, Celano abandons the role of narrator to speak in his own voice, commenting that within the order "we have a greater abundance of weaklings than of warriors." Those who "could not have lived at home except by their sweat" now "feed on the sweat of the poor" without doing any work themselves. Celano is not predicting the demise of the order, though. Echoing the *Scripta Leonis*, he says that God has revealed to Francis that the order will survive even if it is reduced to three brothers.[39]

Who or what is responsible for the present decline? Here too we find an echo of the *Scripta Leonis*. Celano is willing to criticize the superiors to some extent, though the attack is not as sustained as in the *Scripta Leonis*. Some of them are described as drawing friars away from Francis's commands. In fact, when Francis is asked to describe the ideal minister general, he furnishes a job description but remarks that he sees no one currently capable of filling it.[40] Even more interesting, Celano depicts a gravely ill Francis raising himself from his bed and crying, "Who are those who have snatched my order and that of my brothers out of my hands?"[41]

This much is explicitly stated. The implicit criticisms are equally significant. Celano presents an episode in which Cardinal Hugolino suggests to Francis and Dominic that in the future, bishops should be appointed from among their friars. Both reject the idea. Francis says,

> Lord, my brothers are called *minores* so that they will not presume to become greater. Their vocation teaches them to remain in a lowly station and to follow the footsteps of the humble Christ, so that in the end they may be exalted above the rest in the sight of the saints. If you want them to bear fruit for the church of God, hold them and preserve them in the station to which they have been called, and bring them back to a lowly station, even if they are unwilling. I pray you, therefore, Father, that you by no means permit them to rise to any prelacy, lest they become prouder rather than poorer and grow arrogant toward the rest.[42]

In short, Franciscans have been called to serve the church in a way different from that of ecclesiastical authority. The same point is made in a different context in yet another echo of the *Scripta Leonis*, when Francis tells his friars to be at peace with the clergy and win them over.[43] Passages like these are not warnings against future conduct, but implicit criticisms of what is already taking place. Celano writes for an order that has already profited from papal privileges that restrain the clergy, one that is even now seeing its friars promoted to episcopal office.

What other evidence do we have concerning the 1240s? Angelo Clareno tells us that the relaxations encouraged by Crescentius of Iesi, who was provincial minister in the March of Ancona and then minister general of the order from 1244 to 1247, so offended some friars that they sent a delegation to Rome. Their goal was to protest "the changes in location and building projects in the cities and towns, with scandal to the clergy and people"; the "abandoning of solitary poor places and construction of sumptuous buildings"; the struggle for legacies and burial rights, undercutting the rightful claims of the secular clergy; the neglect of prayer and preference for "the curious and sterile knowledge of Aristotle" over divine wisdom; and the multiplication of schools devoted to worldly knowledge.

Crescentius's intelligence services were efficient. He got wind of the plan and sent his own delegation, which spoke to the pope first. Once the pope was on his side, he ambushed the other delegation on its way and punished the brothers severely. They were then sent to remote provinces of the order with letters describing them as troublemakers.[44]

That much is clear enough in Angelo's narrative, but he is less instructive on how widespread the insurrection was. He originally describes the discontent in such a way as to suggest that the protesting delegates came from throughout the order, and that they were a sizable group (Angelo says sixty-two on one occasion, but "sixty-two or seventy-two" on another). Nevertheless, when he rehearses the argument purportedly presented to the pope by those representing the leadership, he has them describe the malcontents as living "in certain provinces," and he suggests that the entire delegation was arrested at the same time, both of which are consistent with the idea of a more localized problem.

Angelo is writing nearly a century later and has an agenda to pursue, but others present stories at least reminiscent of his. One of his contemporaries, Pelegrino of Bologna, describes a similar event, but draws a very different moral from it.[45] Pelegrino, writing in 1305, says that shortly after Crescentius became provincial minister, he discovered "a sect of brothers who, . . . despising the institutions of the order and thinking themselves better than the others, wanted to live as they wished and attributed all to the spirit, wearing cloaks so short that they came up to their buttocks." Angelo and Pelegrino receive some degree of support from Thomas of Eccleston, who, writing around 1258, says without elaborating that Crescentius was having trouble with his province on the eve of his election as minister general.[46]

So far, the sources seem to allow us to believe that Angelo is exaggerating the extent of the trouble and that Crescentius faced a very localized problem, that it was simply a matter of Ancona while he was provincial minister—or at most, of certain Italian provinces once he became minister general. Salimbene, however, tells us that in Germany, "certain solemn brothers, showing contempt for the discipline of the order, did not wish to obey the ministers." They complained to a papal legate, who took them into custody and handed them over to their ministers for punishment.[47] Again, in a work that may have been written during the 1240s, Hugh of Digne stages a literary debate between "a zealot for poverty and his domestic enemy."[48] In the *Dispute*, the "domestic enemy," who seems a poster child for minorite corruption, protests that internal attitude is the essential thing, not external actions; that he can consume without sin as long as he has his superior's permission, since superiors have discretionary power in such matters; that attractive, comfortable buildings serve the purpose of attracting into the order those who might otherwise find it hard to abandon all and follow Christ; and that accepting higher-quality clothing may seem to be a compromise, but is actually more economical in the long run and enables friars to do their jobs more efficiently (e.g., warmer clothing enables them to pray longer in cold churches). The zealot argues that superiors have no more than limited discretion in such matters, because superfluity is forbidden by the Franciscan rule and vow. He defines superfluity as "that which, when taken away, leaves enough to suffice." When the domestic enemy ironically suggests that the zealot talk to his superiors ("and maybe you'll reform the order"), the latter replies that "the superiors are responsible for all the aforesaid abuses . . . and it would be pointless to talk with them, since many not only refuse to listen but cruelly persecute those who speak." He normally discusses such matters only with other lovers of poverty. Yet God is not mocked. The order will be reformed by the very zealots whom current leaders are attempting to suppress.

Still another witness is perhaps provided by a commentary on the prophet Jeremiah, one that most scholars feel was written in southern Italy before 1248, perhaps before 1243. It has been seen as originating in Franciscan circles, but it also has been assigned a Cistercian origin. The evidence is conflicting and confusing. What modern scholars do agree on is that, while in its present form it is not the work of the Calabrian apocalyptic writer Joachim of Fiore (who died in 1205), it nonetheless circulated under that name among mid-thirteenth-century Franciscan Joachites.[49] At any rate, the commentary is a blast aimed not simply at a single order but also at the church, which is portrayed as seeking wealth while neglecting the faithful. The author indicts everyone from the pope down, with the exception of a few *spirituales* who, however dear to the Lord, are unsupported and even persecuted by the hierarchy. God will soon right the matter, however. The church will be laid waste by its enemies, opening the way for its purification. From the *spirituales* will spring a new order. The church will be reborn uncorrupted by wealth, enjoy a new spiritual understanding, and missionize effectively among the Greeks, Jews, and infidels.

That gives us no fewer than six sources for trouble in the 1240s, and they combine to provide a picture oddly prophetic of what we will see in the early fourteenth century. Angelo portrays the troubled brethren as protesting essentially the same abuses that he himself would bemoan in his own time. Pelegrino's preoccupation with the solemn brothers' nonregulation garb and his description of them as "despising the institutions of the order and thinking themselves better than the others" both seem to anticipate the fourteenth-century characterization of the spirituals by the community. So does his suggestion that they relied on the spirit rather than the hierarchy and wanted to live as they wished. Salimbene's description of the "solemn brothers" as "showing contempt for the discipline of the order" and appealing over their leaders' heads to higher authority points in the same direction. Hugh's domestic enemy defends the relaxation of Franciscan rigor with some of the same arguments the community would use in Angelo Clareno's time. Moreover, Hugh and the Jeremiah commentary both forecast the apocalyptic expectation of fourteenth-century spirituals—their sense that despite persecution, their cause would eventually triumph. And Angelo, Pelegrino, and Salimbene all portray not scattered individuals but groups that have enough cohesion to act as such.

There are, of course, obvious difficulties involved. Angelo and Pelegrino may simply be projecting the issues and rhetoric of their own time back onto the 1240s, a period they have no great reason to know intimately. Once their witness is questioned, a good percentage of the other evidence becomes debatable. Thomas of Eccleston is a trustworthy source for the 1240s, but he tells us almost nothing about the nature of Crescentius's difficulties. The Jeremiah commentary, too, is a good reflection of the 1240s, but it does not directly address troubles in the Franciscan order and may not even have a Franciscan author, although it remains significant that Franciscans should have found it so compelling. That leaves us with the Leo materials, II Celano, and the writings of Salimbene and Hugh, all of which are hard to ignore. The first tells us that one element was unhappy about the course the order was taking, but it does not tell us how large that element was or what kind of audience it commanded. Certainly the Leo materials commanded a substantial audience over time, since not only Angelo and Ubertino but also the French spiritual Franciscan spokesman, Petrus Iohannis Olivi, cited them. Moreover, once we turn from documents to oral tradition, we can envisage an even wider audience for Leo's (and the rest of the companions') thoughts on the order. The *Chronicle of the Twenty-Four Generals* tells us that Conrad of Offida hurried to the Portiuncula just before Leo's death and heard from him *multa magnalia* concerning Francis. Salimbene mentions the *multa magnalia* that he and other young friars at Siena heard from Bernard Quintavalle. Angelo Clareno tells us that James of Massa knew Giles of Assisi and other companions; in addition, Angelo says that he himself heard the reminiscences of Giles, Angelo, and other companions.[50]

Who besides Salimbene was paying attention to the companions in the 1240s, though? Obviously Celano was. That II Celano should have included so much criticism is highly significant, since Celano himself was obviously considered a responsible, respectable member of the order or else he would not have been given the assignment of writing the two *legenda*. On the other hand, the fact that the respectable Celano included such criticisms in his work suggests that stating such reservations did not mark one as beyond the pale by that point.

Salimbene's report presents its own difficulties, since he does not bother to explain what those fractious brothers in Germany were complaining *about*. Hugh, however, leaves us in little doubt as to what he is complaining about, at least generically speaking. He offers us a different problem analogous to the one presented by Celano. We learn of Hugh not only from his own writings but also from the chronicler Jean de Joinville, who says that in a sermon before Louis IX, Hugh scolded those members of religious orders he spotted in the royal retinue. He informed them that they ought to be back in their monasteries where they belonged.[51] We also learn about him from Salimbene, who describes a denunciatory address he fired off at the cardinals, "rating them like asses."[52] One gets the impression that Hugh liked to criticize. One also gets the impression that, far from being persecuted for it as the ill-tempered spokesman of a deviant group, he was lionized as a modern-day prophet, a thirteenth-century Bernard of Clairvaux.

This is a point worth emphasizing. Whatever fate Hugh's zealot may have envisaged for those who criticized current laxity, Hugh's own fortunes did not suffer. We know that he himself served as provincial minister,[53] and he announces at the beginning of his rule commentary that he is writing it because he was officially asked to do so. The commentary itself, while it expects friars to observe a serious level of poverty, also expects them to come to terms with the changes in function that have occurred.[54] It bemoans laxity, but essentially the same laxity that the order itself attempted to curb through legislation. Moreover, Hugh's criticism of current behavior is based on the rule, not the *Testament*, which he acknowledges is not binding.[55] His primary focus is not on what Francis desired for the order but on what the rule says. He observes that Franciscans "are bound, not to blessed Francis's intention (which we do not know), but to a common rational understanding of the rule which we vow."[56]

It is rather difficult, then, to reconcile the attitude toward authority found in the *Dispute* with the one suggested by the rule commentary. It can be done, but not to everyone's satisfaction. It would help if we knew the order in which these works were written. Perhaps we should take Hugh seriously when he describes the zealot as "young." We could then treat the *Dispute* as an early work, a product of the idealism and intolerance that often characterize youth. We could place it within Crescentius's generalate, when disenchantment with the leadership would seem more explicable. His rule commentary might then be located early in John of Parma's generalate, a time when serious-minded brothers might entertain some faith in the direction of things.[57] Or the order could be the reverse, and we would have to look for another explanation, perhaps taking refuge in the possibility that when Hugh's zealot blames the leaders, he is looking not at the minister general, but at what he sees occurring on a local or provincial level.

In any case, we are left with the feeling that in the 1240s, scattered groups within the order were unhappy with the direction it was taking, and some were becoming disgruntled enough to seek aid in high places. The latter apparently thought that appeal outside the order was necessary because leaders of the order were themselves responsible for the difficulties. We can be less sure what behavior they were protesting. In Hugh's case, the answer is clearly laxity. II Celano and the Leo materials offer a much more complex critique.

Giles of Assisi

So far, the discussion has proceeded with little attention to another of the original companions. A number of sources refer to Giles of Assisi and quote him at length in ways that seem to make him a witness to discontent, and not simply during Crescentius's generalate.[58] In the collection of sayings attributed to him, we find that "he said frequently, in fervor of spirit, 'Paris, Paris, you have destroyed the order of Saint Francis!'"[59] On another occasion, when someone inquired about predestination, he remarked that the shores of the sea were sufficient for him, and he who inquired about what lay in its depths was stupid. "He does not seek too high," Giles remarked, "for whom the wisdom of how to act well is sufficient."[60] Nor are these the only suggestions that Giles thought the educational program embraced by the order was detrimental to it.[61]

Beyond these comments, though, one finds little in the sayings that could be taken even as indirect criticism of current trends. Certainly Giles emphasizes that being virtuous is more important than talking about it, and criticizes a preacher on that score;[62] certainly he stresses the importance of prayer, poverty, lowliness, obedience, and wretched clothing. But there is little suggestion that the order is being destroyed by a general failure to encourage these things. Nor does the life of Giles attributed to Brother Leo give us any more.[63]

As we move from the thirteenth century into the fourteenth, we find more to go on, but might perhaps trust it less. Ubertino da Casale's *Arbor vitae* (1305) informs us that Giles lamented the decadence of the order through its refusal to follow the rule. In fact, he was so upset abut it that he could not have held on, had Christ not explained to him the part this decadence played in God's plan for the rule, indeed the entire church.[64] Ubertino says that he learned this from "a certain holy man, Masseo, a knight of Perugia."

Angelo Clareno, writing in the 1320s, says that he heard Giles speak of the trouble to which the order was subjected during Elias's generalate.[65] Later he quotes Giles as saying, "The attack is on, and there is neither the strength, time, nor wisdom to repulse it. Blessed is he who, giving ground before the enemy and hiding, can save his soul."[66] Angelo does not mention where he heard this statement, though.

While we cannot dismiss these witnesses out of hand, neither can we simply trust them. Ubertino and Angelo both wrote with polemical intent, and the words they put in Giles's mouth fit their own proclivities neatly. The one bit of information either could claim to have heard directly from Giles is fairly commonplace. Elias's generalate was certainly a time of troubles for the order.

That brings us to another fourteenth-century source, the *Chronicle of the Twenty-Four Generals*. It is even later, completed between 1369 and 1374. The *Chronicle* offers a comment by Giles that, although not quite the same as the one reported by Angelo, reinforces it: "The boat is smashed in and the conflict has taken place, let him who is able flee and get away if he can."[67] Here again we have the sense that the main battle for the soul of the order has been lost, and the only solution is to pursue an eremitical life. The first part of this statement might be compared with Giles's greeting (as reported by Angelo) to John of Parma, when the latter was elected minister of the order: "It's good that you've come, but you've come late."[68] The second part fits Giles's own life from Francis's death on.

It is the *Chronicle of the Twenty-Four Generals* that presents what is undoubtedly the most dramatic story. We hear how Giles, the lover of poverty, living in a little hut made of clay and wattles, heard from Brother Leo that the basilica of Saint Francis was under construction at Assisi and that a marble urn had been placed there to collect money for it. In tears, Giles encouraged Leo to go and smash the urn. Leo and some others did so.[69] We are then informed that Giles himself later visited the church and was given a tour of it. Having looked it over, Giles said, "I tell you, brothers, the only thing still lacking to you is that you have no wives." When the brothers took offense, Giles added, "Brothers, you know well that it's just as illicit for you to dispense with poverty as to dispense with chastity. Once you've rejected the former, it's easy for you to abandon the latter."[70]

Here we have both a strong protest concerning laxity and a genuine confrontation. Note, though, that the issue was not necessarily whether Francis should be accorded a sumptuous church. Ubertino informs us that Giles felt such was justified in Francis's case, although he thought that the Franciscans should build no other expensive churches.[71] The emphasis here is on the means of collection and the luxury of the friars' accommodations.

Unfortunately, the story is being reported well over a century after the fact. The part of the chronicle in which it lies is a full-scale life of Giles, a longer version of the one attributed to Leo. One might imagine reasons why an anecdote in which Leo plays such a controversial role might have been omitted in the shorter version, but the omission does raise some question about its accuracy.

A second anecdote in the longer life is also relevant. It tells how Giles asked Bonaventure what uneducated brothers like Giles himself should do to be saved. Bonaventure replied that it was a matter of loving God, whereupon Giles asked whether an illiterate man could love God as much as a literate one could. Bonaventure assured him that a little old lady could love God as much as a master of theology. At that, Giles rose and went to the part of the garden adjoining the city, crying, "Poor, simple, illiterate old lady, you love the Lord God and can be greater than Brother Bonaventure!"[72]

Anyone who has read much medieval theology will be familiar with the little old lady and the uses to which she was put. Scholars as diverse as Aquinas and Olivi ratified her claim to know more about salvation than Aristotle did, while Ockham imagined her calling a general council. Thus one would hardly be surprised to find that Bonaventure actually said what he is alleged to have said. The more interesting part is Giles's reaction, which seems calculated to put a great scholar in his place. If the story is true, we have yet more evidence of Giles's lack of enthusiasm for scholarly activity, but this time the story has a harder edge precisely because it is aimed at Bonaventure. Since we know nothing of the other scholars who became Giles's targets, we can at least entertain the possibility that they deserved to be chided for prizing scholarship over piety. In Bonaventure's case, that seems harder to believe, and thus we are left with the feeling that—again if the story is true—Giles was profoundly at odds with the Franciscan educational program.[73]

John of Parma and His Generalate

We have seen that there was trouble in the 1240s under Crescentius, although we can be less sure what sort of trouble it was. Was there also discord under his successor, John of Parma? Here we encounter an odd disparity between the 1240s and 1250s. We have several witnesses to trouble in the former decade and only one for the 1250s, Angelo Clareno.[74] Angelo, to be sure, says a great deal. He tells us that the winter of discontent created by Crescentius was made summer through the election in 1247 of his successor as minister general, John of Parma, "a man of God." John spent the first three years of his generalate visiting the whole order, traveling on foot, clad in a single tunic of inexpensive cloth, with a single companion or two. He arrived unannounced, without warning. He ate what was put before him.

It was too late, though. Angelo says that many were already spoiled by the relaxations introduced earlier and, though they hated John for publicly acknowledging Franciscan decadence, they were temporarily constrained to silence by his saintly example and bided their time. Their patience was finally rewarded in 1257, when John stepped down. Angelo suggests two explanations for his resignation. One is that John's defense of Joachim of Fiore, concerning the Trinity, gave them the opportunity to attack him on a different front. The basic issue here was Joachim's criticism of Peter Lombard's views on the Trinity, a criticism which in turn had been condemned by the church. According to Angelo, John argued that Joachim was condemned for misunderstanding the Lombard's view, not for his own formulation. In other words, while Peter Lombard's view was not heretical (as Joachim had claimed), neither was Joachim's own.

The second explanation Angelo provides for John's resignation is that he simply saw the uselessness of continuing. Angelo recites a long harangue by John purportedly delivered at the general chapter of 1257. In it, John announced that he was resigning because he realized that it was impossible for him to bring the entire order back to regular observance. He felt that it was time to step down and let someone else govern the recalcitrant Franciscans. John's jeremiad is filled with particulars. The brothers are guilty of refusing to face even the sins they know exist; they are guilty of looking upon those who do observe the rule as disobedient destroyers of the order; they are not content with two tunics, nor are they content with cheap tunics; they skimp on their liturgical duties; they haggle with the secular clergy over burial rights, wills, and legacies; they seek and receive money, simply being careful not to touch it; and, whereas upon entering the order new brothers should divest themselves of all money by giving it to the poor, they are currently allowed to keep some of it to buy books or encouraged to give it to the brothers for new buildings or other amenities.

Angelo makes it clear that John incurred the wrath not of a few unimportant brothers, but of a majority, including the leaders. He portrays John as recognizing that there were really two groups, a small band of Francis's true disciples and a large mass of people who were Franciscans in name only. In fact, he presents John as a prophet who predicted that the order would eventually split into two groups. Eventually a third, purer order would arise, producing reform and eventually unity.

Angelo is also very explicit concerning John's opinion of the *Testament*. He portrays John as arguing that the rule and the *Testament* are substantially the same, for the same Holy Spirit that spoke in the rule dictated the *Testament*. Francis was never more filled with the Holy Spirit than at his death, and it was then that he not only dictated the *Testament* but also announced that he had received both it and the rule by revelation from Christ. Thus, Franciscans are obliged to observe both. In other words, as far as John is concerned, the question of whether the *Testament* is binding depends not on whether Francis had juridical authority, but on whether he had charismatic authority, and John has no doubt that he did.

If Angelo's portrayal of John is accurate, then he and John had a great deal in common. Both bewailed the same transgressions; both saw the rule and the *Testament* as equally binding; both despaired of any solution short of splitting the order. That brings us back to the critical question: Was the situation in 1257 already much as it would be in the early fourteenth century, or is Angelo simply reading his own situation back into the 1250s? If we try to find the answer in Angelo alone, we will not get far. Certainly some aspects of his story inspire less than complete confidence. His description of Gerard of Borgo San Donnino and the scandal of the "Eternal Gospel," which probably set the stage for John of Parma's fall, is completely garbled. Salimbene, who knew Gerard, presents a very credible and very different version.[75]

Salimbene personally knew not only Gerard but also John, and thus he offers an important check on Angelo's accuracy. We find confirmation of several details offered by Angelo, such as the fact that John visited all the provinces of the order. More important, Salimbene confirms John's love of poverty and his interest in Joachim of Fiore, whose apocalyptic thought was becoming popular throughout Europe.[76] He also acknowledges that John had enemies in the order.[77] Nevertheless, he puts these things together in a much different way. He never suggests that John's love of poverty led to his having enemies, which in turn led to his fall. Instead he attributes the fall entirely to John's passion for Joachite apocalyptic speculation and his refusal to distance himself from it at the moment when, thanks to Gerard of Borgo San Donnino and his Eternal Gospel, it had become an embarrassment to the order. In fact, Salimbene notes that whereas Popes Alexander IV and Nicholas III had once loved John because of his learning and holy life, they and certain ministers of the order eventually turned against him because of his Joachism. Thus he was asked to resign. Salimbene recounts a conversation with another brother who commented, "I tell you, Brother Salimbene, Brother John of Parma disturbed both himself and his order, because he was so learned and holy and lived such an excellent life that he could have called for reform in the Roman court and they would have listened to him; but when he followed the prophecies of fantastic men, he injured himself and did great harm to his friends." Salimbene replied, "That's the way it seems to me, too." He then went on to confess his own previous adherence to Joachite prophecy and his rude awakening when the Emperor Frederick II died in 1250—well before Joachites had scheduled his passing— and when the apocalyptically portentous year 1260 passed without incident. Since then, Salimbene observed, "I'm determined to believe only what I can see." "Good for you!" Salimbene's friend exclaimed. "If Brother John had done the same he would have satisfied the minds of his brethren." "He couldn't," Salimbene said. "Some people are so definite about what they say that afterward they're ashamed to retract it lest they seem to be liars."[78]

The implication is clear. John's love of poverty worked for him rather than against him. It was his Joachism that destroyed him. If, like Salimbene, he had confessed his mistake, the brothers would have forgiven him. Moreover, Salimbene assumes that what needed refurbishing was not the order but the

It was not simply a matter of hypocrisy, though. Angelo portrays Bonaventure as driven by an almost pathological rage. "Then Brother Bonaventure's wisdom and sanctity were eclipsed and obscured, and his gentleness so transformed by an agitated mind into fury and wrath that he said, 'If I were not concerned about the honor of the order I would have him punished openly as a heretic.'" When the hearing was concluded, Bonaventure sentenced John to perpetual imprisonment, the same fate meted out to Gerard of Borgo San Donnino and his colleague Leonard. Fortunately, a sympathetic cardinal intervened, and John was allowed to retire into what the order hoped would be obscurity in a hermitage at Greccio.[82]

By the time one arrives at this story in Angelo's chronicle, one reads it with a sense of *déjà vu*, having already seen it in visionary form a few pages earlier. There, Angelo relates his interview with James of Massa, who had been recommended to him as an expert giver of spiritual advice.[83] James was one of those elder statesmen who spanned the gap between Angelo's generation and the early order, a man to whom Brother Giles went for advice. Like Giles, he was given to mystical transports, and during John of Parma's generalate had once remained in rapture for three days, so long that people began to think he was dead. His visions were occasionally prophetic, providing insight into what would happen to the order. That was the case with the three-day trance. When it was over, the provincial minister summoned him and employed him like a reference work, ordering him to tell what he had seen. The minister later commented that if these revelations were made known, people might not find them all that hard to understand, but they would certainly find them hard to believe.

In the course of relating his visions to Angelo, James included what Angelo describes as "a really stunning one." He saw a tree with golden roots, a silver trunk and branches, and leaves that were silver gilded with gold. Its fruits were the brothers minor, and each main branch was a province. At the top of the tree he saw John of Parma. Next he saw Francis, who passed among the brothers with a chalice containing the spirit of life. When offered the chalice, John drained it, and so did a few others; however, many drank some and spilled the rest, while still others spilled the whole thing without drinking any.

Knowing that a tempest was about to assault the tree, John descended and hid himself in the trunk. While he was doing so, Bonaventure (who had drunk part of the chalice and poured out the rest) ascended to the place John had vacated. Bonaventure, equipped with sharp iron fingernails, impetuously leaped down from his place to attack John, but the latter called out to Christ, who sent Francis with a stone to grind down Bonaventure's nails. Then the storm finally came and destroyed the tree, but from its root there grew another tree entirely of gold, even its flowers and fruits.

This story, which also appears in the *Fioretti*,[84] is bristling with difficulties, not least of which is the question of when Angelo had this conversation with James. Moreover, the fact that James is supposed to have had the vision before John's fall, which probably increased its authority in Angelo's eyes, deflates it before the more jaundiced gaze of modern historians, who would be much happier with the story if it purported to present James's reaction once the fall had taken place. Nevertheless, unless we decide either that Angelo is simply lying about having received the story from James himself or that he twisted the story to reflect his own sense of the order and its problems, we are faced here with an indication that as early as the late 1250s (a formulation allowing us to place the story on either side of the 1257 resignation), there was an element in the order that had despaired of its reform and that looked to an apocalyptic solution in which tribulation would lead to renewal. That is what James's vision suggests, and it is pretty much what Angelo presents John of Parma himself as saying.

Angelo's roller-coaster view of Franciscan reform prospects—relaxation under Crescentius followed by a brief Prague Spring under John, which in turn gives way to the Warsaw Pact tanks rolling in under Bonaventure—receives some support from Ubertino da Casale, who entered the order within a year of Bonaventure's death and became a major spokesman for the spirituals in the fourteenth century. Ubertino suggests in his *Arbor vitae* that Bonaventure's life of Francis, the *Legenda maior,* suppressed certain elements of tradition in order to conceal recent decay in the order.[85] Again, Petrus Iohannis Olivi, probably writing in the early 1280s, complains that brothers in his own time are citing Bonaventure's laxity as precedent for their own.[86] These are interesting items, but we must ask how far they take us. Ubertino, as we will see, implies elsewhere that the real decadence set in *after* Bonaventure; Olivi scornfully rejects his opponents' picture of Bonaventure, arguing instead that, while physical infirmity may have made the Seraphic Doctor a bit self-indulgent, he himself humbly confessed his weakness in this regard and consistently stood for reform within the Franciscan community.[87] Olivi cites Bonaventure heavily in his argument for rigorous observance of the rule.

There is also the evidence provided by Bonaventure's own actions and writings. Rosalind Brooke's study of early Franciscan government suggests that the John-Bonaventure succession produced no radical shift in direction.[88] In 1260, in its first major effort at codification, the order produced the constitutions of Narbonne. The constitutions represented a serious effort to set forth a pattern of life that would respect the rule yet leave Franciscans free to accomplish those tasks the church had ordained for them. They tried to set reasonable standards in food, dress, and other areas, standards based on a plausible reading of the rule. Nor did subsequent legislation under Bonaventure relax these standards. In many respects it tightened them.[89]

This is not to say that Franciscan behavior actually mirrored the legislation, and here we arrive at Bonaventure's writings. He wrote letters to the entire order in 1257 and 1266.[90] Neither makes especially pleasant reading. In both, he announces that the order, once loved and respected, is now regarded with loathing and contempt. He attacks the way in which Franciscans avidly seek money and incautiously handle it; their importunate begging (travelers, he says, now avoid friars as if they were highwaymen); their excessive familiarity with those outside the order; their contentious pursuit of legacies and burial rights; their sumptuous living; their frequent moves to more luxurious quarters; and their tendency to promote the wrong people to office. That is an impressive list of failings, one in many ways reminiscent of the complaints Angelo puts in John of Parma's mouth.

These letters are typical of Bonaventure's writings in their tendency to see the danger as coming entirely from one end of the spectrum. The problem is laxity. Not once does he suggest that he is combating another threat from zealots. This point is an important one, because much modern scholarship has proceeded from the opposite assumption, the idea that Bonaventure's generalate represented a final attempt to defend the *via media* against those centrifugal tendencies that would tear the order into two opposing factions after his death. Nor did modern historians invent that assumption. In Dante's *Paradiso*, Bonaventure, passing posthumous judgment on his successors, announces that a few friars still maintain the old standards—

> But not at Casale or Aquasparta, where
> they come to our rule in such a way that
> one flees it while the other constricts it.[91]

Dante is, of course, directing the defunct Bonaventure's aim at Matthew of Aquasparta, who incurred the poet's wrath by serving Boniface VIII's interests in Florence and thus contributing to Dante's banishment. More surprisingly, he is also censuring Ubertino da Casale, spokesman for the spiritual Franciscans in Dante's time. In any case, these lines suggest that the notion of Bonaventure as defender of the *via media* was already available in the early fourteenth century.

It was, however, a notion that seems to have escaped Bonaventure himself. The problem is not simply that he fails to acknowledge the zealots as a menace. It is also that he uses the notion of the *via media* in a very different way. In one work he describes various sorts of mean applying to different classes of person.[92] In the case of evangelical poverty, the mean consists of renouncing possession while retaining use, and limiting use without rejecting necessity. In other words, it means possessing nothing and using only what is necessary. Necessary for what, though? For Bonaventure, it involves using what is necessary to do what needs to be done—and for the Franciscans, that means teaching and pastoral duties. Thus poverty is not so much an absolute that prevents friars from performing such duties as it is a flexible standard defined by the role one is called upon to play. We will see this idea reoccur in Olivi's thought.

There is, then, little evidence that Bonaventure saw himself as charged with the task of holding together an order being torn asunder by two extreme factions. Moreover, there is an important bit of evidence against that idea tucked away in Angelo's chronicle. It is the purely negative evidence provided by his disinterest in the bulk of Bonaventure's generalate. Once he has described John of Parma's trial, he goes into fast forward, and the next thing we know, Bonaventure is dead. Angelo, patently hostile to Bonaventure, would certainly have reported any serious conflict occurring between the time John was packed off to Greccio and Bonaventure's own demise in 1274, yet he says nothing. His silence concerning this period places him in a category with Sherlock Holmes's dog that did not bark.

We have been speaking of poverty. It is worth remarking that much the same thing can be said of Bonaventure's stance on learning. He was, to be sure, a product of Paris and an enthusiastic defender of Franciscan educational accomplishments. Perhaps his most revealing comment along these lines is a passage in the *Letter on Three Questions:*

> Nor should it disturb you that the brothers were originally simple and illiterate. On the contrary, it should confirm your faith in the order. I confess before God that this is what most made me love the life of Blessed Francis, because it is like the beginning and perfection of the church, which began first among simple fishermen and later progressed to the most renowned and learned doctors. You see the same thing in the order of Blessed Francis, so that God might demonstrate that it was not founded through human prudence but through Christ; and because the works of Christ do not decline with time but

rather progress, that this was a divine work is demonstrated by the fact that the learned did not refuse to descend and join the company of simple men.[93]

Such a remark seems oddly at variance with what we might consider Francis's search for holy simplicity as God's fool. Here again, though, it is worth remembering that however much Bonaventure might have differed from Francis on the issue of learning, he differed a great deal less from some whom historians have labeled "spiritual Franciscans." We have heard Thomas of Eccleston quote John of Parma as saying that the house of the Franciscan order was constructed on two foundations, morality and learning;[94] one would get the same impression from reading Salimbene's remarks on John. We also saw that Hugh of Digne thought it only right for Alexander of Hales to continue teaching at Paris after he became a friar. Nor, as we will discover in the next chapter, did Olivi find the idea of Franciscan scholars all that anomalous.

The point is not that Bonaventure, John, Hugh, and Olivi were all saying the same thing, but that all were participants in the same historical development, and that fact makes it hard to project such a clear opposition between Bonaventure and the other three as to suggest that they represented opposing notions of Franciscanism. It is even harder to imagine a distinction that would place Bonaventure on one side of a great divide with John, Hugh, Olivi, Giles of Assisi, and Brother Leo on the other.

To say this much is hardly to deny that the order was changing, that it was moving away from the poverty and simplicity Francis originally envisaged, and that Bonaventure's generalate was a period in which those changes received noteworthy institutional ratification. The 1260 constitutions of Narbonne were an important element in that ratification. So was Bonaventure's *Legenda maior*, which was commissioned by the 1260 general chapter, approved by the 1263 general chapter, and declared by the 1266 general chapter to be the only version of Francis's life worthy of remaining in existence. In the *Legenda maior* we encounter a Francis more to be venerated than imitated, as several modern historians have observed.[95] Nevertheless, the *Legenda maior* still spoke of those who actually had imitated him, and still offered him as "a model for perfect disciples of Christ."[96] He became, to be sure, a different sort of model, one lying beyond our reach yet drawing us after it, a notion perhaps most perfectly realized in Bonaventure's final statement, the *Collationes in hexaemeron*.[97] On the way to that goal, Franciscans were to be guided in their everyday activity by statutes designed to assure a workable, reachable poverty, given the tasks the order had to face.

The Problem of John's Trial

That should take care of the matter, yet it seems impossible to move on without some word concerning the one event from Bonaventure's generalate on which Angelo does lavish attention: his behavior toward John of Parma. It is, in a sense, irrelevant to the issue at hand, because even Angelo acknowledges that the hearing was aimed at John's Joachism and not at his views on observance of the rule; yet it calls for explanation, because it portrays a Bonaventure driven by something between pathological rage and demonic possession. That is not the man usually encountered in history books or, for that matter, in medieval sources. It may not be entirely wrong, though. The scandal of the Eternal Gospel, which began in 1254 and stretched out over the next decade, played into the hands of the Franciscans' enemies. Parisian masters and secular clergy alike found themselves able to renew their attack on the order as a dangerous innovation. This time they had an excellent target. If our sources for Gerard of Borgo San Donnino's beliefs come anywhere near describing the truth, he was a genuine heretic by medieval standards who thought that Joachim's writings had replaced the Old and New Testaments as sacred Scripture in a dawning third age of world history.[98] The public airing of his beliefs not only cast suspicion on Franciscan Joachites but also forced the order to prove its orthodoxy in ways it might not have wished.[99] John of Parma had been minister general when the scandal broke, and he himself was known to be an ardent Joachite. Thus it is hardly surprising that he was called upon to explain himself, and everyone seems to agree that when he appeared he proved intractable. Bonaventure, faced with an endangered order and an inflexible John, may well have lost patience and done something Bonaventure scholars would later regret. These considerations may fall short of excusing his behavior, but they go a long way toward explaining it.

One more element in the story should be emphasized: John of Parma went from minister general to contemplative, from an active role at the center of the order to an eremitical life at Greccio, and he lived on for a very long time. Here again, as in the cases of Giles and Leo, we have a major figure who stood at the center of Franciscan history but then moved—or was moved—to the margin, where he continued to influence those who chose to visit him.

John thus took his place alongside men like James of Massa and Conrad of Offida as a bridge figure. These were friars who had associated with the companions of Saint Francis and would later offer guidance to the likes of Ubertino da Casale and Angelo Clareno. They were contemplative, eremitically inclined Franciscans who enjoyed the opportunity to observe the rule strictly, without the impediments that came from teaching theology or conducting a parish ministry. It would not be hard to imagine how such an environment might encourage not only contemplative delights but also hard thoughts on the current state of Franciscan life.

It is important to note, though, the role of the word "imagine" in the preceding sentence. When we come down to facts, we have few of them to consider. What we have is a bit like the sort of game book children used to take on long trips: "Connect the dots and a picture will emerge." The problem is that in this case there are few dots and a great distance to cover. They seem closer together in the 1240s, but even here the picture that emerges is at best impressionistic.

The Term "Spiritual"

Having answered our first question—whether there were two basic factions within the order—we should be able to dispatch the second question easily. If there is little evidence of two definable factions before 1274, there is even less reason to believe that one of them was called "the spiritual Franciscans." Nevertheless, it is not that simple. While the term may not have been applied to a distinct faction, it was nevertheless used in a way that would affect its later application.

The word itself played a role in Franciscan tradition almost from the beginning. The 1223 rule told brothers what to do when they found that they could not observe the rule "spiritually."[100] Later, the phrase "spiritual man" was widely used to describe a holy man.[101] Bonaventure's *Legenda maior* used it in that way, noting that the vision of Francis in the fiery chariot was granted in order to show his companions that they followed the new Elijah established by God to be the chariot and driver of "spiritual men."[102] Salimbene referred to Bartolomeo Guiscolo as a "courtly and spiritual man"; to Hugh of Digne as "an unusually spiritual man" and as a "good and spiritual man"; and to Hugh and John of Parma as "great scholars [*clerici*] and spiritual men."[103]

So far the word implies holiness. One might observe at this point, though, that Bonaventure's portrayal of Francis in the *Legenda maior* had strong apocalyptic overtones; that Bartholomew, Hugh, and John were all described by Salimbene as great Joachites; and that Salimbene himself, though he claimed to have renounced Joachism after Frederick II died before his predicted time and the year 1260 passed without apocalyptic incident, was really never more than a recovering Joachite.[104] That brings us to another important source for the term *spiritualis:* Joachim of Fiore. In Joachite rhetoric, the "spiritual church" (*ecclesia spiritualis*) of the third age is guided by "spiritual men" (*viri spirituales*). The pseudo-Joachim commentary on Jeremiah, which had a strong impact on early Franciscan Joachites, accuses prelates of withholding their prayers from "preachers of the truth and spiritual men."[105] Thus one might ask whether the word "spiritual," though used in very un-Joachite primitive Franciscan circles, soon acquired Joachite coloration.

Salimbene's use of the term seems to suggest as much. To be sure, he never simply equates the two notions. Bartolomeo Guiscolo is described as "a spiritual man, but also a great Joachite." The pope informs Hugh of Digne, "We have heard that you are a great cleric and a good and spiritual man, but we have also heard that you are the Abbot Joachim's successor in prophecies and a great Joachite." Hugh and John of Parma are described as "great clerics, spiritual men, and the greatest of Joachites."[106] On the other hand, Gerard of Borgo San Donnino, whose obstinacy earned him perpetual imprisonment, is described as a Joachite, an honest man, and even a good man, but not as a spiritual man.[107] In a brief discourse on I Cor. 12:7–11, Salimbene distinguishes between that which is acquired naturally and that which is infused through the Spirit. Later he quotes the pope as courteously informing Hugh of Digne that the Spirit itself has informed the sustained extemporaneous broadside Hugh has just delivered against the cardinals, a sentiment the cardinals themselves may have had trouble sharing.[108] Thus Hugh is termed "spiritual" because the Holy Spirit moves mightily in him, not because he is a Joachite.

Nevertheless, it is noteworthy that Salimbene, in his disquisition on I Cor. 12, mentions Joachim's illumination when describing the gift of knowledge through the Spirit. It is equally noteworthy that, as Jacques Paul has observed, Salimbene's rare uses of the term "spiritual" are normally applied to those whom he also describes as Joachites.[109] When he speaks of Hugh's four great friends, only the Joachite John of Parma is described as spiritual. The archbishop of Vienne is labeled a holy, literate, honest man, while Robert Grosseteste and Adam Marsh are simply great clerics.[110] Thus, while Salimbene does not equate the two ideas, they do seem to be connected in his mind.

The point is that even before there was a definable spiritual Franciscan faction within the order, the word "spiritual" was accruing certain associations that would mark its later use and to some extent define the later spirituals. It suggested someone who was not merely pious in the conventional sense, but also in a way that put him in close relation to God. It suggested someone with contemplative tendencies and perhaps visionary or apocalyptic tendencies as well. It suggested someone zealous about observing the rule. At least in the case of the Jeremiah commentary, it designated a small group of true Christians who would weather indifference and even persecution by the hierarchy and eventually triumph.

All of this seems to have remained gloriously unfocused before 1274. From that point on, events would ensure a clearer definition of issues and factions.

THREE

THE BIRTH OF THE USUS PAUPER CONTROVERSY
1274–1290

HOWEVER UNCERTAIN THE SITUATION might appear up to this point, once we move beyond Bonaventure's generalate, we seem to enter a new world. Suddenly we have some hope of identifying battles with definable issues and contestants. Our use of the plural is justified. There were a variety of battles, though in the period under consideration they gradually began to merge.

Ancona, 1274–1290

The March of Ancona already had produced its share of discontented minorities. A particularly active one had given Crescentius of Iesi trouble when he was provincial minister there. Later, Ancona provided the order with James of Massa and his vision of a taloned Bonaventure attacking John of Parma. In 1274 it witnessed the beginning of yet another battle that was destined to have serious reverberations. Angelo Clareno, this time speaking from personal experience,[1] informs us that in that year a rumor spread through the March that the pope, in consultation with the general council then meeting at Lyons, was about to make the Franciscans accept property. The story was false, but it produced a major theoretical row over whether one should obey one's vows or the pope when the two seemed at odds. Those who favored obedience to the pope were in the majority and, at the first provincial chapter after the council, they threatened the others with punishment as schismatics and heretics if they refused to renounce their view. By that point it was obvious that the entire dispute was over an event that had not occurred, so most of those faced with the choice decided there was little point in refusing compliance. Three held fast, however. One was Thomas of Tolentino, who would later die a martyr's death at Tana. Another, Peter of Macerata, would eventually become leader of the dissident Anconan faction. The third, a Traimondo or Raimondo, plays a walk-on part in history, since he is known only for his role in this debate.

The three intransigent brethren were condemned as schismatics, deprived of their habits, and sent to hermitages; a year later, though, they were summoned and the debate began anew. This time an older, shrewder brother who sympathized with the dissenters intervened and procured a purely diplomatic solution that saved them for a while. But there was too much at stake for purely diplomatic solutions, because the dispute was branching out to include what would become the major Italian spiritual criticisms of contemporary Franciscanism: establishment of friaries in the heart of the city, heavy involvement in worldly learning, and the relentless pursuit of burial rights, legacies, and privileges. As controversy dragged on and civility declined, neighboring provinces became involved (or at least their ministers did). Five of them met in secret and decided that the proper solution was to frighten the dissidents by condemning their leaders as "schismatics, heretics and destroyers of the order." At the next provincial chapter meeting it was done. The original three "and some others," including Angelo,[2] were sentenced to perpetual imprisonment.

Thus speaks Angelo, and we can provide no check on his report. That seems a shame, because he leaves us with some questions. Not least of these arises from the fact that the events he describes—though they happened to him personally—occurred close to a half-century earlier. Anyone who has reached sixty should recognize that the youth we recall by that age is less historical fact than an artfully constructed myth that supports our image of ourselves. The problem is not so much untruth as selectivity and arrangement. Such is probably the case here. Angelo is remembering a youth that fits the rest of his story as he understands it.

That is not the only problem, though. There is, for example, a chronological haziness about his narrative that makes it impossible to say when the putative life sentences actually began, although it would be hard to place their commencement before 1278.[3] The geographical extent of the problem is equally unclear. If five ministers met and decided on the action to be taken, that seems to imply that the dissident views had gained a foothold outside Ancona; yet, when the condemnation occurred, it took place in a provincial chapter meeting and the only people mentioned by name are the same ones cited earlier. Finally, there is the matter of just how illegal the whole proceeding was. Here the problem is not so much Angelo's unclarity as his clarity. He asserts that the five ministers decided that the dissident leaders should be condemned without trial; that no particular crime was mentioned in their sentence; and that they were convicted of "defying all order of divine or human law." If anyone dared to say that the sentence was unjust, he was to be treated to the same sentence. In fact, when one brother said as much, he was imprisoned and languished in irons until he died. Then they threw him in a ditch and covered him up to hide his fate from the laity. Angelo makes Ancona sound like Stalinist Russia. Were things really that bad?

At any rate, help arrived in 1290 in the form of a new minister general, Raymond Geoffroi, of whom we will soon hear more. Angelo tells us that Raymond became familiar with the case when he came to Ancona during general visitation. Finding no crime specified in the sentence, he asked the reason for the brothers' imprisonment and was informed that it was excessive zeal in the observance of poverty. Raymond expressed his wish that the whole order could be found guilty of that crime and ordered them released. Nevertheless, recognizing that the group might still be less than fully appreciated by their Anconan leaders, he sent them off to Armenia where, according to Angelo, they worked productively until forced back to Italy by the hostility of other Franciscans in the area.[4]

The Anconan conflict of the 1270s is an important milestone in the rise of the spiritual Franciscans, if only because it marks the appearance of Angelo Clareno as a performer in the drama. He was still Pietro da Fossombrone at that stage, and not yet a leader when the conflict began;[5] he would eventually become not only one of the three great spirituals but also one of the major sources read by historians when they try to make sense of the spiritual Franciscans. The most important question for the moment, though, is whether the group persecuted in the 1270s represented a few complainers or a significant movement. Angelo says the dissidents were considered dangerous precisely because their enemies saw that they were gaining adherents and feared that they would eventually be strong enough to set policy. Certainly the meeting of those five provincial ministers implies some degree of notoriety. However, there is no evidence that the five were trying to halt a rigorist move- ment already spreading throughout Italy. One might just as easily conclude that they were considering how the province of Ancona should put its house in order, and the fact that the resultant action is described as taking place on a provincial level makes this possibility even more attractive.[6]

Ubertino da Casale's Formation

Whatever those provincial ministers may have seen as problematic, the move- ment really *was* growing elsewhere in Italy. In 1273, one year before the argu- ment over the Council of Lyons, Ubertino da Casale had entered the order, apparently at the age of fourteen.[7] Casale is in the diocese of Vercelli in north- western Italy, and there is good reason to believe that his early years as a Franciscan were spent in the province of Genoa.[8] Ubertino describes these years as filled with intense spiritual searching—in fact, intense spiritual disci- pline. He makes no effort to identify his original influences, but it seems likely that such influences existed, which would imply a climate at least somewhat favorable to rigorist aims within his home province. Ubertino felt, however, that his early spiritual exercises allowed him to grasp merely the external events of Christ's life, and it was only later that he was able to enter into the per- fections of his heart and inner suffering.[9]

Ubertino studied at Paris for nine years, but did not think that he prof- ited from it. On the contrary, he saw it as deleterious to his spiritual health, and his *Arbor vitae* echoes the pervasive Italian spiritual distrust of education by citing with approval the story of how Brother Giles ridiculed scholarly pre- tensions.[10] The more puzzling question is *when* he was at Paris. What we know of his life suggests that it had to be either ca. 1274–83 or ca. 1289–98. The earlier period is not impossible, but most scholars now favor the latter one.[11]

If we take the latter alternative, then when Ubertino tells us he spent around fourteen years in his "first exercises," he is describing a period spent entirely in Italy. The next stage of his spiritual progress thus occurred in the second half of the 1280s. By that point Ubertino was in central Italy, where he vis- ited the Portiuncula and Greccio. The latter stop was important: there he met and talked at length with the elderly John of Parma, who by then had been at Greccio for nearly a quarter-century. Ubertino's description of this visit, penned two decades later in the *Arbor vitae*, is redolent with spiritual Franciscan motifs. He depicts himself as telling John that he did not know whom to follow, "because leaders of both church and order not only practiced a relaxed life themselves but imposed it on others." John replied with a prophecy, assuring Ubertino that within four years God would show him whom to follow. He accompanied that prediction with an apocalyptic scenario, announcing that the opening of the sixth seal described in Rev. 7:2 had begun with Francis and that tribulation was destined to follow.[12]

John's prophecy was fulfilled when, within four years, Ubertino received word that John had died and immediately, "as if a lance had entered my heart," all that John had said at Greccio came rushing back into his mind. It was as if John was presenting himself to Ubertino, saying, "Behold him whom you should follow."[13] If we accept that John died in 1289, then Ubertino's announcement that he saw John four years before that places the meeting in 1285.

In fact, within four years God offered Ubertino a whole series of guides. Arriving at Florence, he met Petrus Iohannis Olivi, who had come as a lector at Santa Croce in 1287. Ubertino would have two years of exposure to Olivi, and in that period he became a disciple. His encapsulated description in the *Arbor vitae* of just what Olivi taught him says a great deal about their relationship: "In a short time he introduced me to high perfections of the soul of the beloved Jesus and his most beloved mother and to the profundities of scripture and deep matters concerning the third age of the world and renewal of the Christian life."[14] The latter part of the sentence is straightforward enough. Ubertino adopted Olivi's essentially Joachite historical perspective and came to see the present period as one of renewal, the beginning of the third age. The former part of the sentence is easier to ignore but also important. Ubertino describes his spiritual development during those years as a personal appropriation of Christ's inner life and suffering. Olivi was one of his spiritual directors in this process. "He taught me," Ubertino says, "always to feel myself crucified with Jesus in mind and body." Nevertheless, despite his debt to Olivi, Ubertino is determined to leave some distance between them. He emphasizes that Christ was leading the way, teaching him from within whatever lessons Olivi was imparting in an external sense. And he bluntly asserts that he does not follow Olivi in all things, "because even the good Homer sometimes slept, nor are all things given to all people." As we will see, this assertion of independence speaks directly to the climate in 1305, when the *Arbor vitae* was written; that said, we can probably also take it as an accurate description of Ubertino's reaction in 1287. He was in some respects quite different from Olivi. The differences would become clear two decades later at Vienne and Avignon, but even at Florence they were probably discernible. Olivi was an intellectual in a sense that Ubertino was not. (Ubertino's description of Olivi as *doctor speculativus* fits the latter well, but it is hardly a name that anyone would seriously apply to Ubertino himself.) Moreover, in 1309–12, when he was defending the spirituals at Vienne and Avignon, Ubertino rejected a great deal more of thirteenth-century Franciscan development than Olivi ever had—and the *Arbor vitae* shows us that he rejected it even by 1305. While it is impossible to get behind the *Arbor vitae* and see the young Ubertino as he was in 1287, it is conceivable that he had begun to reject it then as well. One would give a great deal to be transported back to Santa Croce long enough to hear Olivi and Ubertino discussing Franciscan history.

It was also in central Italy that he cultivated acquaintances with a series of contemplatives, including Margaret of Cortona, Cecilia of Florence, Angela of Foligno, Clare of Montefalco, Margaret of Città di Castello, and the saintly comb-seller Pier Pettinaio. When he met these people is another matter. If we assume that he went to Paris for nine years when he finished at Florence, then his contacts with Margaret of Cortona must date back at least to the 1280s, since she died in 1297.[15] The same goes for Pier Pettinaio, who died in 1289,[16] and Cecilia of Florence, who moved within the Santa Croce orbit while Ubertino was there.[17] Margaret of Città di Castello, on the other hand, was born around the time Ubertino arrived in Florence and was a much later acquaintance.[18]

Clare of Montefalco and Angela of Foligno, who died in 1308 and 1309 respectively, are harder to locate within Ubertino's biography—but there is no reason to think that he knew either before his putative return from Paris around 1298. In Angela's case, he explicitly says that she came to his attention "in the twenty-fifth year of my state," by which he obviously means his time in the order, therefore ca. 1298.[19] We will return to these matters in the Appendix.

One other thing might be mentioned about Ubertino: he repeatedly alludes to a gap between his ideals and his concrete behavior during these years, and he says that it was obvious to others as well. He says this so insistently that we ought to take him seriously, as his later opponents at Vienne and Avignon certainly did when they accused him of adopting a lifestyle at variance with his spiritual Franciscan pretensions and of having been disciplined for a lapse of the flesh.

When we ask ourselves precisely what sort of depravity Ubertino favored, however, we have a harder time making sense of his confession. Certainly there are hints of sexual incontinence, but nothing overt, nothing carried into action. He comes closest to listing his misdeeds when he says that those who heard him preach poverty knew that he himself enjoyed an ample supply of "tunics, books, food, temporal things and vain honors."[20] We will hear similar charges directed at Ubertino later from his opponents at Vienne.

Common Links

Obviously, by 1289, a spiritual movement was taking shape in Italy. There is no evidence that any except the Anconan rigorists were persecuted in the 1270s and 1280s, but Ubertino's adventures demonstrate that salient features of the movement were discernible elsewhere. These included the feeling that Franciscan leaders were impeding observance rather than demanding it; apocalyptic speculation (including the assertion of a role for Francis and of decline in the order); and cultivation of the contemplative life. The apocalyptic speculation was not necessarily Joachite, although Ubertino's certainly was. In 1285 he received apocalyptic instruction directly from one of Salimbene's great Joachites, John of Parma, and then in 1287–89 he improved his knowledge by listening to Olivi, another great Joachite unfortunately unknown to Salimbene. We first encounter Ubertino's apocalyptic views in the *Arbor vitae*, written in 1305, and there is much in that work that he could not have believed in 1273–89, since it reflects later writings and events. Yet we have every reason to believe that the main lines of Ubertino's Joachism were established by the early 1290s.

Angelo presents a somewhat different picture. The expectation he projects backward in describing his conversation with James of Massa (and in citing other prophecies of the pre-1274 period) is not particularly redolent of Joachim, but consists rather of prophecies concerning the decay and rebirth of Franciscan observance placed in the mouths of Francis and other visionary friars. We will encounter the same pattern later in Angelo's letters, and it suggests another element that did unite him with Ubertino: if Joachim was not a strong connecting link between them, Brother Leo was. Both men were heavily informed by a line of tradition purportedly running from Francis through Leo, then through Conrad of Offida and others who mediated these prophecies to Angelo's and Ubertino's generation. These prophecies assured zealots that Francis had foreseen not only the corruption of his order but also its eventual repair. Ubertino and Angelo both give the impression that almost from the beginning they had had a lively desire to talk with early Franciscans and with those who had known them, and that their interest in the Francis prophecies was a very early part of their formation.

Closely related to this interest in a continuing oral tradition is the common Italian interest in Francis's *Testament* as an authoritative document. Here again we can speak of what Angelo and Ubertino were thinking in the thirteenth century only by identifying it with what they wrote in the fourteenth, but if that identification is valid (and there is every reason to believe that it is), we can say that from the beginning the Italian zealots wanted to supplement the rule with a sense of Francis's original intention—derived from authorities like the *Testament*, the Leo sources, and the oral tradition that preserved the memories of those who had known him.

The contemplative element is also important, though here again it took slightly different form in Angelo and Ubertino. Angelo's ideal seems to have been more eremitical in nature, and would remain that way throughout his life. Ubertino was hardly a stranger to the eremitical life. He visited John at Greccio and later spent some time on Mount Alverna, yet he remained more involved with the world around him.

Southern France, 1279–1289

While Angelo was being criticized and then imprisoned in Ancona, another sort of poverty controversy was developing in southern France. The principal participant there was Petrus Iohannis Olivi,[21] a very different brand of reformer than Angelo. Born in Sérignan, near Béziers, Olivi had entered the order around 1259 or 1260 at the age of twelve. After studying theology in Paris in the 1260s, he was back in southern France by the mid-1270s functioning as a lector. He never became a master, probably due to lingering doubts concerning his orthodoxy. From the beginning, his thought was seen as original and slightly dangerous. Angelo Clareno tells us that Jerome of Ascoli, who was minister general from 1274 to 1279, asked to see some controversial questions on the Virgin Mary that Olivi had written and, after examining them, ordered them burned. Angelo's story is corroborated by other sources, and Olivi himself suggests that Jerome was interested in more writings than the questions on the Virgin.[22]

None of this attention proved fatal, however. Olivi continued to teach, write, and gain a significant reputation at least in his own province. In 1279 he was asked by his provincial minister to contribute a position paper in connection with the deliberations that led up to the bull *Exiit qui seminat*, a major papal statement on Franciscan poverty. He tells us that he was in Rome at the time.[23] During this trip to Italy he apparently met Conrad of Offida and perhaps other Italian zealots as well. When he returned to France he brought with him certain elements of the Leo prophecies. These would echo through his work to the end of his life—although they never played as great a role in his thought as other influences, such as Joachim and Bonaventure, and they were never as important to Olivi as they would be to Angelo and Ubertino.[24]

Common Links

Obviously, by 1289, a spiritual movement was taking shape in Italy. There is no evidence that any except the Anconan rigorists were persecuted in the 1270s and 1280s, but Ubertino's adventures demonstrate that salient features of the movement were discernible elsewhere. These included the feeling that Franciscan leaders were impeding observance rather than demanding it; apocalyptic speculation (including the assertion of a role for Francis and of decline in the order); and cultivation of the contemplative life. The apocalyptic speculation was not necessarily Joachite, although Ubertino's certainly was. In 1285 he received apocalyptic instruction directly from one of Salimbene's great Joachites, John of Parma, and then in 1287–89 he improved his knowledge by listening to Olivi, another great Joachite unfortunately unknown to Salimbene. We first encounter Ubertino's apocalyptic views in the *Arbor vitae*, written in 1305, and there is much in that work that he could not have believed in 1273–89, since it reflects later writings and events. Yet we have every reason to believe that the main lines of Ubertino's Joachism were established by the early 1290s.

Angelo presents a somewhat different picture. The expectation he projects backward in describing his conversation with James of Massa (and in citing other prophecies of the pre-1274 period) is not particularly redolent of Joachim, but consists rather of prophecies concerning the decay and rebirth of Franciscan observance placed in the mouths of Francis and other visionary friars. We will encounter the same pattern later in Angelo's letters, and it suggests another element that did unite him with Ubertino: if Joachim was not a strong connecting link between them, Brother Leo was. Both men were heavily informed by a line of tradition purportedly running from Francis through Leo, then through Conrad of Offida and others who mediated these prophecies to Angelo's and Ubertino's generation. These prophecies assured zealots that Francis had foreseen not only the corruption of his order but also its eventual repair. Ubertino and Angelo both give the impression that almost from the beginning they had had a lively desire to talk with early Franciscans and with those who had known them, and that their interest in the Francis prophecies was a very early part of their formation.

Closely related to this interest in a continuing oral tradition is the common Italian interest in Francis's *Testament* as an authoritative document. Here again we can speak of what Angelo and Ubertino were thinking in the thirteenth century only by identifying it with what they wrote in the fourteenth, but if that identification is valid (and there is every reason to believe that it is), we but if he makes an honest attempt to stay on the path and do the best he can, he need not worry about straying across the line at which *pauper* becomes *dives* and venial becomes mortal.

Once the real difference between Olivi and his opponents becomes apparent, it is difficult not to see Olivi's view as simultaneously more realistic, more adventurous, and more faithful to the original Franciscan spirit. For Olivi (as for Francis), the vow is not so much a contract concerning specific behavior as the beginning of a spiritual quest. That quest may engender some uncertainty and anxiety, but these are the inevitable concomitants of challenge and excitement.

Words like "adventurous" should not obscure the prudential element in Olivi's argument. If, like Bonaventure before him, he feels that the definition of necessity will vary with the circumstances, he is also like Bonaventure in feeling that the circumstances in question are largely those in which the order currently finds itself, those dictated by the mission it has been asked to accomplish. The Franciscans are engaged in teaching, and thus they should have books—in fact, a great many of them, since there are many things to be learned. Olivi acknowledges that, in view of this fact, it is difficult to draw the line between necessity and excess, although perhaps it can be said that books should not be too ornate, nor should the friars have multiple copies of the same work.[27]

Olivi's view of gardens is equally revealing. He arrives at the subject in the course of defining what he means by present necessity.[28] He warns that there is a difference between saying that a thing is necessary *at* the present time and saying that it is necessary *for* the present time. Some things are not necessary for the present moment, but must be procured at present because they will be needed in the future. Bread and wine are readily available, however, and thus there is no reason for the friars to store large quantities of them for the future. Legumes and oil can be harder to find at short notice and thus they can be conserved with a clearer conscience. At this point, Olivi arrives at vegetables and herbs. These are, he says, hard to procure in the necessary quantities without planting a garden, and so the friars can maintain such gardens without violating *usus pauper*.

Now comes an interesting leap in his thought, one that shows how far he was willing to go in accepting the order as it had evolved. "No one doubts," he remarks, "that such gardens are necessary, especially in the case of a cloistered group [*collegii claustralis*], for it is entirely fitting that such groups, to preserve freedom of the spirit and health of the body, should have some open space around their buildings, and gardens can serve that purpose."[29] Olivi has jumped from vegetable gardens to something quite different, something more in line with what we mean when we speak of recreational or pleasure gardens. Remember that by "cloistered group" he is really referring to the Franciscans, and that he is envisaging the present situation in which Franciscan houses were complexes located within the towns. Adding a garden to such a complex would increase its size significantly. This passage should be kept in mind when we arrive at Ubertino da Casale's 1310–12 critique of the order and its building practices.

However moderate Olivi's view of *usus pauper* might seem to us, the commission of seven rejected it. Why they did so is unclear. In fact, they did not even manage to clarify what aspect of his view they were rejecting. Olivi himself was confused. In a 1285 letter to the commission, he attempted to defend his views, and he pointed to the ambiguity of their comments. It was, he observed, impossible to say whether they were denying that the vow entailed *usus pauper* as he defined it or *usus pauper* in any sense whatsoever. One might assume that their rationale was similar to the one just identified with Olivi's opponents, but there is no reason to assume as much, as they had a very different option available to them.

In order to explore that option, we must say something about the concrete situation of the order in Olivi's time. The commission of seven may have taken Olivi's position on *usus pauper* to be not merely theoretically incorrect or spiritually disquieting but also politically imprudent. They approached their task fully aware that the question of whether the Franciscan vow was inherently dangerous constituted one element in a long history of conflict with secular critics and eventually with their fellow mendicants, the Dominicans. On a relatively simple level, the question was whether Franciscans, in renouncing all possessions and regular income, needlessly placed themselves in physical jeopardy, yet there was a subtler form of the accusation that became a part of the so-called *correctorium* controversy. That controversy is normally seen as beginning with the Franciscan William de la Mare's critique of Thomas Aquinas, the *Correctorium fratris Thomae* (hence the name of the controversy), but on some issues it might be said to have begun with Aquinas himself. In the *Correctorium*, written before August 1279 (the date of *Exiit qui seminat*), William takes issue with two statements by Aquinas. In one, taken from the *Summa theologiae*, Thomas asks whether someone who takes a vow sins mortally in transgressing against anything contained in it. He decides that those who profess a rule do not vow to observe everything in it, but rather vow the regular life consisting of poverty, chastity, and obedience. Some orders are more prudent than others: they vow not to observe the rule but to live according to it. The rule becomes an exemplar after which they can pattern their lives. Other orders are even more prudent, and vow obedience according to the rule. In this case, only what is against the precept of the rule constitutes a mortal sin; all other transgressions or omissions are venial. "In one religion, however, namely the order of Preaching Brothers, such transgressions or omissions [against anything other than a precept] do not by their nature entail either mortal or venial guilt, but only that one should sustain the punishment meted out."[30]

In the other passage, this time taken from his *Quodlibeta*, Thomas asks whether one who intends to vow everything in the rule sins mortally in transgressing any part of it. He asserts that, since transgression of a vow entails mortal sin, anyone who vows to obey everything in the rule places himself *in laqueum peccati mortalis*, "in the snare of mortal sin." Thomas also notes that anyone who vows to observe the rule apparently obliges himself to obey everything in it, and thus exposes himself to precisely that danger. Thus the *sancti*, when they instituted orders, saved people from the snares of damnation by requiring them to promise obedience according to the rule—not observance of the rule.[31]

Obviously Thomas was quietly congratulating his own order, but he was doing so at Franciscan expense, since the Franciscan vowed "to observe the rule throughout my whole life."[32] Moreover, the Franciscan rule itself spoke of "promising . . . to observe the rule" and announced that "the rule and life of the friars minor is . . . to observe the holy gospel."[33] Thus Franciscans were apparently required to observe not merely everything written in the rule, but also everything found in the gospels.

William's *Correctorium* attempts to show that the Franciscan vow is more limited. He argues that anyone professing a rule should intend to conform himself with it according to the intention of the author, and no author intends to produce a rule that binds vowers to all its parts equally. This much is particularly obvious in the case of the Franciscan rule, which distinguishes between precepts and admonitions. The Franciscan, in vowing to obey the gospel, merely binds himself to obey those parts of it that are expressed in the rule *praeceptorie vel inhibitorie*, "in the manner of a precept or prohibition."[34]

William's reply was hardly novel. He was quite aware that he was facing an old problem and that his solution to it had been anticipated in previous papal bulls.[35] In fact, it was about to be confirmed by yet another. In May 1279, Pope Nicholas III asked the Franciscan general chapter at Assisi what he could do for the order. The result was *Exiit qui seminat*, promulgated in August of that year. One Franciscan source announces that *Exiit* was promulgated "to settle questions about the rule and to curb certain attackers who were springing and snapping at it," while the bull itself refers to those who "snap at the brothers and tear at their rule with doggy barks."[36] All of this canine imagery tends to evoke the "hounds of the Lord," the *domini canes*—a bad pun on the Dominicans' name that had enough currency to be translated into visual imagery in the Spanish Chapel of Santa Maria Novella in Florence during the fourteenth century. Nicholas certainly had the Dominicans in mind in *Exiit qui seminat*,[37] although the defense offered there extended beyond them to parry secular attacks as well.

Exiit directly confronts the problem of the Franciscan vow as *laqueus* by acknowledging that it "might seem to ensnare the soul of the vower," since a promise to observe the gospel, taken absolutely, could not be kept.[38] Nicholas then assures his readers that it is to be taken *not* absolutely, but according to Francis's intention. In his rule, some evangelical counsels are, in effect, promoted to the status of precepts because they are demanded *praeceptorie vel inhibitorie* or by equivalent expressions. Other counsels remain counsels because they are merely recommended through words of admonition, exhortation, and advice. The Franciscan is more committed to pursue these counsels than the average Christian would be, but is not constrained to pursue them as he is the precepts.[39]

If Nicholas's solution was not original, it did make one important addition. Whereas previous popes had spoken of what was demanded *praeceptorie vel inhibitorie*, Nicholas referred to that which was demanded *praeceptorie vel inhibitorie, seu sub verbis aequipollentibus*, "by precept, prohibition or equivalent words." His phraseology reflects a new sophistication growing out of the debate itself. Like Olivi, Nicholas was aware that if Franciscans were constrained by precept only to that which was enjoined in the rule through explicit commands like *praecipio* or *teneantur*, some of the most central elements in the Franciscan life would disappear—or at least be reduced to the status of counsels. Having noted this fact, however, Nicholas and Olivi drew very different conclusions from it. Olivi used it to reject the notion that the vow bound the Franciscan by precept to do a series of things specifically demanded in the rule. Nicholas, on the other hand, accepted that notion but also added his category of "equivalent words" in order to include more things. His solution created an ambiguity that Clement V would address three decades later at the Council of Vienne.

Olivi had fired his opening salvos in the *usus pauper* controversy slightly before the appearance of *Exiit*, but he delivered another shortly thereafter.[40] This one, aimed at Aquinas and echoing William de la Mare, actually did double service as an installment in both the *usus pauper* and *correctorium* controversies. In it, Olivi follows William in arguing that no legislator binds his subjects to all elements of his law equally, but then adopts a strikingly different criterion for determining the differences. Whereas William, like Nicholas, argues that the rule itself makes the distinction because it demands some things *prae-ceptorie* and merely counsels others, Olivi talks about degrees of obligation based on a hierarchy of ends. The supreme end of all rules is the *cultus dei*, worship of God. Training of the soul and spiritual union with Christ and one's confreres constitute penultimate goals. Below this level are external acts of poverty and chastity, and lower still are things like clothing, fasting, and silence. What, then, should we take as binding the Franciscan by precept? Not only those passages of the rule in which the words *praecipio* and *teneantur* are used, but all those things that are necessary to the substantial integrity of the Franciscan life.

Within the category of precept, Olivi draws his usual distinction between those proffered precisely, which cannot be violated without mortal sin, and those given indeterminately, violation of which is mortal only if the offense is great. How does one know when the offense is great? Olivi invites the reader to consult his earlier comments on the matter. How can one know what is precept and what is counsel? It is hard, Olivi says, but at least we can be sure that we are dealing with counsels when we encounter words like *consulo* or *moneo*.[41]

The main thing to note here is that in 1279, Franciscans were facing three distinct views of *usus pauper* and the vow. According to Olivi's opponents, restricted use was so important that the Franciscan life was worth little without it, but it was nonetheless not an essential part of the vow, as it was not specifically demanded by some word like *praecipio*. Moreover, because there would be no way of determining the point at which it was violated—and because any violation of a vow entailed mortal sin—its inclusion in the vow would mean constant spiritual danger and anxiety. Olivi, on the other hand, was arguing that the Franciscan indeed vowed *usus pauper,* but indeterminately. He was also refusing to accept the notion that every violation of the vow entailed mortal sin.

However desperately Olivi and his opponents tried to claim Nicholas III's support, neither of them really agreed with *Exiit qui seminat.* Nicholas agreed with Olivi's opponents in seeing the rule as a collection of specific precepts and counsels. To this extent, both he and they moved within a continuing tradition developed in earlier papal declarations and Franciscan polemics. Nevertheless, Nicholas apparently agreed with Olivi in assuming that Franciscans were bound by precept to restricted use. He never spelled this point out clearly enough to offer the sort of help Olivi needed, but that is partly because he wrote *Exiit* with other issues in mind. He was responding partly to the charge that the Franciscan vow was dangerous, endangering one's health. Thus he argued forcefully that it did not prevent Franciscans from using whatever was necessary, or even from procuring now what would be necessary in the immediate future. It does not seem to have occurred to him that he might have to address the opposite view, an argument within the order that the vow did not in fact limit use to what was necessary—indeed, that it did not limit use at all. Olivi's problems with Nicholas as an authority were remarkably similar to his problems with previous apologists for Franciscan poverty like Bonaventure and John Pecham. One gets the impression that he was essentially right in citing them, since they would happily have supported his insistence that restricted use was an essential part of the vow; yet here, too, he was dealing with people who never quite said it clearly enough, since they were not writing with the *usus pauper* controversy in mind.[42]

If neither Olivi nor his opponents were entirely at one with *Exiit*, we might ask why it was Olivi alone who underwent censure in 1283. There is ultimately no secure answer to this question, although we can always speculate.[43] Politics and personalities undoubtedly played a role that we will never completely understand. So did the ongoing struggle with the Dominicans. It would be understandable if the commission of seven thought Olivi's reformulation of the problem compromised the gains made by the order through *Exiit qui seminat* by reopening the vow to the charge of being a snare of damnation. Moreover, practical defensive considerations aside, one can understand how the commission itself might have seen Olivi's view as spiritually dangerous. Olivi was more able to live with ambiguity than most of his contemporaries (or, in fact, most people in any age), and thus could live more comfortably with the idea of indeterminate vows than the commission could.

That may explain why the commission censured Olivi's position, but it still sheds no light on why his opponents emerged unscathed. After all, if Olivi's presentation of their view can be trusted, they were divorcing *usus pauper* from the vow and thus splitting asunder what Nicholas III had joined together. Why were they not censured? One could answer that things turned out as they did because along the way the whole affair had turned into an investigation of Olivi's suspect opinions, not a referendum on the nature of *usus pauper*. The commission's task was to decide on the former, not the latter. Nevertheless, it is possible that even if the commission *had* been asked to pronounce on the latter, it would have found little to criticize in Olivi's opponents. By the early fourteenth century (as we will see), leaders of the order had, in effect, implicitly rejected both Olivi and *Exiit* by denying that friars vowed *usus pauper*. The 1283 commission report could be interpreted as a step on the way to that rejection, although their censure of Olivi's view is so vaguely worded as to leave some doubt.

So far we have managed to discuss the reasons for Olivi's censure without ever invoking what casual observers normally have assumed to be the underlying issue: that Olivi, who wanted strict observance of the rule, was crushed by those who preferred laxity. Clearly it was not that simple. Despite their theoretical differences, Olivi and his opponents both said that Franciscans should practice *usus pauper*. Olivi quotes his opponents as saying that "even if [lavish] use of possessions is not directly against the vow or precept of the rule, it is nevertheless against its intention," and as granting *usus pauper* to be "so perfect, useful and, as it were, necessary for the avoidance of vice that the profession of poverty has little or no value without it."[44] Moreover, at one point, Olivi himself seems to accept a major element in his opponents' argument, granting that only lack of property can be considered "poverty itself, or its radical part."[45] Thus, on a theoretical level, the line between their positions seems razor-thin.

Nevertheless, in time—and perhaps even at the beginning—the argument included some defense of current laxity on the part of Olivi's opponents and an attack on that laxity by Olivi himself. If the chronology I offered in an earlier work is correct,[46] this element grew along with the controversy. The *Tractatus de usu paupere* displays it most strongly. It is there that we find Olivi citing his opponents' praise of *usus pauper*, and he treats it there as a bit of camouflage applied to avoid scandalizing others. He claims that they say it "to twist their words and cover themselves with the cloak of deception," and do so "lest they be taxed with contempt for *usus pauper* or with support for laxity." He also depicts his opponents as arguing that *usus pauper* could not be an essential part of the vow, because "today the Friars Minor eat and drink well, frequently dress well, and have big, beautiful dwellings, yet the pope has confirmed their status anyway," and because "Bonaventure and others who wrote about these matters lived very laxly."[47] Olivi replies that the pope has confirmed the rule and vow as it should be observed, not the many violations of it currently seen in the order. He quotes a letter to the order by Bonagratia, the current minister general, in which he reports the pope's threat of punitive action if the order does not improve its performance. As for Bonaventure's purported laxity, Olivi is clearly appalled.

> It was hitherto customary to cite pious men as examples of perfection; yet today, alas, they are cited as examples of laxity by these people, thus at one stroke wounding the men by their accusations, mutilating themselves by the example they draw from it, and infusing poisoned doctrine into others. I say, therefore, what I know of

the aforesaid father. He was of the best and most pious inner disposition, and in his words he always endorsed whatever is consistent
with perfect purity, as is clear from what has been said above; yet he
had a frail body and was perhaps a bit self-indulgent in this respect,
as I often heard him humbly confess. For he was not greater than the
apostle, who said, "We all offend in many things." Nevertheless, he
so grieved at the widespread laxity of this age that in Paris, in full
chapter with me present, he said there was no time since he became
minister general when he would not have consented to be ground to
dust if it would help the order to reach the purity of Saint Francis and
his companions, which Francis indeed intended his order to attain.
Thus the holy man was largely if not entirely innocent of these
charges, for he was not among the number of those defending relaxations and assailing the purity of the rule, nor among the number of
those who seem to enjoy wallowing in the aforesaid impurities. On
the contrary, if he shared any of them he did so with sorrow and
lamentation. Such defects, I believe, are not to be considered mortal
sins unless, all circumstances considered, they are very great.[48]

The statement is characteristic in a number of ways, two of them worth
emphasizing here. First, as the final sentence makes clear, Olivi is presenting
Bonaventure as a demonstration model illustrating his notion of indeterminate
vows. Bonaventure could violate the vow as he did without incurring mortal
sin because his general tendency was in the right direction. His sins against
the vow were limited and profoundly regretted. Thus they were venial. Second,
here as elsewhere Olivi shows the extent to which he accepts the order as it
currently stands, the sort of order for which Bonaventure stood. In fact, as his
reference to "what has just been said" implies, he has just finished citing
Bonaventure, Pecham, and others at length in support of his position. He also
has cited papal declarations, particularly *Exiit qui seminat*. Nor is he simply doing
what he believes he must, what he sees as politically required. He really sees
himself as in fundamental agreement with the direction in which Bonaventure,
Pecham, and Nicholas III wanted the order to move. When he criticizes the
order, he feels he is criticizing it for the same abuses they attacked, and he
is largely correct in that assumption.

It is this fundamental acceptance of Bonaventure that makes the reaction
of the 1283 commission so intriguing. They criticized Olivi's view of *usus pauper*, but so vaguely as to leave him (and us) wondering just what they were condemning. Moreover, they went on to censure three other views: his assertion

that Franciscan bishops were bound to *usus pauper;* his criticism of Franciscan involvement in the burial of laymen; and the restrictions he placed on Franciscan control over the procurators who handled their finances for them. To be sure, it is impossible to identify these three censures as a defense of laxity, since in each case the issue was a complex one with a long prehistory and in no case was the commission all that clear as to what it found offensive about Olivi's position.[49] Yet these were nonetheless issues about which the laxer and more zealous brethren were likely to disagree.

In each case their specific objections raise unanswerable questions. On the subject of bishops, Olivi's flexible notion of *usus pauper* allowed him to grant Franciscans a great deal of latitude in pursuing their episcopal tasks. Like Bonaventure, he saw the allowable level of use as varying with the tasks that had to be accomplished. Necessity comes in many forms. Thus, like Bonaventure, Olivi saw no great problem in asserting that a Franciscan bishop remained bound to his vow of poverty, because like Bonaventure he thought that the vow itself provided the flexibility required in such situations.

The commission members may or may not have understood this aspect of Olivi's view. In any case they did not directly attack his denial that bishops could be dispensed from *usus pauper*. Instead they censured his assertion that bishops "are in some way obliged even more than before to observe *usus pauper,*" then censured his statement that there could be no dispensation. The total effect was to leave Olivi (and us) uncertain whether they were denying what Bonaventure affirmed, namely that there could be no dispensation, or simply denying that bishops were obliged *even more than before* and that there could be no dispensation from that extra obligation. To confuse matters even further, in the process they also censured as false a statement that was not even Olivi's—it had been lifted verbatim from John Pecham.

Their reaction to Olivi's comments on burial were equally problematic. They condemned Olivi's argument that, while burying the dead was a spiritual act, it was less so than other acts like baptism and should be avoided if it impeded the performance of these other things. Here again Olivi was not all that far from Bonaventure and others who criticized the order for engaging in internecine warfare with the secular clergy over burial rights and legacies. Here again the commission leaves us absolutely unclear whether it was registering disagreement with Bonaventure or simply attacking some aspect of Olivi's phraseology.

The situation is somewhat different in the case of procurators, the people who served as buffers between the order and financial reality. They were appointed by the pope to receive and dispense money. Olivi never rejected this arrangement: he simply wanted to clarify who appointed and controlled the procurators. He wanted it made plain that the order did not. Here he was quite in line with the general development on the matter up to 1283, but in that year, Pope Martin IV issued yet another statement on the subject which, though not strongly at variance with Olivi's view, went further than he probably would have wished in giving the order control over procurators.[50] Here again, though, the commission was remarkably vague about what it was attacking.

Once Olivi was censured in 1283, his works were confiscated and his career seemed to have come to an abrupt end around the time he passed his thirty-fifth year. Dante may have considered it midway through life, but for Olivi, it was apparently the end of the road, academically speaking. Olivi was a tenacious man, however. In early 1285 he managed to get his hands on the documents needed to compose a polite but remarkably firm defense of his orthodoxy, which he sent to the very commission that had censured him. His case was also discussed at the general chapter held that year. The minister general chosen there, Arlotto da Prato, had been a member of the commission, and he apparently initiated the process that would lead in 1287 to Olivi being given another teaching position by Arlotto's successor as minister general, Matthew of Aquasparta. In that year, Olivi was sent off to Florence, where he served as lector in the convent at Santa Croce until 1289, when he was reassigned to Montpellier, back in his native southern France.

These were prestigious positions, and Olivi's assignment to them says something about the *usus pauper* controversy in the late 1280s. If Olivi was rehabilitated, it was not because he had recanted his former views. His newly granted respectability suggests that, whatever the commission did in 1283, it did not settle the *usus pauper* question definitively. Olivi could continue to offer his view as a minority opinion with relative impunity.

Equally significant is the identity of the minister general who sent him to Montpellier: Raymond Geoffroi, the man who freed Angelo and his colleagues. Raymond was perhaps a personal friend of Olivi, and he was certainly one of the major spokesmen for the spirituals in the early fourteenth century.[51] One cannot deduce from his election as minister general in 1289 that the rigorists were temporarily in control, since he may have been chosen for reasons that had little to do with the poverty issue.[52] Raymond has been identified as the youngest child in a rich and powerful family, that of Burgondion I, viscount of Marseilles. The viscount's family was connected by marriage with the counts of Provence, and this connection in turn bound it, through a complex web of marriage alliances during the thirteenth century, with such major figures as King Louis IX of France, King Henry III of England, Richard of Cornwall, and Charles I, count of Anjou and eventually king of Naples. Raymond's election represented a triumph of sorts not only for the reformist faction but also for the house of Anjou, which had secured the election of a member of its own family, one who had worked for Angevin interests over the preceding three years. Nevertheless, his tenure (like Olivi's teaching posts) is one more indication that the rigorists were hardly in disgrace, and having Raymond as minister general gave them the best opportunity they had experienced in some time to reform the order.

Olivi's 1283 censure is as interesting for what it did not include as for what it did. In a letter to some friends (possibly including Raymond Geoffroi) written just before Easter of 1282 or 1283,[53] Olivi responds to various charges against him. He is responding to a list submitted by his friends. Toward the end of the letter he remarks that, although his comrades have not asked about it, others have criticized him for his interest in visions and prophecy. He then proceeds to defend his essential moderation on these matters, arguing in effect that he accepts visions as valid only if they are commensurate with Christian dogma and supported by the sort of inner authentication of which Augustine spoke in describing his mother. His acceptance of prophecy extends only to general prediction, never insisting that such and such a person will do some precise thing at a specific time. He does hold as certain that the Franciscan order, after being purged by innumerable temptations, will reform divine worship throughout the world. He does not insist, however, that it will come about in any specific manner.[54]

Here we find several of the elements already noted in connection with the Italian zealots. Like Angelo and Ubertino, Olivi had a lively interest in visionary experience and maintained contacts with contemplatives outside the order, male and female alike.[55] He used their visions in striking ways. In his commentary on John he is willing to reinterpret the crucifixion narrative in a way that seems to contradict any sensible reading of the text simply because a contemplative of his acquaintance has informed him that in her visions Christ was stabbed with the spear before he died rather than after. Even more enlightening is his brief dissertation on the nature of prophecy in his Isaiah commentary, in which he explains the prophetic experiences of Daniel and Isaiah by drawing heavily both on Joachim of Fiore's description of his Easter enlightenment and on contemporary visionaries' reports of their own raptures.[56]

This preoccupation with visionary experience is closely related to the second element, apocalyptic speculation. Olivi's interest in the former is partially explained by his belief that he lived in the dawning new age of history, which would be marked by an *intellectus spiritualis* facilitating just that sort of experience.[57] His apocalyptic expectation is strongly Joachite, although he is also influenced by Franciscan tradition, and especially by Bonaventure. In this respect, as in his relationship with mystics outside the order, he resembles Ubertino more than Angelo. Nevertheless, he resembles both inasmuch as the decay and reform of the order lies at the heart of his apocalyptic expectation. We will return to these matters in the next chapter when we examine his Apocalypse commentary, but it is important to recognize that even in the late 1270s and early 1280s his thought had a strongly apocalyptic dimension.

Neither Olivi's visionary nor his apocalyptic interests drew censure in 1283. This remained the case throughout the rest of his life. The same thing could be said about another aspect of his thought that would later prove troublesome: his view of obedience.[58] In the eleventh of his *Questions on Evangelical Perfection*, Olivi defines the limits of obedience.[59] First of all, one should never obey an order that clearly entails sinning. That applies to venial as well as mortal sin. Second, one should never obey if obedience would imperil one's own salvation. Third, one must not obey an order that compromises the purity of evangelical perfection. That is a very big limitation, and a very vague one.

In the fourteenth question of the same work, Olivi argues energetically that the pope cannot absolve from evangelical vows.[60] If he attempts to do so, he should be cut off as a schismatic and a heretic. In the sixteenth question he goes even further.[61] If the pope

> audaciously and pertinaciously wishes to introduce some profane novelty in opposition to the counsels and examples of Christ and the apostles; and in opposition to the testimonies most worthy of belief, the regular statutes, and the examples of the angelic man Francis . . . ; and in subversion of the whole evangelical state; then in this case he would not act as the vicar of Christ but as the noonday devil, and he should by no means be obeyed but rather resisted with all one's powers as Lucifer and the noonday devil.[62]

Olivi was hardly unique in placing limits on even papal authority to absolve from evangelical vows. The problem was discussed by a series of thirteenth-century scholars who came to various conclusions. The particular vow upon which they focused their attention was that of chastity, not poverty, but the basic issue was very much the same.[63] The differences between Olivi and these other scholars are subtler than simple affirmation or denial. First, there is the sheer amount of attention Olivi gives to what should be done if the pope tries to absolve from them anyway. This attention rests partly on a hidden assumption—namely, that the pope actually will do just that—and the assumption proceeds directly from his apocalyptic scenario. Just *when* Olivi decided that the pope would take his place among the enemies of evangelical perfection remains unclear. Certainly he thought so by the end of his life, as we will see in the following chapter. His earlier works are more problematic, never quite stating that notion. Yet much in these early works suggests anxiety on this score. Brian Tierney has argued that Olivi's interest in affirming papal infallibility under certain conditions, far from signaling faith in coming popes, represents a desire to protect sound papal decisions of the past (such as *Exiit qui seminat*) from being reversed by ungodly decisions in the future.[64]

The other thing that made Olivi's thought on obedience potentially explosive is that he combined it with the inclusion of *usus pauper* as a part of the vow. By doing so he insured that the obedience question would become a genuine crisis of conscience by being linked with a live debate within the order. No one would agonize over obedience in connection with the vow of chastity, because leaders of the order were not ordering Franciscans to be unchaste. No one would agonize over poverty if it simply meant lack of possessions, because everyone in the order assumed that Franciscans should have none. If vowing poverty also meant vowing *usus pauper*, however, every Franciscan who felt that his house was run too laxly had to ask himself whether it was run *so* laxly as to demand protest and then disobedience on his part. A number of them eventually decided that the answer was "yes."

Here again we have a part of Olivi's thought that escaped notice in 1283 and remained unnoticed throughout his life. Eventually, though, the issue would become hard to ignore.

FOUR

OPPOSITION IN HIGH PLACES
1290–1309

IN 1290 THINGS SEEMED to be looking up for rigorists throughout the order. Raymond Geoffroi, sympathetic toward advocates of strict observance, was minister general; Angelo and his zealot companions, released from prison in Ancona, were off to Armenia; Olivi, after his rehabilitation and two-year stint in Florence, was back in southern France, apparently in good odor. A number of friars must have imagined that the 1290s would be a period of reform. The decade soon turned into something quite different, however, and what it did become deserves scrutiny, since events of the 1290s continued to exert significant influence over the next two decades.

Disciplinary Action in Southern France

The first sign of trouble came in 1290 itself when Pope Nicholas IV, the first Franciscan pope, wrote Raymond Geoffroi, telling him (as the *Chronicle of the Twenty-Four Generals* explains it) to look into "certain brothers who seemed to introduce schism into the province of Provence, condemning the state of the other brethren and considering themselves to be more spiritual than the others."[1] The word "spiritual" is intriguing, since it suggests that a party label had emerged. It is worth remembering, however, that the *Chronicle*, a product of the late fourteenth century, may not be taking the word from Nicholas's letter. An investigation was carried out by Bertrand de Sigotier, a Franciscan inquisitor. The result was submitted to the 1292 general chapter at Paris, and several brothers (one source says twenty-nine) were punished for sowing schism. Olivi was spared, but not until he had explained himself before the general chapter. The explanation is interesting in its own right. Olivi was not required to deny that *usus pauper* was part of the vow, but rather to acknowledge that Franciscans were bound to it only in the sense defined by Nicholas III in *Exiit qui seminat*. That was hardly a major concession, since both Olivi and his opponents had been claiming the support of *Exiit* all along. He also promised not to support anyone holding a contrary position.[2]

The affair has a triple significance. First, it suggests that the rigorists in southern France were far from a monolithic unit, and that a significant number of them stood far enough to Olivi's left to make him willing and able to distance himself from them. One wonders whether it was the very brightness of reform prospects that produced the crisis. One can imagine zealots feeling encouraged to make stronger demands, which resulted in a comparable reaction from their opponents.

Second, in this episode we see the *usus pauper* controversy in Olivi's area evolving into a different sort of problem than it had been in the early 1280s. At that time, the problem was Olivi, and the challenge presented by him was primarily not one of behavior but of ideas. Olivi was censured because he held a series of views the commission saw as incorrect. What was going on in the early 1290s was a disciplinary problem in the full sense, involving a threat to good order. In short, it was closer to what already had been occurring in Ancona.

Third, the call to do something had come not from leaders of the order, but, for the first time, from the pope. This is a difficult distinction to make, to be sure, since Nicholas IV was the former Jerome of Ascoli—the man who, as minister general, had ordered Olivi's questions on the Virgin burned and probably investigated other Olivian opinions as well. Thus his intervention was in some sense an in-house affair. In fact, one wonders if this whole story has political dimensions that escape us. The *Chronicle of the Twenty-Four Generals* mentions that when Raymond Geoffroi was elected minister general, Nicholas IV, in whose presence the selection occurred, had preferred another candidate.[3] Whether he was overruled by Angevin influence or by reformist pressure, he was in any case overruled. Thus it may have given Nicholas—who was obviously a good politician but has left no evidence of a strong dedication to the pursuit of Franciscan poverty[4]—some satisfaction to embarrass Raymond by ordering him to enforce discipline in his own home territory and punish members of the very reformist wing with whom he was known to sympathize. Nevertheless, the precedent is important. Nicholas was the first pope to view Franciscan zealots as a threat to good order and demand action.[5]

Celestine V, Boniface VIII, and Italian Unrest

Angelo's group was to fare no better in Armenia. It eventually encountered hostility from other Franciscans and was forced to return. Thus Angelo and his colleagues found themselves back in a very tense relationship with their Anconan superiors. In 1294 it looked for a moment as if their problems might be solved. After a two-year vacancy in the papal office, the hitherto deadlocked College of Cardinals achieved a majority by resorting to one of the oddest choices in church history. They elected a relatively obscure hermit in the Abruzzi, Pietro Morrone, who became Pope Celestine V.[6] The Anconan rigorists saw that this might be their kind of pontiff and, encouraged by Raymond Geoffroi,[7] appealed to him. Celestine established them as the Poor Hermits of Pope Celestine with Pietro da Macerata as their leader and Cardinal Napoleone Orsini as their protector. In essence, they gave up the Franciscan name but kept the Franciscan rule, and they were allowed to observe it according to what they saw as Francis's original intention—their evaluation of the latter being founded on the rule, *Testament*, and Leo sources. At that point not only the group but also its two most famous figures received new names. Pietro da Macerata became Liberato, while the man who had hitherto been Pietro da Fossombrone became Angelo Clareno.[8]

It might have been a workable solution if Celestine had proved more durable, but he soon decided that he and the church would be better off if he returned to his mountain hermitage. There was much to be said for that decision. He had not proved an especially effective reformer or even a competent administrator. In December 1294, just over five months after his election, he resigned and was succeeded by Boniface VIII, who quickly rescinded most of Celestine's legislation, presumably including that concerning the new order. Angelo, Liberato, and the others were technically back in the grasp of their Anconan superiors.[9] Many of them—including Angelo and Liberato—soon decided that it would be better not to be such in actuality, and they departed for Greece. According to Angelo's remarkably diplomatic turn of phrase, Celestine's resignation convinced Liberato that "for our own greater peace and safety we should journey to remote places, where we might serve God freely and without tumult or scandal."[10]

Other Italian Franciscans, many of whom had supported the Poor Hermits and some of whom had probably belonged to the group, stayed at home. Of these, some sided with the Colonna family, Boniface's archenemies, in opposing the legitimacy of Boniface's election. If Celestine's decision to resign and return to his old life had cost the Poor Hermits their freedom from Franciscan superiors, others' decision to question Boniface's legitimacy in turn cost Celestine his freedom to carry out his eremitical project and may eventually have cost him his life. Boniface was not eager to see him back in his hermitage, where he would be all too accessible to the Colonna family. Celestine fled from virtual captivity, escaped to his mountains, and eluded his pursuers for four months. He was finally captured and died in papal custody on May 19, 1296.

Boniface VIII's disputed succession affected the *usus pauper* controversy in three complementary ways. First, opposition to him pushed some rigorists into a more militant stance, prompting an equally strong reaction from the pope. Thus we find Boniface using inquisitors to prosecute Franciscan zealots as rebels against ecclesiastical authority. Second, Boniface's effort to check this genuine threat probably encouraged a heightened awareness of dissidence in general as a danger. The pope was moved to examine all groups more suspiciously, especially those that lacked proper regulation. Third, the disorder and confusion produced by the dispute created an environment in which such small factions and sects might be expected to proliferate.

We see evidence of these three results in Olivi's 1295 letter to Conrad of Offida and in various papal letters.[11] Olivi's letter describes something close to a worst-case scenario. He attacks certain errant brothers who deny not only the legitimacy of Celestine's resignation, but also the lawfulness of previous papal declarations like *Exiit qui seminat*, which, they say, violate the rule and the *Testament*. These brothers are taking Rev. 18:4, "Come out of her, my people," as a call to separate from the carnal leaders of church and order.

Olivi, aghast, delivers a stern lecture on ecclesiology and history, defending everything the rebellious brothers are rejecting—an impressive list, including the receipt of money through procurators, extra tunics in case of necessity, papal interpretations of the rule, and the possibility of papal resignation. He then asks rhetorically whether Brother Leo saw fit to part company with church and order over such matters. In the process, Olivi rejects the rebels' view that Francis's *Testament* is binding upon the order just as the rule is (a subject to which we will return in dealing with the later debate at Vienne). He also warns that their behavior will prove politically disastrous to the order in general and their own cause in particular. It will furnish new ammunition for the enemies of the Franciscan order, who will see the rebels' extreme interpretation of the Franciscan vow as corroborating the old argument that the rule is impossible to observe and is thus dangerous—the very charge countered earlier by William de la Mare and *Exiit qui seminat*. At the same time, it will allow the laxer brethren, the zealots' enemies within the order, to dismiss the entire reform movement as the work of anarchic, heretical extremists.

However Olivi's diatribe may have affected the Italian rebels, they could hardly have reacted more negatively than some modern historians. Several earlier scholars thought him guilty of hypocrisy,[12] while at least one recent writer has leveled that most contemporary of charges, insensitivity. The charge of hypocrisy makes little sense.[13] Olivi was not rejecting the elements that united him with these rebellious Italian spirituals. Rather, he attacked the elements that distinguished them (a point with which we will deal in a moment). The charge of insensitivity is harder to answer, since one is not quite sure what it entails. Lydia von Auw, who describes the letter as "not very generous," protests that "Olivi did not understand or did not wish to understand" the tragedy of the Italian situation. He had not lived through the experiences of Angelo Clareno and his associates, nor did he share the danger they faced if they fell back into the hands of their former superiors. Olivi, von Auw suggests, "wanted to disengage himself from all responsibility in the affair of the Italian spirituals and avoid new difficulties."[14]

On a purely factual level, some of this seems obvious. The real question is what effect it should have had on Olivi's behavior in the affair. He was not attacking Angelo Clareno. He was attacking a much more extreme position than Angelo's, a position that Angelo himself later rejected in strong language. Olivi disagreed with the rebels' views; he thought they were dangerous not simply for the rebels but also for the entire reform movement, as they could be used by the movement's enemies to discredit it. A look at Boniface's actions will show that he was correct.

Boniface's letters describe a wider spectrum of behavior, all of which he finds disturbing.[15] He wants ecclesiastical authorities to take measures against unauthorized groups that dress and behave like approved orders. Some contain both laity and renegades from established orders. Some claim to follow the Franciscan rule. Some wander around, having no stable residence. So far he could be describing Angelo's group, at least, among others. Nevertheless, Boniface goes on to report that some members of these groups have taken on priestly functions, and some feel that they are the only legitimate priests left in the church, since God has taken power away from the pope and the ecclesiastical hierarchy. Some say manual labor is forbidden. Some think it more effective to pray naked. It is an oddly heterogeneous list, but that is precisely its significance. Cut loose from ecclesiastical control, small groups of like-minded zealots might be expected to cultivate their own eccentricities—even their own heresies.

Here we see the confrontation of two important movements that continued across the High Middle Ages. Popular religious enthusiasm, like the runoff from a flash flood, tended to follow its own bent, cutting new courses through the ecclesiastical landscape. The institutional church, ever sensitized to the dangers of erosion, constantly attempted to steer these currents into officially sanctioned channels. The church was a living, growing thing, and it was not necessarily growing from the top. Yet it was also a matter of institutions and dogma, and these *were* officially determined from the top. Leaders had wrestled with this problem at the Fourth Lateran Council in 1214 and the Council of Lyons in 1274. They were partially successful in producing the best solution one could expect, one that kept the two elements in tension like plates on a geological fault line. After Celestine's resignation, the plates shifted slightly, and for a moment, the pope seemed to stare across a widening crevasse at a series of unauthorized groups. Some were deliberately escaping. Others were doing pretty much what they had been doing before, but as the crevasse opened, they seemed to be moving away.

Boniface's reaction was predictable. He called for surveillance—not only of the genuinely rebellious groups, but also of all whose freedom from direct control might possibly hide rebellion. The magnitude of this task becomes touchingly apparent when in one letter he orders his subordinates to take a good look at hermits. One can imagine those subordinates trudging through the mountains conducting their eremitical census. Even Boniface must have seen the limitations of this approach.[16]

Italy was in some ways a more fertile ground for Franciscan deviance than southern France was. It is significant that the eremitical life itself was more characteristic of Italian than of French Franciscans.[17] So was the tendency of individual groups to pursue their own aims without official sanction, at least in the thirteenth century. If we compare the moderate French reformist position (as portrayed in Olivi's writings and later in Raymond Geoffroi's 1309 statement to Pope Clement V[18]) with the Italian rigorists' critique of the order (insofar as we can reconstruct it both from our limited documentary material and by projecting backward from views expressed later at the Council of

Vienne), we will find that the two differed in several ways. Italian rigorists tended to be more critical of thirteenth-century developments in the order, more insistent on returning to the original intention of Saint Francis as seen in extra-legal documents like the *Testament* and the Leo sources, and more willing to solve the problem by splitting the order. In contrast, the southern French rigorist stance as revealed in Olivi's and Raymond's writings saw a much smaller gap between Francis's original intention and the order as it existed. It was more apt to seek sanction in the rule, Franciscan legislation, and papal documents than in extra-legal documents. It wanted to reform the order, not split it.

While these are valid generalizations, one can take them only so far. The 1290–92 difficulties in southern France, when many brothers were punished but Olivi was not, suggest that this area too may have been experiencing centrifugal tendencies among the rigorists, and it is impossible to know what the radical end of the spectrum may have been saying. Moreover, while Olivi sounds absolutely conservative in his letter to Conrad of Offida (and his position there is quite consistent with his attitude elsewhere[19]), his position had its own subversive elements in the long run. The three most important for our purposes were the ones untouched by his earlier censure: his attitude toward obedience, his apocalyptic expectation, and his interest in visionary experience. We have seen that the first was quite traditional in some respects. Olivi placed limits on obedience to Franciscan superiors and argued that the pope could not dispense from evangelical vows, but so did others in his century. What seems more significant is his way of formulating the problem. He was, as we have noted, peculiarly insistent upon asking what should be done if pope and vow differed in their demands. That was the question the Anconan brothers were discussing in 1274 and the refractory Italian brothers were acting on in 1295, but it was not one explicitly broached by preceding Franciscan scholars. Like those rebellious Italians, Olivi was certain that one must follow one's vows even in defiance of the pope. Moreover, as we have seen, Olivi's argument was given special significance by the fact that he saw *usus pauper* as an essential part of those vows. The effect was to raise the stakes in the *usus pauper* controversy, and here, too, he agreed with the rebellious Italians. Thus the difference between Olivi and the rebels was not *whether* one should defy authority but *at what point* one should defy it—and whether that point had been reached.

That brings us to the second matter, Olivi's apocalyptic expectation. Again, he shared ground with the Italian rebels. The difference between them lay not so much in whether a time would come when God's elect would have to evacuate Babylon, but in whether that time had arrived. Olivi's apocalyptic scenario

agreed with the one accepted by the Italian zealots inasmuch as both anticipated a great betrayal in which leaders of church and order would vitiate
the rule and turn its true observers into a persecuted resistance movement. But
Olivi, who accorded greater legitimacy to thirteenth-century changes within
the order, could comfortably project that betrayal into the future, while the
Italian rebels thought that pope and order already had violated their trust. The
difference was a real one, and it allowed Olivi to express righteous indigna-
tion in 1295, but it does not erase the fact that his own apocalyptic predictions raised the stakes in the *usus pauper* controversy by placing the dispute at
the heart of the coming apocalyptic tribulation. If Olivi's discussion of obedience turned a controverted issue into a crisis of conscience, his apocalyptic
scenario gave it major eschatological significance and turned a theoretical
papal betrayal into a nearly certain one. Moreover, though he projected that
betrayal into the future, he did not push it very far into the future—and his
immediate followers caught up with it rather quickly, as we will see.

Olivi's interest in visionary experience has received less attention than his
apocalyptic thought, but it is extremely important and closely related to the
latter. We will examine it in some detail later.

It is not entirely clear how Olivi spent his final years. We can be reasonably sure that he was not manning the barricades in the mid-1290s, nor was
he among those subject to disciplinary action. Nevertheless, an offhand comment in his May 1295 letter to three captive Angevin princes suggests that as
the decade progressed he may have felt less secure in Narbonne.[20] The princes
(who included the future King Robert the Wise of Naples and the future Saint
Louis of Toulouse) had invited him to come and visit them. He took their invi-
tation seriously, remarking that "if I do not come to you I may have to hurry
off elsewhere."[21] One wonders what he meant by that. The letter also shows
Olivi's awareness that he was identified with a group that might cause anxiety. Among the possible arguments against such a trip, he mentions fear on
their father's part that he might "beguinize" them. This is not the first inci-
dence of the word "beguin" being used to designate pious southern French
laity connected with the Franciscans,[22] but it is the first evidence of a connection between Olivi and those bearing that label. We will return to the matter in a moment.

If Olivi did sense that the situation was deteriorating in May 1295, he had
only to wait a few months longer to see it get even worse. In October 1295
Boniface removed Raymond Geoffroi from the office of minister general. Perhaps
attempting to orchestrate a graceful departure for Raymond, Boniface offered
him the bishopric of Padua and then the archbishopric of Milan. Raymond
refused both. The *Chronicle of the Twenty-Four Generals*, which tells only of the offer

concerning Padua, says that Raymond refused it because he felt he was not worthy of such a position; Boniface replied that if that was the case, Raymond was even less worthy to rule the entire Franciscan order.[23]

In May 1296, in an election held at Anagni under papal surveillance, John of Murrovalle (who had been a member of the seven-man commission that censured Olivi in 1283) was chosen as Raymond's successor.[24] One's first impulse is to see this move as further evidence of Boniface's attitude toward Franciscan rigorists, but here, as in the case of Raymond's election, something more may have been at stake. Boniface had reason to look with suspicion not only on Franciscan zealots but on Raymond's French relatives, and he understandably decided to entrust the order to a man who was to some extent Boniface's client and had served him well in the past.[25] Nevertheless, John's election ushered in a new phase in the *usus pauper* controversy.

Raymond's tenure as minister general shows that even at that stage Franciscan rigorists could still garner support from the most respectable circles; it also demonstrates, though, that even those respectable circles would have trouble aiding the rigorists if provincial leaders opposed them. Having freed the Anconan spirituals from prison, Raymond could do little to protect them except point them toward Armenia and then, when that option ran out, point them toward the pope. He had even less power to control hostility from above. When Nicholas IV demanded an investigation of obstreperous brothers in southern France, Raymond, whose tour of the order had now reached the province of Provence, complied. Perhaps he proceeded as gently as possible, and perhaps he was at least partly responsible for saving Olivi from punishment, but the resultant discipline was nonetheless hard on a number of zealots.

Of course, as minister general, Raymond had a complex role to fulfill, one that left him only limited time for the zealots in any case. It is symbolically fitting that in the fall of 1291, while the inquisition in southern France was progressing apace, Raymond, still on tour, was in England receiving the heart of his relative Eleanor of Provence from the hands of her son, King Edward I, so that he could preside over its interment at the Franciscan house in London. Yet Raymond had at least done what he could. So did his successor, but not on the spirituals' behalf.

Olivi's Apocalypse Commentary

Olivi's commentary on the Apocalypse, written just before his death in 1298, provides striking proof that recent events had not increased his optimism.[26] Here we find the same positive apocalyptic evaluation of Francis and his order discernible in earlier works, but this is combined with a negative reading of ecclesiastical authority which, though not inconsistent with what Olivi had said before, spells the problem out with a clarity earlier works had lacked and perhaps consciously avoided. Olivi's interpretive framework is essentially Joachite, but with a particular twist. That twist comes partly from Bonaventure, but is also partly unique to Olivi.

Olivi adopts not only the traditional division of church history into seven periods but also the Joachite division of world history into three ages. He sees his time as hanging between the fifth and sixth periods of church history, which is to say that it also hangs between the second and third ages of world history. The fifth period marks the end of the second age, that of the Son. More particularly, the period has been a time when Christianity attained a degree of internal peace but underwent moral decline. By the end of the period, "practically the whole church from head to foot is corrupted and thrown into disorder and turned, as it were, into a new Babylon."[27] The decay takes a variety of forms, such as ecclesiastical corruption, heresy, an Islamicized Aristotelianism that subverts Christian doctrine, and the denial that *usus pauper* is an essential part of the Franciscan vow. Yet these are simply different symptoms of the same basic malady, a carnality that pervades the church.

Nevertheless, Olivi sees his time as one of overlap between the declining fifth period and the dawning sixth period of church history that will usher in the third age of the Holy Spirit, a time of new spiritual knowledge and peace. This third age began with Joachim and Francis, but it will not be fully actualized until the sixth period of the church cedes to the seventh. In effect, just as Olivi's age represents a time of transition between the fifth and sixth periods, the sixth period itself represents a moment of transition between the second and third ages. It is a time of new spiritual gifts, but it is also the time of Antichrist. More precisely, it is a time of Antichrists, since Olivi expects two of them, the mystical and the great.

If we examine the commentary with an eye to determining who will play these roles and where each will fit into the temporal divisions already outlined, we will discover that Olivi is extremely tentative. This exegetical caution should not blind us, however, to the fact that when he discusses the immediate future he routinely assumes a specific order of events: Continued decay of the church will lead to rule by a pseudopope who, with the aid of secular authority, will support a carnal version of Christianity, persecuting those who observe evangelical poverty. These carnal leaders and the carnal church they represent (Babylon) will eventually be destroyed by a non-

Christian (presumably Muslim) army. Thus will end the persecution of the mystical Antichrist, but that of the great Antichrist will then begin. Another king/pseudopope combination will join in a persecution aimed more explicitly at Christianity itself. Here, too, Olivi seems to anticipate an important role for Islam. Finally, with Christ's aid, this second persecution will end and the seventh period will begin.

Will the king or the pope be the mystical Antichrist? Which will be the great Antichrist? Olivi is not all that concerned about answering such questions. As Warren Lewis shrewdly observes, the king/pseudopope combination is more important to him than the idea of a single evil leader called "Antichrist."[28] Nevertheless, Olivi is inclined to believe that in both cases the label should be applied to the pseudopope, not the king.

How long must Christians wait to see all this confirmed? Olivi's attempts to wring a chronology from the biblical text do not all yield precisely the same result, but all tend toward roughly the same general scenario. The temptation of the mystical Antichrist is in some sense already underway, but it will escalate in the near future under the first king/pseudopope combination. There is no reason to believe that Olivi sees the pseudopope as already present in the shape of Boniface VIII. The worst is yet to come, although it will not be all that far into the future. Some of Olivi's comments suggest that he thinks the mystical Antichrist could arrive anytime after 1300. The great Antichrist should be destroyed and the third age fully operative by the middle of the fourteenth century. It will last until around the year 2000, when earthly history will culminate in the final judgment.

When Olivi attempts to put flesh on this chronological skeleton, he seems painfully aware of the limits imposed by his own experience. He can speak with some authority of the fifth period and the early stages of the sixth because it is his own time, but anything after that involves a world he has not visited. Thus one can hardly expect great detail in his comments on the great Antichrist and the age of peace thereafter. It is arguable, though, that he finds the latter easier to describe than the former, and for a very good reason. His picture of the third age, however sketchy, bears a remarkable resemblance to his idea of Francis and the Franciscan rule, and these, in turn, are closely related to his notion of Christ and the gospels.

Viewed from one perspective, the third age is essentially one of rebirth, a return to the rule as Francis intended it and to the apostolic pattern as Christ intended it. Identification of the rule with the gospel had become a commonplace in not only Franciscan but also papal writings of the thirteenth century, but by the end of the century, the difficulties of this equation were beginning to dawn on the papacy. *Exiit qui seminat* was at least partly an attempt to think the matter through.

Olivi, like the rest of his order, assumes that the apostles rejected both individual and common possessions. Like the rest of his order he is willing to portray the Franciscans as superior to other orders precisely because they follow the apostolic pattern in this respect and other orders do not. Nevertheless, Olivi goes beyond most of his order in the clarity with which he identifies ecclesiastical decline after Constantine with the acceptance of ecclesiastical possessions. He never suggests that this departure from the apostolic pattern was sinful. On the contrary, it was instituted for tactical reasons by God. Nevertheless, in the third age the church will surrender those possessions and return to the apostolic state. It will, in effect, be Franciscanized.

The third age is not simply a return, though. It also involves profound novelty. Olivi's notion of history is essentially progressive. God is working something out, and he does so by instituting real change. Olivi compares the transition from the second to the third age with the earlier one from the first to the second, the transition from synagogue to church. Occasionally he speaks of the "new church" or even the "new world" of the third age.[29]

Will citizens of the third age, then, surpass those of the second in wisdom and virtue? Will they in fact surpass Christ and the apostles? Olivi sees the danger lurking here, and he is careful to advance not only Christ but also the apostles as early models of the evangelical perfection that will characterize the third age.[30] In Christ's case this task is simplified by Olivi's notion of the three advents. Christ comes in the flesh in the first century; in the spirit in the thirteenth; then in judgment around the end of the twentieth. His second coming in the spirit will reveal "the singular perfection of his life and wisdom," and the result will be so striking that "a certain new world or new church will then seem to have been formed, the old having been rejected, just as in Christ's first advent a new church was formed, the synagogue having been rejected."[31] The word "seem" does important service here. The transition to the third age is not a transition to a new, post-Christian dispensation. Christ still rules, and he rules over the same church, now even more closely assimilated to the model of Christ.

Nevertheless, however carefully Olivi might attempt to balance progression with recapitulation and innovation with continuity, the progressive, innovative elements still raise inconvenient questions. Olivi may be able to keep Christ equally relevant to all ages by granting him three advents, but the apostles remain trapped in the first century. The problem does not lie primarily in the area of poverty. Olivi's *viri spirituales* in the final age emulate apostolic poverty without surpassing it because they conform with the model of poverty offered in the Franciscan rule, which is essentially the same one that Christ imposed on the apostles. The real problem lies in the area of knowledge. Olivi is committed to the notion that something very special is happening in his own time. "In the first five periods of the church it was not conceded to the saints, however illuminated they might be, to open the secrets of this book, which were to be opened more fully only in the sixth and seventh periods, just as in the first five periods of the Old Testament the prophets were not given the ability to open clearly those secrets of Christ and of the New Testament which were to be opened and actually were opened in the sixth age of the world."[32]

In the preface to his Apocalypse commentary Olivi offers an image that encapsulates his sense of history as the arena of progressive revelation.

> Three mountains separated by two valleys will strike a man who sees them from a great distance as a single mountain. . . . Then, when he stands on the first mountain, he will see the first valley and two mountains, and when he stands on the second mountain he will see two valleys and three mountains. Just so, the Jews before Christ's first advent, like one standing before the first mountain, did not distinguish the first from the later ones, but took the whole for a single thing. Christians before the sixth period of the church distinguished between the first and the others because they stood on the first and saw an intervening space . . . between the first and final advents, but they did not commonly distinguish between the advent in the sixth period and the one at final judgment. . . . Those, however, who shall be placed in the sixth period or who see it in the spirit distinguish it from the first and the last. Then they see this distinction in the prophetic books, and also in those things said by Christ and the apostles about Christ's final advent and the final age of the world. Then they also see the concordance of various events in the first five ages of the world with those in the first five periods of the church, as well as the concordance of the seven periods under the law with the seven periods of church history.[33]

The passage is remarkable in the way it highlights the roles played not only by increased spiritual illumination but also by sheer accumulation of experience. Olivi is more able than Augustine to see the pattern of history because he has more history to work with, and the development he sees there enables him to read the prophets with new understanding.

The importance of progression and its attendant problems are also seen in Olivi's tendency to draw a parallel between church history and progress through the various grades of purgation, perfection, or contemplation. He himself does his best to avoid the implication that *viri spirituales* of the third age will surpass not only the church fathers but the apostles as well.

> Again, [perfect contemplation] will not be entered into until after the seventh angel pours out [his vial], just as the book will not be perfectly open nor the mysteries of God entirely consummated until the seventh angel begins to blow his trumpet. It should be known, however, that these seven grades of purgation may be perfected (and may have been perfected) in any saints of any period, allowing them to enter into the temple without waiting for the seventh period of the church, for in them [the seventh period] was virtually or spiritually attained, so that it is just as if they temporally belonged to the time and activity of the seventh period.[34]

Here again, as long as we can take Olivi's comments as applying to poverty and perhaps to spiritual gifts in some general sense, he seems to be making an arguable point. When it comes to knowledge, one is less sure. In that area he says too much to avoid the conclusion that something radically different is occurring.

In fact, his comments suggest a remarkable shift even within the third age. When he talks about the sort of *intellectus spiritualis* appearing in the sixth period, he usually seems to be talking about improved biblical exegesis, a fuller knowledge of both the spiritual and literal senses. Greater insight into the shape of church history is an important part of this new knowledge. When Olivi speaks of the seventh period, though, his emphasis shifts away from biblical exegesis toward what might be described as mystical vision.[35] He suggests that Rev. 21:22, "I saw no temple in the city," has been fulfilled to some extent throughout church history, since the church has been bound neither to a physical location like the Jerusalem temple nor to a ceremonial law like that of Judaism. In the church of the seventh period, however, "it will be fulfilled even more fully inasmuch as it will not need many earlier doctrines, since Christ's spirit will teach it all truth without mystery of external voice and book." Olivi does not mean to imply that Scripture and doctrine will become obsolete the moment the seventh period begins. On the contrary, this too will be a progressive matter. The prediction "is being fulfilled and will be fulfilled *secundum quid* in the church militant, but *simpliciter* in the church triumphant."[36]

Note that Olivi feels the prediction "is being fulfilled." The transition is already underway. Where, though? Certainly in Joachim of Fiore. Seeking to locate the beginnings of the sixth period, Olivi remarks that it had "a certain prophetic beginning" in "the revelation accorded to the Abbot Joachim and perhaps to certain others of his time."[37] The term "prophetic beginning" seems to mean here that Joachim and the anonymous others were anticipations of more to come. Nevertheless, Olivi does actually see Joachim not as one more scholar but as a latter-day prophet. Later, dealing with Joachim's suggestion that the fifth period will reach its definitive end in the year 1200, a view that Olivi takes to be manifestly false, Olivi comments that

> on this and similar matters Joachim was offering opinions, not mak-
> ing assertions. For just as, through the natural light of our intellects,
> we know some things unquestionably as first principles, know others
> as conclusions necessarily deduced from these principles, and hold
> still others only as opinions formed on the basis of probable argu-
> ment; and in the latter case we are often wrong, yet the concreated
> light granted to us is not on that account false, nor are we incorrect
> insofar as we recognize that our opinions are not infallible; thus the
> light given freely to us through revelation knows certain things as
> first and unquestionable revealed principles, knows others as con-
> clusions necessarily deduced from those principles, and holds certain
> views merely as probable and conjectural opinions formed on the
> basis of these [first principles and necessary conclusions]. This is what
> seems to have occurred in the case of the knowledge of scripture and
> the concordance of New and Old Testaments given by revelation
> to the Abbot Joachim, as he himself asserts.[38]

Olivi had made a similar remark close to two decades earlier in the work that, among his numerous writings, comes closest to being the Olivian equiv-alent of a scholastic treatise on prophecy.[39] In the prologue to his Isaiah com-mentary—and that work is little except prologue—Olivi considers several of the major issues addressed in such works, such as whether the prophet received his insight by looking into the mirror of eternity, the *speculum aeternitatis*. Olivi, like many before him, rejects this view, then goes on to suggest that "some people" adopt another explanation that is "easy enough to support and under-stand." They say that the principal basis of prophetic certitude lies in a change that occurs in the prophet's mind. That change complements the highest con-templation. "For when the mind is altered in the highest, most intense, and liveliest way by God, one cannot doubt that the alteration is caused by God, and consequently one understands through a most certain sense or taste [*gustus*] that what is said or shown [in the experience] is infallibly true," even though one cannot prove it by human reasoning. Olivi's thought here is less than fully developed, yet two things are clear enough. First, his notion of prophetic certainty is so closely related to his view of contemplation that it seems an extension of it. In both cases cognitive and affective categories seem to combine, allowing Olivi to speak of a state in which "God himself, his truth and his sweetness are tasted." Second, his experience is not a miniaturized *visio dei*. "It is not attained through immediate vision, but rather by means of the created mirror."[40]

Olivi is aware that the Bible offers varieties of prophetic experience. Sometimes God grants prophetic vision without *gustus*, as was true of Balaam, whose case is evidence that prophecy can be accorded to the evil as well as the good. Yet even the good may not always enjoy prophecy with *gustus*. Olivi confides that a "very holy person" has told him in private that the prophetic utterances placed "in an intellectual way" within her heart were at first accompanied by *gustus*, but later were not. Moreover, the prophetic vision is sometimes granted without any certainty that it is from God. In some cases there is limited but not complete assurance. Again, even when the prophet is sure that his vision is from God, he may not know what it means. Here anyone familiar with thirteenth-century discussions of this subject will think of two *loci classici* for the phenomenon of prophetic incomprehension, Nebuchadnezzar and the pharaoh whose dream Joseph interpreted. Olivi obliges by mentioning both, but goes on to observe that in these cases it is not all that clear whether they even knew their dreams were from God. What is more surprising is that he also cites Daniel and John the Divine, contending that they sometimes did not understand the meaning of their own visions.[41]

In some cases the recipient of prophetic vision understands only part of its significance. Thus, at the Annunciation, the Virgin knew that the angel was divinely sent and that she was to bear the son of God, but she did not yet know whether she would do so in a spiritual or carnal way. In other cases God intends the vision to have several meanings, and the prophet may know only some of them.

How does the prophet come to understand these things? Knowledge provided through prophecy can involve a habitual disposition in the mind that facilitates such understanding. Here again Olivi is covering well-explored territory. Earlier writers like William of Auxerre and Philip the Chancellor tended to assume that prophecy should be seen as a *habitus*, but Hugh of St. Cher disagreed. For Hugh, prophecy was not a *habitus* but an *actus*.[42] Both views found later support. The idea of prophecy as a *habitus* is found in a treatise on prophecy that some scholars have attributed to Bonaventure.[43] The most famous spokesman for the opposite opinion is Thomas Aquinas, who argues in his *Summa theologiae* that prophecy is not a *habitus* but a temporary *actus* or *passio*. If it were a *habitus*, it would be a permanent ability and the prophet would be free to prophesy whenever he chose.[44]

Olivi, on the contrary, sees no difficulty in the idea. He can think of three different kinds of habitual disposition that might be involved. The first would produce a sharpening or clarification of the intellect; the second would involve a habitual knowledge leading to the habitual understanding of some truth; and the third would entail a habitual adherence through faith, leading to a firm belief that something will occur or is already true. Daniel offers a good example. When it is said that he was granted understanding of dreams and visions, we can take it that he was granted "a certain intellectual acumen and affective vivacity for the purpose of examining dreams easily and profoundly, so that he could discover whether they were from God and what they meant." Here we are dealing with the first type of habit. Nevertheless, Daniel was given the second type as well. He enjoyed

> a habitual wisdom or knowledge concerning the general laws of divine providence, according to which God rules all things, especially human events. Through this knowledge Daniel judged dreams, just as we use general principles to judge particular conclusions. And in this way Joachim, in his *Liber de concordia* and *Expositio Apocalypsis*, says he suddenly received the entire concordance of the Old and New Testaments in the form of some general rules from which he later deduced certain things, some of which (it seemed to him) he considered himself to know as certain conclusions, while he saw others only as probable conjectures which might be erroneous. It is just the same with the natural light of intellect joined to us from the beginning of our condition. Through it, without any argumentation, we know first principles, and from these we infer some conclusions necessarily, others only probably. In the latter case we are capable of error, yet it does thereby follow that the light itself is not from God, or that it is in itself false. I say this because there are those who wish to conclude that Joachim's whole understanding was from the devil or by conjecture of the human imagination, because in certain particulars what he said was merely opinion and occasionally perhaps even false.[45]

This interpretation of Joachim's vision mirrors not only Olivi's later remark in the Apocalypse commentary but also the autobiographical note inserted by Joachim himself at the beginning of his Apocalypse commentary. In fact, it makes remarkably good sense of that note. One is left with the question of where Olivi sees necessary deductions and where he sees probable conjectures. That question is partly answered in the Apocalypse commentary.

In attempting to clarify the second type of habit, Olivi remarks that when it concerns knowledge of future contingents or truths beyond human understanding, the habit cannot lead to genuine *scientia* or *intelligentia*, for such things cannot be proved syllogistically. Thus the certainty of a prophet's predictions does not rest on their being *scientia* in the scholastic logical sense. How, then, can the prophet be certain that a contingent event will occur when the very fact that it is contingent suggests the possibility of its not occurring? Olivi contends that it is impossible that an event, once promised by God, will not actually occur, but that its nonoccurrence is nonetheless possible *quantum ad potentiam*. The prophet's certitude does not stem from any necessary connection between present cause and future effect, or from a vision of the event as somehow already occurring, or from the fact that the event has in any sense actually occurred, but only from an unshakable faith in God and his revelation. The prophet knows that, although things *could* be otherwise, they will not be, because God has promised this particular result.[46] Such predictions, Olivi says, are always founded upon faith, just as a flower or fruit is founded upon the tree or root.

Obviously we are dealing here with Olivi's third type of *habitus*, but we are dealing with more than that. His earlier allusions to *gustus* and contemporary contemplatives have already forewarned us that he is uncomfortable with any discussion that remains on a strictly intellectual level. He observes that sometimes, through divine intervention,[47] our powers may be altered and applied so strongly that

> certain lively feelings, beliefs and notions [*affectiones et credulitates seu estimationes*] follow in us which we sometimes call instincts or impulses. Thus Caiaphas may perhaps have had some hidden instinct or impulse in both his imaginative and interpretive powers, leading him to say that a man must die, etc. For he did not say this of Christ by intention or through any good will. I believe that without this sort of thing no habitual gift granted to Daniel or Joseph or the other prophets would have sufficed for the understanding and interpretation of all divine visions.[48]

Moreover, Olivi continues, we are all aware that sometimes a number of people can look carefully over the same field, yet only one will see the grain of gold lying in it. In the same way, several people may read the same book and one of them will see some element or implication missed by the rest, even though several of those who missed it are more intelligent. Thus sometimes, through angelic aid, one who receives a vision is made aware of some key element which provides the key to interpreting that vision and immediately begins to see its significance. This is, in fact, one way God teaches us important truths of Holy Scripture in an instant.

Throughout this discussion, Olivi takes standard positions and gives them a characteristically Olivian twist. One obvious difference between Olivi and a scholar like Aquinas is that they concentrate on different books of the Bible. Aquinas, when considering prophecy, prefers to concentrate on the Old Testament prophets.[49] Isaiah and Jeremiah stand at the center of his discussion. He acknowledges that prophecy grew in three stages—before the law, under the law, and under grace—yet he shows little interest in the third category. He cites Jerome's reminder that we read of people prophesying in the book of Acts, then adds, "And John wrote a prophetic book about the end of the church." That is as far as he cares to pursue the matter.[50]

Aquinas's focus on the Old Testament is understandable when we consider that he tends to view the stages of prophecy as a gradual unfolding of doctrine, more precisely of doctrine concerning the Trinity and the incarnation. He accepts the common view that prophecy in its fullest form deals with the prediction of future contingents, yet in the *Summa theologiae* he is remarkably uninterested in prophecy as the prediction of future events except insofar as Old Testament prophets predicted the incarnation. Thus there is really very little room for consideration of the Apocalypse.

Olivi's view of prophecy, like his theology of history, is strongly influenced by his reading of the Apocalypse, yet the difference involves more than greater interest in John the Divine. Olivi looks at prophecy throughout all of church history, including his own century. It is fascinating to watch how easily he shifts back and forth across a spectrum of religious phenomena ranging from Old Testament prophecy through contemporary contemplative and exegetical practice. What other scholar would attempt to illuminate the nature of Old Testament prophecy by alluding to mystics he himself has known, or liken Old Testament prophetic vision to the exegete's discovery of hidden meanings in the Bible? Certainly others in the thirteenth century spoke of preaching or exegesis as prophecy, but not in this literal sense. Olivi is, in effect, constructing a unified field theory of contemplative experience that includes exegesis and prophecy.

Olivi's approach is vividly demonstrated in his treatment of Joachim. His understanding of the Apocalypse, prophecy—and for that matter, history itself—is radically dependent upon Joachim, but the reverse is equally true. Having informed Olivi's theology of history, Joachim is in turn explained by it. He is portrayed as one morning star of a new contemplative age,[51] and as such he forms a link between the Old Testament prophets and the spiritual riches to come. He is moved by the same spirit that moved the prophets, and so there is nothing odd about allowing him to take his place alongside Daniel as an example of prophetic insight. Olivi fully expects the two cases to illuminate one another.

Joachim is equally important for the connection Olivi sees between prophecy and inspired biblical exegesis. Olivi sees the prophetic vision described by Joachim in his Apocalypse commentary as at least partly an exegetical insight, and that is pretty much the way Joachim himself saw it. The spirit that inspired the prophets to write the Bible inspired Joachim to interpret it, and did so not by dictating the significance of specific passages, but by equipping Joachim with general rules of interpretation (just as it once equipped Daniel with the general rules of divine providence, which allowed him to predict the future).

The idea of Daniel proceeding to interpret dreams by applying the general rules of providence is parallel to that of Joachim interpreting the Bible on the basis of his divinely revealed theory of concordances. That observation brings us to a central question: Is Olivi interpreting Joachim in the light of Daniel, or Daniel in the light of Joachim? Obviously influence flows in both directions, but in the final analysis it would seem that the Joachite tail has succeeded in wagging the biblical dog. Joachim's gift has become a model for explaining Daniel's. Much the same could be said of Olivi's appeal to the word of contemporary mystics. The significant element here is that he sees their interpretation of their own experience as clarifying the nature of Old Testament prophetic experience. It can also clarify the meaning of the Bible itself, as we will see later when we turn to one of the odder elements of Olivi's exegetical work, his willingness to alter what seems the obvious meaning of John's gospel in order to accommodate the experience of a contemporary mystic.

Thus the *intellectus spiritualis* of the third age belongs within the tradition of prophetic experience, but it is also in some way a progressive affair. The same tension between progressive and recapitulative tendencies is seen in Olivi's description of church government in the third age. After centuries of possessing temporal wealth, leaders will return to the apostolic model.[52] They will be not only poor but also humble. Prelates will see themselves as ministers and servants and will refuse to be honored. The subordinates will thus honor them all the more, and there will ensue "a blessed contention of evangelical humility in which the superiors prohibit such honors and the inferiors never cease to honor them and subject themselves to them." Thus the hierarchy will remain intact, but its basis will be charismatic rather than juridical.

It might be suggested that the model being applied here is actually Olivi's notion of Francis and the sort of leadership Francis wished to see in his order, which in turn represents, in Olivi's eyes, a thirteenth-century edition of the apostolic model. That would seem to make the change more recapitulative than progressive, but Olivi expects these leaders to be aided in their task by the new, improved *intellectus spiritualis*. The evangelical poverty and humility to be displayed by them will be nurtured by the increased contemplative gifts of the third age. That makes the progressive element hard to ignore.

Another aspect of the third age deserves attention. Olivi sees the seventh period as witnessing the completion of a universal conversion already begun in the sixth. In its sixth-period phase, this conversion was inspired by Francis's own missionary activity and the missionary legacy he bequeathed to his order; in subsequent years, it will be shaped by opposition to evangelical renewal within the church. Just as the apostles, seeing the hostility they aroused within Judaism, directed their missionary efforts primarily at the Gentiles and only secondarily at the Jews, so the spiritual men of the sixth period, seeing the same opposition within the Latin church, will turn to the Greeks, Muslims, Mongols, and Jews. Among the Latins, the laity are more responsive than the clergy. Simple, unlettered men are more easily brought to penance than scholars and monks. Here, too, Olivi draws a parallel between the transition from synagogue to church in the first century and the transition under way in his own.

One possible result of universal conversion is that the capital of Christendom may migrate from Rome to Jerusalem. Olivi is not insistent on the matter, since he sees no clear indication of it in Scripture, yet the idea obviously makes sense to him.[53] Why? There is reason to suspect that he sees it as at least partly a judgment on Rome, but that is not what he actually says. Instead he evokes the ebb and flow of Christian history. The apostles preached first to the Jews, then turned to the Gentiles after the Jews rejected them. Spiritual preachers of the third age, rejected by leaders of the carnal western church, will turn to the Greeks, Moslems, Tartars, and finally the Jews. A shift from Jerusalem to Rome in the first period, and then from Rome back to Jerusalem in the seventh, would reflect the rhythm of conversion. Moreover, in an age of universal conversion, moving the capital to Jerusalem would reflect geographical realities. Olivi suggests that the seventh age will see a *sublimissimus cultus Christi* on Mount Zion. "Nor would it be surprising if the place of our redemption should be exalted over all other places at that time, especially in view of the fact that the highest rulers of the world will find that place more suitable for the conversion and later the governance of the whole world, since it is the geographical center of the habitable world."[54]

Thus the shift to Jerusalem would imply not merely a return to the original center of Christianity, but the progressive advance of conversion. Rome was a convenient capital in the second age, when Christianity was essentially a Mediterranean and northern European phenomenon; in the third age of universal conversion, however, as the geographical center of Christianity shifts east, it would be sensible for the capital to follow it, settling in Jerusalem, which—Olivi might note, pointing to a contemporary *mappa mundi*—is the geographical center of the world.

More could be said of life in the third age, but this much will suffice to reveal some aspects of Olivi's scenario that churchmen found challenging, to say the least. Whether they read that scenario as innovation or recapitulation, a move forward into a new dispensation or backward to the original apostolic model, they recognized its suggestion that the status quo would be swept away (and in fact needed to be swept away). Olivi combined sharp criticism of church life in his own time with a conviction that major changes were already underway and would eventuate in a new age of church history strikingly unlike his own. In his mind, these changes would reach completion not through the good offices of the church hierarchy, but in spite of persecution by it. In saying as much, Olivi left the next generation something remarkable to think about. We will see the conclusions that generation drew from it.

Persecution in Southern France

In March 1298, Olivi died at Narbonne, just in time to miss a dramatic worsening of conditions for the French rigorists. At the Franciscan general chapter meeting of 1299, Olivi's teachings were condemned and anyone using his books was declared excommunicate. His writings were collected and burned. A determined effort was launched to dissolve "the sect of Brother Peter John."[55] Visitors were sent to Olivi's province and investigation led to such extensive results that "a great book was made of the punishments and errors involved." Nor was the effort limited to Olivi's order. Boniface VIII too played an active role. He not only supported John's effort to discipline Franciscan zealots but also commissioned Giles of Rome to produce a refutation of Olivi's

Apocalypse commentary.[56] That seems to imply that Olivi's commentary was already being put to questionable use before 1303, the date of Boniface's death. It would be good to know how Giles's project turned out, but we do not.

The resultant persecution gained enough momentum to survive Boniface's death in 1303 and John's resignation in 1304. "Olivi's sect" was in for a long spell of trouble. The real question is what qualified one as a member of "Olivi's sect." What did John and his colleagues see as the basic issues? The formula of abjuration forced on all brothers in the province seems to have contained three items: *usus pauper* as part of the vow, the wound in Christ's side, and veneration of those who had not been officially canonized.[57] We can take the three in that order.

Poverty as the Basic Issue

It is the first issue that interests us most. Did it in fact interest them most, too? At the Council of Vienne, Ubertino da Casale would report that at some point early in the persecution the Franciscan provincial minister of Provence wrote to his minister general, John of Murrovalle, asking why the whole thing was taking place. John replied that "all those who dare to assert that *usus pauper* is a substantial part of our vow of poverty should be judged superstitious holders of a pernicious doctrine." This represents a bit of special pleading by Ubertino, since it forms part of his attempt to establish that poverty was the real issue underlying all other attacks on Olivi's orthodoxy. Yet there is little doubt that it was a major issue, if not the only one.

Granting that poverty was an important issue, how was it important? Seeing John and his successor, Gonsalvo of Spain, as apostles of laxity who reversed Raymond Geoffroi's attempts at reform would be an oversimplification. Paradoxically, the meager extant evidence shows more reforming activity from John and Gonsalvo than from Raymond.[58] The general impression given by this evidence is that during the first decade of the fourteenth century, while the attack on Olivi's group was progressing, John and Gonsalvo attempted to curb abuses but were only partially successful. It was, after all, a very large order, and the gap between ideal and reality had not narrowed with time. To say this much is not to say that John and Gonsalvo agreed with the rigorists on reform (although the extent of their differences would depend on which rigorists one chooses to consider).

One wonders, though, if by 1299 the differences had as much to do with attitude as with specific beliefs. Like Salimbene's "solemn brothers showing contempt for the discipline of the order" around 1246, or Nicholas IV's "brethren considering themselves more spiritual than the others" in 1290, the errant brothers in 1299 may have offended as much by the style of their criticism as by its content. Their continued protests had marked them in the eyes of their leaders as a stiff-necked, arrogant group, the very existence of which disturbed the harmonious operation of the order. Its members needed to be taught a lesson.

This observation is partly confirmed by the story of Pons Bautugat. His case must have been a famous one, since Ubertino da Casale and Angelo Clareno both mention it. His crime lay in refusing to hand Olivi's writings over to be burned.[59] What seems particularly significant about Pons is that he apparently had no writings by Olivi, but simply told his superiors that even if he had possessed any he would not have surrendered them, although he would gladly have submitted them to the pope for correction. However theoretical his refusal, Angelo reports that he was cast into a foul prison, where he remained so tightly fettered that he sat rotting in his own urine and excrement. Angelo says that they fed him merely by pushing in some bread and water from time to time with their heads averted. Needless to say, he died, and when they removed his body the lower part of it was largely eaten away by worms. They buried him secretly, but those charged with the task reported that they were stunned by the beatific expression on his face, more angelic than human, and by the fact that, despite the poor state of his body, it emitted a sweet odor that triumphed over the stench. Anyone familiar with hagiography would know what that meant.

Obviously we have moved well beyond categories like "debate" or "controversy" by this point. We are dealing in persecution and martyrdom. Ubertino and Angelo mention others punished with similar cruelty for refusing to deny that *usus pauper* was part of the vow. It is worth noting, however, that according to Ubertino these other recusant friars also appealed to the pope, urging that he define the matter. There was, of course, some reason for Ubertino to say as much, since he was doing just that at the moment, but he and Angelo seem credible in reporting such an appeal. At that point the recalcitrant rigorists in southern France still saw themselves as battling their superiors within the order, not the entire ecclesiastical hierarchy.

The second of the three items, the wound in Christ's side, alludes to Olivi's suggestion that despite what Scripture seems to say, Christ's death came after he was wounded with the spear. The claim had received no serious attention from Olivi's opponents up to that point, but it would be subjected to special consideration at the Council of Vienne. We will return to it then. For the moment, we need only comment that if Olivi's enemies had not noticed, his admirers had. That brings us to the third and final item.

The Olivi Cult and the Beguins

The third item, veneration of one not canonized, is a reflection of the fact that a thriving Olivi cult had sprung up at his grave in Narbonne.[60] The cult was growing even as Olivi's disciples were being hounded down. Angelo Clareno seems to suggest that the 1299 attack on Olivi's writings was accompanied by a violation of his tomb and some damage to his remains,[61] but Angelo, subject to occasional chronological leaps, is probably looking ahead to what we know occurred in 1318. At any rate, we know that shortly after Olivi's death it was already being visited by pilgrims. In a 1325 inquisitorial record Na Prous Boneta, a resident of Montpellier, mentions having been at Olivi's tomb twenty years earlier.[62]

Reference to the Olivi cult brings us to an important element in the story after this point, the beguins and beguines. A great deal was written about this group somewhat later when the inquisitors began to turn their attention to it, but we have little to go on in constructing a picture of lay religiosity in Languedoc ca. 1300, and even less with which to form a picture of Olivi's place in that religiosity. Some things *can* be said, though. First, the name "beguin" can be used to include those laypersons devoted to the defunct Olivi, but it cannot be limited to that group. Words such as *béguin* and *bizocco* (a term widely used in Italy, employed by Boniface VIII in describing disturbing Italian phenomena and by Jacopone da Todi in describing himself during the first ten years after his conversion[63]) could be applied to laypersons acting like members of a religious order or simply to very pious laypersons. These laypersons might be considered quite orthodox, as in the case of Douceline, Hugh of Digne's sister, whose community of women lived according to a discipline and referred to themselves as beguins.[64] Or they might be tried for heresy, as in the case of Rixende, a visionary of Narbonne prosecuted in 1288, whose associates are described as beguins.[65] Some beguins were members of the Franciscan third order, while others were not.[66] Such terms, like the phenomena they describe, are not easy to pin down.

One reference to beguins may bear directly on our subject. In 1299 a provincial council at Béziers, presided over by the archbishop of Narbonne, announced that many people, some of them said to be very learned and some members of a praiseworthy established religious group, had been preaching to *beguini seu beguinae* that the end of the world was at hand and that the time of Antichrist was present or nearly so. They were encouraging their audiences to adopt new modes of penitence and distinctive clothing. The result was vows of chastity that were later broken; secret conventicles meeting at night; lay usurpation of the preaching office, concealed by the pretense that they were not preaching but merely consoling one another; and new rites distinct from anything practiced by the rest of the faithful. The council predictably wanted the whole thing stopped.[67]

Raoul Manselli feels that elements like the mention of learned men and a praiseworthy religious group—as well as the allusion to apocalyptic expectation—show that the council was referring to Olivi's followers, albeit imprecisely. He thinks it probable that further examination freed the group from all suspicion.[68] Such a reading seems to limit the possibilities unduly. Rixende's case shows that lay religiosity was pullulating dangerously in the region even earlier. On the other hand, one cannot preclude a connection between this religiosity and Olivi, since as early as 1285 Arnold of Roquefeuil, Olivi's provincial minister, joined with thirty-five other Franciscans from the province in a petition branding Olivi as the leader of a superstitious sect and a sower of discord and error.[69] Nor is connection with Olivi in Rixende's case ruled out by the fact that her specialty, though eschatological, was not explicitly apocalyptic.[70] She was a visionary, and Olivi had interests in that area. The tie between Franciscans and southern French lay visionaries dates back at least to the mid-thirteenth century, when Douceline—beguine, visionary, and Hugh of Digne's sister—maintained connections with her brother as well as other Franciscans. Rixende herself had Franciscan connections.[71] Whether they were at least partly with Olivi is another question, but we know that Olivi did have ties with at least some female mystics,[72] much as Ubertino da Casale did. It is unclear, however, whether the female mystics of Olivi's acquaintance were "lay" in the full sense, since for all we know they could have belonged to a religious order. Nevertheless, Olivi's ties with beguins do seem implied by his suggestion that Charles of Naples might worry about him "beguinizing" his sons.

In the final analysis, what we can discern about Rixende and her friends and what we know about the group attacked in the 1299 provincial council do not rule out a tie with Olivi. But the data do not establish a tie, either. While Olivi was obviously an important man, there is no reason to detect his shadow behind everything that happened. Two other bits of evidence place us on firmer ground. Paul of Venice informs us that around 1300, one Matthew of Bouzigues from the province of Provence fled with some of Olivi's works and arrived in Rome with five male beguins and thirteen women, who elected him pope in Saint Peter's. Then he left for Greece with Liberato, Angelo, and their companions.[73] While one is not required to believe Paul of Venice on all or even any of these points, the part about Olivi's works is interesting. It becomes even more significant when we learn from Angelo Clareno that around 1301, Jerome of Catalonia arrived in Greece with several women (two of whom he said were his mother and sister) and with books he said had been sent to Angelo's group by Olivi. Some days later a priest who had served as confessor to the group warned Angelo's associates to be careful. The two women in question were not Jerome's mother and sister. Angelo says he also heard later that the books were stolen. Thus exposed, Jerome broke with Angelo's group and joined the Franciscan order, then accused Angelo and his colleagues of all the errors he himself had been disseminating. He found a receptive audience among their enemies.[74]

If Paul of Venice is at least questionable concerning Matthew, so is Angelo regarding Jerome, who went on to establish a solid reputation for himself within the order and to emerge as a major detractor of Angelo's associates. There is also at least some question as to whether Matthew and Jerome really did represent different groups entering Angelo's life at different moments, although most modern scholars believe that this was the case.[75] The important thing for our purposes is that we see Olivi's writings traveling in the company of beguins, a demonstration that around 1300 he was already exerting significant posthumous influence on the laity. That is not to say that he was considered a saint by all of them or was leading them all into heterodox byways. Obviously there is something odd about both Matthew and Jerome as presented by their respective sources. Paul portrays Matthew of Bouzigues as being elected pope by his entourage, but he does not seem to know much about Matthew. Matthew's own confession, presumably composed shortly thereafter,[76] does acknowledge that he has been accused of heresy. In this confession, he says nothing to indicate any disloyalty to the pope, but he does back Olivi's view of poverty as an essential part of the vow as well as the notion (also held by Olivi) that Christ was wounded in the side with the spear before his death rather than after, as the Bible seems to state. As for Jerome, he was obviously able to convince the Franciscans of his orthodoxy and went on to achieve a distinguished career,[77] but Angelo claims that he had changed his tune by then. Angelo does seem to have been wrong at least about the sister,[78] so perhaps he was wrong about the rest. In the final analysis, we cannot know what either man was saying when he entered the story. The important thing is that we see Olivi's influence.

What sort of influence, though? What were they reading? Manselli discusses and publishes[79] several devotional treatises that seem to have been popular in southern French and Catalan lay circles. These sources are eminently orthodox, mainly moral exhortation. They discuss visionary experience, but prudently; they include apocalyptic reference, but just barely. Was nothing stronger being circulated? Manselli explicitly denies that Olivi's Apocalypse commentary was widely known or circulated until later; yet one wonders whether that could actually be the case. Certainly the commentary was known among Franciscans quickly enough for Ubertino da Casale to have borrowed extensively from it in his 1305 *Arbor vitae*. It was also considered problematic enough that Boniface VIII, who died in 1303, asked Giles of Rome to refute it. If it spread that rapidly, why should we assume that it remained undiscovered and unused by beguins?

Other evidence of the Apocalypse commentary is hard to find before 1318, but there is some. We might anticipate a bit by noting that a Catalan work probably written in 1318 followed Olivi's commentary closely, yet embroidered it, making Olivi himself the angel of Rev. 10:1.[80] What makes this fact important for our present purposes is that we find an apparent allusion to the same belief in a 1311 document, written by the community, which charges that some of Olivi's followers believe him to be "that angel described in the Apocalypse who came after the angel who had the sign of the living God."[81] There is, to be sure, no indication of whether these particular followers are laypersons or Franciscans, and in any case saying that Olivi's followers identified him with an angel of the Apocalypse by 1311 is not the same as saying that they were reading Olivi's Apocalypse commentary. Indeed, in a perverse mood one might take the 1311 passage as evidence that they were not, since the preceding sentence in that document describes some of his followers as insisting "that Brother Peter's doctrine should be defended as an article of faith," and yet we know that in the Apocalypse commentary Olivi identifies the angel of Rev. 10:1 with Francis, not himself. Nevertheless, demanding that sort of logical consistency would be naive (if not perverse), and it is clear that by 1318 familiarity with Olivi's commentary had combined with belief in Olivi as an apocalyptic angel, so it is possible that they had combined substantially earlier.

What else by Olivi were they reading? Bernard Gui[82] would later say that the beguins possessed translations of Olivi's treatises on poverty, mendicancy, and dispensations, as well as "certain other treatises." In other words, they were familiar with several of his *Questions on Evangelical Perfection*, including those that asserted *usus pauper* to be an essential part of the vow and questioned the pope's authority to compromise Franciscan poverty. Gui was describing what the beguins were like from around 1318 on, however.

Angelo and the Poor Hermits

It is time to ask what was happening to the Italian zealots during this period. Our best source, Angelo, says that he and the other fugitive brethren lived for two years on the island of Trixonia in the Gulf of Corinth, protected by Thomas of Autremencourt, lord of one of the French baronies set up after the fourth crusade had wrested most of the Byzantine Empire from its Greek rulers.[83] Here, as in Armenia, Franciscans in the area did their best to discredit Angelo's group, but (again as in Armenia) they initially found it difficult work. Eventually leaders of the order approached John of Murrovalle, by now a cardinal, and with his support appealed to Pope Boniface VIII. Angelo says that Boniface was originally dismissive, telling the brothers, "Leave them free to serve God, they're doing better than you are," but those wily brothers already had worked out a winning strategy. They told Boniface that Liberato's group was denying the legitimacy of his election. That did it. He dispatched documents calling for their excommunication and arrest.

Precisely what those missives said must remain unsettled, since they did not survive. Yet Angelo, in a 1317 letter to Pope John XXII, offers what seems to be a point-by-point refutation of the charges made by Boniface in the central document, the bull *Saepe sacram ecclesiam*.[84] In this letter, Angelo attempts to deal with two basic accusations. The first was that his group, though not an authorized order, was behaving like one; the second, that according to Angelo, Boniface was not the pope (authority having been transferred from the hierarchical church to Angelo's own group). Angelo tends to dodge the first charge rather than refute it, since it happens to be true. The second charge he rejects clearly, even passionately, insisting that he would refuse to believe such things "even if I heard them announced by angels or apostles, complete with miracles, nor was I ever so flighty or stupid that I would even consent to listen." Here he is quite believable. Given the stakes, it is possible that in the mid-1290s he entertained doubts about the validity of Celestine's resignation and mentioned these doubts to others. Yet everything we know about Angelo suggests that he would have been unlikely to turn his doubts into a full-scale campaign against Boniface's legitimacy. Of course he was not even the leader of the group until Liberato's death around 1306, and it is theoretically possible that others in their society could have been preaching against Boniface, but even that seems unlikely, since according to Angelo the group already had been carefully vetted in response to charges by the Franciscans in Greece.

The bull proved easier to write than to deliver, and during the delay, the group moved on to Thessaly, where they remained for a few more years.

Eventually they decided to return to Italy and lay their case before Boniface himself, but events were outrunning them. Liberato, their leader, went on ahead, yet apparently by the time he arrived, Boniface was no more—and Boniface's successor, Benedict XI, was himself on his deathbed.[85] In any case Liberato saw neither, became ill at Perugia, and died in that vicinity two years later. Most of the group settled into hermitages in the kingdom of Naples, where King Charles II and the local inquisitor conspired to make their lives miserable.

Angelo himself fared better. He missed this whole episode, having remained in Greece making arrangements to transport the rest of the brothers back to Italy. On their arrival, he and some of his companions went to Perugia, where Cardinal Napoleone Orsini befriended him and—had Angelo not become ill—would have taken him to the papal court in France, Clement V having now been elected. Instead, Angelo remained "in Roman parts," where he was forced to defend himself against more accusations. He claims that he and his associates in the kingdom of Naples were found innocent of heresy, but he says little else about his life between 1305 and 1311 when, at the suggestion of Isnardo Tacconi, papal vicar in Rome, he journeyed to France and put the case of the Poor Hermits before the pope.[86]

Ubertino and the *Arbor Vitae*

We have followed Ubertino as best we could through the early years of his life. We know that he was born around 1259 and entered the order ca. 1273. Around 1285 he visited John of Parma at Greccio and, shortly after, spent some time in Florence in the company of Olivi. At some point—perhaps shortly after his novitiate, but more likely in 1289—he was sent to Paris for study and remained there for nine years. In retrospect, he saw his time at Paris as a period of spiritual decay; encouraged by classmates, teachers, and superiors alike, he abandoned piety for sterile philosophizing. By the turn of the fourteenth century, presumably by 1298, he was back in central Italy. He tells us that he "continued to teach for about four years," and then devoted himself exclusively to preaching.

By that point Ubertino had derived a strongly apocalyptic sense of the order from John of Parma, Olivi, and others, and his spirituality had been shaped not only by John and Olivi but also by various mystics. The result was a heady brew, too strong for some of his confreres. In late 1303 or early 1304, having "borne witness to the truth" before the clergy and people of Perugia,

Ubertino was denounced by his enemies and cited before Pope Benedict XI. The inhabitants of Perugia interceded on Ubertino's behalf and Benedict acceded, but Ubertino's superiors ended his preaching and sent him off to Mount Alverna. There he was influenced by a number of pious friars, including his own brother and the Blessed John of Fermo. He was also guided by still another pious woman, this time unnamed, although we can assume that it was Margaret of Città di Castello. It was at this point that he wrote the *Arbor vitae*.[87]

This work, in many ways Ubertino's greatest, is also his most radical. It holds several major Franciscan sources in uneasy tension. The early part depends heavily upon Bonaventure, but the fifth and final book veers dangerously in another direction. There Ubertino displays more immediate influences. On the one hand he leans heavily on Olivi's Apocalypse commentary. The basic pattern he imposes on church history is essentially the one used by Olivi, who in turn derived it from Joachim of Fiore.[88] Ubertino follows Olivi's division of church history into seven periods and of world history into three ages. Like Olivi, he sees Francis as the angel of the sixth seal who inaugurated the sixth period of church history and the third age of world history; he distinguishes between a mystical and an open Antichrist; he identifies the temptation of the mystical Antichrist with Aristotelian philosophy as well as opposition to Franciscan poverty; he places that opposition within the church itself; and he identifies the pope with the mystical Antichrist. Thus he endorses precisely those propositions that would attract the heaviest fire when Olivi's commentary was subjected to ecclesiastical examination in 1318 and thereafter. Moreover, Ubertino manages to go well beyond Olivi on some of these matters. Olivi simply read Francis into the Apocalypse—and he was hardly unique in doing so—but Ubertino does the same for John of Parma, and the role he assigns John is that of calling down judgment on the great whore.[89] Olivi, at least, placed the mystical Antichrist in the future and saw Celestine V's resignation as valid. Ubertino does neither. He identifies the mystical Antichrist with both Boniface VIII and Benedict XI, and he argues that Celestine was a holy but simple man who was misled by those around him. Boniface was never the legitimate pope. He was instead the beast from the sea prophesied in Apoc. 13. The one nearly slain head (13:3) represents the attempt by the Colonna cardinals—described by Ubertino as "soldiers of God"—to contest the legitimacy of his election. That wound could not have been healed, had Boniface not been aided by the beast from the land (Rev. 13:11–17), played in this case by some in religious orders (Ubertino has the mendicants in mind) who, aspiring to ecclesiastical dignity, supported the pseudopope and were believed by the world on the strength of their reputation for sanctity and knowledge.[90]

If the beast from the land stands for ambitious friars, it also represents Benedict XI. After Boniface was struck down by that battler for Christ,[91] Philip IV—Ubertino is thinking primarily of the Paris assembly in June 1303, which struck at Boniface in word, not the physical assault at Anagni, which did so in deed—he seemed dead in body and authority, his works annulled. Yet immediately thereafter, Benedict, a beast from the land of the religious, arose and perpetuated the authority of the first beast. Ubertino knows someone whom Christ personally informed that Benedict's election was not legal because "all the sheep were not called to the flock" (that is, all the cardinals were not summoned).

Whatever one may think of Ubertino's exegesis, his historical grasp is quite adequate. Benedict, who qualified as rising "from the land of the religious" because he was a Dominican, was attached to his predecessor and wanted to punish those responsible for Anagni. The Colonna complained of his failure to right the wrongs committed against them. Nor did the reformers have reason to like him much. As we have seen, he conducted a hearing against Ubertino and imprisoned Arnald of Villanova, who emerged from the experience as hostile toward Benedict as Ubertino obviously was. When the pope died, Arnald was accused of having poisoned him, and Bernard Délicieux (whom we will later encounter defending the spirituals in 1318) was accused of having conspired with him in the act.[92]

So far Ubertino's interpretation seems to suggest that Boniface was the mystical Antichrist and Benedict his chief supporter, but Ubertino really considers them both to be the mystical Antichrist. He narrates a story he heard from two brothers who had been in Greece. One day they were reading Justin Martyr's interpretation of the Apocalypse. There was general merriment when they discovered that according to Justin, the number of the beast (666)—when converted into letters—spelled BENEDICTOS. They assumed that the Holy Spirit had elected to designate Boniface by his prepapal name (Benedetto Gaetani), but Ubertino feels that more is suggested.[93] Benedict XI's decision to take his predecessor's baptismal name showed that the false authority of the first was transferred to the second. That "Benedictos" is singular in Greek but plural in Latin reflects the fact that Boniface was famous for his evil among Greeks as well as Latins, while both did evil among the Latins. Thus they were jointly the mystical Antichrist. Nevertheless, Ubertino suggests that the name refers more literally to Benedict, because he could do more damage, due to his reputation for sanctity.

As we have seen, Ubertino links Boniface's credentials as the mystical Antichrist with his supplanting of Celestine V, who liberated the dissident

Anconan spirituals. The centrality of that episode in the *Arbor vitae* leads us to other ways in which Ubertino was more radical than his model Olivi. First, while Olivi and Ubertino both saw decay in the order, Ubertino saw a great deal more of it. He was less comfortable than Olivi with the developments that had transformed the order during the thirteenth century. For example, while both men connected the temptation of Antichrist with Aristotelian philosophy, Olivi remained a dedicated scholastic theologian who could cite the Stagirite as an authority, even though he recognized that Aristotle's approach to wisdom was in some ways radically opposed to Paul's.[94] He criticized excessive devotion to philosophy, but never reacted to the Franciscan educational program as negatively as Ubertino did. Nor does the difference lie only in the realm of education. It could be extended in any number of directions with much the same result. Olivi argued that Franciscan bishops should continue to observe Franciscan poverty, while Ubertino questioned whether Franciscans should be bishops at all.[95] Olivi cited papal declarations concerning the rule when he thought them useful in shoring up his case, and he discreetly ignored those that militated against it. Ubertino dismissed papal declarations as a concession to imperfection and characterized *Exiit qui seminat*—the very bull Olivi cited at length in the early *usus pauper* controversy—as a millstone tied around the waist of the order.[96] Olivi rested his case for *usus pauper* on the rule, papal declarations, and recent Franciscan masters like Pecham and Bonaventure, but Ubertino was much more likely to cite the *Testament* and Brother Leo.

The latter contrast brings us to the heart of the matter. It never seems to have occurred to Olivi that he should look with suspicion on Bonaventure's *Legenda maior*. Ubertino would have been more than happy to correct him on this score, because he felt that the order in Francis's day was simultaneously better and worse than Bonaventure dared to reveal. In the *Arbor vitae*, Ubertino observes several times that in composing his life of Francis, Bonaventure omitted episodes concerning the high level of poverty practiced by the early Franciscans. Their inclusion would have revealed the extent to which the order in Bonaventure's day had decayed. At the same time, Bonaventure's rosy picture of the early order ignored the extent to which it was *already falling* in Francis's lifetime. Ubertino shared Angelo Clareno's tendency not only to canonize the *Testament* and the early Franciscan experience as seen in the Leo sources, but also to assume that by the end of his life, Francis—having relinquished power because he saw where the order was going—had devoted his energies to prophesying how much worse things were going to get.[97] As Gian Luca Potestà observes, this sense of an early betrayal enabled Ubertino and Angelo to see "an absolute continuity, historical and ideological," between

Francis and themselves, and to discover the roots of their own contemporary conflict in Francis's time.[98] Once Francis had resigned and Elias had accepted authority, the contrast between them was, in effect, analogous to that between the spirituals and their corrupt superiors. In Potestà's words, "Elias becomes for the spirituals the symbol of those superiors responsible for the decadence of the order, and the polemic against him is nothing more or less than the expression of a diffuse antihierarchical sentiment."[99]

This view of Franciscan history as moving steadily along two paths right from the beginning had wider implications that encouraged Italian spirituals to explore possibilities unacceptable to Olivi. For example, it made them much more willing than Olivi to sanction a split in the order as a means of saving the Franciscan life. The difference was hardly absolute. Olivi, having spent some time in Italy, was aware of the currents that informed Italian rigorist thought. He was aware of Brother Leo and of Francis as a prophet of decay. He even cited Conrad of Offida on Francis's possible resurrection.[100] That sort of thing was not central for him, however. Ubertino took the basic structure of Olivi's commentary and filled it with a more radical critique of the order. Thus there is some irony in the fact that it was Olivi's commentary that ultimately faced condemnation—and Ubertino who found himself explaining that, while he utilized Olivi, he did so prudently, accepting the sound parts and avoiding the rest.[101]

It is impossible to say exactly when Ubertino left Mount Alverna, but it was presumably soon after he finished the *Arbor vitae*. He entered the service of Cardinal Napoleone Orsini, then pontifical legate in central Italy. During his period with Orsini, Ubertino preached and served in various ecclesiastical capacities, and it was probably at this time that he carried on his investigation of the heretical sect of the *spiritus libertatis* (an episode that will receive attention later in this volume).[102] He seems to have remained in Orsini's service until 1309, although not always with Orsini himself. In that year, Orsini went to Avignon, and somewhat thereafter, Ubertino did the same.

Jacopone da Todi and the Rebellion Against Boniface VIII

Angelo and Ubertino may have despised Boniface in their hearts, but they did not man the barricades against him. Other spiritual Franciscans did just that, as Olivi's letter to Conrad of Offida testifies. We learn from Olivi that in 1295 some Italian Franciscans were saying that Celestine was still the pope, and they were apparently saying it loudly enough for their voices to carry all the way to Narbonne. They were claiming that those who supported Boniface were part of the synagogue of Satan. Moreover, they were applying to the church under Boniface the injunction to separation found in Rev. 18:4, "Come out of her, my people."

Who were these brave souls? It is tempting to think that Conrad himself was one of them, and that Olivi, in begging Conrad to correct such errant brothers "should you run into any," was being either tactful or ironic. That seems unlikely, though. Angelo informs us that Conrad did run into difficulty during this period. Some of the brethren complained to the newly elected minister general, John of Murrovalle, that Conrad had said neither the declarations nor the rule was being observed in the order, and that those who tried to observe them were impeded in their efforts. They also accused him of having said that another order—we can assume that the reference is to the Poor Hermits of Pope Celestine, since Conrad encouraged its formation, though he did not join it—was the real order of friars minor, and that those who wished to observe the rule should leave the Franciscan order.[103] John confronted Conrad with these charges, then cried, "I can barely restrain myself from tearing all my clothing into shreds, just as you have torn my heart!" Conrad, rapidly shifting from defendant to spiritual counselor, prayed for John and "with a few humble, simple words" so endeared himself to the minister general that the latter called upon him for spiritual comfort until Conrad's death in 1306.

What should we make of this story? The charges seem highly believable, since Angelo himself says that they were well documented, and they fit Conrad as Angelo portrays him throughout the *Chronicle*. He describes Conrad as "content for fifty years and more with one tunic of old, inexpensive cloth, patched with sackcloth and other rags, always barefoot, never wanting anything except a tunic and cord. His bed was the bare ground covered with a bit of straw or a mat or planks, and he never ceased from prayer, vigils and fasting." He goes on to say that Conrad observed all the fasting periods "sequestered from all conversation and activity, insofar as he could." Such a description, in addition to the fact that Conrad was instrumental in the creation of the Poor Hermits, makes it likely that Conrad was guilty as charged.

The dramatic reconciliation with John might strike one as harder to accept, and it is hardly made more credible by its resemblance to other, similar stories Angelo tells about unexpected support in high places for one rigorist or another. Yet there is no reason to doubt it, either. It is probably accurate at least in suggesting that Conrad managed to avoid punishment.

If we accept Angelo's story even to that extent, it becomes highly unlikely that Olivi's letter was aimed at Conrad. If Conrad was saying in 1295 that Boniface was not the legitimate pope (and saying it publicly enough for Olivi to have heard the report), then undoubtedly his enemies would have heard about it too and relayed it to the minister general. The result would have been more or less the same as when enemies of the Poor Hermits made the same charge about them before the pope. Conrad would have found himself in very serious trouble.

Who else might have held the views described in Olivi's letter? Perhaps the closest we can come to putting a face on such sentiments is Jacopone da Todi. Primarily known as a poet—certainly one of the greatest at the turn of the fourteenth century—Jacopone was around sixty years old when Celestine V became pope. Angelo explicitly names him (along with the minister general, Conrad of Offida, and three others) as one of those who encouraged Angelo's group to seek aid from Celestine, which suggests that Jacopone was already considered a key supporter of spiritual aims.

Jacopone is an important witness to the spiritual Franciscan attitude toward Celestine, precisely because he saw from the beginning that the transition from hermit's hut to papal palace might prove disastrous. One of his *Laude* begins, "What will you do, Pietro da Morrone, now that you've been put to the test?"[104] The poem acknowledges the degree of hope placed in Celestine as he takes office and the level of disillusionment that will follow if he does not fulfill those hopes. It recognizes the damage that will be done to Celestine's own reputation if he fails. The papal court is presented as a crucible in which the hermit pope has been placed, testing his mettle.

The fire will be an extremely hot one. The final lines of this poem, found only in some manuscripts, announce that the cardinalate has fallen to a low condition in which everyone intends to enrich his relatives. Nor are the cardinals unique. In *Lauda 35*, Jacopone depicts the church weeping as she sits surrounded by bastard sons; her true sons have disappeared, along with the father and all other legitimate relations. The scandalous lives of these illegitimate progeny lead the world to call the church a whore. The true sons loved poverty, led austere lives, and scorned worldly ambitions. The bastard sons fight among themselves, and their sole interest is in gaining ecclesiastical office in order to make money.

Jacopone's *Laude* are particularly hard on Franciscan scholars. In the poem just cited, he asks rhetorically,

> Where are the doctors, full of prudence?
> I see many raised up in knowledge
> But their lives don't suit me.

Lauda 88 personalizes the same message, aiming it at a specific dead friar.

> Where have you gone, Friar Rinaldo?
> You, who have disputed over quodlibets,
> Tell me if you paid your debts.
> Are you in glory or is it hot where you are?
> God hasn't filled me in.

Here again Jacopone draws a contrast between being raised up to high academic honors, a worldly achievement,

> You were educated at Paris
> With great honor and great expense,

and true Franciscan humility.

> I fear that the honor
> Has drawn from your heart
> Any urge to consider yourself
> the least of despised *fraticelli*.

Much the same sentiment lies at the heart of *Lauda* 31, which begins with the words,

> So it goes, there is no more religion.
> We see a bad Paris that has destroyed Assisi
> With its learning, sending it off on a bad path.

The next few lines go a long way toward explaining the nature of that wrong direction.

> Those with learning eat with the guests,
> While the rest eat greens with oil in the refectory.
> If the lector is off his food he's treated like an emperor,
> But if the cook gets sick no one visits him.
> When they meet in chapter they make many rules,
> And the first to enunciate them is the first to break them.
> Note the great love for one another they cherish in their hearts!
> They wait like mules to kick one another in the chest.

> Try disagreeing with one and he'll prepare a cross for you,
> Setting traps for you until he succeeds in getting rid of you.
> They stand around joking with women
> and if a *fraticello* gives them a look
> they'll put him in prison.
> Even if they're sons of shoemakers or low-born butchers
> they act as if they were the sons of royalty.

This poem moves through a series of observations, some more acceptable to modern ears than others. The closing lines remind us that Jacopone, who was himself from a respectable family, could season his humility with a dash of snobbery. The middle lines suggest that academic fortune seeking can destroy mutual affection, a point that will hardly amaze present-day scholars. It is the early comment about dining arrangements that most impresses, though. The basic thought here is that education has contributed to the creation of an elite with special status and privileges. That is precisely the critique we will hear from Ubertino da Casale at the Council of Vienne.

The problem, then, is partly that involvement in the academic milieu at Paris is part of a much larger accommodation in which the order has come to terms with worldly assumptions, goals, and social structures. A more complete investigation of the matter would have to look seriously at Jacopone's notion of knowledge and how one goes about achieving it. His perspective differs not only from that of mainstream Paris masters like Bonaventure, Pecham, and Matthew of Aquasparta, but also from Olivi as well. It is closer to what one encounters in Italian spirituals like Ubertino and Angelo, but even here one should look much more closely before equating them with Jacopone. In *Lauda* 87, the poet notes that

> In Paris one doesn't see such a great philosophy
> as going mad for Christ.
> He who goes mad for Christ
> Seems afflicted and in tribulation,
> But he is really a master of natural philosophy and theology.

The poem goes on to say, "He who seeks honor is not worthy of Christ's love," but "He who seeks shame needn't go to Bologna to attain some other magistracy."

Again, we see the tie between contemporary education and a worldly orientation that seeks honor or fame, but here it is contrasted with a different sort of knowledge, a divine madness that overturns worldly standards. Such a perspective comes, of course, from traditional Christianity—indeed, straight from I Corinthians, with its distinction between God's foolishness and the wisdom of the world, its recognition that "knowledge puffeth up." In Jacopone, however, this insight is shaped by its connection with a profound mysticism that pushes the *via negativa* far enough for a modern historian like Romana Guarnieri to place Jacopone alongside Marguerite Porète and Meister Eckhardt within the tendency she identifies as the *spiritus libertatis*.[105]

In any case, Jacopone thought the order badly compromised, and the church itself in dire straits. In *Lauda* 29 Christ chastises the Roman church, describing it as "contemptuous and ungrateful for his love." In *Lauda* 17, Jacopone depicts the false religious and proud scholars of his day as new Pharisees, crucifying Christ yet again. *Lauda* 6 uses language from the Book of Revelation to paint the current crisis in apocalyptic hues.[106] *Lauda* 8 portrays the fruits of the spirit as crying out,

> Revenge our injury, high, just Lord,
> The Roman curia has done this evil.
> Let us run at it in fury and drive them all out.
> A limb of Antichrist has called itself the church.
> Watch yourself, Lord, don't take any more of this!
> Purge your church of those who have lived evilly in it.
> Let them be sent to a place where they can purge their sins.

Thus it is hardly surprising that Jacopone was psychologically prepared for extreme measures when Celestine resigned and was replaced by Boniface. Those measures were taken in 1297 by the Colonna. They, like the Poor Hermits, had been left in an exposed position by Celestine's resignation. The papacy would give Boniface VIII extra leverage in his battle with the Colonna, and on May 3, 1297, some of the Colonna family executed a preemptive strike on Boniface, waylaying a convoy that was bringing him 200,000 florins. Three days later, they restored the stolen money, but the battle escalated anyway; on the night of May 9–10, at the Colonna fortress of Longhezza, they drew up a declaration declaring that Boniface was not the legitimate pope.[107] They could hardly call for the return of Celestine, who had been dead for a year, but they did demand a general council to settle the matter. The Longhezza declaration was signed by a number of people, including three Franciscans— one of them Jacopone.

Having signed on with the Colonna, Jacopone earned the opportunity to be besieged with them at Palestrina for a year and a half. It may have been while confined there that he wrote *Lauda* 83, his first poem addressed to—more precisely, aimed at—Boniface. It catalogues his misdeeds and designates him a "new Lucifer on the papal throne, poisoning the world with his blasphemies." Like the attacks orchestrated by the Colonna and later by Philip IV, Jacopone's poem charges the pope with several of the seven deadly sins, but goes beyond that to accuse him of genuine impiety and even heresy (although Jacopone does leave the last matter undecided, allowing the reader to determine whether Boniface is motivated by heresy or despair).

When Palestrina fell in September 1298, Jacopone was imprisoned at Todi, presumably in the Franciscan house. The sentence was perpetual imprisonment, which simply meant imprisonment until the pope should decide to release him. The result was a poem that furnishes us with valuable information not only on the nature of Franciscan prisons, but also on Jacopone's remarkable resilience in the face of adversity. *Lauda* 53 begins as his poem to Pope Celestine had: "What will you do, Friar Jacopone, now that you've been put to the test?" We learn that his cell is underground and that the privy "doesn't smell like perfume." No one can speak to him except the jailer, who must report whatever is said. His fetters make it difficult to walk, although he must do so to fight the cold; when he moves at night, his legs get tangled in the chains. His food consists of bread, onions, soup and apples. None of this sounds terribly inviting, yet the dominant emotion in the poem is a wry, ironic humor. In the middle section of the poem Jacopone observes that his jailers are simply doing for him what he should be doing for himself, aiding him in the penance he seeks. What is happening to him is what he, as a Franciscan, has been seeking for thirty years. They cannot hurt him. "I myself am the only enemy that can stand in the way of my salvation." Toward the end, he sounds almost cheerful as he pictures himself busily ordering his troops to ward off attack. The reader is left with every reason to believe that he will do so.

Jacopone addressed two more poems, *Laude* 55 and 67, to Boniface. In both, he expressed his willingness to stay in prison if the pope would only lift his excommunication so that he could again be considered a Franciscan in good standing and receive the sacraments. No absolution was forthcoming, though. During the jubilee year of 1300, the pope gave out many pardons, but none to the Colonna or their supporters.

Jacopone had to wait for his release until Boniface died in 1303 and was succeeded by Benedict XI. He then spent the last three years of his life as a brother at Colazzone. The fact that Jacopone was reconciled with his order at this point—a time when many other spirituals were enduring a persecution that would abate only when Clement V intervened—suggests that his problem was never primarily with the order but with Boniface. He was imprisoned and then released mainly as a Colonna supporter, not as a Franciscan dissident, although one cannot completely separate the two.

That Jacopone stayed in good standing with the order during his final years indicates that he was not seen as a zealot. How one interprets that fact depends on how one organizes his poems. George Peck places most of Jacopone's great mystical poems in those last three years and thus can see the prison experience as a turning point.[108] The isolation and physical deprivation of this experience enabled the poet to turn inward to a greater extent than ever before. The result was a deeper spirituality. Jacopone more or less transcended the earthly battles still being fought by the rigorists. While it is dangerous to let a theory of spiritual progress dictate chronology, Peck's suggestion makes sense, and a theory of spiritual progress is pretty much all we have to go on in dating many of Jacopone's poems.

Spirituals and Female Mystics

Jacopone's mystical experience brings us to an interesting question, one already raised by Ubertino's close contact with various lay mystics. One might ask whether in certain of these lay mystics we discern an extension of spiritual Franciscan values to the lay sphere, much as we see those values extended in the case of the French beguins. Some scholars have recently asserted that such is the case. They have argued that the friars who were the confidants of Clare of Montefalco, Angela of Foligno, and Margaret of Cortona were largely spiritual Franciscans. In fact, some have gone further than that. They have asked whether the visions attributed to these women were largely spiritual Franciscan productions. A number of historians have been open to the possibility. The question is important enough to rate more serious attention than it can receive here, and thus it will be deferred for the moment and considered in the Appendix.

The Significance of the Period 1290–1308

Before moving on the Council of Vienne, we might pause to consider the significance of the period 1290–1308. Obviously it witnessed increased polarization within the order. Gradual hardening of battle lines had caused persecution, and persecution in turn accelerated hardening. Even in 1308 one cannot speak of two factions with distinct programs. The spirituals by their very nature would remain heterogeneous, and there would always be an indistinct band of brothers with spiritual tendencies lying more or less safely within the order; but by 1308 the split was notable enough to produce the debate that would occur at Vienne.

The period also witnessed attacks on the spirituals coming from a higher level than before. The 1270s and 1280s featured action against the Anconan zealots by their provincial leaders, but by the end of that period, the action had been frustrated by the minister general. In southern France we know of no action at all. Olivi's 1283 censure was a different matter, belonging within the history of processes against individual scholars. In the 1290s, however, disciplinary action against zealot groups was conducted throughout southern France and Italy. In southern France in the early 1290s and again in 1299, it was carried out under the direction of the minister general, either by papal order (1290) or with papal approval (1299). Inquisitors were involved. In Italy, we find Boniface VIII taking a major interest in dissidents, even in eccentrics. Here again inquisitors were involved.

This new attention from the highest levels was closely related to a feeling at those levels that Franciscan dissenters were dangerous to good order within the church. Pope Nicholas IV, a Franciscan himself, called for action in 1290 because he thought that certain southern French zealots were disturbing peace and harmony within the Franciscan family. Boniface VIII called for action against Italian zealots because he felt that some of them were threatening good order, his own position, and Christian orthodoxy. Had some Italian zealots not questioned Boniface's legitimacy, he might have been less concerned about their threat to order and orthodoxy; some did question it, however, and their challenge probably affected the way he looked at other deviant groups. The result would provide an unfortunate precedent for future papal action. By 1308, rigorists might show their loyalty by appealing to the pope against their ministers, but they needed to state their allegiance now in a way that they had not before.

The period also shows a growing alliance between Franciscan zealots and pious laity. Close connections between Franciscans and laypersons can be traced back to the beginning of the order. One might even say that they began with Francis. There was also an old and honorable precedent for close relationships between laypersons and Franciscan reformers with apocalyptic tendencies. Hugh of Digne's circle at Hyères, as described by Salimbene, shows us judges, notaries, physicians, and other learned men gathering in Hugh's room to discuss Joachite doctrine.[109] In the 1270s, 1280s, and 1290s, ties between devout laity and Franciscan rigorists can be seen in Ubertino's relationship with Pier Pettinaio and various holy women; in Olivi's epistolary contact with the captive sons of Charles II; perhaps in Olivi's contact with various mystics; and in a variety of other cases. The major influence did not always run in the same direction. If the French beguins were shaped in significant ways by their relations with Franciscan rigorists, Ubertino may have been more influenced by the female mystics than they were by him.

Left to their own devices, lay-religious combinations like the ones that influenced Ubertino might produce a series of interlocking circles, following their own bent without much concern about higher authority. In some ways their creativity and spontaneity epitomized lay movements during the preceding century. It was a time for new forms of religious expression. One need only look at the rich variety of forms female lay piety took.[110] Unfortunately, spontaneity implied lack of ecclesiastical control—particularly unwelcome during a period when the church was intent on refining its hierarchical structure, extending its authority as far as possible. A hierarchy bent on guiding piety along institutionally approved paths might find the efflorescence of religious experimentation rather frightening, and from the 1274 Council of Lyons on, we see the institution increasingly willing to curb novelty in the interest of predictability.[111] It never did so consistently—indeed, it could not do so. What happened on a local level was still largely in the hands of local and regional authority unless the papacy wanted to make a special issue of it.

Even in cases where the hierarchy came to speak with a single voice, such groups were hardly easy to control; once threatened by higher authority, they possessed remarkable psychological resources to sustain them in resistance or even rebellion, should they think it necessary. Eventually, of course, some did rebel. Most of these groups opted for a fugitive, underground existence, rather than armed resistance. The Apostles under Fra Dolcino took the latter course, though only in the latter stages and apparently only as a last resort.[112]

We should remember that when Boniface and other ecclesiastics looked at Franciscan zealots and their lay companions, they saw them in the light of other phenomena like the Apostles. It is significant that historians have had a hard time deciding precisely which group Boniface was describing in some of his bulls.[113] It is also worth noting that (according to Angelo Clareno) after the inquisitor Thomas of Aversa rounded up a number of Liberato's group in southern Italy around 1305, he wrote King Charles II informing him that he had captured forty heretics from Fra Dolcino's sect. That was untrue, of course, but one of those taken does seem to have been a "brother Apostle" from Lombardy who had been wandering about the area.[114] The designation suggests that he was indeed (or at least had been) a member of the group Dolcino was currently leading; however, that is not quite the same as saying that he believed what Dolcino believed. The Apostles had undergone a remarkable change between their early years under Gerardo Segarelli and their later ones under Dolcino. Thus, when we describe someone wandering around southern Italy in 1305 as an Apostle, we have not thereby defined precisely what sort of Apostle he was.

Nor have we settled the matter of whether this particular Apostle was wandering around with Liberato's people. Angelo's phraseology is confusing at best. He reports that a friendly lord, having been told of the inquisitor's activities by two members of Liberato's group (and perhaps notified about the purported forty Apostles by the inquisitor himself), asked the two informants, "Was there any Lombard brother with you?" They replied, "No, lord, nor did the inquisitor detain anyone born in Lombardy except for a single brother Apostle, whom he found wandering about and detained." The lord then wrote to the inquisitor and told him he had heard from reliable witnesses that "among all the people he had captured he had only one Lombard."

Thus Angelo leaves us uncertain as to whether the Lombard was even traveling with Liberato's group. In the final analysis, however, the answer to this question is really less relevant than the inquisitor's initial tendency to see Liberato's group in that context. It was hardly a good omen for the beleaguered Franciscan rigorists, since during this period the Apostles were seen as dangerous enough to rate destruction by a crusade.

To say that spiritual Franciscans crossed paths with heretical groups like the Apostles or the putative *spiritus libertatis* is not to say that contact led inevitably to influence or that in the first decade of the fourteenth century spiritual Franciscans were significantly swayed by these associations—although there is certainly evidence of mutual influence and confusion at a later date, when the spirituals, pushed beyond the margins of ecclesiastical acceptance, found themselves within what Raniero Orioli describes as "the multiform, convergent, muddled heretical underbrush."[115] The point for the moment is that even coming within range of these groups hindered the spiritual Franciscans in their efforts to gain the love and trust of ecclesiastical leaders.[116]

THE COUNCIL OF VIENNE
The Spiritual Franciscan Position

WHAT EVIDENCE WE HAVE SUGGESTS that the first decade of the fourteenth century was a bad time for those in southern France who adhered to Olivi's position on *usus pauper*, but their travail ended when Pope Clement V intervened in 1309. Why he did so is not entirely clear, but Angelo Clareno may provide part of the answer: Angelo reports that Arnald of Villanova was responsible. Arnald, a Catalan, had served as physician to Peter III of Aragon, Boniface VIII, and Clement V.[1] He was also much given to apocalyptic speculation and in 1299 or 1300 had produced, while on a diplomatic mission to Paris, a work on Antichrist that led to his arrest. While his speculation kept him on the edge of serious trouble for the rest of his life, his excellent contacts and medical reputation constantly prevented him from falling irrevocably into it. Arnald's troubles were primarily with the Dominicans, and his counterattacks on them showed substantial sympathy not merely for Franciscan poverty, but also for Olivi's notion of *usus pauper*. Moreover, he had spent some time in southern France—he taught medicine at Montpellier—and had come to show compassion toward the spiritual Franciscans' plight. Immediately after Benedict XI succeeded Boniface VIII, Arnald attempted to secure a reversal of the persecution against them and, incidentally, protection from attacks against his own apocalyptic thought. The result was another period of imprisonment that ended with the accession of Clement V. Clement valued Arnald as a physician and was apparently indifferent to his theological preoccupations (as well as to the charge that he had conspired to poison Benedict XI). Clement ignored Arnald's requests that his apocalyptic works be submitted to new examination, but his inaction probably saved Arnald from still another condemnation.

Angelo says that Arnald appealed to King Charles of Sicily, and the latter wrote Gonsalvo of Spain, the minister general. Charles threatened to complain directly to the pope if the persecutions did not cease. This seems odd if the Charles in question was the Angevin king of Naples, Charles II. Charles had not hitherto shown any great sympathy for the spirituals and, as Angelo himself indicates, he had aided in the persecution of some Poor Hermits at Gonsalvo's request.[2] He died in May 1309, and some have suggested that Angelo confused Charles with his immediate son and successor, Robert the Wise.[3] Like his brother, the Franciscan bishop-saint Louis of Toulouse, Robert was more than normally interested in religious matters.[4] The suggestion has its difficulties, though, since one recent scholar argues energetically that there is little evidence of any sympathy for the spirituals on Robert's part.[5] So unless in the final months of his life Robert's father, Charles, began to see the spirituals with new eyes, thanks to Arnald, we might look for a third candidate. There is one. Since Angelo says Arnald talked with *Carolo rege Siciliae* and we know that Arnald did have a close relationship with Frederick, King of Sicily, Angelo may really have Frederick in mind.[6] We simply do not know.

Arnald himself appealed directly to Clement.[7] Nor were the voices of Arnald and (whichever) king the only ones speaking on behalf of the spirituals. Clement himself noted in a bull of 1310 that he had been informed "frequently" in both secret and public consistories of the need to correct some things in the Franciscan order.[8] Cardinal Napoleone Orsini (whom Celestine V had chosen as protector of the ill-fated Poor Hermits) had received the spiritual Ubertino da Casale into his service around 1306, employed him in various ways at least through 1308, and by 1309 had journeyed to Avignon and may have used his influence to end the persecution. The two Colonna cardinals, Pietro and Giacomo, also had a history of contact with some of the spirituals, having united with them in opposition to Boniface VIII. Giacomo had been on friendly terms with John of Parma and would serve as Angelo Clareno's patron. Finally, we know that in August 1309 officials from the city of Narbonne petitioned the pope to reverse not only the persecution but also the condemnation of Olivi's writings and the prohibition of the Olivi cult at his tomb in their city. The petition also complained that the Franciscan rule was not being observed in the community.[9]

Clement summoned spokesmen for both factions to a protracted hearing, which moved with him from his summer retreat at Grozeau to the papal court at Avignon, then to the Council of Vienne, and finally back to Grozeau again after the Council ended in May 1312. In April 1310, at the urging of Raymond Geoffroi, Clement temporarily removed from control of the order all those who were serving as spokesmen for the spirituals.[10] It was a wise precaution though perhaps an insufficient one. Raymond Geoffroi died suddenly that summer, and he was followed quickly by two and perhaps three other spiritual spokesmen. Both Angelo Clareno and another source claim that they were poisoned, and Angelo reports that some members of the community actually bragged of having done it.[11] The charge of poisoning was common in the Middle Ages—we already have registered another in this chapter—yet so, apparently, was poisoning. We might find it hard to imagine pious Franciscans engaging in such behavior, but then again we might have equal difficulty believing some of the imprisonment stories recounted by Ubertino and Angelo.

Like a modern conference organizer, Clement issued a call for papers. Both sides were to address four issues: whether the spirituals had been infected by the heretical sect of the *spiritus libertatis,* which recently had been suppressed in Umbria; whether the rule and *Exiit qui seminat* were being observed properly within the order; Olivi's orthodoxy; and the persecution in southern France. The ensuing debate ushered in a new phase of the controversy. First, it applied a brake to the persecution, though it did not stop it entirely. Second, it elevated the spirituals' spokesmen to a position of temporary equality with leaders of the order. Third, it presupposed a single spiritual faction embracing both French and Italian zealots. Certainly, there had been contact before 1309; nevertheless, the French and Italian zealots had moved on parallel tracks, as they were concerned with somewhat different issues and pursued diverse aims. Even in Italy there were remarkable strategic differences from group to group. Between 1309 and 1312, most of the tracks seemed to merge for a while as French and Italian spokesmen combined forces. Fourth and most important for our immediate purposes, the great confrontation of 1309–12 produced another great burst of polemical literature on the *usus pauper* question. It is to this literature that we must now turn, although we can by no means do it justice.

Raymond Geoffroi

The earliest extant reply to the four questions was penned by Raymond Geoffroi toward the end of 1309 on behalf of the French spirituals.[12] After his dismissal by Boniface VIII in 1295, Raymond had renewed his Angevin connections and had become a confidant of Louis, the son of Charles II, Angevin king of Naples. One of the three royal hostages who had sought Olivi's tutelage in 1295, Louis became bishop-designate of Toulouse in 1296, but was on his deathbed in April 1297. Raymond remained with him, was holding Louis's hand when he died, and was a witness in the ensuing canonization process.

In his 1309 missive to Clement V, Raymond deals in order with the four questions posed by the pope. He denies any connection with the *spiritus libertatis* and moves quickly to the more important question of how the rule and *Exiit qui seminat* are being observed. His answer is quite mild. On the whole, he says, they are indeed observed, but with many impurities in the matter of poverty. Large and ornate buildings have been constructed and, although the increased number of Franciscans excuses the practice to some extent, there are certain cases that cannot be explained away on this basis. Some brothers have too many books, while others have garments that are too expensive; these are rare cases, however, and for every brother who has too many clothes, there are many who do not have enough. A greater problem stems from the fact that brothers scarcely dare to use old, patched garments because they fear that they will be condemned as fanatics. There are also excesses in the manner of receiving gifts and legacies. The latter, indeed, are sometimes an occasion for unseemly legal wrangling, "although this abuse has been corrected to some extent in some parts of the order." If Franciscans would only follow the constitutions of the order, all of these problems would be alleviated.

The major cause of these impurities, Raymond observes, is some people's insistence that *usus pauper* is not a substantive part of the rule and vow. The order will deteriorate even more in the future unless the pope corrects this false opinion. *Usus pauper* is like chastity and obedience. A few carnal thoughts or a little mulishness would not constitute mortal sin. Neither would a minor lapse from restricted use. The sin becomes mortal only when "one wishes to live in a style that completely surpasses the bounds of evangelical poverty." Raymond explicitly accepts Olivi's assertion that *usus pauper* is vowed indeterminately, and he has no qualms about doing so. In fact, he argues that Olivi's orthodoxy should need no defense, since on that score Olivi himself managed to satisfy everyone "except perhaps a few rivals" in 1283 and 1292. If anyone still wishes to accuse him, Raymond is confident that the matter can be cleared up easily.

As for the situation in southern France: for the last twenty years, Raymond says, that unhappy province has been burdened with investigations *(inquisitiones)* that have been marred by repeated violations of due process and have led to the punishment of innocent brothers. Raymond obliges legal historians by enumerating the procedural defects, then remarks that the first of these enormities was perpetrated by the provincial minister Arnold of Roquefeuil and the visitors sent by John of Murrovalle immediately after the general chapter at Lyons. Since Raymond is writing in 1309, he thus seems to give us a choice between believing his first statement (that the investigations have been going on for twenty years) or his final one (that the oppression began shortly after the general chapter of 1299). Perhaps he should be interpreted as saying that the investigations have been in progress for around two decades (i.e., since Nicholas IV intervened?) but that there was a serious escalation of oppression after 1299. His catalogue of legal improprieties seems to refer to the latter period.

Raymond's response is disappointingly brief but quite suggestive. If he is characteristic of any large body of opinion in southern France—and his position as spokesman allows us to hope that such is the case—then we can conclude that even in 1309 a number of French spirituals followed Olivi's lead in assuming that the Franciscan order, though besmirched, was still essentially Franciscan. It had sustained damage but could be repaired. The superstructure was still sound. Like Bonaventure and Bonagratia of San Giovanni in Persiceto before him, this former minister general suggests that the machinery for reform is already available in the constitutions. He grants that some reform has taken place; his greatest concern is for the future. His essentially Olivian moderation on this score is all the more striking when we consider that he has lived through a decade in which the situation as Olivi knew it no longer held, a decade in which both Olivi's followers and his memory were subjected to persecution. Like Olivi before him, Raymond locates the mischief in the area of poverty, ignoring other equally striking changes that had occurred during the preceding century. When he turns to specific problems, they are the same ones noted by Olivi, Bonaventure, Bonagratia, and Pecham in the late thirteenth century.

Ubertino da Casale's Response

A second answer to the four questions was provided by Ubertino da Casale, probably at the beginning of 1310.[13] It constituted Ubertino's first word in the controversy but hardly his last. Ubertino's appearance in the lists at this moment marked his debut as a major spokesman for the spirituals, but it was a role for which he had been in preparation over the previous four decades.

Since he himself investigated the *spiritus libertatis*, he is able to offer assurances on that score by referring to another document that the pope will receive. Thus his answer to the four questions leaps quickly over the first one and embarks upon a long answer to the second, the present state of the order in relation to the rule and to *Exiit qui seminat*. Here he is painfully explicit. He argues energetically and at great length that the present state of the order is, quite simply, one of collapse. *Status est collapsus!* After the brief, measured, diplomatic response from Raymond, the former minister general, we encounter a less measured one from Ubertino—a man who never had been and never could be minister general.

In what sense had the order collapsed? In the course of the debate, Ubertino would explain his position in stunning detail, in several works, over and over. Most of these writings were answered by the community, and their responses were answered in turn by Ubertino. Following the debate is a bit like watching a tennis game, provided one can envisage a match in which one player is occasionally able to get off another shot before his opponent manages to return the previous one. Thanks to this situation, practically every issue in the controversy was discussed several times. We will simplify our work here by taking the issues one by one, synthesizing all the works on either side, and dealing simultaneously with Ubertino's charge and the community's response. We will examine a series of specific areas in which Ubertino sees decay, then turn to the more abstract question of *usus pauper* and the vow.

Confessors

Some of Ubertino's charges deal with practices not directly related to restricted use, yet relevant to the controversy insofar as they reflect areas of tension between spirituals and conventuals. For example, Ubertino complains that ministers and custodians use information gained through confession in making assignments and denying promotions. He notes that, according to *Quo elongati*,[14] the minister general should provide "mature and discreet" confessors other than the leaders.

In responding to this charge, the community agrees that it is wrong to break the seal of confession and insists that those who do so are punished, although it protests in the same breath that it knows of no such violations.[15] Here the issue gains its importance from the fact that the sacramental and administrative functions of such leaders inevitably clashed in situations in which they were loyal to the community but found themselves governing spirituals. It is understandable that the spirituals, troubled by the strain such a situation produced on their consciences, would feel the need of a good confessor—and equally understandable that prudence would counsel them to think twice before bringing their problems to their leaders.

Care of the Sick

Ubertino complains that sick brothers are well cared for if they happen to be lectors or leaders, but the rest go unattended and have to provide for themselves by such stratagems as hoarding books to sell in times of illness. The community indignantly rejects the charge, protesting that Franciscan medical attention is the best in the world; that sick Franciscans are better cared for than they would be by their own mothers; and that great doctors often say that they would rather be tended in a Franciscan infirmary than at home by their families.[16]

Work

Ubertino's stand on work is a relatively moderate one.[17] He insists that the injunction to it in chapter 5 of the rule should be considered a precept, but he reads this passage as requiring that those not engaged in other duties (like study or prayer) should be required to perform manual labor in order to keep from being idle. The enemy is *otiositas*. Ubertino insists that he is in step with both *Exiit* and Franciscan tradition on this score. It is his adversaries who are no longer synchronized. "Oh, what a hard saying this is for many who are busy with none of these things, but instead waste most of their time in pointless wandering and idle conversation." He suggests that a good part of the Franciscan collapse is in fact connected with the increasing vice of idleness. Bonaventure noted it in his first letter to the order, but it has reached epidemic proportions only recently. "The state of the order when I entered it so differs from its present condition that one might as well compare a healthy and handsome man with a sick one." Since Ubertino joined the order in 1273, we are invited to infer a radical decay within the last four decades. Nor is there any doubt about who is to blame. Superiors provide neither discipline nor example to correct their underlings. In fact, the idle are rewarded with leadership roles and other offices, especially if they have material wealth and are willing to share it with those in power.

The community spokesmen seem genuinely uncertain as to what they are supposed to be defending at this point. In one reply, they deny that manual labor is required, but they are vaguely aware that Ubertino never said it was.[18] In another, they argue at length that work is neither prescribed nor counseled in the rule, and thus they manage to connect the matter with the *usus pauper* question and with a basic underlying problem in their reading of both the rule and *Exiit*, as we will see. Finally, however, they acknowledge that the central element in Ubertino's complaint is not a theoretical statement about the obligation to engage in work, manual or otherwise, but a concrete indictment of certain elements in the order as *otiosi* and a suggestion that they were made that way by a defective process of formation presided over by bad leaders. Here again they encounter an attack on Franciscan leadership.[19]

Food

A number of issues relate very directly to *usus pauper*. For example, Ubertino complains that the community solicits contributions from lay benefactors to finance banqueting at provincial and general chapter meetings. Even more offensive to him are the special dinners held in the infirmary for the leaders and scholars, not to mention the better treatment such people regularly receive in the refectory. Ubertino accuses the leaders of rewarding with promotion those brothers who are willing to finance special dinners. He laments that this situation sets a bad example for laymen as well as lesser brothers and makes people ambitious to assume leadership roles in order to gain worldly advantage.[20]

The community answers this charge in a number of ways.[21] There is a straightforward *ad hominem* response that Ubertino is hardly in a position to know about dining habits among the brethren, since he himself eats at the curia. In fact, they say, Ubertino has some nerve passing judgment on others when it is well known that he himself could never tolerate the poor food he found in the cloister. As for the special meals at chapter meetings, these are instigated not by the order, but by laymen who want to provide them because they see them as redounding to their own honor. Chapter meetings do not occur all that often and the participants eat temperately, so what is the harm in a bit of banqueting? Nor should it be considered monstrous if those who work hard at administration, teaching, and preaching occasionally receive in their own houses little pleasures not offered to others. If it occasionally happens that brothers who have financed such pleasures gain promotion, that is simply because they happen to be worthy of it. Only if they were unworthy would Ubertino have something to complain about. The community also contests Ubertino's claim that the rule limits the quantity and quality of food used by Franciscans. On the contrary, chapter 3 of the rule tells the brothers to eat whatever is placed before them. And chapter 2 admonishes them not to judge those who partake of delicate food—a bit of advice Ubertino should take to heart. It is not primarily the rule but the statutes of the order that restrict

Franciscan eating habits. Thus, as the community likes to emphasize, thanks to the statutes the order is actually living more strictly than the rule demands, rather than less so, as Ubertino claims. Nevertheless, as the community also likes to emphasize, since such limitations are imposed by the statutes, they can be removed whenever the leadership considers it expedient to do so.

Clothing

Ubertino notes that both the number and the quality of garments are limited by the rule.[22] Francis wanted every brother limited to one outer tunic with hood, but he allowed those who needed it to have a second, inner garment. He explicitly allowed patching, not in case of wear and tear—why waste words giving the brothers permission to do what any poor man is obviously free to do?—but in case of inclement weather, as a form of insulation. He expected the ministers to keep a small supply of extra tunics which the brothers could don while washing their own. The present reality is quite different. Entering novices, if they come from a humble background, find the regulation Franciscan issue more luxurious than what they had been wearing. Thus from the first day they are encouraged not to take the rule seriously.

The situation regarding shoes is similar. The rule prohibits shoes except in case of necessity, and "necessity" means something more than chilly feet. Yet Franciscan masters and those who live among the great (such as papal penitentiaries) wear them steadily in the winter. In fact, only the spirituals do not normally go about shod, and they are persecuted for their effort, just as they are hounded for wearing vile, patched habits. Here we encounter another common complaint. The conventuals do not merely violate the rule but punish the spirituals for observing it. Ubertino tells the story of a spiritual who washed his tunic, hung it out to dry, and next encountered it in the latrine being used as toilet paper. Obviously by this time the spirituals' garments had become a symbol of their quarrel with the community.

The community, however, rejects Ubertino's claim that excessive clothing has become normal throughout the order. In fact, they say, most brothers do not have enough clothing, vile or otherwise, to satisfy their needs. In any case, the rule tells friars to dress in *vilibus vestibus*, not *vilissimis*. Moreover, it gives the leaders authority to adjust the official wardrobe in keeping with the season, climate, and other variables. *Exiit* emphasizes their freedom in this respect.

As for novices, the community asks whether life is really all that pleasant for them. Those who were raised in bourgeois or noble homes find their new living standard greatly diminished, and if there are those who, because of their humble background, have little to surrender upon entering the order, all nevertheless give up their own wills. The leaders do use their discretionary power when it is fitting to do so. For example, it frequently happens that delicate young nobles enter the order. Raised in luxury, they could not immediately undergo the full rigors of Franciscan life without endangering their health, and thus it is reasonable to allow them a period of adjustment under a gentler regime.

The community flatly denies Ubertino's statement regarding shoes. It is public knowledge, they announce, that Franciscans customarily go without shoes. No brother uses them unless it is necessary, even in frigid regions like England or Germany. Nor are masters especially given to wearing them. In fact, Vital du Four continued to go without shoes even after the pope told him to put them on. If the papal penitentiaries occasionally wear them, we might assume that they are doing so through necessity. After all, papal penitentiaries are usually very old men and do a great deal of walking on cold floors. If Ubertino is all that enthusiastic about observing the rule, he might begin with its admonition in chapter 3 to judge oneself instead of others. Here, too, Ubertino's own behavior becomes an issue. The community observes that "he talks about austerities which he himself doesn't wish to touch with one finger."

Another line of defense is used only once, but it is well worth noting, since it appears in other contexts as well. Echoing Augustine,[23] community members suggest in passing that the really sinful thing—the thing to avoid at all costs—is not the *use* of goods but the *desire* to use them. As for persecution of the spirituals, they are not punished for wearing vile garments but for metaphorically waving them in their colleagues' faces. Austerities are applauded as long as they do not become an occasion for showing off or condemning others, and as long as clothing does not depart so thoroughly from the norm that it is unrecognizable as a Franciscan habit. The spirituals are deficient on both counts.

In the process of replying to Ubertino's charge the community makes a few of its own—quite apart from the issue of clothing. The spirituals are condemned, they assert, not only for their behavior in regard to attire but also because they are "proud and contumacious regarding the demands of licit and honest obedience; . . . are followers [*sectatores*] of dreams and fictitious visions; spend too much time talking with women, especially beguins, under the guise of holiness; and are defenders of perverse dogmas, errors, or new and dangerous opinions."[24] The list is an interesting one, because in it the community confirms (if in a pejorative manner) the spiritual Franciscan interest in mystical experience. It also juxtaposes that interest with another factor we will consider further in the Appendix: spiritual Franciscan relations with laywomen.

Buildings

Like others before him, Ubertino criticizes the construction of big, expensive buildings. He is fully aware that he is moving in a great tradition and quotes the standard lines from Bonaventure, Pecham, and the constitutions of Narbonne attacking excesses in this sphere.[25] Unlike his illustrious predecessors, however, Ubertino places the development in a wider context that says a great deal about his reading of Franciscan history. Francis, he asserts, intended that the brothers' dwellings should be located outside settled areas so that they could have peace, quiet, and solitude; however, he also wanted them to be near enough to the cities so that the brothers could visit the parochial churches and preach there, provided they had episcopal permission.[26] Franciscan churches were to be for their own worship and not for crowds of laymen. In describing Francis's intention, Ubertino appeals not only to a mass of documentary sources—including the rule, the *Testament*, Bonaventure, and Brother Leo—but also to physical evidence. The churches built by Francis himself, he says, "are small and not curiously decorated, but they are so strong that it seems as if they would last until judgment day."

In his own time, the brethren are dissatisfied not merely with rural living, but also with houses just outside the city walls. They cannot rest until they are located right in the center of town, where their churches will be filled with laity. The result is friction with the secular clergy, squabbles over land and burial rights, territorial battles with other orders, and fraternization with women. Ubertino is conscious of the economic implications. The order is moving into the high-rent district. It leaves beautiful, well-constructed, economical, quiet places outside town and buys expensive city houses, which it promptly tears down in order to build adequate living accommodations and large churches. The total result requires a scandalous amount of land. Franciscans want a garden, a cemetery, and a big cloister in a part of town where rich burgesses can hardly afford to maintain a house. All of this is financed with alms that should go to feed the poor.

Ubertino dwells on the size and public nature of Franciscan churches as well as on their contents. He agonizes a bit over elaborate paintings and books, but seems particularly struck by chalices, thuribles, vestments, and the like, which would rival those found in the richest cathedral or monastery. He gives some examples, prudently withholding names of the guilty. This sort of extravagance, he says, contrasts not only with the practice of Francis and his companions, but with the constitutions in force a few years ago and only recently relaxed.[27]

The community responds in a number of ways. It observes that for some time now it has tried without success to learn which churches the spirituals have in mind. The order has strong regulations through which those guilty of excesses in building can be punished, and it will be happy to apply them if the spirituals will only be specific. On the other hand, the community notes that there are certain cases where matters are out of their hands. Some churches, such as the basilica of Saint Anthony in Padua, were built by devout laity. The basilica of Saint Francis in Assisi was mandated by the pope. In such cases the brothers have no right to halt the proceedings. In fact, the community goes one step further and suggests that, since the pope owns all Franciscan buildings and the brothers are simply perching in them, as it were, they have no right to destroy or deform anything in them.

Besides, size and splendor have their uses. Franciscan churches are frequented by the laity. The churches must be big enough to hold these crowds so that the order can carry out its preaching mission. Moreover, the laity assemble more willingly and worship more devoutly in beautiful churches. Nor should Ubertino forget that, when one is speaking of churches, there is more at stake than accommodating or dazzling the laity. These buildings are decorated for the greater glory of God. Viewed from that perspective, far from being overstocked with chalices, vestments, and the like, most Franciscan churches do not have enough. Where such things are found, one should offer praise, not criticism—praise for a devotion that leads men to deny themselves in order to adorn God's altar. The community denies knowledge of any spectacular cases like those mentioned by Ubertino, yet does allude to a cross and thurible given by Charles II to the Franciscans at Naples. As for sumptuous paintings, the community claims to have seen such things only at Assisi, where they were commissioned by Nicholas IV in honor of Saint Francis.

In the discussion of buildings (as in a host of other matters), the community is careful to specify that whatever prohibitions may exist are to be found in the statutes and not in the rule. There is also the inevitable attempt to pit the spirituals against *Exiit*. Nicholas III assumed possession of those very buildings—or at least of some like them—now denounced by the spirituals. He must have thought it licit for Franciscans to occupy such structures. This appeal to authority is followed by a reference to changing times. It should not be surprising that the brothers have bigger and better houses than they did when the order was small, its value as yet unknown to the world. Echoing Bonaventure, the community remarks that the order mirrors the church as a whole in this respect, and that its success is an indication of divine approval. Finally, the community again appeals to the Augustinian dictum that guilt lies not in the use of expensive things, but in the desire to use them. Thus, Franciscans do not sin if they dwell like pilgrims in the midst of luxury.

It is worth noting Ubertino's response to some of these arguments. In reply to their apparent confusion as to where the spirituals find excess, he invites them to look in almost any direction. It is, in fact, hard to find a place in which it does not exist. In answer to their assurance that violators are promptly punished, he observes that the same leaders who must enforce the statutes are themselves the greatest violators.[28] Ubertino vigorously rejects the claim that Franciscans are powerless in the face of lay initiative. The latter rarely decide to finance a Franciscan building without being importuned to do so by the brothers. The persuasive techniques used in the process often leave an unpleasant taste in the mouths of the local clergy as well as the laity. In those rare cases when donors take the initiative and offer to build something, think how edified they would be if the brothers politely refused.

Ubertino agrees that the construction of churches is laudable when it is balanced by expenditure for the needy, but he sees nothing praiseworthy about forcing the needy to look elsewhere for their sustenance while the money that should have been used for them is channeled into splendid buildings for an order created to show the virtues of apostolic poverty. The community's appeal to changing times is countered with the observation that the church is a single body, the members of which belong to various unchanging states. The apostles who vowed apostolic poverty should not at some point become rich, nor should the Franciscans be expected to turn into something else as the years pass. Besides, there is that physical evidence. Francis, who was given prophetic knowledge of the future, built his churches not only small and plain but durable as well, so that future brothers could continue to use them and be saved from the temptation to construct newer, bigger edifices.

Other arguments are countered in turn. Ubertino continues to insist that sumptuous buildings are prohibited in the rule because (like Olivi before him) he finds there a blanket obligation to observe *usus pauper*. Like Olivi, he denies that *Exiit* conferred a papal benediction upon every single thing the order was doing in 1279. The issue of *Exiit* remains a touchy one for him, however, as we will discover in a moment.

Books

Ubertino is also concerned about the appropriation of books by individual brothers.[29] Books are useful, he says, but they should be available to all. Instead, some brothers have large boxes of books designated for their personal use and will not let anyone else read them. If they change houses, the books go with them. In some cases, the brothers do not even use their cache. Ubertino says he knows of brothers who, though old and unable to read, hang on to their chests of books. In view of what he has said about the use of books as health insurance, one can hardly blame them.

The community, however, points to the utility of designating books for personal use. If Franciscans are to preach the truth instead of fables, they must read not only divine Scripture but other works as well. Great scholars like Augustine, Jerome, and Ambrose all had many books.[30] Besides this prudential argument, the community offers a legal one. Nothing is said of this matter in the rule, the document by which Franciscans are actually bound. (Here a major issue surfaces briefly, and we will see more of it later.)

Barns and Cellars

Like others before him, Ubertino attacks the notion of barns filled with wheat and cellars filled with wine.[31] He even takes a try at arguing that these excess supplies violate the prohibition against ownership, since they fall outside those things allowed by *Exiit*—and therefore outside the limits of what the pope has agreed to own. If the pope does not own them, then they must belong to the Franciscans.

The community's response is oddly reminiscent of Olivi.[32] In reply to Ubertino's evocation of Matt. 6:34, "Do not think about tomorrow," they remark that all provision for the future is not prohibited, but only provision leading to excess. There is nothing wrong with storing wheat during harvest in preparation for the coming year. If there were, then the order would have to question its right to keep books or live steadily in the same houses. It would seem that the real point at issue here is not whether one should provide for the future but how securely one should guarantee that future. Like Olivi, the community takes present necessity to mean something more than what is needed for use in the present. It includes doing what has to be done now if future necessities are to be satisfied. In the final analysis, Ubertino has no quarrel with this perspective. He simply feels that the community is going well beyond what is required for survival. In doing so, it erases the situation of radical dependence emphasized by Francis and ensures a comfortable future for itself.

Franciscan Income

The question of barns and cellars is intimately connected with other issues.[33] Ubertino mentions houses in which brothers live on permanent incomes established by testators or donors at some time in the past. He also complains that some houses make money by selling agricultural produce. They are given more grain than they need for their own use, store it in their barns until the price rises, and then sell it. In fact, some houses have such extensive gardens and vineyards that they market their own harvest. Nor is produce all that is being marketed. The Franciscans also receive income from the sale of such odd items as horses and armor, which they receive from the families whose burials they oversee.

The question of burial has its own intricacies (as we have already seen in Olivi's 1283 censure).[34] Ubertino takes roughly the same line as Olivi: he argues that burial is a less spiritual act, one that impedes more spiritual ones. Moreover, according to the constitutions of Narbonne, Franciscans should avoid involvement in burial duties whenever they can do so without causing scandal. Ubertino bewails the current situation, in which Franciscans waste huge portions of time competing with the secular clergy for the bodies of wealthy and noble laity.

Here as elsewhere the community's self-defense moves on two tracks. On the one hand, Ubertino is wrong because he defines the requirements of the Franciscan life too narrowly and thus condemns perfectly legitimate activity. On the other hand, he is wrong because, even when he does define the requirements correctly, he sees more violation than actually exists. These two lines of defense are interwoven in complex patterns. In this particular case, the community acknowledges that perpetual incomes are forbidden and insists that the order does enforce its statutes against such things, but it simultaneously defends the legitimacy of converting gifts into money and argues that burying the dead is a pious act allowed to the Franciscans by the pope himself. If the friars receive some contribution for performing it, well and good; however, the order does have strong statutes against actively inducing the laity to accept such burial, and it makes sure that these statues are observed.[35]

Handling Money

The notion of selling things raises a related issue—the Franciscans' handling of money.[36] Ubertino notes that the prohibition against receiving money is honored only to the extent that the brothers do not physically touch it. His examples are plentiful and revealing. The Franciscans accept monetary collections in their churches. Sometimes they sell candles, with each candle being sold ten times over. The faithful place the money in a box that is periodically emptied by a servant, so that the friars need not physically touch it.

When Franciscans travel, they often take along a *bursarius*, a servant who carries the money and spends it as they direct. Though he is said to be controlled by the person who donated the money, only the friars decide on expenditures. In fact, the money is often locked in a chest and a friar carries the key.

When Franciscan leaders travel to chapter meetings, they almost always bring *bursarii*. They go on horseback with great pomp, creating such a bad example in the inns along the way that it is talked about for years afterward. Friars who cannot or will not use *bursarii* find it difficult to beg their sustenance, since people assume that they too are carrying money with them.

Franciscans move about the cities asking for monetary contributions, which are received by their own servants. Yet the brothers portray these servants as the agents of those who donated the money. Brothers who, on the grounds of conscience, refuse to participate in such activities are denounced as schismatics.

These are not the only horror stories Ubertino tells, but they will suffice to convey the general idea. The community again gives a dual response. It acknowledges that selling candles is forbidden, but maintains that instances of it are rare and promptly punished. It also denies that leaders are needlessly extravagant in their travels. Nevertheless, the community defends the rest of the things mentioned by Ubertino as perfectly legitimate (although it acknowledges that carrying the key conveys an unfortunate impression and should be avoided). On the whole, the community defense proceeds along legal lines. However things may look and whatever the participants themselves might think, the man who carries or collects the money is a representative of the giver, not of the Franciscans. Though brothers may make the decisions, the giver technically has authority over how the money is spent. The pope has given his blessing to these practices, and thus in criticizing them, Ubertino is defying the pope.

Procurators

Obviously these issues highlight the problem of procurators as well.[37] We have seen that the order carried on its financial affairs through a series of middlemen (variously called *nuntii* and *procuratores*) who acted in the interests of the brothers but were theoretically controlled by someone else, be he the donor or the pope. Ubertino does not directly challenge the existence of such intermediaries. When he and the community argue explicitly about this issue, they differ not on the procurators' general legitimacy but on the way they are employed—for example, their role in legal processes aimed at gaining something owed the Franciscans, such as a bequest that the heirs refuse to pay. Here again Ubertino resembles Olivi. He objects to the current practice in which a procurator, though theoretically the pope's man, is actually controlled by the order. Franciscans nominate him, give him orders, and even go with him to court, where they "denounce the adversary immodestly."

The community avoids dealing with Ubertino's concrete evocations of courtroom drama. Instead it concentrates on the legality of procuratorial actions.

The Franciscans have no right to pursue such goals, but the pope has every right to do so, and if the property bequeathed to the order is really owned by the pope it is his rights the procurator is defending. The proper procedure has been outlined in *Exiit* and the order is following it. Thus he who critiques the order critiques the pope as well.

In one work, the community constructs a rationale for Franciscan involvement in procuratorial processes that is striking, at least for its ingenuity. Matt. 18:15–17 commands us to correct our brother if he sins against us. No oath can erase this divinely imposed obligation. Moreover, canon law recognizes that the rich are bound by charity to aid the poor when possible, while the poor have a right to denounce to the church those who fail in this duty. The church, in turn, should coerce recalcitrant rich men. Thus, even if the Franciscans did not have a privilege explicitly affirming the legitimacy of procuratorial processes, they would still have not only the right but also the duty to denounce those who are not giving them what is legally owed them—and the church would be obliged to defend them in court. Whatever the value of this argument—and at seven centuries' remove it seems a particularly odd one—the fact remains that, as far as the order is concerned, such a privilege really does exist. That is no small claim and Ubertino must face it.

Some General Observations

We could go on cataloguing specific abuses as seen by Ubertino, but all good things must come to an end (and these are, in any case, most of the major ones). Before proceeding to deal with *usus pauper,* we might pause for a moment to consider what we have seen so far. Ubertino has gone a long way toward explaining how, in his happy phrase, the Franciscan state has collapsed. The standard issues are all there: barns full of wheat; cellars full of wine; big and elaborate buildings; books of excessive worth; the scramble for profit through burial, legacies, or rents; and a variety of seemingly hypocritical practices by which money is amassed even while the prohibition against it is technically observed. Ubertino is at one with Bonaventure, Pecham, Olivi, and others in denouncing these things, though he differs from them in his specificity and in the sheer magnitude of the abuses he describes.

On the other hand, much of what Ubertino says suggests a more radical critique of Franciscan history than Bonaventure, Pecham, or even Olivi would have dreamed of providing. Ubertino sees how the Franciscans' various problems fit together, how one grows out of the other and is nurtured by it. His solution is a return to the starting line, or at least to what he sees as the starting line. His goal is to follow Francis's original intention. Deriving his inspiration from the rule, as he interprets it with the aid of the *Testament* and the Leo sources, Ubertino wants to see his order disengaged from many of those present activities that give it wealth and power. His comments concerning the Franciscan migration to the cities are particularly revealing. Reform involves living humbly, but it also involves living out of town. It involves entering the city as a visitor and moving through it like a stranger, preaching in other people's churches and only with their permission.

Granting that the Franciscan state has collapsed, when did it do so? Ubertino is ambiguous here, and for good reason. At one point he suggests that the real decay has occurred since he joined the order in 1273. He desperately wants to claim support from Franciscan tradition through the time of Bonaventure and Pecham, and he is partly right in doing so, insofar as Bonaventure and Pecham bemoan many of the same abuses he himself attacks. Yet he decries long-term developments that were well underway by their time and that they generally accepted. At times he implies that the collapse has been in progress since Francis's day.

Why did the state collapse? Ubertino refuses to accept the idea of an inevitable development. The order is in trouble because people have made the wrong choices and strayed from Francis's intention. Who, then, are the guilty parties?

Franciscan Leadership

Obviously, Ubertino feels that the order is being destroyed by its own leaders. In discussing individual abuses, he constantly traces responsibility back to those whom he calls the *potentes*, the power elite of masters, lectors, inquisitors, confessors, preachers, guardians, and ministers. According to Ubertino, these people are the principal offenders against prohibitions concerning money and excessive use. By garnishing their offices with special perquisites, they encourage others to live in a similar fashion and to seek office for material gain. Thus, even though Franciscan discipline is relaxed at every level, relaxation at the lower levels seems less culpable to Ubertino because he sees it as encouraged by the leaders. Indeed, "encouraged" is too weak a word. Ubertino portrays the persecution of the spirituals as evidence of how the *potentes* react when someone tries to observe the rule.

Education

This corrupt system is perpetuated not only by constraint and bad example on the part of the leaders, but also by an educational system designed to destroy Franciscan piety. Ubertino's portrayal of the average academic career in his day is not a particularly pleasant one. The budding scholar is put to the study of philosophy immediately after his novitiate. Exempted from the divine office and from humble tasks in order to occupy himself with "curious questions and arid studies," he never gains a foundation in the virtues. Then he goes to Paris in order to prepare the way for his own advancement rather than to seek the truth. A Parisian education is the ticket to power and prestige within the order, and selection for this honor is often based on money or political alliance rather than ability. At Paris, the young scholar is nurtured by a curriculum featuring pagan authors and more of those "questions which are curious rather than devout," with little attention to the fathers or the Bible. This educational program, combined with his own natural unfitness, makes him bored with study, lazy, impious, vainglorious, proud, contentious, envious, and covetous. Thus excellently formed, he returns to his home province and becomes a leader. "So," Ubertino observes, "because the order is ruled by such people and they almost always participate in the provincial and general chapters, the order is getting steadily worse."[38] Ubertino protests that he is not against study itself—only its current misuse. Francis envisaged an order in which study would direct prayer and prayer would illuminate study. The principal goal and occupation of a Franciscan was to be prayer rather than study, however.

Preaching

Ubertino is equally impressed with preaching, another product of the educational system. Francis wanted young Franciscans to subject themselves to spiritual formation through Bible study, prayer, and acts of humility. Such training would produce men who, though few in number, would understand Scripture and practice what they preached. Instead, the order sports an excessive number of preachers but, thanks to their educational program, they are not trained to do themselves what they should be teaching others to do. In fact, they have been trained in a way calculated to destroy not only their effectiveness but their very souls as well. They learn composed sermons and recite them like magpies. The divine word is thus cheapened in the ears of lay listeners, and so is the order. The laity now treat Franciscan preachers with scorn, insisting that they are interested only in fancy oratory.[39]

The significant thing about such behavior is not that Ubertino considers it wrong—most Franciscans would undoubtedly agree with that much—but that he thinks of it as normal procedure. He assumes a basic opposition between Francis's original intention and Franciscan life in his own time. The leaders' flaws are more than individual deficiencies. They have become institutionalized.

Urban Involvement

Franciscan decadence is also perpetuated by involvement in urban life.[40] Having settled into the cities, the Franciscans develop ties with them. Ubertino is painfully aware that the scramble for legacies, the purchase of land, the construction of churches, conversations with women, and all the other concomitants of social and economic immersion in the towns has created a noxious environment for minorite life. In fact, he sees a great deal more. Ubertino notes that once they have established themselves in a town, the Franciscans begin to think of that town as theirs. Unfortunately, it often *is* theirs. Friars frequently return to their old hometowns and convert the Franciscan houses into little enclaves filled with their own people. They discourage outsiders from joining the community and, because their family connections remain intact, they become involved in party strife. In one of his few positive remarks about the existing leadership, Ubertino adds that John of Murrovalle tried to end this tendency by ordering that in some Italian provinces no more than one-third of the brothers in any house should be natives of that area. Faced with widespread protest, John had to back down.

Papal Privileges

There is one more important causal factor in Franciscan decline. Ubertino thinks that the order is being suffocated by the mass of privileges heaped on it by successive popes. It is significant that in his reply to Clement's four questions, having announced the collapse of the Franciscan state, he immediately launches an attack on papal privileges, citing Francis's *Testament* and Brother Leo. His chief target in this passage is Franciscan involvement in litigation, but his words could apply to any number of problems. Of course, he says, he agrees with Pope Gregory IX's statement that Franciscans are not bound to observe the *Testament*, since equals cannot bind equals (thus Francis could not bind his successors), and in any case, by human law, Francis had renounced his authority earlier. It is nonetheless true that in the *Testament* "he wished to explain to us, in the manner of a precept, what he meant to say in the rule, a meaning given him by the Holy Spirit and asserted by him with certainty to be the will of the Lord." Thus Ubertino ostensibly seconds the pope in denying the *Testament* one sort of authority, yet simultaneously grants it another, higher sort. Again and again he emphasizes that Francis's intention should be the central criterion in determining the proper shape of Franciscan poverty.[41]

This attack on papal actions seems an odd way to court Clement's favor, but Ubertino immediately assures him that the real culprit is the order itself. Privileges were granted because the Franciscans sought them. The popes were unaware that such privileges were noxious to the Franciscan state, nor did they foresee how these privileges would be abused. Ubertino later asserts that such relaxations are not binding because "they were not imposed by the Roman pontiff but extorted from him."[42] Thus he relieves the popes of responsibility by undermining their pretension to be knowledgeable and authoritative interpreters of the rule.

Ubertino's attitude toward papal privileges creates an unavoidable problem for him. He must deal not only with Clement V but with Nicholas III, whose declaration was considered so important that Clement had asked respondents to state whether it as well as the rule was being observed. Ubertino is of two minds about *Exiit*. On the one hand, he is profoundly at odds with it. While he criticizes current practice for not measuring up to the standard set by *Exiit*, he sees that standard as itself an occasion for laxity. Nicholas watered down the original standard of Franciscan poverty and thereby encouraged further decline. Ubertino also complains that *Exiit* "contains a lot of complicated Latin, especially on the subject of money." If those who wished to do so were allowed to observe the rule "according to the letter" and all others were constrained to the level set by *Exiit*, he acknowledges that there would be some improvement, but it would be slight and would not last long. The only true reform would be one that returned the entire order to observance of the rule without gloss or privilege, as Francis intended it to be observed. If there is any question about what Francis intended, it can be settled—not by appealing to popes, but rather by attending to Francis's *Testament* and the reminiscences of Brother Leo or other early companions. If some current members of the order are unwilling or unable to meet that standard, let them be given a laxer way of life so that their behavior will harmonize with their words and everyone will know what they stand for. Then let the holy rule instituted by Francis and approved (*bullata*) by Christ himself be given to those who will observe it purely and without gloss or declaration.[43]

Ubertino is intelligent enough to recognize that this view puts him on a collision course with the pope. In fact, the community is all too eager to point this out to him—and to Clement as well. Ubertino and the spirituals are constantly portrayed as denouncing precisely that procedure accepted by *Exiit*, and therefore as denouncing papal authority itself. Of course the matter is not quite that simple. Ubertino thinks that the popes damaged the order by making a series of bad decisions, and he is willing to say as much. He also obviously denies the papal claim to be the authoritative interpreter of the rule, but here he must be more circumspect. Thirty years earlier, Olivi could argue that a pope had to be disobeyed if he ordered Franciscans to violate the rule. Olivi was dealing with a theoretical situation, however, and he was not writing to the pope.

To the extent that Ubertino faces this problem at all, he takes a position that seems to affirm and reject papal authority in the same breath. At times he seems to be placing the pope's authority to grant privileges alongside the Franciscan duty to reject them if they contradict the rule.

> We do not say that the Roman church cannot legislate as it sees fit about bequests made to the brethren. We simply say that when, as a result of such a privilege, the brothers involve themselves in litigation and induce procurators to institute it, attending the proceedings and denouncing the opposition as worldly people do, then they are apostatizing against the rule and giving a bad example to the world. For, despite the pious intention of the popes who have conceded them, these privileges are poison to the rule and a cause of ruin. Thus they should be abolished and we should repudiate them as contrary to the rule. The general chapters of former times thought as much. Thus, for the reasons stated above, the Strasbourg general chapter ordered that these privileges not be used. Now, however, whoever enters into such litigation most is considered the greatest promoter of the order.[44]

On the other hand, Ubertino feels obliged to show that the popes are on his side. Nowhere is this tendency clearer than in his argument for *usus pauper* as part of the vow, and it is to that subject that we finally turn.

Usus Pauper and the Vow

Like Olivi before him, Ubertino tries to show that the Bible, the rule, the great Franciscan masters, and the popes all have considered restricted use a substantial part of the vow. The masters cited by him include Hugh of Digne, Bonaventure, Pecham, William de la Mare, John of Wales, and Henry of Ghent. As for Olivi, Ubertino argues that he not only stayed comfortably within the main line of Franciscan tradition but also demonstrated more moderation than his predecessors did in his willingness to acknowledge the demands of varying circumstance. Here as elsewhere, Ubertino presents his old colleague as a fallible human being, albeit an admirable one. He argues that the attack on Olivi's theology and philosophy was a flanking movement in the poverty controversy, designed to discredit Olivi's forthright championship of *usus pauper*. That said, he also protests that he does not follow Olivi in all things.[45] The subject of Olivi's orthodoxy constitutes a separate topic in the great discussion, one of the four proposed by Clement, and Ubertino deals with it as such. (Respect for logic might suggest that we deal with it in this chapter, but we will defer it until the following one, sticking for the moment to Ubertino's thoughts on poverty and the order.)

The popes summoned to Ubertino's defense inevitably include Nicholas III. Like Olivi before him, Ubertino points to those places in *Exiit* where the pope allows Franciscans necessary use or forbids them superfluous use. Nicholas's assurances that the rule allows necessary use are interpreted as implying that it allows *nothing except* necessary use. All the pope's admonitions that the Franciscans be content with necessary use are taken as suggesting that they must do so because they are bound to do so by their vow. Like Olivi, Ubertino is anxious to call attention to those statements in which Nicholas mentions lack of ownership and limitation to necessary use as if they were two complementary aspects of Franciscan poverty. Like Olivi, he relishes Nicholas's identification of these two things with the Franciscan *professio* and his description of excess (in utensils and so on) as *indicta*.[46] Like Olivi, he takes full advantage of the pope's reference to "precept, prohibition or equivalent words." He interprets "equivalent words" as broadly as possible, including within this category use of the subjunctive in an imperative sense, as in the words, "let them have one tunic with a hood."[47] If one were to exclude such constructions, he avers, there would be almost no precepts in the rule, since very little is demanded through express words of precept or prohibition. He acknowledges, however, that all such constructions cannot be taken as precepts, since it would be foolish to imagine that Franciscans are inevitably bound to say "peace to this house" whenever they enter one.[48]

On the whole, granting the extent to which Ubertino overstates his case by reading every concession of necessary use as a prohibition of superfluous use—and every prohibition of superfluous use as an implied reference to the vow—we must still conclude that, at least on the subject of *usus pauper*, his reading of *Exiit* is not a bad one. Nicholas does seem to see both *usus pauper* and lack of ownership as necessarily entailed in Franciscan poverty, and he does treat statements like "let them dress in vile clothing" as if he saw them as precepts. Unfortunately, Ubertino wants a great deal more, as did Olivi before him. Nicholas, we recall, begins by raising the question of whether the Franciscan binds himself to the entire gospel and answers that he does not. Nicholas sees the mention of poverty, chastity, and obedience in the rule as qualifying the Franciscan's obligation; he qualifies it further by stating that Franciscans are bound by precept only to those evangelical counsels expressed in the rule by precept, prohibition, or equivalent words. Ubertino simply cannot accept this approach. Like Olivi, he wants to find a blanket commitment to *usus pauper* in the vow, and he sees no danger in this position because he does not share their opponents' assumption that any violation of a vow entails mortal sin. With Olivi, too, he distinguishes between those aspects of the vow that are proffered precisely and those proffered indeterminately. The prohibition against owning things belongs in the first category, and that against *usus dives* in the second. In the case of indeterminately proffered vows, only gross violation involves mortal sin. Thus Ubertino accepts Olivi's view that in the matter of *usus pauper,* the point at which venial sin becomes mortal cannot be determined *in puncto,* precisely; yet (again like Olivi) he sees it as involving a violation so great that anyone who pursues his vocation seriously need not worry about inadvertently straying across the dividing line. He also follows Olivi both in quietly abandoning Nicholas's notion that, in the rule, precepts and counsels are neatly labeled as such, and in substituting a more nuanced distinction between precept and counsel based upon a hierarchy of ends pursued in the Franciscan life.[49]

In short, Ubertino conforms to Olivi's thought at precisely those points where Olivi, while claiming support from *Exiit,* rejected some of *Exiit's* basic presuppositions. Olivi, as we have seen, was not particularly eager to face his fundamental disagreement with Nicholas (and consequently with a significant segment of Franciscan and papal opinion prior to *Exiit*). Ubertino too is disinclined to do so, but he feels unable to ignore it entirely. Thus he makes a heroic effort to read his view into *Exiit.* Leaning heavily upon Nicholas's identification of the Franciscan rule with the gospel and with the life of Christ and his disciples,[50] he argues that if Nicholas accepted that identification, he must have thought that the rule bound Franciscans to the entire gospel and therefore to evangelical perfection in its entirety. If Nicholas seems to limit the Franciscan commitment by referring to poverty, chastity, and obedience, that is simply the pope's way of saying that poverty, chastity, and obedience are so basic to the evangelical life that all aspects of it can be reduced to these three headings.[51] If Nicholas seems to limit the Franciscan vow to what is expressed in the rule by precept, prohibition, or equivalent words, that must be because he believes that everything pertaining to evangelical perfection is contained in the rule in one of these three ways.[52] In effect, Ubertino reads *Exiit* in such a way as to reverse the answer to the original question asked in it. Does a Franciscan vow to observe the entire gospel? Nicholas says "no." Ubertino interprets him in such a way as to imply that he really meant to say "yes."

Ubertino, Olivi, and Raymond

A comparison of Olivi and Ubertino, then, reveals both differences and similarities. Ubertino is more deeply alienated from the course of thirteenth-century Franciscan history than his old colleague ever was. He is more negative—not only about the present, but about the past as well. He describes a precipitous fall from virtue after Bonaventure's generalate, but he actually blames the fall on tendencies that were accepted long before then. This difference between Olivi and Ubertino is related to another one in the area of authority. Ubertino rejects papal interpretations of the rule. Olivi did not. Ubertino's critique is rooted in the *Testament* and Leo sources. Olivi's was not. Given his perspective, it is hardly surprising that, unlike Olivi, he should be willing to entertain the possibility of settling the controversy through division rather than reform.

These differences reflect more than two different minds. They also reflect two different areas. Olivi and Raymond Geoffroi represent the main line of southern French spiritual tradition, while Ubertino is more characteristically Italian. Nevertheless, there is also a sense in which the differences illuminate a strikingly changed situation. There is no accurate way of measuring whether the decay in Franciscan standards was objectively greater in 1309 than it had been in 1279, but it seems clear that those who called for strict observance of *usus pauper* did so at greater personal risk during the decade after 1299 than during the preceding twenty years. Not only had the order become increasingly factionalized (and the bonds of fraternal love accordingly weakened), but during the preceding two decades, Franciscan leaders had also experienced some success in presenting critics of current Franciscan life as a disruptive element, one that threatened good order and doctrinal rectitude. Ubertino had reason to be pessimistic about the recent course of Franciscan history.

However Olivi and Ubertino may differ, though, in some ways they are strikingly alike. Ubertino may reject the very notion of papal declarations, but he still finds it necessary to argue that they agree with his position, just as he tries to enlist thirteenth-century Franciscan masters on his side. Above all, he must insist upon support from Nicholas III. Ubertino and Olivi are also alike on the question of *usus pauper* as part of the vow. Ubertino's argument is heavily indebted to Olivi's. Ironically enough, agreement in this area does not help Ubertino come to terms with *Exiit qui seminat*. On the contrary, it intensifies his estrangement from it, because Olivi himself brings to the discussion a conceptual structure different from the one employed by Nicholas. Moreover, it is Nicholas who is closer to the mainstream of Franciscan tradition.

A Silent Participant: Angelo

While there is some virtue in seeing Raymond Geoffroi and Ubertino da Casale as the two major spiritual Franciscan spokesmen (representing the French and Italian positions, respectively), we should note in passing that one other major spiritual Franciscan leader weighed in with an opinion at this stage. Angelo Clareno tells us that he "came to the curia the year the Council of Vienne was celebrated" and that his business was presented to the pope by Isnardo Tacconi, the prefect of Rome, with whom he had traveled to France. The business in question was defending the existence of Angelo's group. He hoped for a reversal of Boniface VIII's judgment regarding it—hardly a chimerical hope, since many of Boniface's acts already had been reversed. Angelo's letters from this period are sparse, and he is silent about this affair in his chronicle. We know little except Clement's general reply: "He was content that we continue to serve the Lord in our present state."[53] Thus Angelo gives us little to place alongside the contributions from Raymond and Ubertino.

The important point for our purposes is that spiritual leaders at Vienne offered three different programs for reform. Raymond was milder than the other two when it came to assessing the current state of the order. His recommendation involved improving the general level of observance within the order and ending persecution of the spirituals. Ubertino and Angelo were less sanguine about the possibility of reforming the order as it stood. Both suggested dividing it, but not in the same manner. Ubertino, whatever he might realistically have anticipated, asked for a division in which the spirituals would emerge with the rule and the name. Angelo asked for confirmation of the more limited division made in 1294, one in which he and his associates had given up the name but kept the rule.

The Council of Vienne
The Community and the Pope

IF UBERTINO WAS STILL ARGUING the case for *usus pauper* as part of the vow in much the same way that Olivi had thirty years earlier, does the inverse hold true as well? Was the community using the same arguments against *usus pauper* that Olivi had rejected?

The Community on *Usus Pauper*

The answer is that to a point they were, despite their occasional attempts to suggest that the controversy was limited to southern France and was merely a battle over terms, hence not worth arguing about at all.[1] They were not disputing directly with Olivi, and thus one occasionally finds them discussing some issue he never raised. Yet on the whole, the continuity is remarkable.

One finds the same basic presuppositions leading inexorably to the same conclusions. The community proceeds from the assumption that violation of a vow entails mortal sin. Thus the obligations incurred through a vow must be precisely definable, known to the vower, and capable of fulfillment by him. *Usus pauper* fails this test, because differing needs and situations make it impossible to establish a secure boundary between observance and violation. *Usus pauper*, then, would be a dangerous thing to vow. The poverty to which a Franciscan unalterably binds himself is a lack of possessions, not limited use.[2]

Like Olivi's adversaries before them, spokesmen for the community assert that the act related to the vow of poverty is a mental one. They too like to quote Augustine's dictum that guilt lies not in the *use* of things, but in the *desire* to use them.[3] Nevertheless, like those earlier adversaries, they grant that the rule does entail some moderation of use. Here, we must look skeptically at the word "they." Like "the spirituals," "the community" is an abstraction. Various people wrote, and it is often hard to tell whether they simply expressed things differently or actually disagreed. One encounters a similar problem in dealing with Olivi's original opponents.[4]

Nevertheless, the documents do display a more or less coherent position that seems to have been acceptable to a large segment of the community. According to this position, only those obligations from which the pope cannot dispense should be considered substantial parts of the vow. This criterion allows lack of ownership to be included within the vow but excludes *usus pauper*, since the pope can legitimately allow or even order individual Franciscans to wear shoes, dress in fine clothes, or ride horses, all of which in fact occur when a Franciscan becomes a bishop.[5]

On the other hand, the rule does speak of wearing vile clothing and not riding horses.[6] Thus, even though the Franciscan does not actually vow such things, he is bound to them *ex voto* in some sense, since he is bound *ex voto* to all that the rule contains in obligatory fashion. Those speaking for the community are somewhat hazy on this point. The term they prefer to use for such things is *usus pauperes*, which might be inelegantly translated as "poor uses," specific types of restricted use. They want to recognize a special category for those *usus pauperes* specifically mentioned in the rule, but they insist on separating them from lack of ownership. Only the latter cannot be suspended by papal dispensation, and thus only the latter is vowed in such a way that violation of it automatically implies mortal sin, although the community acknowledges that mortal sin is incurred when one "notably exceeds" the specific prohibitions in the rule regarding *usus pauperes*. Thus the community seems to settle for a position that offers more precision than Olivi's in one way, but seems remarkably like his in another. By limiting Franciscans' obligation *ex voto* to particular *usus pauperes*—namely, those practices specifically mentioned in the rule—they avoid the vagueness associated with Olivi's insistence that the vow entails a commitment to *usus pauper* in general. Yet by acknowledging that mortal sin is incurred only in cases of gross violation, they neglect to demarcate clearly the border between spiritual safety and mortal sin, and thus they could be accused of fostering the same uncertainties and anxieties that Olivi's opponents claimed were encouraged by his notion of indeterminate vows. In 1311, as in 1279, opposing sides attempted to draw a clear line between their positions on *usus pauper* and the vow, but in both cases key disclosures occasionally alert the reader that the difference between the two views was either less dramatic or more subtle than the contestants admitted or perhaps even allowed themselves to recognize.[7]

Those items explicitly mentioned by the rule are contrasted with other things, such as cleaving to necessity in food, books, and buildings. These fall into a third category. While not specifically enjoined, they are still demanded in some way. The expressions vary—*ex decentia status, ex quadam decentie tentione, de condescentia status, ex bono et equo*—but the idea remains. As Nicholas III says in *Exiit*, "There are some things to which a Franciscan is not bound by precept, but to which he is more obliged than other men by virtue of his status as a Franciscan."

Mention of Nicholas brings us to the issue of authority. The community argues from authority in much the same way that Olivi's antagonists did. They quote the words of the vow taken by Franciscans as well as the parallel opening lines of the rule.[8] They quote whatever in the rule suits their purposes, but they are particularly fond of the line, "Eat whatever is placed before you," and they quote it in both its biblical and Franciscan contexts.[9] They insist that the presence of explicit prohibitions in the rule concerning things like clothing and horses implies the lack of any blanket obligation to limited use incurred by the vow. Their treatment of biblical evidence is equally reminiscent of the 1279–83 debate.[10]

Of course, they cite *Exiit* as well. They make sure that Clement V is fully aware of Ubertino's negative attitude toward papal declarations as well as his fondness for Brother Leo and the *Testament*. The community spokesmen repeat almost *ad nauseam* that they base their understanding of the rule on the firm foundation of papal declarations, while Ubertino and his colleagues want to break loose from this authority and observe the *regula nuda*—interpreting it in one way today, and in another tomorrow, as the mood strikes them. It is pointless, they say, to cite Francis's intention over against the declarations, for it is in the papal declarations that one must seek Francis's intention.[11]

They are equally derisive and equally effective in showing that Ubertino distorts *Exiit* by explaining away its attempt to limit the Franciscan vow.

Ubertino, they say, is reopening the old debate about the safety and observability of the rule by affirming the same vague commitment to the entire gospel—the commitment from which Nicholas was trying to save the order. Again and again they emphasize that, according to Nicholas, a Franciscan vows the gospel not unconditionally, but as specified in the rule: first by the reference to poverty, chastity, and obedience, and then by express statements of precept, prohibition, or equivalent words.[12]

But is their own position really consistent with *Exiit*? As Ubertino and Olivi both recognize, some passages in *Exiit* treat lack of ownership and restricted use as two complementary and equally important parts of Franciscan poverty. These passages can be harmonized with the community position only through an extremely subtle exegesis of Nicholas's words. That, of course, is precisely what the community provides. For example, Nicholas's clearest endorsement of *usus pauper* as part of the vow is probably his announcement that "it is truly fitting for that profession which vows the poor Christ to live in such poverty that it rejects all ownership and is content with necessary use of the things conceded to it." The community fastens on the word "fitting" (*condescens*), arguing from its use that the passage calls for *usus pauper* not as a part of the vow, but *de condescentia status*, as befitting the Franciscan state. This argument has its difficulties. Ubertino rightly notes that if such an interpretation removes *usus pauper* from the vow, it excises rejection of property as well, since both are described as *condescens*.[13]

Three Scholarly Discussions

The *usus pauper* question was also debated in good scholastic fashion during this period. We have three works on the subject attributed to major scholars. Those by Richard of Conington and Pierre Aureole support the community. More surprising, a third—once attributed to Nicholas of Lyra—defends the Olivian view. We will begin with this third work, assuming for the moment that Lyra is the author so that we can at least call him something.

Writing in 1310, "Lyra" follows in Olivi's wake without ever citing him by name.[14] Like Olivi, he examines Christ and the apostles as interpreted by the fathers and the *Glossa*, concluding that what is said of their poverty pertains more to restricted use than to lack of ownership. Like Olivi, he cites Pecham, Bonaventure, and the rule at length. Francis, the constitutions of Narbonne, and *Exiit qui seminat* are mentioned as well. In defending the notion that *usus pauper* is an essential part of the vow, "Lyra" adds to the Olivian legacy in only one notable respect. He argues that all who accept clerical status assume Christ's poverty to some degree. Citing Bonaventure and canon law to show that the secular clergy are obliged to live moderately, he argues that secular clergy, monks, and mendicants are distinguished by increasingly stringent limitations—not only on ownership, but also on use. And even among mendicants, those who vow a higher poverty are, all other things being equal, obliged to more restricted use.[15]

"Lyra" must face the standard objection that *usus pauper* is a vague requirement. He does so very much in the Olivian tradition, even using the magic word "indeterminate" at the strategic moment. Like Olivi, he emphasizes that one must examine particular circumstances and assume a degree of latitude within which self-indulgence is at worst venial. The vow of poverty "is observed more perfectly by one person, less so by another."[16]

Like Olivi, he tries his hand at a few distinctions, contending that (all other things again being equal) a friar can eat better food at the king's table, where he simply takes what is given him, than he can in a situation where he himself is allowed to choose. Liturgical items can be more expensive if donated or bought with money specifically given for that purpose than would be the case if they were purchased from general funds, so to speak. Books are quite acceptable in view of the fact that few outside the mendicant orders are pursuing any except lucrative subjects, but those held in common for study can be multiplied more legitimately than those deputed to the use of individual brothers. Moreover, it is hard to excuse having books with expensive miniatures and impossible to excuse hoarding books for an extended period when others need them. Like Olivi, "Lyra" feels that in the final analysis the criteria for judging such matters must not be sought in a handbook of specific prescriptions and prohibitions, but must instead emerge from the purpose of religious vows: removal of the affections from worldly things, freedom from care and external distractions, and elevation of the mind to God. If a particular use furthers these ends, it is legitimate. If not, not.

In short, "Lyra" resembles Olivi not only in seeing *usus pauper* as part of the vow, but also in his general approach to the vow itself. Neither thinks that the vow must be reduced to a series of clear obligations. Both are willing to live with a great deal of ambiguity. If "Lyra" differs from Olivi in any significant respect, it is in his identification of indeterminacy with the discretionary power given to superiors by the rule and by *Exiit*. It is of course impossible to make too much of this difference, because Olivi too is all for obedience, while "Lyra" is aware that this power can be abused, since we are prone to rationalize laxity by calling it necessity. Nevertheless, it remains true that "Lyra" gives the discretionary power of superiors an important place in his argument for *usus pauper,* while Olivi does not. His interest in doing so is partly due to the fact that the community continually cited that power as an argument in the opposite direction, but it is also perhaps explained by the fact that by 1310, the spiritual cause was seen as a force for disorder, and it seemed a good idea for anyone defending the connection between *usus pauper* and the vow to link the former with established authority as well.

But is the author really Nicholas of Lyra? Probably not. Several scholars have argued that Franz Pelster was wrong in his attribution.[17] On the whole, while the available evidence makes it hard to prove conclusively that the work is *not* by Nicholas, it nonetheless suggests that there is no strong reason to choose him as the author and some difficulty involved in doing so. That is, to say the least, unfortunate; if it is not by Lyra, we cannot say *who* the author might be.

The two other works, Pierre Aureole's *Question on Usus Pauper* and Richard of Conington's *Treatise on Franciscan Poverty,* support the community.[18] Both assume that any obligation incurred through a vow must be readily determinable. In Pierre's words, it must have a *medium solidum et certum.* Otherwise, in Richard's words, it would be a *laqueus animarum,* a snare of souls. This is, of course, a familiar line of attack. So is their insistence that, if *usus pauper* were a substantial part of the vow, those Franciscans who live in the palaces of kings and prelates would automatically be violating their vows. To this extent, both men could be writing in 1279 instead of ca. 1310. Neither comes to terms with the fact that such arguments had been countered by Olivi decades earlier.

They do show some originality in the amount of time they spend arguing for a definition of poverty that utterly excludes use. Poverty becomes what Richard likes to call *expropriatio.* Some of the same arguments appear in each work. Both belabor the example of a rich man who lives austerely and note that John the Baptist was more austere than Christ, yet Christ is considered to have been poorer. Each nevertheless has his own peculiar emphases. Pierre, for example, argues at length that restricted use pertains to the virtue of temperance, not poverty. Richard's treatise, like the polemical documents submitted to the pope by the community and analyzed earlier in this chapter, treads on what would soon become dangerous ground by insisting that only *expropriatio* is a substantial element in poverty because only it is not subject to papal dispensation.[19]

In defining poverty as essentially *expropriatio,* Richard and Pierre are developing an idea already stated (*sotto voce,* as it were) in the earlier arguments as reported by Olivi. Why Olivi made so little of it is unclear. One might infer that his opponents did not make much of it either, but it is at least possible that he trod lightly around it because he found it hard to deny. On one occasion he came close to agreeing that lack of possessions was indeed the central element in poverty.[20]

Richard and Pierre follow the great tradition in granting that *usus pauper* is nonetheless required. The Franciscan vows only poverty, chastity, and obedience, as the rule and *Exiit* insist; yet, while not included in the vow, *usus pauper* is somehow implied in it. The two men work this out in different ways, however. Pierre takes what was by then a familiar route. He argues that whoever vows a virtue is held *ex condescentia* to those things that are connected *(annexa)* with that virtue. For example, he who vows virginity is required to restrict useless conversation with women. Temperance, the virtue expressed by *usus pauper,* is linked with poverty, for there would be something anomalous about a poor man who lived luxuriously *(abusio est pauper delicatus).* Thus the Franciscan, by vowing poverty, commits himself to restricted use in general. In addition, he is held to specific *usus pauperes* through his vow of obedience, because the rule explicitly restricts him in certain areas, such as the reception of money. Since these are matters of obedience, however, they are open to adjustment insofar as the rule gives discretionary power to superiors.

Richard's view is more difficult to describe, and for two different reasons. In the first place, he is at times subtle to the point of being abstruse. This subtlety is seen in the welter of distinctions with which he likes to begin his responses, but it is also manifested in the fact that he sees and tries to neutralize a whole series of problems that Pierre simply avoids.[21] In the second place, Richard's treatise is available in an edition based on a single, apparently defective manuscript, which omits passages here and there and changes the occasional word.[22] Thus, any summary of his thought must be rather provisional.

At one point Richard acknowledges that Franciscans are in some way held, *ex voto,* to eschew lax use of clothes, shoes, and horses—i.e., in that way in which the rule induces them to observe these things strictly. In what way *are* they so induced? Somewhat earlier, Richard has noted that the brothers are necessarily held to some things in the rule simply because they represent virtuous activity. For example, the brothers are told to take care of the sick. Such things are not vowed, since the vow involves only supererogation. Second, they are held to some things because they are demanded by precept, prohibition, or equivalent words. There is some difficulty in the text here, but Richard seems to be saying that in these cases (e.g., not accepting money), the Franciscan is bound by the vow of obedience rather than that of poverty. Third, they are bound to certain things because "the formal nature [*ratio*] of what is vowed" is expressed in them. For example, appropriating no property for oneself is a specific aspect of *expropriatio*, and thus one is bound to it by the vow of poverty. Finally, they are bound to some things because they are necessarily connected (*annexa*) with the vow. Thus the brothers are to move through the world like pilgrims, refrain from litigation, and so forth because such things are vowed as necessary consequences of *expropriatio*, which is the thing that they principally vow. Thus both Pierre and Richard use the word *annexa*, but each seems to give it a slightly different significance. For Richard, one is held *ex voto* to the things necessarily "annexed" to what is principally vowed. For Pierre, one is held *ex condescentia* to things "annexed" to what is vowed. One can see why the community spokesmen at Vienne found their terminology shifting from time to time.

Pierre and Richard reflect the past in any number of ways. In particular, the arguments refuted by them show a remarkable continuity. Pierre refutes arguments that Franciscan poverty is the highest sort and that a poverty including use is higher than one without it; that without *usus pauper*, one would have only a *paupertas mathematica*, a purely abstract poverty; that one vowing poverty is held to *usus pauper* just as one vowing chastity and obedience is held to concrete activity in these areas; that several biblical passages—the same ones used earlier by Olivi—imply *usus pauper*; that a series of passages in the rule (also the ones used by Olivi) demand it; and that *Exiit* constantly emphasizes necessity in use. In each case we can trace a line of descent from the 1279–83 battle to the 1309–12 one.[23] Like the position papers offered by the community at Vienne, Richard and Pierre present more sophisticated arguments than the ones combated earlier by Olivi, but it is hard to say whether the difference is due to greater subtlety on the later polemicists' part or oversimplification on Olivi's.

Exivi de paradiso

We can conclude from what has been said so far that the 1309–12 debate at Avignon and Vienne both differed from and resembled the earlier one in the 1270s and 1280s. We have seen that there were really two *usus pauper* battles in the earlier period. The one in southern France included some argument about laxity in the order, but it was primarily a scholarly controversy that centered on the question of whether *usus pauper* was an essential part of the vow. The one in Ancona began with a very different sort of debate, one involving the question of whether a Franciscan should obey the pope or his vow if the

two stood in conflict, and it soon developed into a confrontation over concrete practices. The stakes were high, with the losers facing not merely censure but harsh imprisonment as well. The debate was not simply over a few
excesses. It concerned the general course of the order's development in the
thirteenth century. The difference between these two battles had much to do
with the fact that Olivi and his supporters in southern France were more comfortable with that course of development than their Anconan brethren were.

At Vienne, the two battles joined, as French and Italian spokesmen made
common cause against the community. The theoretical issue that had characterized the earlier southern French debate now had become everyone's problem. Ubertino da Casale and Raymond Geoffroi alike defended Olivi's position
on the question of whether *usus pauper* was part of the vow. Here the argument had evolved surprisingly little since the early 1280s. Certainly, there
were terminological innovations—and even a few new arguments—by 1312,
but both sides still argued the same positions in much the same ways. In this
respect, at least, Olivi and his adversaries had determined the course of the
entire controversy to 1312. Moreover, the situation of the Anconan spirituals had become everyone's problem. What had happened to Angelo and his
colleagues three decades earlier now had happened elsewhere. Ubertino and
Raymond could join in protesting a general persecution of spirituals in Italy
and southern France.

The differences were still evident, though. Ubertino, reflecting the Italian
zealots, broke ranks—not only with Olivi, but with Raymond Geoffroi as well
in offering a more radical critique of thirteenth-century developments, in
attempting to canonize the *Testament* and Leo sources as indices of Francis's
intention, and in encouraging a settlement of the controversy through division of the order. Angelo agreed with Ubertino on all these matters, but the
division he sought was of a different sort.

It was, however, a debate that Clement V very much wanted to end. That
was why he had solicited all this material. Having collected it, he appointed
a fourteen-member commission to advise him, and then finally issued *Exivi de
paradiso* on May 6, 1312.[24] Viewed from one perspective, it represented a
victory for the spirituals. In it, the pope rehearses Ubertino's charges against
the community, acknowledges that most of the practices censured by Ubertino
are really abuses, and tells the order to tidy up its life.

To be sure, Clement parts company from Ubertino in accepting the validity of papal privileges and papal glosses on the rule as well as in refusing to
countenance a division of the order. In these respects, however, Ubertino
hardly spoke for Olivi, or even for all the spirituals at Avignon and Vienne. It

is possible to argue that in *Exivi* Clement is actually closer to Olivi's position on such matters than Ubertino was. Clement's general thrust is to recall the order to a decent level of poverty that will edify the faithful while enabling the brothers to get on with their work. For example, he describes it as rational and fitting that Franciscans whose strength is sapped by arduous study or prayer should have access to gardens that provide not only necessary items but also a quiet place to restore the soul. Nevertheless, he staunchly denounces gardens so large that brothers can sell the produce. Olivi might have been willing to agree on both counts.

Viewed from another perspective, *Exivi* represents an attempt to end the *usus pauper* controversy by declaring a moratorium on it, at least in its more virulent form. Clement's final word on poverty in the bull is the announcement that it is "presumptuous and temerarious" to denounce as heretical the statement that *usus pauper* is (or is not) included in the vow. He does not mean to suggest that the question is unanswerable—indeed, he has just attempted to answer it—but only to observe that the order would be better off dropping the matter and engaging in more constructive pursuits. His intention is to end the controversy without declaring a winner.

Neither of these perspectives really does justice to the content of *Exivi*, however. Just before calling an end to the debate, Clement asserts that "by the profession of their rule friars minor are especially obligated to restricted or poor uses *(arctos usus seu pauperes)* contained in their rule, and they are bound by that type of obligation under which the rule contains or posits those uses." In 1279 such a statement would have meant papal support for Olivi against his opponents, but by 1312 things were more complicated. After all, by that time the term *usus pauperes* was being used by the community, and the latter recognized a commitment *ex voto* to restricted practice. Which group Clement is really supporting here depends on what he means, and the answer to that question is seen earlier, when he addresses the subject of whether Franciscans are held by their profession both to the precepts and to the counsels of the gospel. Some say yes, he remarks, while others say that they are held only to live in obedience, in chastity, and *sine proprio*, and to those things that are posited by words of obligation *(sub verbis obligatoriis)* in the rule. Clement himself, "following in the footsteps of our predecessor," asserts that because a vow must fall *sub certo*, the Franciscans cannot be held to evangelical counsels that are not specifically mentioned in the rule. That this was Francis's intention is seen from the fact that he included some evangelical counsels in the rule while omitting others, which would have been pointless if he had wished them all to be obligatory.

What, then, is the relationship between the words in chapter 1 of the rule, "living in obedience, in chastity, and *sine proprio*," and the specific obligations scattered throughout the rest of that document? Franciscans are bound by their profession (*ex professione*) not only to the three general obligations "nakedly and absolutely accepted," but also to all those things in the rule that modify the three. Thus the rule as a whole is seen as specifying the three general obligations. Clement goes on to add that Francis did not intend those who profess the rule to be bound equally to everything in the rule that modifies the three general obligations. He intended that some violations should be mortal, others venial. This is shown by the fact that in some cases he used the word "precept" or an equivalent.

Here we arrive at what, for Clement, is clearly the center of the problem. He acknowledges that there has been some uncertainty over whether all imperatives in the rule should be considered to have the weight of precepts, and that the problem of where to find the precepts has been increased by Nicholas III's reference to "equivalent words." The Franciscans, he says, have asked him to relieve their consciences by defining precisely what these equivalent words are, and he now intends to do just that. Thus, "although the brothers are not bound to observe all things demanded through imperatives in the rule as if they were precepts or the equivalent of precepts, nevertheless, if they are to observe the purity and rigor of the rule, they must recognize that they are obliged to observe the following things as equivalent to precepts." Clement then lists a series of obligations: not having more tunics than one with a hood, another without; not wearing shoes; not riding unless it is necessary; dressing in vile clothes; and so on.

In order to appreciate the significance of this list, we must pause for a moment and examine a similar one offered by the fourteen-man commission charged with advising Clement.[25] The commission announces that Franciscans are obliged by their vow to obey the three general vows,

> not only absolutely, but in the ways in which the rule pursues these three, so that by vowing poverty and chastity they are held to all that the rule touches upon pertaining to these two; yet in such a way that, in the case of those things which the rule demands by precept, prohibition or equivalent words, they are held to obedience necessarily, and transgression means mortal sin. And they are held in the same way to other things not pertaining to the aforesaid two, things which are demanded in the rule through words of obligation.

The commission goes on to provide its own list of such obligations. There are a number of things about this list that one might find interesting, but the most significant, from our point of view, is that it diverges from Clement's. Some differences are more apparent than real, stemming from the fact that the commission lists everything it considers "heavily obliging precepts" (*praecepta graviter obligantia*), both those expressed with explicit words of precept (i.e., *teneantur* and *praecipio*) and those in which equivalent words are used. Clement, apparently assuming that the former need no elaboration, lists only the latter. Nevertheless, they really do differ in the latter category. Clement, for example, includes (and the commission omits) passages concerning the clerical obligation to recite the divine office and the lay brothers' obligation concerning the Lord's Prayer, while the commission includes (and Clement omits) passages concerning work, imposition of penances, visitation by the provincial minister, and missions to the infidel. Moreover, the commission report includes dissenting opinions. Some difference of opinion is recorded on nearly one-third of the demands presented as precepts by the commission. Here is a more or less typical item in their list: "'And all the brothers will dress in vile clothing.' All but three of us believe that these words have the force of a precept. Of the three masters who disagree, two think the opposite and the third cannot decide."

We can now indulge in a few general observations. First, Clement and the commission both side with Olivi in believing that the poverty vowed by Franciscans includes more than simple lack of ownership. It involves restricted use as well. The rule explicitly restricts use in some areas, and violation of these restrictions involves mortal sin. Even in the ambiguous climate of 1312 Clement seems at this point more in tune with the spirituals than with the community. In other ways, though, the official view contradicts both the Olivian and community positions. The community, we recall, occasionally suggests a tripartite hierarchy of obligations. Lack of ownership is vowed in such a way that any violation of it automatically implies mortal sin. Those *usus pauperes* specifically enjoined in the rule are binding *ex voto* in some lesser sense, but in such a way that only notable excesses will result in mortal sin. Other *usus pauperes* are demanded as befitting the Franciscan state, but they are not required by precept. At such moments the community offers a significant concession to Olivian indeterminacy. The middle category accomplishes precisely what Olivi's original opponents apparently wanted to avoid.[26] It ties both the vow and mortal sin to some obligations that are not precisely determinable.

Clement and the commission will have none of it. They want to limit the vow to determinable obligations, but they also want it to include practice in such a way that the Franciscan is bound to certain forms of limited use by precept, just as he is bound to lack of ownership. In effect, they combine the first and second categories offered by the community into a single one, placing specific practices alongside lack of property as two complementary aspects of the vow. While this position parts company with both Olivi and the community, it is really harder on Olivi. It implicitly rejects many of his basic presuppositions and accepts those of his adversaries. The vow entails not a general commitment to *usus pauper,* but a commitment to specific *usus pauperes.*

In suggesting that Franciscans are bound by their vow only to those evangelical counsels specifically mentioned in the rule (because a vow must fall *sub certo* and because Francis's explicit inclusion of some counsels logically eliminates the rest), Clement is following a line of thought rejected by Olivi and his original opponents alike. Nevertheless, Clement is hardly original in taking this position. In fact, he is right in step with authors familiar to Olivi and his foes. Previous popes and Franciscan apologists had protected the order from external criticism by taking precisely the same line.[27] Clement is indeed walking in Nicholas's footsteps—but along a very well-beaten path.

At no time in the past, however, had the implications of the traditional argument come into clearer focus. The popes and most Franciscan leaders were unwilling to live with ambiguity on the matter of what was entailed in the vow. They needed specificity in order to defend the brothers against spiritual uncertainty, and they needed it to defend the order against external critics who might be tempted to argue that the rule was a "snare of damnation." Right through 1279 and *Exiit,* when they had to defend the Franciscan vow against these dangers, they spoke as if those specific requirements were there in the rule for the asking. In their own musings on the rule, however, they were willing to recognize that things were not so simple. In this context, Franciscans had long since anticipated Clement in recognizing that every imperative in the rule was not a precept and every precept was not expressed as an imperative.[28] Where, then, were those specific requirements? The *usus pauper* controversy had raised this question in a very pointed way. Olivi's notion of "indeterminate vows" offered one possible answer, but it was a solution that made both Clement and Franciscan leaders very uncomfortable. Another answer was to cut *usus pauper* loose from the vow entirely, leaving Franciscans with a vow in which "poverty" simply meant *expropriatio.* Franciscan leaders were hospitable to that solution, but Clement was not. He wanted real *usus pauperes* included in the vow, so he had to find them in the rule. Only then would friars have the spiritual security they needed.

And find them he did. Now, in 1312, Clement and his commission were bowing to the necessity of telling Franciscans just what the requirements were; yet their very lack of unanimity underscored the fact that the ultimate sanction of Clement's list lay not in the fact that it was an accurate mirror of the rule, but in the fact that it was Clement's list. Franciscans were henceforth to believe that those particular demands had the force of precepts precisely because the pope had selected them and not others for that honor.

Even so, the solution seemed to leave another problem untouched. Opponents of Olivi's view had seen that the quest for precisely determinable requirements, if taken to its logical conclusion, would exclude from the vow not only a blanket commitment to *usus pauper* but commitment to particular *usus pauperes* as well, since one would still be unable to delineate the precise degree required. Thus, for example, one could not safely vow to wear vile clothing because it is impossible to indicate that precise degree of sartorial splendor beyond which such a vow would be broken.

Clement found this conclusion unacceptable. He wanted some *usus pauperes* included in the vow, and thus he promoted to the status of precept the demand that brothers dress in vile clothing. What, then, did he do about the argument (reiterated since Olivi's day) that such a precept would be spiritually dangerous, because one could not draw a sharp line between observance and violation? Perhaps the best reply is that he ignored it. Still, there is a solution of sorts implied in his decree. Clement's final word on vile clothing is to leave its determination in the hands of Franciscan superiors. They will decide how vile the clothing should be in the light of local conditions. Presumably the brothers need only obey and their consciences will be clear. Thus Clement manages to retain some *usus pauperes* within the vow and to have specific requirements as well, but only by making such requirements the responsibility of those in authority. Friars must believe that vile clothing is a precept because the pope has told them that it is. They must adopt a certain level of vileness because their superior tells them that it is the proper level.

There is an odd convergence here. Clement has taken a different path but arrived at the same emphasis on the discretionary power of superiors already attained by Conington and Aureole, who got there by tying specific *usus pauperes* to the vow of obedience rather than the vow of poverty. Even our mysterious "Lyra," the defender of Olivian indeterminacy, points in that direction. In practical terms, Clement's solution means that the average friar's obligation is to obey the rule as interpreted by those in authority. There is little place in such a world for Olivi's notion that the friar has a responsibility to disobey superiors if they demand violation of the rule. Unfortunately, as we shall see, a number of spirituals found the Olivian view rather hard to abandon.

Fidei catholicae fundamento

On May 6, 1312, the same day Clement V promulgated *Exivi de paradiso*, he issued yet another bull, *Fidei catholicae fundamento*. This one dealt with another of the great issues confronted at Vienne, Olivi's orthodoxy, although in an odd way, since it never even mentioned him. The subject had been an important one for decades. During his life, Olivi had weathered repeated attacks not only on his view of poverty, but also on a variety of theological and philosophical views, ranging from his notion of the Trinity to his ideas about the nature of quantity.[29] After the censure of 1283, he had experienced relative peace on all issues except that of poverty. Once he was dead, though, and the attack on the spirituals had intensified, his earlier difficulties were too tempting a weapon to ignore, and the persecution that began in 1299 included an official order to confiscate and burn his writings. (We recall the fate of the unfortunate Pons, whose hypothetical refusal to surrender Olivian works led to his imprisonment and death.)

By the great debate of 1310–12, the community had resurrected a series of old Olivian errors for papal perusal. Raymond of Fronsac and Bonagratia of Bergamo, now spearheading the attack, presented a list of such enormities in March 1311.[30] In the theological and philosophical realm, we find several survivors from the censure of 1283. These rather predictably include Olivi's views on Franciscan bishops and burial of the dead, both of which relate directly to the poverty dispute, but they also include his thoughts on the divine nature, infant baptism, marriage, the sacramental character, and the rational soul as form of the body.[31] In addition, we find two charges untouched by the earlier censure. First, Olivi is described as affirming that it does not contradict the text of John 19 to say that Christ was alive when his side was opened by the lance; on the contrary, such a statement is quite consonant with the mysteries of the church. Second, Olivi is accused of disseminating "false and fantastic prophecies concerning the church" in his writings, especially in the Revelation commentary, "calling the church a great whore and dogmatizing many other things in disparagement of the church." Raymond and Bonagratia consider the counterargument that Olivi was simply presenting these views without asserting them. They find this defense easy to dismiss, because it is heresy to call into doubt what the church already has defined. They also dismiss the objection of some (including Ubertino) that at the end of his life Olivi submitted his works to the papacy for correction. Those who physically submit their works to the Holy See for examination and correction are excused from the taint of heresy if their work contains elements of doubtful orthodoxy.

None of this applies to Olivi, however. He did not physically submit his works, and his views are more than merely doubtful. They openly contradict established truths defined by holy councils and by the universal Church. Raymond and Bonagratia point to the fact that Olivi's works already have been condemned by his own order and by the apostolic see on the advice of Paris masters. This condemnation occurred because the participants recognized that the heresies contained in Olivi's writings were very dangerous and were so thoroughly dispersed throughout the works that it would be impractical—in fact, impossible—to remove the bad and preserve the good.

These charges against Olivi are a bit like the Olivian works as portrayed by them: truth and falsity are so skillfully blended as to make any distinction between the two difficult. Raymond and Bonagratia are right insofar as Olivi's thought was subjected to more than one examination during the 1270s and 1280s, and they are right insofar as his entire *oeuvre* was confiscated twice, after both the 1283 and 1299 condemnations. On the other hand, they conveniently forget that by the end of the 1280s Olivi had been rehabilitated, his works were circulating again, and he had been assigned to teaching positions in Florence and Montpellier. During the early 1290s, when zealots in southern France were disciplined, Olivi was not, despite Raymond and Bonagratia's effort to suggest the contrary. He was apparently asked to clarify his views on *usus pauper,* but seems to have cleared that hurdle nicely and continued to teach. These facts seem to compromise their presentation of Olivi as a well-known heretic. The mixture of accuracy and overstatement in their presentation makes it hard to know what should be done with their insistence that Olivi was condemned not only by Parisian masters and his order but also *by apostolic authority.* Do they know something we do not about the way things occurred in 1299 and immediately thereafter, or are they simply drawing an unauthorized inference from papal involvement in the southern French investigation from 1290 on, and then in the more widespread persecution after 1299? There is no way of knowing.

As Olivi's memory was subjected to attack, at least some spirituals reacted with an escalated appraisal of Olivi's thought. As Raymond and Bonagratia tell us, some described his views as revealed to him by the Holy Spirit and insisted on defending them as articles of faith.[32] Others took a more cautious line, presenting Olivi as a generally orthodox but nonetheless fallible scholar. Ubertino tends to adopt the latter stance in his several polemical works. He states his own willingness to eschew any errors discovered by the pope, but emphasizes that such errors, if found at all, will represent no more than a few rogue assertions in a vast body of otherwise orthodox doctrine. He also underscores his conviction that the denunciation of Olivi's theology is nothing more than a flanking movement in the poverty battle, an effort to compromise the reform movement by discrediting one of its major theoreticians.

Here again one encounters a bewildering mixture of truth and overstatement. Modern scholarship has begun to wade through Olivi's massive scholarly production and has discovered a first-rate mind who deserves to be placed alongside the best in his age, but it is disingenuous to suggest that his detractors attacked his theology and philosophy simply to discredit his thought on poverty. Olivi was bright and at times profoundly original. It is hardly surprising that he worried people. We have reason to believe that his views on the Virgin Mary and perhaps other issues as well were anxiously examined well before he stumbled into the *usus pauper* controversy.

Once he descends to particulars, Ubertino goes a long way toward defending Olivi not merely against his current detractors, but also (implicitly) against the 1283 censure. He argues that when the present minister general was a scholar at Paris, he defended as probable the very opinion on the divine essence that Raymond and Bonagratia now consider heretical, and that the view is in harmony with the Nicaean council, the fathers, and Innocent III. As for marriage as a sacrament, Ubertino notes that Peter Lombard, Hostiensis, and others agree that it differs in many ways from other sacraments. As for the disputed Olivian view on whether infant baptism confers a *habitus* of virtues, it is presented by Olivi without assertion and is more or less consistent with the opinion of Peter Lombard, Gratian, Augustine, Anselm, and others. In the final analysis, the question is an open one. So are the questions of how the soul informs the body and what effect a sacramental character has upon the soul.

On questions related to the poverty issue, Ubertino defends Olivi even more strongly. He argues that Bonaventure and Pecham are even stricter than Olivi on the subject of how Franciscan bishops should live, and that the Olivian view of *usus pauper* as a substantial part of the vow was also held by Bonagratia of San Giovanni in Persiceto, the former minister general. Olivi's only purported offense on the matter of burial is his perfectly justifiable observation that Franciscan involvement in it detracts from the highest perfection if it involves greed, scandal to the clergy, and bad example for the people.

So far, Ubertino has been rehearsing old grievances—and, in the process, defending Olivian views actually censured in 1283. The last two charges by Raymond and Bonagratia explore hitherto uncensured areas of the master's thought. One of them, that Olivi's Apocalypse commentary calls the church a great whore, would necessarily have been ignored by attackers during Olivi's life, since Olivi wrote the commentary just before his death. Olivi's apocalyptic speculation had occasioned comment even before the 1283 censure, but had not excited enough attention to rate a negative judgment. Nor do we see any evidence that this earlier comment saw Olivi's thought as an attack on the church.[33] In any case, Ubertino stoutly denies the charge. On the contrary, he says, in the Apocalypse commentary and elsewhere Olivi spoke of papal authority with the utmost reverence. On his deathbed, he recognized it yet again by submitting all his works to papal correction.[34]

The other new charge, that Olivi placed the spear wound before Christ's death rather than after, elicits a lengthy reply from Ubertino, one that moves in two different directions. On the one hand, he tries to liberate Olivi from the charge by distancing him from the idea. He points out—quite correctly, in fact—that in one of his theological *quaestiones* Olivi bases his argument on the assumption that Christ was already dead when he received the spear thrust.[35] He also acknowledges, however, that Olivi discusses the problem at some length in his commentary on the Gospel of John. There, as Ubertino well knows, Olivi recalls how astonished he was to learn that the opposite order of events had been revealed to "a certain very holy person of our time, used to many raptures and divine revelations." Olivi was aware that the Gospel of John seemed to place the death first, but he nevertheless began to ask himself whether the mystic's reverse reading might somehow be harmonized with the gospel account. He finally discovered that there was a way of doing so, and his efforts were later rewarded when another mystic, whose experiences he himself had witnessed (but with whom he had not discussed this particular issue), informed him that her visions were often based on that same scenario.[36] Olivi's way of reconciling this order with John's apparently explicit statement to the contrary need not detain us here. The important thing for our purposes is that, though highly motivated in his effort to defend the scenario presupposed by his two mystics,[37] Olivi nevertheless leaves the question open.

Ubertino recognizes as much. Olivi, he notes, never affirmed that Christ died after the spear thrust. Had Ubertino left the matter there, his argument would have been much less interesting than it turns out to be, for at this point he begins to move in a different direction. He notes that if Olivi really had intended to affirm the questionable position, he certainly would have cited the authorities supporting it. Ubertino then goes on to invoke those authorities. He visits pseudo-Bernard of Clairvaux, the Gospel of Nichodemus, and, more surprising, Jerome, although the latter is used in a rather complicated way. Ubertino argues that the incident of the side wound is inserted before Christ's death in several manuscripts of the Gospel of Matthew and that he has seen it in one old manuscript that contains the text as corrected by Jerome himself.[38]

Thus Ubertino begins by distancing Olivi from the charge but ends up exposing himself to it. His fascination was shared by several contemporaries who, like Olivi and Ubertino, courted trouble for other reasons as well. These included Raymond Délicieux; Matthew of Bouzigues; four spiritual Franciscans who submitted a notarized statement affirming the presence of this variant in extant manuscripts of Matthew; and any number of beguins who, according to Bernard Gui, argued that the passage originally in Matthew had been removed by the church because it seemed to clash with John's narrative, although the conflict was only apparent since John was simply describing the event as it *seemed* to occur.[39] These later defenses of the Olivian position part company with that position, though; although their claim of a biblical variant has been supported by modern Bible scholars,[40] it is not supported by Olivi himself, who never mentions Matthew and apparently assumes that only John is relevant.

When one examines Ubertino's treatment of disputed Olivian views, it is impressive how many of them he is willing to defend, despite his observation that Olivi undoubtedly erred occasionally and that he is not interested in backing every statement Olivi ever made. In the final analysis, though, Ubertino declares his willingness to follow Olivi's wish and submit the latter's works to the pope for correction.[41] That process was already going on even as Ubertino wrote. Three theologians had been given the task of examining certain questionable elements in Olivi's work (not the entire corpus), and by the time Ubertino penned his major defense of Olivi in late spring or early summer of 1311, they were hard at it. They presumably had finished by late summer of that year, because in a work written then, Ubertino announces that of the many charges leveled against Olivi, the masters had found only three to be important. The three were Olivi's views on the divine nature, the rational soul, and Christ's side wound. Even in these three cases, the masters had concluded that Olivi's intention was pure and without the stain of heretical depravity.[42]

It is unclear how the work of this three-man commission is related to that of another seven-man commission mentioned in an anonymous document that has survived in a single manuscript.[43] According to this document, Clement V gave the seven-man commission the task of examining five articles. We are told the findings of four out of seven masters, who are then listed, one by name and the other three by title or order. Apparently the seven failed to reach unanimity. At any rate, two of the five articles deal with the divine essence, and the remaining three cover the soul, infant baptism, and Christ's side wound. On every issue except the last, the four state their own views in a way that provides room for Olivi's. Only on the latter issue do they seem at variance with him, and even here there is some ambiguity, thanks to the way they phrase their position. They brand as erroneous any view that would consider it less certain to say that the side wound was inflicted after Christ's death than to say the opposite. Such a position, they affirm, is contradicted by the *sancti* and by the Gospel of Matthew! Olivi, of course, made no such assertion.

This is our only witness to the commission of seven and its deliberations. One would feel somewhat better about it if the anonymous author had not gone on to observe that "the decretal was made according to the relation of these four, and thus it was determined that Brother Peter John was catholic and his books were made public throughout the whole world." If we assume— as it seems we must—that the decretal in question is *Fidei catholicae fundamento*, then that seems something of an overstatement. As we will see, the decretal does not mention Olivi by name, and his works emerged from the deliberations without any new stigma being attached to them; but if this document gives us an accurate report of the four commission members' conclusions, then the pope was less tolerant than they were concerning some of the contested views. It is not impossible, though, that the decretal took a harder line than a majority of the seven-man commission did, since the pope presumably enjoyed the guidance of the other three members of that commission, of the three theologians mentioned by Ubertino and others, and of various individual theologians whose views had been solicited. These included Giles of Rome, who was critical of twenty-four articles, and Augustinus Triumphus, who was even less pleased with the twelve he considered.[44]

In *Fidei catholicae fundamento*, the result of all this consultation, Clement pronounces on three issues. First, he states unequivocally that the lance pierced Christ's side after his death. Second, he affirms that the rational soul is the form of the body, and that anyone who denies it is a heretic. Third, he recognizes that there are various opinions among theologians on the effect of infant baptism, but he determines that "the opinion which says informing grace and the virtues are conferred in baptism is to be chosen as more probable and more consonant with the words of the *sancti* and modern doctors of theology."[45] The pope is clear on this much. He is less helpful on how it all relates to Olivi. Three different issues are at stake. First, are the views rejected here really Olivi's? Second, does Clement at least *think* that he is addressing Olivi's views? Third, if so, why does he never mention Olivi by name?

Our answer to the first question depends on which part of the decree is being considered. It is hard to avoid the conclusion that Clement's categorical statement regarding the side wound contradicts Olivi by closing an issue that Olivi leaves open in his commentary on John. Much the same could be said of the judgment on infant baptism. Here again Olivi makes no assertion, but he obviously favors a view that the decree considers less probable. One might protest that Olivi's opinion is protected to some extent by Clement's recognition that theologians differ on the matter, yet the fact remains that whatever differences he sees in the past, he goes on to tell theologians the view they should favor in the future, and it is not the one favored by Olivi. (There is, to be sure, something odd about a doctrinal decree that orders theologians to accept a view not as true, but as more probable and more in line with the thought of past and present scholars, but that is what the pope said.)

Clement's thoughts on the soul present a different problem. Efrem Bettoni is correct in saying that if Olivi had been alive in 1312, "he would have been ready to subscribe to the conciliar definition, convinced that he had never taught the contrary."[46] Here the issue is a complex one. Let it suffice to say that, however real the difference between Olivi and other scholars may have been on this matter, it existed on an entirely different level. Olivi never denied what Clement here asserts.[47]

Granting that Clement is implicitly contradicting Olivi on only two of the three issues, whom does he *think* he is contradicting? Clearly Olivi. After all, he had set a whole stable of theologians loose on Olivi's writings. He had done so because Olivi's orthodoxy had become a bone of contention in the debate. And in two out of three cases he was more or less on target. If he was wrong in the third, he was at least in good company. Almost from the beginning Olivi had found himself attacked on this score.

Why, then, was Olivi not mentioned? The answer to that question died with Clement, but we can still speculate. Omission of Olivi's name was a minor victory for the spirituals, since it corresponded with Ubertino's recommendation that Clement address those aspects of Olivi's thought that needed correction while protecting his reputation as a pious, catholic (though fallible) scholar.[48] After all, in an age when major theologians might be told to change their minds on a list of specific issues and still go on to carve out successful careers in the church, three questionable opinions in an entire *oeuvre* was hardly shameful. Durand de St.-Porçain had had his difficulties in that respect, and then went on to do very well for himself as a theologian and bishop. Giles of Rome, the same man asked by two different popes to pass judgment on Olivi's work, had his own corrections to make early in his career.

In the final analysis, however, the immediate effect was not so much to vindicate Olivi as to neutralize him as an issue, at least for the moment. The idea of omitting his name fit well with Clement's general aim at Vienne. His main purpose was to produce a settlement which would unite the order. Explicitly deciding on Olivi's orthodoxy or heterodoxy would not have aided that project. Nor would anything have been gained by dealing with Olivi's thoughts on Franciscan poverty. Clement apparently considered these three issues important enough in their own right to rate clarification, but he chose to present them in just that way, on their own.

Unfortunately, the pope's neutralization attempt was only briefly successful, as we shall see.

SEVEN

THE COLLAPSE OF THE CLEMENTINE SETTLEMENT

WE SAW IN THE LAST CHAPTER that Clement V's settlement at Vienne conceded some points to the spirituals and denied others. Clement took their complaints seriously, acknowledged grave abuses, and told Franciscan leaders to reform. Yet he refused to divide the order and let the spirituals go their own way. Moreover, he confirmed the key role of ministerial discretion in determining the scope of *usus pauper*, thereby limiting the spirituals' chance to exercise autonomy within the order. It remained to be seen how effective this solution would be.

Angelo's Initial Optimism

Angelo Clareno's correspondence from the period suggests that he was almost pathetically committed to optimism concerning the Clementine settlement, and a number of spirituals may have felt the same. Even in 1312, however, an objective observer might have predicted that, from a practical viewpoint,

Clement's refusals would have greater long-term significance than his concessions. The spirituals were still an embattled minority, vulnerable to their superiors' hostility. If the Franciscan organization was as far off course as Ubertino seemed to think, there was no reason to assume that the leaders would repent simply because Clement told them to do so. In his chronicle, Angelo notes (with the advantage of hindsight) that they pretended to accept *Exivi de paradiso*, but in their hearts, they despised it.[1]

Why, then, were the spirituals hopeful? Angelo offers a partial answer. In a letter of 1312 he announces that Clement is on the spirituals' side and is in the process of punishing wicked superiors. He is already turning his attention to southern France and Angelo hopes that he will go on to do something about Tuscan leaders, who continue to persecute the spirituals.[2] Another letter, written slightly later, is equally optimistic, announcing that "the lord pope has deposed all the leaders who attacked the way of the spirit and the doctrine of Brother Petrus Iohannis [Olivi]."[3] Still another says that pious hermits who live in obedience to their bishops are protected by the constitutions of Vienne from molestation at the hands of "certain persons" and from the inquisitors as well.[4] In these letters Angelo consistently suggests that, much as he would like to go home, he must stay in Avignon to exercise his influence in the ongoing negotiations.

By the 1320s the rosy glow of optimism had long since faded. Angelo would simply write in his chronicle that "when the council was over the friars' business remained unsettled."[5] That is a more sober analysis, yet it still assumes—as do the earlier letters—that when the Council of Vienne was officially dissolved on May 6, 1312, the Franciscan settlement remained a work in progress. The assumption was not a bad one. The council only lasted seven months, and throughout most of it, if Clement slept poorly, it was not primarily because he was agonizing over the Franciscans. His main concerns were Boniface VIII and the Templars. The two problems were related, inasmuch as in both cases Clement had to satisfy King Philip IV without giving him all he demanded. In the case of Boniface, that meant undoing the dead pope's actions against Philip and his associates without acceding to Philip's desire that Boniface be condemned as a heretic. In the case of the Templars, it meant suppressing the order without pronouncing it heretical—as Philip preferred—or acceding to the king's position on how to dispose of its property. The Templars were not officially suppressed until April 3, and negotiations concerning them dragged on even after that date. The process concerning Boniface VIII was closed only on May 6, the same day *Exivi de paradiso* and *Fidei catholicae fundamento* were promulgated. In short, the pope was busy elsewhere and could not have been expected to give the Franciscans all the attention they deserved during the council. Of course, the council relied heavily on commissions that studied particular issues and then submitted their conclusions to the pope. Nevertheless, in the case of Franciscan poverty, as in those of Boniface and the Templars, it was natural to assume that the pope would add his own ingredients to the recipe, particularly since much of the problem involved not abstract doctrine, but practical decisions on governance.

Administrative Shifts

The most immediate decision facing the pope was what to do about the fact that the superiors to whom he had just granted authority to decide on matters of *usus pauper* were the same people who had been persecuting the spirituals for the last decade. Clement saw that part of the problem clearly. He could hardly have missed it with Ubertino da Casale around. Ubertino reminded Clement that the spirituals had obeyed and trusted him. Clement had encouraged them to place their confidence in his protection and, if he now failed to provide it, their blood would be on his hands.[6] Clement, however, was committed to certain assumptions that restricted the range of solutions he would accept. He never doubted that the religious life demanded order and authority. During the great debate, he freed as few spirituals as possible from the discipline of their superiors. Only those explicitly named to represent the cause were so exempted. The rest were left under their normal superiors, although Clement forbade further harassment, warned the leaders that he would punish them severely if they did not obey, and agreed to a streamlined appeal procedure in case of emergency.[7] His solution at Vienne proceeded along the same lines. In effect, Clement rested his hope on a single structure, within which spirituals would obey a revitalized leadership that, in turn, was held in line by obedience to the pope. As Angelo Clareno suggests, this solution relied rather heavily on the assumption that the friars would respect papal authority.[8]

The Tuscan Spirituals

The wisdom of this assumption was open to question even before Clement issued *Exivi de paradiso*. According to Angelo, while the great debate was in progress, spirituals in southern France, Tuscany, and the Val di Spoleto were actually persecuted more harshly than ever.[9] In his 1312 letter, he had voiced his hope that the pope would act against Tuscan superiors, but even as he wrote, the time for preventative action had passed. Early in 1312, a group of Tuscan spirituals assigned to convents in Florence, Siena, and Arezzo had banded together and taken over convents in Arezzo, Asciano, and Carmignano by force. According to Angelo, on the advice of a canon regular from Siena—who promised to represent them before the pope—they "elected for themselves a general and other leaders in accordance with the rule."[10] The group itself claimed to have acted "with the advice of several cardinals and scholars learned in theology as well as in both laws."[11] The size of the rebel group cannot be determined accurately, but the documents mention around eighty coming not only from Tuscany, but from elsewhere in Italy as well. One was from southern France.[12]

In June 1312 the custode of Siena cited eight of the group to answer accusations, warning them in the process not to shelter certain apostates from elsewhere who had been reported as missing.[13] The eight replied that the custode's actions took no account of the proceedings at Vienne. They managed to suggest that pope and council supported the spirituals and that they were covered by the exemption from Franciscan control tendered to spiritual spokesmen at Vienne. They were eventually disabused of any such illusion by Clement.

In July 1313 Clement wrote the archbishop of Genoa, bishop of Bologna, and bishop of Lucca, asking one or more of them to intervene against the Tuscan rebels.[14] He accused the latter of causing scandal and acting as they wished—charges echoed by Angelo and by the Sienese ecclesiastic who eventually conducted the process against them.[15] Angelo recalls in his chronicle that even those who supported the spirituals at the council were disturbed and henceforth more easily disposed to believe all that their enemies had said of them.[16] We will see that Angelo himself upbraided the Tuscan rebels in a letter to his associates.

The process against the Tuscan spirituals advanced slowly yet inexorably. The definitive action did not occur until May 24, 1314, when Bernard, prior of S. Fidelis in Siena (and the man ultimately responsible for dealing with the problem), published a sentence of excommunication against thirty-seven of them.[17] The text of this sentence deserves examination, because it is a portent of things to come. Bernard opens with a lengthy meditation on the centrality of obedience—not only for the church in general but also for the Franciscan order in particular. There is one church, which is obedient to one gospel and one vicar of Christ. The rebels are attacking that unity through their disobedience. They are doing so by their actions as well as by their words, "pertinaciously asserting that questions regarding the rule cannot be settled by the supreme pontiff, the vicar of Christ." In fact, "they assert that by doing so in the past and in the present the Holy See has endangered and sown error in the souls of those who profess the rule." They "deride, judge, reject and condemn" all past and present papal declarations concerning the rule. Thus Bernard declares them to be "notorious apostates, schismatics and rebels; originators and proponents of a superstitious sect; and sowers of pestiferous doctrine." This seems to imply not only disobedience but heresy as well. To be sure, in an earlier letter giving them sixty days to submit, Bernard had threatened to proceed against them "as manifest rebels, enemies of the church, schismatics and heretics."[18]

By that time some of the Tuscan brethren had read the signs and escaped to Sicily, where King Frederick III sheltered them, defying attempts by Alexander of Alexandria, the new Franciscan minister general, to effect their extradition by invoking the spectre of papal wrath.[19] Frederick's support might at first seem odd, but a closer look at the Sicilian situation makes it more understandable. Here again, at the beginning of the fourteenth century, we find a strong current of spiritual renewal and reform that developed on its own, without guidance from or attention to the papacy. In the case of Sicily, the ground had been laid in the period after the Sicilian vespers, when the popes backed the Angevins, excommunicating the Sicilian rebels and the new regime. Benedict XI and Clement V had attempted to place the relationship on a new footing, but the result had not been a happy one. Sicilians continued to see the papacy as meddling in their religious affairs to the detriment of their piety and their economic well-being.[20] Thanks to Arnald of Villanova and others, Frederick was already favorable to reform along spiritual Franciscan lines and, just as important, convinced of his own duty to further it. In fact, his contact with Arnald represents at least a mild anticipation of his role with the Tuscan rebels, since in 1304–5 Arnald himself had taken refuge in Sicily when his situation in northern Europe became increasingly insecure. He had returned to the island in 1309.[21] Arnald's brand of reformist evangelism, akin to that of the spiritual Franciscans (although his apocalyptic program differed from theirs), impressed not only the king but other Sicilians as well. Nor did Frederick's intransigence necessitate a break with his clergy. When the king asked a group of his higher clergy—including the archbishop of Monreale, the vicar of the archbishop of Palermo, and various experts in theology, canon law, and civil law—to pass judgment on the rebels' request for refuge (and, by extension, the minister general's request that they be turned over to him), the clergy replied that, far from teaching heresy or schism, the Tuscan fugitives were "true servants of the Holy Gospel."[22] (Later, however, Frederick did offer at least a partial submission to John XXII, as we will see in a moment.)

The Tuscan spirituals were part of the same Italian spiritual tradition that produced Ubertino da Casale and Angelo Clareno. This much is plain from their appeal to Frederick of Sicily,[23] although it is worth remembering that in this document the group might be expected to present the most moderate self-portrait possible. They acknowledge that the rule was approved by the pope, but they balance that recognition with an insistence that it was revealed to Saint Francis, that they are obliged to observe it, and that Francis clarified how they should do so in his *Testament*. They place heavy emphasis on the word *minores* and warn that, although the pope has given the order privileges that grant it leverage in its struggle with the secular clergy over issues like wills, burials, and preaching rights, they intend to ignore them. If bishops forbid them to preach, they will simply desist. They will not accept money deposited for their use, even if the negotiation is handled by a third party. Nor will they accept and then resell things that they do not need, such as horses, arms, or excessive amounts of grain, and so on. All in all, the Tuscan spirituals seem to be arguing that they are bound to accept only what is necessary for present survival (the latter being sensibly interpreted, presumably).

The Tuscan spirituals proceed through other major issues contested at Vienne—clothing, churches, liturgical paraphernalia, and the rest—taking much the same position Ubertino had taken. The real departure, the moment when we sense we have moved into another time, comes when they deal with the point John XXII would eventually make against the French spirituals: the fact that *Exivi de paradiso* places responsibility for determining the nature of *usus pauper* in the hands of the superiors, and thus the individual friar need only obey and he will fulfill his vow of poverty. The Tuscan spirituals respond that *Exivi* immediately adds, "in such a way however that they observe vileness in clothing," and notes that such should be understood in the light of what is generally deemed "vile" in that locale. Thus, they say, the pope limits the range of decision open to superiors. In short, subordinates are still left with the responsibility of judging whether their superiors are within the accepted parameters.

What, then, about their vow of obedience? Francis, they say, commanded them to obey superiors in all things that they have promised to observe and that are not damaging to the soul or contrary to the rule. A superior has authority only within these limits. If he orders otherwise, "then to disobey is to be truly obedient to God and to the rule."

All this constitutes a ground floor of Italian spiritual Franciscan belief. Beyond it, Angelo Clareno sensed genuine differences and was not shy about identifying them.

Angelo's Reaction

Angelo's reaction to the Tuscan rebels is instructive. On September 9, 1313, he wrote to members of his group in Italy. They were perturbed by the Tuscan events and sought guidance. Angelo's reply to them presents a harsh critique of the rebels. He begins with a sustained celebration of love and its role in Christian life. This celebration evolves along the way into praise of obedience. Angelo goes on to note that "just as the law of grace is succeeded only by Christ's coming in judgment, so authority remains in prelates, whether they are just or sinners, until the Lord's second coming."[24] Moments later he announces that "the state [*status*] of the church remains fixed and unchangeable in its authority and dignity, in good and bad prelates, in the just and in sinners, until the end of this world, and in every age [*statu*] of the church the good are intermixed with the bad."

Shortly thereafter Angelo notes that "only the supreme pontiff, who holds the place of Christ in the church, was able by his plenitude of power to concede to Francis and the Order of Minors the right to elect a general minister." Those who have arrogated to themselves the power to make such a selection have disobeyed the rule, Saint Francis, the ecclesiastical hierarchy, the pope, the fathers, and the decrees of all the councils. They have done so "partly from ignorance, partly from audacity, partly from temerity, and partly from presumptuous contempt of the wise counsel of all their friends and brothers." Through their "depraved and ignorant confidence in themselves and their erroneous interpretation of the rule," they have separated themselves from the body of the faithful and merit just punishment. They are guilty of sacrilege and can legitimately be castigated for it. In the process of making this point, Angelo also asserts that "the rule could have been conceded to Francis and his successors only by the supreme pontiff." Throughout his response, Angelo is free with the word "disobedience" as well as with "heresy." He explains that "where there is division and schism, there also is ignorance of the truth," and "where error is pertinaciously defended as the truth, there heresy is confirmed."

Angelo's praise of obedience might seem odd in view of the fact that he himself had not exactly devoted the previous two decades to implementing the pope's wishes regarding the Poor Hermits. In fact, though, Angelo cherishes a very precise notion of obedience. He hastens to explain that a brother who suffers martyrdom because he refuses to obey an ungodly command does not lose the merit of obedience, but a brother who denies the authority of the prelate in such a situation (and presumes to determine that he is no prelate at all) has rejected humility, taking what is not his. We are required to honor and defend bad prelates, even if they kill us, although we are not required to obey them if they command us to do evil. This is the lesson of Christ's voluntary death on the cross. It is also the lesson of Francis "in the first rule which the Lord Pope Innocent approved and conceded to him." In it, Francis said,

> In the same way the brothers should not have power or domination over one another, for as the Lord said in the gospel, "the rulers of the Gentiles lord it over one another and those who are greater exercise power over them." It will not be that way among the brothers, but whoever among you wishes to be greater, let him be minister and servant of the rest, and the greater among you should become the junior or lesser. Nor should any brother do or say evil to another, but rather in the spirit of love they should voluntarily serve and obey one another. And this is the true and holy obedience of our Lord Jesus Christ.

Angelo informs us that in the beginning, the Tuscan rebels justified their actions by reference to the rule as they misunderstood it, but now, "converted to apocrypha," they fortify their position by appealing to "secret revelations of a certain holy person" and to the writings of Olivi, which they also misinterpret.[25]

Lydia von Auw sees Angelo's judgment on the Tuscan rebels as "illogical and unjust."[26] She compares it with Olivi's letter to Conrad of Offida. History, she says, was repeating itself.[27] Von Auw suggests that Angelo's attack was "inspired by a certain opportunism. The Tuscan rebellion compromised the long campaign . . . to obtain separation of the spirituals from the community by legal means."[28]

It, is, happily, unnecessary to discuss Olivi's letter, since we have considered it in an earlier chapter. As for Angelo, von Auw seems both right and wrong about him. As she says, in 1313 he was a great deal more sanguine about the chances of working things out with the pope than he would be later, and he saw the Tuscan rebels as compromising his efforts. Had he possessed a copy of Olivi's earlier letter, he might have copied the passage about radical elements giving the spirituals' enemies ammunition to use against the entire movement. In this respect at least, he and Olivi were quite correct.

Moreover, von Auw's accusation of illogicality is, if not irrefutable, at least understandable. She protests that "if the rule is identical with the Gospel as he believes, then the pope's assent to it is a secondary affair."[29] Thus it seems odd to emphasize the centrality of papal authority as Angelo does. Odd, perhaps, but not entirely illogical. The problem was a major one for the thirteenth century in general. In that century, the problem of whether solemn vows could be abrogated was given careful consideration inside and outside the Franciscan order, with varying results.[30] Within the order, the discussion took on new urgency once the spirituals found themselves opposing their leaders and once apocalyptic expectation or practical experience encouraged them to believe that the pope himself might constitute a problem in this regard. Here, too, one could come to varying conclusions. It was not an easy problem to deal with, much less solve, and Angelo's attempt to settle it seems as sensible as most.

Angelo is very Augustinian in his solution. His starting point is Paul's admonition in Rom. 13:1, and he proceeds from there to a position not unlike the one Luther would adopt two centuries later. We must refuse to obey an ungodly order, but we must also be prepared to take the consequences. In other words, one who is given such a command is released from the obligation to obey it, but not from the authority of the commander. Nevertheless, Angelo's position seems Augustinian in a slightly different way from Luther's. Luther places heavy emphasis on the sinfulness of humankind and thus accepts the need for strong authority to impose order on a potentially disordered world. Angelo seems to agree that firm restraint should be exerted on those who, like the Tuscan rebels, have arrogantly and illegally seized authority. However, his attitude toward authority goes well beyond the negative element of restraint. Obedience becomes part of the Franciscan higher way. As Gian Luca Potestà recognizes, Angelo's position is closely tied to his Christology.[31] He sees love and obedience as fundamental elements in the incarnation. To follow Christ—or Francis for that matter—means submission to authority.

Angelo's optimism concerning papal support eventually faded, but his advice about obedience remained roughly the same. He repeated it in 1317, as John XXII proceeded to move against the spirituals,[32] and he was still saying it as the 1320s drew to a close.[33] Moreover, he apparently believed it deeply enough to let it affect the governance of his group. All this must wait until we return to Angelo in a later chapter, however.

One more fact about the Tuscan rebels should be considered. Years later, after they had been hounded out of Sicily and some of them drifted back up the peninsula, Angelo's colleagues wrote to him, asking how they should be treated. Angelo replied with yet another attack on their character, yet closed that portion of his letter with the words, "As long as they are able to be with you, sustain those who are such because they are your merit, your test and your mercy."[34] These are remarkable words. They go a long way toward clarifying how love and obedience as seen by Angelo differed from love and obedience as seen by the hierarchy.

Angelo's Apocalyptic Program

Angelo's September 1313 letter also raises questions about his apocalyptic expectation. It is hard to miss his insistence that the pattern of church governance instituted by Christ will continue until the end of the world. This seems an implied refutation of the Joachite (or, more precisely, the Olivian) theology of history as the Tuscan rebels understood it; it seems to favor, instead, an essentially Augustinian pattern. Whether we can move beyond the word "seems" here to state unequivocally what Angelo is denying or affirming is a more complex problem. As Potestà recognizes,[35] a major complication is introduced by the fact that the immediate target is an appropriation of Olivi's apocalyptic vision by a group that Angelo accuses of misunderstanding Olivi's thought. Was he correct, though, or did the Tuscan rebels accept more of Olivian apocalyptic than Angelo did? Ubertino certainly accepted more, and it is interesting that he was at least briefly involved in the case as one of the procurators designated in the defense of nine brothers from the Arezzo convent.[36]

Beyond this difficulty lies another: Angelo speaks briefly and generally here about a subject to which Olivi devoted several hundred pages. In time, he would say a great deal more. We will return to the matter in the final chapter.

Southern France

Clement's pacification program was off to a poor start in Tuscany. It fared no better in southern France. The best we can say is that the situation deteriorated somewhat more slowly there. By the end of the council, no substantial group of spirituals in Olivi's old territory had gone the way of the Tuscans. At least we have no evidence that any such thing had occurred, although even the supposedly exempt spiritual spokesmen seem to have undergone harassment from the community—and, as we have seen, rumors were circulating that members of the community had murdered three and perhaps four of the spiritual leaders who died in rapid succession that year.

With Gonsalvo's death, Clement saw to it that the order should elect a cooperative minister general. He wrote to the 1313 general chapter at Barcelona urging them to choose a *pater benevolus* who would reconcile opposing factions.[37] Alexander of Alexandria, Gonsalvo's successor, seemed willing to do just that. He assigned the houses at Narbonne, Béziers, and Carcassonne to the spirituals, ordering provincial leaders to make sure they received guardians acceptable to them. Clement already had prepared the way by dismissing from office the provincial minister and fifteen others hostile to the spirituals, prohibiting their return to authority, taking disciplinary action against them, and making sure that they were replaced by leaders who would "lean more toward the minority, which had hitherto been afflicted."

So at least we are told by the spirituals of Narbonne and Béziers,[38] and their story is corroborated by other sources.[39] They go on to relate sadder news. After Clement and Alexander died (in April and October 1314, respectively), supporters of the infamous sixteen engineered their return to power and the spirituals soon found themselves in their former state. They sought redress from the provincial minister, but he gave them none, "because he did not wish or did not dare to do so."[40] In fact, what he did give them was a dedicated enemy, Guillaume Astre, as custode.

Having neither pope nor minister general to whom they might appeal, the spirituals undertook their own defense. With lay support, they drove the guardians and their adherents out of the convents at Narbonne and Béziers.[41] These convents then became havens for escapees from other houses in the province and from the province of Aquitaine, until eventually around 120 spirituals had congregated there.[42] For the moment the spirituals were in a strong position. They found supporters not only among the laity but also within the ecclesiastical hierarchy, including some influential cardinals.[43] Physical attacks were blocked by the local citizenry, while ecclesiastical processes were impeded by friends in high places.[44] The lack of a minister general and pope, which had worked against them when they were trying to stay within the law, worked *for* them once they stepped outside it.

The situation would inevitably change when these offices were filled. In order to keep their opponents at bay, the spirituals had to impress the impending general chapter at Naples with the justice of their cause and hope that a more or less sympathetic minister general would be elected there. They failed in both respects. Their carefully crafted apologia either fell on deaf ears or was never received at all, their messenger having been assaulted before he could deliver it, and the new minister general turned out to be Michael of Cesena, whose sentiments lay with the community and who soon warned the spirituals that he would do nothing for them.[45]

Whether Michael was elected precisely *because* he would do nothing for them is another matter. He was not present at the chapter meeting, and Manselli argues that since the meeting was held in the presence of King Robert and Queen Sancia, both sympathetic to the spirituals, one would be surprised if it enjoyed much in the way of anti-spiritual polemics.[46] If, however, Samantha

Kelly is correct in arguing that Robert was not in fact sympathetic toward the spirituals, the whole event becomes easier to imagine.[47] Certainly once Michael took office he quickly made it obvious that he stood with the community, and many at the meeting must already have known where he stood.

The Naples chapter meeting was followed by a new set of general constitutions published the same year. Manselli sees them as an early sign of Michael's sympathies.[48] He highlights two passages. One demands that *vilitas* in clothing be observed, but as determined by the superiors, and with uniformity of dress. The other calls for action against *appropriatores locorum*.[49] What we may be dealing with here, though, is not so much Michael's anti-spiritual bias as the temptation to read too much into a document when one already knows how the rest of the story developed. Viewed on its own terms, the passage on dress seems evenhanded, attacking excesses of every sort;[50] moreover, in his letter to the provincial ministers recommending the constitutions, Michael attacks only excesses in the direction of laxity, demanding that abuses be ended in the areas of clothing, money deposits, the sale of produce, buildings, horseback riding, wearing shoes, and eating meat.[51] Again, viewed from our perspective, the passage concerning *appropriatores locorum* may automatically recall the takeovers at Béziers and Narbonne, but it defines such *appropriatores* as those who, if ordered to leave a place, prevail on seculars to use their influence in getting the order revoked, or who do not welcome into their houses brothers or superiors whom they consider to be outsiders, not "one of their own."[52] It is, in short, a reworking of the 1313 Barcelona statute, which in turn reflects a concern expressed in the Padua legislation of 1310.[53] The *appropriatores* attacked in this earlier legislation were brothers who had dug into their convents (often in their hometowns) and made them closed corporations. The problem was an old one, already recognized by Hugh of Digne. It had been explored at length by Ubertino da Casale at Vienne. Perhaps the 1316 situation, with its defiant southern French houses supported by the local laity, added a new dimension to the statute in the eyes of Franciscan administrators; but the problem had continued to exist elsewhere in its traditional form, and thus one should hesitate before assuming that the 1316 legislation was inspired primarily by spiritual Franciscan activities.

Appeals for Support

In any case, once Michael of Cesena had a chance to respond directly to the situation in southern France, there could be little question concerning how much help the spirituals might expect from him. There was, of course, one more court of appeal. In August 1316, a new pope was elected: John XXII. Both sides tried to enlist his support.[54] Their arguments seem to have been generally consistent with those offered ever since the "liberation" of the two convents. Thus, the time from late 1314 or early 1315 (when the southern French spirituals apparently began their revolt) through early 1317 (when John acted) can be considered as a single period. The sources for this period are sparse, but sufficient to give us some idea of what each side was saying. On the spiritual side, we are especially enlightened by their appeal to the Naples general chapter in May 1316; their appeal to John in late 1316; and Cardinal Giacomo Colonna's sympathetic letter of February 1316.[55] For the conventual position, the best sources are a document from the papal investigation giving the general outline of their argument and Bertrand de la Tour's excommunication of five spirituals who had decamped from their houses in the province of Aquitaine, joining the spirituals at Narbonne.[56]

The conventuals do their best to depict the spirituals as chronic malcontents. Clement V ordered them back to obedience after doing what he could to settle their grievances. He even gave them leaders to whom they could not object. It was all in vain. After Clement's death, as soon as they saw any cause for complaint, they again became fractious, "like a dog returning to its vomit."[57] In defying the Clementine settlement, they have become more than simply unpleasant. In fact, they have progressed beyond simple disobedience and are now schismatics. In effect, the spirituals are trying to establish themselves as a separate group. They dress differently—having adopted a *habitum difformem*—and have adopted their own name, insisting that they be called *fratres spirituales*.[58] They are also taxed with violence: during the takeover at Béziers, they laid violent hands on Brother Jacques Ortolan and locked him up.[59]

In addition, the spirituals are stigmatized as heretics, a charge made on at least three grounds. The first is an old, familiar one: They read, respect and even venerate Olivi, whose teachings were condemned by John of Murrovalle and others in the order as well as by the pope at Vienne. This indictment is actually two-pronged: on the one hand, the spirituals are accused of asserting that Olivi's writings contain no error,[60] and thus they obviously hold the same views for which Olivi was condemned; on the other hand, they venerate Olivi as an uncanonized saint.[61] Second, the spirituals are heretics because they hold a heretical view of ecclesiastical authority. Like the Cathars and Waldensians before them, they make it dependent upon inner purity, arguing that sinful clerics should not be obeyed.[62] Third, they are accused of saying that "marriage is no more than a concealed brothel." Here again they seem to stand in a great heretical tradition.[63]

This hardly exhausts the list of charges leveled by the community. Nevertheless, these accusations seem to be the main ones, and they are hardly inconsequential. Willful disobedience, fractiousness, and violence are no small charges against a Franciscan. Apostasy, schism, and heresy are even greater ones. If all or even some of them had been accurate, then Bertrand de la Tour would have spoken truly (if somewhat inelegantly) when he called for decisive action "to keep the little foxes in sheep's clothing from sneaking in and destroying the vineyard."[64]

The spirituals, of course, denied all, or nearly all. Far from rejecting the Clementine settlement, they protested, they had defended it. Their *antagonists* were the ones who had disobeyed: they had reappointed leaders whom Clement had permanently banned from office, and they had ended the arrangement according to which the spirituals were allotted three houses with sympathetic superiors. Here we encounter the real significance (and, as things turned out, the poignancy) of their appeal to John XXII. He was not simply their last hope; he was the linchpin of their entire defense. They had disobeyed their guardians, custode, provincial minister, and finally minister general, but they had done so, they said, in the name of a higher obedience to a set of papal commands rejected by these leaders.[65] Viewed from this perspective, their actions took on a different meaning. Instead of rebelliously seizing control of the convents, they had honored the Clementine settlement by maintaining those convents as spiritual havens. Far from illegally establishing new leaders, they had reinstated the same old leaders installed under the Clementine settlement and later illegally removed. If Brother Jacques Ortolan was imprisoned, it was because he had impeded those restoring the papal settlement, ferociously beating them with a stick, and thus had to be restrained "according to the rules of the order."

The spirituals also took issue with the community's revisionist explanation of why Clement V had removed the notorious gang of sixteen. He had not simply tried to pacify the spirituals. Had that been the case, there would have been no later disciplinary action against these men.[66] The spirituals also stoutly denied that they had adopted distinctive traits. Rather than insisting that they be called "spirituals," they wished "no other name than the one blessed Francis imposed on them, 'brothers minor.'" Rather than rejecting the habit of their order, they were attempting to conform with the attire worn by Saint Francis himself.[67]

This is an extraordinary argument. In order to appreciate how extraordinary it is, one need only imagine Clement V's reaction if he had been treated to it. The more straightforwardly historical part of it he would have seen as justified. However one looks at *Exivi de paradiso*, one cannot see it as an attempt to satisfy the querulous complaints of a few whiners. Clement certainly felt that something should be done about the old Franciscan leadership. Nevertheless, he would have been aghast at the idea that it could be done by anyone except duly constituted leaders. *Exivi de paradiso* had demanded conformity with the rule, but had given superiors a key role in enforcing it— and even in determining what conformity entailed. It is hard to believe that Clement would have seen much difference between the Tuscan rebels and the French ones.

As for Olivi, the spirituals insisted that he was not condemned at Vienne and that "his work dogmatizes no errors fundamentally opposed to the Catholic faith."[68] Here, they were walking a thin line between truth and falsehood. Olivi had not been mentioned explicitly by the bull *Fidei catholicae fundamento*. Thus it is true that he was not condemned there. Nevertheless, the views rejected in that bull look suspiciously like his. Modern scholars may differ on the precise connection between Olivi and the bull, but it is hard to escape the conclusion that, whatever that connection, Clement at least thought that the views he had rejected were Olivi's.

The Olivi cult presented the spirituals with another delicate task. They had to acknowledge its existence without seeming to have bypassed proper ecclesiastical channels. They denied that they referred to Olivi as "Saint Peter" (*sanctus Petrus*), but granted that they did describe him as a holy (*sanctus*) man or as a holy father. They denied that they accorded him the reverence due a canonized saint. No solemn prayers or offices were recited in his honor, nor did his name appear in the calendar. Nevertheless, they said, "on the anniversary of his death or at other times the people assemble at his tomb. God is praised and glorified, a solemn mass is said in honor of his blessed mother, and signs are brought in of the more evident miracles which occurred by invoking him and through his merits during the past year. Through gifts and tearful voices, people proclaim the benefits they have received and praise God who performs such mighty acts through the merits of his servants."[69] It would be blasphemous, they insisted, to reject such customs. Had they been prohibited in the cases of Francis, Dominic, Anthony of Padua, and Louis of Toulouse, the church would have lacked some of the evidence used in their canonization processes. They also suggested that there was a touch of envy involved in attacks on the Olivi cult, not to mention temerity, since it meant criticizing the devotional practices of bishops, cardinals, and other leaders who appeared at Olivi's tomb.

The spirituals' suggestion that the Olivi cult enjoyed substantial popularity outside their own circles might seem little more than wishful thinking on their part, but Angelo Clareno offers a believable witness to the same phenomenon. In a 1313 letter, he notes that in that year "the feast of Brother Peter John at Narbonne was celebrated by clergy and people so solemnly that never in these parts was a feast so solemnly celebrated, for people assembled at his tomb from all over the province, and in no smaller number, they say, than used to gather at the feast of Saint Mary of the Portiuncula."[70] Nor can the spirituals be accused of hyperbole in speaking of the "miracles which occurred by invoking him." We will see that several beguins subjected to inquisitorial processes in the 1320s mentioned cures wrought at Olivi's tomb.[71]

Tempting as it may be to dismiss the Olivi cult as something of a sideshow, it was substantially more than that. His feast day provided an excellent opportunity for the spirituals to indoctrinate pilgrims through sermons and conversation. When we examine inquisitorial processes from the 1320s, we will see how the friars used this opportunity to apply Olivi's thought to their situation and win adherents to their cause. The tomb became a rallying point—a visible symbol of their resistance—and the miracles occurring there served as the spirituals' validation.

Another heading in the heresy charge, denial of authority to sinful clerics, was vigorously rejected. The spirituals even rejected the notion that superiors should be disobeyed whenever they violated papal commands. They did insist "that one should not obey lesser authorities (*inferiores prelati*) who notoriously and openly show contempt for ecclesiastical authority, explicitly vilifying its commands." They had said as much in the past because they were faced with just such a situation. Rebellious lesser authorities had freed, reinstated, and promoted men whom the pope had deposed, tried, and incarcerated. "Otherwise, we have said, still say, and have put in writing that any carnal superior should be obeyed as long as the church puts up with him, unless, as has been said, he is illegitimately installed and demands that his subordinates openly transgress the rule and what has been established by the apostolic see."[72]

At first glance, this passage seems to limit disobedience even further, confining it to situations in which three separate conditions are met. Illegitimate installation must be combined with a demand for patent contempt not only toward the pope but toward the rule as well. One naturally wonders whether they could have meant it that way and, if not, whether the various conditions might be taken in a disjunctive sense. If the latter, and any of the three conditions could stand alone as a mandate for disobedience, then reference to the rule becomes disturbingly suggestive. That is certainly not the impression the spirituals wished to convey, however. They wanted to talk about disobedience in the name of a higher obedience to the pope. If the rule entered this discussion at all, it was to come safely accompanied by the papal *instituta*.

The same tendency can be seen in what little evidence we possess concerning a group whom this defense did not entirely fit—the renegades from the province of Aquitaine. They had escaped from their duly appointed local superiors, and then defied an order to return issued by their duly appointed provincial minister. Why? According to Bertrand de la Tour, they sent back letters explaining that they had fled because "the rule and declarations not only were not observed, but were held in contempt in Aquitaine, and those wishing to observe them were persecuted."[73] Here, observance became the chief issue, but it was carefully anchored to papal authority through the declarations. Thus the appeal to higher obedience was adopted, though in somewhat attenuated form, by the Aquitainian spirituals as well.

The third heading in the heresy charge, marriage as a concealed brothel, was curtly dismissed with the observation (reminiscent of the Vienne proceedings) that the accusation was false and, if any individuals actually said such a thing, they should be punished. Thus the spirituals disassociated themselves from the view without excluding the possibility that some in their midst might have held it at one time or another. In fact, it is possible that some did.

Here we enter upon admittedly dangerous territory, since our evidence comes from later inquisitorial records and there is probably no moment at which modern historians are inclined to trust these records less than when they begin to discuss sexual practices. Nevertheless, there is evidence that some beguins did speak of marriage in that way, though it is difficult to decide precisely what to make of it. Guillaume Martin, a defendant in an inquisitorial investigation sometime after 1319 and before 1325, recalled having heard someone read from a book by Olivi and having heard the person say that Olivi called marriage a private brothel (*lupanar privatum, gallice Bordel Privat*) in that book.[74] The defendant said he himself later repeated the sentiment to others. That is a hard claim to assimilate, since we know of no work by Olivi saying anything like it. His thoughts on marriage as a sacrament were censured in 1283, but not for this reason.[75] It is interesting that Guillaume did not say that he heard it read from the book, but instead that the reader assured him that it was in the book.

Other evidence is puzzling but intriguing. In a 1323 process, Guillaume Lacourt confessed that one day, moved to wrath against his wife, he hit her in the presence of other people. Admonished for his conduct, he replied that "marriage was nothing but a *lupanar privatum*." He was immediately informed that he had spoken badly, withdrew the comment, and went to confess it to a priest.[76] In another process, from 1325, a priest named Raimond Sacourt said that he was talking with some people about elderly women who contracted a second or third marriage long after they were past childbearing age. Raimond observed that he did not believe such a marriage was pleasing to God or that it was a true marriage; in fact, he believed that it was a *lupanar privatum*. He too insisted to the inquisitor that he was immediately reproached by those who were with him, withdrew his comment, and went to confess his sin.[77]

In both of these cases we get the feeling that the reaction of those present had less to do with the context in which the term was purportedly being used than with their common recognition that the term had a deeper, more dangerous significance. The inquisitor obviously felt the same way. He immediately asked Raimond why he had used just that expression.[78]

These charges and countercharges are as significant in what they omit as in what they include. Most striking is the complete avoidance of what had been a principal bone of contention in earlier polemics, the question of whether *usus pauper* was an essential part of the vow. The omission is understandable in view of Clement's attempt to settle the issue and his virtual ban on future name calling in connection with it. The matter could not be ignored completely, though. We can infer from the spiritual Franciscan position papers that the limits of legitimate practice were still being debated. These writings brand as false the assertion that Franciscans can regularly store up wheat and wine. They also seem to support the Olivian position on procurators, although their comments are negatively phrased and too brief to support anything much in particular.

Rare and allusive they may be, but such passages offer an important corrective to the impression created by contemporary documents from the community. The latter completely lack the defensive element noticeable in their arguments at Vienne, where Franciscan leaders were forced to justify current practice at some length. Lack of such material might lead to the conclusion that these issues were no longer being debated. Nevertheless, spiritual Franciscan allusions to wheat, wine, and procurators, however cursory, offer evidence that some defense of current practice was still considered necessary by the community in 1316, although one would guess that it formed a very minor element. Certainly the spirituals were not asking John XXII to render a definitive judgment on such matters. Their appeal to him really asked for two things. They wanted him to confirm the Clementine settlement and to acknowledge their orthodoxy.

The debate over *usus pauper* as part of the vow haunted the proceedings nonetheless. The community was at pains to present the spirituals as a threat to good order, but the question of whether they really were such could not be untangled from that of why they were disobeying their superiors. As we have seen, the spirituals were wary of any suggestion that their recalcitrance was based on a higher obligation to their vow. They recognized that it was more politic to invoke a higher obedience to the pope. That explanation was at least tenable as long as John was still deliberating. Eventually he would come to a decision and tell them to do something. Then their loyalties would finally be clarified.

John Acts

JOHN DID NOT INHERIT A SINGLE spiritual Franciscan problem. Rather, he fell heir to a series of them: the Tuscan rebels, the Narbonne and Béziers rebels, Angelo's associates, and miscellaneous others, such as Ubertino, who fit within none of these groups. The whole matter required thought. Once John had absorbed the evidence, however, he acted swiftly and decisively.

The Tuscan Rebels

The problem of the Tuscan rebels—now the Sicilian renegades—must have seemed relatively straightforward to him. We find him raising in consistory the questions of whether schismatics should be supported, and whether those who fled from Tuscany to Sicily should be regarded as schismatics,[1] yet it is hard to imagine that he found either question very perplexing. Clement V had decided against the Tuscan rebels and they had defied his authority. There was little left to consider. John's main problem was really not whether to condemn them but how to pry them loose from Sicily. He wrote King Frederick on March 15, 1317, exposing the serpentine cunning that lurked beneath the refugees' dovelike exteriors and ordering the king to hand them over to their superiors for correction.[2] On April 5 he sent Frederick the same letter, adding only that he had decided to write again because he was very anxious to see the matter settled and was unsure whether Frederick had received his first epistle.[3] On the day the pope first wrote, some cardinals corresponded with the Sicilian bishops and archbishops. They underscored the schismatic nature of the Tuscan revolt. Having elected their own minister general, provincial ministers, custodes, and guardians, the renegades were receiving new members, appointing preachers and confessors, and generally carrying on as if they were an independent order.[4]

However Frederick himself may have felt about the refugees, he soon discovered that a good number of his citizens wanted him to obey the pope. According to a report sent to Frederick's brother, James II of Aragon, the citizens of Messina told their king that they would suffer death for him but would not consent to be branded as supporters of heresy. However rocky Sicilian relations with the papacy had been during the previous two papacies, at least they had stayed on the right side of excommunication and interdict. That was precisely what the Sicilians now faced if they openly defied the pope, and it was a bad moment to face any such radical break with John. A complex series of circumstances had encouraged Neapolitan military activity and given the Angevins a better hope of success. Should John excommunicate Frederick, place Sicily under interdict, and call for a crusade, Neapolitan chances would improve remarkably.

Thus Frederick partially capitulated to John's demands. He worked out an arrangement with the Muslim ruler of Tunis whereby the spirituals were allowed to settle in his territory as long as they did not preach. This must have been a painful solution for members of an order that valued missionary activity so highly, particularly if they shared Olivi's apocalyptic expectation regarding conversion of the heathen through spiritual men who had been forced out of Christendom by the carnal church. How many actually took advantage of the arrangement is another matter. Some apparently did, but others returned to the mainland, settling in the kingdom of Naples. A good number remained in Sicily. Of these, some were hidden out of the way in existing monasteries and others in monastic houses especially created for them, while a few continued their ministry in the cities.[5]

Frederick had managed, at least momentarily, to avoid a seriously damaging confrontation, but John eventually became aware of the situation and attempted to do something about it.[6] By the early 1320s, he was again applying pressure, but by this time Sicily was already under interdict again for confiscating church lands to finance the war with Naples—so Frederick had less to lose by defying the pope.

John Summons the Spirituals

Even if he had not surrendered his visitors to the proper authorities, as the pope had directed, Frederick was at least not openly protecting them by late 1317 when John began to rain bulls down on the spirituals and their supporters. By that time, the pope had begun to sort things out in southern France. He had told two cardinals to compose a letter calling the spirituals of Narbonne back to obedience.[7] "Impeded for certain reasons"—presumably by their own sympathy toward the spirituals[8]—they had failed to complete the task. On April 22, 1317, three other cardinals wrote to the minister general and provincial minister relaying the news that they had waited so long to hear. The pope had thought the matter through and had decided to support the community.[9]

On first reading, this letter seems an almost ludicrous corruption of the issues. One might infer from it that the *usus pauper* controversy was an argument about fashion. The word *habitus* (in the sense of "attire") is used seven times. When the cardinals finally get around to mentioning that the spirituals are no longer entitled to their own houses, it seems almost an afterthought. In reality, the operative sentence in the letter comes at the beginning: "It is wisely established by sacred canons that, among those who preach a single gospel and are of the same profession, there should be no difference in attire or observance, but all should conform to the same regimen and honest attire, for otherwise unity is destroyed and much scandal generated." The cardinals are ignoring historical specifics and going back to first principles. The whole tortuous history of debate over proper observance of the rule, the whole welter of charges concerning oppression and countercharges concerning disobedience, all disappear from view, leaving the cardinals free to carry a single hypothesis through to its logical conclusion. A single order should wear common dress and obey a single group of leaders. Therefore, the spirituals must stop wearing their distinctive garb and consent to be fully integrated within the order.[10]

Five days later, on April 27, John wrote to Narbonne and Béziers. He summoned sixty-two spirituals by name (or perhaps sixty-one, since the same name appears twice in the letter to Narbonne). These brothers, he said, had responded to his attempts to settle unrest in the order by launching "certain appeals and protests which not only detract from the state of the order but are plausibly thought to have encouraged dissension and scandal and derogated from the honor of the apostolic see." They were ordered to select procurators and explain themselves to the pope in ten days.[11] Even before they arrived, John was interrogating their potential supporters. Inevitably Ubertino da Casale was included. Angelo Clareno, a participant, tells the story so dramatically that he should be allowed to do so here.

> And when Ubertino da Casale had refuted all the charges made by the brothers, showing how all they had said proceeded from malice and envy, the pontiff questioned Brother Ubertino as to whether he sided with the brothers of Narbonne and Béziers and whether he wished to defend the doctrine of Petrus Iohannis [Olivi]. Ubertino replied, "Holy father, all that I formerly did in that way was carried out through obedience to your predecessor, and nothing was done through my own initiative. Thus, if it is now the holy father's pleasure that, through his command, I should speak on behalf of the brothers from Narbonne or Brother Petrus's doctrine, then behold, I am ready to obey your will in all things." To which the pope replied, "We do *not* wish you to involve yourself. We do not wish it at all!"

Thus Ubertino was eliminated as a potential spokesman. The pope then asked Geoffroi de Cournon and Philippe de Caux whether they wished to support the brothers from Narbonne and Béziers. The former said that he would not, since he was not directly involved in the affair and was not completely informed about it. The latter said that he was not personally involved, but wanted to support them anyway in their quest for reform.

Angelo himself was next to be interviewed. John immediately set about intimidating him.

> When Brother Angelo had come before him, the pope asked whether he was a Franciscan and he replied that he was. And the pope asked him, "Why have you then left them?" Brother Angelo replied, "Holy father, I have not left them. Ask them why they have rejected me." The pope was silent, then said to him, "I order you to tell me whether you ever have heard confessions." Brother Angelo responded, "Holy father, I am not a priest, and one of the reasons why I have not wished to become one is because I did not wish to hear confessions. Thus I

have not heard a single confession." After some other interrogations the pope ordered the brothers to read some letters from Pope Boniface and the Lord Patriarch of Constantinople.[12] When they had been read, he said to Brother Angelo, "Brother Angelo, you are excommunicated." Brother Angelo replied, "Holy father, I am neither excommunicated nor excommunicable, because I always have obeyed Pope Boniface, the patriarch, and other leaders of the church." And he began to speak, showing how the letters had been obtained and preserved both maliciously and deceitfully. . . . But the pope could not bear to hear him and prevented him from completing what he had begun to say. Then Brother Angelo said, "Holy father, you have listened to the brothers' lies, yet you could not bear to hear the truth which I have spoken to you." But it was around the sixth hour, and the pope ordered that Brother Angelo be detained on account of that excommunication.[13]

Angelo's *Epistola excusatoria*

Obviously John had come to this interview armed with damning evidence. A letter from Francesco da Norcia to Gentile da Foligno informs us that the pope had been given a dossier on Angelo by leaders of the order.[14] As a result, he was detained briefly in the custody of Cardinal Arnaud d'Auch.[15] Thanks to the influence of other, friendlier cardinals, Angelo was soon released and back in the home of his patron Giacomo Colonna, but not before he had penned his *Epistola excusatoria* to John XXII.[16] This long narrative of his travails to that point constitutes, along with his later chronicle, the major source for our knowledge concerning Angelo's adventures before the Council of Vienne. It also gives us a good idea of the charges that had led to his recent brief confinement. In fact, it may give us insight into the contents of *Saepe sacram ecclesiam*, Boniface VIII's letter to Greek church leaders condemning Angelo's group (the letter that Angelo had avoided receiving for around two decades, but had now caught up with him).

Angelo begins the *Epistola excusatoria* by affirming that he and his associates are not heretics "unless it is a heresy worthy of excommunication to believe and confess . . . what Saint Francis believed and confessed concerning the observance of his rule." If so, "I confess that I have always subscribed to that heresy, and that I still do so." As for "the other things contained in the letters of Pope Boniface, that of Peter, patriarch of Constantinople, and the brothers' petition against me and my group," the charges contained therein are entirely false. Angelo lists what apparently constituted the main items in the dossier presented to John. He now proceeds to answer the charges point by point. First, Boniface's letters were incorrect because "we have never said nor do we now say that we observe the rule of the Brothers Minor, but rather that we are Poor Hermits living the life conceded and granted to us by the Lord Pope Celestine." This seems an odd claim, considering his initial statement of faith in the Franciscan rule, but it makes sense. From 1296 on, Boniface VIII wrote a series of letters warning churchmen to be on guard against those who belonged to no approved order yet attempted to wrap themselves in the legitimacy of some other group by wearing its habit and claiming to observe its rule.[17] Angelo is insisting that his group does not attempt to gain legitimacy by feigning a connection with the Franciscans.

Angelo next rejects the charge that they have built residences. On the contrary, they live like pilgrims and paupers in other people's buildings. Nor do they preach or hear confessions unless ordered to do so by ecclesiastical authority, in which case they are bound to obey. These are interesting comments. They reveal the delicate balance Angelo had to strike in setting a course for his group after they left Greece. He could not afford to act as if his order had been dissolved—in that case there would be little to do except obey—but it would have been equally disastrous to ignore what had occurred and behave like an established order. He steered a middle course, assuming the role of perpetual petitioner. It was important to establish that the Poor Hermits were running on a more or less emergency basis while Angelo, an obedient son of the church, attempted to gain papal recognition of their legitimacy.

That brings Angelo to what were potentially the deadliest charges of all against his group. He recites six opinions he and his associates are accused of holding: that papal authority has ceased; that Pope Boniface was not really pope; that authority has long since been taken from the church and given to his own group until such time as the church is reformed; that only his group and those who have the spirit as they do are true priests; and that the Eastern Church is superior to the Western. His judgment on these ideas is that "I would not believe such things even if I heard them announced by angels or apostles, complete with miracles, nor was I ever so flighty or stupid that I would even consent to listen."

Angelo requests that the charges against him be presented in writing, along with the names of witnesses, so that he can clear himself. He declares that he is ready to undergo the ordeal in order to prove that he is not a heretic. As for obedience, he protests that "I have never contemptuously or defiantly refused obedience to any prelate, although sometimes, as was proper, I have been unwilling to obey orders involving manifest sin." He goes on to narrate how dearly his superiors have made him pay for that stance. We hear of his early troubles and imprisonment in Ancona; of his rescue by the minister general, Raymond Geoffroi; of his time in Armenia, unfortunately ended by a Franciscan smear campaign that turned secular leaders against the group; of their return to Italy, where the provincial vicar told them that he would rather receive a group of fornicators; and of a second timely intervention by Raymond Geoffroi, who sent them to Pope Celestine V. Celestine invited them "to observe our life and rule in his habit." Then he "accepted our vow before all those present and ordered us to observe the rule and *Testament* all the days of our lives according to Saint Francis's will and command, but without the name of Brothers Minor. And he absolved us before all those present from any obedience or responsibility to the order, saying, 'it is my wish that you should henceforth be bound in obedience only to me and to Brother Liberato as if to me.'" Then he ordered the leader of the Celestinians to accept them and provide them with hermitages. That brings Angelo to his real point:

> And that is why, right up to today, we do not know or consider ourselves to be apostates from any order; but we believe that we really would be apostates before God and would be renegades from such an eremitical life if, of our own volition, we should abandon the way of life to which, by divine inspiration and papal concession, we have been called, and should instead be found among those who have committed perjury before Christ and are worthy of damnation. And that is why we beg Your Holiness to provide us with some way of observing the vow made by us and received as well as confirmed by the supreme pontiff.[18]

Thus Angelo, like practically everyone else, presents the issue as a matter of obedience. He has taken a vow, and then been given an order by the pope himself, and he desperately wants to obey. He is pleading with John to make it possible by granting the legitimacy of the Poor Hermits.

There is, of course, one more problem to be dealt with. So far he has taken his story only up to the interview with Celestine. There is still the unfortunate sequel with Boniface to be explained. Why was Angelo so much less eager to respond to that other papal order, *Saepe sacram ecclesiam*? Angelo turns to that problem next.

> We are not and were not excommunicated, both because we have
> never shown contempt toward any order to us and because no cita-
> tion or process was ever sent or delivered to us, or at least if one was
> sent it was not delivered. We waited for a year and requested that the
> pope's commands concerning us be carried out; then we were mali-
> ciously expelled and only at that point was the process against us
> begun, when it was no longer possible to present it to us. For after
> the patriarch's death we were scarcely able to travel to a single place
> and convene in a group. Moreover, even if the excommunication was
> put into effect, we were absolved from it.[19]

The enigmatic final sentence refers to an event that Angelo has not yet
mentioned, the visit of one Jacobus de Monte. We will turn to it later, but at
the moment there is still something left to explain. Why did Angelo and his
colleagues flee to Greece in the first place? Certainly not in obedience to anyone's orders. Angelo replies that they were moved by Christ's command, "Flee
from the face of persecutors" (Matt. 24:16), and by their own deep love for
peace and quiet, the penultimate goal of all God's children.

> For when the brothers heard that Lord Celestine had absolved us from
> obedience to them and their order, they immediately came armed in
> order to capture us, contemptuously neglecting the fear of God as
> well as reverence for the pope and his command. Thus, when the
> pope renounced his office, it struck Brother Liberato that, for the sake
> of our own safety and the brothers' peace, we should travel to some
> remote location where we could freely serve the Lord without tumult
> and scandal.[20]

Angelo describes how, once they had settled on a remote island, their relentless Franciscan detractors renewed the smear campaign, accusing them of
Manichean tendencies. In the process of showing how these charges were
proved groundless, Angelo manages to mention that in the masses they conducted they included prayers "for the Lord Pope Boniface," one more reminder
that they recognized his legitimacy. Having failed to poison the minds of bishops and princes in Greece, the enemy proceeded directly to Boniface, whose
initial response was, "Leave them alone, they're doing a better job than you
are." At that point the frustrated Franciscans embarked upon what proved an
effective strategy. They said,

"Lord, Holy Father, they are heretics and schismatics, and they are preaching throughout that land that you are not the pope, and that there is no authority left in the church," and other similar things which are manifestly contained in the letters of the Lord Pope Boniface and the Lord Patriarch of Constantinople and the brothers' petition presented to you on behalf of the minister general and the whole order. Deceived by these falsehoods, the Lord Pope Boniface sent to three prelates of that province the letters which I heard read for the first time before Your Sanctity, and a rumor came to our ears that very severe letters had emanated from the Lord Supreme Pontiff. Hearing this, we all gathered in a group and agreed to obey the letters of the Supreme Pontiff thoroughly in all their aspects, to the death, whatever they commanded. Whence, after the letters had been received by the lord executors, we waited for a year against the wishes of the secular powers, who said they had been told by the lord bishops to expel us. We presented ourselves not once but twice to the archbishop of Athens and even more often to the archbishop of Patras. The latter told us that he would remove himself from the episcopate before he proceeded against us on the basis of letters so mendaciously obtained, for he was certain of our faithfulness and innocence. We begged the lords of the land to hold us as if imprisoned in some place and write to the Supreme Pontiff concerning us, but failed to get either action. Thus we were forced to leave and, since no one would provide us with a way of crossing the sea since we were deprived of all human counsel and aid and on every side the brothers were preparing traps to capture us, we entered the territory of the Sebastocrator, which was closer to that island in which we had been serving the Lord. Now that we were dispersed, the Lord Patriarch came from Venice and the brothers all flocked to him with a certain perverse brother named Jerome.

At this point, Angelo gives the pope a report on Jerome of Catalonia's duplicitous career, then notes (delicately leaving the reader to draw his own conclusions) that the Patriarch, having fulfilled his commission against the Poor Hermits, promptly died.[21]

Around the same time, Angelo and his colleagues were treated to a six-month visit by one "Jacobus de Monte" (probably Giacomo da Monterubbiano[22]) and other brothers sent by the Roman province of the Franciscan order as missionaries. Jacobus, who was vicar of the orient (comprising Armenia, Georgia, and Persia),[23] decided that the Poor Hermits were orthodox and innocent of the charges against them. Thus, on the basis of the papal privileges with which he had been armed before departing from Rome, he absolved them *ad cautelam*. The Poor Hermits immediately sent two brothers to Boniface VIII with letters submitting the group to his will, and then sent another two, whom the Franciscans captured and detained to keep them from delivering their message. At that point, Liberato left secretly for Italy, and later the whole group did the same, as we have seen. Since even Liberato arrived too late to present their case before Boniface—or, for that matter, Benedict XI—it was a matter of waiting for Clement V to be elected. Clement, considering the matter, decided "that we should serve the Lord in the state in which we found ourselves, but my heart was not made quiet by this."[24] Thus, despite his detestation of life at the papal court and desire to return to his colleagues, Angelo remained in Avignon in order to see the business of his order carried through to completion.

"And now that I have been detained by Your Holiness, my heart is glad and my soul rejoices in God, because I am cared for, guarded under the hand and obedience of the shepherd." Certain in his heart that he is neither an apostate nor a heretic, Angelo does not ask that his innocence be accepted on the basis of his own testimony, but that he and his group be subjected to a thorough investigation in which the charges against him are presented to him in written form. Such an investigation is important, he feels, because Angelo's detractors are subverting an entire tradition. In an anticipation of the structure guiding his later chronicle, Angelo mentions some prominent representatives of that tradition, a list running from Bernard of Quintavalle, Francis's first follower, through John of Parma and Olivi.

It is hard to read the *Epistola excusatoria* without admiring Angelo's skill as a raconteur and a skillful rearranger of awkward details. Some might wonder if he is doing more than merely rearranging. Some might wonder if he is lying. If so, it would be a rather hard thing to prove. On the whole, one is inclined to believe him when he denies that he and his associates openly attacked Boniface's legitimacy or, *a fortiori*, that they claimed that ecclesiastical authority had shifted from a discredited hierarchy to themselves. In order to claim that Angelo did either, we would also have to believe that the rest of his letters represent a concentrated attempt to conceal his true feelings, since what we find in the other letters is more or less consistent with what we see in the *Epistola excusatoria*. Angelo took obedience seriously, and the object of that obedience was the established ecclesiastical hierarchy. The hierarchy had been instituted from the beginning, and Angelo saw no evidence that God had changed His mind or was about to do so. He harbored no illusions about virtue inevitably accompanying authority, but felt that, good or bad, prelates should be obeyed. Failure to do so not only suggested a mistaken notion of whom God had placed in authority, but pride on one's own part as well. Thus, humble obedience was a spiritual duty in a double sense. The only real exception involved refusal to obey a sinful command, and then Angelo felt that the individual should humbly submit to the consequences.

Nor is it likely that Angelo and his group worked against Boniface personally. He himself says that in conducting mass they prayed for Pope Boniface, and the group did attempt an appeal to him in the wake of *Saepe sacram ecclesiam*. Here again Angelo's letters are significant, particularly those written in the years after John fell out with the Franciscan leaders. Their basic message is to stay out of such conflicts.

To say this much is not to say that in the dark days after Celestine's resignation, Angelo never wondered aloud whether a pope could resign and thus whether Boniface VIII was really only Benedetto Gaetani after all. Who knows what he might have said? There is one bit of evidence that at least some of his group, when they were together in the privacy of their own circle, flirted with the idea of Boniface as the beast from the land in Rev. 13. As we saw in Chapter 3, Ubertino da Casale recounts an interview with "two truly evangelical men, one of whom knew Greek well and the other to some extent," who were part of a group that had fled to Greece in order to escape persecution. They told of sitting at dinner while the one who knew Greek well read from the pseudo-Justin Martyr commentary on the Apocalypse. When he came to the number of the beast, he discovered that, according to the commentary, the numbers could be translated into letters spelling out the name *Benedictos*. On hearing this the whole congregation laughed and the reader, laughing as well, said to the brothers, "If Benedict of Anagni, who now reigns, knew this, he would send all his forces to seize and burn this book, because it clearly and openly displays his falsity."[25] It seems quite possible that the two evangelical men were connected with Angelo's group, although Greece afforded a handy sanctuary for various religious refugees in the period. (It was an abortive attempt to get there that led to Celestine V's capture, ending his post-pontifical fugitive phase.) It is also at least possible that the one who told the story to Ubertino was Angelo himself, who certainly knew Greek well, although what little we know of Angelo's itinerary on the one hand and the composition of the *Arbor vitae* on the other would make it a rather tight fit. In any case, the important point to be grasped is that there is a great distinction between saying such things on occasion and becoming part of an anti-Boniface faction based on a belief in his illegitimacy. Angelo may have done the former, but it seems impossible that he did the latter. Arsenio Frugoni summarizes the worst that might be said on this score:

> It is not hard to believe that even the Poor Hermits of Celestine were against Boniface, before whose menace they had fled. And that in their hearts they considered him illegitimate for a while or, perhaps better, they desired him to be such. And if we see that desire contradicted in the prayers at mass or in Liberato's appeal, we should not thereby invoke the principle of noncontradiction and accuse the Poor Hermits of duplicity, but only of that compromise which is to some extent the drama of concrete existence, from which the best extricate themselves, not through exercise of logic, but through brilliant action when circumstances call them to assume a precise responsibility.[26]

Nevertheless, there is still room to wonder whether the basic inconsistency goes well beyond Angelo's attitude toward Boniface and lies at the heart of his entire self-defense. He and his group may not have doubted ecclesiastical authority, but they proved remarkably adept at getting out of its way. There is an element of unintended humor in Angelo's explanation of why *Saepe sacram ecclesiam* never reached him. Any bill collector or process server would recognize the genre. In the final analysis, though, Frugoni's comment on "the drama of concrete existence" applies here as well. Angelo believed in obedience to duly constituted authority; not only was it safer to obey, but he also identified obedience with humility, charity, and orthodoxy. Yet he also thought that he was required to obey Francis as he had spoken in the rule and *Testament*. When these requirements clashed and he was faced with two incompatible demands, he avoided the conflict as best he could, salvaging what he could of both loyalties. If his effort proved less than completely successful, neither was it completely unsuccessful. He was able to remain true to his sense of Franciscan poverty while never breaking flagrantly with the pope. We will return to the matter in a later chapter.

The French spirituals were to be less fortunate. They would soon have to choose openly between the two sorts of obedience.

NINE

CENSURE AND CONDEMNATION

AROUND PENTECOST, SIXTY-FOUR BROTHERS from Narbonne and Béziers arrived at Avignon.[1] Instead of going to the Franciscan house, they went directly to the papal palace and stood outside the doors all night, eager to present themselves and state their case (or perhaps simply afraid to go to the local house). They had accepted Bernard Délicieux as their spokesman—an unfortunate choice, both for them and for him.

Bernard Délicieux

Bernard was a well-known, even legendary figure who had spent much of his life battling the Dominican-run inquisition at Carcassonne and Albi.[2] In the process, he had assisted in remarkably risky ventures, including forcible liberation in 1303 of the prisoners held at Carcassonne and, in 1304, a plot to transfer rule in the region from Philip IV of France to Ferrand, son of the king of Majorca. The conspiracy against Philip, once discovered, had put Bernard in a delicate situation and forced him to end his political activities. That he emerged from the affair as well as he did—several other plotters paid with their lives—was due to many of the same factors that had produced a temporary hiatus in the spirituals' suffering during the pontificate of Clement V.[3] Just as the spirituals had powerful defenders in the curia whose intervention led Clement to investigate the debate within the Franciscan order, so Bernard had equally prestigious supporters whose influence helped encourage Clement to open an investigation of inquisitorial excesses in Languedoc, place a relatively benign interpretation on Bernard's conspiratorial activities, and do what he could to secure him royal favor, or at least an end to royal disfavor.

In the matter of Bernard and the inquisition, as with the spirituals, Clement's intervention produced temporary relief for certain individuals while leaving intact larger structures that would ensure more trouble in the future. The inquisition in Languedoc remained under Dominican control, but Bernard eventually found himself at liberty. Clement told him to find a convent that agreed with him, and Bernard chose Béziers, where the bishops had long supported his battles with the inquisition.

Once in Béziers Bernard became an important figure among the spirituals. The Dominican Raymond Barrau, who presents himself as one of Bernard's major attackers at Béziers, reports that he was frustrated in his persecutory project by the fact that the bishop and canons treated the spirituals and their leader Bernard as if they were "saints of God and the foundation of His church." In fact, Barrau says the entire town not only protected Bernard and his group but also accepted their guidance.[4]

That Bernard should have been sympathetic with the spirituals has puzzled most historians, who feel that he had shown no interest in them earlier. As statements go, that seems a dangerous one, since most of the light illuminating Bernard's career comes from his 1319 trial. That process tells us about certain of Bernard's pursuits and ignores the rest. His support for the spirituals constituted one of the four charges on which he was examined, but it was the one that interested his judges least. They questioned him only briefly on the matter and their sentence ignored it entirely. Moreover, those few bits of evidence that historians do cull from the process are often analyzed in a relatively superficial manner. For example, Bernard's political maneuvering is sometimes cited as evidence that he was not a spiritual; however, political connections and an ability to exploit them can be seen in several important spiritual spokesmen, including Ubertino da Casale, Angelo Clareno, and Raymond Geoffroi. To be sure, none of them ever engaged in political activities with the gusto or bravado suggested by Bernard's career, but that could simply suggest that Bernard represents one more variety of spiritual Franciscan in what we are beginning to recognize as a very heterogeneous group. It is also sometimes suggested that Bernard's personal property—he sold his books and other possessions to further the anti-inquisitorial cause[5]—and his handling of money stand in sharp contrast with Olivi's radical espousal of poverty, yet Olivi, while radical on a theoretical level in claiming that the vow entailed a blanket commitment to *usus pauper*, was relatively moderate in defining the limits of concrete behavior.[6] Olivi's writings, like Raymond Geoffroi's position paper for Clement V, can be taken as evidence that French spiritual leaders sought the sort of poverty that would allow Franciscans to perform without luxury (but also without extreme hardship) the functions assigned to them during the thirteenth century. It is easy to understand how Alan Friedlander, Bernard's most recent biographer, can assert that "nothing in this last chapter of Bernard's career . . . is inconsistent with Bernard's earlier life."[7]

In fact, some elements in the process might be taken as evidence of a long-standing sympathy with the spirituals on Bernard's part. There is his early association with Arnald of Villanova, which went back at least to 1304; the protection he received from some of the same cardinals who befriended the spirituals, notably Napoleone Orsini and Pietro Colonna; and Bernard's own statement that he has suffered for Olivi's cause. Bernard may well have known Olivi personally and certainly was heavily exposed to his memory, since he became lector at Narbonne shortly after Olivi's death. Béziers, where he resided before his fateful journey to Avignon, was the scene of Olivi's novitiate—and the city outside of which Olivi had been born and raised.[8] It is significant that he shared Olivi's fascination with the idea that Christ's side wound was inflicted before his death rather than after, although (like Ubertino) he appealed to a variant gospel text as evidence, whereas Olivi assumed that on the face of it the Bible was against his view. Bernard's apocalyptic interests, particularly his apparent admiration for Joachim of Fiore, offer yet another similarity, although what little we know of Bernard's apocalyptic suggests involvement in traditions other than those that dominated Olivi's thought[9]—and in any case, apocalyptic speculation was hardly an exclusively spiritual Franciscan activity.

In the final analysis, however, one has to admit that there is little in Bernard's career before 1313 that would prepare us to expect his leadership of the spirituals at Béziers or his appearance at Avignon as their spokesman. The real question to be asked is what he saw in them. Perhaps he had come to agree with them on strict observance of the rule, although the record does not say as much. He probably saw them in the context of his interest in apocalyptic speculation, although the record does not say that either. But it is worth noting that in some ways his 1317 activities did resemble his earlier ones. His defense of the spirituals was, to some extent, a continuation of his old involvement with the citizenry in their battle against religious suppression, since many citizens of Narbonne, Béziers, and Carcassonne backed the spirituals, just as they had once backed those that they claimed were falsely condemned by the inquisition. Bernard could be seen as serving not only the spirituals but also their families and lay supporters, just as he had earlier supported the family and friends of inquisitorial victims. And there is still another significant parallel. One important thing the spirituals shared with the victims of inquisitorial oppression was their equally beleaguered state, and it is possible that some of their appeal for Bernard lay in precisely that. The element of risk offers another similarity. Bernard had thrown himself into the earlier battle with a zeal that inspired him to play very dangerous games, defying established authority at considerable personal risk. He did it again in 1317. He must have been intelligent enough to see which way the wind was blowing at Avignon: it was blowing in much the same direction as it had at Carcassonne, when he plotted against Philip IV (and especially when, after managing to avoid the fate of his co-conspirators, he continued to seek royal support for his campaign against the inquisition).[10] If Bernard was half as able a politician as historians have claimed, he must have recognized that he was pursuing politically improbable goals in both contexts, but he pursued them nonetheless. Either he felt an uncontrollable desire to aid the oppressed, or he was a man who liked to live dangerously, or both. One suspects it was both.

At any rate, Bernard fared even worse than the other would-be champions of the spirituals. Once he began his attempt to defend them, representatives of the community catalogued his previous purported crimes—an impressive list, which included not only defiance of the inquisition and treason against the king but also conspiring with Arnald of Villanova in the assassination of Pope Benedict XI. John ordered that he be imprisoned. We will return to Bernard later. For the moment, we must hear Angelo's description of what happened once he had been led away.

> When he [Bernard] had been eliminated in this way, Brother François Sans wished to assume the task of explaining his colleagues' position. Then the brothers cried out in a similar way, "Lord, this one should not be heard either, for he has presumed to teach and preach and impugn the order with all his power, against the orders of his minister." Because of this, the pope ordered the brothers to incarcerate

him. But when Brother Guillaume de Saint-Amans then wished to put forth those things which seemed expedient for their case, the brothers interrupted and accused him, claiming that he had squandered and dissipated goods conceded to the order by the pope for their use, and that he had run away from the Narbonne convent. On the strength of these accusations, the pope immediately detained him.

By this time it was obvious that anyone who chose to defend the spirituals had better be above suspicion himself. There was such a man, Brother Geoffroi de Cournon. He had done his best to stay out of the battle, but he now saw his responsibility and assumed it. This time, the accusing chorus of brothers remained silent. The pope had to become both prosecutor and judge.

> "Brother Geoffroi," he said, "I am more than a bit surprised that you demand strict observance of the rule, yet you yourself have five tunics." Geoffroi replied, "Holy father, you are deceived in this matter, for it is not true that I have five tunics." The pope said, "Then in other words, we are lying?" Brother Geoffroi said, "Holy father, I did not say (nor would I say) that you are lying. I merely said (and still say) that I do not have five tunics." The pope said, "We will detain you and find out whether you have five tunics." The others, seeing that they would receive no hearing, cried out, "Justice, holy father, justice!" Then the pope ordered them all to return to the house of the brothers, and he ordered the brothers to watch over them until he had thought more carefully about what should be done with them.

John's treatment of potential spokesmen seems to have been inspired as much by the desire to keep them from testifying as by any real interest in their individual failings. He simply did not want the old complaints rehearsed. Once he had placed the rebels from Narbonne and Béziers under the supervision of the community and felt free to deal with them at his own speed, he could afford to be merciful toward those who, like Ubertino da Casale and Angelo Clareno, had powerful protectors and were at least temporarily willing to stay out of trouble. Angelo was allowed to transfer to the Celestinians, whether they wanted him or not, and Ubertino became a Benedictine.[11] Bernard Délicieux was less fortunate. Like Angelo, he had been handed over to Cardinal Arnaud d'Auch, but two days later he was subjected to close confinement in the papal prison. The Dominicans had a score to settle, and so did his own order. His story after that point is a complex one. Let it suffice to say that the charges against him, though numerous, were quite different from those lodged against the spirituals from Narbonne and Béziers. In fact, little in Bernard's process had much to do with his recent appearance in Avignon. He was confronted anew with all the old accusations. The actual trial took place two years later, when an investigation concluded in the summer of 1319 led John XXII to impanel three judges to hear the case in a three-month trial that led to a verdict in December. By the end of the process, Bernard had confessed to aiding the spirituals, impeding the inquisition, and plotting against Philip IV, but he never admitted to conspiring in the murder of Benedict XI. The judges ignored the matter of aiding the spirituals and concluded that there was insufficient evidence to convict him of murdering Benedict, but they found him guilty on the other two counts.[12] He was degraded from spiritual office and sentenced to perpetual imprisonment at Carcassonne. Within a year, he was dead.

Quorumdam exigit

Meanwhile, John's policing of the order proceeded apace. While the Narbonne and Béziers spirituals languished in the care of their leaders at Avignon, the pope fortified his case against them and the Sicilian rebels with a series of bulls. The first of these, *Quorumdam exigit,* appeared on October 7, 1317 and prepared the way for his action against the southern French group.[13] It begins by announcing that John has been forced to take pen in hand and to settle the doubts of a few Franciscans whose blind, uninformed scrupulosity has led them to withhold obedience on the pretext that they are following their consciences. In the first place, they insist on wearing "short, tight, unusual and squalid habits" when previous papal declarations have made it clear that the choice of clothing is up to their superiors. To be sure, these popes added the important qualification that *vilitas* should nonetheless be maintained, and the spirituals defend their intransigence on the ground that their superiors are not adhering to this requirement. In answer to their objection, John asserts that it is up to the superiors to decide not only what should be worn but also whether *vilitas* is being maintained. In the course of the bull, John announces—three times—that he and his predecessors have "burdened the consciences" of the superiors with this responsibility, as well as that of determining what constitutes true poverty in granaries and wine cellars.

There is, then, a single right course to be followed. It involves exchanging those "narrow, short and peculiar habits" for others of the superiors' choosing. "For poverty is good, and chastity is greater, but obedience is greatest of all if preserved intact." The first involves mastery over things, the second mastery over one's body, and the third mastery over one's mind and soul. John is echoing an argument by Thomas Aquinas (one already refuted by Olivi in the late 1270s or early 1280s).[14] Thus, nearly four decades later, Aquinas had his revenge.

Now that the pope had spoken, the next step was up to the Franciscan leadership. Five days later, on October 12, Michael of Cesena began to interrogate the spirituals detained at Avignon. In the presence of a notary and witnesses, he asked them whether they would accept *Quorumdam exigit* on the subjects of clothing, wheat, and wine. Some said they would, but others said they would not. A few tried to temper their refusal with qualifications, asserting, for instance, that they would not don the habit currently worn by the community, or that they would wear the habit but would not concur with storage of wheat and wine. Those who refused, when asked why, answered variously that what the pope required was contrary to their vow, the gospel, Christ's precepts to his apostles, or the rule "in which the whole evangelical life is contained." Some made explicit what most of them must have assumed: Their refusal was a matter of obligation. They could do nothing else.

Those who withheld assent were asked a second question: Did they think that the pope had the authority to command what he had in fact commanded in *Quorumdam exigit*? Most said that he did not, although at least one said that he simply did not know. Required to explain themselves, they replied in different ways: it was because he had no power to change the gospel; because he could not absolve from virtue and demand vice; because he could not order anything opposed to the evangelical counsels; or because he could not order the violation of an evangelical vow.[15]

Now it was up to the inquisitor. On November 6, John XXII placed the twenty-five brothers who had refused assent in the hands of Michel Le Moine, O.F.M., who was no stranger to the spirituals. He was one of the sixteen leaders removed from office by Clement V. John XXII had appointed him an inquisitor in 1317. In the letter setting Michel to work, John, who constantly referred to the recusant friars as *pseudofratres*, also branded them as heretics. Thus Michel's task was simplified for him. It was not so much to decide whether they were heretics as to define their particular genus and species. He was given a generous hint in this direction, as well, when John announced that some of the accused had replied to his commands with "appeals and protests" and the rest had gone along with them.

Was this really heresy? John made sure of the answer by submitting three questions to a panel of thirteen scholars. Was it heretical, he asked, to assert pertinaciously that Franciscans should not obey their superiors when commanded to remove their "short, narrow and peculiar" habits, since such commands demanded transgression of the rule and therefore of the gospel; that the pope did not have the authority to order what he had in fact ordered in *Quorumdam exigit*; and that neither pope nor superiors were to be obeyed regarding the contents of that bull, since it violated both the rule and Christ's counsels? Sometime in early 1318 the experts said "yes" to all three questions. The assertions were manifestly heretical, because they were contrary to evangelical truth as well as to the authority of pope and church.[16] Thus the scholars gave John just what he wanted. The spirituals were heretics: not only were they reading the gospel wrong, but their disobedience also displayed a heretical view of ecclesiastical authority.

Two More Bulls

Meanwhile, John hammered out two more bulls. On December 30, 1317, he issued *Sancta romana*.[17] The precise target of this one is hard to determine, although the general thrust is obviously against unauthorized religious groups. John speaks of those in Italy, Sicily, and southern France who call themselves *fraticelli, pauperes de paupere vita, bizzochi, beghini,* or other things. Contrary to canon law, which requires all who enter the religious life to choose one of the established orders, these people form their own new groups, choose leaders, build convents, receive members, and generally act as if they were an approved body. Many try to cover their tracks by claiming to observe the rule of Saint Francis literally, even though they do not place themselves under the authority of the general and provincial ministers. They insist that their course has been sanctioned by a privilege of Pope Celestine V, even though all such privileges were later cancelled by Boniface VIII. Some claim that they have received authorization from their superiors, their bishops, or other church leaders; however, such approval, even if really granted, is illegitimate, because it contradicts canon law. Some claim to belong to the third order of Saint Francis, but the rule of the third order makes no provision for organizations like theirs. Some have progressed beyond disobedience and are beginning to deviate from the faith in other ways, despising the sacraments and disseminating other errors. Such is often the case, John observes, with people who prefer their own ideas to established ecclesiastical practice. Moving from narrative to commandment, John revokes all permission for such groups, from whatever source. Any bishops or other ecclesiastical leaders granting such permission in the future can consider themselves *ipso facto* excommunicated.

This bull was obviously something of a catch-all, covering Franciscans and non-Franciscans, Italians and French alike. It is probably dangerous to read the descriptive section too carefully, expecting it to yield accurate information about any particular group. John's major purpose was to nullify all attempts to bypass established organizations by appealing to special privileges or by claiming membership in some legitimate group without actually obeying its leaders.

Within a month, on January 23, 1318, John issued another bull on roughly the same subject, though this one was more specific.[18] John begins *Gloriosam ecclesiam* with a brief tribute to the Franciscan order, then goes on to decry some of its recent deviants. He speaks of those in southern France who have displayed their vanity by insisting that they alone are observing the rule. His illustrious predecessor, Nicholas IV, wrote letters demanding that these people be brought to heel,[19] but the error revived in the time of Clement V, when certain elements in France and Italy bombarded the pope with complaints against the rest of the order.

Clement, trying to solve the problem through kindness rather than severity, responded with remarkable patience. He submitted the complaints to various ecclesiastics and masters, and then, advised by their wisdom, settled the doubts that had arisen. Finally, he ordered the querulous brothers to return to their assigned convents and humbly obey their superiors. That should have ended the matter, but it did not. Somewhat later, Clement ordered that action be taken against those Tuscan friars who had rebelled against their leaders. These friars then escaped to Sicily and, breaking entirely with their old superiors, established a separate order with its own leaders and convents. They adopted their own "short, narrow, unusual and squalid" habits. Since pride leads to contention, contention to schism, and schism to heresy, it is not surprising that they soon complemented their odd attire with a few doctrinal peculiarities.

John lists five such errors that, he says, the group is reported (on good authority) to hold. First, they say that there are two churches. The carnal church, rich and worldly, is led by the pope and other lesser prelates. The spiritual church, poor and virtuous, is composed of themselves and their supporters. This view of oneself as spiritual and everyone else as carnal is, John observes, hardly an unusual one among heretics. John's refutation of this first error naturally leads him to assert the unity of the church expressed in the Petrine succession, and to emphasize the mixed nature of the church in history, with good and bad growing up cheek by jowl within it until judgment day. He also underscores the legitimacy and usefulness of ecclesiastical wealth.

Their second error is to assert that the priests and other ministers of the church, having been deprived of jurisdiction, can no longer confer the sacraments or instruct the faithful validly. Here, they follow the error of the Donatists. In opposition, John asserts that, by God's immutable will, ecclesiastical authority will remain with the Roman Church until the end of time. Their third error is that, like the Waldensians, they denounce all oaths as sinful. Their fourth is that, also like the Waldensians, they believe that a sinful priest is devoid of power to confer the sacraments. Their fifth is that, somewhat like the Manicheans and Montanists before them, they see the gospel as fulfilled for the first time in them, declaring that the promise of the Holy Spirit has been fulfilled in them rather than in the apostles at Pentecost—and thus that the gospel has been opened to them alone. These presumptuous people also attack the sacrament of marriage, spin out dreams about "the course of time and the end of the world," and say that the time of Antichrist has just begun.

John comments that such assertions, which he considers "partly heretical, partly insane and partly fabulous," should simply be condemned rather than seriously refuted since, devoid of any reason, authority, or likelihood, they stand as their own refutation. He notes that he has admonished King Frederick of Sicily to aid the order in capturing these pseudo-friars, and his majesty, an obedient son, has done so. Some, however, have escaped to pagan lands, while others are being protected by supporters in remote parts of Sicily.

We finally arrive at the operative part of the bull. John implores all and sundry, ecclesiastics and laymen alike, to give the rebels no aid, but rather to hunt them down like the rapacious wolves they are and turn them over to their Franciscan superiors. Their organizational structure and activities are to be regarded as without validity. Those recruited into their group are to be examined by the ecclesiastical authorities, who will sniff out heresy and impose the fitting punishments, invoking the aid of the secular arm if necessary.

Some General Observations

Thus John's bulls manage to encompass all the major brands of rebellion within the Franciscan order, including the southern French spirituals and their third-order supporters, the Tuscan rebels, and Angelo's group. This seems a heterogeneous collection, but they all agreed on one issue. All were either members or supporters of the element in the order that wanted to observe *usus pauper* strictly and criticized Franciscan leaders for condoning (in fact, enforcing) violation of the rule on this score. Moreover, all felt moved to act out their dissent.

This fact tells us a good deal about the progress of the *usus pauper* controversy. The theological debate about *usus pauper* probably continued somewhere in the second decade of the fourteenth century, but we are hard pressed to discover where. After Vienne, at least the theologians seem to have obeyed Clement in that they laid the issue to rest, but the activists struggled on. The decade was not without its major issue, but that issue was obedience, not poverty. One of the most striking things about John's three bulls is their relative indifference to the question of how poorly Franciscans should live. What they *are* concerned about is establishing that Franciscan leaders should decide the matter and should expect unquestioning obedience once they have done so. John is also trying to establish that, having said as much, he himself is to be obeyed. The debate is over. The spirituals should stop protesting, stop appealing, and return to being good subordinates.

Scholars often explain John's attitude by referring to his essentially legalistic mentality.[20] There is some truth in this characterization, although other aspects of his character seem equally important. His handling of the spirituals at Vienne does not simply display legalism, but a rather brutal decisiveness as well. Nevertheless, in fairness to John, some observations must be made. The first is that John's concentration on the issue of obedience is partly explicable in terms of his situation. He did not think of *Quorumdam exigit* as supplanting *Exiit qui seminat* and *Exivi de paradiso*, but as supplementing them. Those earlier bulls had established that it was the leaders' responsibility to determine the proper level of *usus pauper,* but they also had stressed that it must indeed be *pauper.* According to John, rebellious spirituals had tried to evade the first point by appealing to the second. His present task was to inform them that it was not their prerogative to make such judgments. It was ridiculous for subordinates to assume that they could measure their superiors' decisions on specific practices against some theoretical standard of poverty, for it was up to their superiors to define the latter as well as the former.

This brings us to a second observation. John is often compared unfavorably with Clement V, yet in some respects, he was simply carrying Clement's program through to its logical conclusion. Certainly John distorted history when, like the community, he portrayed the Clementine settlement as nothing more than an attempt to deal gently with a whiny minority and their misplaced scruples. On the contrary, Clement seems to have felt that the spiritual complaints were justified in part. Even so, it was Clement who decided against the Tuscan spirituals. In fact, he displayed a remarkable willingness to think the worst of them, dismissing their complaint of persecution out of hand and accusing them of capitalizing on the unstable situation in order to follow their own willful bent. His interpretation of their conduct may seem surprising, but his rejection of it is understandable. Their complaints (echoed by Angelo Clareno) may have been just, but clearly no pope could countenance a group that created an alternate leadership structure—from minister general down—as the Tuscan spirituals had. Angelo himself condemned them in words disturbingly similar to those used by John XXII.[21]

At first glance, the French situation might strike us as very different. The rebels had reacted to a patent violation of papal orders by the community and, unlike the Italians, were not interested in setting up an alternate order. They emphasized as much and publicly looked forward to the day when, the order having returned to the Clementine settlement, they could end their defiance. Here one sees a continuing difference between the French and Italian spirituals. The Italians were readier to consider a split in which the spirituals and the community went their own separate ways. Nevertheless, the Council of Vienne had moved the French spirituals closer to the Italian goal by granting them, not reform of the entire order, but relative freedom within the order, their own little corner of it to themselves. It was an unwieldy arrangement and would have required substantial papal oversight in order to remain viable, if indeed it could ever have been viable. A significant number of influential Franciscans did not like the spirituals. Every time a custode of Narbonne, provincial minister of Provence, or minister general was elected, there would have been cause for anxiety. Moreover, the arrangement applied only to southern France. How could one avoid applying it to Italy as well? In short, the Clementine solution was so fraught with difficulties that one wonders whether Clement himself would have been willing to maintain it for long.

John certainly was not. His opening words in *Ad conditorem canonum*, written later to address a different situation, could have been applied to this one as well: "When he who creates canons sees that statutes produced by him or his predecessors are doing harm rather than good, it is undoubtedly within his authority to see that they do no more harm."[22] The neatest solution was to recognize that Clement's southern French settlement was unworkable—and end it. Franciscan leaders already had taken steps toward doing just that, and John ratified their action by ignoring its illegality and adopting their mythology concerning the nature of the struggle to date. Viewed from that perspective, the problem lay not in Clement's solution but in the spirituals' refusal to accept it. Such a perspective enabled John to employ a time-honored practice of administrators and reverse his predecessor without explicitly admitting that he had done so. This was certainly hard on the spirituals, but it simplified John's task enormously. He could dispense with further appeals and wrangling. Any tidying up could be left to the inquisitor.

Thus we arrive at a third observation. In searching for parallels to the present crisis, John turned not simply to the preceding decade, but also to the 1290s. He was partially correct in doing so. Like Boniface VIII, he had to deal with a situation in which Franciscan spirituals had rebelled against authority. The scenario was slightly different, since in the 1290s the rebellion was aimed partly at Boniface himself, whereas the Narbonne and Béziers spirituals were appealing to John against their superiors. Yet the Tuscan rebels were already defying papal authority when he took office, and he recognized that the French spirituals were capable of following the same course. A number of them eventually did. In other words, John was right to imagine that the spirituals were a menace to the clean, orderly chain of command he sought. They had inherited from Olivi a theory of poverty that justified (in fact, demanded) disobedience when a superior—be he local guardian, provincial minister, or pope—ordered a violation of *usus pauper*. They had become convinced that their superiors were doing just that, and they had disobeyed. At least some of them had also inherited from Olivi a theology of history that made their superiors' behavior only too explicable. This element had not escaped John either, as we learn from *Gloriosam ecclesiam*. The apocalyptic dimension of the affair is important, and we will return to it in a moment.

Moreover, we do John some injustice if we confine our discussion to the spirituals. By 1317, ecclesiastical authorities could place such cases in a much wider context. Italy pullulated with localized religious movements. Left to themselves, they could take bizarre and even dangerous turns, a point amply illustrated by the Apostles under Fra Dolcino. These movements continually crossed lines with one another, sending their messages in new directions through unexpected channels. Dolcinists became fellow travelers with the tattered remnants of the Poor Hermits, while orthodox Tuscan mystics rubbed shoulders with adherents of the *spiritus libertatis*. If this situation worried John XXII, it also had worried Boniface VIII and Clement V. It would have worried any pope devoted to the principles on which the medieval church had been built. John saw the spirituals from this wider perspective, and it was not one calculated to highlight their best features.

Mention of their best features leads us to a fourth point about John and his three bulls. Modern historians sometimes interpret his treatment of the spirituals as evidence of his massive insensitivity to the spiritual value of Franciscan poverty. It is true that John was not sympathetic, and that his lack of sympathy extended beyond the spirituals to include poverty as the rest of the order understood it. Franciscan leaders would learn this painful lesson shortly thereafter, and they might have divined it even from these earlier bulls, in which

John praises the order and its virtues without paying the least attention to poverty. Nevertheless, it is hard to call John insensitive to poverty without accusing Aquinas of the same failing. John's attitude toward the spirituals is quite explicable in terms of Thomist theology. It is important to take seriously John's decision, at a key point in *Quorumdam exigit,* to echo Aquinas on the superiority of obedience to poverty and chastity. John is, to some extent, passing a judgment not only on the *usus pauper* controversy but on the *correctorium* controversy as well, and his judgment should have made Franciscan leaders nervous. Thus one might ask whether John's actions proceeded from insensitivity or informed disagreement.

A fifth point: In choosing to concentrate on the question of obedience, John can hardly be said to have yanked the controversy violently off course. It was, in fact, the main issue for the participants as well during the period after Vienne. The polemical war waged in the period between Clement V's death and the moment John acted was primarily a battle over who was disobeying whom. Even the French spirituals felt required to dwell on obedience, arguing that it was the community—not they—who had defied the Clementine settlement. Thus, while it may well be true that John's essentially juridical approach to the controversy showed his insensitivity to the deeper spiritual issues in the poverty dispute, it is also true that those issues were not being examined very deeply by the contestants at the moment when John became involved. The terms in which he solved the problem were, to a surprising extent, those in which it was presented to him.[23]

Nor—and here we add a sixth and final point—was it John who first branded the zealots as heretics. Angelo Clareno[24] says that the five Italian provincial ministers who met around 1279 decided to punish the Anconan zealots as schismatics, heretics, and destroyers of the order, and then he tells us that they were actually sentenced as heretics and destroyers of the order. Angelo is writing at a much later date, and his recollection of the event may reflect the polemics of his own time. We know, however, that bulls by Boniface VIII leveled the charge of heresy against various dissident groups, including Angelo's, and that the Tuscan rebels were attacked in similar terms, as were the spirituals in southern France.

The Spirituals as Heretics

At any rate, armed with the pope's bulls and his blessing, Michel Le Moine could proceed against the errant twenty-five. Twenty of them recanted. As part of their penance, they were forced to abjure their errors publicly in the very places where they had formerly preached them.[25] Of the other five, one held out almost to the end, and then finally recanted—but so late that he was sentenced to wear crosses front and rear, be degraded from all orders, and spend the rest of his life in prison. His four colleagues went to the stake impenitent.

We have the inquisitorial sentence.[26] In it, Michel says that the accused are guilty of pertinaciously asserting that the pope does not have the authority to command what he commanded in *Quorumdam exigit*; that what he commanded was against Christ's evangelical counsels and their own vow of evangelical poverty, which is the very vow Christ himself observed and imposed on his disciples; and finally, that in such a case they could obey no mortal with a clear conscience. Michel reports that they clung stubbornly to these illusions even when it was explained to them that their stance contained certain errors, "such as that what is contrary to the observance and meaning of the Franciscan rule is therefore contrary to the gospel and the faith . . . ; and that no one can force them to remove their short, narrow habits and wear those of the community; and that those who criticize their short, narrow habits are by that very fact criticizing Christ's gospel and his rule; and that orders to remove these habits and wear others are not binding because they are contrary to the gospel."

These errors challenge not only papal authority but also the gospel itself, since the latter says that Christ gave Peter the power to loose and bind. They also contradict evangelical doctrine, which tells us that Christ had a purse; that it is consonant with the gospel for those who profess the rule to save for future necessities; and that no religious rule can be identified with the gospel, since the Roman Church obediently submits to the gospel without correcting or confirming it, whereas all religious rules owe their legitimacy entirely to the Roman Church. "Thus the Roman pontiff would not violate the gospel and faith of Christ if he contradicted, changed or even abolished the [Franciscan] rule; nor is that rule identical with the gospel, but is instead a certain laudable way of life approved and confirmed by the Roman pontiffs and simply and absolutely subject to interpretation, alteration or any other sort of action on their part."

Much of what we find here should be quite familiar by now, but there are some surprising additions. The most striking one—particularly since Michel is himself a Franciscan—is his repeated assertion that the Franciscan rule is distinct from the gospel and is thus subject to modification by the pope. In saying this, he seems to be putting asunder what had been joined together by Francis in the opening lines of the rule and by Nicholas III in *Exiit qui seminat*. In addition, he is paving the way for the attack on this identification spearheaded by John over the next few years.

One is also struck by Michel's assertion that Christ carried a purse. This was hardly a novel idea, even among Franciscans. Olivi had acknowledged as much. Nevertheless, earlier writers like Bonaventure, Pecham, and Olivi had discussed the matter in the process of replying to secular and Dominican charges that Franciscan poverty was not rooted in the gospel. They found themselves discussing the subject because it had been raised by their opponents and had to be explained away. Although those who rejected *usus pauper* as part of the vow in Olivi's time did allude to Christ's purse, they do not seem to have done so often, possibly because they knew that the purse could be invoked against poverty as they themselves understood it. Here again, in raising the issue, Michel was setting the stage for outside attack.

Toward the end of his sentence, Michel names the source of the spirituals' heresy. It flows from a "poisoned fountain of doctrine": the thought of Petrus Iohannis Olivi. In his Apocalypse commentary and elsewhere, Olivi temerariously attacked the honor and authority of the Roman Church. His writings were condemned and burned by his own order. Nevertheless, since John XXII has submitted them to certain cardinals and masters for still another decision, Michel simply warns all and sundry that in the meantime, they are not to read them, nor are they to revere Olivi as a saint or as a "catholic and approved man."

Once the sentence had been pronounced, results followed swiftly. The four were given one last chance to recant. They did not. Indeed, they felt that they could not. Thus they were degraded from all orders, turned over to the secular authorities, and burned, all on the seventh of May, 1318. Angelo Clareno notes their passing and summarizes the reason for it.

> They were burned because they asserted that the rule of Saint Francis was the same as Christ's gospel; that, once solemnly promised, it enters the category of precept in such a way that the vow has the force of a precept, especially in those things which the rule demands by precept or inhibition; and that it is thus beyond anyone's power of dispensation. They also asserted that the supreme pontiff could not concede cellars, granaries and storage facilities for oil to the brothers minor, who had promised to observe Christ's gospel; and that the pope had sinned in conceding such things, as had the brothers in accepting them.

The four men who died for these ideas were Jean Barrau, Deodat Michel, Pons Rocha, and Guillem Sancton. We know little else about them.

Olivi's Apocalypse Commentary

While Michel Le Moine was busy condemning those living spirituals, their dead hero was also undergoing examination. John had entrusted Niccolo da Prato, cardinal bishop of Ostia, with the task of examining Olivi's Apocalypse commentary. The cardinal had extracted certain passages and turned them over first to a single theologian, then to a commission of eight, which included Bertrand de la Tour and another Franciscan. The individual theologian reported in 1318, the commission of eight in 1319.[27] In the spring of 1319, before the commission delivered its verdict, the Franciscan order held its general chapter meeting at Marseilles and used the occasion to insulate itself against the ongoing process by carrying out its own condemnation of Olivi's works. The decision was approved by a commission of twelve Franciscan masters.[28] Moreover, during roughly the same period, two other theologians—the Carmelite Guido Terreni and the Dominican Pierre de Palu—censured a Catalan work that seems to have been based heavily on Olivi's Apocalypse commentary (although it went beyond that work, including Olivi himself in the apocalyptic scenario as the angel of Rev. 10:1).[29] Thus, although the commentary was not actually condemned by the pope until substantially later, there was ample support for such a decision by the end of 1319.

It is easy to spot the linkage between these activities and the process against the spirituals. The commission of eight, in its report to John, echoes *Gloriosam ecclesiam* in rejecting the idea that the fullness of revelation through the Holy Spirit is reserved for the sixth and seventh periods of church history, and in attacking the notion that a new, spiritual church, which is coming to birth and replacing the old one (just as the church once replaced the synagogue), is being opposed by the carnal church, identified as none other than the Roman Church.[30] Nor are the parallels limited to *Gloriosam ecclesiam*. Take, for example, their reaction to Olivi's identification of the Franciscan rule with the gospel. The commission remarks that

> if he means by this what *Exiit qui seminat* meant, then he is right. If, however, he means what he himself declares elsewhere and his followers assert, namely that the rule of blessed Francis is truly and properly the same as the gospel of Christ and the reverse, and that the lord pope has no power over it just as he has none over the gospel, or that Christ literally observed everything in the rule of blessed Francis and ordered his apostles to do the same, then we consider what he says to be simply heretical, ridiculous and insane.[31]

We recall that when Michael of Cesena asked the spirituals to obey *Quorumdam exigit*, they backed their refusal with arguments similar to those attributed here to Olivi and his followers. Michel Le Moine explicitly addressed this problem in his sentence. In fact, the Olivi commission implicitly rejects the identification of rule and gospel in words similar to Michel's. In parrying what they take to be Olivi's belief that the Roman Church will attack the rule, they comment that the church would never condemn such a holy rule, "although it can nullify the rule of blessed Francis or any other rule which it has approved and confirmed, disbanding the order founded upon the rule just as it has disbanded others previously confirmed by it."[32]

A brief statistical excursus will suggest which elements in Olivi's commentary bothered the commission most. Of the 60 articles censured by the commission of eight, 33 deal directly (and another 5 indirectly) with Olivi's apparent identification of terms such as the "carnal church," "Babylon," and "harlot" with the Roman Church. Fifteen of the 60 articles are devoted to the preeminence of the sixth and seventh periods of church history over the five preceding periods, and 3 more to the superiority of the third age of world history over the first two. Of these 18 articles, 15 involve the notion that the sixth and seventh periods (or the third age) will enjoy knowledge and virtue superior to that of the apostles, while 8 include the assertion that these periods are related to previous ones as the church was related to the synagogue. These ideas, then, lie at the heart of the censure.

That is hardly to say that other articles are merely window dressing. For example, several of them are of central importance: they focus on the way in which Olivi works Francis and his order into the apocalyptic scenario. One senses a certain amount of embarrassment on this score, because two of the commission members were Franciscans, and the order itself had made some strong statements in this regard. Indeed, 2 articles deal with the notion of Francis as the angel of Rev. 7:2 and yet, since that identification had a long and honorable history in the order (having been sanctioned by Bonaventure himself), the notion is never explicitly challenged. Again, while the commission notices Olivi's suggestion that the Franciscan rule is identical with the gospel observed by Christ and imposed by him, it is painfully aware that the identification can not only be found in the writings of respectable Franciscans, but also in *Exiit qui seminat*, so the best they can do is suggest that in Olivi's work, the identification is given a new, incorrect sense. At these moments, we sense the difficulty experienced in trying to contain the censure, allowing it to condemn Olivi and the spirituals without letting it spill over to contaminate the order as a whole. The diplomatic problem thus entailed becomes even more clear when we compare the commission report with the Catalan process. The latter process (conducted by a Carmelite and a Dominican) attacks Olivi's Franciscan boosterism continually and with gusto, remarking twice that it is perverse to interpret the gospel, a document meant for the whole church, as if it applied to a single order. Nor does the Catalan process have any trouble deciding that the identification of Francis as the angel of Rev. 7:2 is bad exegesis.

Nevertheless, even the commission report offers some limit to Olivi's ambitions for his order. It rejects his suggestion that the order will play the dominant role in future missionary activity. It strongly condemns any implication that the pope has no more power over the Franciscan rule than he has over the gospel. It rejects the idea that Francis is the highest observer of evangelical perfection after Christ and his mother (a view it sees as slighting the apostles and other New Testament saints). It denies that Francis is, after Christ, the first and principal founder of the sixth period, and it vigorously attacks the idea that Francis will complete the parallel with Christ by experiencing a resurrection.

These criticisms are varied, in one sense, but in another, they seem all of a piece. The commission report and the Catalan process both take issue with a theology of history that is essentially dynamic and progressive, one that sees the world as entering a new stage in the present or immediate future. That theology of history sees Francis and the Franciscans—or at least a righteous remnant among them—as point men of the new order. It assumes that the institutional church, led by the pope, will act toward this new age as the synagogue did toward the early church, and that the result will be persecution followed by ultimate vindication.

The only question is whether that theology of history is really Olivi's. It is clear that after 1318 the spirituals and their lay supporters used Olivi's Apocalypse commentary to justify rebellion against the church, and it seems likely that some spirituals were doing so well before that date.[33] We cannot say definitely when the Catalan document censured by Guido Terreni and Pierre de Palu was produced, but what their report says about it seems to suggest that when it spoke of the carnal church it really meant the Roman Church. The question is whether the Catalan document and those who censured it were correct in assuming that Olivi himself made that identification.[34]

While the Catalan document, its judges, the Olivi commission, and the later rebels all distorted Olivi's meaning to some extent, there is still a sense in which they read him quite correctly. The distortion comes in their oversimplification of his use of terms like "carnal church" and "Babylon." The carnal church in his commentary does not simply refer to the Roman Church, but encompasses the totality of anti-Christian forces operating in the guise of the true church, yet actually seeking completely different ends. It takes on different guises at different times. It is like all the other symbols Olivi utilizes in his commentary. Olivi maintains them in all their richness and complexity as he weaves them into an inexhaustibly fascinating pattern. It seems almost insulting to reduce them to a series of aliases.

Nevertheless, the fact remains that Olivi did expect a radical transformation of the church, including the ecclesiastical hierarchy, in the near future. He saw a remarkable new *intellectus spiritualis* being born around him, and he expected it to mature in the new age until it arrived at a state where the church "will not need many earlier doctrines, since Christ's spirit will teach it all truth without mystery of external voice and book."[35] He also anticipated a new type of leadership in the church. Leaders would be eminent exemplars of the new *intellectus spiritualis*. They would renounce their possessions and return to the apostolic model. Their insight, poverty, and humility would encourage subordinates to obey them, and the result would be a hierarchy founded on charismatic rather than juridical authority.

As we noted earlier, such a vision of the third age makes it a mixture of progression and renovation. It returns to the apostolic model while moving into a realm of genuine novelty. Certainly the renewal aspect bothered Olivi's censors, since it assumed an apostolic church that looked remarkably like the Franciscan order as Olivi understood it. It was, however, the progressive aspect that most disturbed them. The problem was hardly that they could see no way in which the church had evolved over the centuries. An ecclesiastically acceptable way of envisaging such change is found in Henry of Ghent's question dedicated to the refutation of a Joachite third age.[36] Henry sees a gradual clarification of doctrine proceeding through the Old Testament, gospels, apostles, and doctors. "Thus the Lord wants each to add what he can so that the whole edifice, gradually growing, is perfected in both doctrine and works."

When we ask how Henry's notion of progress differs from Olivi's—or, in this case, from Joachim's—we will find his own explanation less helpful than we might have hoped. He rejects Joachim on two grounds. First, in equating Christ's promise of the spirit with a third age of the Holy Spirit, Joachim ignored the fact that the promise was fulfilled in Acts 1. Second, there can be no state more perfect than that of Christ's new, evangelical law, which will endure to the end of time. Both of these objections refute views held neither by Joachim nor by Olivi. They both had heard about Pentecost and both saw the third age as unfolding within the Christian era.

The real distinction between Henry's view and Olivi's is that in Henry's, the Spirit is leading the church to greater knowledge under the guidance of the ecclesiastical hierarchy, while in Olivi's it is not—at least in the present crisis. Olivi accepts that the transformation will be opposed by a carnal element that will capture the highest offices in the church, including the papacy, and will persecute the elect. The commission that censured Olivi's commentary saw that much quite clearly and reacted as one might expect.

Moreover, on the question of obedience—and we have seen that this was a vital question for all participants—there was little misunderstanding. The view attacked by John XXII, Michel Le Moine, and the 1318–19 Olivi commission was in fact the one sustained by Olivi in his Apocalypse commentary and elsewhere.[37] Here, we encounter an issue growing not only from Olivi's apocalyptic thought but also from his writings on poverty: Olivi felt that even the pope could not abrogate evangelical vows, and if he tried to do so, he should not be obeyed. This meant that the vow of poverty was inviolable, and Olivi argued that the vow of poverty included an obligation to observe *usus pauper*. It takes little imagination to see where this line of argument led. The Olivian apocalyptic scenario added assurance that a papal attack on *usus pauper* was certainly coming and supporters of Franciscan poverty should be ready for it. They should be ready to suffer for their principles. The scenario also provided reassurance that one's disobedience and consequent punishment, far from being an unexpected and perplexing turn of events, was in accordance with a pattern already predicted by John the Divine in the first century, a pattern that would end in heavenly reward for the oppressed and ultimate earthly victory for their cause. For these reasons, Olivi did in fact offer a clear and coherent rationale for spiritual Franciscan recalcitrance, and thus it is hardly surprising that when the spirituals went to trial, Olivi was named as a co-conspirator.

One might expect the commission report to have led to an immediate papal condemnation, but it did not. By that time, though, as we have seen, the Franciscan general chapter meeting of 1319 had condemned a series of errors from the Apocalypse, and another side of the problem also had received attention. Sometime in 1318, the Olivi cult at Narbonne suffered a rude shock when his body was removed and disposed of so discreetly that we still do not know what was done with it. Bernard Gui says that it was hidden away elsewhere, "and there are various opinions as to where it is now located."[38] Gui is certainly correct about the various opinions. Angelo Clareno informs us that they dug up Olivi's remains and burned them.[39] Nicholas Eymerich provides two choices.[40] Some say the body was burned, presumably at Narbonne, along with all the wax images and clothing left at his tomb by the faithful; others claim that it was taken to Avignon and tossed into the Rhône in the dark of night.

SOUTHERN FRANCE
Four Case Histories

BY THE END OF 1318, the spirituals' situation had changed dramatically. The pope had decided, and he had done so in a way that made further resistance equivalent to heresy. Since this turn of events meant triumph for the community and defeat for the spirituals, one might consider it the end of our story. Few stories ever end completely, though. The community soon discovered that its victory bore a huge price tag, and the spirituals found themselves presented with more options than simple capitulation to their superiors.

Spirituals, Beguins, and Inquisitors

We begin with the aftermath in southern France. Here, the task of dealing with recalcitrant spirituals had fallen into the hands of inquisitors, and it is mainly from inquisitorial documents that we gain a picture of what happened next. By the time Michel Le Moine had berated and then burned the four hold-outs at Marseilles, the others had returned to obedience. In time, though, some of the latter began to rethink their options, and for a variety of reasons. We can infer from comments in later inquisitorial processes that some felt pangs of conscience; that the superiors to whom they returned could be vindictive; and that some continued to keep an anxious eye on Michel Le Moine. Michel, they feared, had not forgotten them (and in fact he had not). Eventually a number of French spirituals followed the example already offered by their Tuscan brethren and continued their defiance as fugitives. By the end of 1319, we find Michel Le Moine writing to the inquisitor of Tuscany with the announcement that certain of the friars who had abjured at Avignon had since returned to their error and were at large.[1] Better yet, we have an earlier report of the farewell note some of them left behind.[2] They announce that they are leaving "not the order but the walls; not the habit but the cloth; not the faith but its shell; not the church but the blind synagogue; not a shepherd but a devourer." They predict that after John's death "we and our companions who are now suffering persecution by Christ's adversaries will come forth and bear away the victory." It seems that the inquisitors still had a great deal to do.

Once they found themselves at large, these escapees would have had little chance of survival if they had not been supported. The close ties between French spirituals and the urban laity already had born fruit in the support that cities such as Narbonne and Béziers had given the spirituals against their leaders prior to and immediately after John XXII's election.[3] Raymond Barrau, writing two decades later, claims that the bishop, the cathedral chapter—in fact, the whole city of Béziers—backed the spirituals.[4] In Narbonne, as late as February 1317 the consuls of the bourg publicly affirmed their solidarity with their local Franciscans, emphasizing that they went to their church regularly to hear masses and pray for those family members who were buried there.[5]

Once John had clarified his stand, residents of those cities had to make hard choices. The sort of open, corporate support once given the spirituals no longer seemed possible. Nevertheless, inquisitorial records suggest that a surprising number of townspeople continued to aid the fugitive friars by hiding them and attempting to transport them out of France. Soon the protectors too became targets. On October 14, 1319, three lay supporters were burned at the stake in Narbonne.[6] More would follow as the investigations spread across a good deal of Languedoc and down into Catalonia.

We encounter these remarkable people under the worst possible conditions. They are under examination, and their interrogators include some of the most famous inquisitors of the period. One is Bernard Gui, well known to readers of Umberto Eco's *The Name of the Rose*. Gui's *Practica inquisitionis*, a manual for inquisitors, includes a very full section on this group. In at least one series of investigations, Gui is assisted by Jacques Fournier, bishop of Pamiers and future Pope Benedict XII, whose investigations into heretical activity in his own diocese provided the raw material for Emmanuel Le Roy Ladurie's *Montaillou*, one of the few serious historical studies to become a best-seller.

The interrogators want what interrogators always want in such situations. They could be FBI agents tracking down a ring of domestic terrorists or CIA agents trying to unravel an international espionage system. They want confessions, but they want a great deal more. They need information. The defendant knows that little is gained by simply implicating oneself. Genuine confession involves genuine contrition and cooperation, which entails naming names. Thus we find the defendants doing what defendants normally do. They provide the requisite information but try to limit disclosure as much as possible, preferably mentioning only those people they think are already known. As for themselves, they readily admit to less serious actions and to actions about which they assume the inquisitor already has heard, but they are less forthcoming about other matters.

Historians normally refer to this group as "the beguins." So did the inquisitors, and so will we, though with reservations. The beguins as presented in Bernard Gui's manual for inquisitors are a more homogeneous body than extant inquisitorial processes actually suggest, a matter to which we will return in the next chapter.[7] We will ignore the Catalan beguins[8] and concentrate on southern France, where lay response to the pope's action is dramatically indicated in a series of inquisitorial processes stretching from 1319 into the 1330s. We will begin by exploring four case histories—those of a spiritual Franciscan and three beguins—in order to get the flavor of the investigations. Then in the next chapter, we will proceed to some general observations.

Raymond Déjean

Raymond is important, because he provides us with a vivid picture of what life after Avignon could mean for a spiritual Franciscan. He was born in Montréal and probably entered the order around 1292.[9] Thus he was a Franciscan well before Olivi's death and could easily have known him. In fact, his name (Raymundus Iohannis, which we could just as easily render as "Raymond Jean")[10] allows us to believe that he may have been a relative, though perhaps not a close one. Before the spirituals seized control of the Béziers and Narbonne convents, he was apparently at Carcassonne, but was one of those who gravitated to Narbonne thereafter.[11]

He was one of the approximately sixty-two brothers summoned to Avignon in April 1317, and one of those who conformed to papal orders in October.[12] In time, he was sent to the Franciscan house at Anduze. The transfer to such a remote house was hardly unusual. Relocation of the former rebels was so common that inquisitorial processes almost reflexively speak of the spirituals summoned to Avignon as "those friars who had been given a penance by the inquisitor at Marseilles, then sent to various places."[13] One process neatly encapsulates their history by speaking of "those spirituals who wore short habits and appealed to the Roman curia and later were given penances by the inquisitor at Marseilles and sent to remote houses."[14]

Raymond stayed at his new house "for a while," but eventually escaped with another friar when he received a letter citing him to appear before Michel Le Moine at Marseilles.[15] That Raymond, who seems to have cooperated at Avignon, should receive such a letter is less odd than one might imagine. The decision elicited by John from the thirteen scholars in 1318 was broad enough to make people in Raymond's position suspect for what they already had said. Note that the processes just mentioned speak even of the brothers who capitulated at Avignon as having "received a penance from the inquisitor at Marseilles," and these are hardly the only processes to speak of them as having been so treated.[16]

Raymond went to Béziers and stayed hidden in a home there for over three years. Then—probably after a brief stay in Toulouse—he went to Sauvian, just outside Béziers. At Sauvian he probably stayed with a relative: Olivi's niece, Alarassis Biasse, of whom we will hear more in a moment. If we are right in assuming that he is the friar Alarassis describes as related to her, then he probably left Sauvian with other renegade friars. Some of them went all the way to Sicily, but two—one of them apparently Raymond—turned back at Majorca and returned to Sauvian.[17] From there he sent a message to his nephew (also named Raymond Déjean) in Montréal. The nephew came and, once Friar Raymond was provided with secular clothing, took him to Montréal. When Raymond left there, the nephew accompanied him as far as Ginestas. Later, hearing that he was at Narbonne, the nephew went and brought him back to Montréal where he stayed for a year, living with the nephew and others; then, when he left again, the nephew accompanied him to his next stop. Later the nephew visited Raymond at Narbonne.[18]

During his period of wandering, Raymond also spent time at Carcassonne, Cintegabelle, and Montpellier,[19] and made yet another trip outside France— this time all the way to Sicily and then back to Montpellier.[20] He must have left Montpellier soon after, shortly before the beguins there were arrested. Jean Orlach, a resident of the town, accompanied him to his next destination.[21] Eventually Raymond moved on yet again, this time into Gascony. Orlach was eventually arrested, asked about Raymond's location, and finally revealed it.[22] Once he did so, Raymond was captured and brought to the inquisitorial prison at Carcassonne.

Raymond's confession is dated October 1325, but certain passages seem to be from a later date. It was some time before he was willing to tell the inquisitor everything the latter wanted to hear, but eventually he surrendered on all issues. On some matters he retreated gradually, but he did retreat. On November 11, 1328, he completely abjured his heresy. Among the twelve sentenced to prison that day, four—whose crimes deserved special punishment—were singled out. One of them was Raymond, and he was then in turn named as rating special punishment even among those four. Stripped of ecclesiastical orders, he was assigned to the worst part of the prison, where he was to be kept in irons.[23]

If we ask why Raymond was considered exceptional, the answer is partly that he was the only apostate Franciscan sentenced that day,[24] but there is more to it than that. Raymond was considered a heresiarch, and he was one of the people the inquisition most wanted to capture. If we had only his own process, we would not find it easy to see why they thought him so dangerous. The man who appears there is aging (certainly no younger than his early forties, more likely in his fifties) and worn down by years as a fugitive followed by time in the inquisitorial prison. We can only guess what had been done to him.

In any case, in his confession, Raymond is remarkably subdued. He is ready to acquiesce on some of the most fundamental issues in the poverty controversy, such as the pope's right to grant the Franciscans granaries and wine cellars. He denies ever totally accepting that the executed spirituals and beguins were holy martyrs, a belief that was common currency among the beguins. He even acknowledges the pope's right to give the Franciscan order common possessions, and he is willing to agree with the pope's assertion that Christ and the apostles had possessions. On these last two issues he is surrendering ground that even leaders of the order were still defending against the pope in the 1320s, as we will see; yet Raymond denies, not only that he questions papal authority on such matters, but also that he ever questioned it.

There are moments in the process when Raymond seems to take a stand. For example,

> he said he already had heard that Bernard Léon of Montréal had been condemned and burned because he said if the lord pope gave him, who had vowed chastity, a wife, or wished to make him, who had vowed poverty, a canon at Carcassonne and give him a regular

clerical income, he did not know if the pope could do that and he would not obey. If, [Raymond] said, Bernard Léon was condemned for this and nothing else—and he had no doubt that Bernard was in fact condemned for the aforesaid—then he believed Bernard was saved and in Paradise because, as he said, [the pope] cannot make a man who has vowed chastity take a wife or make a man who has vowed poverty accept a regular clerical income.[25]

Here Raymond is defending the notion of vows as inviolable and thus placing himself in the great tradition running through Hugh of Digne,[26] Olivi, the twenty-five friars who refused to submit at Avignon, and the four finally burned at Marseilles. In fact, we have seen that the question of whether the pope could dispense from such vows was a subject for debate among thirteenth-century theologians, and not all of them decided that he could.[27] Nevertheless, Raymond himself had submitted on this matter at Avignon, and he eventually submitted at Carcassonne. "Finally, though, he said that he is ready to believe what the supreme pontiff says on this matter and whatever the latter has said should be accepted."

Raymond's apocalyptic views are equally subdued in the confession. He acknowledges that he "once read to a certain person whom he names, and later to another person, from Petrus Iohannis's Apocalypse commentary, that the church was adulterous. He believed that, he said, particularly because of its simony. It was not entirely such, but only a part of it." That much was dangerous, but not necessarily very dangerous. It depended on which part of the church he had in mind. Three more allusions to the commentary come close to providing an answer. "Again, he read to many people (whom he names) from the commentary that someone would be like Herod who persecuted the children. He sometimes thought this would be . . ." Here the passage breaks off. A second passage says, "Again, he read to other people (whom he names) this line from the commentary: 'The wild boar from the forest lays it waste, and the beasts of the field feed upon it' [Ps. 80:14]. And he was somewhat of the opinion that this one was the boar, and he would have believed this firmly had evidence not shown him that the contrary was true, for example maintenance of divine worship, attention to justice, love of honor and other things which are evident, as he said." And a third passage says,

> Again, when he was reading the aforesaid commentary and was asked by a certain person listening to him who that mystical Antichrist was, he replied that it was he who did good and bad at the same time. In

reality he does not believe he knows; yet he said that it was . . . [again something seems to be omitted], because, as he said, he had read long ago in a theological work that the mystical Antichrist would provide the Friars Minor with regular income. It was perhaps this that prevented him from believing [that this person was the mystical Antichrist], because this person took such away in doing as he did concerning the Clementine decretal, for he took away their procurators and humiliated them.

Raymond seems to be admitting that he accepted Olivian apocalyptic speculation and applied it to John XXII. In each case the precise identification is missing,[28] but it is hard to imagine that he had anyone else in mind. These were beguin commonplaces. Comparison of John with Herod, for example, is also found in Bernard Gui's description of the beguins and in Na Prous Boneta's confession.[29] Identification of John as the mystical Antichrist was even more common.[30] Raymond never quite says that he believed these things, though. He simply says that he considered the possibility, but ruled it out when he considered John's positive accomplishments.[31]

We find the same hesitation to admit strong convictions in Raymond's explanation of why he left Anduze and became a fugitive. He says he did so not to defend a principle, but because he feared persecution. "Again, he said he did not consider himself to be excommunicated or irregular or apostate from his order because, as he said, he did not leave his order with the intention of apostatizing, transgressing his vow and rule, or forsaking his obedience, but only with the intention of fleeing the malice of his ministers, of his order, and of the inquisitor at Marseilles."[32]

Thus the confession gives us, at best, a muted sense of Raymond's career as a heresiarch. To improve upon it, we must look at the confessions of all those beguins who came into contact with him during the years when he was on the run. His period at Montréal is illuminated by a series of such reminiscences, and we can assemble them into a picture of his life there. Jacquelline Sobiran—whom Raymond had entrusted with his clothing when he left for the papal court—says that she visited him at Montréal.[33] Another defendant, Flours, in a confession dated March 1325, says that she saw Raymond there in the home of her father, Pierre Baron, and often ate with him.[34] Five other women, all testifying in 1325, say that they too visited Raymond at Pierre's home.[35] They brought him food and money. Flours and three others say that they confessed to him. Thus he was more than a fugitive; he was conducting a ministry, and it included the sacraments. Pierre Montlaur, testifying in 1326, tells us that he heard mass from Raymond at Narbonne, and we know from Raymond's own confession that "he commonly celebrated mass and engaged in the care of souls in Gascony."[36] Presumably he did so at Montréal, too.

He also taught, if only through informal conversation. Some beguins are quite specific in their recollection of things he told them.[37] Their testimony, too, is muted. They knew that it was dangerous to admit having heard, let alone believed, too much, and were often anxious to distance themselves from Raymond as much as possible in retrospect;[38] yet the total impression given by their testimony is anything but muted. Raymond was a man they liked, trusted, and risked their lives to protect.

One of the most significant anecdotes about Raymond comes from a priest named Mathieu who was sentenced on November 11, 1328, the same day as Raymond. He recalls hearing Raymond preach a public sermon at Montréal seven years earlier. In it, Raymond described persecutions of the faith continuing down to the present. After the sermon, Mathieu asked Raymond what he had meant when he said in the sermon that he, Raymond, would suffer for the faith. He was not, after all, going overseas among enemies of the faith. Raymond replied to him and others that "enemies of the faith are among us, for the church by which we are ruled is what is signified by the great whore of which John speaks in the Apocalypse, and it persecutes Christ's ministers and the poor. Can you not see that we do not dare to appear openly before our own brothers? Later Brother Raymond Déjean said that there had been no true pope in the Roman Church since Celestine."[39]

Here we find a remarkably strong indictment of the church in the Olivian tradition and, more surprising, the view of Celestine's successors vigorously attacked by Olivi in his 1295 letter to Conrad of Offida. If Mathieu is remembering correctly, Raymond was focusing Olivi's apocalyptic on the present situation and announcing that what Olivi predicted was now occurring. Nevertheless, he was going well beyond Olivi, combining him with completely different influences that directly contradicted him. Olivi, after all, had put some effort into arguing that Celestine's resignation was valid and that Boniface VIII was a legitimate pope.

The most interesting question, though, is *when* Raymond said all this. We know from his process that the friars summoned to Avignon in April 1317 were held there until October, when they were asked what they thought of *Quorumdam exigit*. Raymond accepted it and was eventually sent to Anduze, where he remained "for a while." He left when he received the summons from Michel Le Moine and he went to Béziers, where he was in hiding "for more than three years." Vague as these indications may be, they make it hard to imagine Raymond leaving Anduze before the end of 1317, and adding "more than three years" suggests that Raymond's heretical mission in secular garb cannot have begun before early 1321. The testimony of Raymond's nephew complicates the story to some extent, suggesting that the Béziers stay may have ended as early as 1320. But these are minor details. The important thing is that Raymond was probably either at Anduze or in hiding between late 1317 and around 1320.[40]

Mathieu says he had heard the sermon seven years earlier. Earlier than what, though? Mathieu and Raymond were part a group sentenced on November 11, 1328. Mathieu's confession is dated *anno domini millesimo trecentesimo vicesimo*, but the evidence strongly suggests that the notary left off the final number and that he was actually interrogated in late 1325 or early 1326.[41] If so, then in recounting something that occurred "seven years ago," he was speaking of an event that took place around 1318 or 1319. If we are to make his testimony fit with Raymond's movements, however, we must assume that he heard Raymond preach either slightly earlier than that—i.e., just before the summons of April 1317—or slightly later, i.e., shortly after Raymond's nephew brought his uncle from Sauvian to Montréal. Raymond's comment that he cannot appear openly before his brothers seems to suggest the latter, and the sermon did, after all, take place in Montréal, a city where he spent some time after leaving Anduze; but if Raymond was a fugitive fresh from three years in hiding, it seems odd that Mathieu would have heard him preach a public sermon. Moreover, he is described as "then of the Friars Minor," suggesting a contrast with what he had become, an apostate. Thus there is much to be said for placing the sermon before April 1317.[42]

If so, then the anecdote provides us with some explanation of how the beguins were able to change from apparently loyal churchmen into rebels from 1318 on. Even before the spirituals were summoned to Avignon, some of them already had a good idea of what would happen to them and, in sermons to the laity, applied Olivi's apocalyptic speculation to their situation in such a way that their hearers were encouraged to expect the worst of present ecclesiastical leadership.

Pierre Tort

This suggestion receives striking confirmation from another process, that of Pierre Tort. Pierre's confession is dated May with no year given, but it was probably 1322.[43] The son of a cutler from Montréal, Pierre was a third-order

Franciscan. His confession says little about his activities as a heretic but much about what he believed. Concerning the former, we merely learn that he harbored fugitive spiritual Franciscans and beguins in his home. Other processes shed light on his capture, which occurred in Cintegabelle. After being arrested and imprisoned, he refused to cooperate for a few days, but finally confessed and was sentenced to perpetual imprisonment.[44]

Pierre provided a huge list of ideas he once accepted. These included the convictions that neither Christ, nor his apostles, nor the Franciscans owned anything, either privately or in common; that the Franciscan rule was evangelical; that it was the only rule that could be considered entirely such, since the others, by allowing common possessions, observed something less than the evangelical standard of poverty; and that the pope could not alter the rule any more than he could alter the gospel, nor could he order the friars to violate their vows.

Pierre granted that he had accepted the pope's right to dispense friars from their duty to wear the customary Franciscan habit, but in a remarkably limited context.

> If some Friar Minor, through the malice of his leaders or through some defect in himself, could not remain peacefully and quietly among the Friars Minor, the lord pope could give him dispensation to transfer to some other order, in such a way however that even though he was in the other order he still observed the vow he promised according to the rule of Saint Francis, and still had nothing either privately or in common, and he should not obey his new leaders if they ordered him to act contrary to that vow. Thus according to his habit he would be a monk of that other order, but in his heart he would still be a Friar Minor.

Here Pierre echoes a common theme among beguins, many of whom were apparently distressed by the transfer of spirituals like Ubertino da Casale and Angelo Clareno to other orders.

Pierre also revisited the long-standing controversy over Franciscan bishops. He admitted having believed

> that a Friar Minor who had been made a bishop should not feel he had any right to whatever mobile or immobile goods of his church were normally claimed by the bishop. He should regard these goods as if they had nothing whatsoever to do with him, but were com-

pletely extraneous, although he could use them for his own necessities. He should commit the care and regime of temporal goods and incomes to someone else and devote himself to prayer, contemplation, preaching and the administration of the sacraments.

Like many beguins, Pierre considered the four friars burned at Marseilles to be holy martyrs and the inquisitors to be the real heretics. So were those who consented to the executions. That obviously raised the question of what he thought about the pope. Here Pierre was cautious. He made it clear that he had thought the pope wrong in ordering the spirituals of Narbonne and Béziers to submit to their superiors, "because, as he said, he turned them over before they had a chance to state their case before him." Nevertheless, he was substantially less comfortable about including John in his heresy charge.

> He said he had believed that if the present lord pope consented to or welcomed the condemnation of the four Friars Minor by the inquisitor, he himself became a heretic, because he acted against the gospel of Christ and condemned the life of Christ; but—so he said— he did not believe the lord pope knew the truth about why the inquisitor condemned these friars as heretics. He suspected that the inquisitor mendaciously informed the pope of errors the friars had never held or confessed to holding. Thus he did not believe the lord pope had lost his papal authority, or that he should not be obeyed.

Here he was being much kinder toward John than any number of other beguins, who had no trouble at all identifying him as a chief instigator of the executions and equally little trouble believing that he had thereby lost his pontifical authority. (We will see, though, that Pierre himself eventually acknowledged believing something even worse about John.)

However sure he had been about the four friars, Pierre was more measured in his attitude toward subsequent executed beguins.

> He said he had believed that those beguins who were condemned as heretics in two sermons at Béziers and burned—beguins he himself heard judged and saw burned—died faithful catholics, and he considered them glorious martyrs. Nevertheless, concerning those beguins who were first burned at Narbonne, and those burned at Capestang and Lunel, he was in doubt as to whether they were saved or not, and whether they were martyrs or not, because he was not present when

they were condemned and burned, nor did he know with any certitude concerning which articles they were condemned, although he did know that they were condemned as heretics by the prelates and by the inquisitor at Carcassonne. He believed that those who were condemned at Pézenas and those condemned the last time at Narbonne died as genuine heretics, though, because the former did not suffer their persecution patiently but said a great many injurious things to the lord bishops and inquisitor, while the latter refused to swear.

One of the most striking things about this statement is the role Pierre assigned to his own experience and judgment. We will return to this matter later. For the moment, we should note that Pierre expected those who had died unjustly to be vindicated in the near future. "Concerning the others, however, whom he thought had died as faithful catholics and glorious martyrs, he believed that once the carnal church was destroyed—which it would be in a short time—the spiritual church to reign after its destruction would recognize that those Friars Minor and beguins had been condemned unjustly by the carnal church, consider them glorious martyrs, and accord them a feast day just as there is now a feast of the martyrs of Christ."

Here again, Pierre had to face the problem of how to regard those who consented to the executions.

He said he had believed that the inquisitor at Carcassonne and all the prelates who had condemned those beguins as heretics had become heretics themselves on that account, but he did not believe that the prelates thereby lost the power to loose and bind or confer orders. Again, all the prelates and others—secular clerics, religious and laity alike—who knew what these beguins believed, especially those articles for which they were condemned, and did not believe these articles represented the truth were heretics outside the church of God, members of the carnal church. Those who believed what the condemned beguins believed were faithful catholics and within the church of God. As for simple folk who neither believed nor disbelieved these articles but would believe them if informed concerning them and the beguin faith, he thought they were faithful catholics and were not outside the church of God.

Once again Pierre spared the pope, this time by simple omission, but the total effect of his statement is striking. It sets up a clear demarcation between sheep and goats based on one's attitude toward these executions.

Pierre had much to say about Olivi and his orthodoxy. He reported to the inquisitor that "he had heard someone named in his confession preach a public sermon at Narbonne in which he said the whole doctrine of Petrus Iohannis Olivi and all his writings were good, faithful and catholic, and at the Council of Vienne they and his own person had been excused from all error and praised, except for five doubtful articles which the pope reserved to himself, although even these five he did not declare erroneous." This allusion to Vienne, far from being unique, was repeated in a series of beguin testimonies, although with variations. Some simply stated that Olivi's writings had been approved as holy and orthodox at Vienne; others deduced from this that those who condemned Olivi were themselves guilty of heresy; and still others acknowledged that, while most of Olivi's thought had been approved, some of it had not. Of the latter group, some spoke of three articles, some of five, and some merely rounded it off at "a few."[45]

Pierre offers a ringing endorsement, not only of Olivi's apocalyptic scenario, but also of Olivi himself as an apocalyptic figure.

> He also said he had heard in sermons by Friars Minor at Narbonne during the feast of Friar Petrus Iohannis that his doctrine and writings were more necessary to the church of this final time than those of any other holy doctor except the apostles and evangelists, because, as he said, more had been revealed to Friar Petrus Iohannis than to any other holy doctor about what would happen toward the end of the world. The whole world would be in darkness and ignorance of the truth, especially regarding this modern age, were it not for Friar Petrus Iohannis and his writings. They considered him to be on a par with Augustine, Jerome, Gregory and Ambrose.

What Pierre heard from spiritual Franciscans in sermons and conversation was supplemented by what he himself read. He was one of the few beguins who seems to have been literate, or at least one of the few who spoke of having read things as well as having heard them read. His reading included a narrative of Olivi's death also cited by Bernard Gui. Gui says the beguins "frequently and willingly read or have read to them" from "a certain small work entitled *The Passing of the Holy Father.*" According to this document, Olivi, on his deathbed, "after he had received holy unction and with the entire convent of Brothers Minor of Narbonne standing about, said all of his knowledge had been infused in him by God, and that in the church at Paris at the third hour he had suddenly been illumined by the Lord Jesus Christ."[46] Pierre's version is fuller. He reports that "just before he died Olivi called the friars minor together and told them that while he was in Paris, at the moment when he was washing his hands to administer the eucharist to a certain priest, the entire truth concerning the gospel and Christ's life was revealed to him, and that all his writings were true and had been revealed to him, and that he had put nothing in his writings on his own, but had written only what had been revealed to him by God."[47]

Pierre's reading also included Olivi's own writings translated into the vernacular, particularly the Apocalypse commentary, which he said he read frequently. Here the problems begin, though. On one occasion he mentions having read that Olivi "was that angel of whom it is said in the Apocalypse that his face was like the sun, and he had an open book in his hand, because he clearly had knowledge of the truth." We have seen that this identification, while not traceable to Olivi himself, was accepted by some of his followers even before Vienne, and was incorporated into the Catalan apocalyptic work condemned by Guido Terreni and Pierre de Palu in 1318 or 1319 (a writing that consisted mostly of Olivi's Apocalypse commentary, but with additions like this one). Thus we have reason to wonder if what Pierre read was Olivi's commentary in its pristine state or something like the Catalan work. Other comments by Pierre raise the same question.

Part of the problem is that Pierre often combines what he heard with what he read in such a way as to leave us uncertain which of the two he is drawing from in stating a particular belief. For example, he notes that, "informed by others and by the writings of Friar Petrus Iohannis, he had believed the Preaching Friars were pharisees." Olivi never explicitly said that, but perhaps those "others" did. Elsewhere Pierre observes that he

> believed for two years something he had heard from certain apostates and fugitives of the Order of Friars Minor and from certain beguin associates whom he names, and which he himself had read in the books of the aforesaid Petrus Iohannis translated into the vernacular, namely that the Roman Church as far as the reprobates within it was Babylon the great whore, of which it is said in the Apocalypse that she had a gold chalice in her hand filled with abominations and was drunk with the blood of the martyrs of Jesus Christ, taking the Roman Church to mean the church which is in Rome and also diffused throughout the world as far as the Roman Empire extended. It was the great whore, according to them, because it involved itself in carnal delights, pride, luxury, cupidity and simony. It was called "Babylon" because of its great power, and because it sinned confusedly and all

things were confused in it. It was said to be drunk with the blood of the martyrs of Jesus Christ because it persecuted those who maintained the poverty and life of Jesus Christ, and killed them. This Roman Church would be destroyed and rejected in this time, they said, through the ten kings, some of whom he names.

The passage goes on to identify John XXII with the mystical Antichrist and predict that the great Antichrist will arrive while John is still reigning. There will be two popes for a while. The great Antichrist, he says, "will be an apostate from the Order of Friars Minor, because it is the highest state in the church, as they say. They say it will be Friar Angelo, who is an apostate from the order. Others say the Lord Philip of Majorca is Antichrist. Many of them say Frederick the King of Sicily will be emperor and persecute the Roman Church, causing the Antichrist to be adored by all. Some of them say the Antichrist will finish his career within three years, others say within thirteen." This scenario reflects Olivi in one way (the Antichrist as an apostate Franciscan); expands him in another (the application of that general prediction to a specific Franciscan, Angelo); and straightforwardly contradicts him in still others (the two Antichrists as concurrent, and the king who aids the great Antichrist as arising from within the Christian realm, instead of being from Islam, as Olivi implies). Yet Pierre rounds off this prediction by noting that he believed all this "informed by the aforementioned apostates and beguins and by Petrus Iohannis' commentary on the Apocalypse."

In short, even the literate Pierre was far more reliant on what he heard than on what he read, and it is not at all clear what sort of thing he read. As for what he heard, we might ask in what context he heard it. The priest Mathieu cites both a sermon he heard Raymond Déjean preach and a lengthy conversation they had while traveling together. Pierre, too, seems to have absorbed his beliefs in both conversational and sermonic form. He draws our attention especially to sermons delivered at Narbonne on Olivi's feast day. On that day, he heard a friar say that the poverty prescribed by the rule had been hidden from those in the community, even though Olivi had made it clearly evident; that the pope could not relax the demands made by the rule; and that if he attempted to do so he should not be obeyed. Pierre provides the reasoning behind this claim, and it is straight out of Olivi's *Questions on Evangelical Perfection*.

Pierre does not date these sermons, but it seems likely that they were delivered no later than March 14, 1317, the last Olivi feast day before the call to Avignon. He says that he has believed many of these things for five years, which seems to mean since 1317. Moreover, the whole scene—spiritual Franciscans preaching public sermons at Narbonne on Olivi's feast day in which they warn the laity that in the approaching hour of trial, they must observe their vows, even in the face of papal commands to the contrary—seems to fit the period between the time the house was forcibly taken over by the spirituals and that last feast day in 1317. In succeeding years, after Olivi's tomb at Narbonne had been destroyed and John had transformed the spirituals from dissidents into heretics, one is hard pressed to imagine too many defiant public sermons being preached by spirituals at Narbonne on March 14, although Olivi's feast continued to be celebrated in private.[48]

Others heard similar sermons. Marie de Serra says that she heard a sermon at Narbonne on Olivi's feast day in which she was told that Olivi was an uncanonized saint. It was not important whether he was canonized by humans, because God had canonized him.[49] Marie, Pierre, and others confront us with the picture of an embattled spiritual group at Narbonne applying Olivi to their current situation in a way that radicalized his message—not only by applying his general predictions to specific people and events, but also by mixing in elements that were not Olivian at all. Thus Pierre Tort heard from the Narbonne spirituals something they said had been revealed to Saint Francis, namely that the order would be divided into three parts. Two of them, the community and the Tuscan rebels in Sicily under Enrico da Ceva, did not observe the rule and would be destroyed, while the third, the spiritual Franciscans and beguins, would survive their many persecutions and endure until the end of the world. All of this had been revealed to Saint Francis.[50] Here the matter is confused by Pierre's failure to designate this assertion explicitly as one of the ideas he encountered five years earlier, but whenever he heard it, we can be sure it did not come from Olivi.

Alarassis Biasse

Alarassis Biasse's testimony tells us little about beguin doctrine and much about beguin commitments.[51] Olivi's niece, she lived in Sauvian, five miles from Béziers and a short walk from Sérignan, Olivi's birthplace. Her testimony was probably given in 1325,[52] yet it deals with events that occurred "four years and more" earlier.

Alarassis confesses that she received into her home two friars who said they had been sent to far-off houses by their superiors, but had opened the sealed letters they carried with them and discovered that they were to be imprisoned once they arrived. These fugitive friars reported that six of them had been hiding in Toulouse. One of the two who arrived at Alarassis's door was a relative, and we have seen that it may have been Raymond. These two stayed from Easter into June, cared for by Alarassis and her mother. During that time two more of the six appeared. Alarassis gave them cloth for secular garments, and eventually the more recent two returned to Toulouse.

One day, two men appeared at Alarassis's door and she gave them something to drink. They announced that they had come from Sicily in search of fugitive spirituals, hoping to transport them there. Uncertain whether she could trust these purported rescuers enough to tell them about the two friars currently hiding in her attic, she went to Narbonne and sought the advice of Pierre Trencavel, a beguin leader. He reassured her, and she informed the two renegades that their hour of deliverance was at hand. Fifteen days later the two men from Sicily returned with a boat, she produced her two guests, four other friars appeared, and the entire group left for Majorca. Once they had arrived there, two of the friars returned and reported the outcome to Alarassis.

The latter admits having received many beguins into her home and here, as with all the apostate spirituals mentioned so far, the record duly notes that she has identified them by name. She also reports having heard Pierre Trencavel say on occasion that the friars burned at Marseilles were condemned unjustly and should be considered holy martyrs. She heard one of the fugitives say that they believed the same thing. When asked by her interrogators if she herself believed it, she replies—and here we begin to wonder if Alarassis is not only shrewd but also given to irony—that it is women's nature to believe anything new when it is first presented to them. Asked how long she believed it, she apparently senses danger and replies that she does not remember. She does report that she eventually became uncertain about the matter and confessed her doubt to the rector at Sauvian. He told her that Christ had given his power to Saint Peter, that whatever the latter bound on earth would be bound in heaven, and that if the pope had condemned the friars, he must have done so justly. From that point she abandoned any doubt on the matter.

As seems almost inevitable, Alarassis is asked what she thinks of her uncle. Here again she becomes cautious. She says she believes what the church decides or will decide. The answer is more evasive than modern readers might imagine. Her allusion to a future decision by the church seems to ignore the decisions already made in this area and, as Bernard Gui notes, when heretics pledge their loyalty to the church it is always wise to wonder which church they have in mind.[53] The record closes with the observation that she is confessing events that occurred four years or more earlier and made no effort to denounce the spirituals and beguins named here to the authorities until she herself was arrested and imprisoned at Carcassonne. Nevertheless, "she says she repents."

Alarassis's case presents a strong contrast to Raymond's and Pierre's. She was hardly a heresiarch like Raymond; neither, probably, was she an avid listener and reader like Pierre. She was essentially an operative. She managed one station in an escape route. One wonders how many people really passed through it.

Alarassis was among a series of heretics sentenced on March 1, 1327, at Carcassonne. She is included among those sentenced to imprisonment.[54] Nevertheless, another sentence delivered on November 11, 1328, begins with a list of people who are to be released from prison and given the lighter penance of going on pilgrimages and wearing crosses. One of the names on this list is "Aladayci Biassa de Saluiaco,"[55] which one can assume is our Alarassis. The new arrangement, though substantially better than prison, was still rigorous. It included wearing crosses sewn on her clothes front and rear, inside and outside the home; going on pilgrimage at least once to each of a long list of churches in France, Spain, Italy, and England; going to her cathedral church every year for the major feast day; confessing to her own parish priest three times per year, namely before Easter, Pentecost, and Christmas; taking communion at these feasts unless told to abstain by the priest; attending mass on Sundays and feast days; presenting herself to the priest at these masses with rods in hand for discipline; following processions with rods in hand to receive discipline at the final stop; and aiding in the pursuit of heretics or their supporters.

Na Prous Boneta

On August 6, 1325, Na Prous Boneta gave her testimony at Carcassonne. A resident of Montpellier, she had been arrested along with her sister Alisseta and another woman, Alisseta (or Alarassis), who lived with them. They had been hiding fugitive spiritual Franciscans and beguins in their home, Raymond Déjean among them. Her testimony is strikingly different from any of the three we have seen so far—in fact, from any in the entire corpus of beguin processes. Prous distinguished herself by the extremity of her views and by the openness with which she espoused them. When she finished, the inquisitors could have no doubt that they were speaking with a heretic, and an unrepentant one at that. Her claims were so bold that one might have expected the fires to be kindled immediately. Nevertheless, only three years later was she finally handed over to the secular authorities (three years in which, according to the inquisitor who sentenced her, she was continually shown the error of her ways but refused to acknowledge it).[56]

Prous tells the inquisitor that she made a vow of virginity around 1305 and nine months later was at Narbonne for Olivi's feast day. Christ later informed her that on the day she vowed virginity she had been conceived in the spirit in a reprise of the immaculate conception, since all her sins had been forgiven, just as Mary's were in her mother's womb. On Olivi's feast day she had been born spiritually.[57]

The next major step in her development occurred around 1321, when she was attending mass in the Franciscan church at Montpellier on Good Friday. She was transported in the spirit to the first heaven and saw God's divinity. The experience continued and intensified the next day. In fact, it continued over several days. By the time it was over, Prous had received the entire Trinity in a unique way. Her special relationship was with the Holy Spirit, though. Just as the Virgin Mary was donatrix of the Son, she was designated donatrix of the Holy Spirit. Just as John the Baptist was herald of Christ's advent, she heralded the advent of the Holy Spirit.[58]

Prous provides us with an extreme version of the Olivi cult. Like Pierre Tort, she identifies him with the angel of Rev. 10:1, but that is only the beginning. Olivi's writing—Prous continually refers to his *scriptura*, which could refer to his entire corpus, although she seems to be thinking primarily of the Apocalypse commentary—was dictated by the Holy Spirit and must be believed if one is to be saved. Instead, it has been assaulted by the powers of evil, notably Thomas Aquinas and John XXII. Aquinas and Olivi are like Cain and Abel, for Aquinas spiritually slew his brother Olivi by attacking his writing.[59] John XXII too became a Cain, but also an Adam, a Caiaphas, a Simon Magus, and a Herod. Prous works these parallels out with some care. They all proceed from John's persecuting ways. By condemning Olivi, the spirituals, and the beguins, John abandoned the truth and became Antichrist. This brings us to Prous's most striking comparison. Just as the noblest name among angels was assigned to Lucibel, so the noblest name among men, "apostle" or "pope," was given to John; and just as, after his fall, the former received the most terrible name among all the demons, "Lucifer," so after John's fall Christ gave him the most terrible name among men, "Antichrist."

He received that name on the next-to-last Friday before the preceding Christmas, thus presumably on December 14, 1324.[60] Why then? Prous offers no explanation except that on this date God told her such was the case. Christ told her that John and everyone else had lost the grace of the sacraments. One might conclude from the way these two statements are run together that both messages were delivered on that fateful penultimate Friday before Christmas; but this may not be the case, since the next sentence in the process describes a completely different conversation with Christ that took place "on a certain feast of the purification of the Blessed Virgin." At that time she had intended to take communion, but Christ had advised her not to do so, because the sacraments did not confer salvation. The chronological uncertainty is intensified by two other passages in which Prous says that on the next feast of Christ's nativity, it will have been two years since the sacraments lost their power.[61] Thus it would seem to have occurred in December 1323. In one of these passages the loss is explicitly identified with the condemnation of Olivi's *scriptura*.

We see here three closely related events: the condemnation of Olivi's writing; John's fall from supreme pontiff to Antichrist; and the loss of sacramental power within the church. Prous periodically suggests that all three happened at the same time; yet in two places, she pictures the first and third events as occurring nearly two years earlier, while in another, she announces that the second event happened less than a year earlier. There is no obvious way that these statements can be reconciled, but good reason to wish we could do so, since the result would have some impact on our chronology of the process against Olivi's Apocalypse commentary. Previous scholarship on that subject has tended to leap from 1322, when John XXII announced that he was reserving final judgment on the matter for himself, to February 8, 1326, when according to Bernard Gui, the commentary was condemned in papal consistory.[62] Prous's confession suggests that there must have been an intermediate, relatively well-publicized step in December 1323 or 1324.

Some evidence seems to suggest that the significant date was really December 1323. If Prous received the revelation in 1324 and was captured in time to testify in August 1325, she would have had little time to disseminate it, but it seems to have been generally known. A beguin named Ermessende, an inhabitant of Gignac who testified in November 1325, says that while she was at Montpellier, she heard that Prous held a number of fatuous beliefs, including the notion that the sacraments no longer conferred grace.[63] Raymond Déjean, in his confession of October 1325, acknowledges having heard from Prous that the sacraments were no longer valid.[64] He probably received the news in Prous's home, since we know from Prous's sister, their friend, and Ermessende that Raymond stayed there,[65] though none provides a date.

We recall that Raymond left Montpellier with Jean Orlach, traveled about with him for a while, and then went to Gascony, where he stayed until he was captured. The latter occurred only after Orlach himself had been arrested and spent a year in prison before revealing Raymond's location. If all that occurred by the time Raymond testified in October 1325, he must have left Montpellier well before December 1324. Thus the decisive revelation would have come in December 1323.

Unfortunately, there are two more bits of evidence to consider. First, that the Olivi investigation was still considered underway as late as November 1324 is implied by the fact that one of the opinions on the commentary solicited from individual consultants cites the papal bull *Quia quorumdam*, and thus was written after November 24, 1324.[66] Second, a Catalonian inquisitorial process discovered by Josep Perarnau records that sometime between Christmas 1324 and the beginning of Lent in 1325, a notary in Girona named Guillem des Quer destroyed incriminating documents in his home after he received a letter saying that Olivi's Apocalypse commentary had been condemned.[67] Unless the mail in Catalonia was slower than we would expect, it would seem that the condemnation referred to here occurred in December 1324 and is the same one noted by Prous.

There is something wrong here, and it is hard to say precisely what. The problem deserves more attention than it can receive in this context. In any case, it is clear that according to Prous, John has fallen and, more important, he will not get up again. The parallel with Lucifer holds in this respect, too, although it need not have been true in either case. Christ has informed Prous that he is willing to forgive Antichrist if he repents, just as he would have forgiven Cain, Caiaphas, Simon Magus, and Herod. They did not seek forgiveness, however, and Prous makes it clear that John will not do so either.

If John has lost grace permanently, has the church as well? Prous replies with a history of God's various dispensations. Buried in her testimony is a hint of Joachim's (and Olivi's) three ages. She speaks of one situation—what sort is unclear, since the record seems to omit something important here—enduring from the fall until the incarnation. God created the angels in the heavenly paradise and Adam and Eve in the terrestrial one. Both lost the grace originally given them. God then ordained that men and women should be given both sorts of grace, that is, they should be awarded the celestial paradise given to angels and the terrestrial one given to Adam and Eve. Thus the Son was placed in the womb of the Virgin Mary. Christ created a new terrestrial paradise, the church, with its seven sacraments. In it he placed Elijah and Enoch, known to us as Saint Francis and Olivi, both bearing witness to Christ. Francis bore witness concerning the poor life inaugurated by Christ, while Olivi witnessed to the divinity in Holy Scripture. Antichrist, in the person of John XXII, killed them both, ending the old dispensation.

This turn of events marks not the frustration of God's intentions, but their fulfillment with the birth of yet another dispensation. The Trinity has invested all its power in the Holy Spirit and placed the Holy Spirit in Olivi. This parallelism between Mary and Olivi seems to place him in the position Prous assigns herself elsewhere, but even here she edges in beside Olivi, noting that God had once told her of two women mentioned in Holy Scripture, Mary and herself, who were to receive the Son and Holy Spirit respectively.[68] This identification of Prous's role with Olivi's extends to both being unquestionable authority figures. To be saved, one must believe that God gave Olivi the Holy Spirit in its entirety—and, since Prous claims that she herself shares that same Spirit with Olivi, one must believe not only Olivi but Prous as well.

Thus the church has not lost grace, but merely relocated it. The transition has not been an easy one. From the moment the sacrament of the altar lost its power, the gates of heaven have been closed and no one has entered. The souls of those ultimately bound for glory have been placed in limbo, where they are to stay until Christ dies a second time. That is exactly what is happening, though. Just as the Son of God was sent to the Jewish legal experts and, not recognizing him, they crucified him, so in the present the Christian legal experts have failed to recognize (and are therefore crucifying) the Holy Spirit in the person of Prous herself.[69] Like the Jewish leaders who crucified Christ, modern church leaders have simultaneously put an end to their own authority and helped to effect the new dispensation.

However much of the old dispensation disappears in the new one, much remains. The church remains, although its sacraments vanish and its leadership changes. Nor is Christ somehow replaced by the Holy Spirit. Nevertheless, Prous emphasizes that the two ages are marked by two passions atoning for two different sins. Radical as such claims may be, they are not unconnected with the other testimony we have seen so far, and they are certainly not unrelated to Olivian apocalyptic.

Prous's confession closes with the announcement that "having been warned, asked, and exhorted many times in judicial proceedings and on other occasions to revoke and abjure all the things reported above as erroneous and heretical, she persevered in them, claiming that in the aforesaid, as in the truth, she wishes to live and die." She was impenitent and remained so until she was finally turned over the secular powers for judgment (i.e., execution) in November 1328.

Like Raymond Déjean, Prous is described as a heresiarch in inquisitorial documents. One can see how Raymond earned the title, but did Prous qualify? She seems so extreme that it is hard to imagine other beguins taking her seriously. Moreover, while her confession describes her as in almost constant conversation with God, it reveals substantially less human contact. Nevertheless, other confessions show that she was indeed taken seriously, though it is less clear how widely she was believed.

We have a decent body of evidence, because a question about Prous was routinely included among those posed to a specific group of suspects who had enjoyed contact with the Montpellier beguins. The aim of this question was to determine whether they knew of Prous's beliefs, which beliefs they had heard about, and whether they had believed them.[70] Raymond Déjean, who had been Prous's houseguest, was asked that question. He granted that he had heard her say that the Holy Spirit was given to her just as the Son had been given to the Virgin Mary; that the sacraments no longer brought salvation; that the church was spiritually dead; that one no longer needed to receive the body of Christ, because this was the era of the Holy Spirit; and that in order to be saved, one had to believe what Prous had said on these matters. Raymond emphatically denied that he ever believed any of these things.[71] Another woman named Sybil admitted that ten years earlier she had been familiar with various beguins at Montpellier, including Prous, her sister, and their friend, had visited them in their home, and even had seen one of them in her own home. She also admitted to having heard a certain person speak of the errors held by Prous, but contended that she did not believe these errors.[72] A third beguin, Ermessende, said that while she was in Montpellier she had heard that Na Prous Boneta held a fatuous set of beliefs. Since others did not wish to go with her, she went alone to Prous's home in order to correct her. It proved a difficult task. Prous replied that she was speaking the truth, for she had been certified by God as having the Holy Spirit. Hearing this, the would-be instructor crossed herself, commended herself to the Lord Jesus Christ, and left.[73]

So far we have little reason to conclude that Prous had a following, but also little reason to be confident that she did not. The inquisitors themselves observed that Sybil, however she may have felt about Prous's beliefs, had not reported them as she should have, and that Ermessende not only told no one but also continued to deny that she had heard about them, even after she was arrested; she admitted it only when she knew that the inquisitor had received the information from someone else. Why, then, assume that they were being entirely truthful about not believing Prous? Raymond Déjean, too, was less than honest about his former beliefs, although we might suspect on a more or less *a priori* basis that an educated Franciscan like Raymond would have been unlikely to accept Prous's self-appraisal.

Jean Orlach, the man who cared for Raymond Déjean, also knew Prous, but his testimony is hard to assess. He admitted that he visited Prous in prison, but the process says nothing more, and he visited other imprisoned beguins as well, so we have no reason to infer any special devotion to Prous.[74] More interesting are the testimonies by Prous's sister and their housemate. The housemate, "Alisseta or Alarassis," admitted to having helped shelter Raymond Déjean and various fugitive beguins in their home; having heard Prous enunciate a series of heretical beliefs; having believed them; and having believed that not only the friars burned at Marseilles but also the beguins executed at Narbonne, Lunel, and elsewhere were—with the single exception of one genuine heretic burned at Narbonne—unjustly condemned and currently in paradise. She still accepted all this when she was captured, and the process says that she continued to do so for some time thereafter, though she finally announced to the inquisitor that she was ready to believe whatever he told her to believe.[75]

Prous's sister, Alisseta, presented a slightly different problem. Even before she was captured, she said, she had been unable to decide whether Prous was receiving genuine revelations. At one time she believed such was the case, but at another she began to think that it was all an illusion, the devil's work. By the time she was arrested, she had decided that the best course was to avoid any strong opinion on the matter. "She concluded she would not dare to say or believe definitively that it was a demonically caused illusion or temptation, because if she said so she feared God would punish her. She wished to believe definitively that on the whole it was God's work and the Holy Spirit's work rather than the devil's; yet insofar as it might be against the holy church of God, she did not want to hold to it, as she said." The authorities naturally found that conclusion unsatisfactory. "It was explained to her by the inquisitor's representative that what she heard from her sister was erroneous, heretical, against the faith and Holy Roman church, and the work of the devil. She was ordered, asked, admonished and begged to reject and abjure all of the aforesaid, consider her sister a heretic and heresiarch, and acknowledge that those who had been condemned and burned were heretics." Yet Alisseta proved hard to convince. "She replied that she would not swear this because she did not have knowledge of God's judgments, nor did she know to what end He might bring the aforesaid."[76] It took them another year to move her from this position, but they finally did so, and in October 1325 she signed a document that said what the inquisitor wanted to hear. It was none too soon. One month later, she was sentenced to perpetual imprisonment, and her sister was turned over to the secular authorities. Their friend, too, was given perpetual imprisonment.[77] One year later, on September 10, 1329, the two were released from prison and their sentences were commuted to wearing crosses and going on pilgrimages.[78] On that same day, one Stephana Boneta, probably another sister, was sentenced to perpetual imprisonment.[79]

Two more mentions of Prous show that her influence extended outside her own household. In September 1325, one month after Prous's confession, Guillerma, an inhabitant of Narbonne, was interrogated at Carcassonne.[80] She had proved remarkably uncooperative, had been saved from burning earlier simply because at the last minute the inquisitor chose to give her more time to repent, and even then had spent a substantial period in prison before making a confession that the inquisitor would accept. When she finally made that acceptable confession, she informed the inquisitor that she would have told the truth much earlier had she not been placed near Prous in the prison.[81] Guillerma was not the only one deterred by Prous. Another resident of Narbonne, Guillermus, in a confession dated 1325 (the month is omitted), said that previously he had denied the charges against him because he was induced to do so by Prous.[82]

ELEVEN

SOUTHERN FRANCE
Some Generalizations

WHILE IT WOULD BE AN OVERSTATEMENT to say that the four cases exam-ined in the last chapter present spiritual and beguin life after 1318 in all its complexity, they at least give us a start in that direction. We are now in a posi-tion to make some generalizations.

Socioeconomic Considerations

The first message that these cases convey concerns the limits of generaliza-tion. Gui's presentation of the beguins inevitably tends to homogenize them. He describes them as a distinctive (if unauthorized) religious group. They claim affiliation with the Franciscan third order, dress in brown or grey habits, engage in characteristic behavior, and adhere to a specific body of doctrine heavily reliant on Olivi's thought. Gui grants that there are "simpler beguins of both sexes who do not know explicitly all the doctrine described here," but he is primarily interested in the ones who do. The "order" of beguins that emerges from Gui's description is hardly his own invention. We find something similar in the Catalan beguin communities described by José Maria Pou y Marti and Josep Perarnau,[1] and the cases prosecuted by Gui himself did reflect much of what he describes in his manual.[2]

The verbal processes enshrined at Paris in the Collection Doat offer a slightly different picture, but it is hard to say how different, since we must recognize—as Gui forewarns us—that there were many things the defendants preferred not to mention if they could avoid doing so. Even when we make allowance for this factor, though, we still seem to encounter a wider spectrum of motivation and belief than Gui would have us believe. Some defendants were pious members of the Franciscan third order who had received advice, penance, and communion from many of the same brothers who now needed protection. In other cases, however, we are given no reason to assume that they either belonged to the third order or wore distinctive clothing; moreover, they became involved for a greater variety of reasons than Gui suggests. We also find a range of status. Not all of the defendants were laity. Jean-Louis Biget estimates, from the surviving processes, that around 32 percent were priests, or at least clerics.[3]

The resultant picture is a complex one, leaving us with the problem of how we should use the word "beguin." We can limit it to those actually in the third order, or we can extend it to all those pious clerics and laity who defended the spirituals—and eventually one another. Gui prefers to use it in the first way, but we will use it in the second, less precise sense.

In any case, the beguins were overwhelmingly townspeople. The movement involved rural knights and peasants only peripherally.[4] Moreover, they were from a limited geographical area. Narbonne formed the center of the movement, which encompassed around twenty towns, forming a band measuring around 200 kilometers by 50 kilometers.[5] Narbonne was the center not only geographically but also numerically, accounting for over a third of the beguins known to us. Biget estimates that even where they were strongest, they would have compromised only around 3 percent of the population at best. Thus the beguins were hardly a mass movement.

In 40 percent of the processes, we are told the defendant's occupation. Besides the 32 percent who were priests or clerics, we find artisans (51 percent), merchants (7 percent), and notaries (5 percent). Of the artisans, a large number were connected with the textile industry, which is hardly surprising in view of the fact that the towns involved tended to be important in the cloth trade. These particular artisans seem to have been well-off, on the whole. Thus the beguins came largely from the upper socioeconomic range of urban society. In this sense, at least, they were a homogeneous group.

Around 37 percent of the extant processes are directed at women.[6] Nevertheless, the few beguins who stood out as principal figures in the movement were mostly men. Prous was the only exception, and the nature of her influence was different. Renegade Franciscans like Raymond Déjean or influential beguins like Pierre Trencavel, Guillaume Serallier, and Guillaume Doumergue moved around a great deal, spreading the beguin message and strengthening beguin resolve. Prous's testimony describes one missionary trip on her part, but by and large one gets the impression that her message was transmitted within Montpellier—often within her own home—and in prison after her arrest.

Reaction to Persecution

Not all beguins acted in the same manner when placed before an inquisitorial tribunal. It is impossible to read the last two processes in the previous chapter without realizing that we are seeing two radically different people react to their interrogators in disparate ways. Alarassis, like most defendants, was being careful. She wanted to emerge from the process alive. Here, as in most processes, the questioners were very much in charge. Alarassis was at least superficially pliant, though specific aspects of her testimony (such as her vagueness on chronology) are perhaps indicative of the subtle contest being waged in her responses. Interrogations often seem like deadly chess games. In the case of Bernard Maury, a priest of Narbonne, it gradually becomes clear to us that the extent of his guilt hinges not only on what he thought but also on when he thought it, and we watch his defense unravel as the inquisitors carefully maneuver him into admitting that by his own testimony, he was still a heretic well after the date when he had theoretically recanted.[7]

Prous was very different. She did not even seem to take the problem of survival into consideration. She saw herself not as being judged by the inquisitors, but as instructing them, witnessing to the truth, although she did not expect them to recognize it as such. Prous was also exceptional in the way she continually managed to wrest the initiative away from her questioner and direct the course of her own interrogation.

Prous was unique in any number of ways, though. She was the only beguin with whom God seemed all that interested in conversing, the only one who enjoyed continuous visionary experience,[8] the only one whose opinions had to be taken as true—not because they accorded with the gospels or with Olivi, but because she herself had enunciated them as an instrument of the Holy Spirit.

Family and Social Commitments

What drove these people to defy the church, even at the cost of their lives? Those who presented the matter from an ecclesiastical perspective, like Bernard Gui, tended to emphasize doctrinal deviance, and there was certainly a great deal of that; yet another element is hard to miss.

It is hardly irrelevant that Alarassis was Olivi's niece; that her mother was also involved in hiding the fugitives; and that one of the fugitives who arrived at her door was a relative. If that relative was Raymond Déjean, then we can add him and his nephew to the family tree, and we are witnessing an activity that encompassed two or three generations. Thus presumably family solidarity played a role in Alarassis's decision making. What role, though? The way the story is told may mislead us by encouraging us to think of Alarassis as dragged into the beguin network by the appearance of her relative, yet she acknowledges that she entertained beguins in her home. She admits that she knew Pierre Trencavel and, even more important, where to find him. The inquisitors would have liked to know as much. Perhaps she was told these things by her guests, or perhaps she was already active in the resistance. We will never know. As a result of these ambiguities, her original motives are hard for us to sort out, and she herself might have found the task equally difficult.

One finds the same mixture of familial loyalties and religious beliefs elsewhere. Bernard Durban, a blacksmith living in Lodève, went to Lunel in 1322 to see his sister Esclarmonde burned along with sixteen other beguins. He returned with some of her bones and flesh. Did he keep these relics because she was his sister, or because she was considered a holy martyr? He says both at the hearing, and both are probably true. We know that Bernard's brother Raymond was also present that day, and he too took some of his sister's body. In fact, it seems that on that day at least two members of the Durban family were at Lunel to see two others die at the stake.

Other examples are readily available. Manenta, the wife of Bernard Arnaud, a cobbler from Lodève, admitted that she sometimes displayed devotion toward the executed beguins, considering them saints "because of the asperity of the life they led"; but she also acknowledged that she had been given a volume that had belonged to her sister-in-law, one of those burned at Lunel, "although she claimed that she displayed no devotion toward it."

In such cases it is impossible to say whether motivation was primarily religious or familial. Prous, Alisseta, and Stephana Boneta were raised in a beguin family. Otherwise, Prous would not have found herself visiting Olivi's tomb before she was ten years old. Alarassis Biasse was from a similar family. In such cases, family loyalty probably walked hand in hand with belief.

Note that Raymond Durban's brother lived at Clermont rather than Lodève. Thus family ties facilitated communication and movement between towns. His case is hardly unique. Pierre Baron's home was an important beguin center at Montréal. The inquisitors also pursued Bernard Baron of Mazères, Agnès Baron of Carcassonne, and Bernard Baron of Narbonne.[9]

Social ties could bind as well. When Jacquelline Sobiran, presumably still in possession of Raymond Déjean's clothing, went from Carcassonne to Montréal and visited the fugitive friar, one can assume that she was propelled by more than heretical belief. He was her former confessor and, one assumes, her friend. The interrogation of Bernard Maury often concentrates less on his beliefs than on questions such as why he dined with Pierre Trencavel, a fugitive heretic, rather than reporting the latter's whereabouts to the inquisitor. The inquisitor's assumption was undoubtedly that Bernard did so precisely because he shared Pierre's beliefs, and we can assume that such an explanation is at least partly correct. Nevertheless, when we try to imagine Bernard, Pierre, and other friends at table, as he describes them in his testimony, we begin to imagine what else might have been involved.

Economic connections were also important. The major beguin cities were important in the manufacture and distribution of cloth, and a good percentage of the beguins themselves were active in it. The relationships already formed in their professional lives probably aided communication and reinforced loyalty when it came to defying the church.

Levels of Offense

Inquisitorial sentencing practices offer at least an indirect tribute to the complexities of motivation. As even the four case histories suggest, people met with different fates on sentencing day. Some were judged to be *fautores*, people who had aided heretics (if only by not reporting them), while others were sentenced as *credentes*, believers in heresy. Those in the former group were given penances principally consisting of pilgrimages and crosses worn front and rear. *Credentes* who repented were sentenced to perpetual imprisonment, while those who refused to repent were turned over to the secular courts for sentencing, and that normally meant death. There were also the *relapsi*, those *fautores* and *credentes* who had previously recanted and received their penances, then either had not carried these penances out—for example, had removed their crosses without permission or had not undertaken the required pilgrimages—or had returned to their old heretical associations. They too were turned over to the secular courts, although in some cases they were given perpetual imprisonment rather than executed.

Despite words like "perpetual," no sentence except death was really final. Those sentenced to life imprisonment might hope to see their sentences commuted to crosses and pilgrimages after as little as a year. Those given crosses and pilgrimages could hope to see their crosses removed once they had shown their good intentions by completing the assigned pilgrimages. Once they had confessed themselves guilty of something, heretics began a lifetime of progression or retrogression, moving up and down the ladder of punishment, at the inquisitor's discretion. Their world became a Dantean purgatory, though it differed from Dante's in being multidirectional.

Thus death at the stake played a much smaller role in inquisitorial processes than popularly imagined. The processes themselves give us a skewed perspective because they concentrate heavily on the defendants' attitudes toward those previously executed. Again and again we find them being asked whether they consider these people to be unjustly condemned, or martyrs, or even saints. We hear the succession of places where executions occurred. It is certainly an impressive list. A beguin named Bernarda, confessing in March 1322, speaks of three burned at Narbonne on one occasion and twenty-one on another; of seventeen who died at Lunel; of two killed at Béziers in one sentencing and seven in another; of two specific people "and some others" executed at Capestang, and of unspecified numbers burned at Lodève and in the diocese of Maguelonne.[10] If Bernarda's count is accurate, it is hard to imagine that fewer than sixty died within the first three years the beguins were being prosecuted. This figure receives rough confirmation from another sentence of 1322, which tells how Pierre Doumergue composed a litany containing, alongside canonically valid saints, the names of around seventy beguin martyrs.[11] At that date, the persecution still had a long way to go, so we might assume that in the course of the persecution substantially more beguins were executed.[12]

Nevertheless, when we examine extant processes, we discover that the percentage of beguins relinquished to the secular arm is very small. However many beguins were burned, most went not to the stake but on pilgrimage or to prison. Which of the two they were assigned depended, as we have seen, on whether they were considered *credentes* or *fautores*, and that should in theory have depended on whether they were seen as believing in heresy or merely aiding and abetting heretics; yet it is not quite that simple. To some extent, the two categories were tied to the sort of punishment received rather than to whether the defendant had been a believer or not. That is, certain people who were clearly believers were nonetheless sentenced as *fautores* for one reason or another.

We can follow this process in the Lodève sentences of July 3, 1323,[13] in which six defendants were given crosses and pilgrimages, two were sentenced to perpetual imprisonment, and one was declared a lapsed heretic to be surrendered to the secular arm. We know the logic behind this distribution because we have not merely the sentence but also the recommendations from the panel of experts that advised the inquisitor.[14] In this particular case, the inquisitor, Jean de Beaune, heard from a panel of twenty-five experts. We learn from their recommendations that one of those sentenced to crosses and pilgrimages was recognized to have confessed and been absolved previously, which should have qualified him as a lapsed heretic; two others were described by the panel as *credentes* yet sentenced as if they were *fautores*. In the case of the person who had confessed previously, Bernard Durban, the panel acknowledged procedural flaws in his earlier abjuration. It had been made without witnesses and had not been duly recorded by a notary. Thus, "leaning in the direction of mercy rather than toward the rigor of justice," the panel recommended that the original abjuration be ignored. It still disagreed on whether he should be considered a *fautor* or a *credens*. Even within the group that thought he should be sentenced as a *fautor*, there was disagreement, with some recommending that he be given a harsher form of that punishment, others a milder one.[15] One gets the impression that the difference here was between those who felt he must be judged strictly on the evidence of this process and those who felt that giving Bernard extra pilgrimages or sentencing him as a *credens* was the least they should do to a man who really deserved to be executed. The majority voted for strict procedural rectitude, though, and that is what he received.

The other two cases are also instructive. In one case, that of Berenger Jaoul, the panel noted—presumably with some regret—that Berenger was clearly a *credens*, but he had been promised grace before he came to confess and had provided the inquisitor with certain valuable information. Thus he should be sentenced as if he were only a *fautor*. In the other case, Berenger Roque was described as a *credens* but a repentant one, so he was given double crosses and increased pilgrimages. This last sentence defies rational explanation since, of the two who were given perpetual imprisonment, one was judged a penitent heretic and the other a believing heretic.

Excellent as the Lodève sentences may be in demonstrating the intricacies of inquisitorial decision making, they are misleading in one important respect. The panel of experts was atypical in its bias toward assigning crosses and pilgrimages. Most extant recommendations seem to have been weighted in the other direction. On the day Alarassis Biasse, Raymond Déjean, and Jacquelline Sobiran were sentenced, twelve people were given crosses and pilgrimages, and nineteen perpetual imprisonment. On the day Na Prous Boneta, her sister, and their friend were told their fate, six people received crosses and pilgrimages while twelve went to prison. These distributions are not all that different from what we find in other cases.[16]

Disobedience and Heresy

It is not surprising that panels tended to designate more *credentes* than *fautores*. The decision to aid or not report heretics seemed in itself a sign of heresy—and the beguin heresy was an extension of the spiritual Franciscan heresy. That much seems obvious from the way beguin processes center on issues such as whether the four spirituals at Marseilles were unjustly condemned, whether the pope can alter or dispense from a vow, whether he can give the friars granaries and cellars or make the spirituals discard their characteristic clothing, and other questions already contested by the spirituals. Yet it is also an extension of the spiritual Franciscan heresy in a deeper sense. If beguins were normally expected to say how they felt about the four spirituals burned at Marseilles, the point of this query was not unlike that of the questions that led those four unfortunate friars to the stake. In both cases, the basic assumption justifying inquisitorial action was that denial of papal authority involved a denial of the Nicene Creed's statement of belief in one church, and thus constituted heresy. The four spirituals actually died at Marseilles for refusing to recognize the pope's right to decide what he had decided in *Quorumdam exigit*. Later, the beguins died for refusing to recognize the pope's right to make a whole series of decisions: *Quorumdam exigit*, seen by beguins as licensing large granaries and wine cellars in violation of the Franciscan vow; condemnation of the four Franciscans, who had simply witnessed to the immutability of solemn vows; and condemnation of those beguins who had been executed since 1319. In a curious way, then, inquisitorial action against the spiritual Franciscans and against the beguins resembled that against anti-papal Ghibellines in Italy during the same period. There too the charge of heresy was partly based on the assumption that disobedience implied a denial of papal authority and thus a denial of the Nicene Creed.[17] Viewed from this perspective, any deliberate failure to aid the inquisition in its search for beguins might be interpreted as heresy. The wonder is not that so few people were sentenced as *fautores*, but that any were at all.

Beguin Saints

It is, of course, misleading to speak of the beguins simply as denying papal authority. They were denying the authority of the entire ecclesiastical hierarchy, and theoretically that left them free to rethink a great deal of the faith. How thoroughly they did so depends on which beguin one has in mind. Prous constitutes the most extreme example. Unlike Prous, most beguins displayed little interest in doctrine and ecclesiastical structure, limiting their revisionism to specific areas like sainthood.

We have seen that Pierre Doumergue produced a litany that placed recently martyred beguins alongside canonically approved saints. One gathers from other processes that the roster of beguin saints was both greater and smaller than Pierre's list might suggest. It was greater in the sense that it included Olivi and the four friars executed at Marseilles. Olivi constitutes such a special case that we will reserve consideration of him for a moment. As for the four Franciscans and the beguins, defendants were asked whether they saw them as glorious martyrs unjustly condemned and whether they thought they were now in Paradise. Many acknowledged that they had so believed, although with notable variations. The four who died at Marseilles were normally seen as martyrs, although the processes of Raymond Déjean and others function as evidence that some defendants hesitated to admit that they had believed even that much.[18] The inquisitors were correct in thinking that the question was an important one. It is impossible to read the confessions without recognizing that the execution at Marseilles constituted a defining moment within the beguin community. When beguins decided that John XXII had become a heretic or that he had lost papal authority, they were very likely to identify that transformation with his treatment of the four spirituals.

Attitudes toward the executed beguins varied more. One sees a tendency to make distinctions. As we have seen, some beguins distinguished between those who were martyrs and those who were genuine heretics. Even among the ones considered martyrs, some were singled out for special veneration. We have seen that relics of Esclarmonde were particularly prized at Lodève, and they may have made their way elsewhere as well.[19] At Montréal, the memory of Bernard Léon was especially treasured. Among those who died at Narbonne, people there and elsewhere continued to celebrate Friar Mai and Pierre du

Fraysse.[20] Beguins occasionally stipulated that while they admired these people, they did not venerate them as saints; however, in many cases, what we see is clearly the latter. We read of people keeping body parts in their homes, kissing them, and otherwise venerating them. Some processes refer to them straightforwardly as relics and to their containers as pixes. Nor did the relics consist only of human remains. Raymond d'Antusan admitted to having bits of wood from the stakes on which Friar Mai and Pierre du Fraysse were burned.[21]

Olivi might be considered the beguin saint *par excellence*. The order paid grudging tribute to his status by destroying his tomb, and the inquisitors implicitly acknowledged it by the regularity with which they asked what people thought of him. There was no single beguin view on the matter, though. Opinions extended downward from Prous's notion of Olivi (and herself) as incarnating the third person of the Trinity; through the more widespread picture of him as receiving all his knowledge by revelation; all the way to a presentation of Olivi as essentially correct in his thought, though guilty of some error. Or perhaps one should extend the spectrum to the Lodève processes, where he is barely mentioned.[22]

Olivian Apocalyptic and Beguin Expectation

Granting that the beguins were faithful to Olivi's person, how faithful were they to his ideas? John's behavior had given those ideas new relevance. His decision to throw his weight behind the Franciscan leaders had produced precisely that worst-case scenario envisaged in Olivi's *Questions on Evangelical Perfection*, one in which the pope orders violation of the vow. Or at least that is how the spirituals and beguins saw it. Olivi was very clear on what should be done in that case. Moreover, his apocalyptic thought explained to the embattled spirituals and beguins not only why they must resist, but also why they were being put in a position where they had to do so. It made sense of the event and thus assured them that, however terrible the consequences, everyone was playing his or her assigned role. The problem any authority structure faces in dealing with groups motivated by such a scenario is that any attempt to suppress them has the effect of validating the scenario. Whether we look at inquisitors prosecuting beguins at Narbonne in 1325 or FBI agents storming the Branch Davidian compound at Waco in 1993, we see that by acting just as the group expects them to act, the authorities seem to confirm that they are precisely the persecutors that group anticipated, and that the whole event thus means just what the group thought it would mean.

If it is obvious that beguins made use of the Olivian apocalyptic scenario, it is less clear whether they used it responsibly or seriously distorted it. On the whole, most scholars have favored the latter position, but the truth seems more complicated. In saying that the pope should not be obeyed if he ordered the Franciscans to violate their solemn vow of *usus pauper,* they were reading Olivi correctly. He said this much explicitly and rather insistently, not only in his *Questions on Evangelical Perfection* but in his Apocalypse commentary as well. The only real question is whether Olivi would have recognized the particular behavior demanded by the pope in 1317 as so obviously in violation of the vow as to demand disobedience—and that, of course, is an unanswerable question.

Much the same thing could probably be said of Olivi's apocalyptic scenario as reflected throughout the beguin processes. Olivi saw the church as becoming increasingly corrupt, and expected that in the near future, corruption would reach the highest possible levels. He saw a new age dawning with Francis and his order and expected that a future carnal pope would join a carnal secular ruler in opposing it. He tended to think that some pope would be the mystical Antichrist, but was willing to grant that the secular ruler might fill that role. In the final analysis, he was more interested in the king-pope combination than in labeling either as the mystical Antichrist. This "persecution of the mystical Antichrist" would end when the carnal church was destroyed by a non-Christian army—a force whose goal was actually to destroy Christianity, not to save the suffering righteous from persecution. The righteous would still find themselves persecuted, but by a new oppressor, the Great Antichrist. Here again Olivi anticipated a king-pope combination, this time a non-Christian ruler collaborating with an apostate friar. And here again, Olivi was more interested in the combination than in which of the two would be the Great Antichrist, although he again tended to favor the pope for that role.

To put the matter this concisely is to be a great deal clearer than Olivi himself was. He was fond of the word "perhaps" and enjoyed offering alternative scenarios. In the final analysis, though, it is hard to read him without deciding that the above scenario is the one he himself favored. He offered no precise timetable, but assumed that the mystical Antichrist might begin work anytime after the beginning of the fourteenth century and that the great Antichrist would be dead at least by the middle of the century.[23]

The beguins were a great deal more specific. Once they identified the spirituals and themselves as the vanguard of the new age, their persecutor John XXII automatically became the carnal pope—and thus, by extension, the mystical Antichrist.[24] They were not unanimous on this point. Some would go no further than to assert that John was wrong, perhaps misinformed by the inquisitors,[25] while others were willing to call him a heretic but did not assign him any apocalyptic status.[26] Nevertheless, the heavy number of references to John as the mystical Antichrist, combined with the likelihood that many defendants would temper their views in the presence of the inquisitor, suggests that the belief was an extremely popular one.

Here again Olivi's prophetic word had become solid flesh, and here again it is impossible to say whether he himself would have made the same identification. In fairness to the beguins it should be recognized, though, that whether Olivi would have recognized John's credentials as the mystical Antichrist or not, he would have had to acknowledge that John was occupying the position Olivi had expected the mystical Antichrist to hold; that in undermining Franciscan poverty as Olivi understood it, he was doing pretty much what Olivi had expected the mystical Antichrist to do; and that he had appeared just about when Olivi would have expected to see him. Nor was the idea of the beguins as defenders of the new age against prelates and theologians totally at variance with Olivi's expectations. He had predicted that the new age would be rejected by the wise and powerful, but accepted by the simple.

Once we move beyond the mystical Antichrist to the great one, we find it easier to see a tension between the Olivian prediction and its beguin application. At least some of the beguins, including Pierre Tort, saw the temptation of the Great Antichrist in terms of the Angevin-Aragonese rivalry that characterized European politics at the moment. The destruction of the carnal church and mystical Antichrist would be carried out by a powerful king (Frederick III of Sicily) and a false pope (either Angelo Clareno or Enrico da Ceva, leader of the Tuscan rebels then in Sicily). Once they had vanquished and humiliated John XXII, the way would be opened for the great Antichrist, Angelo Clareno or Philip of Majorca.[27]

The curious thing about this scenario is that it is made up of people who were sympathetic to the spiritual cause. The Majorca-Sicily connection reminds us of the escape route just mentioned. That is perhaps part of the explanation. These identifications attest to the fact that, however good the intentions of a Frederick III or a Philip of Majorca may have been, the realities of their situation made it impossible for them to offer the French spirituals sustained, long-term help. Eventually, inevitably, the beguins felt betrayed by their Italian and Majorcan brethren.

That is, at any rate, the explanation offered by Raoul Manselli, and there is much to be said for it. It should be added, however, that no verbal process actually says as much, and Alarassis's case suggests that the escape route was still in operation as late as 1321, only a year before beguins were testifying that they had identified Majorcan and Sicilian leaders with the persecution of Antichrist. We have every reason to assume from Raymond Geoffroi's career that it was operative even later. Thus it seems that the route was open even as the identification was forming. Moreover, there were a number of other historical considerations that tended to encourage the beguins' interpretation.

For one thing, the Angevin-Aragonese rivalry could be seen as a continuation of the Angevin-Hohenstaufen rivalry. Frederick III carried on the old battle against a papal-Angevin alliance and consciously identified with his Hohenstaufen precursors, with whom he was in fact tied by blood. That enabled French Franciscans to identify him with the widespread notion that Antichrist would spring from the seed of the Emperor Frederick II. He even had the right name. Olivi himself had not paid much attention to the "seed of Frederick" tradition, but he had paid some attention to it, and his almost reflexive pro-Angevin stance is seen in his 1295 letter to the three captive princes.[28] Thus the tradition identifying the Aragonese with Antichrist, while it did not stem directly from Olivi, was not completely at odds with him either—and it proved a durable one, reappearing years later in the prophecy of Jean de Roquetaillade, who updated it to target a subsequent member of the Sicilian royal house.[29] Of course, at the turn of the fourteenth century, those whose expectations were developed in a more Ghibelline environment could show the same interest in the Aragonese Frederick, but assign him a more positive role. Thus Fra Dolcino expected Frederick to arrive in Rome in 1304 and set the scene for the election of a holy pope.[30]

Enrico da Ceva's appearance in the scenario also has a history. As we saw in the last chapter, Pierre Tort reported having heard from the Narbonne spirituals that the Franciscan order would be divided into three parts: the community, Enrico da Ceva's group, and the spirituals (along with the beguins). The first two groups would be destroyed, but the third would last until the end of the world, although it would have to undergo the many persecutions already revealed to Saint Francis.[31] This negative attitude toward the Sicilian spirituals is hardly surprising. The Tuscan rebels broke with the papacy and took refuge in Sicily at a time when other spirituals were still hoping to work something out. Their behavior was roundly condemned by Angelo Clareno, and beguin testimony suggests that the French spiritual Franciscans shared Angelo's opinion.

The only surprising elements in this scenario, then, are Angelo himself and Philip of Majorca. In Angelo's case, we might be speaking of betrayal in a rather complex sense. We will see that Angelo resolutely attempted to avoid even the appearance of rebellion against John XXII, and that was not a posture calculated to impress many French beguins. Moreover, Angelo was transferred out of the Franciscan order, and we have seen that beguin processes from 1321–22 show a preoccupation with the question of whether such a transfer was truly possible. On the whole, the beguin answer was that friars could be placed in another order, but they would still have to honor their Franciscan vows in all their rigor. Angelo did just that, but he did it in Italy and it is doubtful that the beguins had any sense of what he was doing down there. In any case, we have seen that according to Pierre Tort, beguins expected Angelo to be the Antichrist because (according to Olivi) the latter would be an apostate Franciscan, and Angelo was seen as such.

As for Philip of Majorca, here again we have a complex problem.[32] Philip was the younger son of King James I of Majorca and thus a member of the Aragonese royal family, itself remarkable for its piety. His grandfather, James I of Aragon, had abdicated and become a Cistercian; his elder brother had chosen to become a Franciscan rather than king; his sister Sancia had thought of leaving her husband, King Robert of Naples, to enter a religious order; and his nephew Ferdinand II of Majorca would vow perpetual chastity when he was eleven. Philip himself joined the Dominican order but found it unsatisfactory. He eventually became a member of the Franciscan third order, a proponent of beguin ideals, and a great admirer of Angelo Clareno, who in turn admired Philip. In Majorca, Philip surrounded himself with a group of likeminded friars and laity who felt, as he did, that the rule must be practiced in all its rigor. Philip's status made Majorca a haven for spirituals long after they were being persecuted in southern France, and his position as regent of the kingdom from 1324 to 1329 (during the minority of his nephew James II) put him in an especially strong position.

Nevertheless, even Philip's influence had its limits. He pleaded insistently and at times aggressively with John XXII to grant Angelo's group and his own some sort of recognition, but the pope refused. John attempted to deflect Philip by offering him two bishoprics, both of which he refused, but did succeed in giving him some benefices. After 1329, when Philip and some of his group moved to the kingdom of Naples—and Majorca found itself under the control of a king who did not share his uncle's tastes in piety—the situation of the beguins became more precarious. The process against Philip's friend and fellow beguin sympathizer, Adhémar de Mosset, which began in 1332, shows how the wind had changed.[33] Philip eventually attempted to gain from Pope Benedict XII what he had failed to receive from John XXII, but he was rebuffed once more.

What might a French beguin have found offensive about this *curriculum vitae?* The worsening of the beguin situation thanks to his departure in 1329 might seem a good answer, but Philip's candidacy as Antichrist was being considered long before that. Here again one wonders how much the French beguins knew of Philip, but if they knew anything, they must have been aware of his Aragonese family connections—which put him in the same class as Frederick of Sicily. Moreover, like Angelo, he attempted to observe evangelical perfection while remaining obedient to John XXII, and the French beguins followed a strikingly different path.

When we ask how this beguin expectation regarding the Great Antichrist compares with Olivi's original thoughts on the matter, we might be excused for suspecting that Philip of Majorca and the Aragonese-Angevin confrontation simply cannot bear the weight of Olivi's expectation, which involves the destruction of the carnal church by a non-Christian force, followed by an unholy alliance between a pagan ruler and an apostate Franciscan pope. Olivi was painfully aware that he was projecting the discussion into a time beyond his own imagining. His understanding of the church in his own time gave him some sense of what the temptation of the mystical Antichrist might be like, but with the Great Antichrist, he was moving into unexplored territory. Nevertheless, what he seems to have had in mind, insofar as he could envisage it at all, was too monstrous to be translated into anything as prosaic as an alliance between Frederick III and Angelo Clareno, although it is impressive that beguins like Pierre Tort respected Olivi's text enough to be on the lookout for an apostate Franciscan.

On the other hand, the beguin expectation of life after Antichrist seems essentially in harmony with Olivi's. That is partly because Olivi preferred to leave that period undefined, and they said little about it either. There is, however, an attractively Olivian ring to Bernard de Na Jacma's suggestion that at that time, a young virgin would be able to go from Rome to Santiago da Compostella without anyone making any evil plans concerning her along the way.[34]

Nor was the beguin timetable totally out of step with Olivi's. We have seen that Olivi expected the mystical Antichrist to show his hand any time after the beginning of the fourteenth century, so John XXII was none too early for that appearance. The rest of the timetable also has points of contact. Though he was cautious about it, Olivi tended to assume that the Great Antichrist would rule sometime during the first four decades of the century.[35] We find various beguins saying in 1321–22 that the Antichrist is now over twenty years old; that he will be in Jerusalem by 1325; and that he will be dead in either three, thirteen, or fourteen years.[36] While these numbers do not mirror Olivi's, they are not at variance with his, either. It is hard to say how much they differed on the length of the third age. Olivi thought it would last until around the year 2000. Bernard Gui claims that the beguins expected it to last approximately a century, and perhaps many of them did. Those whom we meet in inquisitorial processes simply do not say. They and their questioners were too preoccupied with the present tribulation to worry much about the future peace.

In the final analysis, the important thing is that, even if the beguins radicalized Olivi's thought by giving it concrete application and distorted it by combining it with traditions Olivi himself rejected, they were very much in tune with central themes in his writing, such as his sense that the church was heading into a new age and that the pope would stand against it. They were formed by Olivi's strong sense that Christ's age and his own age represented two major turning points of history, and that they were generally similar in structure, with Francis and his order playing the role of Christ and the contemporary church hierarchy cast as the chief priests, scribes, and pharisees. They were informed by Olivi's notion that in this new period, Christ was suffering a new passion in his people, prior to being resurrected in a new age. These were powerful images that sustained and united the beguins, even when their presentation of the details varied.[37]

The Exercise of Personal Judgment

It is important to emphasize that in speaking of "the beguin timetable" and the like we are speaking very broadly indeed. The beguins insisted on making up their own minds concerning things that the church thought it had decided for them. We recall Alisseta Boneta informing the inquisitor that she did not dare to second-guess God on the question of her sister's visions, and the inquisitor replying that the church had, in effect, already done just that. Such decisions were for it—not her—to make. This sort of exchange was repeated again and again. One can imagine a similar reaction from the inquisitor when, examining Pierre Tort, he asked whether Pierre thought that the beguins burned at the stake were heretics or martyrs, and Pierre, instead of delivering the ecclesiastically correct response, proceeded to answer on a case-by-case basis. Some were, some were not, and in still other cases he simply could not say.[38] The same dangerous tendency to make personal decisions echoes through the processes at Lodève. Martin de Saint-Antoine, the person who collected the bits of Esclarmonde that were later distributed, was asked why he chose her rather than someone else. His reply includes a widespread story about something she said before her execution, something that allowed bystanders to see her as unjustly condemned. Nevertheless, Martin also says that he knew her personally and felt she had lived a good life. Bernard Maury said much the same thing about Pierre Trencavel. "Asked if, in the last three years, a period when he still associated with Pierre Trencavel, he considered (or still considers) Pierre to be a good man or an enemy of God, he said he never heard Pierre say or saw him do anything that would make him think Pierre should be considered a bad man or mortal sinner, and so he considered him a good man and a faithful catholic."[39]

One can appreciate why the inquisitors found such exchanges frustrating. Historians looking for a definable set of beguin beliefs will find it equally frustrating. Nowhere does this insistence on making up one's own mind become clearer than in the process of Berenger Roque.[40] When Berenger explained that he left Lunel with a bit of flesh belonging to one of those burned there because of the devotion in which he then held the condemned, "because he himself had experienced their holy lives and behavior," the bemused inquisitors might well have observed that there was little left for Berenger to decide once the church had proclaimed these people heretics, but Berenger obviously saw it otherwise. Nor did he think that his task ended there. Having taken the purported relic home with him, he explained, "He put this piece of flesh on a table in his house in a vessel and left it there two or three months. Having been told by others that it could not be corrupted, he inspected it after that time and, seeing that it was rotting, he removed it from his house and threw it into a field when he was on the way to his garden." What we have here is a do-it-yourself home canonization process. Berenger preferred to make his own decisions—not only about heretics, but about saints as well.

This pattern is, of course, characteristic of dissident movements in general. Once people entered the heretical briar patch, they were doomed to begin making more personal choices. Whether this was more true of the beguins than, let us say, the Cathars just before the Albigensian crusade or the Apostles under Fra Dolcino is another matter. This is hardly the moment to begin comparing heresies. What we can do, though, is acknowledge the symmetry between this tendency and Olivi's thoughts on the historical moment. He had announced that Christianity stood at the gates of a new age, and how one regarded the Franciscan rule was a central element in whether one stood for the new age or against it. In this moment of crisis, those in positions of authority would deliver a deceptive message, but a few *viri spirituales* would preach the truth and a number of simple laity would recognize it as such. By the 1320s, those *viri spirituales* were in short supply, and the laity were increasingly forced to work things out for themselves. They considered Olivi's works authoritative, but their knowledge of what these works actually said had been mediated largely through the spiritual Franciscans, and after 1317 the latter were not widely available for consultation. Prominent beguins like Pierre Trencavel obviously exerted influence over what others believed, but they too were only sporadically accessible.

Naming Names

Faced with people who insisted on thinking matters through for themselves, the inquisitors found it essential to reassert ecclesiastical authority. This was done—as it was in dealing with other heresies—partly by insisting that the beguins not only abandon a series of heretical beliefs but denounce their fellow beguins as well. Doing so became an inescapable part of abjuring heresy. The most repeated phrase in these processes is probably "whom he/she named," as in, "He went to the home of a person whom he named." Such disclosures had a series of uses. They pointed heresy-hunters in the direction of new suspects; furnished the inquisitors evidence of the repentant beguin's sincerity; and, theoretically at least, had a psychological effect on denouncer and denounced alike, shaking their faith in the strength of old personal loyalties to the cause and to one another. One recalls Winston and Julia, the failed lovers and New Age heretics in George Orwell's *1984*, whose commitment to one another and to the battle against Big Brother ended when they were forced to recognize that at some point each was willing to sacrifice the other for purposes of self-protection.[41]

The Perils of Life After Reconciliation

In the beguins' case, fact never emulated theory as neatly as it did in Orwell's novel. Those who had already gone through the cycle of confession and reconciliation with the church were now committed to avoiding the company of heretics and reporting them if any came their way. That often proved easier to promise than to do. Jacquelline Amouroux, one of those who received crosses and pilgrimages at Lodève, later met Guillaume Serallier, a beguin fugitive, "and gave him some of the sausages she was carrying, as well as three or four *sous*, for the love of God as she says."[42] On March 1, 1327, she was sentenced to perpetual imprisonment for her kindness. Manenta, another beguin who had received crosses and pilgrimages at Lodève, was arrested again, died in prison, and then in November 1328 was sentenced to be exhumed and burned. After receiving her first sentence she had sent, by means of Berenger Jaoul (yet another of those who had received crosses and pilgrimages at Lodève), two *sous* to a woman who was known to be a fugitive. She also had heard Berenger make heretical statements and, although she claimed to have reproved him for it, had not reported him.[43]

It is hard to read such cases without reopening the question of motivation. Jacquelline and Manenta both imply that they had renounced their heretical beliefs but found it harder to renounce their heretical friends. It appears from Manenta's testimony that Berenger renounced neither. That would hardly have surprised the consultants who advised the inquisitor concerning his first sentence. It was Berenger who, even though the judges at Lodève considered him "a believer and a protector [*credentem et fautorem*] who should be punished according to the rigor of the law," was given only crosses and pilgrimages "because he was promised grace before he came to confess and because he revealed certain hidden things." Nevertheless, we must remind ourselves (as we can be sure the inquisitors did) that the two women might well have presented themselves as compelled by compassion rather than heretical belief simply because they considered it a less damning motivation.

Whatever their subsequent fates, at least Jacquelline, Berenger, and Manenta could take comfort in having shown themselves consistently loyal. Other beguins, presented with similar dilemmas, acted differently. Raymond d'Antusan of Cintegabelle, after abjuring his heresy and promising to cooperate with the inquisitors, went home one evening to discover two beguins talking with his wife Bernarda, who was in the same situation as he.[44] One of the two was our old friend Pierre Tort. Raymond says in his testimony that he scolded his wife for not reporting them. Hearing that they had been captured shortly after leaving his house, he apparently spent a very bad night. The next morning he hurried to the castle at Cintegabelle, where they were being held, and urged them to repent. As they were being led away, he fell in with the group and advised one of the beguins to come clean about the relic Raymond had seen in the man's house.

Raymond's behavior may strike the modern observer as anything from pitiful to despicable, but it is certainly comprehensible.[45] We can imagine the panic he must have felt when he heard that the fugitives had been captured. The trail of association led back to his house, and if the authorities retraced it, he could go to the stake. His wife, Bernarda (who appears in her own verbal process), provides yet another perspective on the event. She says that she gave the two beguins food and told them to leave. Later the same night, when officers of the court came to her home in search of the fugitives, she belatedly attempted to cut her losses by revealing their escape route.[46]

The same two heretics caused yet another moral crisis that evening. Like Raymond and Bernarda, Guillaume Roux had already had a brush with the inquisition and abjured, but when he heard that his old associates were in Cintegabelle, he hurried over to see them.[47] In his testimony Guillaume describes the warm reunion and provides a remarkably creative explanation of his thinking at the time. He decided that his promise to report beguins to the authorities somehow did not apply to these two because, "although they thought and felt as the beguins did and were called such by the inquisitor, nevertheless they were not beguins."[48] He concluded that his vow to report heretics applied only to more dramatic cases, such as apostate Franciscans, fugitive beguins who had escaped from the inquisitorial prison, or recalcitrant beguins who had been given a penance and refused to carry it out. If any of these people came along, he would certainly turn them in. In fact—and here we see Guillaume at his most creative—he thought one *might* come along at any moment. If he did nothing about the two birds in hand and simply waited with them, "in a little while Pierre Trencavel of Béziers might come, or some other great apostate, and then he could assist in their capture."

In the meantime, Guillaume sat and drank with his friends. He told them his situation and they told him how bravely the beguins recently condemned at Narbonne had faced execution. Finally he said good-bye to them and left. Once he was out of the house, though, the fresh air seems to have cleared his mind. He began to contemplate what might happen to him if they were captured and mentioned his name. He went straight to the town authorities and reported them.

Raymond d'Antusan presents himself as a man who wants to break with his past but discovers, to his horror, that his past has paid him a call. Guillaume Roux is more complicated. Unable to commit himself either to his old life or his putative new one, he provides poignant testimony to the fact that old habits are hard to break, even when they threaten to destroy us. But it was all the same for Pierre Tort and the other fugitive: impelled by fear, Raymond, Bernarda, and Guillaume all eventually betrayed their old associates in one way or another.

It did not end the same way for Raymond, Bernarda, and Guillaume. The first two were sentenced to perpetual imprisonment, while Guillaume Roux was turned over to the secular arm. The inquisitor clearly felt that his betrayal

of the fugitives was the result of a momentary panic at variance with his real
convictions. (He also had attempted to take sexual liberties with a woman by
convincing her it was a form of spiritual exercise.[49])

The Price of Resistance

The inquisitorial records introduce us to a few remarkable beguins like Prous,
genuinely exceptional people who seem slightly larger than life. Yet on the
whole, those we encounter strike us as earnest, rather ordinary people whose
beliefs and practices were not that different from anyone else's in their era,
but who were enticed into defying the hierarchy by a complex mixture of
social, familial, and religious factors. It is hard to think about them without
recalling William Butler Yeats's poem, "Easter, 1916." Like Yeats's improbable
revolutionaries, they were caught up in a great event and transformed by it
into something remarkable.

They impress us with their courage, but we read with full knowledge that
they were fighting a losing battle. By the 1320s, inquisitors had become efficient at persecuting marginal groups, whatever they believed. They were especially so in southern France, because they were operating close to the papal
court and were more or less supported by the crown. Even so, the French
beguins were hard to eliminate, and in Catalonia they were apparently even
more tenacious. The *Little Summa or Brief Word on the Concord of the New and Old
Testaments*, one of our clearest insights into the heavily Joachite ideology which
sustained the Catalan beguins, was produced in the early 1350s, and we also
know of processes from that decade.[50]

Ubertino da Casale and the Controversy over Christ's Poverty

EVEN AS JOHN'S INQUISITORS were crushing the beguins and French spirituals, John was turning on the Franciscan order itself. Moreover, he was doing so with at least some help from a man leaders of the order detested, Ubertino da Casale.

Ubertino's Escape to the Benedictines

We last encountered Ubertino at Avignon in 1317, telling the pope that he would willingly speak for the spirituals if asked to do so. He was, we remember, informed that no such request would be forthcoming. If John wanted to keep Ubertino from testifying, it was obviously because the pope wanted to get on with the task of bringing the recalcitrant friars into line and did not want Ubertino complicating the process. One wonders, though, if his rejection of the offer might also have revealed a degree of sympathy for Ubertino himself. Angelo portrays John as saying, "We don't want you to involve yourself in this business." It was, to be sure, a dangerous business in which to be involved.

Angelo reports that Ubertino heeded the pope's warning and stayed out of the affair, but the Franciscan leaders wanted to see him ruined anyway, because they were afraid that he would speak out against them in the future—and indeed that might have been the case. At any rate, he had said enough in the past to keep any leader with a decent memory on his scent for a long time to come. Once the French spirituals had been placed on a path that would eventually lead them back to their superiors (or, if they chose, to the stake), those superiors found it troubling that Ubertino was still living with his patron Napoleone Orsini at the papal court. According to Angelo, they wore the pope out with their incessant requests that Ubertino be returned to obedience. John, hoping to satisfy the order, finally summoned Ubertino and suggested that he spend a few days with the Franciscans while the pope worked out a permanent solution to his problem. Ubertino replied that if the leaders managed to get their hands on him for just one day, there would be no need for John or anyone else to worry about his future. John saw the point and gave Ubertino a choice: he could go back to the Franciscans or join a completely different order. Ubertino chose the second alternative, although he was not happy with it and hoped that he could persuade the pope to find yet another solution. The pope had decided, however, and on October 1, 1317, he officially made Ubertino a Benedictine, assigning him to the monastery at Gembloux. John saw that it was a solution the Franciscan leaders could tolerate, and Angelo affirms that they were jubilant when Ubertino assumed the Benedictine habit as if he were taking up the cross. Moreover, as Angelo also observes, his assignment to Gembloux would keep him well out of the way. In reality it did not. The assignment seems to have been a purely notional one, with Ubertino staying in Avignon under the protection of Cardinal Orsini. Angelo observes that he was treated with honor and respect by the cardinals. Nor did Ubertino's transfer change the overall plan of the Franciscan leaders. Angelo says that they continued to seek Ubertino's death, digging a pit for him into which they themselves eventually fell.[1]

The Controversy over Christ's Poverty

The nature of that pit is another story, and one that must be told here at least in outline. We have seen that by the 1320s, inquisitorial attention had broadened from the spiritual Franciscans to their lay supporters. It was a hearing concerning one such supporter that spread the net even wider, sending heresy-hunters beyond distinctively spiritual Franciscan doctrine to examine what had hitherto been considered orthodoxy throughout the order. The story, as related by Nicholas the Minorite,[2] is that the Dominican inquisitor Jean de Beaune had been examining a beguin at Narbonne. As was customary, he consulted with a number of local experts concerning the process, and one of these was Berengar Talon, lector in the Franciscan house. One of the purportedly heretical beliefs held by the beguin was the idea that Christ and his disciples possessed nothing, either individually or in common. Upon being confronted with this belief, Berengar observed that far from being heretical, it was accepted by the entire Franciscan order, and had been sanctioned in 1279 by Nicholas III in *Exiit qui seminat*. Jean de Beaune promptly accused Berengar, too, of heresy, and the latter appealed to Rome. John reacted vigorously and, one suspects, enthusiastically. He sought opinions from the cardinals and from various theologians, but he probably already had a strong opinion on the subject himself.[3]

The story of Jean de Beaune and Berengar Talon has an almost mythic quality. We see a single statement in an otherwise unremarkable heresy investigation ignite a fuse leading straight to the explosives hidden not under the spiritual Franciscans, but under the entire Franciscan order. We find that Berengar, the otherwise unremarkable friar who made it all possible was, as if by magic, the current occupant of Olivi's old teaching position at Narbonne. It seems almost too good to be true, and many historians have concluded that it is not. They have suggested (without any real evidence) that the story is apocryphal or that the event really occurred but was, in effect, a set-up designed to force the issue. It seems easier to believe that the whole thing occurred pretty much as described, although it is equally likely that the issue confronted by Jean and Berengar was already very much on people's minds. Both the process against the spirituals and that against Olivi's Apocalypse commentary had sensitized John and those around him to the fact that there was something odd about the Franciscan self-understanding—not only odd, in fact, but a bit insulting to the rest of the church. The Franciscans were saying that they and only they were completely emulating the poverty of Christ and his original disciples, and therefore that they attained a higher degree of perfection than other orders. It was a message that had gone down hard with the Dominicans throughout much of the thirteenth century, and it is not surprising to find a Dominican inquisitor challenging the Franciscans on it.[4]

If it was an old complaint for the Dominicans, they were making it in a very new situation. Heretofore Franciscans could expect papal protection. *Exiit qui seminat* was intended (in Nicholas III's own words) to silence "barking dogs" who were snarling and snapping at the Franciscans' heels, and I have suggested that the beasts Nicholas had in mind were at least partly *Domini canes*.[5] John XXII had a great deal more in common with those barking dogs. He admired Aquinas as a theologian and the Dominican rule as an organizational pattern. He had little sympathy with either Franciscan piety or Franciscan pretensions. None of this might have mattered as much as it did if events had not forced him to think a great deal about the Franciscan order, but they had done just that.

The processes against the spirituals and against Olivi's Apocalypse commentary had been instrumental in training John's attention on the order, but they had done so in slightly different ways. In order to see how the spiritual-conventual battle had sharpened the issue, we need only recall the reasoning of those Franciscans who in October 1317 told Michael of Cesena that they would not accept *Quorumdam exigit*. They refused to accept the pope's solution, because they felt that it violated the gospel pattern that had been imposed on the apostles by Christ and later accepted by the friars when they vowed the Franciscan life. We have seen that the whole question of whether the pope could abrogate a solemn vow had its own private history in the thirteenth century, quite apart from the Franciscan poverty question, but in this particular case the spirituals' willingness to place their vows beyond papal control had given the issue a new significance. Of course, the spirituals were doing the defying at this point, and it is noteworthy that in his sermon to the condemned at Marseilles, Michel Le Moine (a Franciscan himself) explicitly granted the pope's right to alter or abrogate the Franciscan rule, or any other rule for that matter. Nevertheless, the fact remained that the tradition celebrated even by the community saw the Franciscans as distinct from and superior to other orders precisely because they conformed more fully to the life of Christ and his disciples.

It is arguable that the spiritual-conventual dispute encouraged papal attention in still another way. The spirituals' notion of the Franciscan life was by no means identical with Francis's own notion, no matter how fondly they may have imagined it to be such. They did have one thing in common, though: like Francis, the spirituals saw the Franciscan life as one that many might admire but few would actually care to emulate. Had the spirituals, *per impossibile*, succeeded in making the entire order follow their example, it would have been a much smaller order and perhaps a more secure one. An elite detachment of friars who witnessed with their disciplined lives would, if kept in obedience to the pope, have made a very poor target for carping from other orders.

The community, on the other hand, made a remarkably good target. It emerged from the spiritual-conventual controversy victorious and apparently prosperous, yet claiming to follow the way of the cross and to be poor. It had spent four decades arguing that the vow of poverty did not bind Franciscans to living moderately, but simply to lack of possessions. However tenable that view may have seemed when elucidated by theologians, when it was baldly stated, there was something ridiculous about it. The reaction it inspired in contemporaries must have been similar to that evoked by a modern television commercial in which a slim, gorgeous young woman appears holding a huge dish of ice cream and announces that her new diet allows her to eat whatever she likes. The viewer instinctively feels that, whatever the value of the product being sold, this particular young woman is an actress who does not eat whatever she likes. Likewise, when a Franciscan lector invited a few influential clergy and laymen to join him and the rest of the power elite in that convent for a substantial meal in their own private dining quarters, and then told his guests that Franciscans were the poorest of all men, the clerics and laymen might well have been excused for reflecting that although some Franciscans somewhere might fit that description, these Franciscans certainly did not.

One can appreciate how, before 1317, the bemused guests might have found it easier to hold on to both ends of that thought. After 1317, thanks to the pope and leaders of the order, the first part of it seemed harder to believe. I use the word "seemed" advisedly. It is hardly true that after 1317 every Franciscan with integrity was dead, in prison, or hiding in someone's attic. A number of friars managed to live disciplined lives within the community. We are speaking of perception here. The community had fought a long, very public battle, and won it, yet even many of those who aided in its victory might have seen the spirituals as witnessing to traditional Franciscan values that the community itself had betrayed. It is worth remembering that when leaders of the order approached Boniface VIII, complaining about the spirituals, his immediate response (according to Angelo Clareno) was "Leave them alone, they're doing better than you are!" Angelo has a weakness for morally edifying but historically dubious anecdotes, and this may be one of them, but the point of his story seems valid. If Boniface eventually threw his support behind the leaders, it was not because he somehow admired them more than he admired the spirituals, but because he had become convinced that the danger to order posed by the spirituals outweighed their virtues. We see something similar in the next two popes. Clement V went far in accepting the spirituals' critique of the community; nevertheless, he recognized the threat to discipline presented by their protest, and tried to neutralize it with a solution that would, despite his best intentions, eventually lead to the spirituals' defeat. John XXII moved decisively against the spirituals, but his subsequent evaluation of the community sounded oddly like Ubertino da Casale's assault on it at Vienne.

In other words, however differently these three popes may have acted, all recognized that there were two sides to the matter. The spirituals were dangerous because they threatened duly constituted authority, but their criticism of the order was valid to some extent. After 1317, a great many people might have found it easy to conclude that in defeating the spirituals, the order had won a victory over its own conscience. Having reached that conclusion, those who had resented Franciscan pretensions for decades could decide that the emptiness of those pretensions was more apparent than ever before, and it was an excellent time to expose them.

The process against Olivi's Apocalypse commentary laid the groundwork in a slightly different way. Joseph Koch argued in 1933 that all three processes—that against the spirituals, that against Olivi's commentary, and the subsequent one concerning Christ's poverty—were causally related. The attack on Olivi's commentary was a result of John's assault on the spiritual Franciscans. It represented one weapon in that assault. In the process of censuring the commentary, however, the papal commission discovered a disturbing overlap between Olivi's purportedly heterodox views and what had hitherto passed for orthodoxy within the Franciscan order. In identifying the rule with the life of Christ and his disciples, and in claiming total lack of possessions as an important part of that identity, Olivi was stating what the order as a whole believed and, unfortunately, what Nicholas III had promulgated in *Exiit qui seminat*. The commission contained two Franciscans and thus slid over this difficulty by suggesting that, whatever Olivi and Nicholas meant by this identification, they could not have meant the same thing; but John, unsatisfied, was determined to pursue the matter.[6]

Koch's theory, in its strongest form, ignores the fact that John, a man on good terms with the Dominicans, did not need the commission's report to alert him to the problems inherent in the traditional Franciscan self-understanding.[7] The Dominicans had been saying for years what John was about to say, and we can reasonably assume that they also had been saying it to John. In an attenuated form, however, Koch's argument makes good sense. The peculiar overlap between Olivi's claims and the community's might well have heightened John's sense that something had to be done about the Franciscans, and once he began to do it, that same overlap turned the Olivi process into a missile that could be pointed at the order as a whole. John could use Olivi against the order in much the same way the order had once used him against the spirituals. The Apocalypse commentary could be depicted as illustrating the heretical implications of accepted Franciscan doctrine concerning evangelical poverty.

Thus it is hardly surprising that in the early 1320s, when John followed up the commission report on Olivi's commentary by seeking further illumination from individual theologians on specific issues, one of the statements from the commentary on which he sought advice was the assertion that the pontificate assumed by Peter originally involved evangelical poverty and only later was converted to a state of owning temporal property. Another targeted assertion was Olivi's identification of Saint Francis as the revealer of the evangelical life and rule to be observed in the sixth and seventh periods of church history and (after Christ and his mother) as its highest observer. It is impossible to say how many theologians were asked to consider these statements, but we have the reactions of two to the first. Both take issue with the implication that the apostles had neither common nor personal possessions, and one calls it heretical.[8] Only one response to the second statement has survived. It recognizes the special claims for the Franciscan order inherent in the passage; curtly announces that the Franciscan rule is no more evangelical than the Augustinian or Benedictine; and affirms that, despite Franciscan claims to the contrary, the apostles had common possessions—as do the current Franciscans, however much they wish to deny it.[9] These responses show how the Olivi process was moving in tandem with John's effort to change Franciscan views concerning the apostles and themselves. In fact, both theologians fortify their critique of Olivi by citing 1323 and 1324 bulls aimed at the order, bulls to which we will turn in a moment.

In the early 1320s, then, even as theologians registered opinions on Olivi's commentary, they were also registering opinions on the question of Christ's poverty for an entirely different investigation. Numerous opinions on the latter subject were gathered together in a single codex, which has survived.[10] It is not surprising that all the Franciscans who weighed in with views—except one—insisted that Berengar Talon's opinion was orthodox, while most of the others said it was heretical. The only real cause for amazement is the one atypical Franciscan: It was Ubertino da Casale.

Ubertino and Christ's Poverty

Ubertino's selection as a consultant might seem odd in view of the fact that the order had continued to hound him after his theoretical switch to the Benedictines. In 1319 he had been caught up in the Olivi process when

Bonagratia of Bergamo, now procurator of the Franciscan order, filed a series of charges against him at Avignon, and he was asked to tell papal auditors how he felt about those theses from Olivi's commentary censured by the papal commission. Ubertino argued that though the "bare articles" (*nudos articulos*) examined by the commission might seem heterodox when read alone, anyone who viewed them in the context of Olivi's total commentary would see that they were orthodox.[11]

On that occasion, Ubertino escaped Bonagratia's clutches yet again, but the incident is significant nonetheless. Bonagratia's precise charges showed the nexus between the Olivi process and the process against the spirituals, since he attempted to identify Ubertino with Olivi's purported heresy in identifying the Franciscan rule with the gospel. Bonagratia not only cited Olivi's Apocalypse commentary but cited the eighth of his *Questions on Evangelical Perfection* as well,[12] and observed that some of Olivi's followers had already been executed for adhering to Olivi's views as Ubertino did. He was apparently referring to the 1318 burning of the four spirituals at Marseilles. Unfortunately, as Bonagratia would soon discover, the area in which he chose to bind Olivi to Ubertino and the spirituals was one in which others could see a connection between Olivi and the entire order. The procurator would soon learn the lesson he was already teaching Ubertino: that one had to speak very carefully when discussing the relationship between Christ's original followers and contemporary Franciscans.

At any rate, Ubertino must have emerged from the experience very much aware that the topic was a dangerous one, and he soon learned that the pope's opinion on the matter was not identical with Bonagratia's. When John broached the matter at a consistory in March 1322, even before he had the benefit of all the opinions he would receive, he attacked the Franciscan position vigorously. Ubertino, still in the service and under the protection of Napoleone Orsini, would have known what was said. When he was asked, almost immediately thereafter, to state his thoughts on Christ's poverty, he knew what he was supposed to say.

His first reply, probably delivered in person before the pope by Easter 1322, was neither what the pope wanted him to say nor what we might expect him to have said. It was, in fact, elusive. In good academic fashion he drew two distinctions. First, he distinguished between Christ and the apostles as leaders of the church and as examples of religious perfection. As leaders of the church, they possessed goods in common. This was the traditional Franciscan position, held not only by earlier apologists like Bonaventure and John Pecham, but also by both sides in the *usus pauper* controversy. The Franciscans, confronted from the beginning by the objection that Christ and his disciples had a purse, always had acknowledged that leaders of the early church held common possessions in some sense. Even Olivi had agreed to that much,[13] although it is dangerous to push this point too far, since Olivi was writing in the midst of another battle and thus asking himself a slightly different set of questions. The contrast of Olivi's comments on ownership in 1279 and Ubertino's in 1322 reminds us of the differences between Bonaventure's comments on *usus pauper* and Olivi's.[14] Some passages in Bonaventure had seemed to support Olivi's assertion that *usus pauper* was an essential part of the Franciscan vow, but any aid they might have furnished was always compromised by the fact that Bonaventure, innocently pursuing his pre-conflict agenda, had not been forced to trace the logical conclusions of his stance, as Olivi and his opponents were required to do. We see a similar characteristic in Olivi's comments on ownership. Like Ubertino, he distinguished between the apostles as prelates and as exemplars of evangelical perfection, yet his focus was always more on use than on ownership. The question that interested Olivi most was why the apostles found themselves carrying a purse, not whether they owned its contents in one sense but not in another. His focus was on function. He argued that the apostles did not compromise evangelical perfection by carrying a purse, because in their role as prelates, they used the money to provide for the faithful. Moreover, when moving through hostile territory in which no one would provide for them, they were justified in carrying money to purchase supplies. This is not to say that Olivi never discussed ownership. He did, just as Bonaventure discussed *usus pauper*. He simply did not do so in a context that forced him to be very technical. It is for this reason that, when we read in the Apocalypse commentary that the pontificate assumed by Peter originally involved evangelical poverty and only later was converted to a state of owning temporal property, we need not ask whether somewhere between 1279 and 1298 Olivi had changed his mind on the question of property in the early church.

But we return to Ubertino. Having offered his first distinction and having cheerfully granted that as prelates, the apostles had possessions, he turns to the second category, the apostles as exemplars of evangelical perfection. Here he makes his second distinction, between possession in the sense of civil or legal right and possession of necessities according to the law of nature. They lacked the first, so they had no right to defend their goods by legal process, but they enjoyed the second.

Here Ubertino seems to be going slightly beyond other Franciscan apologists of his time.[15] They granted that the apostles had a natural right to use (*ius utendi*) things necessary for their survival, but that fact did not give them dominion over such things. What they had was *simplex facti usus*, precisely what Adam and Eve had in the garden before the fall. Property came later, as a result of the fall. When the Franciscan order met at Perugia in May–June 1322 and issued an official position, that was it. Here again it is important to underscore the remarkable corporate claim implied in this apparently antiquarian discussion. Since the Franciscans assumed that they and they alone among contemporary orders fully embodied this state, they were describing an exclusive group composed of the pre-fall Adam and Eve, Christ and his apostles, and themselves.

The implication was hardly lost on other orders, and they opposed it with a different view of the relationship between use and dominion. Dominican theologians such as Hervé Natal and Durand de St.-Pourçain insisted that Adam, Eve, Christ, the apostles, and the Franciscans had not only *simplex facti usus*, not only *ius utendi*, but also genuine dominion or lordship (*dominium*) over what they consumed in use.[16] Such distinctions may seem little more than empty theorizing, and it is hard to study the poverty debate of the 1320s very long without concluding that the empty theorization quotient in it was rather high; yet the difficulties of measuring *dominium* against *ius* (or even of decoding such terms) should not blind us to the serious implications of the battle. A papal decision in favor of the Franciscans would have endorsed their claim to membership in that exclusive club. A decision against them would endorse the charge—launched not only by the Dominicans but also by earlier secular critics, such as Gerard of Abbeville—that the Franciscan claim to superiority was hollow and pretentious, that they had in fact been living a lie.

We are again losing sight of Ubertino. What, exactly, was he saying about this issue? It is rather hard to decide. He avoided using the phrase *simplex facti usus* but, as Charles Davis points out, in saying that Christ and his apostles possessed what they needed for subsistence "according to the law of nature and of common fraternal charity," he did echo a passage from Bonaventure that Michael of Cesena would also put to use in defending the Franciscan position.[17] In the final analysis, as Davis also observes, Ubertino's words were ambiguous enough to have been used in succeeding years to support very different positions. They were also ambiguous enough to make the pope decide that he needed a clearer statement from Ubertino. The result was his longer, written document, *Treatise on the Highest Poverty Practiced by Christ, His Apostles, and Apostolic Men*.[18]

The *Treatise* consists of a long argument and a short summary.[19] Here again Ubertino joins the Franciscan tradition in agreeing that the apostles possessed goods insofar as they were prelates. Again he allows that they possessed "insofar as natural sustenance is concerned." That is, they possessed what they needed, avoiding excess. In this work, however, Ubertino finally clarifies the question of *dominium*. The apostles had *dominium quantum ad usum*, dominion over what they used, but they did not have "civil dominion which would allow them to litigate."

In allowing the word *dominium* entrance into the Franciscan camp, Ubertino breaks ranks with tradition and with current Franciscan leaders as well. As for tradition, he parts company with Bonaventure, with Michael of Cesena, and even with Olivi. The extent of his apostasy can be measured by comparing this treatise with the eighth of Olivi's *Questions on Evangelical Perfection*, from which Ubertino borrows extensively. Charles Davis has traced the limits of his borrowing, and he demonstrates the significance of Ubertino's departures. He notes that, although Ubertino copies extensively from question eight, he reorders its parts and leaves out one section entirely. The section he omits is the last one in Olivi's argument for poverty, which deals with its role in the history of salvation. Here as elsewhere, Olivi had attempted to argue that Franciscan poverty and its revival of the apostolic model could be read as a key development in the birth of a new era. In other words, he had placed Franciscan poverty in an apocalyptic context. Ubertino quietly removes that context. Poverty, as he describes it in his treatise, has no obvious apocalyptic significance. Neither does the Franciscan order.

The elimination of Olivi's apocalyptic musings, involving as it does the omission of an entire section, is hard to miss. As Davis shows, however, Ubertino differs from Olivi in a subtler way, through smaller changes in the sections that he does reproduce. In these sections, Olivi had argued that the highest poverty—Franciscan poverty—is superior both to individual and to communal ownership. Ubertino discreetly eliminates the argument concerning communal ownership. Thus, the implication that so disturbed not only critics of Olivi's Apocalypse commentary but also everyone who listened carefully to the Franciscans when they celebrated their own superiority—the idea that they and only they manifested the poverty observed by Christ and the apostles—is absent from Ubertino's treatise. He suggests that Franciscans, Dominicans, Benedictines, and other groups that renounce private property can claim to observe evangelical poverty, as long as they avoid litigation and use only what is necessary. This latter element is important. Far from weakening Olivi's emphasis on *usus pauper* as an essential part of evangelical poverty, Ubertino fortifies it.

It might strike the reader that Ubertino has executed a remarkable retreat from his old position, and it might seem equally tempting to attribute this withdrawal to his new institutional affiliation, his need to please John XXII, or to both. Certainly his position in the treatise fits both. He is redefining evangelical poverty in such a way that he can observe it as a Benedictine; in addition, his argument against the Franciscan notion of *simplex facti usus* echoes a notion dear to John's heart, the idea that in the area of consumables, use is inseparable from dominion. It is, in other words, impossible to eat one's dinner without having dominion over it. Nevertheless, before attempting to turn either factor into an explanation, one should consider two things.

First, Ubertino's silence on apocalyptic matters was less recent than either his Benedictine connection or John's request for an opinion on poverty. We think of Ubertino as a heavily apocalyptic thinker because of the *Arbor vitae*, but the latter was written in 1305 and represents Ubertino's last serious apocalyptic utterance of which we have any record. Thus, between the *Arbor vitae* and the *Tractatus de altissima paupertate*, we have a seventeen-year interval with no indication that he was still thinking in these terms. This period includes a sizable polemical offering from him in connection with the Council of Vienne.

To be sure, one could argue that at Vienne, as later at Avignon, his political instincts kept him from mentioning anything that controversial. Thus the fact that he said nothing about it does not prove that he was not still thinking about it. The question then, is this: Do we have any reason to think it likely that his silence was any more than tactical, that he would actually have changed his mind?

Very little, but Charles Davis offers one interesting observation. In 1305, Ubertino identified both Boniface VIII and Benedict XI with the mystical Antichrist. In doing so, he went well beyond Olivi, who avoided such concrete identifications. Various scholars have recognized this difference without pondering its possible effect on Ubertino's faith in the Olivian timetable. As Davis recognizes (without spelling it out in detail), taking what Olivi predicted and actually plugging it into the present would have encouraged Ubertino to evaluate Olivi's scenario in the light of what happened next. What Olivi expected to happen immediately after the mystical Antichrist appeared was persecution of the elect, followed by the destruction of the carnal church (probably by a non-Christian army), and then the arrival of the Great Antichrist. What actually happened after 1305 was persecution of the elect (the spirituals), followed by an attempt on Clement V's part to protect the spirituals by reforming the order. The carnal church, instead of being destroyed by a non-Christian army, was entrusted to the care of a well-meaning (if wrongheaded) pope who attempted to shelter the spirituals from their oppressors.

It would be understandable if Ubertino, weighing Olivi's scenario against these events, had decided that either the scenario was incorrect or he had been incorrect in thinking that history had already arrived at the stage of the mystical Antichrist.

If this is the case, then Ubertino makes an interesting contrast with an Occitan beguin like Na Prous Boneta. Prous saw the situation from 1317 on as a credible setting for the persecution of Antichrist—and John XXII as a credible Antichrist. These were days in which history fit the Olivian scenario rather well, and Prous's process leaves us with little doubt that by the time history began to depart in any significant way from the scenario, she was no longer alive to witness its divergence. Ubertino arrived at the same events after having read the program into history much earlier and having seen it fail to reflect reality after a certain point. Thus he may have come to the drama of 1317 already disillusioned with apocalyptic interpretation. Moreover, as an insider at Avignon who had developed an oddly intimate relationship with John XXII, he would have seen these events from a much different perspective than Prous and would have found it hard to recognize the Great Beast in the cantankerous old pope.

The second point to be considered is that Ubertino's critique of the Franciscan insistence on complete expropriation echoes his earlier complaints at Vienne in a significant way. While none of Ubertino's writings from that era ever explicitly questioned the basic notion that Franciscans were entirely without possessions, he was relentless in his effort to expose the rationalizations that allowed his coreligionists to enjoy substantial control over the resources at their disposal without acknowledging ownership of them. One need only remember the images he invoked of friars traveling with their bag boys so that they would not have to violate their vow by actually touching money, or the money boxes in Franciscan churches being emptied by someone other than a friar. Ubertino had a clear sense of the hypocrisy underlying such expedients.

Even at Vienne, Ubertino was aware of the connection between the friars' hypocrisy and their peculiar relation to the pope. He argued that the decline of Franciscan poverty had occurred because a succession of pontiffs had conspired with leaders of the order to create a situation in which Franciscans controlled substantial resources that were technically owned by the pope. These resources were theoretically managed by procurators under papal control, but by the fourteenth century, such procurators answered largely to the order. If the resources were threatened in any way, the order could not take the matter to court, but the pope could and would, since he owned those resources.

Ubertino wanted the system reformed in a way that largely eliminated the papacy from involvement. Goods donated for the friars' use would remain under the ownership and control of the donor. The Franciscans' hold over buildings, books, wine, and everything else would remain precarious until the moment they were consumed by use. If donors wanted to take them back, they would be free to do so.

The major issue here is Ubertino's attitude toward papal patronage of the order, and it is a point on which he was absolutely consistent, whether we read the *Arbor vitae,* the polemics of ca. 1310–12, or the 1322 *Tractatus.* He did not question the pope's right to act as protector, if he chose to do so, and even cited key papal bulls when they suited his purpose; but he made no secret of his conviction that the total effect of these bulls had been negative and that they constituted a violation of Francis's plea to avoid seeking privileges and to observe the rule literally, *sine glossa.* The 1279 bull *Exiit qui seminat,* which Olivi had cited in the *usus pauper* controversy and which, according to Brian Tierney, Olivi had regarded as such a safeguard of Franciscan poverty that he had elaborated the first doctrine of papal infallibility in order to protect it against the ravages of a future evil pope,[20] was described by Ubertino as "like a great millstone tied around the waist of the order."[21] It had given Franciscans the sort of power and security Francis himself had wanted them to avoid, and it had done so in a way that made them hypocrites as well.

If the 1322 treatise offers something new to this viewpoint, it is that for the first time, in the process of rejecting such hypocrisy, Ubertino rejects the Franciscan doctrine of total expropriation as well. The doctrine emerges as a fiction that the order would be better off abandoning. It is hard to believe that Ubertino takes this line for purely tactical reasons, to curry the pope's favor or to avoid his wrath. On the contrary, he seems to believe what he is saying, and there is no reason why he should not. It is a logical extension of what he had been saying over the previous two decades. For this reason, the treatise should be seen as an important document in the continuing discussion of poverty. In it, Ubertino sustains Olivi's legacy (and indeed his own) in celebrating *usus pauper* as the indispensable cornerstone of apostolic poverty, but goes beyond Olivi in compromising what Olivi would have seen as the other cornerstone, total lack of possessions.

Nevertheless, even if Ubertino moved away from Olivi and toward John XXII in granting that Christ, the apostles, *and* the Franciscans owned property, he was still much closer to Olivi than he was to John. His treatise lauds an apostolic life that held little interest for the pope. John, in fact, saw Christ and the apostles much differently, and not only credited them with common property, but also conferred upon them the right to litigate about it.[22]

John's Decision and Its Aftermath

By the time Ubertino wrote, events were moving at a rapid pace.[23] The year 1322 was one of confrontation between John and the Franciscan leadership. In March, the pope issued *Quia nonnunquam*,[24] which freed theologians to state their opinions by lifting the ban *Exiit qui seminat* had placed on discussion of its contents. *Exiit* had been written to solve a problem once and for all, but John wanted that problem reconsidered. As he explained in the opening lines of *Quia nonnunquam*, there is often a gap between the goal of legislation and its actual result. When a lawmaker sees by experience that what he or his predecessor thought would be beneficial has turned out to be harmful, he has the right and the duty to change it.

Leaders of the Franciscan order were thoroughly alarmed. *Exiit* was their shelter from all those vicious beasts that would otherwise have been snarling at them. When, at Pentecost, they met at Perugia for their annual general chapter, they sent a letter to John asking him to restore the ban. More important, they issued two encyclicals to the faithful defending the position on Christ's poverty found in *Exiit*.[25] John was not amused. In effect, the order had defied him by taking its case to the universal Church.

John's response came in December. *Ad conditorem* restated his right to do what he had done in *Quia nonnunquam*.[26] Again he explained that when a lawmaker sees laws working out badly, it is proper for him to do something about them. Thus he had a right to change that clause of *Exiit* that banned discussion about it. In the process of saying all this, however, John changed yet another clause of *Exiit*, the one in which the papacy assumed ownership for everything the Franciscans used. John refused to accept responsibility for any goods arriving at Franciscan doorsteps from that point on, and thus he refused to appoint any more procurators. The order had denied steadfastly that it held *dominium* over these goods. John now announced that he didn't either.

Who did, then? John's bull contained an answer, one that went straight back to the middle of the thirteenth century. Echoing early secular critics of the Franciscan order, John announced that it was nonsense to claim that one could consume goods without holding *dominium* over them. It was silly to insist that every bean, every egg, and every piece of bread given to and eaten by every Franciscan in the world actually belonged to the pope. Nicholas III couldn't have meant to affirm as much, because he was simply too intelligent to say anything that foolish.

Anyone who takes the trouble to read John's thoughts on this score—or for that matter to examine other, earlier thoughts on the same issue—may begin to wonder if the important element in them was not so much a carefully crafted, subtle, intellectually convincing argument about the relationship between dominion and consumable goods as an exasperated protest that the emperor had no clothes on. Whether one inevitably exercised *dominium* over goods consumed in use was a question that could be (and was) argued either way. It was possible for Franciscans to erect a theoretical structure that gave the pope ownership over goods that they received directly from donors, consumed, or dispensed with as they saw fit. But one look at the result was sufficient to convince John and others that it left the pope with a purely theoretical ownership and the Franciscans with a purely theoretical poverty.

John's bull contained another, almost perversely effective argument. In their encyclical, the Franciscans had argued that lack of ownership kept them from solicitude concerning material goods. John replied that the remarkable solicitude shown by the order concerning the acquisition of material goods demonstrated that, if this was the result of renouncing ownership, it hadn't worked. Here again the main point was the one John had now made in two bulls: If experience shows that past legislation has not produced the expected effect, it should be changed.

The pope had thus established that the Franciscans had property. That left Christ. In November 1323, he settled the question in the bull *Cum inter nonnullos*.[27] This time he was brief: It would henceforth be considered heretical to affirm that Christ did not own anything either privately or in common. It would also be heretical to assert that Christ and his disciples had no right to use, sell, or exchange the things that they had. That seems clear enough, but John himself probably recognized that it was not completely so. There was, for example, no mention of *dominium* or *simplex usus facti*. John may have wanted the bull to contradict the Perugia encyclical without explicitly contradicting *Exiit qui seminat*.[28]

Franciscans continued to protest, and they received aid from a surprising quarter. The Emperor Ludwig of Bavaria, at odds with the pope, saw a potential weapon against his enemy and seized it gratefully. The April 1324 Sachsenhausen Declaration supported Franciscan claims, announcing that Nicholas III and a host of preceding popes had already settled the question of Christ's poverty. What had been solemnly determined by Christ's vicar on earth was unchangeable. Thus John was not merely wrong but heretical.

However much the Sachsenhausen Declaration might have warmed Franciscan hearts, it must also have caused discomfort to those leaders who recognized that it echoed the writings of Olivi.[29]

This turn of events presented Michael of Cesena with new possibilities, though it is hard to tell when he began to take advantage of them. The general chapter held at Lyon in 1325 produced a statute ordering Franciscans to speak of John XXII with the proper reverence.[30] Nevertheless, Michael was in Italy in the summer of 1327, and that spring, Ludwig had gone to Rome with some Franciscans in his cortège. Was Michael already negotiating with Ludwig by summer? There is no way of saying for sure, but John thought so. In fact, he was soon told as much by the Guelfs of Perugia, who informed him that Michael was planning to become Ludwig's antipope. Summoned to Avignon, Michael pleaded illness and delayed his trip. When he finally arrived in December 1327, he found that the papal court was easy to enter but hard to leave. The pope and minister general must have coexisted there under some tension until, at a consistory in April 1328, they publicly shared their feelings toward one another. Michael was again ordered not to leave Avignon. Six weeks later he, William of Ockham, Bonagratia of Bergamo, and Francesco d'Ascoli quietly did just that. They were escorted to Italy by imperial troops and began their period as a Franciscan government in exile.

Ubertino was not directly involved in the Avignon confrontation. Indeed, by the time the summer of 1325 had ended, Ubertino had fled the papal court. In September of that year, the pope sent a letter to leaders of the Franciscan order informing them that Ubertino was wandering through the world like a vagabond and should be apprehended—but he was not apprehended. According to a contemporary chronicler, he was present in Rome for the coronation of Pietro di Corbara, Ludwig the Bavarian's antipope, and busied himself preaching against John XXII. Some historians have viewed this notice with skepticism, but we have another record of him preaching against John XXII at Como in 1329. The chronicler Nicholas Glassberger, writing in the early sixteenth century, says that Ubertino was reconciled with the pope in 1330, but there is no other evidence for such a happy ending. In a 1341 letter from Pope Benedict XII, he is referred to as deceased, and a tradition describes him as having met a violent end, but there is no way of saying how or precisely when he died.[31]

ANGELO CLARENO AND BEYOND

WHILE UBERTINO DA CASALE was working out his destiny with the aid of John XXII and a hostile Franciscan leadership, Angelo Clareno was following a much different path. In 1317, the year in which the spirituals were flattened by a first wave of bulls from John's chancery, Angelo, like Ubertino, was allowed to transfer to another order—in his case, the Celestinians.

Two Letters

In the summer of 1317, just before that transfer took place, Angelo wrote two significant letters. One looked backward, the other forward. The former was the *apologia* addressed to John XXII around the early summer of 1317,[1] a work that we have already considered here. In it he replied to accusations against him by leaders of the Franciscan order. These accusations had brought into question the odd relationship between the Franciscan rule and Angelo's own apparently defunct order, the Poor Hermits of Pope Celestine; in addition, they had urged examination of Angelo's attitude toward the papacy.

We need not rehearse the discussion here. Suffice it to say that he denied all. His letter to John closes with a request that the pope rescue him and his colleagues from the wrath of their persecutors and provide them with a way of observing the Franciscan rule outside the Franciscan order.[2] As we have seen, that did not occur. The more interesting question is whether at this late date Angelo still saw any real possibility of its occurring, or whether his plea was by this time largely *pro forma*.

Here lies the interest of the other letter, written at roughly the same time, but to some colleagues in Italy.[3] In it Angelo seems to be warning brothers at home not to expect too much from the current situation. He announces that "virtue and power, the thing and its name, will exist together in the same entity when that which you deem already fulfilled is in fact fulfilled," but at present the two are unconnected.[4] In the eyes of the decretists and legists, the names themselves are quite adequate. Thus if you have a minister, a cardinal protector, and an order, you have the reality ordained by Saint Francis. The truth is otherwise, though. These offices were created for the sake of the rule, not the reverse. The rule is from Christ and continues even in the absence of these offices, just as during the time between Good Friday and Easter Sunday, the church continued to exist in the Virgin Mary alone. Obedience to the rule is greater than obedience to the ministers and cardinal protector. The rule can retain its substantial being in its loving observers even when the name of the order, its walls and roofs, and all its external ceremonies are absent.[5]

Angelo reminds his readers that this is more than a theoretical discussion. Through his prophetic gifts, Francis foresaw that leaders of the order would begin to decide on the basis of human prudence and ambition rather than the rule, and would settle for the name rather than the reality. For that very reason Francis himself preferred to speak not of the *ordo minorum* but of the *vita minorum*, thus emphasizing behavior rather than the institution. For that reason, too, Francis warned the order that it should rejoice more in having a few ardent observers than in attracting large numbers. He knew that if the order grew to a size of just three devout brothers, Christ would protect it.

Angelo's negative evaluation of the Franciscan leaders is hardly new, but Gian Luca Potestà is nonetheless correct in suggesting that in this letter Angelo, without admitting it, abandons the strategy that he has been pursuing for some time.[6] He seems to have given up hope of negotiating an institutional solution and is warning his colleagues that they must go on with the business of observing the rule even though they can expect little support from the ecclesiastical hierarchy. That is perhaps putting the matter too positively. Angelo reminds his followers that Christ's passion precedes his resurrection and predicts that it must be thus with Francis. Like Christ, Francis must be rejected in the person of his followers before he arises in those three symbolic good brothers.[7] Here again we encounter the theme dear to spiritual Franciscan hearts—Francis's passion and resurrection—and here again it would be dangerous to examine it too closely, trying to judge precisely what Angelo has in mind.[8] Viewed from a distance it is clear enough. The basic theme is repeated in other letters probably written around this time. In them, Angelo comes to terms with the fact that obedience to the rule may be on a collision course with ecclesiastical authority. The rule is the evangelical form of life sanctioned by Christ himself, and Christ must be obeyed, rather than men. This will, however, mean submitting to persecution.[9]

His instincts were in good working order. On December 30, 1317, *Sancta romana* explicitly attacked those who claimed to operate on the basis of a privilege from Celestine V. The bull was aimed at those "commonly called *fraticelli seu fratres de paupere vita.*" John's bull robbed Angelo's group of any remaining hope that their dubious legal claim would finally be acknowledged, yet simultaneously (almost as a consolation prize) he awarded them the name by which historians would later refer to them. The term *fraticelli* had been used to designate those who followed a religious life, often an eremitical one, outside any established order or as third-order Franciscans; it was also used by the spirituals or their critics to designate the spirituals themselves.[10] It would become the scholars' term of choice both for the Italian spirituals (the *fraticelli de paupere vita*) and for those who stood with Michael of Cesena against John XXII (the *fraticelli de opinione*), but in the fourteenth century it continued to be used to designate others as well.

Subiaco

John's bull erased much of Angelo's reason for staying at Avignon. Another powerful impetus to leave came in August 1318 with the death of Giacomo Colonna. It was a good moment to disappear, and by the end of that year Angelo was back in central Italy, where he was given protection by Bartolomeo, abbot of Subiaco, a tough, aggressive warrior-monk who at some point in the 1320s experienced a conversion and become a model abbot.[11] Under his wing Angelo had the leisure—around sixteen years of it—allowing him to write extensively. His *oeuvre* included a commentary on the rule, his *Chronicle or History of the Seven Tribulations of the Franciscan Order,* and numerous letters. Most of what we have from Angelo comes from this period.

The rule commentary combined the official rule, the previous *Regula non bullata*, the Leo sources, and the Francis prophecies from the *Verba fratris Conradi* to produce a reading of early Franciscan history establishing direct continuity between Francis and the persecuted *fraticelli*. The latter's travails were seen as not only anticipated in early tensions but also predicted by Francis himself, who foresaw that the order would stray from its appointed path and that the few faithful would have to seek abandoned places or take refuge among the infidels.[12] Compared with the earlier commentaries by Hugh of Digne and Olivi, it shows the distinctiveness of Angelo's project.

Important though the rule commentary might be, it pales to insignificance beside another work on which Angelo labored from around 1322 to 1326: his *Chronicle or History of the Seven Tribulations of the Franciscan Order*. While the *Chronicle* may be less instructive than his letters, it is certainly Angelo's best-known work and the one most likely to be cited. Its purpose is to narrate the history of the Franciscan order as a continuous story with a central plot. In that story Francis, Brother Leo, Gerard of Borgo San Donnino, John of Parma, Peter Olivi, Bernard Délicieux, Ubertino da Casale, Angelo himself, and a host of others become one movement, while Elias, Crescentius of Iesi, Bonaventure, John of Murrovalle, Michael of Cesena, and the rest become another. They represent, to put it bluntly, the good guys and the bad ones, and the aims of each group remain remarkably consistent.[13] The good want to follow the rule and *Testament* literally. The bad ones think it more important to follow worldly prudence. They want the order to be a success in worldly terms. The unity of the story is seen not only in the continuance of these two identifiable factions, but also in the fact that one faction is continually persecuting the other. In the early years, the attack was punctuated by periods of relative peace, but by Angelo's day, the pace of persecution has increased. The worldly, profoundly un-Franciscan faction has been able to effect so much damage precisely because it is successful at playing worldly games and gaining leadership positions within the order. From time to time, good men have risen to the top, men such as John of Parma and Raymond Geoffroi—but both John and Raymond were opposed and eventually deposed. In this battle, as in others, the children of Mammon have all the heavy artillery.

Angelo breaks Franciscan history down into seven periods characterized by seven tribulations visited upon the good by the bad. In effect, he offers an apocalyptic program within an apocalyptic program within an apocalyptic program. He accepts the Augustinian notion that there are seven ages of world history, and that church history unfolds within the sixth of these ages, but he also accepts the sevenfold division of church history that dominated exegesis of the Apocalypse throughout the thirteenth century—and he accepts it, at least partly, in its Olivian form, with Francis ushering in a sixth period of church history that combines renewal and persecution.[14] The seven tribulations are stages within that sixth period and will lead to a final, seventh period of church history, a time of relative peace and fulfillment.

The seven periods of church history as Olivi envisaged them—in fact, as scholars from Bede on envisaged them—were progressive in the sense that each introduced an element of genuine novelty into church history. Angelo's seven miniperiods of Franciscan history, on the other hand, show remarkably little development. The sort of thuggery practiced by Elias as minister general during the second tribulation bears a strong resemblance to the kind exercised by Crescentius of Iesi, minister general in the third, or John of Murrovalle, who occupied the same office in the fifth. Leaders of the order constantly approach popes and gain their support by presenting misleading analyses of the situation within the order. Spirituals repeatedly deliver stinging rebukes in which they accuse the leaders of more or less the same offenses in more or less the same language. Francis, John of Parma, Olivi, and Angelo could listen to one another's complaints with an overwhelming sense of *déjà vu*. And they all prophesy. Francis, John of Parma, Olivi—everyone prophesies. Indeed, they all prophesy the same future in approximately the same terms. There is some development in the sense that things get worse, but this theme is a muted one.[15] Angelo is so obsessed with underlining the basic similarities that he has little time to stress decline.

Angelo on Antichrist

The idea of tribulation in the sixth period was an exegetical commonplace. Various scholars saw current laxity within the church as inspired by the precursors of Antichrist, who were preparing the way for his arrival.[16] Olivi built upon that notion. His idea of a mystical Antichrist preceding the great one might be seen as a variation on the common idea of Antichrist's precursors.[17] Angelo, like Olivi, heavily identifies the tribulation preceding Antichrist with the attack on Franciscan poverty (and thus on the life of Christ and the apostles), but he is less communicative than Olivi when it comes to describing Antichrist himself.

The difference is a significant one. Whereas Olivi spoke constantly of the Antichrist, Angelo seldom does so. In the *Chronicle*, during his presentation of the first tribulation, he alludes to the "precursors of Antichrist" who combated the evangelical life introduced in the church by Christ through Francis; in his presentation of the fifth tribulation, he refers to the Franciscan leaders as passing a decree that established a likeness of Antichrist in the temple of God in advance of his coming; and later he describes the inquisitor Thomas of Aversa as a preacher of Antichrist.[18] That is the extent of his thought on the matter in the *Chronicle*. In other passages, employing the language of the Apocalypse, he speaks of the dragon, the serpent and the beast. His treatment of these figures displays a studied temporal ambiguity that would seem familiar to New Testament scholars. He can announce that Christ *will kill* the beast, but then in the next breath assert that Francis and others *have defeated* the serpent.[19] In short, allusions to future victory are combined with a sort of realized eschatology in which the victory is seen as already achieved.

Much the same thing can be said of the letters. The most striking thing about them is how seldom the word "Antichrist" appears. When it does, it is used in one of two ways. First, it may be employed in a relatively nontemporal, moral sense, as when Angelo says that "spurning Christ's counsels is a work of Satan and of antichristian pride"; or when he says that he who is displeased by Christ's commandments is an adversary of Christ and an Antichrist; or when, following I John 2:18, he says that many have become Antichrists under the name of Christ.[20]

Second, it may be used in reference to a future event involving a specific figure, as when Angelo says that "he who shows true obedience fears his own body and its senses more than he fears Antichrist with the armies of the impious, and is more terrified of the rationalizing of his prudence and the counsels of his senses than of the pseudo-prophets and unclear spirits who are already loosed and soon to be loosed with Antichrist";[21] or when he says that before Christ comes in judgment, Elijah will come to resist Antichrist and convert the Jews and Gentiles; or when he speaks of "that desert in which the elect will be saved during the time of Antichrist."[22]

If this distinction seems to be supported with too many examples, we can at least take solace in the fact that there could not have been many more. We have cited practically every explicit allusion to Antichrist in the entire letter collection, and that in itself is an interesting bit of data, since the collection runs to 364 pages in von Auw's edition. (There is one other reference, and it is an intriguing one, but we must wait a moment before considering it.)

In Angelo's failure to offer a sharply focused portrait of Antichrist, we encounter, in one more form, the basic difference between him and Olivi. In his Apocalypse commentary, Olivi attempted to make a coherent theology of history emerge from line-by-line exegesis of Scripture. He showed little concern with labeling a particular individual as Antichrist, but was intensely interested in discovering what the temptation of Antichrist would be like, when it would occur, and how it would be related to general threats like Islam or contemporary Parisian philosophy.

In Angelo—at least as we encounter him in the *Chronicle*—we see the opposite phenomenon. We see a *raconteur* whose major accomplishment lies in presenting a dramatic epic history of the order organized according to a few general principles. His story has a simple plot and a huge cast. The major lesson illustrated by it is not how things have changed, but how much they have stayed the same from Francis's day to Angelo's—and how miraculously Christ will snatch victory from defeat in the near future. His thought on Antichrist goes no further. Just as Angelo's apocalyptic program does not extend far beyond affirming that Francis was sent by God on a crucial historical mission and that God's intention will not be frustrated, so his thought on Antichrist does not extend beyond projecting a largely undefined temptation of Antichrist into the future but seeing previous and present persecution of the spirituals as a dress rehearsal for that persecution. That is the burden of his message. If we persist in reading more into it, that is partly because he punctuates his narrative with passages that seem more Sybilline than Joachite, more dithyrambic than philosophical, passages that invite us to read what we will into them.

Angelo and Joachim of Fiore

Angelo shares with most contemporary exegetes the notion that the great tribulation will be followed by a seventh period of church history, one in which God's people will finally be free to serve Him. He entertains this notion in its Olivian form, insofar as he describes the tribulations in the sixth period and the victory celebrated in the seventh period as a persecution and triumph of the values introduced by Saint Francis.[23] Does he accept it in a *completely* Olivian form, though, positing Joachim of Fiore's division of history into three general ages of Father, Son, and Holy Spirit, the third of which is born in the sixth period of church history and comes of age in the seventh? Here we must finally face the thorny problem of Angelo's Joachism.[24]

The real question is not whether Angelo was a Joachite, but what he would have had to say to qualify as one. If citing Joachim with approval on some particular issue made one a Joachite, then a good number of scholars were Joachites. Thirteenth- and fourteenth-century exegetes quoted him periodically in commentaries on the Apocalypse. Some did so in contexts that had nothing to do with his theology of history (for example, citing him on the meaning of a particular word in the text), but others went further, appropriating bits of his historical vision as well.[25]

If, at the other extreme, we reserve the term "Joachite" for those who fully appropriated Joachim, then Joachim himself was the first and last Joachite. Should we broaden the criteria slightly, and admit only those who adopted what we now consider the most distinctive elements in his theology of history—such as his concordance between the seven Old and seven New Testament periods, and his division of history into three ages of Father, Son, and Holy Spirit—then we would find some Joachites, but not many. Olivi would qualify, but few others would.

In the middle, we have that great sea of individuals who spoke enthusiastically of Joachim and who appropriated specific aspects of his theology of history while ignoring others. Those mid-thirteenth-century figures whom Salimbene labels "great Joachites"—preeminently John of Parma, Hugh of Digne, Gerard of Borgo San Donnino, and Salimbene himself—probably would have qualified by that standard. We know so little about them that it is hard to say what they actually believed. But the general impression derived from what we do have is that their peculiar concerns and interest in what we now know to be pseudo-Joachite works not only set them apart from essentially Joachite doctrine, but also set them apart from Joachism as Olivi would have understood it.[26]

Angelo belongs, at best, somewhere in the vicinity of this latter group. It is hard to discover the three ages of history in his work. There are passages in Angelo's letters that at least imply a new age of major proportions,[27] and such passages are not entirely absent from the *Chronicle*, either.[28] Yet in the final analysis, with the exception of two very ambiguous passages,[29] there is little evidence that Angelo has any real interest in the Joachite threefold division. (He does place Francis's triumph in the seventh period, though, as we will see in a moment.)

The same is true of Joachite concordances. Angelo is not above using them,[30] but he does so rarely. He is mainly interested in recruiting Joachim's services as a prophet of thirteenth-century Franciscan events, and in pursuing this project, he is willing to echo pseudo-Joachite prophetic works without analyzing them very deeply (as when he announces that Joachim "and others before him who had the spirit of prophecy" predicted Olivi).[31] In this particular case Angelo goes on to mention the Cyrillic prophecy and the Erythrian Sybil. He is thus paying a brief visit to the world of thirteenth-century pseudo-Joachite prophecy, not that of genuine Joachism.[32]

In fact, precise references to Joachim's genuine works are hard to find in Angelo's writings. There is certainly one at the end of his rule commentary, where he contrasts Olivi's view of the angel of the sixth seal with what Joachim says about that figure in his Apocalypse commentary;[33] but such passages are rare.

Those moments in the *Chronicle* at which Angelo discusses Salimbene's "great Joachites" tend to reinforce our sense that his own interest in Joachim was slight. He grants that John of Parma not only looked for reform in the order but also appealed to Joachim in support of his position; that is hardly surprising, since Salimbene, who knew John well, assures us that John's enthusiasm for Joachite apocalyptic led to his fall. Nevertheless, when Angelo himself deals with the issue on which John came to grief,[34] he does not speak of Joachite apocalyptic, but of Joachim's disagreement with Peter Lombard on the Trinity. He does the same with Gerard of Borgo San Donnino. Salimbene thinks that Gerard's real offense was an extension of Joachite apocalyptic to ridiculous (in fact, heretical) lengths, and the evidence supports his view.[35] Angelo, however, pictures Gerard as condemned for conducting a valiant defense of Joachim concerning the Trinity.[36] Again, Salimbene tells us how Gerard infuriated the French friars by predicting, on the basis of the pseudo-Joachite Jeremiah commentary, that if Louis IX went on crusade it would turn out badly for him. Angelo transforms the story into one about a visionary experience that allowed Gerard to announce Louis's capture at the very moment when it occurred. The closest he comes to presenting apocalyptic speculation as an issue in Gerard's case is when (without explicitly naming Gerard) he says that two of John's colleagues wrote two sermons, one of which praised Joachim excessively, while the other praised the Franciscan rule yet criticized the relaxations permitted by Franciscan leaders.[37] The point to be derived from these passages is not simply that Angelo knows little about these people (although that in itself seems significant) but also that he links them with Joachim without tying them very strongly to Joachite apocalyptic expectation.

The Popes and Antichrist

So far we seem to have established that Angelo was apocalyptic without being particularly Joachite, and that he expected Antichrist, but was not preoccupied with describing him or fixing a date for his arrival. We do have one bit of secondhand information that suggests a more precise application of the Antichrist label sometime between 1294 and 1303—namely, the story Ubertino da Casale reports having heard from the two brothers who had been in Greece.[38] If at least some members of Angelo's group read the number 666 in Rev. 13:18 and saw Boniface, then perhaps they considered Boniface to be Antichrist, though one would not inevitably follow from the other. The real question is whether those two brothers belonged to Angelo's group, and whether, even if they did, they represented a view held by Angelo himself.

No such identification of Antichrist is found in the *Chronicle*, nor is it found in any other work by Angelo. In his letters, however, we do find certain elements traditionally associated with the Antichrist legend adapted in a way that says a great deal about Angelo's appropriation of that material for his own purposes. Throughout his letters—indeed, throughout his life—he wrestled with a very concrete problem occasioned by his particular sense of what was entailed in Franciscan poverty. For Angelo, it was inseparable from humility, which in turn was inseparable from obedience. How seriously he took this connection is evidenced by the way in which the communities in Ancona under his influence during the 1320s handled the problem of leadership. According to Gentile da Foligno, who says that he visited Angelo and spent several days discussing such matters with him, individual groups "rule themselves through the counsel of one member whose authority is derived, not from the authority of prelacy which commands others, but from the bonds created by counsels based on love, while the others accept these counsels because they are thus provided with the pleasure of humbling and submitting themselves." In this way, through negation of their own wills, they put themselves on the road leading to Christ.[39]

Gentile reported to Angelo that many were scandalized by the arrangement, deeming it contrary to the pope's orders. Angelo replied that this method of governance, if observed along with obedience to the church and its prelates, led to perfection and was forbidden by no Scripture, tradition, or decree, but was in fact endorsed by the early fathers.[40] It is worth remembering that, as Potestà observes,[41] the situation of these groups made it difficult for them to claim any other sort of leadership. They were not prepared to submit themselves to the duly constituted leaders of the order. To choose their own leader with juridical authority, however, would have been equivalent to taking the path already traveled by the Tuscan rebels (albeit without the necessity of ejecting hostile superiors). Nevertheless, it is clear from Gentile that Angelo and his colleagues did not adopt this method of governance simply because it was tactically advantageous for them to do so. They believed in it.[42]

Angelo's emphasis on obedience as an important spiritual exercise made the prospect of being forced to choose between it and poverty a grim one.

Unfortunately, John XXII seemed intent on placing him before just that choice. This occurred in 1317, when John summarily dismissed spiritual Franciscan appeals and sided with leaders of the order; it occurred again from 1322 on, when John turned against the leaders as well, announcing that Christ had property and so did the Franciscans. If there was ever a series of decisions that, in Franciscan eyes, might conjure up the image of Antichrist, this was it. And on at least one occasion Angelo came very close to saying as much.

Here we come to that one other instance of his using the word "Antichrist" in his letters. In this particular letter, he comments that anyone who says that Christ and the apostles had property blasphemes Christ and his life, introducing heresy and the blasphemies of that lying son of perdition, Antichrist.[43] The letter is dated 1329, well after Pope John XXII had asserted just that. It is, however, the closest Angelo ever came to putting the name "John" and the word "Antichrist" together in the same sentence. Even here he identified the anonymous perpetrator not as Antichrist but, in effect, as a precursor or perhaps an emulator of Antichrist.

It is not difficult to decide what he thought of the pope. In 1329, after Philip of Majorca had asked John XXII for permission to form an order that would observe the Franciscan rule in its purity, Angelo wrote to Philip, saying, "I do not find that any of Christ's disciples sought the opinion of some priest or leader of the synagogue. Thus I doubt if anyone of sane mind, after receiving a certain illumination of the Holy Spirit, could without offense seek advice on how to run his life from those who live and teach in carnal fashion."[44] When Philip informed him that he intended to send the pope a strong statement of his views on poverty, Angelo replied, "Writing to the supreme pontiff or to kings does not seem a fruitful course, for avarice, love of visible things, and ambition to rule distances them from recognition of Christ's heavenly perfection and life, and from love of the highest poverty." He compared the present situation with that in Christ's time, when rulers, priests, and scholars all united against him.[45] One hardly needs to read between the lines to see that by this point Angelo expected little from those in power.

That is perhaps putting the matter too mildly. He was quite clear in defining the nature of John's offense. Later in the same letter to Philip, he noted that "if the supreme pontiff calls that which is true and certain into doubt and defines as heretical what the church, the doctors and the rules of holy men teach to be catholic and the height of perfection, no one judges him, but he judges and damns himself." Angelo goes on to specify the doctrine in question: "He who excommunicates and declares heretical the highest evangelical poverty is himself excommunicated by God and is a heretic before Christ."[46]

In a letter to some of his colleagues written in 1329, the previous year, he had been even more specific, characterizing the question of Christ's poverty as an issue already settled. "Ecclesiastical decisions on matters not of the substance of faith, determined by councils and holy doctors, should be left to the church; but this question was determined and defined by Christ, the apostles and holy doctors, the supreme pontiffs, and three councils."[47]

The Abomination of Desolation

Thus the pope had damned himself on the poverty issue. Where did that leave him, though? Obviously, there were three possibilities: (1) John was not the pope, but Antichrist; (2) he was not Antichrist, but he was not the pope either; or (3) he was wrong and morally corrupt, but still the pope. As for the first, we have seen that Angelo preferred not to bring the word "Antichrist" into juxtaposition with the word "pope," but that does not mean he was completely unwilling to place John's actions in apocalyptic perspective. Here we arrive at what may be the most significant thing about Angelo's discussion: his preference for a completely different apocalyptic framework than the one favored by Joachim and Olivi, one based on a different biblical source. Joachim and Olivi clearly proceeded from the Book of Revelation.[48] In Angelo's letters, when he wants to use apocalyptic language to characterize his situation, his favorite source is not Revelation but Matt. 24, the "little apocalypse."[49] That choice allowed him to proceed in a somewhat different way than Olivi (or, for that matter, the French beguins) when it came to dealing with John.

Within the little apocalypse, he favored two passages. The one he quoted most often was 24:12, "since iniquities abound, the love of many will cool," which he obviously considered a succinct statement of current reality. The second-most-quoted passage was 24:13f., "when you see the abomination of desolation foretold by the prophet Daniel standing in the holy place [let the reader take note!], let those who are in Judea flee to the mountains." The passage allowed him to come as close to an assessment of John as he ever wished to come, and it suggested a strategy for dealing with his situation.

As for the first benefit, it allowed Angelo to use terminology that, though traditionally associated with Antichrist, did not have to be—and in Angelo's case, probably was not. Cut loose from identification with Antichrist, it was evocative yet undefined. Certainly calling John "the abomination of desolation" labeled him as wrong and corrupt. And certainly Angelo's use of the phrase makes it hard to deny that he was thinking of John. It is not clear that he was thinking *only* of John, though. The expression allowed him to be somewhat more general than that, alluding to evil in high places; but John certainly was included.

Was John then illegitimate? Did Angelo actually endorse the second of our two possibilities? One passage seems to suggest that he did. In one of the letters to Philip of Majorca already cited above, Angelo mentions a prophecy by Francis: that the papal throne would be occupied by one not elected in a catholic manner, one who would have a mistaken understanding of Christ's life and the Franciscan rule.[50] While it is theoretically possible to imagine that he did not see the prophecy as currently being fulfilled, this seems almost astronomically unlikely.

The problem, though, is that irregular election was not a flaw easily assigned to John, and elsewhere Angelo always seems to consider him legitimate at least from that perspective. Arsenio Frugoni has suggested that Angelo is not speaking of John, but of the antipope Nicholas V, the Franciscan Pietro di Corbara, who was established at Rome by Ludwig the Bavarian but had renounced his papal crown and submitted himself as a penitent to John XXII by the time Angelo wrote the letter.[51] In fact, shortly after citing this prophecy, Angelo speaks of Pietro and says in effect that he held a misguided notion of poverty. Nevertheless, Gian Luca Potestà finds Frugoni's argument insufficient, and he offers impressive counterarguments.[52] The best one can say is that if Angelo was referring to John, he was using the phrase "not elected in a catholic manner" so oddly as to make it impossible to leap from it to the conclusion that he was questioning John's legitimacy.

Most of what Angelo says elsewhere in his letters suggests that he thought his group was dealing with a hierarchy that, though morally bankrupt and wrong about poverty, was nonetheless legitimate. Even in this missive to Philip, shortly after invoking the "pope not elected in a catholic manner," he notes that Christ taught his disciples to "heed and honor avaricious and illegitimate priests, invidious and lying scribes, hypocritical and fraudulent pharisees, because of the dignity of their status and to conserve peace and unity among God's people." How much more then should Christians "show obedience and honor to prelates who, however sinful they may be, occupy the place of Christ and his apostles?"[53]

Here as elsewhere in Angelo's letters, the duty to obey ecclesiastical superiors takes on a basic, bottom-line quality. The rationale behind it is complex, though. There are at least three reasons for obedience. The first is practical: openly challenging the authorities will gain nothing and endanger much. Angelo's letters to Philip are remarkably realistic about the latter's chance of success if he attempts to change the pope's mind. Nor is it simply a matter of wasting energy. Angelo is aware that he must at least try to change the pope's attitude toward his group, even if he cannot change the pope's mind on Franciscan poverty. In his letters to his colleagues, Angelo emphasizes that good behavior on their part is necessary "to show your innocence and disprove the evil stories and lies told about you."[54] Seen from this perspective, obedience becomes a viable strategy for one in Angelo's position.

The second reason for obedience is that, as the passage quoted above suggests, the ecclesiastical hierarchy is divinely established and Christians must obey it. What is involved here for Angelo is more than just the duty to follow the dictates of a juridically valid superior. He constantly stresses the relationship between obedience and "the unity which the faith and charity of Christ produce in the faithful and in the church."[55] Obedience is an expression of that unity. The connection allows him to speak of "rejecting and judging the authority and lives of prelates, breaking and sundering the unity of the faith and the church," as if he were describing two aspects of a single evil mindset.

Third, those bound by Franciscan vows are obligated to obedience in a special way. For Angelo it goes substantially beyond the fact that he has vowed obedience. It involves his whole conception of the Franciscan life, a life of self-emptying. Humility, poverty, and obedience are to a great extent the same thing, seen from different angles. Thus submission to authority is a basic part of one's Franciscanism.

Yet observing the rule was also a basic part of one's Franciscanism. We have returned to the essential problem. If Angelo's friends and colleagues had to obey the pope, but also felt that they had to observe the rule in a way forbidden by the pope, what were they to do?

Flee to the Mountains

The answer lay in Angelo's apocalyptic text of choice. His references to it go back a remarkably long way, considering that we have little written by Angelo before 1317. As early as 1314, in a letter bewailing the dangers produced by the cardinals' failure to act promptly in replacing the deceased Clement V, Angelo noted that he had delayed fleeing from Judea to the mountains—but still had time. In 1317, in the course of explaining to John XXII why his group left for Greece after Celestine V's death, Angelo cited Christ's instructions to "flee from the face of persecutors."[56] From that year on, as he saw John XXII take his stand first against the spirituals and then against the order as a whole, Matt. 24:13f. would become the key text upon which much of his advice hinged, and his interpretation of it deepened.

The result is seen in a letter written to some of his colleagues around 1323.[57] It is a carefully wrought position paper that Angelo valued enough to send it to two different groups. It begins with an extended, rather general meditation on what it means to be a Christian. Suddenly, though, he places his readers squarely in the present and before a rather ugly reality.

> Every religious order, every congregation, every state—whether cler-
> ical, religious or lay, whether leaders or subordinates—is placed by
> apostolic authority under a single rule or law of faith and love of
> Christ so that all may be ordered through Christ to the destruction
> of sin and the nurturing of virtue in the Holy Spirit. Since, however,
> in every religious order and every state—whether clerical, lay or reli-
> gious, whether leaders or followers—all is done now for the accom-
> plishment of sin and destruction of virtue, either openly or occultly,
> and no one cares about obeying, honoring or glorifying Christ, and
> by authority of every religious order or congregation human will and
> sense are pertinaciously placed above God's will or serving God, "then
> those who are in Judea," as the Savior counsels, "should flee to the
> mountains" since the abomination of desolation is clearly seen to be
> standing in the holy place. Then "it is time for the Lord to act,"
> according to the prophet,[58] "because they dissipate the law" of Christ.
> Then it is time to say, "It is more important to obey God than men."[59]

What does it mean, though, to "flee to the mountains"? Angelo answers that question directly.

> Then it is time to return to the example furnished by the lives of
> Christ and the saints in heaven and on earth, dedicating one's soul to
> Christ and the unity of faith and church, that is, by verbal confession
> and actual life; adhering to the doctrine of Jesus Christ. That is what
> is meant by fleeing to the mountains. It occurs according to the exi-
> gencies and opportunities of the situation, sometimes with a change
> of place and sometimes without. The disciple of Christ who adheres
> to the unity and faith of the church before all things as the substance
> of eternal life and is ready to die for the confession of it, always nur-
> turing within himself Christ's patience, humility, piety, peace, chastity

and love, standing among evils and yet separating himself from evils, flees to the mountains according to the Savior's counsel.[60]

Thus, whatever else it was, fleeing to the mountains involved a basic orientation. It meant living in the world, but for Christ, rather than for the world. On at least one occasion, Angelo extended this inner sense of Matt. 24 far enough to assign an inner sense to the abomination of desolation.[61] In one of the few passages combining the Apocalypse with Matt. 24, he noted (we have seen the passage earlier) that to one who exercised real obedience, the beast of the abyss, "that is, our body and senses," was more terrible than Antichrist and his armies, and to such a person his own will was the abomination of desolation.[62]

Yet Matt. 24 was not simply about attitude. It was about what to do in a concrete situation—in fact, the one in which the church found itself. What was a serious Christian to *do*? What, concretely, did the situation demand? Angelo was hardly reticent in suggesting precedents, and they were not encouraging. In his 1330 letter to Philip of Majorca, Angelo spent a great deal of time drawing out the parallel between those who joined Herod in crucifying Christ on the one hand and the contemporary church on the other. In another letter to Philip, Angelo found himself talking about the need to emulate the martyrs and confessors in the early church. In yet another letter to some of his associates he proposed another parallel, that of the church during the time when the emperors and church leaders were Arian and the true church remained alive in just a few catholics. The ultimate parallel was, of course, Christ. As he informed his disciples, to be like Christ was to suffer like him.[63]

That argument seems to imply that their task was to witness with the martyrs, yet it was never that simple for Angelo. Immediately after drawing the parallel between Herod's associates and current church leaders, he told Philip, "Nevertheless, these things are not to be communicated to many people, because it behooves us to show great gravity and discretion in such matters, and to be slow in believing them. It is more useful and much better to keep them in our hearts and ruminate on them in silence, for men of this period are very fraudulent. They display a bovine innocence on the outside, but within they conceal a lupine ferocity." He granted to Philip that he should firmly and freely confess the faith, yet in the next breath, he asserted (as we will recall) that if the pope called truth heresy and denied what the church already had established as doctrine, then he did not need to be judged by Philip, because he had condemned himself. "We, however, occupying the place of humility and confession of the truth, must not speak or write anything to kings or masters but should rather leave judgment and examination to Christ and church leaders, attending rather to ourselves, confessing the truth by work and word, justly and humbly going about our business and not presuming beyond our station."[64]

In the 1329 letter to his own colleagues, cited earlier, he said much the same thing. There, as we have seen, he stated at great length that John XXII was wrong in denying Christ's absolute poverty, a doctrine already established by the church. He advised them that, if circumstances demanded it, they must confess the truth, and they would be rewarded for it in heaven. He added, however, that "silence, discretion, isolation and patience are singularly opportune in these days, . . . insofar as is possible during the time of this confusing tribulation."[65]

In short, whether advising Philip or his own associates, Angelo discouraged aggressive witness. His advice was to keep one's head down and wait it out if possible.[66] The word "patience" was a popular one with him, and that is hardly surprising. If Francis predicted tribulation, he also predicted victory for those who defended his rule, and not simply in heaven, either. Nor by 1330 did Angelo feel that it would be long in coming.

Matt. 24 allowed Angelo to justify a lifetime of disappearing into hard-to-reach corners of the Christian world where he could observe his vow of poverty without feeling that in the process he had violated his vow of obedience. He could go to Greece, as he and his colleagues did in 1294; to Subiaco, as he did in 1318; or into the Basilicata, as he did shortly before his death in 1337. He could flee to the mountains.

The Birth of Benjamin

The question is how long he thought he had to stay in the mountains. That is not easy to determine, but toward the end of the *Chronicle* we find an intriguing assertion. The Latin reads, "Denique vigintiocto annorum revolutionibus attributis laboribus revolutionis sextae rotae circuli animalis pauperis viatoris in iudicium reprobati, superadditis novem ad eiusdem rotae revolutionem septimam distinguendam, alterius temporis aurora, cum sancta in melius immutatione clarebit rex regum."[67] We might translate that literally: "Thus twenty-eight revolutions of years attributed to the labors of the revolution of the sixth wheel of the animal circle of the poor pilgrim called into judgment, nine more superadded to the revolution of the same wheel, the seventh is to be distinguished, the dawn of another time [*temporis*], with a holy change for the better, the king of kings will shine forth." This passage has puzzled scholars. The twenty-eight years are relatively straightforward. Earlier, Angelo had alluded to a prophecy that the sixth tribulation would begin with Celestine V's resignation and last for twenty-eight years.[68] Thus we have a period running from 1294 to around 1322.

The nine years seem problematic, though. Lydia von Auw suggests that they represent a truce separating the sixth and seventh tribulations,[69] but since the years 1322–31 contained John's battle with the Franciscan order, the persecution of the beguins and spirituals in Languedoc, and John's continued unwillingness to recognize the legitimacy of Angelo's own group, that would seem an odd sort of truce. Moreover, Angelo explicitly says that the seventh persecution began in the twenty-ninth year.[70]

Gian Luca Potestà offers another, better explanation: Just as Joachim and Olivi saw the seven periods of church history as overlapping, with the new period developing in the womb of the preceding one, so Angelo saw his tribulations.[71] Thus the nine years represent a watershed period in which the sixth and seventh tribulations run concurrently, after which the seventh goes on alone.[72]

Potestà's reading of the passage makes better sense than von Auw's, but it still does not do justice to that reference to "the dawn of another time." Perhaps we should take the word *tempus* in the sense Olivi would have taken it—and the way Angelo takes it earlier in the *Chronicle*[73]—as meaning a period of church history rather than a tribulation. That is also the way in which he uses the image of a revolving wheel earlier.[74] If we do so, and then read that meaning back into the preceding references to the sixth and seventh wheels, we will be able to paraphrase the passage as follows: "Once twenty-eight years have been added to the sixth period (i.e., once the twenty-eight-year sixth tribulation has been added to the previous five tribulations within the sixth period of church history) and nine more years (i.e., the seventh tribulation within the sixth period) have been added to that, the dawn of the seventh period can be seen, with a great change for the better. Christ will shine forth."

In short, the seventh and final tribulation will end ca. 1331, and the seventh period of church history will begin. This reading not only makes sense of the passage but fits with other evidence as well. There is a certain logic to Angelo's hope for relief in the near future. The seventh and last tribulation had begun in 1322, was largely orchestrated by John XXII, and John was a very old man. (Angelo would have to wait somewhat longer than he might have hoped, but he did manage to outlive John.) Moreover, Angelo's letters point in the same direction. They too support the notion that he was prepared for the seventh period to dawn in the 1330s. In one clearly from that decade, he says that after sixty years of watching the labor pains connected with reformation of the order, he finally sees Benjamin being born, along with his mother's death.[75]

A seventh period of what, though? In his *Chronicle*, as elsewhere, Angelo is extremely vague on the subject. Certainly he thinks that it is not far off, and he anticipates a return of Saint Francis—not physically, but through a "full and perfect multiplication of the seraphic status in Jews, Greeks and Latins."[76] That is, he expects the rule to triumph, though probably not in its old institutional form; moreover, he expects the conversion of the Jews, which had become a traditional element in apocalyptic programs. Perhaps he expects a great deal else, but he does not share it with us. Nor does he say how long he expects the seventh period to last.

We can draw one important inference from the Rachel-Benjamin metaphor. Its use as a symbol for the birth of a new spiritual order has a long history,[77] but in Angelo's case, it must be seen in light of the prophecies he assigns to James of Massa and others in the *Chronicle*.[78] The Franciscan order as it previously existed (Rachel) is to be replaced by a more perfect, contemplative life (Benjamin). This expectation is linked with Angelo's warning in his letters that Francis was primarily concerned with establishing a way of life, not an order in the institutional sense, and that one should not confuse the latter with the former.[79] Angelo's emphasis on way of life rather than order helps to explain why in 1294 he and his companions felt free to escape from their differences with Franciscan leaders by forming a new order, the Poor Hermits of Pope Celestine, which would observe the Franciscan rule. It also helps us understand how he could see the new age of Franciscan observance dawning even at a time when the order remained unreformed. And perhaps this emphasis, plus the sense of entering a new era, makes it marginally easier to believe the evidence from inquisitorial processes in the mid-1330s that Angelo's group had developed into something resembling an independent order. More of that in a moment, though.

Note that if Angelo did indeed think that he was seeing the end of tribulation and the dawn of the seventh period, he differed sharply from Olivi and Ubertino on this score. Olivi died assuming that, like Moses, he had been called to point toward the Holy Land without actually entering it. Ubertino simply stopped talking about it, and perhaps lost interest in apocalyptic speculation after 1305, as we have seen.

In fact, Angelo would have differed from Olivi and Ubertino in still another sense. If what has been said so far is correct, he must have expected the Antichrist (as opposed to Antichrists) to appear at the end of the seventh period rather than at the end of the sixth. In doing so, he would have been tapping into a respectable exegetical tradition. Indeed, Joachim of Fiore can be read in that way.

The Role of Individual Conscience

Thus the new age was dawning, but only just. In the meantime, the best thing to do was to stay out of the way. Angelo's behavior was quite consistent in that respect. His basic strategy involved remaining slightly out of reach, placing himself where he could follow the dictates of his own conscience without directly challenging a pope who obviously had other plans for him. His actions seem to imply that in the final analysis, obeying those in authority meant little more than not openly defying them.

Where, then, did one look for guidance? Who was really in charge? One can deduce from the sort of advice Angelo gave that in this situation, fleeing to the mountains meant relying more on individual conscience and less on ecclesiastical authority. He said as much in the letter telling his disciples that fleeing to the hills could mean escaping or staying where one was. How did one know which was required? The individual disciple had to decide "according to the Savior's counsel." That was equivalent to making it a personal decision.

He also said as much in a letter to Philip of Majorca probably written between 1324 and 1328. Philip, then serving as regent of Majorca, was perplexed about how he should deal with a case of excommunication (probably that of Adhémar de Mosset, who had been excommunicated for ordering the execution of two clerics caught while engaged in criminal activities).[80] Angelo's response in the letter was that the times were unsettled and that learned men often differed, since their judgments were based less on divine guidance than on human prudence and love of worldly things. It seemed a good moment to give wider scope to one's own conscience. "Remember," Angelo announced, "that the Redeemer's mercy wipes our sins away, not in one way alone, but in many ways."

Angelo's Favorable Situation

Angelo's apocalyptic views combined with his situation to produce a relatively viable strategy for survival. To appreciate the truth of this statement, one need only compare his case with that of the spiritual Franciscans and beguins in southern France. Olivi had identified the temptation of Antichrist with the sort of thing that John XXII eventually did. Once John turned on the spirituals and denied their cherished assumptions about Franciscan poverty, they and their beguin supporters, armed with Olivi's Apocalypse commentary, knew precisely how to interpret John's behavior and the duty it placed on them. Their urban environment aided them to some extent, yet it was also a terrain on which the inquisitors could work effectively, and in Languedoc, the latter were aided by cooperative ecclesiastics and royal officials.

Angelo's case was very different. Both his ideology and his situation allowed him more possibilities. As for the former, thinking in terms of the abomination of desolation rather than Antichrist allowed him to think of John's policy as not only wrong but even heretical and evil, yet never deny that he was the pope and thus was owed allegiance. We may be tempted to say that it allowed Angelo to defy the pope without admitting it even to himself, but there is more involved. His reliance on Matt. 24 allowed him to develop a subtle notion of obedience that arguably came closer to reconciling it with the demands of poverty than was the case with the French spirituals and beguins. It is also arguable that his position was much closer to the original Franciscan vision than that of the Occitan spirituals.

As for his more favorable situation, the abomination of desolation might have been sitting on the papal throne, but that throne was located in Avignon, not Rome. Moreover, Ludwig the Bavarian's involvement in Italy kept the pope from doing much about the Italian spirituals by remote control, so to speak, for a considerable time. That partly explains the odd peace enjoyed not only by Angelo but also by his colleagues. Other factors were important, though. The eremitical bent of Angelo's movement helped enormously. A series of hermits scattered throughout the Val di Spoleto and elsewhere made a much poorer target than the urbanized spirituals of Narbonne and Béziers did. The very different situation of the bishops in central Italy also insulated spirituals from the dangers they would have faced in southern France. Mario Sensi publishes a document of 1333 in which Bartolomeo Bardi, bishop of Spoleto, grants four laymen living in a hermitage near Pissignano (and any others who might join them in the future) the right to pursue "the evangelical life." That is as specific as the bishop chooses to be. No mention is made of any need for them to place themselves under the control of an established order or vow an approved rule. In short, what the bishop is sanctioning seems to be more or less what John XXII was attacking in *Sancta romana*. The only recognition of this difficulty in the entire document comes in the form of a postscript (as Sensi rightly calls it) added after the date and place have been supplied. In it, the bishop simply notes that he does not intend "to derogate in any way from the papal constitution *contra fraticellos*."[81]

Such episcopal benevolence was hardly universal, but it was far from an isolated phenomenon.[82] It gave not only Angelo's colleagues but other hermits as well the sort of protection they would not have received in Languedoc. Angelo's letters suggest that his group was secure enough for them to receive new members and, in general, to act as if they were sanctioned by ecclesiastical authority.

The Departure from Subiaco

The era of relative calm could not last forever. In 1330, Ludwig abandoned Italy for good. John was freer to move against the *fraticelli* and other dissenters. The process unrolled slowly, however. In early 1334 the pope wrote to the inquisitor, Simone da Spoleto, and to the guardian of the Franciscan house of Santa Maria in Ara Coeli at Rome admonishing them to move against Angelo and his group.[83] *Fraticelli* began to be interrogated. One brother informed his questioner that when the order to surrender Angelo finally reached the Abbot of Subiaco, the latter replied that he would not turn Angelo over even if they rewarded him by making him pope.[84] The inquisitors were also told that the abbot did nothing without Angelo's advice.[85]

The depositions of these *fraticelli* provide a picture of the group in which, as Potestà remarks, "what remained prudently indeterminate in Angelo's letters is fixed in concise, univocal formulae."[86] What appears in Angelo's letters as a loosely connected series of communities emerges as a full-blown order with local guardians, provinces, and a general minister, Angelo, who has a *socius* charged with visitation and correction and sends letters with his own seal affixed. John XXII—whom they call by his pre-papal name, Jacques de Cahors—is a heretic, the church has become a whore, and the *fraticelli* are the only true friars minor.

One might be tempted to imagine that these notices reflect not reality but inquisitorial assumptions. And it should be noted that we have, in fact, the testimony of only three witnesses, one of whom claims not to be a *fraticello* but merely to have conversed with them. Nevertheless, even if we choose to be skeptical concerning the part about John XXII, the detail in describing institutional arrangements does make one wonder. The *socius* has a name, Nicola di Calabria, and the seal is minutely described.[87] One of the brothers says that he himself was ordered by Angelo to go somewhere three years before, and that only fifteen days earlier he had been present when the brothers received a letter from Angelo announcing that Philip of Majorca would be pope.[88] Only eight days earlier Angelo's *socius* had visited his group and corrected the brethren.

One particularly odd note is sounded. A single witness recalls hearing from several *fraticelli* that fornication is not a sin. In fact, he names some of the brethren from whom he heard it.[89] One is reminded of the *spiritus libertatis*, but it should be added that this same witness reports other statements that sound like hyperbole. He portrays one brother as saying that Francis must be in hell, because if he were in heaven, he would chase out all the fat brothers. Another, he claims, said that the bones of the Emperor Constantine and Pope Sylvester should be burned, because they enriched the church and then used the wealth to conduct wars.[90] Moreover, what he actually quotes the brothers as saying— that "fornicating with women or the act of fornication itself is not a sin"—is stated so generally as to have a perfectly orthodox meaning.

In any case, Angelo saw the danger and decided to flee. One of the *fraticelli* being interrogated at the time announced that he was headed back to the Marches, his native soil.[91] It is hard to tell whether that was part of a disinformation campaign intended to throw pursuers off the scent or if Angelo had really entertained that idea. In any case, he went in the opposite direction, into the kingdom of Naples, where Philip of Majorca and many others would be happy to give him aid.[92] He probably spent his final days in the hermitages of Santa Maria de Aspro and San Michele in Basilicata. Angelo died in 1337. His tomb at Santa Maria de Aspro quickly became a pilgrimage site and the scene of reported miracles.

One might assume that Angelo's group, if a group it was, would have disappeared when he did. Thus it comes as a shock to discover, in the fifteenth century, an orthodox congregation called the Clareni who are seen as descending from Angelo's Poor Hermits. The transition to legitimacy is not entirely surprising, though. Mario Sensi, piecing together the sparse surviving evidence, shows how episcopal protection and encouragement could have led at least some descendants of Angelo's group to regularize the situation by vowing the rule for third-order Franciscans that was promulgated in the thirteenth century by Pope Nicholas IV. As Sensi recognizes, the internal logic of their situation from the 1320s on gave Angelo's group a different relationship to possessions, effectively pushing them in the direction that Ubertino was traveling in his reply to John XXII. *Usus pauper* became the important thing, while complete lack of possessions became harder (if not impossible) to achieve.[93]

The Complexity of the Italian Situation

Among Angelo's other accomplishments, he had outlived his papal nemesis by three years. John XXII died in 1334, but that did the Franciscans little good: his successor, Benedict XII, was the former Jacques Fournier. As bishop of Pamiers and then of Mirepoix, Fournier had taken his place alongside Bernard Gui and Jean de Beaune as a major heresy-hunter of the era,[94] and he was more than ready to continue the work on a higher level. Thus the spirituals could expect little relief from him. Nor could leaders of the order look forward to better days. Shortly after his election he informed the minister general, Guiral Ot, that he really preferred the Dominicans.[95]

If the new pope offered little hope to the battered *fraticelli,* neither did Guiral Ot. He had risen to power in the wake of Michael of Cesena's defection and was very much John XXII's man. Nevertheless he remains something of a puzzle. In 1331, he suggested that the pope do away with Franciscan prohibitions concerning money; abrogate both *Exiit qui seminat* and *Exivi de paradiso,* which had become sources of confusion; and give superiors authority to dispense from provisions of the rule at their discretion.[96] His idea was rejected not only by leaders in his own order but also (indirectly) by the pope himself who, in a bull issued shortly thereafter, ordered certain Italian ministers to observe the rule, *Exiit,* and *Exivi* on the question of money.[97] Modern historians have treated his idea no more gently, yet Duncan Nimmo is probably correct in suggesting that there was something to be said for Ot's suggestion.[98] If John XXII's bulls had rendered much of *Exiit* and *Exivi* untenable and a good deal of the order had been living by a lower standard of poverty anyway, it seemed hypocritical to continue acting as if Franciscan behavior was defined by the words of Nicholas III and Clement V.

At any rate, however sensible Ot's suggestion may have been, it represented an effort to move the order in a direction diametrically opposed to the one traditionally favored by the spiritual Franciscans. Thus it comes as no surprise that the Italian *fraticelli* continued their resistance.[99] By that point, though, the word *fraticelli* had become an umbrella term covering a great many things. Descendants of the spiritual Franciscans persevered as the *fraticelli de paupere vita,* while the descendants of those who had followed Michael of Cesena into exile in 1328 were identified as the *fraticelli de opinione.* Since Michael had joined with John XXII in persecuting the spirituals before his own spot of trouble with the pope, one might expect these two varieties of *fraticello* to be easily distinguishable, but they soon became muddled. Neither group could remain homogeneous in organization or belief, although both seemed to agree in execrating the late John XXII as a heretic. In fact, the situation is even more complicated, since the term *fraticelli* continued to be applied to other groups as well. Even if we concentrate on the lineal descendants of the *fraticelli de paupere vita* and *fraticelli de opinione,* we will find that their story from this point on is the story of small groups faring well or poorly in specific places. It is the story of citizens in Rieti, Narni, Todi, and Perugia intervening, sometimes violently, to rescue dissidents from the inquisitors, though for a variety of reasons; it is the story of towns such as Florence alternating between toleration and persecution. Why a city government should act one way or another toward the *fraticelli* is a complicated problem. Political considerations certainly played a part,[100] but so did conviction. The Franciscan dissidents struck a familiar chord in Italian spiritual life.[101]

The Observants

The most efficient weapon to be deployed against the *fraticelli* was not the inquisitor. Rather, it was another group emerging from within the Franciscan order, a group that struck a familiar chord. Surprisingly enough, it was Ot who agreed in 1334 to provide John of Valle, an earnest brother in the convent at Foligno, with permission to settle at Brugliano, where he and four associates could observe the rule literally. Thus the minister general who might stand as a quintessential conventual sanctioned the creation of the Observants and set the stage for a separation within the order, a solution that would have made sense to many of the spirituals at Vienne.

Why should Ot have agreed? Not because he wanted to get rid of reformers by sending them where they wouldn't bother him. Ot was more intelligent than that. Duncan Nimmo is probably correct in suggesting that the minister general himself, like others in the order, recognized the need for reform and saw the Brugliano venture as a start in that direction. He is probably also correct in seeing Ot's decision as a flanking movement in his campaign against the *fraticelli*. On the one hand, the order combated them by participating in inquisitorial processes against them, "but is it not possible that they hit on a far better response: to show that within the Order too the rule was observed to the letter? If so, there could be no more suitable place to start a counterattack than the hill-side of Brugliano: as it were an outpost overlooking the very heartland of Fraticelli success, the region of the Camerino." Nimmo points out that according to the *Chronicle of the Twenty-Four Generals*, Ot drove a group of *fraticelli* out of the Carceri in 1340, then established there his own group of brothers who would follow a strict observance.[102]

The Brugliano venture probably offended any number of Franciscans and seems to have caused alarm in Avignon as well. In 1343, Pope Clement VI wrote Ot's successor, informing him that "certain men" claimed to be members of the order yet departed from established practice in "habit, way of living, doctrine, and other approved observances." The new minister general was told to avoid doing anything that would imply approval of this group until the pope had time to make suitable arrangements for them.[103]

Nevertheless, when Clement did in fact speak on the subject (in a 1350 bull allowing strict observance in four hermitages lying in the dioceses of Assisi and Spoleto), his authorization was worded in such a way as to suggest that by that point, the movement was facing opposition from leaders of the order and needed aid from the pope.[104] The bull was apparently composed in response to a request not by John of Valle but by Gentile of Spoleto, one of John's original four associates at Brugliano, and it led to a temporary setback in the development of the Observant movement. Gentile proved less diplomatically astute than John, and his group did all the things most likely to produce a crisis. They adopted short habits similar to those favored by the spirituals; apparently consorted with *fraticelli*, allowing some to join their group; and, worst of all, refused to recognize the minister general's authority over them. As a result, the pope's concession was revoked in 1355 and Gentile was imprisoned. Fortunately, in 1368, the Observants were more or less reborn when Paoluccio dei Trinci was given permission to occupy the currently deserted hermitage of Brugliano with four or five companions. They sought a degree of freedom to pursue a life of simplicity and poverty, the sort of life Angelo Clareno had sought. As Mario Sensi observes, Paoluccio succeeded in gaining from the order what Angelo Clareno had fruitlessly requested earlier.[105] Yet one must add that what happened next partly recapitulated the course of Franciscan history in the thirteenth century. From that starting point at Brugliano, the Observant movement would grow, prosper, and evolve from a simple group of lay hermits into an order sophisticated enough to produce great preachers like Bernardino of Siena. Eventually, it would further arm the church against the *fraticelli*. It not only offered a rival, orthodox model of strict observance, but also furnished determined persecutors like John of Capistrano.[106] That, however, is another—later—story.

CONCLUSION

WE HAVE FOLLOWED THE STORY of the spiritual Franciscans through a series of phases. Up to the 1270s, we can only point to isolated cases that seem to anticipate what we see emerging in that decade. From the 1270s to around 1290, we see a genuine movement begin, but in separate dramas whose diverse plots unfolded in southern France and Italy. In southern France, the poverty debate surfaced with the *usus pauper* controversy, a theoretical dispute over whether restricted use was an essential part of the vow. This issue was one of several on which Peter Olivi, one of the most remarkable intellectuals of the age, was attacked by his contemporaries. When he was censured in 1283, his stand on *usus pauper* was one of the targets, but there were others—and they involved such serious philosophical and theological issues as to make us hesitate before proclaiming that poverty was the *real* bone of contention and the other complaints simply red herrings. Moreover, his dispute with his antagonists over *usus pauper* was not explicitly one over whether Franciscans should practice restricted use, or even how restricted that use should be. In the opening rounds of the debate, the distinction between Olivi's and his opponents' views was razor-thin. They agreed that Franciscans were obliged to practice restricted use. It was the precise *source* of that obligation that was at issue. As the debate heated up, Olivi combined a defense of his theoretical position with suggestions that his opponents were justifying lax behavior, but the focus remained on theory, not practice. Olivi's connection with his leaders, however strained, never snapped; by the end of the 1280s he was back in harness as a lector.

Another sort of poverty dispute had been percolating in the March of Ancona since 1274. According to Angelo Clareno, it originally involved obedience. If the pope ordered the Franciscans to accept possessions, should they obey him, or were they bound by their vow to refuse? Very quickly, however, the controversy apparently became one about humility: how humbly Franciscans should live and how far off course current standards were. The zealots thought that those standards were widely off course. Things turned out wretchedly for the zealots, and in time several of them (including Angelo Clareno) were in prison. How soon they arrived there is an open question, but that is where the minister general Raymond Geoffroi found them in 1290.

If we were to characterize the level at which the battle was occurring during these years, we would say that most of the serious strife took place on a provincial level. Olivi's conflict was originally with other lectors in his province, and Angelo was disciplined by leaders in his. Olivi's 1283 censure came from a commission appointed by the minister general, but he was rehabilitated by the next two ministers general (and in the case of the Anconan zealots, it was the minister general who ordered them released from prison).

The 1290s saw the controversy enter a new stage. At this point, popes began to show an interest in the zealots, and much of the action taken against them was by papal order. In southern France, this occurred at the beginning of the decade, due to the intervention of Nicholas IV; in Italy, toward the middle of the decade, under Boniface VIII. In each case, the pope had become alarmed at the disruptive possibilities of zealot behavior. The minister general throughout the first half of the decade was Raymond Geoffroi, who was personally sympathetic toward the zealots but deferred to papal requests. From 1296 on, Boniface had a more willing accomplice in John of Murrovalle.

To say this much is not to say that papal action was leveled at the spirituals indiscriminately. When the investigation in southern France resulted in the disciplining of several spirituals at the general chapter of 1292, Olivi was not among them, although he was required to clarify his stance on *usus pauper*. In Italy, the accession of Boniface VIII resulted in a variety of experiences for a variety of zealots. Conrad of Offida found himself in trouble but seems to have talked himself back into John of Murrovalle's good graces. Angelo Clareno and his associates, whose brief apparent salvation at the hands of Celestine V had—once it was abrogated by Boniface—left them even more detested by their Anconan superiors and thus at greater risk than ever before, avoided trouble by the simple expedient of leaving for Greece. Jacopone da Todi stayed in Italy, sided with those who denied the validity of Boniface's election, and wound up in prison. Heaven knows what happened to that even more radical faction attacked by Olivi in his 1295 letter to Conrad of Offida.

Nor is it to say that there was even a recognizable group to be characterized as "spirituals." There was some communication and some recognition of common interests. Olivi, who had been south in 1279 and a decade later spent two years teaching at Florence, knew Conrad of Offida enough to cite him in his works and to write him an angry letter. Ubertino da Casale came to know Olivi at Florence and admired him enough to plagiarize him in the *Arbor vitae*. Angelo, too, admired Olivi, without necessarily knowing much about him, and eventually turned him into a major saint of the movement in his *Chronicle*. Nevertheless, Olivi's aims were not the same as Angelo's or even Ubertino's. Olivi wanted a united and reformed Franciscan order. His program for reform was not stunningly different from the one Bonaventure had advocated. He was comfortable within an order that produced bishops and university professors. Olivi simply wanted those bishops and university professors to observe *usus pauper* according to his own moderate definition of that term. He found little to criticize in the way Franciscans had taken root in the cities, constructed residences, and taken on pastoral duties. He merely wanted the order to scale those residences to his own (flexible) notion of necessity and avoid squabbling with the secular clergy over things like burial rights. The growing crisis of the 1290s had its effect on this program, however. By the time of his death in 1298, Olivi seems to have adopted a darker view of the immediate future and perhaps a more radical notion of the new dispensation that would emerge. There is no evidence, however, that he thought the time had come when it was impossible for a conscientious friar in Narbonne or Béziers to go through his normal round of activities without betraying his vows.

By 1298, Angelo had gone beyond all that. He had renounced any hope of observing the Franciscan rule within the Franciscan order. The evanescent Poor Hermits of Pope Celestine technically died with Celestine himself, but they furnished Angelo with an ideal he would spend the rest of his life pursuing. That ideal contained few of the duties accumulated by the Franciscan order during the thirteenth century, duties largely accepted by Olivi. Angelo was perfectly content to see his group renounce those tasks and pursue an eremitical life.

During the first decade of the fourteenth century, what had previously been a sporadic persecution of zealots became a sustained, organized one that sharpened the line between spirituals and community. Indeed, by 1309, when Clement V intervened and temporarily rescued the spirituals, one can think of the latter as a discernible group that *needed* rescuing. Yet even here, one must be careful not to overstate the matter. Clement sharpened the distinction between spirituals and community by orchestrating a debate between spokesmen for both sides.

Moreover, even at that point, the programs advocated by spiritual spokesmen varied widely. Raymond Geoffroi still cherished Olivi's ideal of a united, reformed order that would continue to perform most of the functions entrusted to the Franciscans during the preceding century. Ubertino da Casale's more thoroughgoing critique of the order called many of those functions into question and abandoned the hope of a unified, reformed order, suggesting instead that the pope sanction a division in which the spirituals would inherit the name and the rule while the rest continued to practice their lax behavior in a new order that had the common decency not to call itself Franciscan. Our third, less public spokesman, Angelo Clareno, advocated another sort of split in which he and his colleagues could form a separate group that observed Francis's rule to the letter without being a part of the Franciscan order.

Clement's way of sorting the problem out doomed the spirituals. He concurred with the spirituals in seeing *usus pauper* as an essential part of the vow, but agreed with the community that the vow should be limited to specific things. Since the rule was less informative in identifying these things than anyone might have wished, he offered a list. The result was a solution that underscored the role of authority in deciding such matters (which was further intensified by his emphasis on the role of Franciscan leaders in determining how much *usus pauper* was enough).

Equally important, Clement rejected Angelo's and Ubertino's plea that the order be split, concurring instead with Raymond Geoffroi's vision of a united and reformed Franciscan order: enlightened superiors would give the spirituals room to practice strict observance, and the spirituals would, in return, acknowledge their place within the organization. Such a program underestimated the divergence in aim that separated many spirituals from the main body of the order *and* the degree of animosity felt toward the spirituals by many of the leaders. Clement's solution of setting aside special houses for the spirituals in southern France ignored the fact that Italian spirituals, too, needed protection, and his attempt to secure a kinder, gentler leadership was fated to achieve only temporary success. In fact, it was scheduled to last only as long as Clement did. After his death the old leaders seeped back into office and the spirituals were again in dire straits, where indeed some had remained throughout the period of purported reconciliation.

The question is whether Clement could have done much else. Certainly he could have followed Ubertino instead of Raymond and split the order, recognizing that he had two very different groups on his hands. That would have been a far from easy way of settling the problem, because by that point there were in reality not two different groups but several. It is hard to imagine what a newly constituted spiritual Franciscan order would have been like with Ubertino, Angelo, the Tuscan rebels, and the southern French all in it. Nevertheless, ungainly as that solution might have been, it would have given the various zealots substantially more protection than they were about to enjoy during the next few years. It might also have spared Franciscan leaders a great deal of trouble, since John XXII's effort to crush the spiritual Franciscans put him on a path that eventually led to the critical reconsideration of ideas held sacred by the order as a whole.

What actually did occur, of course, was not pleasant. Clement's attempt at reconciliation led instead to deeper division and then to straightforward persecution under John XXII. After Clement's death, some southern French spirituals, despairing of any assistance from their leaders, resorted to rebellion (as the Tuscan spirituals had earlier). John, who inherited this situation, settled it by rejecting the spirituals' self-justification, ordering them to conform, and branding those who refused as heretics. He has received his share of criticism for taking this course, yet we have seen that to some extent he moved within a developing tradition. From the 1290s on, popes had been concerned about the spirituals' disruptive potential. Nicholas IV, Boniface VIII, and Clement V all had acted against one group of spirituals or another. Moreover, even as Clement V tried to give spirituals room to pursue their ideals within the order, he had redefined the question of *usus pauper* in a way that highlighted the role of superiors in determining what it entailed. In the interval between Clement's death and John's 1317 blitzkrieg, spirituals and Franciscan leaders conducted their publicity war against one another—each group seemingly intent on accusing the other not primarily of laxity but of disobedience. It is hardly surprising, then, that John should have seen the controversy in these terms as well.

John's 1317 offensive marked an important point in the debate, however. Up to that moment, southern French spirituals had been operating in overt defiance of their superiors, but they could seek justification for their action by appealing beyond those superiors to the pope. After 1317, they could continue their rebellion only by defying the pope as well, thus severing their ties with the institutional church. That many spirituals did so, and that many of the laity supported them, serves as remarkable testimony to the depth of their conviction and of lay loyalty to them. Yet their resistance has to be seen in context. Franciscan leaders made flight more attractive to the French spirituals by continuing to harass them even after they had submitted. Moreover, in the course of his pontificate, John inspired a great deal of opposition; much of that opposition found itself defying him while under ban of excommunication or accusation of heresy. The variety of John's opponents and the fact that many of them labored under religious sanction made it easier for at least some spirituals to preserve both their integrity and their lives during the 1320s. Nevertheless, John's action against them marked the end of a very long era in which the spirituals had functioned as an embattled but theoretically loyal dissenting movement within the order and church.

Was there a spiritual Franciscan movement at all, though? Or is the spiritual movement about which historians write essentially a trick played on us by Angelo Clareno? Certainly that movement attained its clearest outlines and greatest coherence in the pages of Angelo's *Chronicle,* where it became an old and honorable tradition running from Francis and his companions through Angelo himself. Once we turn from Angelo to the evidence, the contours of the movement blur. It is hard to trace any definable movement before the 1270s, and from then on we see different individuals and groups with notably different agendas.

Nevertheless, we do discern some degree of family resemblance. French and Italian spirituals were united in believing that the Franciscan vow bound friars not only to renouncing possessions but also to observing *usus pauper.* They were united in believing that the order needed reform in this regard, although they differed on just how bad things had become and on what aspects of thirteenth-century Franciscan development would have to be jettisoned in order to make things right. Increasingly, they shared a remarkable lack of confidence in the current leadership, both in the order and in the church as a whole, but combined their pessimism about their leaders with a strong faith that God would effect the necessary reforms anyway (and that he would do so in the relatively near future).

Their pessimism *and* their hope were articulated in the form of a scenario that was apocalyptic without being notably eschatological. That is, there was great attention to the succession of eras and little to the proximity of final judgment. In Olivi's case, the end of the world was rendered uninteresting by the fact that he projected a dawning third age of around seven hundred or eight hundred years.[1] Bernard Gui tells us that some beguins expected it to last one hundred years—which is fewer than eight hundred, but certainly long enough to relieve eschatological tension. We do not know how long Prous thought that it would last, a fact that is significant in itself. It was a question that simply did not interest her. The end that concerned her was not that of the world but that of the old dispensation.

Angelo gives the same impression, though he offers a less detailed scenario and is interested only in the fate of Francis's immediate family. His general message is that Francis's heritage has been, is being, and will be attacked as Francis himself predicted, but a reformed observance will soon emerge from the tribulation. In all the apocalyptic scenarios analyzed in this book—Olivi's, Ubertino's, Prous's, and those favored by the rest of the beguins—except Angelo's, the persecution of Antichrist is presented as a stage leading to a new era, not as the ultimate historical evil leading to final judgment. Angelo may reverse the equation, projecting an Antichrist to come at the end of time, but he is too vague on the matter for us to decide with any confidence, and in any case his notion of the abomination of desolation offers an equivalent of the others' placement of Antichrist on the road to the new age.

Another remarkable similarity in all these factions—closely related to the apocalyptic scenario and the pessimism about ecclesiastical leaders—is the recognition that in the final analysis, people must now make their own decisions, often at some cost. In Olivi's case, that recognition remained theoretical, but his statement on the limits of obedience functioned as a harbinger of things to come. By the third decade of the fourteenth century Ubertino, Angelo, and renegade French spirituals were all following their diverse paths, paths they had chosen without notable ecclesiastical reinforcement. Each developed his or her own particular style of challenging papal authority. Ubertino seems to have joined forces with John XXII's major institutional rival, the emperor, in public opposition. French spirituals like Raymond Déjean joined with beguins in an underground resistance movement, remaining clandestine when they could but, when finally captured, facing the choice between submission and death. Angelo Clareno continued to praise obedience and managed to preserve at least the appearance of it by developing an uncanny ability to slip just out of official reach whenever it seemed necessary. However different these paths may seem, they all stood in stark contrast to the essentially institutional, hierarchical model of decision making offered by Clement V and John XXII.

Supporters of the spirituals showed a notable inclination to set their own courses. In inquisitorial processes, perplexed inquisitors kept asking their victims why they had continued to support renegade beguins even when they knew them to be such. The victims, in response, kept appealing to their own personal experience of these people and to the conclusions that they had drawn from that experience. When the priest Bernard Maury was asked why he continued to consort with the beguin leader, Pierre Trencavel, even though he knew that the church considered Pierre a heretic, the answer—insofar as Bernard managed to articulate one—was that he himself judged Pierre to be a good man and never heard Pierre say anything he himself thought to be heretical. When Berenger Roque, a parchment-maker, was asked why he left Lunel with a bit of flesh belonging to one of those burned there, he said he did so because of the devotion in which he then held the condemned, "because he himself had experienced their holy lives and behavior." The inquisitors thought it an argument dangerous to ecclesiastical authority, and it was.

Another theme uniting some (if not all) of the spirituals is an intense interest in mystical experience and the association of it with a dawning new age. Certainly such interest can be found in the three major spokesmen. As for the spirituals' lay supporters, Prous certainly fits the description (as does Queen Sancia of Naples, who, in her 1331 letter to the Franciscan general chapter at Perpignan, claimed that what she said there had been dictated to her by God).[2] Nevertheless, despite the fact that most of the Occitan beguins subjected to inquisitorial processes credited Olivi with mystical illumination, they showed little evidence of expecting to see it in themselves. Nevertheless, that may have something to do with the sorts of questions asked them by the inquisitors.

A further bond uniting French spirituals, beguins, and various Italian spirituals was a common symbolic patrimony. Olivi and the Italian spirituals he attacked, Angelo and the Tuscan rebels he attacked, all shared a number of common themes such as the resurrection of Francis, though they employed these themes in different ways and with endless variations. In many cases, the images were left relatively undefined. If forced to spell out precisely what sort of resurrection they anticipated, Olivi, Ubertino, Angelo, and Conrad of Offida might have found that they expected drastically different things, but they never needed to be that explicit. Scholars delegated to examine Olivi's Apocalypse commentary close to two decades after his death found the idea of Francis's resurrection bizarre and wanted to know precisely what he meant by it, but by that time it was too late to demand precision of him. In studying the spirituals—in trying to decide whether any such entity as the spirituals actually existed—it is important to acknowledge both sides of the coin, the symbols and the concrete expectations, and to recognize the complex relationship between them.

Obviously much of what has been said so far cannot be limited to the spiritual Franciscans. We see certain basic tendencies that cut through the entire period, involving more people than the spiritual Franciscans and beguins. In the late thirteenth and early fourteenth centuries, the church had to deal with any number of individuals and groups whose inner compasses pointed them in directions at variance with the official papal road map. One discovers a certain community of themes in these groups. Stephen Wessley,[3] for instance, sees the spiritual Franciscans, beguins, Guglielmites, and Dolcinists as all connected by their common reliance on the thirteenth-century themes of *ecclesia spiritualis*, *imitatio Christi*, and *vita apostolica*. One might add that all these groups displayed the same interest in heralding a succession of eras rather than announcing an imminent final judgment, though they might differ in how they estimated the duration of the final era and where they placed Antichrist.[4]

We could extend the web of connections in a number of directions. It was an era in which pious clergy and laity pursued spiritual transformation in a variety of forms, some of which the church managed to bring under control and some of which it did not. The affinity between these movements and the spiritual Franciscans is epitomized in Ubertino's involvement with Italian female mystics.

Still, despite their diversity and the way the things that did bind them were reflected in other movements as well, there is a sense in which the spiritual Franciscans and beguins were a particular movement within these more general trends. However separate the various factions might have been, they were aware of one another and of their common concern about the decay in Franciscan life. They shared enough concerns to compel Clement to structure the great negotiations of 1309–12 as an attempt to mediate between two groups, the spirituals and the community; for Italian as well as French Franciscans to be considered (and rejected) as possible spokesmen for the Béziers and Narbonne spirituals when they were summoned to Avignon in 1317; and for southern France to be united with Sicily in the 1320s as opposite ends of an ambitious escape route. Olivi, Ubertino, Clareno, and the rest were never so close as they became in Angelo's *Chronicle*, but they were close enough for their followers to share a common persecution—and, to some extent, the common dream of a revived Franciscan observance on the other side of persecution.

APPENDIX:
SPIRITUALS AND MYSTICS

IN THE FOURTH CHAPTER A QUESTION was raised and temporarily evaded: Can one document any clear tie between the spirituals and certain female mystics, particularly Clare of Montefalco, Margaret of Cortona, and Angela of Foligno? It is time to consider that subject. We will begin with Clare.

Clare of Montefalco

Clare's Life and Saintly Nachleben

A brief biographical sketch is in order.[1] Born in 1268 at Montefalco, Clare spent her entire life there. She had two sisters, one younger (who died as an infant) and one older, as well as a brother. The latter, Francesco, followed the broad hint offered by his name and became a Franciscan. The older sister, Giovanna, pursued the life of a recluse.

Clare showed her vocation early. At four, she was constantly disappearing into the most secret places of the house to pray. Her mystical experiences began at that age, although she was still too young to recognize them as such. At six, she left her family home and joined her sister in the latter's *reclusorium*, which by that point contained others as well. The group followed no established rule at first. Giovanna, as founder and leader, provided direction.

During the seven years following Clare's entry, the community grew enough to require a change of houses, which occurred in 1281. It was not an easy move. The new building was big enough and its inhabitants numerous enough to make the commune wonder if it already had too many religious establishments requiring support from the faithful, and it did its best to defeat the project. Its best extended to physical violence aimed at the building and active discouragement of contributions, leading to some hungry times for the sisters. In 1283 Giovanna attempted to remedy the lack of donations by sending a few sisters out to beg, and Clare did so eight times.

The group endured whatever discouragement the commune visited upon it, and by 1290, it was an accepted fixture. In that year, its mode of existence was challenged in another way, this time by the church, though the way in which that challenge came about is unclear. We do know that in 1290, Giovanna formally requested a rule from the bishop of Spoleto, and he assigned them the rule of Saint Augustine. We also know that he gave other groups of recluses in the area the same rule. Giovanna now became an abbess.

The group did not join the Augustinian order. It simply adopted the Augustinian rule while remaining under the direct authority of the bishop. As Enrico Menestò says, it "passed from a free and particular form of eremitical life to a free and particular form of mendicant cenobitic life under the guidance of the Augustinian rule."[2]

In 1291, Giovanna died, and Clare, now barely twenty-three years old, became abbess. One can understand why a young woman constantly open to intense mystical experiences might want to avoid administrative duties, but she seems to have been a good abbess and held the position until her death in 1308. During that period the experiences continued, but she combined them with wise spiritual direction of her charges and, perhaps more surprisingly, sound decisions concerning internal organization.

The campaign to canonize Clare began on a local level almost immediately after her death. It soon received powerful support, first from the bishop of Spoleto's vicar, Berengar de Saint-Affrique, then from the cardinals Pietro Colonna, Giacomo Colonna, and Napoleone Orsini. By the end of 1309 an official investigation was underway, and within a decade, her credentials were under consideration at the papal court. After that point the process slowed considerably. It ground on until 1333, when it was suspended. Revivified in the eighteenth century, it was again suspended and brought to completion only in 1881, 572 years after it was begun. The interviews compiled for the canonization process provide us with most of what we know about Clare's views and associations.[3]

Significant Associations

The first thing to be said about Clare is that, whereas Angela of Foligno and Margaret of Cortona were third-order Franciscans, Clare had vowed the Augustinian rule (although throughout the modern period, a series of determined Franciscans have argued that she too was a tertiary). In reality, the fact that Clare's convent followed the Augustinian rule is somewhat less important for our purposes than one might at first imagine, since it was adopted when her sister Giovanna was in charge and it seems to have been the result of an administrative choice by the bishop of Spoleto, not of an ideological one by Giovanna. Nor did it produce any close relationship to the Augustinian order.[4] Least of all did it preclude close contact with the Franciscans. When we examine the dossier, we find it filled with anecdotes involving them. Her relationships with them were obviously numerous and close.[5]

One element that merits attention is Clare's continuing relationship with the same cardinals who served as protectors of the spiritual Franciscans: Napoleone Orsini, Giacomo Colonna, and Pietro Colonna.[6] She also had at least some relationship with a major spiritual Franciscan spokesman, Ubertino da Casale, who later testified to having been cured of a hernia by her[7] and was in Orsini's service at the time of the canonization process.[8] When Ubertino would have known her is another matter. He presumably had some contact with her when he was investigating the heresy of the *spiritus libertatis* at the behest of Napoleone Orsini, a matter to which we will turn in a moment. In any case, her absence from the *Arbor vitae* suggests that he met her after 1305.

Clare's Franciscan connections were hardly limited to the spirituals and their protectors, though. She enjoyed personal contact with Franciscans who held important positions within the order, at least on a provincial level. Her brother is a case in point, since we know marginally more about him than we do about most of the others. Some scholars have asserted that Francesco was himself a spiritual. There is no evidence that he was. He was a custode in 1318–19,[9] a moment when spiritual Franciscan fortunes within the order were arguably at their lowest.

The problem, though, is what we are asking when we ask whether Francesco was a spiritual. Certainly he did not match the meaning of the term as found in inquisitorial documents, where the spirituals were portrayed as a group of arrogant malcontents who, driven by their own misguided scruples, destroyed good order by challenging their superiors and were thus disciplined by the pope. Francesco certainly was not one of these people, or he would not have moved smoothly through the Franciscan *cursus honorum*.

On the other hand, if we forego protest and defiance as qualifications for inclusion and, lowering the bar considerably, we simply ask whether Francesco lived the sort of life recommended by spiritual spokesmen, the answer is that we know very little about what sort of life Francesco led or what sort he thought a Franciscan *ought* to lead. There is, to be sure, Francesco's story of how as a student he was scolded by his sister for what she perceived as unwarranted self-indulgence. The anecdote implies that, at least at that age, Francesco was not overly concerned with asceticism, but we have no way of knowing how effective the intervention proved. Again, we have seen that we have not one but several models of spiritual Franciscan life from which to choose, even among its major spokesmen. Olivi, who had no essential quarrel with either university education or an extensive Franciscan urban ministry, might have seen Francesco as a true Franciscan, while Ubertino da Casale and Angelo Clareno might have been less enthusiastic.[10]

When we stop talking about major spokesmen and turn to the problem of what beliefs or behavior might have qualified one as a spiritual Franciscan in the Montefalco area during the final years of Clare's life, we can be excused for wishing that the question had not been asked. The various Franciscans who consorted with Clare while holding significant positions within the order may not have been spiritual Franciscans in the sense that they protested decay in the order and were persecuted for it, but they may well have been pious, virtuous individuals who were serious about Franciscan poverty and practiced it in their own lives. We have no reason to believe that cultivation of traditionally Franciscan virtues was an absolute bar to institutional advancement in the province of Saint Francis.

Clare's Poverty and Humility

Mention of Franciscan poverty encourages us to approach the same problem from a slightly different perspective. According to various witnesses, Clare chose to live in poverty.[11] In practice, her way of life was similar to the one treasured by the spirituals, particularly the Italian ones with an eremitical orientation, such as Angelo. Whatever her justification of *usus pauper,* she did practice it. Adoption of the Augustinian rule, the evolution of Clare's group toward a more ordered cenobitic life, and the responsibilities consequent upon serving as leader of that group all undoubtedly moderated this asceticism to some extent, but did not end it.[12]

The problems begin when we try to extend Clare's connection with the spirituals beyond that point. It is difficult to make any serious case for an attachment to the spiritual Franciscan theory of poverty—or, for that matter, to the Franciscan theory of poverty, spiritual or otherwise. Clare was, in this sense at least, a product of the Augustinian rule. She did not see herself as subjected to an apostolic poverty that demanded lack of communal property, as the Franciscans did. Nor did she reject any direct contact with money. These observations not only separate her from the spirituals but also from the Franciscans in general. As for the spirituals in particular (and their characteristic insistence that the Franciscan vow demanded not only lack of ownership but *usus pauper*), if Clare herself voluntarily practiced such limited use, she did so as a form of penance, an ascetic practice. There is no evidence that, like the spirituals, she thought it was required for imitation of the apostolic model.[13]

In fact, one could ask to what extent the poverty noted in various depositions was a matter of necessity rather than choice. As we have seen, communal hostility resulted in some hard times for her convent. And as Giovanna Casagrande has noted, the emphasis in the depositions falls on the patience and humility with which she bore these deprivations. Clare's final advice to her sisters was to be humble, obedient, patient, and united in love, a formulation that completely omitted poverty.[14]

If Clare's poverty is worth discussing, so is her humility. Especially notable is her insistence on performing menial tasks even when she became abbess. One is reminded of the mid-thirteenth-century minister general, John of Parma, as described by Salimbene da Parma and Angelo Clareno. Angelo and Salimbene both describe John as plain in his dining habits, and Salimbene also praises his willingness to pitch in and help with simple tasks like cleaning and preparing vegetables.[15] It is a portrait that stands in stark contrast with the situation at the turn of the fourteenth century as described by Jacopone da Todi and Ubertino da Casale, both of whom emphasized the extent to which those who held prestigious positions within the order formed an elite and used their status to gain special favors.[16]

On first glance, this contrast, with its implied link between Clare and the spiritual ideal of leadership, may seem easy to demolish. After all, John of Parma is considered a precursor of the spirituals largely because Angelo Clareno portrays him as such in his chronicle and because Ubertino lays claim to him in the *Arbor vitae*. Angelo's chronicle is a remarkably tendentious document that turns John into a spokesmen for Angelo's own views, and Ubertino's description of leadership in his time is even more tendentious. Nevertheless, it is not Angelo who tells us about John helping out in the kitchen but Salimbene, whom no one has ever accused of being a spiritual Franciscan. Moreover, Ubertino's stark portrait of a Franciscan elite jealously guarding its own privileges receives at least some support not only from his fellow spirituals, but also from the very people Ubertino is indicting. In response to Ubertino's attack, the leaders protest that it should not be considered all that wrong if those who work hard at administration, teaching, and preaching occasionally receive little pleasures not offered to others.[17]

Here again, however, it is one thing to cite the defensive strategies pursued in the first decade of the fourteenth century by leaders of the order at Avignon, and quite another to ask what sort of life individual custodes, guardians, or lectors around Montefalco might have been leading. Any number of those who knew and admired Clare might have been much closer to the ideal Ubertino defends than to the behavior he rejects. We simply do not know.

Clare, Scholarship, and Mystical Experience

Like many of the Italian spirituals, Clare was sensitized to the dangers of scholarship. There are statements that suggest a suspicion of and even a disdain for higher learning, as when she is reported to have told her brother, an educated Franciscan, that she would be happier if he were a lay brother and a cook than if he were one of the greatest scholars in the order. Her dossier repeatedly presents her as possessing, through unction, a more valuable access to the truth, one so impressive that scholars came to consult her. Nor were the witnesses above making invidious comparisons with Parisian scholarship.[18] Here we have the theme dear not only to a protospiritual, such as Giles of Assisi, but also to genuine spirituals, such as Jacopone da Todi or Ubertino da Casale.

Nevertheless, it must also be noted that we find the witnesses, not Clare herself, making those invidious comparisons. Moreover, the notion of a mystical piety tapping resources of wisdom unavailable even to the most accomplished scholar, while particularly relished by the Italian spirituals, was hardly unique to them. It goes back to the image of Francis enshrined in Thomas of Celano.[19] In fact it goes back a great deal further than that—to the Apostle Paul. It became a familiar theme in writings about female mystics of Clare's time.

Clare's knowledge was said to come directly through mystical experience. That in itself might seem to connect her with the spirituals, since such experience was prized by the spirituals and by those who favored them, such as the Colonna cardinals and Napoleone Orsini. It is arguable that during the half-century after Bonaventure's death it was the spirituals who made the greatest contribution to the Franciscan mystical tradition. Moreover, the spiritual Franciscan connection with female mystics is well established. On the other hand, the spirituals were hardly the sole guardians of that tradition during the period, and there is no reason to think that they were the only Franciscans interested in lay mystics.

Clare and the Spiritus Libertatis

One element that deserves more than passing mention in dealing with Clare is the puzzling role played by the heresy of the *spiritus libertatis* in her life. We know less than we would like to know about this group—if indeed we can call it a group at all—although it is mentioned in several contemporary sources aside from the Clare of Montefalco canonization process, including Angelo Clareno, Ubertino da Casale, and Angela of Foligno. Livarius Oliger, who produced a book-length study of the sect (if, indeed, we can call it a sect),[20] emphasizes that there is no reason to identify the heresy particularly with the spirituals. The central figure of the *spiritus libertatis* as we see it passing through Montefalco was Bentivenga da Gubbio, a Franciscan of Umbria who is reported by Angelo Clareno to have been a member of the Apostles before he became a friar.[21] The core of his teaching was that since whatever we do is caused by God, we are unable to sin and it is best not to feel remorse for our actions. He and his followers managed to insinuate themselves briefly into Clare of Montefalco's circle, but when he told Clare his views, she was disturbed enough to notify the authorities. The inquisitor for the region expressed his sympathy but said that he could do nothing if Bentivenga did not confess his views openly, so Clare appealed to Cardinal Napoleone Orsini, who arranged for Bentivenga to be apprehended. Ubertino da Casale, then in Orsini's service, feigned interest in the heresy. When Bentivenga enthusiastically explained his ideas to Ubertino, whom he saw as a potential disciple, the latter relayed them to the inquisitor, who eventually sentenced Bentivenga and his genuine disciples to perpetual imprisonment.[22] Oliger observes that Bentivenga's ideas hardly disappeared when he did. They fell back into the general sea of heretical possibilities, then surfaced in various forms and combinations during succeeding years.

Oliger's reconstruction of the affair, while excellent, leaves us with some questions. One of them is whether the *spiritus libertatis* should be seen as a heretical group alongside the Cathars and Waldensians, or whether the name points to something more pervasive and more poorly defined, a set of general tendencies in the religious life of the time that surfaced in both orthodox and heretical form. In a massive article on the subject, Romana Guarnieri argues that it was more the latter than the former,[23] and she is probably right. Guarnieri offers a huge dossier of materials on the subject—materials that include Meister Eckhart, Marguerite Porete, Jacopone da Todi, Angela of Foligno, and a host of others. While it is impossible to take this dossier as demonstrating any clearly defined view—in fact, some of the data point in very different directions and cry for distinctions that Guarnieri herself does not attempt to make—she has done an invaluable service in presenting the materials with which historians must come to terms if they are to speak sensibly about the matter.

No one can read through the Clare materials without recognizing that the experience with Bentivenga was traumatic for her. Various witnesses testify that she reacted with horror and vigorously sought his conviction. Clare's connection was clearly an embarrassment both for her and for those who compiled her dossier. Both were apparently determined to distance her from Bentivenga's heresy. The violence of her reaction is most clearly seen in her brother's recollection of the event,[24] but it is reflected by other witnesses as well. Certainly the way Bentivenga presented the matter to her was calculated to sharpen the radical nature of his message and cause maximum offense, since he focused on the moral permissibility of fornication. Yet the dossier makes it clear that the basic stance could be stretched in other directions as well, and more people of Clare's acquaintance than Bentivenga were involved. His views were shared by several Franciscans who were on more or less familiar terms with her. It must have been unsettling for her to discover that her moral radar had so malfunctioned that she had allowed these relationships to develop. The witnesses in the process partially correct the oversight by allowing Clare at least some prophetic warning of the danger, but her reaction, as her brother describes it, is so strong as to suggest genuine shock and dismay. Her reaction to this affair reverberates throughout the dossier. There is perhaps an echo of it in Clare's careful formulation, "I see God's justice in all things, and I see that all things created by God are good, and I see nothing evil except sin."[25]

That brings us to the basic question of whether these wolves disguised as sheep were, in fact, spirituals. If we assume that they were discovered and dealt with in 1306–7, then it is interesting that shortly thereafter we find the community attempting to convince Pope Clement V of a connection between the spirituals and the *spiritus libertatis*.[26] Of course the charge did not become true simply by virtue of the community making it, and in the polemical exchanges leading up to the Council of Vienne, Ubertino da Casale, speaking for the spirituals, denied any connection. Still, although the first decade of the fourteenth century—the decade in which Clare encountered the *spiritus libertatis*— offers no evidence of such a tie (other than unsupported charges by the Franciscan leadership), it is also true that inquisitorial processes from the third decade of the century make the same connection.[27]

Clare and Southern French Beguins

Another intriguing aspect of Clare's story is her connection with southern French beguins. The most obvious of these associations is her relationship with one Margaret of Carcassonne,[28] who is said to have come to Italy as a pilgrim, met and conversed with Clare (without either knowing the other's language), and then settled in the area, presumably to continue their dialogue. Unfortunately there is little about Margaret, as we encounter her in the process, that suggests spiritual Franciscan connections. Less often mentioned, but more promising, is Clare's role in establishing a group of tertiaries from Toulouse at the monastery of San Rocco. As Mario Sensi reports the story, she heard that they had arrived in the area and wished to meet them. This occurred in 1295, "three years after the *beata* and her nuns had accepted the rule of the third order of Saint Francis."[29]

Should we assume that these connections demonstrate sympathy toward the spirituals? Obviously we cannot assume that reference to Toulouse or Carcassonne in itself establishes spiritual Franciscan leanings simply because the spirituals were strong in Languedoc. A more promising fact is that the document informs us of the tertiaries' arrival and labels them "beguins." Of course, everyone called a beguin in 1295 did not move in the spiritual Franciscan orbit, but many beguins in southern France did.

Sensi supports the connection with reference to the codices in Occitan found at Assisi and Todi.[30] These two codices are certainly germane to our story, since the Assisi manuscript contains the confession of Matthew of Bouzigues, an admirer of the spiritual Franciscan leader Petrus Iohannis Olivi, and the Todi codex contains works by Olivi himself. One must ask what these facts contribute to our knowledge of Clare, though. Certainly the story of Matthew of Bouzigues shows that French beguins with spiritual Franciscan sympathies were traveling in Italy around the turn of the fourteenth century, but citing these manuscripts constitutes little more than an attempt to establish guilt by association unless one can show their relevance to the particular case of Clare's tertiaries.

Clare's Canonization Process and Other Factors

There has been some interest in viewing the failure of Clare's canonization process to reach fruition under John XXII as a result—and indeed, as evidence—of her spiritual Franciscan connections. The same has been said about Margaret of Cortona's process. In neither case can the possibility be dismissed out of hand, but in neither case is there much evidence for it. Canonization processes did not automatically succeed unless some flaw was discovered in the candidate's credentials. They could wither along the way for any number of reasons, and a large number did.

Given world enough and time, other factors that evoke the spirit of Francis might be considered. For example, something might be said of her begging (although she does not seem to have done much of it) or her attitude toward lepers (she kissed them). At this point, though, we are finding that her connection with the Franciscan tradition is more easily established than her connection with the spirituals. Chaucer's friar begged, but he was no spiritual Franciscan.

Conclusion Concerning Clare

Where do these considerations leave us? While no particular bit of evidence cited so far establishes a strong link between Clare and the spiritual Franciscans, the totality of the evidence does exert a cumulative effect. The least we can say is that Clare, as the various witnesses present her, had more in common with an eremitically and contemplatively inclined spiritual like Angelo Clareno than with a Paris-educated Franciscan administrator like Bertrand de la Tour, who as provincial minister of Aquitaine established a reputation as one of the spirituals' most prominent enemies within the order. That is not equivalent to saying that an Angelo would have been more inclined than a Bertrand to celebrate Clare's virtues, though. In fact, some years after his encounter with the spirituals, Bertrand was one of three cardinals who, in the early 1330s, wrote the favorable report on Clare presented to Pope John XXII. She was, after all, a potential saint, a special case. One could revere her without feeling that one had to emulate her, just as one could revere Francis without feeling that the whole Franciscan order had to act like him. Nor—and this is perhaps the more important point—can one conclude from the greater similarity between Clare and Angelo that Clare herself thought that the Franciscan order should live like Angelo's conception of Francis or that the order was, in its present state, corrupt. Her dossier simply does not address that problem. What we do know from the dossier is that she spent a great deal of time with "establishment" Franciscans, with lectors and administrators, without feeling moved to reform them, at least as far as we know. Ubertino da Casale was hardly her only visitor.

Again we ask: Where does that leave us? Certainly it leaves us with the feeling that Clare's credentials as a spiritual Franciscan fellow traveler are not entirely beyond dispute. But perhaps it should also leave us with some shred of suspicion that our tendency to treat the spiritual Franciscans as a well-defined group within the order is in itself an oversimplification, one that works against us when it comes to analyzing specific situations like this one. We know what Olivi believed; we know what Ubertino da Casale believed; we know what Angelo Clareno believed. And we know that they did not believe precisely the same things. When we take that difference among the major spiritual Franciscan spokesmen and extend it to a local scene like Montefalco, a small place in a remote area at a time of incredible spiritual ferment, we might be excused for asking precisely what we think we are comparing Clare *with* when we ask whether she resembled the spiritual Franciscans.

Margaret of Cortona

Life and Canonization Process

What we know about Margaret of Cortona comes largely from the *legenda* composed by the Franciscan Giunta da Bevegna sometime between Margaret's death in 1297 and early 1308.[31] It gives us little to work with by way of dates. Some modern scholars offer 1247 as the date of Margaret's birth at Laviano, but that claim is very hypothetical.[32] We know little of her family, except that her mother died when she was small, her father married again, and her brother was a third-order Franciscan. On the other hand, we do know that she ran away from home and lived nine years with a man from Montepulciano, presumably someone of higher social status. They never married, and she had one child by him. After he died, she returned to Laviano but was rejected by her father, who was spurred on by the stepmother. The legend offers a brief but striking description of Margaret sitting under a fig tree in her father's garden, deciding what to do next. Her choices, as she saw them, were to live by her still young and beautiful body or to strike out on a new and different path.

She chose the latter alternative and went to Cortona, where she stayed with two women and supported herself by performing various domestic tasks for aristocratic women of the town. At the same time, she entered into close relations with the Franciscans there, and several times requested admission into the order of penitents. The Franciscans hesitated because they saw her as too young and pretty to display the necessary constancy. Some sources suggest that she was made to wait three years before she was finally given the habit in 1275 or 1277.[33] Eventually she settled into a cell near the home of the two women and went every day to the Franciscan church, where she heard mass and the brothers' sermons. They served as her spiritual guides, and her son, after being educated by a master of Arezzo, became a Franciscan. The traffic in advice eventually flowed in both directions: various Franciscans began to consult Margaret.

During this period, Margaret was involved in charitable activities, such as aiding the poor and working for civic peace. She was also involved in establishing a hospice. Eventually, however, she decided to pursue a more eremitical existence, moving to another cell at the top of the hill on which Cortona is located. The move was opposed by the Franciscans, who felt that her new cell was too far from their church and feared that they might lose claim to her body when she died. Margaret retaliated with the revelation that her external masters, the friars, had been overruled by her internal master, Christ himself, who wanted her to relocate. When this occurred is not entirely clear. It has been dated as early as 1288 but could be slightly later. It is significant that a provincial chapter of the order dictated (probably in 1288) that Margaret should be visited by her confessor and amanuensis, Giunta da Bevegna, no more than once every eight days; in 1290, Giunta was transferred to Siena. Perhaps it is also significant that in 1289–90 Pope Nicholas IV promulgated the bull *Supra montem,* which defined the Franciscans' supervisory role over the penitents.

The Franciscans' fears proved at least partly justified. While Margaret retained some contact with them, she moved closer to the secular clergy and busied herself with the rebuilding of the nearby church of Saint Basil. After her death in 1297, the commune—not the Franciscans—took the lead in promoting Margaret's cult, and her body was eventually placed in a new church near the church of Saint Basil.

The canonization procedure was a remarkably slow one. Instigated by the commune in 1318, it had no success under John XXII and none immediately thereafter. In 1515 Pope Leo X permitted churches in the city and diocese of Cortona to celebrate Margaret's feast day, and in 1623 that permission was extended to all Franciscan churches. Shortly thereafter the canonization process began again, although it was not completed until 1728.

The most extended case for a tie between Margaret and the spiritual Franciscans is made by Maria Caterina Jacobelli, who suggests that Margaret's *legenda* is largely spiritual Franciscan polemic that says more about her amanuensis than about Margaret herself.[34] That is, indeed, the significance of Jacobelli's title, *Una donna senza volto,* "a woman without a face." In Giunta's work we find what Jacobelli describes as "a constructed saint," designed "according to the exigencies of those who stood around her." Jacobelli's case is built largely on her interpretation of specific names found in the legend and references in it to the Franciscans. We will take these in order.

Margaret's Associations

An annotation at the beginning of the earliest manuscript announces that the legend was compiled "at the command of Giovanni di Castiglione, inquisitor of heretical depravity."[35] The same annotation goes on to name various notables who had seen (and presumably approved) the work. Among those named is "Ubertinus de Ianua," who is, we can assume, the spiritual Franciscan leader Ubertino da Casale, although he is inexplicably listed among the provincial ministers, a position there is no reason to believe he ever held. Why an inquisitor ordered the *legenda* written is not explained, but the implication is not necessarily ominous. Giovanni knew Margaret and is mentioned several times in the legend itself. The annotation also notes that Cardinal Napoleone Orsini took the work with him to the papal court and kept it there for several months. Orsini is identified as a legate, and he was indeed such in central Italy in 1304–5 and 1306–8. In February 1308 he returned the legend and, in the presence of several notable friars (including Ubertino), he ordered Giunta to preserve it without making any changes and to allow anyone who wanted to copy it to do so. He also told them to preach it, and the annotation says that Ubertino did just that. So here again we find Ubertino, and we find a cardinal who was identified as a protector of the spiritual Franciscans.

If we find a great many names in this introductory annotation, we discover many more in the legend itself. Among the friars mentioned in the legend, we find a Friar Conrad, "lovable to God," coming to visit Margaret "from a remote province" and receiving advice from her. It is hardly unquestionable that this reference is to the spiritual leader Conrad of Offida, but it is not impossible either. More significant, Ubertino himself is described in the legend as escorting Margaret's son—by that time a Franciscan—to see his mother.[36]

While most of the chronology connected with Margaret is fuzzy, we can focus sharply enough on this incident to give it at least a rough date. Margaret died in 1297, so if we accept that Ubertino was in Paris between approximately 1289 and 1298, we must date the anecdote 1289 or earlier—and that seems likely in view of the anecdote itself. Margaret's son was the issue of her nine-year relationship, and she became a Franciscan tertiary in 1275 or 1277, after having had to wait for three years. Even if we accept that the date was 1277 and assume that she applied for entry as soon as she arrived in Cortona—which seems unlikely—the son could not have been younger than three when she was admitted, and he was undoubtedly older. The son was sent elsewhere to be educated and then became a Franciscan, presumably as soon as the order considered him old enough to accept, or shortly thereafter. A little reflection suggests the impossibility of the latter having occurred much after 1290 at the latest.

The anecdote establishes that it occurred even earlier than that. In it the son, already a Franciscan, oversleeps and misses matins. When the guardian of the house arrives with a rod to administer punishment "like a father," the son reacts dramatically, wresting the rod away and beating himself in the face with it. He is summoned to an accounting by his mother and arrives, accompanied by Ubertino. Margaret, weeping, informs her son that she has mystically eavesdropped "as you took the rod and childishly lacerated your face. Where, son, is the solicitude you should show toward divine praises? Where is the gratitude you should display toward such a God, the author of our salvation?" Stripped of its hagiographic implications, this is a story about an adolescent who, like many adolescents, tends to sleep a lot and get erratically emotional. It is a story about a parent who, like many parents, tells her son to grow up and take some responsibility. There is even an attempt to appeal to the gratitude and obedience he should show toward his father, in this case his heavenly one. The story thus belongs early in the son's Franciscan life. If Ubertino was off to Paris around 1289, the incident must predate his departure; even if we schedule his Parisian trip substantially earlier, as some historians have done, the incident could not have occurred all that much later. The point to be gained from these considerations is an important one: Ubertino would seem to have enjoyed close contact with Margaret at a relatively early date.

Even if we grant that the Conrad mentioned in the legend may not be Conrad of Offida, and even if we grant that Napoleone Orsini might have approved of Margaret's legend regardless of whether it displayed spiritual Franciscan leanings, we will find it hard not to be impressed by the way Ubertino da Casale's name winds in and out of the story. Nevertheless, if we take those names seriously, we must take equally seriously Margaret's acquaintance with other Franciscans who seem to have been leaders in the order. We should particularly note that the legend was produced at the command of an inquisitor. We cannot say precisely when he ordered it, but it must have been between 1298 (when Margaret died) and late 1307, when it would already have been in the hands of Napoleone Orsini. In other words, it would have been commissioned during a time when leaders of the order were carrying out a determined persecution of the spirituals. We cannot say much about the impact of that persecution on Tuscany, but we can assume that it was felt there—not only because Angelo Clareno tells us as much, but also because early in 1312, even after Pope Clement V had ordered leaders to suspend their anti-spiritual campaign and was close to forging an attempted settlement of the problem at the Council of Vienne, a group of Tuscan spirituals found their situation so unbearable that they banded together and took over three convents by force.

Thus we must reconcile three facts: (1) the legend was ordered and approved during a time when leaders of the order were persecuting spirituals; (2) it was ordered by an inquisitor, thus presumably a man in good odor with leaders of the order; and (3) Ubertino da Casale, an eminent Italian spiritual Franciscan leader, was involved in approving and publicizing the legend. It seems hard to do much of anything with these three ideas on the basis of any simple theory of the relations between the spirituals and the community; yet—and this is the important point for our purposes—it seems impossible to reconcile them on the assumption that the legend was a piece of spiritual Franciscan propaganda.

Endorsement of the Franciscans

If the Margaret legend offers us many names, it also offers us much in the way of comments that might be construed as pointing to a strong Franciscan affiliation. The order is given a remarkable endorsement. Christ, in his conversations with Margaret, repeatedly states his love for the order. He observes that people murmur against the friars just as they did about his own miracles and teaching. On another occasion he warns Margaret that, precisely because this order imitates Christ more than any other, it must prepare for tribulation.[37]

It is this theme of tribulation that Jacobelli finds most redolent of spiritual Franciscan preoccupations. Although the Antichrist is not yet born, the tribulation could not be all that far off, for Lucifer's special legate already has left Hell to unleash it. It will be so intense that many religious will leave their orders and many monks their monasteries.[38] The expectation of apocalyptic tribulation—even imminent tribulation—was not, of course, in itself a signal of spiritual Franciscan leanings. In the late thirteenth century it was hardly unusual to imagine that Antichrist's precursors already were preparing the way for him, and that he himself would not be long in coming.[39] The striking element in Margaret's prediction is her suggestion that the pope will be on the wrong side. At one point, Christ (speaking through Margaret) warns the Franciscans to prepare and then adds that, "even if they have no pope to console them," Christ himself will be with them. Lest one imagine that the lack of a consoling pontiff will be due to a papal vacancy, in another place he explicitly announces that "they will have a pope who will seem to be putting the whole world in good order but will actually be wrecking it." Here again, though, Christ promises that he will aid the order and, once the tribulation is over, "will magnificently exalt it."[40] One thinks of Olivi's apocalyptic program in his Apocalypse commentary and thus, by adoption, Ubertino's program in the *Arbor vitae*.

There is one important difference between Olivi's program and Ubertino's: Olivi had no particular pope in mind and Ubertino did (two, in fact). Jacobelli assumes that Margaret is more in Ubertino's camp and that the passage points directly at Boniface VIII. She must then face the chronological difficulty involved in that assumption: While Margaret was predicting during the 1290s, Giunta was presumably writing after Boniface's time. Jacobelli suggests that the prediction is an *ex eventu* prophecy placed in Margaret's mouth by Giunta, whose point is that, although Boniface is dead, the battle continues.

Margaret's *legenda* also contains at least one clear indication of a remarkable spectrum of observance within the order (if not a split between community and spirituals). Christ remarks to Margaret that "there were never so many holy men in the order as there are today, nor so many weak ones."[41] In fact, we might pause to recall that between 1288 and 1290, Fra Giunta's relationship with Margaret seems to have been seen as problematic by some Franciscans. He was required to limit his visits to her and was later transferred to Siena. As we will discover, his experience was not unique. Around 1294, Angela of Foligno's amanuensis was forbidden to speak with her for a while—and after that point, he visited her less often than before. One might be tempted to see a parallel between these phenomena and the community's comment in 1311 that the spirituals were disciplined for "concerning themselves with dreams and false visions" and "spending too much time conversing with women, especially beguines, under the pretense of sanctity."[42] The temptation becomes all the greater when—to anticipate our next mystic—we find the phrase "dreams and visions" echoed in Angela of Foligno's *Memorial*.[43] It becomes greater still when we recall that the same phrase was used in the southern French context from the early 1280s on, when Olivi was accused of "following dreams and fantastic visions." We should also remember that Olivi's interest in visions brought him into contact with female mystics.

Of course, adding Olivi to the mix reminds us that the 1311 charge could have been aimed at the situation in southern France, not Italy, but one suspects that it was not. The community makes the remark in direct response to a complaint by Ubertino and, as we have seen, the community responses to Ubertino at Vienne were often *ad hominem*. This one may be, too: the community may be referring to Ubertino's own contact with various female mystics. In any case, the comment suggests that by 1311, spokesmen for the order saw a special tie between spirituals and female mystics.

Unfortunately, beyond this point there is little to go on in making a case that Margaret's legend was a spiritual Franciscan production—and there is much to suggest that it was not. In the first place, working backward through the last few points, we must say that even if leaders of the order wanted to suggest the existence of a dangerous connection between spirituals and female mystics, it does not follow that only spiritual Franciscans enjoyed close contact with such mystics. Indeed, as we see in Margaret's *legenda*, such was not the case.

As for Christ's observation that there were never so many holy or weak friars, this passage is the only one in the *Legenda* that suggests such a split. Moreover, in that passage, Christ goes on to express his wish that those who are strong sustain the weak by their prayer and example. Such a suggestion seems wildly at variance with what we have come to consider the standard

Italian spiritual Franciscan program: split the order and let those who want to be genuine Franciscans do so unencumbered by those who seek a lax life. Equally at variance is Christ's repeated wish that, given the contemporary dangers of remaining in the secular world, the friars admit those who want to join and then do the best they can in shaping them to be true Franciscans.[44]

As for Christ's fondness for the Franciscan order, it seems to work against a spiritual Franciscan connection rather than for one. There is little in the legend that could be interpreted as a judgment on current Franciscan life. Certainly Christ addresses a few individual friars and some of his advice could be seen as critical; but remarkably little of it finds fault, and none of it comes close to the barrage he levels at the bishop of Arezzo or the citizenry of Cortona.[45] There is no hint of such common spiritual Franciscan themes as that the order has fallen into decay,[46] that it is divided by controversy, or that its superiors are leading the order astray. We have seen that some of Margaret's intimates held leadership positions, and they are hardly criticized for it in the legend.[47]

Moreover, the sorts of things Christ seems genuinely concerned about emphasizing are compatible with the program stressed by leaders of the order. He reassures the friars about their current church expansion, explaining that it will give them more privacy for their prayers. He is concerned about the Muslims and stresses not only the importance of crusading but the need to preach a crusade as well. He asserts the validity of the Portiuncula indulgence and condemns those who attack it.[48] The total impression given is that Christ has fixed his attention and approval on the whole order, not a righteous remnant within it, and that he expects it to keep playing more or less the same role it currently plays within society—the very role that the spirituals found questionable.

Thus we are left with a single element in Christ's conversations with Margaret that calls for explanation: his dire prediction about a future lack of papal support. This is, in fact, the most effective part of Jacobelli's argument. The problem is not that Margaret predicts apocalyptic tribulation. Spiritual Franciscans had no monopoly on that subject, nor were they the only ones to suggest that it was just around the corner. The problem is that Margaret's prophecy suggests an imminent confrontation in which the pope will attack Franciscan values. While most of the church experienced notable difficulty in saying aloud that the pope might join the forces of Antichrist, a number of spiritual Franciscans and beguins were so ready to see him in the role that some of them were willing to identify first Boniface VIII, then Benedict XI, then John XXII as the Antichrist himself. Here we begin to see the problem, though. In the succession of popes between Boniface and John, the only one whom no one identified with Antichrist—in fact, the only one in whom the spirituals invested a great deal of hope—was Clement V, and it was probably Clement who presided over the church at the moment when Giunta compiled Margaret's *legenda*. It was an odd moment to expect the worst from the papacy, which leads us to wonder if the pessimism was actually Margaret's rather than Giunta's and reflected the general malaise of the later 1290s. If so, then on this matter, at least, Margaret acquires a very discernible face.

If Margaret's prophecy stems from a period of disillusionment with Boniface VIII, we should nonetheless think twice before assuming that such anti-Boniface sentiments would inevitably imply strong commitment to spiritual Franciscan ideals. After all, a great many people disliked Boniface. Philip the Fair detested him enough to have him accused of heresy, while Dante called him the prince of the new pharisees and reserved a spot for him in Hell. Yet neither Philip nor Dante displayed any great sympathy with the spiritual Franciscans.[49]

If we choose the opposite alternative and read the passage as part of a posthumous attempt to vilify Boniface, then here again, we are not automatically led to the spiritual Franciscans. Perhaps the underlying aim was less spiritual than political. In 1308, the Colonna were still busy trying to gain territory from the Caetani, Boniface's family, and 1307 witnessed the appearance of the two longest appeals ever launched against Boniface, both probably emanating from Colonna circles.[50]

There is another problem, though, and it lies in the nature of the fear projected in Margaret's prediction. It is innocent of any notion that the pope in question will attack a small group of Francis's true followers within the order. Rather, it seems to imply that the order itself is in for trouble. The controlling thought in the various predictions of tribulation is that Christ sees the same parallel between himself and the order that he sees between himself and Margaret. Because Margaret seeks to conform herself with Christ, the world—stirred up by the Old Enemy—will criticize and oppose her just as it did Christ, but after her death it will repent of its error and exalt her, just as it did Christ. In the same way, the order, because it seeks to emulate Christ, will be criticized and opposed; after tribulation, though, will come exoneration and exaltation. The way of suffering and rejection is the way of salvation. No cross, no crown. Christ bluntly tells Margaret to prepare herself for tribulation because heaven is not something she is going to find in this life.[51]

Conclusion Concerning Margaret

What do we have here, then? Something not all that different from what we discovered in Clare's case. We have a series of names pointing to a spiritual Franciscan connection and several lines suggesting the same; yet other names—particularly those with titles attached—suggest a connection with non-spirituals. The total message reputedly imparted by Christ to Margaret does not reflect characteristically spiritual Franciscan concerns, if in the latter we include a critique of the order for compromising Francis's ideal.

Nevertheless, if by the latter we mean the kind of spirituality displayed by men like Peter Olivi, Ubertino da Casale, and Angelo Clareno, then that is precisely what we are seeing here. French and Italian spirituals were not only similar in their insistence on observance of *usus pauper,* but also alike in their fascination with contemplative experience in their own time and their encouragement of contemporary mystics. It was a characteristically spiritual Franciscan concern in the sense that it was evidenced by a broad spectrum of spirituals.

That does not mean, however, that it was an *exclusively* spiritual Franciscan concern. In fact, documents like the Margaret *legenda* suggest that it cut across spiritual-community battle lines and was shared with those less judgmental in their evaluation of current Franciscan life. In the Margaret legend, we see an Ubertino da Casale who, whatever he might have been thinking or saying about leaders of his order, coexisted with them at least to the point of sharing Margaret with some of them.

Mario Sensi's Alternative Hypothesis

There is, however, one more possibility recently explored by Mario Sensi.[52] Sensi essentially reverses Jacobelli's argument and pictures Giunta as attempting to put the best face possible on Margaret's drift away from the Cortona Franciscans toward the spirituals. The argument is built on three elements. First, there is the fact that she knew Ubertino and Friar Conrad, whom Sensi unhesitatingly identifies with Conrad of Offida. The latter identification is important, because Sensi opines that Margaret's move from near the Franciscan house up to her cell above the city should be seen as an event connected with the 1294 formation of the Poor Hermits.

Second, there is the church of Saint Basil, at the top of the town, where Margaret's body was laid to rest. Sensi argues that the group presiding over it, the group of tertiaries found at the Celle (the hermitage just outside Cortona), and the group that ran the hospital in Cortona founded by Margaret were three segments of a single group of tertiaries—and that they were all spiritual sympathizers. Third, there is the fact that sometime between 1288 and 1291, Margaret left her cell near the Franciscan church and, probably contrary to the Franciscans' advice, moved up to her new location.

Any of these three elements can be questioned. Sensi recognizes that Conrad's degree of involvement with the Poor Hermits is not clear,[53] and that the dates do not quite match. Thus there is a studied ambiguity about his statement. He says Conrad "adhered to" Angelo's group, and "Margaret's choice should probably be read in parallel with Conrad's."[54] The Celle–Saint Basil connection also has its difficulties. Sensi, very much aware that the tertiaries at the Celle cannot be seen as spiritual sympathizers simply because they are called *fraticelli* in extant documents, nonetheless sees them as such because they were ejected in 1318 (the moment when John XXII was taking action against the spirituals). Why, then, was the other part of the group not ejected from Saint Basil's? Because, Sensi asserts, they had powerful support, including that of the commune.[55] Finally, the notion of Margaret as moving away from the Franciscan house because of her adherence to the spiritual cause cannot be accepted without coming to terms with the host of other reasons why she may have chosen her new location. Many have been suggested,[56] including the one presented by the *legenda* itself: She felt called by Christ to move beyond the sort of spiritual life she had led in the middle of Cortona and experience a new one in a more eremitical setting.

In the final analysis, though, Sensi's scenario seems very possible. If Margaret influenced Ubertino and perhaps Conrad of Offida, there is no reason why they should not have influenced her, too. Thus it is not impossible that in the early 1290s she decided to explore the option Conrad himself exercised: to maintain distance from a lax, worldly Franciscan community by choosing a more eremitical existence. If this is what actually occurred, there is no reason why Giunta should not have attempted to whitewash Margaret's rejection of the community. Nor, given our knowledge of how individual Italian towns protected the spirituals, is it impossible that Cortona may have favored a group of them at Saint Basil's. None of this is impossible. There is simply very little evidence for it.

Angela of Foligno

Biography: An Optimistic Assessment

Angela of Foligno's case is simultaneously the most problematic and most promising of all, partly because the Angela materials are quite complex. The materials one works with in compiling a biography consist of two writings from her era presumably describing the historical Angela—the *Memorial* and the *Instructions*—plus a certain amount of tradition. Of the two writings, the former describes her inner development as a mystic, while the latter shows her as the leader of a spiritual circle.

The one certain date is 1309, the year of her death. Beyond that point we find some historians who seem relatively optimistic about what we can know and others who are the opposite. A best-case scenario is provided in the reconstruction of M. J. Ferré.[57] According to this scenario, Angela was born in 1248 at Foligno and married around 1270. In 1285, tortured by guilt stemming from a sin she had committed (one tradition identifies it as adultery), she prayed to Saint Francis and he, appearing incognito in a dream, granted her request. The next morning she entered the cathedral of San Feliciano and encountered a Franciscan who was chaplain to the bishop. He was also related to Angela. The Franciscan heard her confession and absolved her. She left the church a changed woman. Hitherto proud and worldly, she now entered upon a life of penance that involved poverty, service to the poor and infirm, and contemplative experience.

In 1291 Angela went to Assisi on pilgrimage. There, at the church of Saint Francis, she was favored with a strong feeling of divine presence and, when it departed from her, she collapsed in despair at the door of the upper basilica, shrieking. One of the friars who came to see what had happened was a relative, Brother Arnaldo, presumably the same man who had heard her confession in 1285. He was appalled by her behavior and told her to stay away from Assisi in the future. The following year, though, Arnaldo was transferred to the Franciscan house at Foligno. The move gave him an opportunity to ask Angela what had occurred in Assisi. Though initially skeptical about whether her experiences were from God, he eventually decided that they were, and he became her amanuensis. The result was the *Memorial*.

Recording Angela's experiences was not an easy task for Arnaldo. His regular interviews with her made some of the friars suspicious, and around 1294, the provincial minister decreed that he should see her only occasionally. Moreover, even when he was present he often felt that he did not understand what she was telling him. There was the additional problem of his having to translate her narrative from the vernacular into Latin. Nevertheless, God himself eventually testified to the veracity of the *Memorial*.

Biography: A Less Optimistic Appraisal

The worst-case scenario is provided by Jacques Dalarun. In a 1995 article he puts the matter as provocatively as possible by asking: "Angèle de Foligno at-elle existé?"[58] Dalarun is willing to grant that she did, though just barely. That is, there was a woman named Angela who lived in Foligno and died in 1309, but she is not the woman we encounter in the book we fondly imagine to be a record of Angela's mystical experiences. There is undoubtedly a "distant echo" of the historical figure, but no more. The rest is, Dalarun says, "the 'mystical fable' of a group of spiritual Franciscans."

Dalarun's argument proceeds along several paths. On the one hand he—like others before him—is struck by the peculiar anonymity of the *Memorial*. A brief notice prefacing the *Memorial* assures us that it was read and approved by Cardinal Giacomo Colonna and "by eight well-known lectors of the Order of Friars Minor," one of whom had held that post at Milan. Two others had been inquisitors in the Province of Saint Francis; four more had served as minister of that province; and one had been custode in several areas.[59] The only person named in the *Memorial* itself is Pope Celestine V. The friar who wrote the visions down consistently refers to himself as "brother scribe" or something similar; the mystic herself is described as "a certain faithful follower of Christ," "Christ's faithful," or merely "she." In fact, the text of the *Memorial* as we find it in Assisi 342, the earliest manuscript of the work, never uses the name "Angela." The work is given a title in that manuscript, *Liber sororis Lelle de Fulgineo de tertio ordine sancti Francisci*,[60] but this notice is a later addition, a late fourteenth-century notation on an early fourteenth-century manuscript. Another notation antedating the one about Lelle—this one presumably by a frustrated reader—states that the manuscript was presented to him as an anonymous work "and I have not yet been able to figure out what it is."

It is noteworthy that the only two persons mentioned by name in the *Memorial* and its prefatory notice are Pope Celestine V and Cardinal Giacomo Colonna (the favorite pope of the Italian spirituals and a cardinal who befriended the spirituals) and that Angela of Foligno herself is mentioned by a single contemporary: Ubertino da Casale. Ubertino gives an important place to Angela when, in his *Arbor vitae*, he lists the various mystics from whose company he profited.

Dalarun also pays ample attention to style and theological formation. Both, he thinks, point in the same direction. The *Memorial* is the work of educated friars. These considerations lead him no closer to the spiritual Franciscans, but they lead him away from the notion that the document reflects Angela herself. (The manuscript history of the Angela material, on the other hand, *does* lead him closer to the spirituals, but he does not extend his investigation far in that direction.)

Angela and the Spiritual Franciscans

Dalarun has made a significant contribution to our knowledge of the manuscript history of the Angela materials, but has he succeeded in making a case that what we find in these materials is a spiritual Franciscan polemic? The problem with his argument as it stands is that once we get beyond the three names and his limited forays into manuscript history, we have very little to go on in connecting Angela with the spirituals. Dalarun makes no effort to demonstrate that what we find in the Angela material is specifically *spiritual* Franciscan (rather than simply Franciscan).

Others are willing to give Angela a more significant role in producing the Angela materials, but they also go further than Dalarun in building a case for some tie with the spiritual Franciscans. Mario Sensi and others have drawn our attention to the whole religious environment in Foligno, noting its economic connections with Provence and, more important, suggesting that what little we know about the Franciscan house at Foligno points toward rigorist leanings.[61] The main connection, as Sensi develops it, is with Angelo Clareno. Although we have little evidence of any significant connection between Angelo's group and Foligno before Angela's death, there is plenty of evidence for such a connection during the 1320s and 1330s. Sensi rightly points to the important relationships Angelo enjoyed, not only with Franciscans identifiable with Foligno, but also with Augustinians and perhaps Olivetans there as well. Moreover, there is a close connection between the Foligno Franciscans and the later founding of the Observance.

Some scholars have cited the second part of the Angela materials, the *Instructions* (especially chapters 3 and 4), in which Angela evokes Francis and his love of poverty.[62] Mariano d'Alatri, for example, notes Francis's commendation of "those of his sons who burned with zeal to observe the poverty prescribed by the rule,"[63] and suggests that the word *zelus* evokes *zelantes*, "a technical term indicating the spirituals." He also sees significance in the fact that Angela twice evokes the necessity for deeds, *opera*. Nevertheless, he also suggests that Angela is addressing the spirituals—this time critically—when she tells the friars to preach "more by the mortification of your lives than by contentious discourse" and to seek humility so that "you will no longer be prone to disputes and quarrels."[64]

Others, such as Costanzo Cargnoni, claim to discover stylistic and conceptual parallels between the Angela materials and the writings of the spirituals. Cargnoni announces that there are "precise and often literal correspondences with the inspiration of the *Sacrum Commercium* and of many writings of the spirituals, especially those of Angelo Clareno, Ubertino da Casale, Jacopone da Todi, and other spiritual authors, some not even Franciscan." That is a very big claim, and a very important one if it turns out to be true.[65]

Romana Guarnieri expands the argument considerably.[66] She adds to the link between the spirituals and the manuscript history. She also invokes the parallels already suggested by Cargnoni between the Angela materials and works of Ubertino da Casale, Angelo Clareno, and Jacopone da Todi (though neither Cargnoni nor Guarnieri pushes the subject very far). Most important, she focuses attention on a remarkable passage at the very end of the Angela materials, the final "peroration or epilogue" (*peroratio vel epilogus*) that follows the notice of Angela's death. Guarnieri is not the first to note that this epilogue, found only in some manuscripts, is substantially more confrontational than the rest of the Angela materials, nor is she the first to see it as evidence that these materials served as ammunition in the struggle between the spirituals and the community.[67] Guarnieri's contribution is to develop the suggestion considerably, pointing to terminological and conceptual parallels between the epilogue and spiritual Franciscan documents like the *Arbor vitae* and *Mirror of Perfection*. The epilogue draws a contrast between "worldly wisdom, which is animal, earthbound and diabolical, coming from pride-filled teachers who talk big but do nothing" and "the wisdom of gospel perfection" renewed by an unlearned, frail woman, a member of the laity, "through the holy foolishness of the cross of Christ." It praises Angela for having shown us "the way of Jesus Christ" and having proved that it was possible "after the high and mighty had told us, by their words and deeds, that it could not be followed."[68] Here, Guarnieri says, we have the same critique of contemporary learning found in Ubertino and others, as well as their affirmation that, contrary to the leaders from Elias on who insisted that it was impractical (even impossible) to follow the rule *sine glossa*, that is precisely what Francis did and what Franciscans must do. Guarnieri strongly suggests that the author is Ubertino himself. She hypothesizes, moreover, that Ubertino was one of the two friars referred to at the end of the *Memorial*: "The Lord saw to it that two other trustworthy friars acquainted with Christ's faithful one read the text and heard directly from her everything which I had written. They examined everything and even engaged in frequent discussions with her. And what is more, God granted them the grace to be certain of its validity and, by word and deed, they bear faithful witness to it."[69] It is only a step from here to Guarnieri's further suggestion that it was Ubertino who brought Angela to Giacomo Colonna's attention.[70]

When did all this occur, though? Although Angela herself did not die until 1309, the notice prefacing the *Memorial* says that it was approved by Giacomo

Colonna "before he suffered disgrace at the hands of the sovereign pontiff"—thus probably earlier than May 1297, although it is hard to say exactly what might have counted in the author's eyes as Giacomo's disgrace, since official papal sanction came as early as the spring of 1297 but military defeat and surrender was delayed until the fall of 1298.[71] Guarnieri assumes that the epilogue's exhortation of the faithful to conquer their uncertainties ("may all shame be gone from the offspring of this holy mother") and affirm their allegiance ("be proud in being called to such a school"), as well as its willingness to refer to Angela by name, suggests a period when there was no actual persecution in progress. The only such period, Guarnieri says, was the brief time in 1294 between the accession of Celestine V and the moment when Boniface VIII turned on the spirituals. She concludes that the epilogue dates from the second half of 1294, thus perhaps before the *Memorial* was completed.

The Evidence Evaluated

When we ask ourselves how convincingly these authors argue their case for a connection between Angela and the spirituals, we again find ourselves impressed by the cumulative weight of the evidence but less impressed when we look closely at specific parts of it. The "precise and often literal correspondences," for example, are suggested rather than demonstrated by Cargnoni (who promises that they will be the subject matter of another article yet to be written) and by Guarnieri (who says that she awaits such an article). In the meantime, in a study he himself describes as far from definitive, Alfonso Marini has cast serious doubt on those correspondences, provisionally concluding that the divergences are significant, while the similarities stem from "the common terrain of religious tradition."[72]

As for the peculiar anonymity of the *Memorial* and its prefatory notice, which name Giacomo Colonna and Celestine V but no one else (not even the mystic or her amanuensis): It certainly gives one pause, but how far it leads us is another matter. Maria Pia Alberzoni is correct in emphasizing that our lack of knowledge concerning those "eight well-known lectors" and other trustworthy friars who stand witness to the book's acceptability stems not from any tragic gap in the manuscript tradition or other misadventure but from the writer's conscious decision not to provide names.[73] Yet does it necessarily follow (as Alberzoni suggests) that the notice should be read as a coded message aimed at and decipherable by a specific group aligned with the spiritual Franciscan wing of the order? We may not be told their names, but we are given specific information about their positions in the order. Whoever they were, they were part of the administrative elite about whom Ubertino and Angelo Clareno had such pronounced reservations.

Certain passages from chapters 3 and 4 of the *Instructions* do have considerable resonance. One of the most striking of them is a vision in which Angela sees her spiritual sons kiss the wound in Christ's side one by one, and "there seemed to be varying degrees of intensity in the way her sons were embraced and placed at Christ's side. He thrust some of them into his side more, some less, some more than once, and some he absorbed deep into his body. The redness of his blood colored the lips of some and the whole face of others, according to the varying degrees mentioned." The narrator comments, "I believe that the friars whom the Most High gave her as sons of her heart should pay close attention to what this holy mother told me."[74] It is hard to read the passage without thinking of John of Massa's vision in which the sons of Saint Francis were given a cup and some drank more, others less. John's vision is reported in two notably spiritual Franciscan sources, Angelo Clareno's *Chronicle* and the *Fioretti*, and in both sources it becomes a dagger aimed at the heart of current Franciscan leaders.[75]

Nevertheless, if Angela's praise of poverty and recognition of differences in observance within the order might be said to suggest an association with the spirituals, other aspects of Instructions 3 and 4 seem to distinguish her from spirituals such as Ubertino da Casale and Angelo Clareno—or, for that matter, from all Italian spirituals of whom we have any knowledge. Her praise of those who observe the rule fully never turns into a condemnation of those who do not. The vision of Franciscans kissing the wound in Christ's side demonstrates this point well. In the John of Massa vision, Bonaventure, who did not drink from the cup, eventually attacked John of Parma, who had drained it, and Francis himself had to restrain Bonaventure from doing John considerable damage. In other words, the vision suggests a strong antagonism between true Franciscans and false ones, as well as the persecution of the former by the latter. In Angela's vision, the redness of the blood from Christ's side "colored the lips of some and the whole face of others," so there is certainly a difference; but the next sentence says, "To each one he extended abundant blessings and said, 'My sons, make manifest the way of my cross, my poverty, and my contempt—for especially now, those abound who keep these concealed. I have chosen each of you especially for the purpose of manifesting, by your example and word, my truth which is trampled and hidden.'" There is an ambiguity of reference throughout this passage, but it seems clear that the various degrees suggested in it refer to differences, not in the whole Franciscan order, but among Angela's "sons," the intimate group around her. Thus, by Guarnieri's logic, it would denote differences, not between spirituals and others, but *among* spirituals. As for those others who keep Christ's poverty concealed, there is no indication that they are in the order, much less that they are running it. The aim here is not polemical but hortatory. The narrator encapsulates the point of the vision by saying, "Although she had seen the degree each one was in, she did not wish to divulge it of any of them individually. And it did not seem to me to be appropriate to ask, for only one thing matters: that each one strive to the utmost to be joined to the blessed Crucified One."[76]

Here, Mariano d'Alatri's point is worth repeating. While it might be possible to argue that the *Instructions* support a view of poverty consistent with the one endorsed by the spirituals, it would be much harder to see the work as a spiritual Franciscan polemic against the rest of the order. The basic message of the *Instructions* is that Franciscans should concentrate on their own spiritual progress rather than judging others.

As for Guarnieri's comments on the epilogue, she offers a very strong argument, though one might be excused for believing some parts of it to be stronger than others. For example, the 1294 dating of the epilogue is based on the fact that Angelo Clareno's group was harassed at all other times, but that, in turn, seems to assume either (1) that the particular spiritual Franciscan coterie responsible for the epilogue was in fact Angelo's group, or (2) that the fate of Angelo Clareno's group was shared by all Italian spirituals. There is little to recommend either option. Guarnieri's efforts are directed toward connecting Angela not with Angelo but with Ubertino da Casale, and Ubertino's experience in the 1290s seems—understandably—to have been quite different. At that moment Angelo and his associates were seen by their superiors as deserters, or at least AWOL, but Ubertino was making his way within the order (albeit with some friction). Nevertheless, the importance of a possible connection with Angelo's group should not be underestimated, as we have seen.

In any case, these considerations expand the time frame within which the epilogue might be placed. That may be just as well, because a 1294 date, when combined with the notion of a major role by Ubertino, would lead to other problems. There is the obvious one: The epilogue suggests something approaching an Angela cult. By the time it was written, she had developed a following so dedicated as to see acceptance of her as a test indicating whether one stood among the sheep or the goats. It is hard to imagine that such a cult should have developed not only before the cardinal and others had stated their approval, but even before the *Memorial* had been completed.[77]

And then there is a less obvious but equally vexing problem. If, as seems likely, Ubertino left Italy for Paris ca. 1289 and returned only in 1298, his encounter with Angela could not have occurred before 1298. In fact, Ubertino explicitly says that Angela came to his attention "in the twenty-fifth year of my state," by which he obviously means his time in the order, therefore ca. 1298.[78]

As for the content of the epilogue, one problem faced by Guarnieri and others in search of spiritual Franciscan polemic is that the sort of argument that went on between spirituals and the rest of the order bore a strong structural similarity to the one being carried on, during the same period, between the order as a whole and those outside it—particularly the secular clergy and the Dominicans. Franciscan scholars at Paris, such as Bonaventure and Pecham, feared that certain non-Franciscan Parisian scholars were plighting their troth to Aristotle in such a way as to obscure the true wisdom of Christ. Spirituals such as Ubertino felt the same way about the Franciscan scholars at Paris. Franciscans like Bonaventure and Pecham protected themselves against the charge (leveled by seculars and Dominicans alike) that Franciscan poverty was unobservable and thus the Franciscan rule was dangerous; similarly, spiritual Franciscans defended themselves against charges by the rest of the order that poverty, as they wished to practice it, was unobservable and therefore dangerous. Thus, when the epilogue praises Angela for having shown "the way of Jesus Christ" and having proved that it was possible "after the high and mighty had told us, by their words and deeds, that it could not be followed," it is not all that obvious that the reference is to the smaller, intra-order Matryoshka doll and not the larger, inter-order one.

Nevertheless, Guarnieri seems absolutely right in asserting that the epilogue suggests a convergence between Angela's mystical experience and spiritual Franciscan aims. The connection is emphasized in the final paragraph of the epilogue, which says, "Remember, most dearly beloved ones, that the apostles, who first preached Christ's life of suffering, learned from a woman that his life was raised from the dead. In a similar manner, most beloved sons of our holy mother, our rule has been dead in carnal men since the suffering-filled observance of it by our first apostolic parents, Francis and his companions. Now, learn along with me that this rule, preached by the observance of our holy mother, is immortal."[79] Thus Angela becomes the symbol of a resurrected rule.[80]

It is important to remember, though, that we are speaking here of the epilogue, not the *Memorial* or the *Instructions*—and that the epilogue is not found in all manuscripts, nor does every manuscript that includes it contain all of it. The most we can derive from it is that some spiritual Franciscans saw Angela as a symbol of their cause, not that spiritual Franciscans influenced the writing of the *Memorial* and *Instructions* (or even that Angela sided with the spirituals).

One final element should be considered. Margaret and Clare were accorded canonization processes shortly after their deaths, but Angela was not. As one would expect, there were important institutions behind the processes. The respective towns were involved, as were some elements of the ecclesiastical establishment (though not precisely the same elements in each case). In Angela's case, no such institutions swung into action. Here again we see evidence that her following was not diffuse—that it amounted to a small, dedicated group of "spiritual sons."

If we seek a reason for this difference, we can choose from at least two possibilities. On the one hand, we can see it as pointing to a qualitative difference in their mystical experiences. Angela pursued a complex path of mystical ascent which was, in some ways, a very personal affair, one available only to the spiritually disciplined. Margaret and Clare offered visions that were directly relevant to (and easily absorbed by) those about them. In fact, Edith Pásztor notes that Clare's visionary experience was a shared enterprise in the sense that she functioned "as center and intermediary of the experience of a community of women joined together in various ways,"[81] women who themselves had visions. Closely related to this difference is another: Margaret and Clare had both performed posthumous miracles, while Angela had not.

On the other hand, one can also ask whether the institutional support accorded to Margaret and Clare but not to Angela has something to do with their adherents, whether it was recognized that, in Enrico Menestò's words, "Angela's little group of followers became at an early date a point of reference for spirituals from Umbria and the Marches."[82] If so, then we are entitled to see Angela's *cenacolo* as, if not anti-establishment, certainly capable of being perceived by the establishment as slightly dangerous. That would offer another explanation of the odd notation in Assisi 342, "This book was presented to me as anonymous, and I have not yet been able to figure out what it is." Menestò's judgment—"this caution would be inexplicable if reading of the work had not become a semiclandestine activity"[83]—might be judged something of an overstatement, since one can envisage other explanations, yet it is one that invites serious consideration.

The real question, though, is why the work might have been perceived as dangerous. Quite apart from any possible connection with the spiritual Franciscans, Angela's visions moved her perilously close to the stance identified with the *spiritus libertatis*.[84] For that reason alone the Angela materials might have been viewed with suspicion.

Conclusion Regarding Angela

In the final analysis, a connection between the spiritual Franciscans and Angela seems much more arguable than one between them and either Clare or Margaret, but a great deal of work must be done before its nature or even its existence can be demonstrated. What we seem able to assert at the moment is a clear parallel between Angela and the sorts of ideals embraced by the spirituals. What we cannot as yet assert is that Angela saw herself as a partisan of the spirituals in their battle with the community.

That brings us to a final (and by now familiar) problem: what we mean by the term "spiritual Franciscans." If we think of the distinction between the spirituals and the community (the latter taken broadly as those Franciscans not numbered among the spirituals) as one between, on the one hand, a small group of friars who thirsted after true Franciscan values and tried to express them through a devotion to *usus pauper* and contemplative experience, and, on the other hand, a large body of friars who had turned away from traditional Franciscan values in favor of relaxed observance and involvement with the world, then we will have no trouble assuming that, whether or not Angela actually felt an affinity for the former group, she *should* have done so. We can, however, assume a slightly different model. We can see the community as encompassing a broad range of positions joined together, not by a dedication to worldly pursuits or loose living, but by obedience to duly appointed superiors. We can then picture the spirituals as a self-conscious opposition group that condemned the current state of the order and rejected the papal concessions that had made it what it was by the end of the thirteenth century. If we accept this second model, we can imagine that there were any number of friars who resembled the spirituals in their aspirations but did not consider themselves part of a spiritual faction. We might therefore envisage Angela's admirers as including, not only spirituals such as Ubertino, but others who shared some of Ubertino's ideals yet eschewed his tactics as counterproductive. Here we come face to face with the disconcerting fact that, despite Sensi's contribution, we know remarkably little about the composition of a Franciscan house like that at Foligno ca. 1300.

A Provisional General Conclusion

What we have said of Angela applies, *mutatis mutandis*, to Clare and Margaret as well. What sort of connection we see depends on what we mean when we speak of the spiritual Franciscans. To the extent that we imagine people such as Angelo Clareno and Ubertino da Casale as spirituals because they were committed to asceticism and the contemplative life, we can affirm a general resemblance between the spirituals and our three mystics. Indeed, we can go somewhat further and say that spirituals and mystics were attuned to the same spiritual currents that were reshaping piety at the turn of the century, currents the ecclesiastical hierarchy found intriguing yet also terrifying—precisely because it saw them as in danger of spinning out of control without firm guidance. That guidance often involved attempting to limit new trends by forcing them into existing organizational structures and submitting them to the direction of established authority. As church leaders might have discovered from reading their Bibles, however, new wine often sits uncomfortably in old wineskins. In the case of the female mystics, gender produced an additional complication. The papacy acted on the basis of stereotypes that produced an almost grotesque contrast between the view of women animating papal documents in the thirteenth and early fourteenth centuries and the one we derive from available documents concerning Clare, Margaret, and Angela.[85]

Viewed from this perspective, Ubertino's report on his female mystic acquaintances in the *Arbor vitae* speaks volumes about the bond that united them. Ubertino was an educated member of a major order, and they were uneducated women; yet the *Arbor vitae* concentrates not on how he guided them but on how he was enriched by them. Here we see a way in which the spirituals acted as a counterweight to prevailing thirteenth-century developments. The original Franciscan fellowship was neither lay nor clerical. Laymen and clerics were both admitted without any sense that one group was more desirable than the other, and the group was guided by a layman whose authority was charismatically based. As the century progressed, the first order became largely clerical (and its leadership structure completely so). Relationships with laity outside the first order—whether these laity were in the third order or no order at all—were conceived in terms of an authority structure in which friars directed laity. That tendency was mitigated among the spirituals. Ubertino and presumably Olivi still thought of themselves as exercising a preaching function and presumably other pastoral functions as well, but their apocalyptic and contemplative convictions combined to encourage a lively interest in what the laity could teach them. (The latter could also be said of Angelo Clareno, who was himself not a priest.)

Moreover, Ubertino's encounters with female mystics seem to have taken place not in the context of well regulated institutions but in more local, informal, unstructured environments.[86] One might oversimplify the matter by saying that spirituals such as Ubertino and Angelo were like mystics such as Clare,

Margaret, and Angela, insofar as they lived on the frontiers of early fourteenth-century spirituality and were thus among those who needed to be watched rather than those institutionally designated to do the watching. (It must be remembered, though, that in the case of the *spiritus libertatis*, Clare and Ubertino joined the watchers.) On the other hand, to the extent that we characterize Angelo and Ubertino as spirituals because they belonged to a faction that opposed the direction of Franciscan development in the thirteenth century, thought of themselves as the true Franciscans, and condemned their leaders as corrupters of the rule, then it is hard to discern anything similar in these three mystics. In fact, Angela seems to speak against such contention. Margaret and Clare offer us less to go on, but their contacts with Franciscan leaders suggest that they hardly saw them as agents of decay.

In the final analysis we are reminded once again that a term like "the spiritual Franciscans" is a construct—a construct that is useful insofar as it enables us to order available evidence, but dangerous when we begin to make the evidence fit the construct. We know roughly where Olivi, Ubertino, and Angelo stood on major issues facing the order because they wrote a great deal. We know, too, that they were hardly of a single mind on these issues. They represented various brands of spiritual Franciscanism. When we turn from these major figures to all the friars who wind in and out of the Margaret, Clare, and Angela materials—those named in the Margaret and Clare materials as well as those left unnamed in the Angela materials—we might be excused for wondering if we know much of anything about where *they* stood on such matters. In fact, we might be led to conclude that we know remarkably little about the nature and composition of Franciscan houses in places like Montefalco, Cortona, and Foligno.

We do know some things. We know that a number of the aforementioned friars had successful careers in the same Franciscan power structure that Ubertino, Jacopone, Angelo, and others viewed with such misgivings. Yet they were nonetheless on friendly terms with Margaret and Clare, and some of them gave their blessing to the Angela materials. Some are even seen more or less in juxtaposition with Ubertino. We are reminded that before ca. 1300, Ubertino himself lived within a more or less normal Franciscan environment, as had Olivi before him. Later he lived at odds with leaders of the order, but not all those who cherished poverty and piety followed that path. One again, we are back to the question of what we mean when we speak of spiritual Franciscans.

NOTES

Abbreviations

In the notes, the following abbreviations identify frequently cited works.

I Celano	Thomas of Celano. *Vita prima s. Francisci*. In *Legendae s. Francisci Assisiensis saeculis XIII et XIV conscriptae*. In *Analecta franciscana*. Vol. 10. Quaracchi: College of Saint Bonaventure, 1927.
II Celano	Thomas of Celano. *Vita secunda s. Francisci Assisiensis*. In *Legendae s. Francisci Assisiensis saeculis XIII et XIV conscriptae*. In *Analecta franciscana*. Vol. 10. Quaracchi: College of Saint Bonaventure, 1927.
AF	*Analecta franciscana*. 12 vols. Quaracchi: College of Saint Bonaventure, 1885–1983.
Archiv	Denifle, Heinrich, and Franz Ehrle. *Archiv für Literatur- und Kirchengeschichte des Mittelalters*. 7 vols. Berlin: Weidmannsche Buchhandlung, 1885–1900.
AFH	*Archivum franciscanum historicum*
BF	*Bullarium franciscanum*. Rome: Vatican, 1759–1904.
CD	Collection Doat, Bibliothèque Nationale, Paris
Lectura	Petrus Iohannis Olivi. *Lectura super Apocalypsim*. Edited by Warren Lewis in "Peter John Olivi: Prophet of the Year 2000." Ph.D. diss., Tübingen University, 1972.
OFP	Burr, David. *Olivi and Franciscan Poverty*. Philadelphia: University of Pennsylvania Press, 1989.
OPK	Burr, David. *Olivi's Peaceable Kingdom*. Philadelphia: University of Pennsylvania Press, 1993.
Persecution	Burr, David. *The Persecution of Peter Olivi*. Philadelphia: American Philosophical Society, 1976.

Preface

1. Processes in the Collection Doat [hereafter CD] in the Bibliothèque Nationale at Paris often refer to "those friars minor who were called 'spirituals'" or to "spiritual friars minor." See, for example, CD 27:11r, 28:121r, 189v–190r, 207r, 208v, 222v, 226v, 231r, 232v.

2. Livarius Oliger, "Fr. Bertrandi de Turre processus contra spirituales Aquitaniae (1315) et Card. Jacobus de Columna littera defensoria spiritualium provinciae (1316)," *AFH* 16 (1923), 339, 341–42; Franz Ehrle, "Die Spiritualen, ihr Verhaltniss zum Franziskanerorden und zu den Fraticellen," in *Archiv*, 4:52.

3. *Rotulus*, in *Archiv*, 3:101.

4. Ibid., 3:102.

5. Anicetus Chiappini, "Communitatis responsio 'Religiosi viri' ad rotulum Fr. Ubertini de Casali," *AFH* 8 (1915), 62–63.

6. Ibid., 76; Geroldus Fussenegger, "Relatio commissionis in concilio Viennensi institutae ad decretalem 'Exivi de paradiso' praeparandam," *AFH* 50 (1957), 158.

7. Thus we will see in Chapter 4 that the *Chronica XXIV generalium*, in *AF*, 3:420–22, speaks of a process against brothers in southern France who claimed to be "more spiritual than others."

8. As we will see, however, it was used for others besides those we think of as the spirituals.

Chapter 1

1. *Passio sanctorum martyrum*, in *AF*, 3:593.

2. I Celano, 33. Francis confirms this in his *Testament*. See Francis of Assisi, *Opuscula*, ed. Kajetan Esser (Grottaferrata: College of Saint Bonaventure, 1978).

3. *Regula non bullata*, chapter 5, in Francis of Assisi, *Opuscula*.

4. Ibid., chapter 4; *Admonitio* 4 in Francis of Assisi, *Opuscula*.

5. *Regula non bullata*, chapter 6.

6. This element is noted by Théophile Desbonnets, *De l'intuition à l'institution* (Paris: Editions Franciscaines, 1983), 60–63.

7. *Regula*, chapter 10, in Francis of Assisi, *Opuscula*.

8. Malcolm Lambert and others argue that this statement is aimed not at the church, but at those "among the ministers who wished him to affiliate the order more closely to some existing rule." See Lambert, *Franciscan Poverty* (St. Bonaventure, N.Y.: Franciscan Institute, 1998), 29. Even so, that would not lessen the impact of an appeal to direct revelation from God.

9. Privileges by Pope Honorius III in 1222 and 1224 inaugurated the process through which the order would eventually gain a remarkable degree of independence, enabling it to challenge hostile parish and diocesan authorities (ibid., 81).

10. *BF*, 1:68. The phraseology, like that of the 1223 rule, assumes that Francis technically remained the leader of the order throughout his life, with Peter Catanii and Elias simply acting as vicars.

11. On Franciscan inquisitors, see Mariano d'Alatri, *L'inquisizione francescana nell'Italia centrale nel secolo XIII* (Rome: Istituto Storico dei Frati Minori Cappucini, 1954), and d'Alatri's numerous later articles, now published as *Eretici e inquisitori in Italia*, ed. Clement Schmitt (Rome: Istituto Storico dei Frati Minori Cappucini, 1986–87). On Franciscan bishops, see Williell Thomson, *Friars in the Cathedral* (Toronto: Pontifical Institute of Mediaeval Studies, 1975). The first Franciscan cardinal dates from 1273; the first inquisitors, from the 1250s; the first bishops, from even earlier. (Thomson, *Friars*, 27 suggests a date as early as 1226.)

12. For a good survey and bibliography on the relationship between the friars and Italian cities, see Antonio Rigon, "Frati minori e società locali," in *Francesco d'Assisi e il primo secolo di storia francescana*, ed. Maria Pia Alberzoni et al. (Turin: Einaudi, 1997), 259–81. For examples of Franciscan political involvement in Umbria, see Stanislao da Campagnola, *Francesco e francescanesimo nella società dei secoli XIII–XIV* (Assisi: Edizioni Porziuncula, 1999), 65–118.

13. William Jordan, *Louis IX and the Challenge of the Crusade* (Princeton: Princeton University Press, 1979), 51–64.

14. Giovanni Villani, *Cronica* (Florence: Sansone, 1844), 1:297, 300. Two years earlier, when the Aretines entered Cortona by night and sacked it, the signal to open a gate and admit them had been given by a bell-ringing Franciscan friar. MS Cortona, Biblioteca Communale 423, fol. 231–32, quoted in Maria Caterina Jacobelli, *Una donna senza volto* (Rome: Edizioni Borla, 1992), 52–53.

15. Anna Imelde Galletti, "Insediamento e primo sviluppo dei frati minori a Perugia," in *Francescanesimo e società cittadina*, ed. Ugolino Nicolini (Perugia: Centro per il Collegamento degli Studi Medievali e Umanistici nell'Università di Perugia, 1979), 21–23.

16. Francis of Assisi, *Opuscula*.

17. On clericalization, see Lawrence Landini, *The Causes of the Clericalization of the Order of the Friars Minor* (Chicago: Pontifica Universitas Gregoriana, 1968). Landini modified his position in a series of later articles, but I find his original presentation more convincing. For a concise introduction to mendicant education, see Dieter Berg, *Armut und Wissenschaft* (Dusseldorf: Pädagogischer Verlag Schwann, 1977).

18. Dino Compagni, *Dino Compagni's Chronicle of Florence*, trans. Daniel Bornstein (Philadelphia: University of Pennsylvania Press, 1986), 25. Latin text in *Cronica* (Florence: Successori Le Monnier, 1917), 51.

19. For example, see Gerolamo Biscaro, "Eretici ed inquisitori nella marca trevisana (1280–1308)," *Archivio veneto* 62 (1932): 148–72.

20. Decima Douie, *Archbishop Pecham* (Oxford: Clarendon Press, 1952), 49.

21. T. S. R. Boase, *Boniface VIII* (London: Constable, 1933), 205. Boase says that the money was "half gift, half fee."

22. II Celano, 108.

23. *Dino Compagni's Chronicle*, 25 (translation of *Cronica*, 51).

24. *Louis IX and the Challenge of the Crusade*, 185.

25. Hugh of Digne (Hugo de Digna), *Rule Commentary* (Grottaferrata: College of Saint Bonaventure, 1979), 187.

26. Salimbene da Parma, *Cronica* (Bari: Laterza, 1966), 247.

27. Salimbene provides the menu for one of them (ibid., 322).

Chapter 2

1. *Liber chronicarum sive tribulationum ordinis minorum*, ed. Giovanni Boccali and trans. Marino Bigaroni (Assisi: Edizioni Porziuncula, 1999). On the date, see Gian Luca Potestà, *Angelo Clareno* (Rome: Istituto Storico Italiano per il Medio Evo, 1990), 22.

2. I will normally speak of *legenda*, "those things which are to be read," rather than *vita*, "life," although the latter term is hardly wrong. Using *legenda* underlines the fact that the primary function of works like I Celano was not to provide a biography of Francis in the modern sense of that term, but rather to explain Francis's significance to a particular community.

3. *Liber chronicarum*, 296.

4. This fear is seen in efforts to limit new orders as much as possible and, when they were allowed, to give them already existing rules. It is especially seen in papal statements concerning new female movements (e.g., note Innocent IV's complaint in *BF*, 1:541).

5. For the later date, see Duncan Nimmo, *Reform and Division in the Franciscan Order* (Rome: Capuchin Historical Institute, 1987), 79.

6. John Moorman, *Sources for the Life of S. Francis of Assisi* (Manchester: Manchester University Press, 1940), 59: "It is impossible to believe that, with Ugolino in his exalted position to support him, Elias could have lost an election."

7. See Jacques Dalarun, *La malavventura di Francesco d'Assisi* (Milan: Edizioni Biblioteca Francescana, 1996), 89. Dalarun notes that in the years 1228–30, Gregory IX was struggling with the Emperor Frederick II, and thus his fortunes too were at a low ebb. On Elias, see Giulia Barone, *Da frate Elia agli Spirituali* (Milan: Edizioni Biblioteca Francescana, 1999), chapters 1–2, and see especially the extensive analysis by Rosalind Brooke, *Early Franciscan Government* (Cambridge: Cambridge University Press, 1959), book 1.

8. *Malavventura*, 86.

9. I Celano, 96.

10. *De adventu fratrum minorum in Angliam*, in *Monumenta franciscana*, Rerum britannicarum medii aevi scriptores, no. 4 (London: Longmans, 1852–82), 1:80. Eccleston also credits Elias and his

followers with violently attempting to make him minister general—in Giovanni Parenti's place—at that general chapter.

11. See Barone, *Da frate Elia*, 45. Brooke (*Early Franciscan Government*, 138–42) offers a sensible argument on the matter.

12. *Regula*, chapter 4.

13. *BF*, 1:69.

14. For example, Moorman (*Sources*, 85) writes: "Thus Gregory, in gentle and persuasive terms, and with many indications of the love and respect which he bore for the memory of S. Francis, quietly destroys the very foundations upon which Francis had built, and shatters his whole ideal."

15. The full range of charges is discussed by Brooke, *Early Franciscan Government*, 151–62.

16. *Cronica*, 146.

17. One might suggest that Parenti's election in 1227 marked an earlier stage in the same process. It is significant that in 1230 Elias invited all the brothers who were coming to Assisi for the translation of Francis's remains to attend the general chapter meeting as well, but the permission was countermanded by Parenti. See Brooke on Parenti's generalate (*Early Franciscan Government*, 123–36). Perhaps the 1227 election was a wake-up call for those who opposed a more clericalized order in which decisions were made by a small group of leaders. The disgruntled then backed Elias and were temporarily successful—but ultimately defeated.

18. That does not mean that Celano ignored him entirely. In fact, II Celano could be seen as an effort to reaffirm, albeit ambiguously, Elias's place in the story without naming him. See II Celano on the wound in Francis's side and on Francis's final blessing (138 and 216; cf. I Celano, 95 and 108).

19. See Dalarun, *Malavventura*, 122. The manuscript no longer exists.

20. *Anonymus perusinus*, in "L'Anonimo Perugino tra le fonti francescane del secolo XIII," by Lorenzo di Fonzo, *Miscellanea francescana* 72 (1972), 19c.

21. Ibid., 47c.

22. Dalarun, *Malavventura*, 130.

23. Critical edition in *AFH* 67 (1974), 89–144.

24. Thus Dalarun, *Malavventura*, 139.

25. These two sections are also found in MS Rome, Collegio San Isidoro 1/73, where they are labeled as *Intentio regulae* and *Verba S. P. Francisci* respectively. For a concise tour through the complex history of editions, see Théophile Desbonnets's introduction to *Saint Francis of Assisi: Writings and Early Biographies* (Chicago: Franciscan Herald Press, 1972), 959–71.

26. The contents are described in detail by Rosalind Brooke in *Scripta Leonis, Rufini et Angeli Sociorum S. Francisci* (Oxford: Clarendon Press, 1970), 26–32.

27. *Arbor vitae crucifixae Jesu* (1485; reprint, Turin: Bottega d'Erasmo, 1961), 445.

28. *Declaratio*, in *Archiv*, 3:168, 177–78. That could mean either the Sacro Convento or the Portiuncula.

29. *Scripta Leonis*, 57–66.

30. *St. Francis of Assisi*, 1970.

31. See, for example, *Scripta Leonis*, sections 70, 73, 74, 76, 77, and 113.

32. See ibid., sections 71, 75, 76, 70, and 116. On Francis's renunciation of leadership, see section 76. Section 87 does say that he resigned because of illness, while section 105 says that he did so in order to pursue humility.

33. Ibid., section 115.

34. These numbers are taken from Dalarun, *Malavventura*, 92, although Dalarun says "come from" rather than "reflect" and "echo."

35. *Legenda trium sociorum*, 4; II Celano, 4.

36. II Celano, 32–34, 152–54, for example. These passages remind one of the opening sections of the Benedictine Rule.

37. Ibid., 21, 33–69, 129–31. For the references to learning mentioned in this and the following paragraph, see ibid., 52, 102–5, 185, 194, and 195–96; for Francis's visionary sense of opposition within the order, see ibid., 23.

38. See ibid., 157–58. This seems to echo the reason for his resigning authority given in *Scripta Leonis*, as does 188, although in II Celano we also find illness and humility given as motives (see 143, 148).

39. See ibid., 158, which reflects *Scripta Leonis*, 86. For the reference to those who "feed on the sweat of the poor," see ibid., 162.

40. Ibid., 184 (although Celano puts it in such a way that it is possible to read him as saying that the problem lies in the nature of the task itself, not in the poor quality of current friars).

41. Ibid., 188. The passage is not dependent on *Scripta Leonis*.

42. See ibid., 148. Celano also criticizes those who desire to hold offices (145).

43. See ibid., 146; this is a watered-down version of *Scripta Leonis*, 115.

44. *Liber chronicarum*, 338–52. Their banishment "to remote provinces" with defamatory letters anticipates the fate of French spiritual Franciscans disciplined in 1317, as we will see. Either leaders of the order showed remarkable consistency in their treatment of dissidents, or Angelo is reconstructing what may have happened in the 1240s on the basis of what he knows happened in 1317. The former is not impossible, but neither is the latter.

45. *Chronicon abbreviatum de successione ministrorum*, published as Appendix II of Thomas of Eccleston, *De adventu fratrum minorum in Angliam* (Paris: Librairie Fischbacher, 1909), 142–43. Pelegrino's comment is later repeated in the *Chronica XXIV generalium*, 3:261.

46. *De adventu*, chapter 12. Brooke also cites the papal bulls procured during Crescentius's generalate concerning apostates (*Early Franciscan Government*, 253). The problem here, though, is twofold. First, some of the bulls allow one to suspect that the apostates in question might not be disappointed zealots; second, as Brooke acknowledges (267), the problem seems to have continued into John of Parma's generalate.

47. *Cronica*, 574. The names and events mentioned place the anecdote within Crescentius's generalate.

48. *Disputatio inter zelatorem paupertatis et inimicum domesticum eius*, in *Figure del primo francescanesimo in Provenza*, by Alessandra Sisto (Florence: Leo S. Olschki, 1971), 341–70.

49. Pseudo-Joachim of Fiore, *Super Jeremiam* (Venice: Bernardinus Benalius, 1525). Some scholars are at least open to the idea that a writing by Joachim lies at its core. See Robert Moynihan, "Development of the 'Pseudo-Joachim' Commentary 'super Hieremiam,'" *Mélanges de l'École Française de Rome: Moyen Âge, temps modernes* 98 (1986): 109–42; Stephen Wessley, *Joachim of Fiore and Monastic Reform* (New York: P. Lang, 1990).

50. *Chronica XXIV generalium*, 428; Salimbene, *Cronica*, 54; Angelo Clareno, *Liber chronicarum*, 292, 320, 418, 422–24. Thomas of Eccleston narrates a revelation to Francis on Mount Alverna that his order would last until the end of time (*De adventu*, chap. 12). Francis, he says, told Rufino about it. *Chronica XXIV generalium*, 67 makes it Leo, not Rufino, but the relevant thing here is that Eccleston, writing in the late 1250s, records a bit of oral tradition that will then endure as part of his chronicle.

51. Jean de Joinville, *Histoire de Saint Louis* (Paris: Hachette, 1874), 362–63.

52. *Cronica*, 325.

53. Pierre Péano, "Ministres provinciaux de Provence et spirituels," in *Franciscains d'Oc: Les Spirituels, 1280–1324* (Toulouse: Editions Privat, 1975), 44.

54. For an elaboration of this point, see my *OFP*, 19–20.

55. *Rule Commentary*, 97.

56. Ibid., 189. He is not happy about papal privileges, however (see 116).

57. Jerome Poulenc, "Hughes de Digne," in *Dictionnaire de spiritualité*, ed. Marcel Viller (Paris: G. Beauchesne, 1932–69), 7.1:876–79 arranges them in this order. There are, in fact, three works in need of ordering, the third being the *De finibus paupertatis*. See my *OFP*, 18–24.

58. On the various sources for Giles's life, see Stanislao da Campagnola, *Francesco e frances-canesimo*, 369–402.

59. Aegidius Assisiensis, *Dicta Beati Aegidii Assisiensis* (Quaracchi: College of Saint Bonaventure, 1939), 91–92.

60. Ibid., 107–8.

61. We read that he once told a preacher that he should say, "Bo, bo, multo dico, poco fo," meaning, "I say a lot and do little." On another occasion he gave this advice: "Act, act, don't talk." Again, he once said in front of some scholars, "I want to do two things: Love God for the benefits he has conferred on me, and grieve for my sins. These two suffice until the day of my death." *Dicta*, 91–92, 97.

62. Ibid., 91–92.

63. Edited and translated by Rosalind Brooke in *Scripta Leonis*, 318–49. Brooke argues that this shorter life is the original one and is very open to the possibility that it is by Brother Leo, since we can be confident that he wrote a life of Giles.

64. *Arbor vitae*, 433.

65. *Liber chronicarum*, 320: "Quam tribulationem invidia illius, qui de caelo ruit, in Ordine suscitavit; et qui passi sunt eam socii fundatoris, fratres Aegidius et Angelus, qui superarant, me audiente, referebant."

66. Ibid., 420.

67. *Chronica XXIV generalium*, 88. See also the advice given to another friar on 286.

68. *Liber chronicarum*, 360.

69. The *Speculum vitae Sancti Francisci et sociorum eius* (Venice: Simon de Luere, 1504), as cited in Edouard Lempp, *Frère Elie de Cortone* (Paris: Fischbacher, 1901), 163 embellishes the story by having Elias then order that Leo be flogged and driven from Assisi. Brooke rightly dismisses this version (*Early Franciscan Government*, 150).

70. *Chronica XXIV generalium*, 3:89–90.

71. *Arbor vitae*, 433.

72. *Chronica XXIV generalium*, 101.

73. As Stanislao da Campagnola observes, Bonaventure's presentation of Giles in *Legenda maior* is also symptomatic of the distance between them (see *Francesco e francescanesimo*, 375). Bonaventure concentrates on Giles's contemplative experiences, ignoring his earlier involvement in manual labor and itinerant mendicancy, both of which were characteristic of an earlier, less structured order. Bonaventure remarks further that Giles's experiences were achieved "though he was simple and unlettered."

74. Principally in *Liber chronicarum*, 354–88.

75. See my *OPK*, 14–21, and Chapter 13 of this work.

76. For the spread of Joachim's thought, see Marjorie Reeves, *The Influence of Prophecy in the Later Middle Ages* (Oxford: Clarendon Press, 1969).

77. *Cronica*, 332–46 and 449–50. Pelegrino da Bologna, *Chronicon*, 144 also mentions enemies.

78. *Cronica*, 440–41.

79. *De adventu*, in *Monumenta franciscana*, 1:50. Eccleston says of John's departure merely that, no longer able to bear the burden of ministry, John obtained release from the pope.

80. Salimbene, *Cronica*, 435, 450–51; Angelo, *Liber chronicarum*, 386–88.

81. *Liber chronicarum*, 416.

82. Ibid., 452–54.

83. Ibid., 422–34.

84. *Fioretti di San Francesco da un codice quattrocentesco* (Rome: Paoline, 1992), 48.

85. *Arbor vitae*, 437, 445, 449. Angelo says much the same thing in *Liber chronicarum*, 368–70.

86. *Tractatus de usu paupere*, in *De usu paupere: The Quaestio and the Tractatus* (Florence: Leo S. Olschki, 1992), 130.

87. Ibid., 138.

88. *Early Franciscan Government*, 258–84. Malcolm Lambert concurs; see *Franciscan Poverty*, 109–31.

89. See my comments in *OFP*, 8–9.

90. *Opera* (Quaracchi: College of Saint Bonaventure, 1882–1902), 8:468–71.

91. *La divina commedia*, ed. Natalino Sapegno, 2d ed., 3 vols. (Florence: La Nuova Italia, 1968). See *Paradiso* 12.

92. *Apologia pauperum*, 12:18–20, in *Opera*, 8:322–23.

93. *Epistola de tribus quaestionibus*, in *Opera*, 8:336.

94. *De adventu*, 50.

95. See, for example, Chiara Frugoni, *Francesco e l'invenzione delle stimmate* (Turin: Einaudi, 1993), 26; Dalarun, *Malavventura*, 161–62.

96. *Legenda maior*, prologue.

97. *Collationes in hexaemeron*, in *Opera*, vol. 5. See Joseph Ratzinger, *Die Geschichtestheologie des heiligen Bonaventura* (Munich: Schnell and Steiner, 1959), translated by Zachary Hayes as *The Theology of History in St. Bonaventure* (Chicago: Franciscan Herald Press, 1971), and my comments in *OPK*, 33–44.

98. See my *OPK*, 14–21.

99. For example, it may not be coincidental that the order, which had previously avoided inquisitorial duties, assumed them under Bonaventure. Mariano d'Alatri offers the scandal precipitated by Gerard as one reason for the change. See "S. Bonaventura, l'eresia e l'inquisizione," *Miscellanea francescana* 75 (1975), 320.

100. *Regula*, chapter 10. The importance of this passage for later spirituals is clear from Angelo Clareno, *Expositio regulae fratrum minorum* (Quaracchi: College of Saint Bonaventure, 1912), 203–15, as well as his *Liber chronicarum*, 250–54.

101. See, for example, *Scripta Leonis*: "quidam frater spiritualis homo et antiquus in religione" (94); "quidam frater spiritalis homo et antiquus in religione et familiaris beato Francisco" (96); "quidam frater, spiritalis homo, cui nimis erat familiaris beatus Franciscus" (110); "quodam fratre spiritali" (140); "quidam frater, spiritualis homo et amicus Dei" (142).

102. *Legenda maior*, IV, 4.

103. *Cronica*, 324, 331–32, 334, 340.

104. Ibid., 441 states his disillusionment, but he remained interested and continued to note when events fulfilled Joachim's prophecies.

105. *Super Jeremiam*, 22rb–va.

106. *Cronica*, 332, 334, 340.

107. Ibid., 340.

108. Ibid., 307–11, 331.

109. Paul, "Le Joachimisme et les joachimites au milieu du XIIIe siècle d'après le témoignage de Fra Salimbene," in *1274: Année charnière: Mutations et continuités*, Colloques internationaux du Centre National de la Recherche Scientifique, no. 558 (Paris: CNRS, 1977), 801.

110. *Cronica*, 334–35.

Chapter 3

1. For the following, see *Liber chronicarum*, 151–56.

2. He says as much in a letter to John XXII. See *Opera: I. Epistole* (Rome: Istituto Storico Italiano per il Medio Evo, 1980 [hereafter *Epistole*]), 241.

3. See my *OFP*, 28; see also Lydia von Auw, *Angelo Clareno et les spirituels italiens* (Rome: Edizioni di Storia e Letteratura, 1979), 21.

4. *Liber chronicarum*, 156–59.

5. Von Auw, following Livarius Oliger's introduction to his edition of Angelo's *Expositio regulae fratrum minorum* (Quaracchi: College of Saint Bonaventure, 1912), xxii–xxiii, estimates that

Angelo was born ca. 1255, entered the order around 1270, and was thus too new for a leadership role in 1274 (see *Angelo Clareno*, 6). Yet such a late entry is hard to reconcile with Angelo's claim that he heard Giles and Angelo—presumably Angelo Tancredi, another of Francis's companions and, according to von Auw, *Angelo Clareno*, 39–40, the man after whom Angelo named himself—tell about the order during Elias's generalate, since they were both long dead by 1270. In fact, a 1255 birthdate would mean that Angelo was around three when Angelo Tancredi died. Even the 1260 entrance date offered by Ehrle, Sabatier, and others would be too late for him to have met Angelo Tancredi after joining the order. But before pushing his entrance back any further, we should recall that he died in 1337. If he entered the order in 1260, at around fifteen, he would have been around ninety-two when he died.

6. Von Auw applies to this period the passage in *Epistole* (80–81) in which Angelo speaks of being imprisoned in Ancona, Forano, Rome, Viterbo, Assisi, Terranuova, and Messina, and then mentions troubles in Calabria, Cyprus, and Armenia (see *Angelo Clareno*, 17–18). It is hard to say what one should do with this passage, and I suspect that in it, Angelo is looking back over a lifetime of difficulties, not such a limited period; however, either reading of it seems consistent with the conclusion reached here.

7. He says that he was drawn to the Franciscan order "from the fourteenth year of my life," and presented *(oblatum)* to it by his father and mother *(Arbor vitae, 3)*. The year 1273 is derived from the fact that he tells us (ibid., 6) that he wrote the *Arbor vitae* in 1305, during his thirty-second year in the order.

8. In the *Arbor vitae*, Ubertino furnishes substantial autobiographical information, but leaves some doubt as to the order in which events occurred. Frédégand Callaey, *L'Idéalisme franciscaine spirituel au XIV siècle* (Louvain: Bureau de Recueil, 1911), is still useful, but must be considered in the light of Decima Douie, *The Nature and the Effect of the Heresy of the Fraticelli* (Manchester: University of Manchester Press, 1932), 120–27; Gian Luca Potestà, *Storia ed escatologia in Ubertino da Casale* (Milan: Università Cattolica del Sacro Cuore, 1980), 22–24; and Marino Damiata, *Pietà e storia nell'Arbor Vitae di Ubertino da Casale* (Florence: Edizioni "Studi Francescani," 1988), chapter 1. A lengthy consideration of dating problems can be found in Philip Caliendo, "Ubertino da Casale: A Re-evaluation of the Eschatology in the Fifth Book of his *Arbor vite crucifixe Jesu*" (Ph.D. diss., Rutgers University, 1979), part 1.

9. *Arbor vitae*, 4.

10. Ibid., 433.

11. See Caliendo, "Ubertino da Casale," part 1 for the problems involved in either thesis.

12. *Arbor vitae*, 422–23.

13. Ibid., 423. Ubertino was apparently still in Italy—but where? He was told of John's death by Solomon, minister of Ancona, who came to the house where Ubertino was apparently serving as lector *(lectionis officio pressus)*.

14. Ibid., 4.

15. The same conclusion might be drawn from the story in Giunta da Bevegna, *Iunctae Bevegnatis Legenda de vita et miraculis Beatae Margaritae de Cortona*, ed. Fortunato Iozzelli, Bibliotheca Franciscana Ascetica Medii Aevi, no. 13 (Grottaferrata: College of Saint Bonaventure, 1997), 389. See the Appendix to this volume.

16. On Pier, see Raoul Manselli in *Dante: Enciclopedia dantesca* (Rome: Istituto della Enciclopedia Italiana, 1996), 4:492–93. He is mentioned by Dante in *Purgatorio* 13:125–29.

17. See Anna Benvenuti Papi, "L'impianto mendicante in Firenze, un problema aperto," in *Les Ordres mendiants et la ville en Italie centrale* (Rome: École Française de Rome, 1977), 595–608.

18. On Margaret, see Enrico Menestò, "La 'Legenda' di Margherita di Città di Castello," in *Il movimento religioso femminile in Umbria nei secoli XIII–XIV*, ed. Roberto Rusconi (Florence: La Nuova Italia, 1984), 217–37. The *Arbor vitae* explicitly acknowledges Margaret's aid in writing that work (6).

19. *Arbor vitae*, 5. Some textual variants make it plain that such is the meaning, although the text as found in the printed version is open to the other interpretation, i.e., that he met

Angela when he was twenty-four or twenty-five. The problem with this interpretation is that it would front-load Ubertino's various religious conversions, packing his introduction to Angela, John of Parma, and Olivi (as well as his experience at the Portiuncula) all into the period 1284–87. Delaying acquaintance with Angela until 1298 would allow us to interpret him as saying that the good start he made in the pre-Parisian era—thanks to the Portiuncula experience, John, Olivi, and various other mystics—was lost during his spiritually arid time at Paris, leaving him ready to be converted yet again by Angela upon his return to Italy. Besides, Angela was just beginning her spiritual journey and virtually unknown in 1284–85, but she had established a solid reputation by 1298.

20. Ibid., 4.

21. The "Iohannis" is genitive singular, thus suggesting a patronymic, "Peter, Son of John"; however, here (as in the case of Raymundus Iohannis, whom we will encounter much later) it is probably better to consider it a family name and the "Olivi" as designating one branch of the family. François-Régis Durieux says that Olivi's name should be rendered in French as "Pierre Jean-Olieu" or "Pierre Janolieu" (see his "Approches de l'histoire franciscaine du Languedoc au XIII siècle," in *Les Mendiants en pays d'Oc au XIIIe siècle,* Cahiers de Fanjeaux, no. 8 [Toulouse: Editions Privat, 1973], 92). His suggestion is seconded by M.-H. Vicaire in his introduction to *Franciscains d'Oc: Les Spirituels ca. 1280–1324,* Cahiers de Fanjeaux, no. 10 (Toulouse: Editions Privat, 1975), 11–12. I am grateful to Alan Friedlander for his aid on French names.

22. See *Responsio quam fecit P. Ioannis ad litteram magistrorum praesentatam sibi in Avinione,* in "Fr. Petri Ioannis Olivi, O.F.M., tria scripta sui ipsius apologetica annorum 1283 et 1285," by Damasus Laberge, *AFH* 28 (1935–36), 127, where, speaking of his view on marriage as a sacrament, he says, "et de hoc domino Hieronymo satisfeci." Angelo—who seems to know remarkably little about Olivi's life—tells us that much later, after Jerome became Pope Nicholas I, he announced that the burned questions were orthodox and that the command was simply an exercise in humility. Edith Pásztor attacks the entire scholarly tradition—from Ehrle to my own work—for expressing skepticism concerning the part about it being an exercise in humility yet accepting the idea that a work on Mary was burned "without offering the least proof for it" (see "Girolamo d'Ascoli e Pietro di Giovanni Olivi," in *Niccolò IV: Un pontificato tra oriente ed occidente,* ed. Enrico Menestò [Spoleto: Centro Italiano di Studi sull'Alto Medioevo, 1991], 60). In fact, we do offer evidence.

First, Angelo, thoroughly committed to thinking the best of Olivi, would hardly introduce the story of the burning if he did not know that it was true. Second, Angelo is not the only source informing us that some of Olivi's writings were burned in Jerome's time. See Raymundus de Fronciacho, *Sol ortus,* in *Archiv,* 3:13; Ferdinand Delorme, "Notice et extraits d'un manuscrit franciscain," *Collectanea franciscana* 15 (1945), 86; Leo Amorós, "Series condemnationum et processuum contra doctrinam et sequaces Petri Ioannis Olivi," *AFH* 24 (1931), 502. Third, Victorin Doucet, "P. J. Olivi et l'Immaculée Conception," *AFH* 26 (1933): 560–63 offers at least a plausible argument that Olivi's offense was rejecting in strong language the doctrine of Mary's immaculate conception. Pásztor argues that, due to Jerome's diplomatic activities (at papal command) between his election as minister general and early 1279, the meeting between Jerome and Olivi could not have taken place before 1279 (thus slightly before Olivi was allowed to participate in the preparation of *Exiit qui seminat*), and that "excludes all possibility of a condemnation" (64). Yet, busy as Jerome might have been before early 1279, he certainly could have found time to work Olivi in sometime earlier, particularly since he was elected at the Lyons general chapter (1274) and was in France again from 1276 to early 1279.

23. *Peter Olivi's Rule Commentary* (Wiesbaden: Franz Steiner Verlag, 1972), 159.

24. On echoes of Conrad, see my *OPK,* 122–23.

25. See my lengthy analysis in both *Persecution* and *OFP.*

26. See my *Persecution,* 39–41 for the other issues.

27. *De usu paupere: The Quaestio and the Tractatus,* 49.

28. Ibid., 39–49.

29. Ibid., 48.

30. *Summa theologiae*, 2a 2ae, q. 186, a. 9.

31. *Quodlibet* I, a. 20.

32. See Michael Bihl, "Statuta generalia ordinis edita in capitulis generalibus celebratis Narbonae an. 1260, Assisii an. 1279 atque Parisiis an. 1292," *AFH* 34 (1941), 40.

33. *Regula*, chapters 1 and 12.

34. *Correctorium corruptorii "quare"* (Kain: Le Saulchoir, 1927), 302–8, 405–7.

35. Gregory IX, *Quo elongati*, in *BF*, 1:68; Innocent IV, *Ordinem vestrum*, in *BF*, 1:400. For use of the same approach in earlier Franciscan defenses of the rule, see my *OFP*, 161 n. 53.

36. *Chronica XXIV generalium*, 369; *Exiit qui seminat*, in *Corpus iuris canonici* (Graz: Akademische Druck- u. Verlagsanstalt, 1959), 2:1110. For other instances of the canine metaphor, see my *OFP*, 161 n. 50.

37. See *OFP*, 149–55.

38. For explicit Franciscan mention of the charge that the rule is a *laqueus*, see ibid., 159 n. 23.

39. *Exiit*, 1112.

40. "Fr. P. J. Olivi quaestio de voto regulam aliquam profitentis," *Antonianum* 16 (1941): 131–64.

41. See *OFP*, 155–56.

42. See ibid., 57–60.

43. I have done so in ibid., chapters 6 and 7.

44. *De usu paupere*, 131–32.

45. *De perfectione evangelica*, q. 15, in MS Florence, Bibl. Laur. 448, 98rb.

46. See *OFP*, chapter 2.

47. *De usu paupere*, 130.

48. Ibid., 138.

49. For an extended discussion of the following, see *OFP*, 93–102.

50. For more on this bull, see ibid., 100–101. It was not officially adopted by the order until the 1285 general chapter.

51. On his relation to Olivi, see *Persecution*, 37. On his later involvement, see Chapter 4 of this volume.

52. For the following, see Pierre Péano, "Raymond Geoffroi ministre général et défenseur des spirituels," *Picenum Seraphicum* 11 (1974): 190–203.

53. See *OFP*, 39–42, where I favor the latter date. The letter, normally simply called the *Epistola ad R*, is published in "Petrus Ioannis Olivi, epistola ad fratrem R," *AFH* 91 (1998): 133–71.

54. "Petrus Ioannis Olivi, epistola ad fratrem R," 169–70.

55. On the following, see my "Olivi, Apocalyptic Expectation, and Visionary Experience," *Traditio* 41 (1985): 273–88, and "Olivi on Prophecy," *Cristianesimo nella storia* 17 (1996): 369–91.

56. See *Peter of John Olivi on the Bible*, ed. David Flood, O.F.M., and Gedeon Gál, O.F.M. (St. Bonaventure, N.Y.: Franciscan Institute Publications, 1997), 196–98; also see my "Olivi on Prophecy."

57. See *OPK* for extended treatment of the following.

58. On the following, see *OFP*, 163–72.

59. MS Florence, Bibl. Laur. 448, 101ra–110ra.

60. Ibid., 116va–124vb. See the background and discussion provided in Marco Bartoli, "Olivi et le pouvoir du pape," in *Pierre de Jean Olivi (1248–1298): Pensée scolastique, dissidence spirituelle et société*, ed. Alain Boureau and Sylvain Piron (Paris: J. Vrin, 1999), especially 181–88. Bartoli's argument presents a survey of Olivi's thought on papal power as found in all his relevant works.

61. David Burr and David Flood, "Peter Olivi: On Poverty and Revenue," *Franciscan Studies* 40 (1980): 18–58.

62. Ibid., 58.

63. See my *OFP,* 167–68 and 185 nn. 21–26.

64. Brian Tierney, *The Origins of Papal Infallibility* (Leiden: Brill, 1972). But also see Bartoli, who argues that Olivi speaks of *inerrabilitas,* not infallibility, and that the two are not equivalent ("Olivi et le pouvoir du pape," 180).

Chapter 4

1. *Chronica XXIV generalium,* 420–22.
2. See my *OFP,* 108–11 for fuller discussion of both investigation and confession.
3. *Chronica XXIV generalium,* 419.
4. On Nicholas, see Otto Schiff, *Studien zur Geschichte Papst Nikolaus IV* (1897; reprint, Vaduz: Kraus Reprint, 1965) and, more recently, the articles in *Niccolò IV: Un pontificato tra oriente ed occidente,* ed. Enrico Menestò (Spoleto: Centro Italiano di Studi sull'Alto Medioevo, 1991) and *La "Supra montem" di Niccolò IV,* ed. Raffaele Pazzelli and Lino Temperini (Rome: Analecta TOR, 1988).
5. Was he also instrumental in getting Bertrand de Sigotier appointed minister of Olivi's province after the investigation? Or was it the result of Raymond Geoffroi's influence? One can imagine Nicholas wanting the investigator to stay on and police the province; but Bertrand, like Raymond, had close connections with the house of Anjou and had been guardian of the Franciscan house at Marseilles when Raymond was lector there. See Pierre Péano, "Les Ministres provinciaux de la primitive province de Provence (1217–1517)," *AFH* 79 (1986), 31–32, and idem, "Raymond Geoffroi," 197.
6. On Celestine's pontificate and its aftermath, see Peter Herde, *Cölestin V* (Stuttgart: Hiersemann, 1981).
7. Angelo Clareno, *Liber chronicarum* (554–60) and *Epistole* (243).
8. The names are probably references to saintly earlier Franciscans, Liberato da Lauro and Angelo Tancredi. See von Auw, *Angelo Clareno,* 39–40.
9. In reality, the evidence concerning the legality of the Poor Hermits is ambiguous. No actual bull by Celestine exists, and some historians (see particularly Potestà, *Angelo Clareno,* 31) think it probable that his recognition of the new group was exclusively verbal. Moreover, no extant bull by Boniface explicitly denies the legality of the Poor Hermits, although this seems implied by Boniface's 1295 general revocation of all privileges and concessions granted by Celestine except those to be personally confirmed by himself.
10. *Epistole,* 245. See also *Liber chronicarum,* 560–62. Angelo says that even before Celestine's resignation, when their Franciscan leaders heard that the pope had absolved the group from obedience to the order, they had sent an armed posse to capture them.
11. On these sources, see my *OFP,* 112–24.
12. See, for example, Franz Ehrle, "Petrus Johannis Olivi," in *Archiv,* 3:438.
13. See my fuller comments in *Persecution,* 70–72, and *OFP,* 115–16.
14. Von Auw, *Angelo Clareno,* 48–49.
15. See *OFP,* 119–23.
16. Nevertheless, they did it. A life of the Blessed Angelo, a recluse living in remote parts, says that in response to Boniface's order he was checked and judged by the bishop and inquisitor to be legitimate. See Mario Sensi, *Le osservanze francescane nell'Italia centrale* (Rome: Istituto Storico dei Cappuccini, 1985), 82.
17. See Raoul Manselli, *La "Lectura super Apocalypsim" di Pietro di Giovanni Olivi* (Rome: Istituto Storico Italiano per il Medio Evo, 1955), 218–19.
18. See Chapter 6.
19. For this point and the following, see my *Persecution,* 69–72; *OFP,* 115–16 and chapter 7.
20. The letter is in *Archiv,* 3:535–40.
21. Ibid., 539.

22. See, for example, the cases of Douceline and Rixende discussed later in this chapter.

23. *Chronica XXIV generalium*, 431. The offer concerning Milan was made and rejected early in 1296.

24. For the following, see *OFP*, 124–28.

25. See Boase, *Boniface VIII*, 21–22 and 203.

26. For an extended treatment of the following, see *OPK*.

27. Text translated from Warren Lewis's edition in "Peter John Olivi: Prophet of the Year 2000" (Ph.D. diss., Tübingen University, 1972), 52. Following references will be to Lewis's edition, designated here as *Lectura*.

28. *Lectura*, 231.

29. See ibid., 51 and 97, for the third age as a return to the rule; on the "new church" and "new world," see ibid., 48, 55, 57, 102, and 882.

30. See the passages cited in the previous note. His view of the Franciscan rule as embodying the life observed by Christ and the disciples fits with this emphasis.

31. *Lectura*, 57: "Vetustas prioris temporis est sic universaliter repellenda, ut videatur quoddam novum seculum seu nova ecclesia tunc formari veteribus iam reiectis, sicut in primo Christi adventu formata est nova ecclesia veteri synagoga reiecta." For the three advents, see ibid., 46–47, 57, and 101–2.

32. Ibid., 564: "Nam in prioribus quinque ecclesie statibus non fuit concessum sanctis, quantumcumque illuminatis, aperire illa secreta huius libri, que in solo sexto et septimo statu erant apertius reseranda, sicut nec in primis quinque etatibus veteris testamenti fuit prophetis concessum clare aperire secreta Christi et novi testamenti in sexta etate seculi reserandis et reseratis." The passage is confusing, but makes sense if the phrase "in primis quinque etatibus veteris testamenti" is taken to mean "those five ages of world history that constitute the Old Testament period," although the grammar still seems odd.

33. Ibid., 101–2: "Sicut enim viro distanti a monte magno, duas magnas valles seu planities intra se continente ac per consequens et trino, videtur mons ille non ut trinus sed tantum ut unus mons, nullis vallibus distinctus; ex quo vero vir ille stat super primum montem videt primam vallem et duos montes vallem illam concludentes; ex quo vero stat in monte secundo seu medio videt duas valles cum montium ipsas includentium trinitate, sic Iudei, qui fuerunt ante primum Christi adventum quasi ante primum montem, non distinxerunt inter primum et postremos, sed sumpserunt totum pro uno. Christiani vero sextum statum ecclesie preeuntes distinguunt quidem inter primum et ultimum, tanquam iam positi super primum et tanquam videntes medium spatium conversionis gentium, quod est et fuit inter primum adventum et ultimum. Communiter tamen non distinguunt inter illum, qui erit in extremo iudicio, et inter illum, qui erit in statu sexto, quando, secundum apostolum, Christus illustratione sui adventus interficiet antichristum. Qui autem statuentur in sexto vel in spiritu vident ipsum, distinguunt ipsum a primo et postremo. Videntque tunc hanc distinctionem in libris propheticis, et etiam in hiis que a Christo et apostolis dicta sunt de finali Christi adventu et de finali statu mundi. Tunc etiam vident, quotlibet opera quinque priorum etatum concordet cum quinque primis ecclesie statibus et septem prelia seu signacula sub lege completa concordent cum septem ecclesie statibus."

34. Ibid., 791: "Item communiter non intrabitur plene nisi post effusionem septimi angeli, sicut nec liber erit perfecte apertus nec misteria dei omnino consummata, usquequo septimus angelus ceperit tuba canere. Sciendum tamen quod in quibusdam sanctis cuiuslibet status possunt hii septem gradus purgationum perfici vel fuisse perfecti et sic in hoc templum intrasse, non expectando septimum tempus ecclesie, quia in ipsis fuit virtualiter seu spiritualiter completum, ita quod perinde est ac si temporaliter pertigissent ad tempus et opus septimi status."

35. Nevertheless, this distinction must be qualified in view of what will be said in a moment about the coalescence of prophecy, contemplation, and exegesis in Olivi's thought.

36. *Lectura*, 979. The passage draws a parallel between knowledge and use of material things. For further discussion and citations of this point and the next, see my "Olivi, Apocalyptic Expectation, and Visionary Experience."

37. *Lectura,* 395–96.

38. Ibid., 512: "Super quo et consimilibus advertendum quod ipse plura dicit non asser-torie sed opinative. Sicut enim ex naturali lumine intellectus nostri quedam scimus indubitabiliter ut prima principia, quedam vero ut conclusiones ex ipsis necessario deductas, quedam vero nescimus sed solum opinamur per probabiles rationes et in hoc tertio sepe fallimur et pos-sumus falli, nec tamen ex hoc lumen nobis concreatum est falsum nec pro tanto fallimur pro quanto opiniones nostras scimus non esse sententias infallibiles; sic lumen per gratuitam reve-lationem datum quedam scit ut prima et indubitabilia principia revelata, quedam vero ut con-clusiones ex ipsis necessario deductas; quedam vero ex utrisque solum probabiliter et conjecturaliter opinatur; et sic videtur fuisse in intelligentia scripturarum et concordie novi et veteris testamenti per revelationem abbiti Ioachim, ut ipsemet asserit, data."

39. The following represents an abridged version of my article, "Olivi on Prophecy."

40. *Lectura super Isaiam,* in *Peter of John Olivi on the Bible,* ed. Flood and Gál, 195: "Quando enim mens altissime et intentissime et vivacissime immutatur a deo, non potest dubitare illam immu-tationem esse a deo, ac per consequens et illa que sibi tunc ostenduntur vel dicuntur quodam certissimo sensu vel gustu sentit esse a deo, et eo ipso est certissima quod illa infallibiliter sunt vera. Ex secundo vero sumit hoc modo certitudinem. In ipsa enim visione seu allocutione et in ipsa re, prout est obiectum talis revelationis, sentit aliquando mens prophetica quendam gustum veritatis et divinitatis aut cuiusdam divinissimi ordinis, in quo quiddam ineffabile divine sapi-entie hoc apprehendit esse, ita quod non potest dubitare quin illud quod videt sit verissimum et divinissimimum, et tamen cum hoc bene videt quod nullo modo posset illud probare per rationem humanam." And see 196: "Nec per hoc nego quin tunc vere Deus ipse et eius veritas et suavitas gustetur. Sed quod non attingitur per immediatam visionem creati speculi mediationem."

41. Ibid.: "Rursus sciendum quod non semper visio prophetica certificat cor videntis, ymmo aliquando dubitat vel ignorat an sit a deo, aliquando vero semiplene certificat. Constat enim quod deus et angeli eius sic possunt immittere aliqua quod ex modo immissionis non poterit apprehendi an sit a bono spiritu vel a malo, alias donum discretionis spirituum non esset ali-quando necessarium in huiusmodi examinandis et discernendis. Rursus sciendum quod etiam quando certificat se esse a spiritu bono, non semper illustrat ad intelligentiam eius quod per eam significatur. Unde Daniel viderat et audiverat visionem et allucuciones angelicas et divinas, quamvis certus esset quod a Deo erant, adhuc tamen querit intelligentiam visionis et aliquando dicit se ignorare eam. Et idem invenies de Iohanne in Apocalypsi et clarius in Nabuchodonosor et Pharaone, quamvis nec de illis constet an scirent sompnia sua esse a deo. Aliquando etiam illu-stratur mens ad intelligendum aliquid de significatione eius, sed non ad totam."

42. Published in Jean-Pierre Torrell, *Théorie de la prophétie et philosophie de la connaissance aux environs de 1230* (Louvain: Spicilegium sacrum Lovaniense, 1977), 23. Hugh does grant that prophecy leaves in the mind a *quidam habitus* by which, once the vision is over, the prophet knows what he saw, but this is the effect of prophecy, not prophecy itself.

43. Edited by Jean-Pierre Torrell in *Recherches sur la théorie de la prophétie au Moyen Âge* (Fribourg: Editions Universitaires, 1992), 251–313.

44. *Summa theologiae,* 2a 2ae, q. 171, a. 2; *De veritate,* q. 12, 1.1. Nevertheless, in *De veritate,* q. 12, a. 1, Thomas accepts the idea of a certain *habilitas,* a greater facility in prophesying, which comes through having prophesied. Albert the Great accepts the notion of a *habitus,* but in a qual-ified form: it is *quasi habitus. De somno et vigilia,* I, 3 in *Opera omnia* (Paris: Vivès, 1890–95), 9:181.

45. *Lectura super Isaiam,* 197–98: "Habitus vero qui ad hoc valet triplicis generis esse potest. Aut enim dicit solam exacuitionem et clarificationem aciei ipsius intellectus. Sicut enim alibi ostendi quidam habitus sunt in intellectu qui non dicunt nisi quandam habitualem exacuitionem et clarificationem ipsius intellectus, aut dicit aliquam scientiam habitualem, ita quod datur homini habitualis intelligentia alicuius veritatis, aut dicit adhesionem habitualem per modum fidei adher-entem, utpote quod homo habet firmissimam estimationem et credulitatem quod ita sit aut erit. Et hoc ut credo est unum de his que generalius et magis continue certificant mentes

prophetarum. Unde et hoc est magis commune bonis et malis prophetis. Medius autem modus circa contingentia aut super intellectualia, que rationibus sillogisticis probari non possunt, non credo quod habeat rationem scientie vel intelligentie nisi iuxta modum in principio huius positionis premissum. Et ille modus fundatur in fide, sicut flos vel fructus in arbore vel radice. Primum habitum credo quod habebat Daniel quando dicitur quod dederat ei Deus intelligentiam somp-niorum et visionum. Erat enim sibi datum quoddam clarum accumen in intellectu, et quedam vivacitas in affectu ad faciliter et profunde examinanda sompnia, an essent a bono spiritu vel non, et an hoc vel illud significarent. Estimo etiam quod data erat ei aliqua habitualis scientia seu sapi-entia generalium legum seu regularum divine providentie, secundum quas regit omnia et spe-cialiter humana, secundum quas iudicabat de sompniis illis, sicut suo modo per principia universalia iudicamus de particularibus conclusionibus. Et hoc modo Ioachim, in libro de concordia et in expositione Apocalypsis, dicit se subito accepisse totam concordiam veteris et novi testamenti quantum ad quasdam generales regulas, ex quibus ipse postmodum aliqua quasi argumentando deducit, et ut sibi videtur, aliquando sic quod ex hoc extimat se habere certam intelligentiam conclusionis sic deducte, aliquando vero non nisi probabilem coniecuturam in qua plerumque potuiit falli. Et est simile in naturali lumine intellectus nobis ab inicio nostre conditionis iuncto. Per illud enim sine aliqua argumentatione apprehendemus et scimus prima principia, et deinde aliqua conclusiones necessario inferimus per illa, aliquas vero solum probabiliter. Et in his plerumque fallimur. Non tamen ex hoc sequitur quod lumen illud non sit a Deo aut quod in se sit falsum. Quod signanter dico quia quidam ex hoc volunt concludere quod tota intelligentia Ioachim fuerit a dyabolo vel a coniectura spiritus humani, quia in quibusdam particularibus loquitur opinabiliter et forte aliquando fallibiliter."

46. Ibid., 199. Olivi notes that he has dealt with this problem in his question on God's prescience.

47. Olivi actually speaks here and elsewhere of angelic intervention. Throughout the work he assumes that God normally works through angelic mediation.

48. *Lectura super Isaiam*, 198: "Ultra hoc autem aliquando per angelos convertuntur et appli-cantur potentie nostre sic efficaciter quod ex hoc quidam sensus et quedam vivaces affectiones et credulitates seu estimationes sequuntur in nobis quas aliquando instinctus seu impulsus voca-mus. Unde Caiphas habuit forte aliquem occultum et subditum instinctum seu impulsum tam in imaginativa quam in interpretativa ad dicendum quod expedit unum hominem mori etc. Non enim ex intentione aut aliqua voluntate bona illa dicit de Christo. Credo autem quod sine hoc nullum donum habituale datum Danieli vel Ioseph vel aliis prophetis sufficeret ad omnes divinas visiones intelligendas et interpretandas."

49. Aquinas, too, mentions contemplative experience in the prologue of his Isaiah com-mentary, but only to distinguish it sharply from prophetic vision. In fact, he contrasts the lat-ter with three different kinds of contemplation: that of invisible truths through the principles of natural reason, that to which the mind is elevated through the light of faith, and that enjoyed by the blessed through the light of glory. See *In Isaiam prophetam expositio*, in *Opera* (Parma: Fiaccadori, 1853–73), 14:431.

50. *Summa theologiae*, 2a 2ae, d. 174, a. 4.

51. Francis of Assisi is the other.

52. *Lectura*, 51; for what follows, see ibid., 892, 994.

53. On the missionary efforts of the men of the sixth period, see ibid., 974; on Jerusalem, see 751 and 858. Robert Lerner asserts that "Burr overlooks" a third passage on p. 945 in which Olivi "removes doubt by stating that Jerusalem will be 'the principal city and seat of God and the saints'" (see "Peter Olivi on the Conversion of the Jews," in *Pierre de Jean Olivi (1248–1298)*, ed. Boureau and Piron, 214). It seems odd that Olivi, after refusing to decide the matter in two passages where he considers it at some length, should later suddenly commit himself in a single line. In fact, p. 945 discusses not where the new center of Christendom will be located, but why the Book of Revelation refers not only to the new spiritual church of the third age but to the

blessed in heaven as *civitas*, as *Jerusalem*, and as descending from heaven. Why does John use these words? If Olivi were thinking geographically, one would expect him to answer that John says "Jerusalem" because that is where the new headquarters of the church will be. Instead he says it is called a *civitas* because "there is a remarkable unity of all the saints there," and "Jerusalem" because "a vision of the highest peace and of the principal metropolis and seat of God and of the saints will occur there." When he says "there" Olivi is speaking about the new, purified church in the sense of a people, not a place.

54. *Lectura*, 751: "Nec mirum si locus nostre redemptionis super omnia loca terre tunc temporis exaltetur et maxime quia ad conversionem totius orbis et ad gubernationem totius iam conversi ille locus erit congruentior summis rectoribus orbis tanquam centrale medium terre habitabilis."

55. Leo Amorós, "Series condemnationum et processuum," 504–5; Raymundus de Fronciacho, *Sol ortus*, 15–16.

56. Leo Amorós, "Aegidii Romani impugnatio doctrinae Petri Ioannis Olivi an. 1311–12, nunc primum in lucem edita," *AFH* 27 (1934), 403.

57. Raymundus de Fronciacho, *Sol ortus*, 17.

58. See my comments in *OFP*, 127–28.

59. Ubertino, *Sanctitati apostolicae*, in *Archiv*, 2:384–87; Angelo, *Liber chronicarum*, 520–40, 750.

60. On the Olivi cult, see Jean-Louis Biget, "Culte et rayonnement de Pierre Déjean Olieu en Languedoc au début du XIVe siècle," in *Pierre de Jean Olivi (1248–1298)*, ed. Boureau and Piron, 277–308.

61. *Liber chronicarum*, 488.

62. Published in William May, "The Confession of Prous Boneta, Heretic and Heresiarch," in *Essays in Medieval Life and Thought*, ed. John H. Mundy et al. (New York: Biblo and Tannen, 1965), 10–11. We will meet Na Prous Boneta at greater length later.

63. For Boniface, see the documents in *Archiv*, 2:155–58, and *BF*, 4:435–36. For Jacopone, see the *Laude* (Bari: Laterza & Figli, 1974), *Lauda* 55, line 65. The term is also used in a letter by Charles II of Naples published in *Archiv*, 2:335–36. For the context, see *OFP*, 120–21. To streamline the presentation here, I shall normally use the term "beguin" for both sexes, rather than saying "beguins and beguines."

64. See Sisto, *Figure del primo francescanesimo*, 35–36.

65. See Ignaz von Döllinger, *Beiträge zur Sektengeschichte des Mittelalters* (Munich: Beck, 1890), 2:706–11.

66. The story of the third order is itself a complex one. Francis did not found the first lay order of penitents, since the penitent status already had been canonically recognized (for example, in the Humiliati). Nevertheless, by the 1230s and 1240s we have Franciscan sources like Julian of Speyer, the *Perugian Anonymous*, and the *Letter of the Three Companions* connecting Francis— or at least his order—with the formation of a third order of laity. Prior to 1289, some groups of lay penitents were associated in various ways and to various degrees with the Franciscans; some were instead associated with the Dominicans; and some merely operated under the authority of their bishop without any obvious relationship to either order. Nor was the activity of such groups uniform. Some sought a higher level of religious discipline while living at home with their families; others entered into communal living arrangements; and still others became hermits. In 1289 a strong relationship with the Franciscans was not only recognized but required by the bull *Supra montem*, in which Nicholas IV, the first Franciscan pope, depicted Francis as institutor of the third order and placed penitent fraternities under Franciscan guidance. Even then the nature of the third order was not closely defined. For the laity the bull represented, in the words of Giovanna Casagrande, "a big, protective umbrella in the shade of which varied and diverse forms of religious life found shelter and refuge in the form of a canonical-juridical-ecclesiastical regular status." See "Un ordine per i laici: Penitenza e penitenti nel duecento," in *Francesco d'Assisi e il primo secolo di storia francescana*, ed. Alberzoni et al., 251. Casagrande's article provides a brief but excellent summary of the problem with recent bibliography.

67. Johannes Mansi, *Sacrorum consiliorum nova et amplissima collectio* (Florence: A. Zatta, 1759–98), 24:1216–17.

68. *Spirituali e beghini in Provenza* (Rome: Istituto Storico Italiano per il Medio Evo, 1959), 41.

69. Raymundus de Fronciacho, *Sol ortus*, 14. See Ubertino da Casale, *Sanctitati apostolicae*, 388. Arnold of Roquefeuil was again made provincial minister in 1297, thus facilitating the persecution. See Pierre Péano, "Ministres provinciaux de Provence et spirituels," 51. The 1299 council uses the word *superstitio* twice, but it was a common word in such circumstances.

70. She knew the state of souls after death.

71. A copy of the letter that she claimed to have received from St. John was given to the sisters of St. Clare and was, for a while, in the hands of a Franciscan.

72. See the citations discussed in my "Olivi, Apocalyptic Expectation, and Visionary Experience," 279, and the comments of the "very holy person" cited earlier in this chapter from *Lectura super Isaiam*, 196.

73. Paul says this in both his *Historia satirica* and his *Chronologia magna*. See Girolamo Golubovich, *Biblioteca bio-bibliografica della Terra Santa e dell'oriente francescano* (Quaracchi: College of Saint Bonaventure, 1906–48), 2:80–81, 96–97. Paul places the departure of Angelo's group in 1301, but von Auw seems right in saying that they were already gone by then (see *Angelo Clareno*, 46). On Matthew, see Ferdinand Delorme, "La Confessio Fidei du Frère Matthieu de Bouzigues," *Études franciscaines* 49 (1937), 224–39; D. Zorzi, "Testi inediti francescani in lingua provenzale," *Miscellanea del Centro di Studi Medievali*, ser. 1 (Milan: Vita e Pensiero, 1956): 249–324; and most recently, Robert Lerner, "Writing and Resistance Among Beguins of Languedoc and Catalonia," in *Heresy and Literacy, 1000–1530*, ed. Peter Biller and Anne Hudson (Cambridge: Cambridge University Press, 1994), 191.

74. *Epistole*, 247–48. On Jerome, see von Auw, *Angelo Clareno*, 66–67.

75. Von Auw (*Angelo Clareno*) and Manselli (*Spirituali e beghini*) both see them as separate, but Georges Digard, *Philippe le Bel et le Saint-Siège* (Paris: Librairie du Recueil Sirey, 1936), 2:6 n. 2 suggests that Paul of Venice is relaying defective information and that Matthew was really Jerome's companion. Manselli resolutely battles this view, but his arguments are less than decisive.

76. Published in Zorzi, "Testi inediti," 249–68.

77. See José Pou y Marti, *Visionarios, beguinos y fraticelos catalanes (siglos XIII–XV)* (Vich: Editorial Seráfica, 1930), 209–31.

78. See von Auw's comment in Angelo, *Epistole*, 248 n. 1.

79. In an appendix to *Spirituali e beghini*.

80. On this work, see *OPK*, chapter 9, and Chapter 8 of this volume.

81. Published in *Archiv*, 2:371.

82. Bernardus Guidonis, *Practica inquisitionis heretice pravitatis* (Paris: Alphonse Picard, 1886), 265. Beguin confessions from that period verify as much.

83. On Thomas and Angelo's stay in Greece, see von Auw, *Angelo Clareno*, chapter 4, and the more concise presentation in Douie, *Nature and the Effect*, 56–58.

84. See my *OFP*, 117–24.

85. *Epistole*, 249–50, and its companion passage, *Liber chronicarum*, 594–604, are ambiguous in their description of Liberato's activities at this point.

86. On Isnardo's role, see von Auw, *Angelo Clareno*, 78–79 and 83.

87. Ubertino claims that he wrote it in three months and seven days, but also that it was written over a period of seven months beginning in March, though with four major interruptions (*Arbor vitae*, 6). The former claim might be interpreted as the time for actual composition within the seven months. The fact that Ubertino borrows heavily from others would certainly accelerate the process of composition, but even so, such a short period of time would entail remarkable writing speed. Angelo Clareno improves even on that, saying that Ubertino wrote the *Arbor vitae* "in a few days" (*Liber chronicarum*, 650). Potestà (*Storia ed escatologia*) and Damiata (*Pietà*) provide good analyses of the work. Scholars differ on whether what we have represents

a second redaction of the work, but even those who deny that theory are open to the idea that he may have inserted a number of his previously written sermons and treatises (e.g., see the list of such offered by Damiata, *Pietà*, 75–77). The forthcoming edition by Carlos Martinez Ruiz promises to settle the matter in favor of two redactions.

88. Potestà (*Storia ed escatologia*, 96–101) shows, however, that Ubertino too was familiar with Joachim and did not simply absorb his Joachism from Olivi.

89. *Arbor vitae*, 423. John is the angel of Rev. 17:1. John is also identified with an angel of Rev. 19, and that would make sense, since the angel of 19:9 is the same as the one in 17:1. The angel tells John, "Write this down," and John falls at his feet, just as Ubertino tells us he did with John of Parma at Greccio. If so, then John is giving Ubertino his commission to write the *Arbor vitae*. Yet Ubertino's reference to the angel as having come down from heaven makes one wonder if he is really thinking of Rev. 18:1.

90. *Arbor vitae*, 461–63.

91. Ubertino calls him a *pugil Christi*.

92. See Michel de Dmitrewski, "Fr. Bernard Délicieux, O.F.M.: Sa lutte contre l'inquisition de Carcassonne et d'Albi, son procès, 1297–1319," *AFH* 17 (1924), 331–35, and, more recently, Alan Friedlander, *Processus Bernardi Delitiosi: The Trial of Fr. Bernard Délicieux, 3 September–8 December 1319* (Philadelphia: American Philosophical Society, 1996). The accusations against Bernard suggest sorcery as much as poisoning.

93. Contemporary scholars regularly read this passage as if Ubertino were reporting that the brothers who had been in Greece applied the number of the beast both to Boniface and to Benedict. The passage seems to say, however, that they applied it only to Boniface, leaving Ubertino to clarify its true meaning. The latter reading seems justified not only by Ubertino's phraseology, but also by the fact that, if we take Angelo's chronology of events seriously, those in his group—and contemporary scholars also assume that the brothers in question were in fact members of Angelo's group—would have had neither the time nor the motivation to think that harshly of Benedict.

94. See my "Petrus Ioannis Olivi and the Philosophers," *Franciscan Studies* 34 (1971): 41–71.

95. *Arbor vitae*, 423–25.

96. Ibid., 432–47.

97. Even at the time that he wrote the *Arbor vitae*, Ubertino still had not read the Leo sources themselves, and he actually feared that they had been lost (see *Arbor vitae*, 445). He received his information about them through intermediaries like Conrad of Offida. By August 1311 he had discovered that they were still extant. See *Declaratio*, 168, 177–78.

98. *Storia ed escatologia*, 130–31.

99. Ibid., 134–35.

100. See *OPK*, 122–23.

101. *Arbor vitae*, 4. As we will see, he said the same thing at Vienne.

102. See the Appendix, "Spirituals and Mystics."

103. Angelo, *Liber chronicarum*, 554; for the description of Conrad that follows, see ibid., 566–68.

104. Jacopone da Todi, *Lauda* 74, in *Laude* (Rome: Laterza & Figli, 1974), 218–20. Subsequent references to individual *laude* will follow the enumeration in this edition. George Peck's *Fool of God* (Tuscaloosa: University of Alabama Press, 1980) offers a very readable biography with great sensitivity to Jacopone's status as poet and mystic. For Angelo's reference to Jacopone, see *Liber chronicarum*, 556.

105. See "Il movimento del libero spirito," *Archivio italiano per la storia della pietà* 4 (1965): 351–708; Jacopone is considered at 400–403. See his mystical lauds, like 36, 90, and 92.

106. Here again, he sees twin temptations: some are tempted by avarice, others by the vanity of knowledge. Still others who escape these two may succumb to a third peril, though; they are tempted to pursue spiritual gifts like performing miracles, healing, speaking in tongues, and prophesying.

107. Heinrich Denifle, "Die Denkschriften der Colonna gegen Bonifaz VIII und die Cardinäle gegen die Colonna," in *Archiv*, 5:510.

108. *Fool of God*, 153–55.

109. *Cronica*, 343.

110. See, among the more recent publications, Mario Sensi, *Storie di bizzoche tra Umbria e Marche* (Rome: Edizioni di Storia e Letteratura, 1995); Giovanna Casagrande, *Religiosità penitenziale e città al tempo dei communi* (Rome: Istituto Storico dei Cappuccini, 1995); and Anna Benvenuti Papi, *In castro poenitentiae* (Rome: Herder, 1990).

111. Grado Merlo, "Controllo ed emarginazione della dissidenza religiosa," in *Francescanesimo e vita religiosa dei laici nel '200* (Rimini: Maggioli, 1981), 365–88 provides a useful overview. On the dilemma posed by new movements among women, see Edith Pásztor, "I papi del duecento e trecento di fronte alla vita religiosa femminile," in *Il movimento religioso femminile in Umbria nei secoli XIII-XIV*, ed. Rusconi, 29–65.

112. I follow Raniero Orioli, *Venit perfidus heresiarcha* (Rome: Istituto Storico Italiano per il Medio Evo, 1988), in seeing Dolcino's banditry—and eventual confrontation with a crusading army—not as proto-Marxist social protest, but as a purely practical reaction to the demands of his situation. He had abandoned the plains, where his followers had been able to find sustenance and protection among the laity, and had concentrated his group in a mountainous area where they could ward off starvation only by becoming outlaws (and even by that means could expect to do so only temporarily).

113. See Orioli, *Venit*, 78–80; Burr, *OFP*, 119–22, 124.

114. *Liber chronicarum*, 604–22. According to Angelo, the letter spoke of forty, but he himself sets the figure at forty-two. Tempting as it might be to use this figure as a rough estimate of how many Poor Hermits there actually were, Angelo makes it clear that the inquisitor had not captured the whole group and, equally important, that not everyone he captured was a Poor Hermit.

115. See, for example, Orioli, *Venit*, 142, 296–97, and 314; Oliger, *De secta*, 83–84; and Chapters 11 and 13 in this volume. For the "heretical underbrush," see Orioli, *Venit*, 299.

116. Actual contact between groups might not even have been necessary. Orioli provides a fascinating description of how Jacques de Thérines's 1306 *quodlibet* at Paris confused the Dolcinist and spiritual Franciscan platforms (*Venit*, 270–71).

Chapter 5

1. For a recent brief survey of Arnald's difficulties and his self-defense from 1300 to Clement's election, see Gian Luca Potestà, "Dall'annuncio dell'Anticristo all'attesa del pastore angelico: Gli scritti di Arnaldo di Villanova nel codice dell'archivio generale dei Carmelitani," *Arxiu de Textos Catalans Antics* 13 (1994): 287–344. But see also the various conflicting views on the authenticity of some works by Jaume Mensa and Josep Perarnau in ibid., 379–408.

2. *Liber chronicarum*, 592–94, 640.

3. Thus Lambert, *Franciscan Poverty*, 194. For a survey of other opinions, see von Auw, *Angelo Clareno*, 87. Von Auw herself stands by Angelo's assertion.

4. Moreover, while Louis, Robert, and their brother Raymond had been hostages in Aragon, they had written Olivi asking him to come and advise them (although, as we have seen, Olivi had graciously declined, citing among other reasons their father's fear that he might "beguinize" them). Letter printed in *Archiv*, 3:534–40. Olivi says, "pater vester timuerat vos inbeguiniri."

5. While Ronald Musto, Darleen Pryds, and others present King Robert and Queen Sancia as supporters of the spirituals, Samantha Kelly introduces strong evidence that Sancia supported them but Robert did not. See Musto, "Queen Sancia of Naples (1286–1345) and the Spiritual Franciscans," in *Women of the Medieval World*, ed. Julius Kirshner and Suzanne Wemple (Oxford: Basil Blackwell, 1985), 193; Pryds, "Clarisses, Franciscans, and the House of Anjou," in *Clarefest*,

ed. Ingrid Peterson (St. Bonaventure, N.Y.: Franciscan Institute, 1995); and Kelly, "King Robert of Naples (1309–1343) and the Spiritual Franciscans," *Cristianesimo nella storia* 20 (1999): 41–80.

6. See von Auw, *Angelo Clareno*, 87–88, and Clifford Backman, "Arnau de Vilanova and the Franciscan Spirituals in Sicily," *Franciscan Studies* 50 (1990): 3–29. Thanks to the 1298 treaty of Caltabellotta, he was technically king of Trinacria, but by 1308 his chancery was occasionally issuing documents that referred to him as "king of the island of Sicily." See Clifford Backman, *The Decline and Fall of Medieval Sicily* (Cambridge: Cambridge University Press, 1995), 66–67. Nevertheless, Angelo's one definite reference to Charles II in the *Liber chronicarum* (594) refers to him as *Carolus rex Siciliae*.

7. For Arnald's plea, delivered in 1309 in secret consistory, see Pou y Marti, *Visionarios*, 67–84.

8. *Dudum ad apostolatus*, in *BF*, 5:65–66.

9. The petition is mentioned in Raymundus de Fronciacho, *Sol ortus*, 18.

10. *BF*, 5:65–68.

11. Angelo, *Liber chronicarum*, 664. The other document is MS Florence, Biblioteca Nationale [Magliabecch.] XXXIVV, 76, fols. 110v–111r. The relevant passage is quoted in von Auw, *Angelo Clareno*, 91 n. 23. Angelo had not yet taken up his observation post at the papal curia by the time they died, since he says that he went there the year the Council began, and it commenced in October 1311.

12. Raymundus Gaufridi, *Ad primum articulum*, in *Archiv*, 3:142–44. For the dating, see Ehrle's introduction (*Archiv*, 3:138–40). A relatively complete list of the various documents is provided by Albanus Heysse, "Anonymi spiritualis responsio 'Beatus vir,'" *AFH* 42 (1949): 213–16. For the names of the spokesmen, see the two sources cited in note 11; the community document *In nomine domini*, in *Archiv*, 2:372; and von Auw, *Angelo Clareno*, 89.

13. *Sanctitas vestra*, in *Archiv*, 3:51–89. For the dating, see Ehrle's introduction (see *Archiv*, 3:48–49).

14. *BF*, 1:69.

15. See *Rotulus*, 120–21; *Sapientia aedificavit*, in *Archiv*, 3:121; *Religiosi viri*, *AFH* 8 (1915), 74. In fact, the 1310 general chapter at Padua called for such confessors. See Giuseppe Abate, "Memoriali, statuti ed atti di capitoli generali dei frati minori inediti dei secoli XIII et XIV," *Miscellanea francescana* 33 (1933), 31.

16. *Sanctitas vestra*, 73, 80; *Rotulus*, 120; *Sapientia aedificavit*, 120; *Religiosi viri*, 62, 73–74. Books must have been an ideal form of nest egg, more or less excusable and very expensive. For the relative value of books, see Carlo Cipolla, *Moneta e civiltà mediterranea* (Venice: Neri Pozza, 1957), 75. It is hard to evaluate the accuracy of Ubertino's strictures concerning health care, but provincial statutes of Aquitaine produced sometime between 1280 and 1312 did find it necessary to mention that the ill should receive care and medicine without being required to pay for it. A. G. Little, "Statuta provincialia provinciarum Aquitainiae et Franciae (saec. XIII–XIV)," *AFH* 7 (1914), 471. The 1300 Umbrian statutes edited in Cesare Cenci, "Ordinazioni dei capitoli provinciali umbri dal 1300 al 1305," *Collectanea franciscana* 55 (1985): 5–31 suggest that part of the problem arose from attempts to evade financial responsibility in situations in which it was at least contestable (e.g., in the case of a brother who fell ill while away from his home convent or just after being assigned to a new one). See Cenci, "Ordinazioni," 15–16.

17. *Sanctitas vestra*, 78; *Rotulus*, 109.

18. *Sapientia aedificavit*, 110.

19. *Religiosi viri*, 62–63.

20. *Rotulus*, 102–3, 121; *Declaratio*, 187.

21. For the following, see *Infrascripta dant*, in *Archiv*, 3:147–48; *Religiosi viri*, 674–75; *Contra quasdam responsiones*, *Collectanea franciscana* 15 (1945), 78.

22. For the following, see *Rotulus*, 98, 100–102; *Sanctitas vestra*, 65–66; *Declaratio*, 176–78, 181; *Sapientia aedificavit*, 103; *Infrascripta dant*, 148–50; *Religiosi viri*, 668–69, 672–74, 71.

23. *De doctrina christiana*, II, 28.

24. *Rotulus*, 102.

25. For the following, see *Rotulus*, 115–17; *Sanctitas vestra*, 68, 70, 76, 84; *Declaratio*, 163–72; *Infrascripta dant*, 145–47; *Religiosi viri*, 70–71; *Contra quasdam responsiones*, 78. See Bonaventure, *Epistola* I, in *Opera*, 8:468–69; *Epistola* II, in ibid., 470–71; Peckham, *Tractatus pauperis*, chapter 10 in *Tractatus tres de paupertate* (Aberdeen: Typis Academicis, 1910), 21–87; Michael Bihl, "Statuta generalia ordinis," 48.

26. Jacques de Vitry, *Lettres de Jacques de Vitry* (Leiden: Brill, 1960), 75–76 supports Ubertino: "De die intrant civitates et villas, ut aliquos lucrifaciant operam dantes actione; nocte vero revertuntur ad heremum vel loca solitaria vacantes contemplationi." For varieties of opinion on the accuracy of this view, see Grado Merlo, *Tra eremo e città* (Assisi: Edizioni Porziuncula, 1991), chapter 2. Merlo agrees with those who see the early Franciscans as characterized by a *pendolarismo eremo-città*.

27. In support of Ubertino's claim regarding recent legislation, see Ehrle, "Die altesten Redactionen der Generalconstitutionen des Franziskanerordens," in *Archiv*, 6:33–34.

28. See *Declaratio*, 164 where he attempts to explain away the fact that some leaders responsible for building excesses actually *have* been disciplined by the minister general.

29. For the following, see *Rotulus*, 111, 117; *Sanctitas vestra*, 73–75; *Declaratio*, 176–81; *Infrascripta dant*, 148; *Religiosi viri*, 67; *Sapientia aedificavit*, 114, 119; and *Responsiones ad obiectiones*, in "Notice et extraits d'un manuscrit franciscain," by Ferdinand Delorme, *Collectanea franciscana* 15 (1945), 71.

30. Ubertino replies in a later work that Augustine, Jerome, and Ambrose were not Franciscans.

31. For the following, see *Rotulus*, 115; *Sanctitas vestra*, 67, 84; *Religiosi viri*, 68; *Contra quasdam responsiones*, 81; *Responsiones ad obiectiones*, 71.

32. See *OFP*, 68–69.

33. For the following, see *Rotulus*, 115, 133; *Sanctitas vestra*, 66–67, 84; *Religiosi viri*, 66–68; *Contra quasdam responsiones*, 79–80; *Responsiones ad obiectiones*, 71; and *Quidam casus*, in "Notice et extraits d'un manuscrit franciscain," by Ferdinand Delorme, *Collectanea franciscana* 15 (1945), 53–54.

34. For the following, see *Rotulus*, 114; *Sanctitas vestra*, 69, 72; *Religiosi viri*, 66, 78.

35. The community offers a fuller response to these charges, but Franz Ehrle omitted it from his edition of the key document, *Sapientia aedificavit*, and I have not seen the relevant manuscript.

36. For the following, see *Rotulus*, 104–7, 121–22; *Sanctitas vestra*, 67, 71; *Religiosi viri*, 56–59, 75; *Contra quasdam responsiones*, 78–80.

37. For the following, see *Rotulus*, 113; *Declaratio*, 182–83; *Infrascripta dant*, 150–51; *Religiosi viri*, 64; *Quidam casus*, 54–58.

38. *Sanctitas vestra*, 73–74; *Rotulus*, 111, 118, 127.

39. See *Sanctitas vestra*, 75–76; *Rotulus*, 122, 127.

40. For the following, see *Rotulus*, 111–13; *Sanctitas vestra*, 81.

41. See *Sanctitas vestra*, 53–56, 71, 74, 76.

42. Ibid., 86.

43. See ibid., 67, 69, 76, 79, 85–86; *Rotulus*, 105.

44. *Declaratio*, 182–83. See also *Sanctitas vestra*, 76: "Licet autem declaratio domini papae possit concedere ex plenitudine potestatis, sicut sibi placet, et optima intentione id fecerit dominus papa; ego tamen obedientia artatus dico." Ubertino is right in claiming that in the thirteenth century, anxiety about papal privileges was strong enough to have an impact on the legislation of general chapter meetings. See my *OFP*, 100.

45. See *Sanctitas vestra*, 56–65, 88; *Rotulus*, 94, 117; *Super tribus sceleribus*, in Albanus Heysse, "Ubertini de Casali opusculum 'Super tribus sceleribus,'" *AFH* 10 (1917), 125–29, 136–43, 156f.; *Declaratio*, 190–91.

46. *Rotulus*, 132–33.

47. Ibid., 131; *Contra quasdam responsiones*, 76; *Super tribus sceleribus*, 134. Ubertino appeals not

only to the text of *Exiit* but also to personal conversations with those who were present when it was written.

48.　*Super tribus sceleribus*, 134–35; *Contra quasdam responsiones*, 134–35.

49.　*Rotulus*, 135; *Super tribus sceleribus*, 112, 124, 130, 158, 159–61, 162–63, 168.

50.　*Super tribus sceleribus*, 129, 132; *Contra quasdam responsiones*, 72.

51.　*Rotulus*, 94; *Super tribus sceleribus*, 147. Olivi offers a similar argument in *Rule Commentary*, 118.

52.　*Super tribus sceleribus*, 129, 133.

53.　*Epistole*, 251.

Chapter 6

1.　*Infrascripta dant*, 153–54: "Hec disputatio solum est verbalis."

2.　*Declarata*, in Albanus Heysse, "Ubertini de Casali opusculum 'Super tribus sceleribus,'" 116–18; *Sapientia aedificavit*, 96; *Religiosi viri*, 665.

3.　See, for example, *Declarata*, 119–20; *Infrascripta dant*, 155.

4.　See *OFP*, 81, 136.

5.　*Infrascripta dant*, 154, 156; *Sapientia aedificavit*, 130.

6.　For this and the next paragraph, see *Sapientia aedificavit*, 96; *Contra quasdam obiectiones*, 75–76; *Responsiones ad obiectiones*, 69–70; *Religiosi viri*, 69, 671, 675.

7.　See *OFP*, 137–38 on this problem as it concerns Olivi and his opponents.

8.　*Sapientia aedificavit*, 95; *Religiosi viri*, 664, 670; *Contra quasdam responsiones*, 73, 75; *Declarata*, 116.

9.　E.g. *Declarata*, 118, 121. See Lk. 10:8 and *Regula*, chapter 3.

10.　For instance, they, too, emphasize that Christ ate with the rich. See *Declarata*, 118.

11.　*Sapientia aedificavit*, 99, 136; *Religiosi viri*, 666.

12.　*Religiosi viri*, 664–65, 670; *Responsiones ad obiectiones*, 67–69; *Sapientia aedificavit*, 95, 98; *Contra quasdam obiectiones*, 73.

13.　*Contra quasdam obiectiones*, 76; *Super tribus sceleribus*, 135.

14.　Edited by Franz Pelster, "Nikolaus von Lyra und seine Quaestio de usu paupere," *AFH* 46 (1953): 211–50. The dating is discussed in ibid., 225–26.

15.　Ibid., 236–38; 243–44.

16.　Ibid., 247.

17.　For the best argument, see Philip Krey, "Nicholas of Lyra: Apocalypse Commentary as Historiography" (Ph.D. diss., University of Chicago, 1990), 37–47.

18.　Richard's work is published by Albanus Heysse, "Fr. Richardi de Conington, O.F.M., tractatus de paupertate fratrum minorum," *AFH* 23 (1930): 57–105, 340–60. Aureole's work is published in the *Firmamenta trium ordinum* (Paris: Johannis Petit, Francisci Regnault et Johannis Frelon, 1512), pars IV, 116r–119r, and by Ephrem Longpré, "Le Quodlibet de Nicolas de Lyre, O.F.M.," *AFH* 23 (1930): 42–56. Longpré proceeds on the mistaken assumption that it is by Nicholas of Lyra. For its proper identification, see Pelster, "Nikolaus von Lyra," 213. Apparently the *Firmamenta* edition is based on an early redaction done before *Exivi de paradiso* (May 6, 1312), while Longpré's edition is of a redaction after *Exivi*. I shall cite the Longpré edition.

19.　He provides himself with an escape clause, adding, "Et intelligo quod papa non potest, salva semper plenitudine potestatis, quam tamen non exercet nisi ex magna et necessaria causa." For Richard's reaction when John XXII attacked his beloved *expropriatio*, see Decima Douie, "Three Treatises on Evangelical Poverty," *AFH* 24 (1931), 343–44. Douie describes his attitude as "dismayed resignation."

20.　*OFP*, 73.

21.　For example, he recognizes (Heysse, "Fr. Richardi," 355) that *Exiit*'s apparent limitation of the Franciscans to the necessary use of things—a phenomenon duly noted by "Lyra" as well as by Olivi—presents a challenge to his view. He tries to counter it with a fairly straightforward argument, then follows it up with a second, very murky one, in case the first should be refuted.

22. An omission is seen in a. 9, for instance, where Richard ends by responding to more arguments than he reported in the *videtur* section. As for the incorrect readings, the editor has done his best to catch them, but obviously has not entirely succeeded.

23. For all this, see *OFP,* chapter 3.

24. In *Corpus iuris canonici,* 2:1193–200.

25. In Geroldus Fussenegger, "Relatio commissionis in concilio Viennensi institutae ad decretalem 'Exivi de paradiso' praeparandam," *AFH* 50 (1957): 145–77.

26. Whether they succeeded is unclear. Olivi's explication of their position in the *Tractatus de usu paupere* suggests that they did, but it is too brief to allow certainty.

27. See *OFP,* 61–63, 154–57.

28. See, for example, Hugh of Digne, *Rule Commentary,* 96, 120.

29. See Burr, *Persecution,* chapters 5–7.

30. *In nomine domini,* 367–72.

31. See my *OFP,* 93–98, and *Persecution,* 44–54.

32. *In nomine domini,* 371. For what follows, see *Sanctitati apostolicae,* 384–88, 389–98, and 400–402.

33. *OPK,* 63–66.

34. *Sanctitati apostolicae,* 407–8.

35. Ibid., 402. The work in question is *Quaestiones in secundum librum sententiarum* (Quaracchi: College of Saint Bonaventure, 1921–26), q. 50, and the passage is found at 2:32.

36. Olivi's words on the matter are omitted in some manuscripts of the John commentary, but are published as an appendix in Ferdinand Doucet, "De operibus mss. Petri Io. Olivi Patavii," *AFH* 28 (1935): 428–41.

37. His interest stems from more than personal esteem. As I argue in "Olivi, Apocalyptic Expectation, and Visionary Experience," it fits well with the strong parallel he builds between Francis and Christ. (For a condensed explanation of Olivi's reconciliation of the mystic's reading and the gospel account of Christ's wounds, see p. 274.)

38. *Sanctitati apostolicae,* 404.

39. See Manselli, *Spirituali e beghini,* 42–44; Dmitrewski, "Fr. Bernard Délicieux," 464; Zorzi, "Testi inediti," 274; F. Doucet, "De operibus," 441–42; Bernardus Guidonis, *Practica inquisitionis,* 273.

40. See F. C. Burkitt, "Ubertino da Casale and a Variant Reading," *Journal of Theological Studies* 23 (1922): 186–88.

41. *Sanctitati apostolicae,* 412–13.

42. Ubertino, *Declaratio,* 191. On the three-man commission, also see Ubertino, *Sanctitati apostolicae,* 382, 416; Bonagratia de Bergamo, *Nuper controversia,* in *Archiv,* 3:36; and Raymundus de Fronciacho, *Sol ortus,* 20–21.

43. Published by Geroldus Fussenegger, "Relatio commissionis," 176–77.

44. Leo Amorós, "Aegidii Romani impugnatio," 399–451; Augustinus Triumphus, *Tractatus contra divinatores et sompniatores,* in *Unbekannte kirchenpolitische Streitschriften aus der Zeit Ludwigs des Bayern,* by Richard Scholz (Rome: Loescher & Co. [W. Regenberg], 1911–14), 2:485–90. For other Olivian opinions criticized by these two theologians, see *Persecution,* 79. On the whole, these works represent a reconsideration of the views attacked in the 1280s, plus the issue of the side wound.

45. *Corpus iuris canonici,* 2:1132. There is some disagreement among fourteenth-century authors as to how many issues were addressed in the decretal. See *Persecution,* 79. Nevertheless, the evidence points to these three and only these.

46. *Le dottrine filosofiche di Pier di Giovanni Olivi* (Milan: Società Editrice "Vita e Pensiero," 1959), 376.

47. On this and the following, see *Persecution,* 52–54.

48. See Ubertino's comment on the commission of three in *Declaratio,* 191. For the similar reaction of later spirituals, see Amorós, "Aegidii Romani impugnatio," 418.

Chapter 7

1. For Angelo's optimism, see *Epistole*, 104–6. For the hindsight, see *Liber chronicarum*: Angelo, comparing *Exivi* with the Gospel of John, describes it as "the fourth of the papal declarations, like a soaring eagle, coming closest [of the four] to the founder's intention" (690–92).

2. *Epistole*, 104–5.

3. Ibid., 174.

4. Ibid., 110. Lydia von Auw dates this letter from 1317, but it seems to fit the period immediately after the Council better. See Potestà, *Angelo Clareno*, 39–42.

5. *Liber chronicarum*, 696.

6. Ibid., 700; Johannes Mansi, *Stephani Baluzii Tutelensis Miscellanea* (Paris: Riccomini, 1761–64), 2:278.

7. See his bull of April 14, 1310, *Dudum ad apostolatus*, *BF*, 5:65–68.

8. *Liber chronicarum*, 702: "Summus vero pontifex ostendit se confidere de obedientia fratrum."

9. Ibid., 688–96.

10. Angelo tells us little else. Most of our information comes from a series of other documents presented by Heinrich Finke, *Acta aragonensia* (Berlin: Rothschild, 1908), and Anna Maria Ini, "Nuovi documenti sugli spirituali di Toscana," *AFH* 66 (1973): 305–77. They also tried to seize control at Colle Val d'Elsa, but failed.

11. I.e., canon and civil law. For this claim, see their petition to Frederick III for sanctuary in Finke, *Acta*, 2:661–66.

12. Ini, "Nuovi documenti," 316.

13. Ibid., 328–29.

14. See *BF*, 5:96, where it is dated July 13, 1313. *Regestum Clementis Papae V* (Rome: Typographia Vaticana, 1885), 197 dates it July 15, 1313. Niccola Papini, *Notizie sicure della morte, sepoltura, canonizzazione e traslazione di S. Francesco d'Assisi*, 2d ed. (Foligno: Presso la Tipografia del Tomassini, 1824), 245 mistakenly dates it July 15, 1312. Ini accepts Papini's date and the *BF* date and thus reports two letters (see "Nuovi documenti," 331).

15. Angelo, *Liber chronicarum*, 692–96, and *Epistole*, 121–31; Papini, *Notizie*, 246. Clement repeated these charges (and the call for action as well) in another letter written at the same time to the bishops of Arezzo, Lucca, and Pistoia. *BF*, 5:96–97 and *Regestum*, 232–33 agree in dating it July 15, 1313. In this letter, Clement accuses the rebels of taking advantage of dissension in the order to act illicitly "once the reins were loosed."

16. *Liber chronicarum*, 694.

17. See Papini, *Notizie*, 253–64.

18. Ibid., 249.

19. See the relevant documents in Finke, *Acta*, vols. 2 and 3 (as listed by Ini, "Nuovi documenti"). In the letter to King Jaime II of Aragon published in Finke, *Acta*, 667, Alexander says that there were about forty of them and that they "escaped by night." He calls them wolves in sheep's clothing. King Jaime advised Frederick to eject the fugitives. See Pou y Marti, *Visionarios*, 104–6; Backman, *Decline and Fall*, chapter 5.

20. Backman, *Decline and Fall*, chapter 5 covers the situation well.

21. Backman's "Arnau de Vilanova," 3–29 deals extensively with this matter, as does his *Decline and Fall*, chapter 5.

22. Backman presents an edition of their response in "Arnau de Vilanova" (27–29).

23. Finke, *Acta*, 2:661–66.

24. *Epistole*, 121. The letter in question is number 25.

25. Ibid., 131.

26. Ibid., 124 n. 3.

27. *Angelo Clareno*, 115.

28. *Epistole*, 124 n. 3.

29. *Angelo Clareno*, 115.

30. See my *OFP*, 167–68.

31. See Potestà's *Angelo Clareno*, 98.

32. *Epistole*, 307.

33. Ibid., 228.

34. Ibid., 280.

35. *Angelo Clareno*, 100–101.

36. See Ini, "Nuovi documenti."

37. *BF*, 5:93–95.

38. See their letter to the general chapter held at Pentecost, 1316, published in *Archiv*, 2:159–64. They take the same line in their 1316 letter to John XXII refuting the charges launched by Guillaume Astre (see *Archiv*, 4:52–57).

39. It is partly corroborated by Clement's bull of July 23, 1312 (*BF*, 5:89) and entirely corroborated by a letter from Giacomo Colonna written February 27, 1316, to church leaders in Narbonne and Béziers. For this letter, see Livarius Oliger, "Fr. Bertrandi de Turre processus contra spirituales Aquitaniae (1315) et Card. Jacobus de Columna littera defensoria spiritualium provinciae (1316)," *AFH* 16 (1923): 323–55 (especially 352–53).

40. Giacomo Colonna uses the same formula, but obviously does so on the authority of the spirituals themselves. See Oliger, "Fr. Bertrandi," 353–54.

41. Ehrle, "Die Spiritualen," in *Archiv*, 4:36, places the takeover in 1314, citing the *Chronica XXIV generalium*, 469, but the *Chronica* seems uncertain. Under the year 1314, it mentions Clement's death, then says that Alexander died *eodem anno*, and then states that *eodem tempore* (some manuscripts do say *anno*), both positions being vacant, the takover occurred. Later, it says "plures etiam alii fratres annis Domini MCCCXV et XVI de eadem et aliis Provinciis ad eos contra Superiorum suorum obedientiam accesserunt." Early 1315 seems more appropriate than late 1314 for the uprising, since some time would have been required for the old enemies to regain authority, and the decisive event in that process was a provincial chapter that the spirituals themselves seem to place in 1315 (see note 56 below).

42. Raymundus de Fronciacho, *Sol ortus*, 26–27; Angelo, *Liber chronicarum*, 704.

43. Oliger, "Fr. Bertrandi," 338, 350–55; Ehrle, "Die Spiritualen," in *Archiv*, 2:162–63, 4:56, 4:60, 4:62.

44. Guillaume Astre joined with Raymond Rouvier, *custode* of Montpellier, in a process against the brothers who had taken over the houses at Béziers and Narbonne, while Bertrand de la Tour, provincial minister of Aquitaine, launched one against five friars of his province who had gone to join the rebellious brothers. Both processes were quashed, however, through the influence of sympathetic cardinals, including Giacomo Colonna. See Oliger's "Fr. Bertrandi," which publishes Bertrand's process and Giacomo's letter; its introduction summarizes key events.

45. Their apologia is published in *Archiv*, 2:159–64. Michael's response to their plea is mentioned in their later self-justification to John XXII, published in *Archiv*, 4:52–62 (see p. 54). Their messenger's difficulties are described by Michael Bihl, "Aventures du messager envoyé par les spirituels de Narbonne et de Béziers au chapitre général de Naples en mai 1316," *AFH* 5 (1912): 777–79. Bihl notes, however, that there are discrepancies in the story and questions its trustworthiness—a charge vigorously rejected by Manselli, *Spirituali e beghini*, 122.

46. Manselli, *Spirituali e beghini*, 123.

47. Kelly ("King Robert of Naples") offers interesting observations on the royal couple's continuing good relations with Michael.

48. Manselli, *Spirituali e beghini*, 123.

49. See Armandus Carlini, "Constitutiones generales ordinis fratrum minorum anno 1316 Assisii conditae," *AFH* 4 (1911), 278–79 and 282. The sections in question are 2:1 and 2:14.

50. Section 2:1 says "deformitatibus, singularitatibus, pretiositatibus, et superfluitatibus penitus resecatis."

51. See Nicholas Glassberger, *Chronica*, in *AF*, 2:122–23.

52. Section 2:14 attacks those "quibus si dantur obedientie recedendi procurant eas per preces secularium revocari, vel qui alios, non de suis seu quos extraneos reputant subditos vel prelatos secum nolunt habere vel pacifice substinere."

53. See my comments in *OFP*, 128 and 134 n. 90. For the legislation at Padua and Barcelona, see Giuseppe Abate, "Memoriali," 31–35.

54. Michael of Cesena offered the five supplications outlined in Raymundus de Fronciacho, *Sol ortus*, 27. The spirituals produced the apologia published in *Archiv*, 4:52–63.

55. See notes 38 and 39. Manselli rightly observes that Giacomo Colonna was not the only cardinal who wrote on their behalf (*Spirituali e beghini*, 117 n. 3). See Oliger, "Fr. Bertrandi," 338.

56. The first document is published in *Archiv*, 4:62–63, and the second by Oliger, "Fr. Bertrandi," 339–49. The latter document carries the date of February 13, 1315, and is usually so placed by historians, including Oliger (p. 325); however, it is hard to make sense of this date. It is difficult to date the provincial chapter of Carcassonne, where the spirituals lost a vital round, earlier than 1315. In their May 1316 appeal they refer to it as *ultimo celebratum* (p. 161) and as *isto anno* (p. 163). The sources imply that the spirituals ejected their unsympathetic superiors in Narbonne and Béziers after the Carcassonne chapter. Bertrand de la Tour seems to suggest (p. 346) that the Aquitaine escapees left in order to join their apostate colleagues at Narbonne and Béziers. Some time must have elapsed between their departure from their convents and Bertrand's official act (as their provincial minister). Bertrand says that he ordered them to return within twenty days. When they did not show up within that time *or afterward* (p. 348), he excommunicated them. One is hard pressed to imagine all this taking place by February 13, 1315. It seems more sensible to assume that it was 1315 by their reckoning of the new year but 1316 by ours. Bertrand's official action was thus part of a flurry of activity in early 1316 leading up to the Naples general chapter.

57. Bertrand uses the expression. Oliger, "Fr. Bertrandi," 341.

58. Ibid., 339, 341–42.

59. Ibid., 354.

60. *Archiv*, 4:63. Oliger, "Fr. Bertrandi," 339–40 does not go that far.

61. This charge is not made in extant sources stemming from the community, but it is answered by the spirituals, as we will see.

62. Oliger, "Fr. Bertrandi," 344–45, 347–48; *Archiv*, 4:63. The spirituals are variously described as asserting that one should not obey superiors who transgress the gospel, their vows, or the pope's commands.

63. *Archiv*, 4:54. For such a view among the Cathars, see Malcolm Lambert, *The Cathars* (Oxford: Basil Blackwell, 1998), 160–61.

64. Oliger, "Fr. Bertrandi," 348–49.

65. *Archiv*, 4:54–55, 60. Giacomo Colonna makes the same point in Oliger, "Fr. Bertrandi," 354.

66. *Archiv*, 4:58.

67. Ibid., 52, 55.

68. Ibid., 53.

69. *Archiv*, 3:443.

70. *Epistole*, 175 (letter 34).

71. The significance of his tomb is explored in Biget, "Culte et rayonnement."

72. *Archiv*, 4:56.

73. Oliger, "Fr. Bertrandi," 347.

74. CD 28:126v–127r. Guillaume also admitted to having believed that intercourse with one's own wife was a mortal sin. On this matter, see Jean-Louis Biget, "Autour de Bernard Délicieux," in *Mouvements franciscains et société française, XIIIe–XXe siècles*, ed. André Vauchez (Paris: Beauchesne, 1984), 87 n. 54.

75. See Burr, "Olivi on Marriage: The Conservative as Prophet," *Journal of Medieval and*

Renaissance Studies 2 (1972): 183–204, and Burr, *Persecution*, 44–46. He simply denied that it was a sacrament in the full sense, a view shared by other respectable theologians in his time. Pou y Marti sees a causal connection between denial of marriage as a sacrament and the slighting comments about it by beguins, but that connection seems strained (see *Visionarios*, 156).

76. CD 28:200r–200v.

77. Ibid., 215r–216v. There is nothing in Raimond's process that explicitly identifies him as a beguin, but every other heretic in this section of the Collection Doat is such. Nor is this the only seemingly Cathar view attributed to a beguin examined in this section. A woman named Raymunda is shown to have extensive beguin connections, but is also accused of having said that there were two gods (ibid., 210r).

78. Ibid., 216r. He replied that he did so because one of those present had argued with his wife, who was very old, and had used these words. Thus Guillaume's story interlocks with Raimond's in an odd way. Note too that a Dominican, Raymond Barrau, claimed to have heard a Franciscan at Villeneuve-les-Béziers preach that "matrimonium erat proscribile." Pierre Botineau, "Les Tribulations de R. Barrau O.P. (1295–1338)," *Mélanges d'archéologie et d'histoire publiés par l'École Française de Rome* 77 (1965), 506. A final bit of evidence is found in Nicholas Eymerich, *Directorium inquisitorum* (Venice: Marcus Antinius Zalterius, 1595), 266, where Nicholas says that during John XXII's papacy, Durandus de Baldach civis Gerundensis was condemned for holding that "matrimonium non erat nisi meretricium occultatum." Biget, "Culte et rayonnement," 291–92 connects the beguins' attitude toward sex with the desire of their social class (merchants and artisans) to protect family prosperity by limiting the number of births. He suggests that here, as in the case of usury, the spirituals provided pastoral counseling particularly in tune with the needs of that class. On this matter, see also Sylvain Piron, "Marchands et confesseurs," in *L'Argent au Moyen Âge* (Paris: Publications de la Sorbonne, 1998), 289–308.

Chapter 8

1. Raymundus de Fronciacho, *Sol ortus*, 28.

2. *BF,* 5:110–11.

3. *BF,* 5:111 n. 1, given more completely in Ini, "Nuovi documenti," 355–56.

4. Ibid. It is indicative of the general attitude toward the Sicilian rebels that Giacomo Colonna and Napoleone Orsini, who had been more or less sympathetic toward the spirituals, were among those cardinals who signed this letter.

5. Finke, *Acta*, 2:671–72. On the agreement and its aftermath, see Backman, "Arnau of Vilanova," 22–23 and *Decline and Fall*, 224–27. He observes that the boat engaged to transport them to Tunis was too small to hold all the spirituals then in Sicily (*Decline and Fall*, 225).

6. We find John continuing to pursue the spirituals through the pages of *BF* (e.g., 5:285, 320). Girolamo Golubovich, *Biblioteca bio-bibliografica*, 3:190–92 discusses relevant documents. See also Pou y Marti, *Visionarios*, 504 for a possible allusion to the African venture. For the spirituals in the kingdom of Naples, see Clement Schmitt, *Une Pape réformateur et un défenseur de l'unité de l'Eglise: Bénoit XII et l'ordre des frères mineurs* (Quaracchi: College of Saint Bonaventure, 1959), 177–92, and Backman, "Arnau de Vilanova," 23–25.

7. Raymundus de Fronciacho, *Sol ortus*, 28.

8. Thus Lambert, *Franciscan Poverty*, 224.

9. *BF,* 5:118–20 n. 4.

10. The spirituals' clothing had been a subject of comment throughout the controversy, but from this moment on, along with their rejection of granaries and wine cellars, it was almost reflexively mentioned whenever the spirituals were discussed. The spirituals themselves found it necessary to discuss the matter at length. See, for example, Angelo Clareno's detailed description in *Liber chronicarum*, 758–60 of the habit as envisaged by Francis.

11. *BF,* 5:119–20. After this point, the "appeals and protests" become a recurrent theme. John mentions them on November 6, 1317, in a letter to an inquisitor, Michel Le Moine (*BF,* 5:132–33); Michel mentions them on April 7, 1318, in his sentence (see Mansi, *Stephani Baluzii Tutelensis Miscellanea,* 2:248). Manselli, *Spirituali e beghini,* 131 takes this to mean that when the provincial minister transmitted the cardinals' letter to the spirituals, they replied with a formal appeal. Given extant documents, that seems an attractive interpretation. However, it is hard to believe that the letter could reach the provincial, who could relay it to two convents, which could respond with a formal appeal, which could then be sent to Avignon, and that John could respond in turn by summoning the spirituals to Avignon—all in the space of five days. Either he is referring to some orders he gave before then, or the cardinals' letter is dated incorrectly.

12. On these letters, see what has been said earlier regarding Boniface and the Italian zealots. See also Ehrle, "Die Spiritualen," in *Archiv,* 2:155–57; Angelo Clareno, *Epistole,* 246; von Auw, *Angelo Clareno,* 46, 54, 61–62.

13. *Liber chronicarum,* 714–16.

14. Angelo, *Epistole,* 108.

15. As were Geoffroi de Cournon, whose attempt to distance himself from the matter was only temporarily successful; Guillaume de Saint-Amans, vicar of the Narbonne convent; and Bernard Délicieux. See Raymundus de Fronciacho, *Sol ortus,* 29. For the charges against them, see ibid. as well as Angelo's *Liber chronicarum* (as summarized in Chap. 9 below).

16. Angelo, *Epistole,* 236–53. For his denial of the charges, see 239.

17. For some of these letters, see *OFP,* 120–21.

18. For the preceding points, see *Epistole,* 240, 244. On *Epistole,* 244: "Quare usque hodie nos alicuius Ordinis apostatas nec cognovimus nec sentimus sed credimus quod essemus vere coram Deo apostate et a tali statu heremitico profugi si de nostra voluntate modum vivendi ad quem, Deo inspirante, et summo pontifice concedente, vocati sumus, relinqueremus et invenire-mur coram Christo periuri et dampnatione digni. Quare supplicamus Sanctitati vestre quatenus provideatur nobis modus aliquis per quem, facta de nobis ab impositis purgatione legitima, pos-simus emissum votum et a summo pontifice susceptum et confirmatum servare."

19. Ibid., 245: "Movemur autem ad tenendum et credendum quoadusque per Vestram apos-tolicam Sanctitatem auditi fuerimus, his rationibus quod non sumus neque fuimus excommuni-cati: tum quia nunquam contempsimus aliquod preceptum nobis ab aliquo executore factum, tum quia nunquam aliqua citatio vel processus missus vel datus est nobis, quod si missus non datus, tum quia uno anno expectavimus et postulavimus quod fieret de nobis quid Dominus papa man-daverat; tum quia malitiose expulsi sumus et post dispersionem factus processus quando non erat possibile dari nobis. Nam post obitum patriarche per multos dies vix nos potuimus ad aliquem locum reducere et in unum convenire. Tum etiam quia si illa excommunicatio taliter facta aliq-uid fuisset, ab ipsa fuimus absoluti."

20. Ibid., 245: "Si vero queratur quare de partibus ita recessistis, sit persecutio fratrum ani-mosa pro ratione querenti et consulta a Christo *fuga a facie persequentium* et quietis et pacis amor qui est finis prefixus ante finem ultimum omnium filiorum Dei. Cum enim audissent fratres quod Dominus Celestinus nos a sua obedientia et a suo Ordine absolverat, statim manu armata venerunt nos capere, Dei timore et summi pontificis reverentia et mandato contempto. Quare ipso renun-tiante, visum fuit fratri Liberato quod pro nostra salute et fratrum pace ad loca remota iremus ubi absque omnium hominum tumultu et scandalo Domino libere serviremus."

21. See ibid., 246–47, 249. For Jerome, see Chapter 4 of this volume.

22. Thus Golubovich, *Biblioteca bio-bibliografica,* 3:56.

23. See Lydia von Auw in *Epistole,* 249 n. 2.

24. Ibid., 251.

25. Ubertino, *Arbor vitae,* 465.

26. See *Celestiniana* (Rome: Istituto Storico Italiano per il Medio Evo, 1954), 143.

Chapter 9

1. The number is from Angelo Clareno, *Liber chronicarum*, 720. The discrepancy between the number summoned and this figure may simply be due to the addition of Bernard Délicieux and one or two other (unnamed) friars.

2. On Bernard, see especially Michel de Dmitrewski, "Fr. Bernard Délicieux"; Alan Friedlander, "Jean XXII et les Spirituels: Le Cas de Bernard Délicieux," in *La Papauté d'Avignon et le Languedoc* (Toulouse: Editions Privat, 1991), 221–36; and Friedlander, *The Hammer of the Inquisitors: Brother Bernard Délicieux and the Struggle Against the Inquisition in Fourteenth-Century France* (Leiden: Brill, 2000). Friedlander also has edited the process against Bernard in *Processus Bernardi Delitiosi*. I am indebted to Friedlander for his generous counsel on Bernard before his books appeared.

3. As Friedlander observes, Bernard's survival hinged on Benedict XI's death in July 1304 and the election of Clement V in his stead (see *Hammer of the Inquisitors*, 230). Already in April 1304, the Dominican Benedict had called for Bernard's arrest and transfer to the curia for trial.

4. See especially Botineau, "Les Tribulations de R. Barrau," 502–6. Nevertheless, Bernard was not among the Béziers Franciscans cited to Avignon in John's letter of April 27, 1317 (*BF*, 5:120).

5. See the charges in Dmitrewski, "Fr. Bernard Délicieux," 318, 472, 482.

6. See Chapter 3 for his attitude toward books. On money, see Giacomo Todeschini, "Olivi e il *mercator* cristiano," in *Pierre de Jean Olivi (1248–1298)*, ed. Boureau and Piron, 217–37.

7. *Hammer of the Inquisitors*, 239.

8. Dmitrewski, "Fr. Bernard Délicieux," 7.

9. Bernard was influenced by the Pseudo-Joachim papal prophecies beginning with *Genus nequam*, and his preaching showed a parallel with the later papal prophecies, beginning with *Ascende calve*. See Orit Schwartz and Robert Lerner, "Illuminated Propaganda: The Origins of the 'Ascende Calve' Pope Prophecies," *Journal of Medieval History* 20 (1994): 157–91, and Friedlander, *Hammer of the Inquisitors*, 242–49.

10. Friedlander, *Hammer of the Inquisitors*, 232.

11. On Angelo's transfer, see "Angelus Clarinus ad Alvarum Pelagium Apologia pro vita sua," by Victorin Doucet, *AFH* 39 (1948), 119; *Epistole*, 327. On Ubertino's, see *BF*, 5:127; Angelo Clareno, *Liber chronicarum*, 752–56. As we will see, both transfers proved largely theoretical.

12. In his introduction to *Processus Bernardi Delitiosi*, 39–45, and in *Hammer of the Inquisitors*, 273–88, Alan Friedlander finds the evidence for the murder charge more compelling than Bernard's judges did, and he argues the case convincingly.

13. See *BF*, 5:128–30; Johannes XXII, *Extravagantes Iohannis XXII* (Vatican City: Biblioteca Apostolica Vaticana, 1983), 163–98.

14. Petrus Iohannis Olivi, *Quaestiones de perfectione evangelica*, q. 11, 109va (MS Florence, Bibl. Laur. 448); *Lectura super Mattheum*, commentary on 10:9–10, as published in Marie-Thérèse d'Alverny, "Un Adversaire de Saint Thomas: Petrus Ioannis Olivi," in *St. Thomas Aquinas, 1274–1974* (Toronto: Pontifical Institute of Mediaeval Studies, 1974), 2:217.

15. The interviews are alluded to by Raymundus de Fronciacho, *Sol ortus*, 30, and twenty-one of them are published by Manselli, *Spirituali e beghini*, 291–96. Of these twenty-one, only four were willing to conform to *Quorumdam exigit*.

16. Published in Heinrich Denifle and Emile Châtelain, *Chartularium universitatis parisiensis* (Paris: Delalain, 1891), 2:1:215–16. Michael Bihl shows that the document must be dated between February 14 and May 3, 1318. See "Formulae et documenta e cancellaria Fr. Michaelis de Cesena, O.F.M.," *AFH* 23 (1930), 118–19.

17. *BF*, 5:134–35; Johannes XXII, *Extravagantes*, 198–204.

18. *BF*, 5:137–42.

19. See Chapter 4 of this volume.

20. For an excellent analysis of previous opinion, see Malcolm Lambert, "The Franciscan Crisis Under John XXII," *Franciscan Studies* 32 (1972): 123–43.

21. *Epistole*, 121–31. Angelo calls them *sacrilegi* who have received just punishment for their "depraved and stupid confidence in themselves and erroneous interpretation of the rule." He observes that division and schism leads to ignorance of the truth, error, and finally heresy if the error is pertinaciously defended.

22. *BF*, 5:233–34; Johannes XXII, *Extravagantes*, 228–29. The same thing is said in the opening sentence of *Quia nonnunquam*, in *BF*, 5:224–25; Johannes XXII, *Extravagantes*, 217–18.

23. I refer here to the extant polemical literature of the southern French spirituals and their opponents. Angelo Clareno (who in *Epistole*, 121 celebrates obedience as enthusiastically as John himself) does provide a rich discussion of that virtue and its relation to poverty in the course of his letters, although even here it must be noted that most of Angelo's letters were written after 1317.

24. *Liber chronicarum*, 536.

25. Ibid., 732–34.

26. Published in Mansi, *Stephani Baluzii Tutelensis Miscellanea*, 2:248–51.

27. The single theologian's judgment is found in MSS Paris, Bibl. Nat. lat. 3381A and Rome Vat. lat. 11906, fols. 63r–188v. See my discussion of it in "Exegetical Theory and Ecclesiastical Condemnation: The Case of Olivi's Apocalypse Commentary," in *Neue Richtungen in der Hoch- und Spätmittelalterlichen Bibelexegese*, ed. Robert Lerner and Elisabeth Müller-Luckner (Munich: R. Oldenbourg Verlag, 1996), 149–62. The commission report is in Mansi, *Stephani Baluzii Tutelensis Miscellanea*, 2:258–70.

28. Leo Amorós, "Series condemnationum et processuum," 509. Joseph Koch suggests that MS Florence, Bibl. Laur. Santa Croce Plut. 31 sin. cod. 3, 175rb–va, gives the first five articles condemned at the chapter, but there seems little evidence for this theory. See his "Der Prozess gegen die Postille Olivis zur Apokalypse," *Recherches de théologie ancienne et médiévale* 5 (1933): 302–15.

29. Published in Pou y Marti, *Visionarios*, 483–512. Manselli, *Spirituali e beghini*, 164–69 argues that the Catalan work was written after May 7, 1318, and that the judgment on it came in late 1318 or early 1319.

30. Published in Mansi, *Stephani Baluzii Tutelensis Miscellanea*, 2:258–70.

31. Ibid., 261.

32. Ibid., 262. See also 263. The recent fate of the Templars undoubtedly crossed their minds at this point.

33. See my comments in the next two chapters on Franciscan preaching at Narbonne ca. 1317. Manselli, *Spirituali e beghini*, 155–56 tries to minimize the impact of Olivian apocalyptic on the spirituals before 1318. However, if it was unimportant, it is hard to imagine why the pope, the inquisitor, and the order should have been so interested in suppressing it. In addition, we have seen that rebellious Italian spirituals in the 1290s were already apocalyptically oriented; we know that Boniface VIII commissoned Giles of Rome to refute Olivi's Apocalypse commentary; and we learn from Angelo Clareno, *Epistole*, 131 that as early as 1313 the Tuscan rebels justified their action by appealing to Olivi's writings. Saying this much is not equivalent to demonstrating that rebels in the 1290s were reading Olivi or that the 1313 rebels were appealing to his Apocalypse commentary. Nevertheless, the total mass of evidence suggests that Olivian apocalyptic thought in general—and his Apocalypse commentary in particular—appealed to any number of people well before 1318.

34. What follows is explored in much greater detail in *OPK*, chapters 8–11.

35. *Lectura*, 979. Olivi expects this prediction to be fulfilled *secundum quid* in the church militant, then *simpliciter* in the church triumphant.

36. Henricus Gandaviensis, *Summa quaestionum* (Paris: Iodicus Badius Ascensius, 1520), art. 8, q. 6, fols. 68r–69v.

37. See *OFP*, 163–72. For an opposing view, see Manselli, *Spirituali e beghini*, 154–55.

38. *Practica inquisitionis heretice pravitatis*, 287.

39. *Expositio regulae*, 233–34.

40. See the *Directorium inquisitorum*, t. 2, q. 26, p. 313, where the commentator, Francisco de

Pegna, notes that the Barcelona edition that he is discussing (the text of which is carried over into the Venice, 1595 edition) is defective at this point. He provides a fuller text based on other manuscripts, and it is his addition that contains this passage.

Chapter 10

1. J.-M. Vidal, *Bullaire de l'inquisition française* (Paris: Librairie Letouzey et Ané, 1913), 38–39.

2. It is cited in an anonymous document from the archives of the archbishop of Narbonne, published in Mansi, *Stephani Baluzii Tutelensis Miscellanea*, 2:271–72. The author says that he found the spirituals' words in a letter sent by Michel Le Moine and read by the author in 1318. He also says that the spirituals *transierunt ad gentes infideles.*

3. See Manselli, *Spirituali e beghini,* 154.

4. Botineau, "Les Tribulations de R. Barrau," 505.

5. CD 61:468r. I owe this citation to Sylvain Piron, "Marchands et confesseurs," 289–308. Piron points to the spirituals' role as confessors to the commercially oriented townspeople and indicates the connection between that role and Olivi's economic thought. On the theoretical nexus between Olivi's thought on Franciscan poverty and his economic thought, see Piron's "Voeu et contrat chez Pierre de Jean Olivi," *Cahiers du Centre de Recherches Historiques* 16 (1996): 43–56; see also Giacomo Todeschini's *Il prezzo della salvezza* (Rome: La Nuova Italia Scientifica, 1994) and his "Olivi e il *mercator* cristiano," 207–37.

6. Bernard Gui, *Practica inquisitionis,* 264 says that the laity were under suspicion as early as 1315 and seems to say that they were being convicted and burned from 1317 on; however, on 265, he speaks of laity condemned in 1318. Harold Lee, Marjorie Reeves, and Giulio Silano show that beguins in Catalonia were regarded with suspicion as early as 1312; see their *Western Mediterranean Prophecy* (Toronto: Pontifical Institute of Mediaeval Studies, 1989), 57–59. Nevertheless, the verbal processes from Languedoc contained in the Bibliothèque Nationale in Paris in the Collection Doat—as well as the ones published in Philippus a Limborch, *Historia inquisitionis cui subjungitur Liber sententiarum inquisitionis tholosanae* (Amsterdam: Henricus Wetstenius, 1692)—all suggest that the execution of lay supporters began well after the four spirituals were burned at Marseilles.

7. *Practica inquisitionis,* 264–87. Gui speaks of *beguini et beguinae,* but we will simplify by calling all of them, male and female, beguins.

8. In fact, we know a great deal about the situation in Catalonia. We know that Arnald of Villanova maintained in Barcelona a scriptorium that produced books for beguins, and that after his death in 1311 his influence continued to be felt. This was not entirely beneficial to the beguins, since thirteen of Arnald's works were condemned at Tarragona in 1316. In 1318, a council at Tarragona criticized the beguins and prohibited them from owning books. See Josep Perarnau, *Alia informatio beguinorum d'Arnau de Vilanova* (Barcelona: Facultat de Teologia de Barcelona, Seccio de Sant Pacia, 1978), and Robert Lerner, "Writing and Resistance," 186–204. After that point, the evidence is scanty when compared with that for southern France. But see also Agustín Rubio Vela and Mateu Rodrigo Lizondo, "Els beguins de València en el segle XIV: La seua casa-hospital i els seus llibres," in *Miscel·lània Sanchis Guarner,* edited by Antoni Ferrando (Barcelona: Publicacions de l'Abadia de Montserrat, 1992), 185–277, and the following by Josep Perarnau: "Noves dades sobre beguins de Girona," *Annals de l'institut d'estudis gironins* 25/1 (1979–80): 237–46; "Una altra carta de Guiu Terrena sobre el procés inquisitorial contra el francescà Fra Bernat Fuster," *Estudios franciscanos* 82 (1981): 383–92; "El bisbe de Barcelona Fra Bernat Oliver (1345–1346) i els framenors de Vilafranca del Penedès: Un episodi de la 'Qüestió Franciscana' a Catalunya," *Estudios franciscanos* 83 (1982): 277–306; "La butlla desconeguda de Joan XXII 'Ut vester religionis ager' (Avinyó, 19 de febrer de 1322) sobre l'examen dels aspirants al Terç Orde de St. Francesc," *Estudios franciscanos* 83 (1982): 307–10; "Opere di Fr. Petrus Johannis in processi catalane d'inquisizione della prima metà del XIV secolo," *AFH* 91 (1998): 505–16.

9. His process, published in Manselli, *Spirituali e beghini*, 302–6, says that he is from Montréal (as does another process in Limborch, *Liber sententiarum*, 311) and that he has been in the order for thirty-three years. If that is counting from October 1325, the date of his confession, we have ca. 1292. If it is counting from the date of his sentence in November 1328, we have ca. 1295, but this seems less likely. For fuller discussion of Raymond's chronology, see my "Raymond Déjean, Franciscan Renegade," *Franciscan Studies* 57 (1999): 57–78.

10. We will use "Déjean" simply because that is the way Jean Duvernoy rendered the name in *Spirituels et béguins du Midi* (Toulouse: Editions Privat, 1989), his French translation of Manselli's *Spirituali e beghini in Provenza*. Calling him Raymond Jean would follow the pattern long recommended in Olivi's case. See Chapter 3, n. 21 above.

11. His name appears among those summoned from Narbonne (*BF*, 5:118–20). Yet Jacquelline Sobiran, a resident of Carcassonne testifying before the inquisition in 1325, says that she used to confess to Raymond before the friars were cited to Avignon, and when he departed for the papal court he left some of his clothes with her (CD 28:211r–v). His own process simply says that he was one of those cited (Manselli, *Spirituali e beghini*, 302).

12. *BF*, 5:132–33 gives the names of those who were sent on to Michel Le Moine, and Raymond is not among them.

13. See, for example, CD 28:211v, 232v.

14. CD 28:207r.

15. Jacquelline Sobiran, who talked with Raymond after he became a fugitive, says (CD 28:212r) that he told her he had received the letter and feared imprisonment. His own confession simply says that he heard Michel was summoning his companions and forcing them to abjure heresy.

16. See CD 27:84v and 28:222v, for instance. Angelo, *Liber chronicarum*, 732–34 explicitly presents the spirituals at Avignon as renouncing opinions judged to be heretical and thus liable to condemnation as relapsed heretics, should they continue their protests.

17. On the possible connection with Alarassis Biasse, see my "Raymond Déjean."

18. CD 27:197v–198r.

19. Jacquelline Sobiran says that she later saw him at Carcassonne, though when he told her at Montréal that he intended to come, she begged him not to visit her (CD 28:212r). Raymond d'Antusan, described as from Cintegabelle, is accused of having received Raymond in his home (see Limborch, *Liber sententiarum*, 311). At Montpellier, he stayed with Na Prous Boneta and her sister, as we learn from Prous's sister Alisseta, from a friend named Alisseta or Alarassis who lived with them, and from another beguin, Ermessende La Grosse (CD 27:14v, 26v, 32r). Jean de Petra, another Montpellier beguin, invited him to dinner (CD 27:22r).

20. See the testimony of Pierre Tournemire in A. Germain, "Une Consultation inquisitoriale au XIVe siècle," *Publications de la Société Archéologique de Montpelier* 25 (1857): 334–38, where the trip is dated 1324.

21. CD 27:25r.

22. Raymond's process (Manselli, *Spirituali e beghini*, 305) simply says that he was captured in Gascony. Jean Orlach's process (CD 27:26r) explains the circumstances.

23. CD 27:93r.

24. The other three singled out for harsher sentences were clerics, but not friars.

25. Manselli, *Spirituali e beghini*, 305. Bernard was apparently a local hero in Montréal. A beguin named Flours describes how she stood in the place at Capestang where the beguins were burned and, finding there an iron ring with which they were bound, held it in her hand and showed devotion to it on account of Bernard Léon, whom she believed to have been burned there and whom she believed to be *sanctus* (CD 28:231r). Miracle, another beguin who visited and talked with Raymond at Montréal, says that he told her that the executed Bernard was saved (CD 28:191r–v). He said the same thing to still another beguin, Arnaude Mainie (CD 28:197r). Moreover, he told Miracle that just as a married woman could not be given another husband by the pope as long as the first husband lived, so he could not give a husband to a virgin who had vowed virginity (CD 28:191v).

26.   Claudia Florovsky, in her introduction to Hugh's *De finibus paupertatis*, labels him the father of the spirituals on precisely these grounds (see *AFH* 5 [1912], 279).

27.   See Chapter 3 of this volume.

28.   Inquisitorial records do not normally display this sort of reticence. One wonders if Raymond himself avoided using John's name.

29.   Gui, *Practica inquisitionis*, 281–82; May, "Confession of Prous Boneta," 12. In the passage that Raymond was reading, Olivi does anticipate a new Herod who will oppose Franciscan poverty. See *Lectura*, 407.

30.   See, for example, CD 28:206r, 214v, 221v–222r, 225v, 236v; Limborch, *Liber sententiarum*, 312, 316, 318, 330, 388.

31.   Raymond is obviously straining to find these accomplishments. "Maintenance of divine worship, attention to justice, love of honor and other things which are evident" seems at best notably generic and at worst very vague. The reference to taking away the Franciscans' procurators actually reverses the significance of what John did, as we will see.

32.   Miracle and Jacquelline Sobiran (CD 28:191v, 211v–212r) both say that he gave that explanation, although Jacquelline also says that it was due to the four brothers burned at Marseilles because they wanted to observe poverty. Jeanne Jouconne (CD 28:199v) seems to say that Raymond told her that he left the order only to do greater penance, but she also attributes it to the fact that "the others persecuted him because he wanted to observe poverty as Saint Francis did."

33.   CD 28:211v. The passage is doubly interesting in its suggestion that some French spirituals were moderate enough to have extra garments that they could leave behind.

34.   CD 28:231r. Flours also provides a *terminus ante quem* for Raymond's arrival, since her process notes that she had already testified in August 1322 and failed to tell the truth about these matters.

35.   CD 28:191r, 192r–v, 196v–197r, 198v, 199v.

36.   CD 28:223r; Manselli, *Spirituali e beghini*, 302.

37.   See, for example, the recollection of his views on Bernard Léon in note 25 above.

38.   Jeanne Léon (CD 28:192r–v) acknowledges having visited Raymond twice in Pierre Baron's home, confessed to him, and given him food and money, but insists that she had doubts about him because he was in secular attire and had no *socius*. "She sorrowed and still sorrows that she was thus deceived by him." Jeanne Jouconne (CD 28:199v) says that, "induced to do so by Pierre Baron," she visited Raymond in the latter's home and found him in secular clothes, "which displeased her."

39.   CD 27:85v–86r.

40.   For fuller discussion of the chronological problems, see Burr, "Raymond Déjean."

41.   Ibid.

42.   One might be tempted to adduce as further evidence that Raymond said that he dared not appear *before his brothers*, which would make more sense in the period just before April 1317 (when the spirituals were simply defying the order) than afterward, when they also had the pope, the inquisition, and the law to avoid. Raymond seems to have had a special fear of the community, though. He told his nephew (CD 28:198r) that he would rather be in the inquisitors' hands than in those of his brothers.

43.   Limborch, *Liber sententiarum*, 325–29. Pierre's confession is one of a group of thirteen, some undated and some dated 1321. Another of the undated ones is that of Marie de Serra, which will be considered later. Pierre, Marie, and some of the confessions dated 1321 all refer to the May 1318 execution of the four spiritual Franciscans at Marseilles as having taken place *four years earlier*. The confessions dated 1321 are all from before Easter, so it was probably 1321 by their reckoning and 1322 by ours. In fact, two confessions, including Marie's (CD 28:313, 314, 318), refer to executions that, according to Richard Emery, *Heresy and Inquisition in Narbonne* (New York: AMS Press, 1967), 132–33, occurred on February 28, 1322. On Pierre, see my "Did

the Béguins Understand Olivi?" in *Pierre de Jean Olivi (1248–1298)*, ed. Boureau and Piron, 309–18.

44. Limborch, *Liber sententiarum*, 331–32.

45. For varieties of interpretation, see Manselli, *Spirituali e beghini*, 321, 326; Limborch, *Liber sententiarum*, 301, 302, 306, 308, 316, 318, 329.

46. Gui, *Practica inquisitionis*, 287. See also the variant versions noted by me in *OFP*, 109–10 and 130 n. 18.

47. Limborch, *Liber sententiarum*, 329. Reference to washing his hands is also found in another process (308).

48. For example, at Montpellier, as attested in CD 27:21v. In 1325, according to witnesses, its observance included a meal, after which Pierre Tournemire, a priest and a beguin, read from Olivi's Apocalypse commentary. See A. Germain, "Une Consultation inquisitoriale," 333–34.

49. Limborch, *Liber sententiarum*, 319.

50. Ibid., 326.

51. Process in CD 28:216v–219v, edited in Manselli, *Spirituali e beghini*, 319–21. (French translation in Manselli, *Spirituels*, 299–301.)

52. The sentence of March 1, 1327, which includes her process, contains a total of thirty-five processes. Two are undated, one is from 1323, twenty-six from 1325, four from 1325–26, and two from 1326.

53. Gui, *Practica inquisitionis*, 286–87.

54. Her process is found in CD 27:216v–219v. The processes of those to be given lighter sentences, i.e., wearing crosses and going on pilgrimages, run from 189v–203v, and the processes of those to be imprisoned begin at that point.

55. CD 27:4v.

56. The text of Prous's verbal process is found in CD 27, fols. 51v–79v. It was edited by William May in "Confession of Prous Boneta," 4–30. The text of her sentence is in CD 27:95r–96v. It was edited by Henry Charles Lea, *History of the Inquisition of the Middle Ages* (New York: Harbor Press, 1955), 3:653–54.

Recent secondary material on Prous includes Barbara Newman, *From Virile Woman to WomanChrist* (Philadelphia: University of Pennsylvania Press, 1995), chapter 6; Claudia Rattazzi Papka, "Fictions of Judgment: The Apocalyptic 'I' in the Fourteenth Century" (Ph.D. diss., Columbia University, 1996), chapter 2; Daniela Müller, "Der Prozess gegen Prous Boneta," in *Ius et Historia: Festgabe für Rudolf Weigand zu seinem 60. Geburtstag*, ed. Norbert Hühl (Würzburg: Echter, 1989), 199–221; Daniela Müller, "Les Béguines," *Heresis* 13–14 (1989): 351–89; Michèle Fournié, "Deux femmes dans l'erreur: Rixende de Narbonne et Prous Boneta de Montpellier," *Perspectives médiévales* 21 (1995): 7–17; and Louisa Burnham, "The Visionary Authority of Na Prous Boneta," in *Pierre de Jean Olivi (1248–1298)*, ed. Boureau and Piron, 319–39. I deal with Prous in "Olivi, Prous, and the Separation of Apocalypse from Eschatology," in *That Others May Know and Love*, ed. Michael Cusato and F. Edward Coughlin (St. Bonaventure, N.Y.: Franciscan Institute, 1997), 285–304, and in "Na Prous Boneta and Olivi," *Collectanea franciscana* 67 (1997): 277–300.

57. May, "Confession of Prous Boneta," 10–11. Christ may have told her this substantially later, since she was probably only eight or nine at the time. Her testimony begins "Naprous Boneta, daughter of Durand Boneta of Saint-Michel de la Cadière in the diocese of Nîmes, an inhabitant of Montpellier since the age of seven." Her sister Alisseta's (dated November 1325) begins, "Alisseta Boneta, daughter of Durand Boneta of Saint-Michel de la Cadière in the diocese of Nîmes, who has been an inhabitant of Montpellier for twenty-two years" (CD 27:26r). Unless Alisseta was born in Montpellier, that would make Prous around twenty-nine in 1325.

58. Ibid., 7–8, 26.

59. Ibid., 24.

60. Ibid., 16.

61. Ibid., 12, 20.

62. *OPK*, 204.

63. CD 27:14v.

64. Manselli, *Spirituali e beghini*, 305.

65. The sister mentions Raymond's stay at CD 27:26v, the friend at 32r, and Ermessende at 14v.

66. *OPK*, 222–25.

67. Perarnau, "Opere di Fr. Petrus Johannis," 509.

68. May, "Confession of Prous Boneta," 20.

69. Ibid., 23.

70. The first two parts of the question were not simply informational. Even if they had not believed Prous, beguins would still be guilty if they heard clearly heretical beliefs without reporting them.

71. Manselli, *Spirituali e beghini*, 305.

72. CD 27:16v–17r.

73. CD 27:14v–15v.

74. CD 27:25v. He also visited the beguins burned at Lunel, and says that he thought them good people who had lived a good life and made a good end.

75. CD 27:30r–32r.

76. CD 27:26v–27r.

77. CD 27:93r.

78. CD 27:194v.

79. CD 27:225r, 228r. Whether she was a sister or not, that she was a family member seems almost certain, since the panel of experts that recommended the sentence described her as from Saint-Michel de la Cadière yet living in Montpellier, precisely the way Na Prous is described in her confession. Celestin Douais, *L'Inquisition* (Paris: Librairie Plon, 1906), 350.

80. CD 28:226v–228r.

81. CD 28:228r: "Dicens quod citius dixisset veritatem nisi fuisset Naprous Boneta detenta in muro prope ipsam quae a confitendo retraxit eandem."

82. CD 28:230v–231r: "Negavitque multotiens veritatem contra proprium iuramentum quam postea recognovit. Inductus fuit primo, ut asserit, ad negandum praedictam per Naprous Boneta de Montepessulliano detentam in muro." Burnham, "Visionary Authority," 336–37 suggests two more cases, Guillaume Verrier and Guillaume Serralier. The first recanted his beguin beliefs and then reasserted them. The second did the same, but even more dramatically, shouting out his beguin convictions before the crowd just as he was about to be absolved and sentenced. Burnham's argument is based largely on the fact that Prous would have been in the prison at Carcassonne while both men were there, and that according to the testimony of Prous's sister, Alisseta, both had often dined in their home. While it is possible that Prous was instrumental in their change of heart, it is hardly certain. Unlike the other two who acknowledged Prous's influence, Verrier and Serralier were themselves major figures in the movement and deeply committed to it. Whatever the specific conditions that led to their recantations, it would be understandable if, once they had acquiesced and the pressure was off, they should have felt uncomfortable with their choice and returned to their original position.

Chapter 11

1. Pou y Marti, *Visionarios*, 100–101, 155–56; Perarnau, *Alia informatio*, 107–44. In the latter case, the main connection was not with Olivi but with Arnald of Villanova.

2. See the cases in Limborch, *Liber sententiarum*, 298–333. On the manuscript of Gui's register, see James Given, *Inquisition and Medieval Society* (Ithaca: Cornell University Press, 1997), chapter 1.

3. "Culte et rayonnement," 302. Priests might be tertiaries, however. For example, see

Nicholas Eymerich, *Directorium inquisitorum* (Rome: In Aedibus Populi Romani, 1585), 283; Pou y Marti, *Visionarios*, 196–98.

4. We do know of some noble involvement. J.-M. Vidal, "Procès d'inquisition contre Adhémar de Mosset," *Revue d'histoire de l'église de France* 1 (1910): 555–89, 682–89, 711–25 presents the inquisitorial process launched against a Roussillonnais noble. Adhémar also moved in the orbit of another noble supporter of the spirituals, Philip of Majorca, whom we will discuss later. These two were themselves active in the towns, however. Of course, this predominance of towns-people in the processes may also be influenced by the fact that inquisitorial attention could most effectively be pointed in that direction.

5. For these and most of the following statistics, I am dependent on Biget, "Culte et rayonnement," 300–305.

6. Of the forty-four whose marital state we know, nineteen were married, seven were wid-ows, and eighteen were unmarried. Biget suggests that the high percentage is due to the popu-larity of the Franciscan third order among women, but, considering the family nature of beguin involvement, one wonders whether the figure of 37 percent is high enough to need such an explanation.

7. Manselli, *Spirituali e beghini*, 328–45.

8. May, "Confession of Prous Boneta," 29: "Item dixit quod omni die et nocte et omni hora vidit Deum in spiritu, et numquam ab ea recedit."

9. See Biget, "Culte et rayonnement," 303–4; Richard Emery, *Heresy and Inquisition in Narbonne*, 166.

10. Limborch, *Liber sententiarum*, 313.

11. Ibid., 385.

12. An anonymous document that we can date between November 1324 and February 1326 says that eighty-two had been executed by that date. See MS Paris, Bibl. Nat. lat. 4190, 40r. Biget observes, however, that after 1322 the number of executions apparently decreased (see "Culte et rayonnement," 297).

13. CD 28:8–37.

14. Published by Douais, *L'Inquisition*, 289–94.

15. One could be assigned single or double crosses and more or fewer pilgrimages.

16. A panel advising the inquisitor Jean de Prat on August 9, 1324, advised that two defen-dants be considered *fautores* and eleven be judged *credentes*. All the latter were to be given per-petual imprisonment. On February 22, 1325, a remarkable fifty-four counselors advising Jean de Prat suggested that one person be given crosses and pilgrimages, while six should be sen-tenced to prison and four more sent there until they had done a more thorough job of con-fessing. One other person was held over until it was determined with certainty whether he had abjured heresy earlier, and one person was judged not guilty of heresy at all (Douais, *L'Inquisition*, 294–300, 307–13).

17. See, for example, F. Bock, "I processi di Giovanni XXII contro i ghibellini delle Marche," *Bulletino dell'Istituto Storico Italiano per il Medio Evo e Archivio Muratoriano* 57 (1941): 19–70; Stefano Brufani, *Eresia di un ribelle al tempo di Giovanni XXII* (Florence: La Nuova Italia, 1989).

18. Statements on the four are often carefully nuanced. Raymond says (Manselli, *Spirituali e beghini*, 304) that he never *totally* believed them to be martyrs. Ermessende says (CD 27:15v) that when she was first told that they were martyrs, she was stunned, but after thinking it over, she did not consent to believe it. Sybil says (CD 27:17r–18r) that after hearing it, she sometimes believed it, but more often did not. Jacquelline Sobiran says (CD 28:212r) that when she first heard of their condemnation, she was filled with wonder at how such a great light should suddenly be turned into smoke, but she did not believe that they were unjustly condemned or *sancti* and actually argued with another beguin when the beguin said that they were. Yet here, as elsewhere, a peculiar vagueness pervades her confession, leading the inquisitors to conclude that she was not telling the whole truth. Galharda says (CD 28:125r–v) that she heard it and does

not know whether she believed it. Pierre Esperendieu flatly says (Manselli, *Spirituali e beghini*, 308) that he did not. The majority of beguins say that they believed it, though. Guillerma says (CD 28:227v) that of all those burned, she believed most in the four burned at Marseilles. One suspects many others did likewise.

19.   Bernard de na Jacma of Belpech speaks of beguins bringing bones of those burned at Lunel; Raymond d'Antusan of Cintegabelle says that he saw in someone's home the head and other body parts of a certain woman burned at Lunel; Bernarda, his wife, reports hearing her husband speak devoutly of this experience, and specifies that he saw the relics at Narbonne. See Limborch, *Liber senteniarum*, 307, 310, 313.

20.   Ibid., 307, 310, 320; Manselli, *Spirituali e beghini*, 327; CD 27:27v.

21.   Limborch, *Liber sententiarum*, 310.

22.   He is mentioned there by Berenger Jaoul, who simply states that other beguins informed him of Olivi's apocalyptic prophecies. Manselli, *Spirituali e beghini*, 313.

23.   See Chapter 4.

24.   Limborch, *Liber sententiarum*, 308 (with reservations), 312, 316, 318, 330, 388; CD 28:206v, 214v, 220v, 225v, 236r (prepares way for Antichrist); Manselli, *Spirituali e beghini*, 322–23, 325.

25.   Limborch, *Liber sententiarum*, 307, 328.

26.   Ibid., 309, 317, 323.

27.   Ibid., 309, 319, 326, 330; Manselli, *Spirituali e beghini*, 160–65.

28.   Robert Lerner observes as much in his introduction to Johannes de Rupescissa, *Liber secretorum eventuum* (Fribourg: Editions Universitaires, 1994), 61.

29.   See ibid., 138–39, 152–217, and Lerner's introduction, 54–63.

30.   Orioli, *Venit*, 53, 120–26, 226, and elsewhere.

31.   For another prediction concerning the threefold division, see Limborch, *Liber sententiarum*, 303.

32.   On Philip, see J.-M. Vidal, "Un Ascète de sang royal, Philippe de Majorque," *Revue des questiones historiques* 45 (1910): 361–403.

33.   See Vidal, "Procès," 555–89, 682–99, 711–24. Even so, Adhémar probably was not convicted.

34.   Limborch, *Historia*, 308. The same idea is repeated in the investigation concerning Adhémar de Mosset. Vidal, "Procès," 579.

35.   See *OPK*, chapter 7.

36.   Limborch, *Historia*, 319–20, 330, 388.

37.   Prous is a special case. I have considered her testimony in "Olivi, Prous, and the Separation of Apocalypse from Eschatology," and especially in "Na Prous Boneta and Olivi," both of which deal explicitly with the similarities and differences between the two.

38.   Remember, too, the decision of Prous's and Alisseta's housemate to see just one executed beguin as a heretic and the rest as martyrs.

39.   Manselli, *Spirituali e beghini*, 340.

40.   Ibid., 311–12.

41.   Orwell, *1984* (New York: Harcourt, Brace and Company, 1949), 294–95.

42.   CD 28:233v–35v.

43.   CD 27:79v–82r and 97r–98r. In both Jacquelline's and Manenta's cases, their retrials also involved things that they had done before their first processes but failed to include in their confessions.

44.   Limborch, *Liber sententiarum*, 310–12.

45.   Even to the captured beguins, perhaps. The process goes on to say that he not only accompanied them but also dined with them on the way.

46.   Limborch, *Liber sententiarum*, 313–14.

47.   Ibid., 381–86.

48.   Perhaps Guillaume is saying that while these fugitives supported the cause, they

were not actually third-order Franciscans. Yet we know that Pierre Tort, one of the fugitives, actually was in the third order.

49. Ibid., 331–32, 381–83.

50. See Lee, Reeves, and Silano, *Western Mediterranean Prophecy*. Pou y Marti, *Visionarios*, 200–206 describes the trial of Jaime Just and his associates in 1353, though it represents the continuation of an investigation launched more than a decade earlier.

Chapter 12

1. *Liber chronicarum*, 752–56. Ubertino was not the only spiritual transferred to the Benedictines.

2. *Nicolaus Minorita: Chronica* (St. Bonaventure, N.Y.: Franciscan Institute, 1996), 62–63.

3. See Andrea Tabarroni, *Paupertas Christi et apostolorum* (Rome: Istituto Storico Italiano per il Medio Evo, 1990). Malcolm Lambert, *Franciscan Poverty*, chapter 10 provides a useful overview of the controversy.

4. For two striking examples of earlier Franciscan-Dominican tension, see *OFP*, 151–53.

5. See Chapter 3 above. See also *OFP*, 154.

6. Koch, "Der Prozess," 302–15.

7. For a lengthier discussion of Koch's theory, see *OPK*, 244–47 (and, more generally, chaps. 9–10 of that volume).

8. See *OPK*, 224–25.

9. Ibid., 232–33. The writer is the same theologian who calls the first statement heretical.

10. Vat. lat. 3740, which contains marginal annotations in John's own hand. See Annaliese Maier, "Annotazioni autografe di Giovanni XXII in Codici Vaticani," *Rivista di storia della chiesa in Italia* 6 (1952): 317–31; Tabarroni, *Paupertas Christi*, 22 n. 15.

11. For bibliography, see Charles Davis, *Ubertino da Casale and His Conception of "Altissima Paupertas"* (Spoleto: Centro Italiano di Studi sull'Alto Medioevo, 1984), 4 n. 15.

12. Published by Johannes Schlageter in *Das Heil der Armen und das Verderben der Reichen* (Werl/Westfalen: Dietrich-Coelde-Verlag, 1989).

13. See Olivi, *De perfectione evangelica*, q. 8, in Schlageter, *Das Heil der Armen*, 181–82; see also *De perfectione evangelica*, q. 9, in *De usu paupere*, 51–52.

14. See *OFP*, 57–60.

15. For an excellent summary, with references, see Davis, *Ubertino da Casale*, 9–11.

16. For bibliography, see ibid., 10–11.

17. Ibid., 11–13.

18. *Tractatus de altissima paupertate Christi et apostolorum eius et virorum apostolicorum*. For bibliographical data, see Davis, *Ubertino da Casale*, 15–16.

19. The summary is edited by Davis in *Ubertino da Casale*, 43–56. In the only manuscript, the summary is at the beginning, but seems to belong at the end.

20. Tierney, *Origins of Papal Infallibility*. But also see Bartoli, "Olivi et le pouvoir du pape."

21. See Chapter 4 above.

22. See his bull *Quia vir reprobus*, in *BF*, 5:447–48.

23. For the following, see the excellent summary in Lambert, *Franciscan Poverty*, 225–42, and (most recently) Nicolaus Minorita, *Nicolaus Minorita: Chronica*.

24. *BF*, 5:224–25; *Extravagantes*, 217–18.

25. *BF*, 5:234–35; Mansi, *Stephani Baluzii Tutelensis Miscellanea*, 3:208–11.

26. *Extravagantes*, 228–54.

27. Ibid., 255–57.

28. Thus Lambert, *Franciscan Poverty*, 261–62 (although, as Lambert recognizes, the contradiction was there by implication).

29. See the text and Ehrle's comments in *Archiv*, 3:540–52.

30. Angelo Mercati, "Frate Francesco Bartoli d'Assisi Michelista e la sua ritrattazione," *AFH* 20 (1927), 272, 288; Nicholas Glassberger, *Chronica*, *AF* 2:135.

31. For the citations of the above letters and chronicles, see Decima Douie, *Nature and the Effect*, 131–32, and von Auw, *Angelo Clareno*, 162–65.

Chapter 13

1. *Epistole*, 239–53. See Chapter 7 above; see also Potestà, *Angelo Clareno*, 123–28.

2. *Epistole*, 253. He makes the same request on 244–45.

3. Ibid., 68–81. See Potestà, *Angelo Clareno*, 128–37, who dates the letter in this period.

4. *Epistole*, 72.

5. Remember that in their farewell letter, the renegade French spirituals claimed to leave not the order but the walls, not the habit but the cloth, not the faith but its externalities. Cf. Mansi, *Stephani Baluzii Tutelensis Miscellanea*, 271–72.

6. Potestà, *Angelo Clareno*, 134.

7. *Epistole*, 74–75, 78. For the three good brothers, see *Scripta Leonis*, 86 and II Celano, 158.

8. On this theme in Conrad of Offida, Olivi, and Ubertino da Casale, see my *OPK*, 121–24.

9. See letters 3 and 31 as discussed by Potestà, *Angelo Clareno*, 149–51.

10. See Giampaolo Tognetti, "I fraticelli, il principio di povertà e i secolari," *Bulletino dell'Istituto Storico Italiano per il Medio Evo e Archivio Muratoriano* 90 (1982–83): 77–145 for its use by Jacopone da Todi, Ubertino da Casale, Angelo Clareno, Paul of Venice, and Raymond of Fronsac. On the ambiguities connected with its use, see Raffaele Pazzelli, "Movimenti e congregazioni con la regola di Niccolò IV," in *La "Supra montem" di Niccolò IV*, ed. Pazzelli and Temperini, 256–57.

11. On Bartolomeo, see von Auw, *Angelo Clareno*, 149–51. The area was largely dominated by the Colonna. See ibid., 79, 149–50.

12. See *Expositio regulae*, 45–48, where he cites still another prophecy by Francis of a pope who will be either heretical or not canonically elected, but fails to say whether he thinks the current pontiff is the pope in question.

13. There is room for some ambiguity. *Liber chronicarum*, 462 describes Jerome of Ascoli as "a gentle man, modest enough, slow to anger or inflict injury, but remiss and tepid when it came to promoting the good." Note, too, the comment on Haimo of Faversham (330).

14. See ibid., 628, where he notes that the seven tribulations of the order are to be completed within the sixth period of the church; the implicit reference at 670, which alludes to the fulfillment of the sixth period in the seventh; or the explicit one at 682–84, which speaks of the contest between Francis and the serpent in the sixth period. Angelo also alludes to the seven periods in his letters. See *Epistole*, 164–66, where he refers to *septem tempora*. In ibid., 234 he alludes to the sevenfold pattern again (this time more indirectly) when he says that neither Jews, Gentiles, heretics, Saracens, nor the Antichrist can extinguish the light of Christ. In speaking of the sixth period, Angelo occasionally links Dominic's name with Francis's. See *Liber chronicarum*, 468, 648, 684; see also *Epistole*, 165, where they are strikingly characterized as "quasi unus homo ex corpore et anima subsistens et invicem sicut corpus et anima adversantes." Angelo notes, too, that vain envy has destroyed the original harmony between the two orders (ibid., 221).

15. See Angelo's description of a vision that appeared to Saint Francis (*Liber chronicarum*, 48–52). He saw an angel with a head of gold, arms and chest of silver, midsection of brass, legs of iron, and feet of clay. The angel then explained in brutal detail how the order would proceed from gold to clay over the following century. The vision is an adaptation of Dan. 2:32–45. The appearance of the image in various Franciscan documents has been studied by Edith Pásztor, "S. Francesco e l'espansione del francescanesimo: Coscienza storica e problemi emergenti," in

Il francescanesimo in Lombardia. Storia e arte (Milano: Silvana, 1983), 9–16, and more recently by Felice Accrocca, "Angelo Clareno: Riflessioni e nuove ricerche," *Collectanea franciscana* 62 (1992): 311–36.

16. See *OPK*, chapter 2.

17. On his double Antichrist, see ibid., chapter 6.

18. *Liber chronicarum*, 270, 542, 624. He also uses the adjective *antichristianus* three times (638, 648, 686).

19. E.g., ibid., 680–82.

20. See *Epistole*, 164; 362, part of a letter in Italian to Giacomo da Foligno (note that his use of the vulgar tongue enables us to be quite specific about the article); and 264.

21. Ibid., 37–38.

22. Ibid., 164–65, 329. Another case: Angelo says that he who fears and loves only God could not be defeated by Dioclitian or Antichrist, which probably qualifies as yet another reference to a specific future figure despite its lack of explicit future reference (265).

23. See, for example, ibid., 193 and 198, both of which show the centrality of Franciscan problems in the victory of the seventh period.

24. There are those who affirm it and those who deny it. Among the affirmers are Lydia von Auw (*Angelo Clareno*, 224 and elsewhere) and, more recently, Ronald Musto. See his "Franciscan Joachimism at the Court of Naples, 1309–1345: A New Appraisal," *AFH* 90 (1997): 419–86. For a denial, see especially Gian Luca Potestà, *Angelo Clareno*. Felice Accrocca has written widely and effectively on Angelo, but has not addressed this issue. His review article on Potestà's book, "Angelo Clareno: Riflessioni e nuove ricerche," begins by identifying the question as one of the central problems in research on Angelo, but does not come to terms with Potestà's discussion of it.

25. See my *OPK*, chapter 2.

26. We know somewhat more about Gerard, thanks to the process against him. His new "Eternal Gospel" spotlighted three authentic Joachite works (the *Liber de concordia, Expositio super apocalypsim*, and *Psalterium decem chordarum*) built on Joachim's threefold division of history, and included *concordia* in some sense that we cannot adequately define. But according to Salimbene, he also prized the pseudo-Joachite commentary on Jeremiah, and the process suggests that his reading of Joachim was skewed enough to allow a belief that the third age would involve supercession of both Old and New Testaments by a new body of scripture, consisting of the aforementioned three authentic Joachite works. For discussion and bibliography, see my *OPK*, 14–21.

27. E.g., *Epistole*, 165, where Francis and Dominic are sent to prepare the way, just as John the Baptist was.

28. E.g., *Liber chronicarum*, 670: "Misericordiae fontem aperiet parvulis, et gratis odientes et impugnantes iustitiam legis eius a longe respiciens in sex temporum revolutionibus seminata, et septima suorum seminum fructus eos recipere pie discernet, ut temporum vices considerent et distinguant, quibus retrogrado motu a caelestibus ad terrena, a summis ad ima, ab incorruptibilibus ad corruptibilia et a perpetuis ad transeuntia et temporalia sunt conversi."

29. See ibid., 680: "Nota secunda maris secundi saeculi meta, aeris initia tertia rota ponit, stat proles virginea, fulget resurrectio prima, vetera transibunt" (a hard passage to decipher); see also *Epistole*, 164–66, where he refers to *septem tempora* and shows how Elijah, Jeremiah, and John the Baptist are spiritually present in them. Tempting as it might be to see this passage as a reflection of the Joachite threefold pattern of history (particularly since he speaks of Elijah as *Spiritus Sancti personam figurans*), Angelo gives no indication that he is thinking in these terms. Other cases cited by Musto, "Franciscan Joachimism," seem less promising. At *Epistole*, 151–52, where Musto reads Angelo as "using yet another Joachite concordance, setting up a threefold progression from Moses to Christ to the Spirituals," I read Angelo as saying that just as the church is more worthy than the synagogue and Christ than Moses, so we are more obligated to obey the prelates of the church, however sinful they may be. At *Epistole*, 297–99, which Musto says deals with "a threefold process of concordances and fulfillments," Angelo actually says that the church is to be renewed *tripliciter in tribus temporibus*. He does not elaborate, but he seems to be thinking of

Christ, Francis, and the coming renewal. In all these cases, to the extent that we are dealing with Joachism at all, we seem to be encountering a casual, somewhat opportunistic use of him.

30. See Musto, "Franciscan Joachimism," 428–29, 445–46, where he makes a case for Angelo's use of Joachite concordances. Musto is certainly right in seeing a concordance between the Old and New Testaments at *Epistole*, 165. Other examples cited by him are more problematic. At *Epistole*, 101–2 Angelo uses the word *concordare* twice, but on the first occasion, he is simply saying that he and the recipient of the letter agree on the issue at hand. On the other occasion, while considering the various numbers in Dan. 8–12, Angelo says that they have various beginnings and endings according to various mysteries, so that the various temporal patterns found in the Old and New Testaments should agree *(concordent)*—a thought that, though not un-Joachite, stops well short of affirming Joachite concordances in their full sense. See also the examples cited in note 29 above.

31. *Liber chronicarum*, 470.

32. See Potestà, *Angelo Clareno*, 204–7.

33. *Expositio regulae*, 227.

34. *Liber chronicarum*, 412–16. For the Salimbene references to John, see my *OPK*, 7–14.

35. For Salimbene on Gerard, see *OPK*, 14–21.

36. *Liber chronicarum*, 446–50. Angelo describes Gerard as presenting brilliant, unanswerable arguments.

37. Ibid., 380–82, 416.

38. See Chapter 4 of this volume.

39. *Epistole*, 359–60. Note that in *Liber chronicarum*, 228–32, Angelo—echoing the Leo sources (see Chap. 2 of this volume)—has Francis deny that his own leadership was ever based on juridical authority.

40. Angelo, *Epistole*, 359–60.

41. *Angelo Clareno*, 51.

42. Von Auw notes (*Epistole*, 354) that they may have been influenced not only by early Franciscan tradition but by Greek monasticism as well.

43. Ibid., 218.

44. Ibid., 179.

45. Ibid., 143.

46. Ibid., 150–51.

47. Ibid., 221.

48. Kevin Madigan, "Peter Olivi's *Lectura super Matthaeum* in Medieval Exegetical Context" (Ph.D. diss., University of Chicago, 1992), shows how Olivi brought to his exegesis of Matthew an apocalyptic sense informed by his understanding of Revelation, despite the fact that his commentary on the former antedates his commentary on the latter by two decades.

49. Parallels in Mk. 13 and Lk. 21, though Angelo is following Matthew. In his letters, Angelo cites Matt. 24 alone more often than he cites the entire Book of Revelation.

50. *Epistole*, 150.

51. Frugoni, *Celestiniana*, 163–64.

52. *Angelo Clareno*, 242. He notes, among other things, that later *fraticelli* actually did refer the prophecy to John.

53. *Epistole*, 151.

54. Ibid., 15.

55. This and the following quotation are from ibid., 14.

56. Ibid., 338, 45.

57. Ibid., 57–67. The date is that suggested by von Auw, *Epistole*, 257 and Potestà, *Angelo Clareno*, 219. The letter itself is undated.

58. Ps. 118:126 (Vulgate), 119:126 (New American Bible).

59. Acts 5:29.

60. *Epistole*, 265.

61. Ibid., 37–38. The recipients and date are not given.

62. The basic thought here is repeated throughout Angelo's letters: Our real problem is not what others may do to us but the nature of our basic spiritual orientation. He tells his colleagues in ibid., 17, "quod nemo potest nisi a semetipso offendi et quod causa omnium malorum preteritorum, presentium et futurorum et temporalium et spiritualium et eternorum fuit et est et semper erit non recipere et non habere caritatem veritatis."

63. Ibid., 148; 179; 208 (letter from June 1329); 13 (von Auw dates the letter between 1318 and 1323, a date that seems justified by the contents).

64. Ibid., 149, 150ff.

65. Ibid., 223–24.

66. Note that Angelo offers a precedent for this behavior in *Liber chronicarum*, 310–14 by telling how Bernard of Quintavalle, in accordance with the advice of both the gospel and Francis, fled from Elias's wrath by staying for two years in a mountain hermitage.

67. *Liber chronicarum*, 762–63. Boccali's edition says *ac tributis* rather than *attributis*, but the latter reading is possible and makes better sense. It is, in fact, the reading chosen by previous editors.

68. Ibid., 628–30, 644. On 628–30, Angelo confuses the matter by saying that the period will end around the close of Pope Boniface's seventh year in office, but that too makes sense if we assume that he really meant Pope John XXII.

69. *Angelo Clareno*, 226: "une sorte de trêve." Yet on p. 227, von Auw notes, "Après 1331, Angelo espérait un changement favorable."

70. *Liber chronicarum*, 632.

71. Angelo says as much at ibid., 628: "medio cursu praecedentis tribulationis, sequentis initia inchoantur."

72. *Angelo Clareno*, 209. The break between pope and Franciscan leaders is given little attention, Potestà suggests, since "nella periodizzazione proposta essa si trovi a segnare lo spartiacque fra sesta e settima tribolazione." On p. 211, Potestà says explicitly that, starting with the break between pope and order in 1322, the sixth and seventh periods run concurrently for nine years. Thus 1330 witnesses not the beginning of the new age, but the point at which the seventh tribulation goes on without the sixth (see p. 212).

73. *Liber chronicarum*, 682.

74. Ibid., 670, where the periods of church history are referred to as *temporum revolutionibus*.

75. *Epistole*, 204: "Iam fere sunt anni XL elapsi quod Pater misericordiarum et luminum decreverat in homine Dei P[etro] ponere spiritum fundatoris, ideo subesse, sequi et conformare me ei tanquam nunctio signato primi lapidis angularis Francisco, integre et cordaliter amo. Sed post annos quasi LX cum contradictionibus et pressuris in quibus ferventer concupivi videre reformationis Christi vite principia, Benjamin ortum cum doloribus et morte matris conspicio, et in divisione nunc presenti, previsa olim et prophetata, aorosia Pentapolitas percussos et quasi in nocte, ita et in meridie querere hostium et palpare et non invenire video." Von Auw dates the letter between 1334 and 1337, Ronald Musto in 1330. Potestà, while dating it around 1334, agrees with von Auw that it was probably written from the kingdom of Naples. *Liber chronicarum*, 102, refers to "hic Beniaminus Franciscus." Thus for Angelo's *Chronicon* as for Eliot's *Four Quartets*, our end is in our beginning.

76. *Liber chronicarum*, 686.

77. See Joachim, *Liber de concordia novi ac veteris testamenti*, IV, 1, 3, ed. E. R. Daniel (Philadelphia: American Philosophical Society, 1983), 322, where Rachel is identified with the spiritual church; see also *Liber concordiae novi ac veteris testamenti*, V, 49 (Venice, 1519; reproduction, Frankfurt am Main: Minerva, 1983), 84vb, where Benjamin's birth is linked with that of a new spiritual order. For Olivi, see *Lectura super Mattheum*, MS Vat. lat. 10900, 27va, where Rachel is the contemplative church, mother of spiritual children, and Benjamin is "superexcessum contemplativi status

seu cetum extaticorum virorum." Ubertino, *Arbor vitae*, 1:425 identifies Benjamin with Francis, as does Angelo, *Liber chronicarum*, 102. On Bonaventure, see Joseph Ratzinger, *Theology of History in St. Bonaventure*, 42 and 186.

78. *Liber chronicarum*, 422–34.

79. E.g., *Epistole*, 72, examined earlier in this chapter.

80. Ibid., 181–83. For historical background, see Lydia von Auw, *Angelo Clareno*, 172–73; Potestà, *Angelo Clareno*, 224–25. During the 1332 process against Adhémar, the king of Majorca testified that he had heard Adhémar say that he confessed the execution to Angelo and was told by him, "Go, you are absolved before God and are not excommunicated before him." The passage seems to suggest a personal interview, which would be hard to imagine; nevertheless, it supports the idea that the letter to Philip was directed at Adhémar's case.

81. *Le osservanze francescane*, 140 and 312–13.

82. See ibid., 297–98; Livarius Oliger, "Documenta inedita," *AFH* 6 (1913), 267–69.

83. *BF,* 5:565–68.

84. L. Fumi, "Eretici e ribelli nell'Umbria dal 1320 al 1330 studiati su documenti inediti dell'Archivio segreto Vaticano," *Bollettino della R. Deputazione di storia patria per l'Umbria* 3 (1897), 420. The testimonies are published on pp. 412–22 of Fumi's mammoth article and are republished in Renzo Mosti, "L'eresia dei 'fraticelli' nel territorio di Tivoli," *Atti e memorie della Società Tiburtina di Storia e d'Arte* 38 (1965): 103–10. On this and the following, see Potestà, *Angelo Clareno*, chapter 12.

85. Fumi, "Eretici," 415.

86. *Angelo Clareno*, 283. For bibliography, see ibid., 281.

87. Fumi, "Eretici," 414–15, 420. Nothing that has survived corresponds to it, although we do have another seal used by Angelo during the same period. See Livarius Oliger, "De sigillo fr. Angeli Clareni," *Antonianum* 12 (1937): 61–64.

88. Fumi, "Eretici," 413–14. Musto contends that King Robert and Queen Sancia of Naples actually supported Philip's election (see "Queen Sancia of Naples," 197, 201).

89. Fumi, "Eretici," 419. There is an odd connection here with the process against Paolo Zoppo at Rieti in 1334, given in ibid., 349–412. Paolo attempted to lure women into bed by presenting what was about to happen as a spiritual exercise. The significant thing for our purposes is that Robert Brentano, in *A New World in a Small Place* (Berkeley and Los Angeles: University of California Press, 1994), 256–64 succeeds in establishing a clear connection between Angelo's group and the names that appear in the Rieti process. Note that Galeozzo Visconti was accused of believing the same thing. See Merlo, "Controllo ed emarginazione," 385.

90. Fumi, "Eretici," 418. The comment about Saint Francis echoes similar statements concerning Saints Anthony and Benedict.

91. Ibid., 420.

92. Who the "many others" might be is another question. See the comment on King Robert in Chapter 6 above.

93. See Sensi, *Le osservanze francescane*, particularly chapter 4; also see Sensi's "La regola di Niccolò IV dopo la costituzione 'Periculoso,'" in *La "Supra montem" di Niccolò IV*, ed. Pazzelli and Temperini, 147–98; Duncan Nimmo, *Reform and Division*, 248–52; Decima Douie, *Nature and the Effect*, 223–25.

94. The record of his inquisitorial activities, edited by Jean Duvernoy, is found in *Le Registre d'inquisition de Jacques Fournier, eveque de Pamiers (1318–1325)* (Toulouse: Editions Privat, 1965), which furnished the raw material for Emmanuel Le Roy Ladurie's *Montaillou, village occitan de 1294 à 1324* (Paris: Gallimard, 1982). Fournier was also one of the three judges in the trial of Bernard Délicieux.

95. Von Auw, *Angelo Clareno*, 195–96.

96. For this and the following, see expecially Nimmo, *Reform and Division*, part 2, chapter 1.

97. *BF,* 5:503.

98. Nimmo, *Reform and Division*, 207–9.

99. Douie, *Nature and the Effect*, chapter 7 is still valuable; but see also Nimmo, *Reform and Division*, 248–73.

100. See the strong argument for their role made by Marvin Becker, "Florentine Politics and the Diffusion of Heresy in the Trecento," *Speculum* 24 (1959): 60–75, and the equally strong rebuttal by John Stephens, "Heresy in Medieval and Renaissance Florence," *Past and Present* 54 (1972): 25–60.

101. But see Tognetti, "I fraticelli," 132–44, which seems to deny precisely this point. Perhaps a compromise position is possible: Lay interest involved admiring, protecting, and supporting the *fraticelli*, but did not extend to forming lay conventicles similar to those of the French and Catalan beguins.

102. *Reform and Division*, 376, 377 ("but is it not possible . . ."), 377–78 (citing *Chronica XXIV generalium*, 3:530).

103. *BF,* 6:139.

104. *BF,* 6:245–46.

105. *Le osservanze francescane*, 296.

106. On Gentile and Paoluccio, see Nimmo, *Reform and Division*, 382–429. For John of Capistrano's campaign against the *fraticelli*, see the brief notice and bibliography in ibid., 586.

Conclusion

1. The length of the third age depends on whether one dates it from its inception in the early thirteenth century or its full separation from the second age by the mid-fourteenth century.

2. See Musto, "Queen Sancia of Naples," 205 and 213–14.

3. "The Thirteenth-Century Guglielmites: Salvation Through Women," in *Medieval Women*, ed. Derek Baker (Oxford: Basil Blackwell, 1978), 289–303.

4. Dolcino's 1300 letter to the faithful suggested a scenario in which Antichrist would come just before final judgment, and his 1300 and 1303 letters alike stated that the golden years leading up to Antichrist would contain only a single pope. Elena Rotelli, *Fra Dolcino e gli Apostolici nella storia e nella tradizione* (Turin: Claudiana Editrice, 1979) provides a good outline of Dolcino's letters.

Appendix

1. I follow Enrico Menestò, "Chiara da Montefalco," in *Umbria: Sacra e civile*, by Enrico Menestò and Roberto Rusconi (Turin: Nuova Eri Edizioni Rai, 1989), 137–64, but could cite any number of other authors, since the basic facts of Clare's life are not in question.

2. Menestò, "Chiara da Montefalco," 146.

3. *Il processo di canonizzazione di Chiara da Montefalco* (Florence: La Nuova Italia, 1984).

4. Thus Menestò, "Chiara da Montefalco," 146.

5. Giavanna Casagrande, *Religiosità penitenziale*, 331 observes that while there were many orders in the area, only the Franciscans appear frequently in the Clare process. Casagrande also furnishes a useful list of ways in which connections with the Franciscans are strongly indicated.

6. See especially Silvestro Nessi, "Chiara da Montefalco, Angela da Foligno e Iacopone da Todi," in *S. Chiara da Montefalco e il suo tempo*, ed. Claudio Leonardi and Enrico Menestò (Florence: La Nuova Italia, 1981), 14–25. See also Enrico Menestò's descriptions of the canonization process in *Il processo di canonizzazione*, 25–35, and "Il processo apostolico per la canonizzazione di Chiara da Montefalco (1318–1319)," in *S. Chiara da Montefalco e il suo tempo*, ed. Leonardi and Menestò, 269–301. Menestò shows that Orsini and the Colonna enjoyed close contacts with Clare before her death and played a role in her canonization process. Note, too, that during the period when

the Colonna were being attacked by Boniface, a notary of Montefalco threatened to denounce Clare as a familiar of the Colonna. See Nessi, "Chiara," 16–18.

7. *Il processo di canonizzazione*, 32.

8. See Menestò in *Il processo di canonizzazione*, 27 n. 16 for the ambiguity of evidence concerning Ubertino's role. Yet, in the final analysis, that role seems well established.

9. See, for example, ibid., 266.

10. On Francesco's self-indulgence, see ibid., 281–82. With the question of whether he was a "true Franciscan," we enter a huge quagmire. For example, Ubertino criticized the way in which Franciscans conducted their urban ministry, yet he himself seems to have moved comfortably within the cities, whereas Angelo gravitated toward an essentially eremitical Franciscanism. Again, when the church proceeded against the Tuscan spirituals, Ubertino offered to defend them; Angelo roundly condemned them. One could go on.

11. Ibid., 3, art. XIII: "Item quod sancta Clara predicta et alie domine socie ipsius vivebant in maxima paupertate." See her brother's testimony (ibid., 268), which speaks of her having only one tunic and going about without shoes; see also the testimony of Sister Tomassa (ibid., 178): "Erant multotiens in tanta paupertate quod inter eas in quinque partes dividebant unum panem satis parvum duorum denariorum." She says that Clare was content, although "nil aliud haberet ad manducandum quam panem, nisi forte herbas silvestres que erant infra monasterium," and she has seen Clare give even her small portion of food to other sisters who seemed to have better appetite, or to the poor.

12. See Sister Tomassa, for example (ibid., 178): "Interrogata de temporibus, mensibus et diebus, dixit quod frequenter, multis annis, et maxime dum erant in reclusorio secundo, antequam haberent regulam, licet semper ipsa Clara ante et post fuerit pauperrima."

13. Her brother testifies that "nil quasi portabat in dorso nisi solum unam tunicam duram et asperam, et semper discalciata incedebat, et lectum nullum habebat, et quando dormiebat sedens sine lecto, sicud ipsa Clara et etiam dicta Iohanna sibi disserunt ad inducendum ipsum testem ad penitentiam, et continue quasi in oratione stabat" (ibid., 268).

14. *Religiosità penitenziale*, 339, 340–41. See also *Il processo di canonizzazione*, 74, 240.

15. *Cronica*, 449–50.

16. For Jacopone, see *Lauda* 31: "Those with learning eat with the guests / While the rest eat greens with oil in the refectory." For Ubertino, see his constant attack on the leadership in the various treatises he wrote just before the Council of Vienne, in which those whom he calls the *potentes*—the power elite of masters, lectors, inquisitors, confessors, preachers, guardians, and ministers—are portrayed as garnishing their offices with special perquisites.

17. See, for example, *Infrascripta dant*, 147–48; *Religiosi viri*, 674–75, 75; *Contra quasdam responsiones*, 78.

18. For her remark to her brother, see *Il processo di canonizzazione*, 272. On her access to the truth, see ibid., 68–69, where her brother and another Franciscan consult her about the Bible and announce that Solomon could not have given them a better answer; or ibid., 146–47, which says that many teachers and other scholars came to consult her (and here the list includes Pietro Colonna). Another passage (ibid., 199) not only gives names but also offers them as a validation of Clare's orthodoxy: "Interrogata quomodo scit quod verba ipsius sancte Clare essent verba suctilia, profunda et consonantia Scripture divine et sanctorum Patrum, respondit et dixit ipsa quod ipsa testis fuit presens in huiusmodi locutionibus, quas aliqui religiosi et clerici seculares, stantes ad rotam et cratem, audiverunt eam loqui multotiens, qui postea vere dicebant et iudicabant quod sua verba sic erant viva et profunda et suctilia et Scripture divine et sanctorum Patrum consonantia." See also ibid., 233, which speaks of Clare responding "suctiliter et profunde" to scholars who came to consult her. On the comparisons to Parisian scholarship, see ibid., 165 and 259, for example.

19. See, for instance, the comment of the Dominican scholar (II Celano, 104) who consults Francis and exclaims that the latter's knowledge soars like an eagle on the two wings of purity and contemplation, while his own crawls along on its stomach.

20. *De secta spiritus libertatis in Umbria saec. XIV* (Rome: Edizioni di Storia e Letteratura, 1943). See, more recently, Gordon Leff, *Heresy in the Later Middle Ages* (New York: Barnes and Noble, 1967), 1:308–407; Robert Lerner, *The Heresy of the Free Spirit in the Later Middle Ages* (Berkeley and Los Angeles: University of California Press, 1972); Jean Orcibal, "Le 'Miroir des simples âmes' et la 'secte' du Libre Esprit," *Revue de l'histoire des religions* 176 (1969): 35–60; Marino Damiata, *Pietà*, 127–31; Potestà, *Storia ed escatologia*, chapter 9; and the massive study by Romana Guarnieri, "Il movimento del libero spirito," *Archivio italiano per la storia della pietà* 4 (1965): 351–708, of which more will be said shortly.

21. "The Apostles," in this case, seems to mean the group orginally formed around Gerardo Segarelli and eventually headed by Fra Dolcino. It is at least thought-provoking that the Apostles appear in connection with the spiritual Franciscans in other contexts, as we saw in Chapter 5. Note, though, that according to the Clare materials, Bentivenga was called "The Apostle" because of his ostensible piety (e.g., *Il processo di canonizzazione*, 287). Thus it is not entirely impossible that Angelo, writing in the 1320s, might have drawn a faulty conclusion from the nickname and Bentivenga really had no connection with Dolcino's group.

22. On Ubertino's role, see Angelo, *Liber chronicarum*, 654–56.

23. Guarnieri, "Il movimento del libero spirito."

24. *Il processo di canonizzazione*, 287–91.

25. Clare knew several people involved in the heresy: the depositions pertaining to Bentivenga include other names. See her conversation with Giovanuccio da Bevagna as well (ibid., 45–46, 225). For her remark about God's justice, see ibid., 236–37.

26. We saw in Chapter 7 that, in the welter of position papers leading up to the Council of Vienne, one of the four issues that Pope Clement V asked spiritual Franciscan spokesmen to address was precisely the heresy of the *spiritus libertatis*.

27. Processes from the mid-1330s offer sparse evidence, but evidence nonetheless. In the processes discussed in Chapter 13 of this volume, one witness says that he heard from several *fraticelli* that fornication is not a sin. In fact, he names some of the brethren from whom he heard it. Fumi, "Eretici e ribelli," 419. We have, moreover, the connection with the process against Paolo Zoppo at Rieti in 1334 (given in ibid., 349–412) *and* the tie between Angelo's group and the names appearing in the Rieti process as established by Robert Brentano, *A New World in a Small Place*, 256–64 (again, see Chap. 13 for the citations). Paolo attempted to lure women into bed as a spiritual exercise. The whole matter is a complicated one, since there is also evidence that some Italian *fraticelli* and French beguins saw the practice of lying naked with members of the opposite sex not as an occasion for intercourse (as purportedly condoned by the *spiritus libertatis*), but as a test of piety, the assumption being that the participants would *not* have intercourse. The question of where Bentivenga and his associates lived is also relevant. Menestò suggests that these brothers did not reside in the house of San Francesco at Montefalco, as Oliger thought, but in the one at Camiano, which became a center for rigorist Franciscans (see "Chiara da Montefalco," 158).

28. *Il processo di canonizzazione*, 14, 489–90, 64–65, 215.

29. Sensi, "Incarcerate e recluse nei secoli XIII e XIV: Un bizzocaggio centro-italiano," in *Il movimento religioso femminile in Umbria nei secoli XIII–XIV*, ed. Rusconi, 107. The document cited by Sensi speaks of *religiosi* and *beghini*, not *beghine* (i.e., it uses the masculine rather than the feminine). Sensi quotes without comment the part about Clare vowing the rule of the Franciscan third order, a passage on which some prior Franciscan scholars placed heavy reliance in making their case for Clare as a Franciscan tertiary.

30. E.g., see ibid., 108.

31. Giunta da Bevegna, *Iunctae Bevegnatis Legenda*.

32. I follow Fortunato Iozzelli's biographical profile in chapter 3 of his introduction to the *Iunctae Bevegnatis Legenda*.

33. For the dating problem, see Mario Sensi, "Margherita da Cortona nel contesto storico-sociale cortonese," *Collectanea franciscana* 69 (1999): 223–62.

34. *Una donna senza volto* (Rome: Edizioni Borla, 1992).

35. Cortona, Archivio del Convento di S. Margherita, MS 61 (text published in *Iunctae Bevegnatis Legenda,* 477).

36. For Conrad, see *Iunctae Bevegnatis Legenda,* 385 and 425. See also Fortunato Iozzelli's comment on Conrad's whereabouts at that time (ibid., 66 n. 58). For Ubertino and Margaret's son, see ibid., 389.

37. See ibid., 255 (the parallel of the Franciscans with Christ reappears elsewhere, as on p. 368) and 276.

38. Ibid., 382, 384–85, 392.

39. See my "Olivi, Prous, and the Separation of Apocalypse from Eschatology," 285–304.

40. *Iunctae Bevegnatis Legenda,* 382, 404.

41. Ibid., 404.

42. *Sapientia aedificavit,* 102.

43. *Memorial,* chapter 1, where Friar Ar says: "Et de somniis et visionibus retulit unam de multis."

44. Ibid., 305, 405. Compare Angelo Clareno, *Epistole,* letter 26 (pp. 133–34), where Angelo, advising his associates on the selection of new brothers, reminds them that Christ chose only twelve, and even one of them went bad. "While we seek to grow in numbers, we are not magnified but diminished in virtue." Thus it is important, he says, that even those who truly want to join the group not be admitted unless they can measure up to the demands of the vow. The opening chapters of Angelo's *Liber chronicarum* make the same point, showing how, as the order increased in number, it drifted away from the path laid out by Francis. See, for example, 230, where Francis is quoted as saying precisely that.

45. *Iunctae Bevegnatis Legenda,* 401–2, 417.

46. However, in the coming period of tribulation, "they will seem to have fallen from their pristine state."

47. On the contrary, see Christ's comment on the importance of accepting administrative office (ibid., 377).

48. See ibid., 392–93 on the expansion (at the same time, Christ explicitly criticizes Elias's motives in beginning the church); 387, 393, and 404 on the crusade; and 405 on the indulgence. Olivi, to be sure, weighed in with a defense of the indulgence, and there are those who see the indulgence as originally championed by the spirituals, but there is no evidence that such was the case. See Bartoli, "Olivi et le pouvoir du pape," 180.

49. See *La divina commedia: Inferno,* cantos 19 and 27. *La divina commedia: Paradiso,* canto 12 seems to place Dante equidistant from the Franciscan leaders on the one hand and the spirituals on the other.

50. See Boase, *Boniface VIII,* 366. On the political situation in Cortona, see F. Cardini, "Una signoria citadina 'minore' in Toscana: I Casali di Cortona," *Archivio storico italiano* 181 (1971): 241–55 (which notes the generally Ghibelline orientation of the Casali and the Cortonan *popolo* in the second half of the thirteenth century, but does little to clarify the precise situation around 1308). See also, more recently, Joanna Cannon and André Vauchez, *Margherita of Cortona and the Lorenzetti* (University Park: The Pennsylvania State University Press, 1999), part 1, chapter 1, and Sensi, "Margherita da Cortona."

51. Ibid., 272–74, 280, 277. See the similar allusion to tribulation in Angela, *Memorial,* chapter 5.

52. "Margherita da Cortona."

53. Angelo, *Liber chronicarum,* 554 simply mentions him as among those who encouraged them to present their case before Celestine V. When Angelo chronicles the charges made to John of Murrovalle against Conrad, he pictures Conrad's accusers as saying that he praised and counseled the group, not that he joined it (570).

54. "Margherita da Cortona," 256.

55. Ibid., 248–50. Sensi must also neutralize Livarius Oliger, who argues not only that the members of the group at the Celle were not rigorists on the issue of poverty but also that they actually *owned* property (see "Documenta inedita," 290).

56. See, for example, the considerations offered by Iozzelli (*Iunctae Bevegnatis Legenda*, 80–84) or by Benvenuti Papi (*In castro poenitentiae*, 376–90). Again, there are various reasons why the Franciscans of Cortona should have been upset by her move and why Giunta should have found himself exercising damage control, a problem Benvenuti Papi explores in an interesting way.

57. "Les Principales Dates de la vie d'Angèle de Foligno," *Revue d'histoire franciscaine* 2 (1925): 31–34. His reconstruction is summarized by Paul Lachance in the introduction to his translation of the two principal sources, *Angela of Foligno: Complete Works* (New York: Paulist Press, 1993).

58. "Angèle de Foligno a-t-elle existé?" in *Alla signorina: Mélanges offerts à Noëlle de La Blanchardière* (Rome: École Française de Rome, 1995): 59–97.

59. See *Complete Works*, 123. The notice is in few manuscripts, but they are the earliest. The earliest of all, Assisi 342, is dated 1308–9 by Dalarun and others, including Attilio Bartoli Langeli, "Il codice di Assisi ovvero il *Liber sororis Lelle*," in *Angèle de Foligno: Le Dossier*, ed. Giulia Barone and Jacques Dalarun (Rome: École Française de Rome, 1999), 7–27. The critical edition of the Angela materials, prepared by Ludger Their and Abele Calufetti, is *Il libro della beata Angela da Foligno* (Grottaferrata: College of Saint Bonaventure, 1985), but the material is also available on the Internet at <*http://sismel.meri.unifi.it/mistica/ita/TestiStrumenti/fullTextAngela.htm*>. I cite the excellent Lachance translation here, but have checked it against the Internet Latin edition.

60. "Lelle" is a nickname for "Angela."

61. For instance, see Mario Sensi, "Angela nel contesto religioso folignate," in *Vita e spiritualità della Beata Angela da Foligno*, edited by Clement Schmitt, atti del Convegno di Studi per il VII Centenario della Conversione della Beata Angela da Foligno (1285–1985) (Perugia: Serafica Provincia di San Francesco O.F.M. Conv., 1987), 43–44, as well as his *Storie di bizzoche*, chapter 8, and, most recently, "Foligno all'incrocio delle strade," in *Angèle de Foligno: Le Dossier*, ed. Barone and Dalarun, 267–92.

62. Giovanna Casagrande, "Il terz'ordine e la beata Angela," in *Angela da Foligno, terziaria francescana*, ed. Enrico Menestò (Spoleto: Centro Italiano di Studi sull'Alto Medioevo, 1992), 17–38.

63. Angela of Foligno, *Complete Works*, 250.

64. Mariano d'Alatri, "Francesco d'Assisi visto dalla beata," in *Vita e spiritualità della Beata Angela da Foligno*, ed. Schmitt, 149–50. See Angela of Foligno, *Complete Works*, 251, 254.

65. Costanzo Cargnoni, "La povertà nella spiritualità di Angela," in *Vita e spiritualità della Beata Angela da Foligno*, ed. Schmitt, 353–54.

66. "Santa Angela? Angela, Ubertino e lo spiritualismo francescano: Prime ipotesi sulla 'Peroratio,'" in *Angèle de Foligno: Le Dossier*, ed. Barone and Dalarun, 203–65.

67. For example, Paul Lachance, in *Complete Works*, adds a note suggesting a spiritual Franciscan origin for the epilogue (see 415 n. 186).

68. Ibid., 317.

69. Ibid., 218.

70. Guarnieri does not discuss the chronological problem involved here. See Giacinto d'Urso, "La B. Angela e Ubertino da Casale," *Vita e spiritualità della Beata Angela da Foligno*, ed. Schmitt, 160. I have ignored the question of whether Ubertino was the recipient of one or even two of Angela's letters, as some have supposed. Lachance sees no real evidence for this claim, and his conclusion seems well founded (see *Complete Works*, 110).

71. Ibid., 123. The Latin text says "antequam cum summo pontifice in scandalum incideret."

72. "Ubertino e Angela: 'L'Arbor vitae' e il 'Liber,'" in *Angèle de Foligno: Le Dossier*, ed. Barone and Dalarun, 333. Even earlier, Stefano Brufani underlined significant divergences in "Angela da Foligno e gli spirituali," in *Angela da Foligno, terziaria francescana*, ed. Menestò, 83–104.

73. See "L'Approbatio: Curia romana, ordine minoritico e *Liber*," in *Angèle de Foligno: Le Dossier*, ed. Barone and Dalarun, 310.

74. *Complete Works*, 246–47.

75. See Chapter 2 of this volume.

76. *Complete Works*, 246–47.

77. The *Memorial* says that the torments of the sixth supplementary step began "sometime before the pontificate of Pope Celestine" (ibid., 201), thus before July 1294, and lasted over two years. If, with others (see, for example, Ferré, "Les Principales Dates," 24 and Lachance, *Complete Works*, 62), we assume that Angela's remarkable identification with the crucified Christ (an identification that brought the fifth step to a climax) took place on Holy Saturday 1294, then the sixth step could not have ended before Easter 1296, with the seventh and final step following close on its heels.

78. See Chapter 3 of this volume. Note that the 1298 date would also make it hard to believe that Ubertino played a major role in Giacomo Colonna's "discovery" of Angela, since we are told at the beginning of the Angela materials that Colonna and those well-known lectors approved her book before Colonna's disgrace.

79. Ibid., 318.

80. See ibid., 318: "Anyone who fights against Angela—or rather against the way of Christ, and his life, and his teachings—has no love for anyone." The Latin, however, is: "Et vere neminem diligit, qui Angelam, immo viam et vitam Christi et doctrinam impugnat."

81. "Chiara da Montefalco nella religiosità femminile del suo tempo," in *S. Chiara da Montefalco e il suo tempo*, ed. Leonardi and Menestò, 265–66. The same point is made by Casagrande, *Religiosità penitenziale*, 320–21.

82. "Angela da Foligno: Da donna del popolo a maestra dei teologi," in *Umbria sacra e civile* (Turin: Nuova Eri Edizioni Rai, 1989), 112.

83. Ibid., 120.

84. See Paul Lachance's comments in Angela of Foligno, *Complete Writings*, 98–99 and the accompanying note at 354 n. 195.

85. See especially Edith Pásztor, "I papi del duecento," 29–65. Pásztor (61) contrasts the women who appear in papal letters—"fragile, in need of defense, protection, and custody in strict enclosure"—to women celebrated in local cults who appear to us as "strong, confronting difficulties of all kinds, both political and religious (as with the battle against heresy); accepting poverty (whether voluntary or otherwise); taking on the hardest penance and asceticism; experiencing bodily illness and spiritual aridity; carying in their bodies the signs of Christ's passion and, in their hearts, the suffering of the *mater dolorosa*."

86. See Giovanna Casagrande, "Forme di vita religiosa femminile nell'Area di Città di Castello nel secolo XIII," in *Il movimento religioso femminile in Umbria nei secoli XXII–XV*, ed. Rusconi. She speaks of the *vita microassociativa* which flourished alongside institutional forms, manifesting *la fluidità religiosa* of the period (147).

BIBLIOGRAPHY

Abate, Giuseppe. "Memoriali, statuti ed atti di capitoli generali dei frati minori inediti dei secoli XII et XIV." *Miscellanea francescana* 33 (1933): 15–45; 34 (1934): 248–53; 35 (1935): 101–6, 232–39.

Accrocca, Felice. "Angelo Clareno: Riflessioni e nuove ricerche." *Collectanea franciscana* 62 (1992): 311–36.

Aegidius Assisiensis. *Dicta Beati Aegidii Assisiensis.* Quaracchi: College of Saint Bonaventure, 1939.

d'Alatri, Mariano. *Eretici e inquisitori in Italia.* Edited by Clement Schmitt. Rome: Istituto Storico dei Frati Minori Cappucini, 1986–87.

———. "Francesco d'Assisi visto dalla beata." In *Vita e spiritualità della Beata Angela da Foligno,* edited by Clement Schmitt, 143–54. Atti del Convegno di Studi per il VII Centenario della Conversione della Beata Angela da Foligno (1285–1985). Perugia: Serafica Provincia di San Francesco O.F.M. Conv., 1987.

———. *L'inquisizione francescana nell'Italia centrale nel secolo XIII.* Rome: Istituto Storico dei Frati Minori Cappucini, 1954.

———. "S. Bonaventura, l'eresia e l'inquisizione." *Miscellanea francescana* 75 (1975): 305–22.

Alberzoni, Maria Pia. "L'Approbatio: Curia romana, ordine minoritico e *Liber.*" In *Angèle de Foligno: Le Dossier,* edited by Giulia Barone and Jacques Dalarun, 293–318. Rome: École Française de Rome, 1999.

d'Alverny, Marie-Thérèse. "Un Adversaire de Saint Thomas: Petrus Ioannis Olivi." In *St. Thomas Aquinas, 1274–1974,* 2:179–218. Toronto: Pontifical Institute of Mediaeval Studies, 1974.

Amorós, Leo. "Aegidii Romani impugnatio doctrinae Petri Ioannis Olivi an. 1311–12, nunc primum in lucem edita." *Archivum franciscanum historicum* 27 (1934): 399–451.

———. "Series condemnationum et processuum contra doctrinam et sequaces Petri Ioannis Olivi." *Archivum franciscanum historicum* 24 (1931): 495–512.

Analecta franciscana. 12 vols. Quaracchi: College of Saint Bonaventure, 1885–1983.

Angela of Foligno. *Angela of Foligno: Complete Works.* Translated by Paul Lachance. New York: Paulist Press, 1993.

———. *Il libro della beata Angela da Foligno.* Prepared by Ludger Their and Abele Calufetti. Grottaferrata: College of Saint Bonaventure, 1985.

Angelo Clareno. *Apologia.* In "Angelus Clarinus ad Alvarum Pelagium Apologia pro vita sua," by Victorin Doucet. *Archivum franciscanum historicum* 39 (1948): 63–200.

———. *Expositio regulae fratrum minorum.* Edited by Livarius Oliger. Quaracchi: College of Saint Bonaventure, 1912.

————. *Liber chronicarum sive tribulationum ordinis minorum*. Edited by Giovanni Boccali and translated by Marino Bigaroni. Assisi: Edizioni Porziuncula, 1999.

————. *Opera: I. Epistole*. Rome: Istituto Storico Italiano per il Medio Evo, 1980.

Anonymus perusinus. In "L'Anonimo Perugino tra le fonti francescane del secolo XIII," by Lorenzo di Fonzo. *Miscellanea francescana* 72 (1972): 435–65.

Augustinus Triumphus. *Tractatus contra divinatores et sompniatores*. In *Unbekannte kirchenpolitische Streitschriften aus der Zeit Ludwigs des Bayern*, by Richard Scholz, 2:485–90. Rome: Loescher & Co. (W. Regenberg), 1911–14.

Auw, Lydia von. *Angelo Clareno et les spirituels italiens*. Rome: Edizioni di Storia e Letteratura, 1979.

Backman, Clifford. "Arnau de Vilanova and the Franciscan Spirituals in Sicily." *Franciscan Studies* 50 (1990): 3–29.

————. *The Decline and Fall of Medieval Sicily*. Cambridge: Cambridge University Press, 1995.

Barone, Giulia. *Da frate Elia agli Spirituali*. Milan: Edizioni Biblioteca Francescana, 1999.

Barone, Giulia, and Jacques Dalarun, eds. *Angèle de Foligno: Le Dossier*. Rome: École Française de Rome, 1999.

Bartoli, Marco. "Olivi et le pouvoir du pape." In *Pierre de Jean Olivi (1248–1298): Pensée scolastique, dissidence spirituelle et société*, edited by Alain Boureau and Sylvain Piron, 173–91. Paris: J. Vrin, 1999.

Bartoli Langeli, Attilio. "Il codice di Assisi ovvero il *Liber sororis Lelle*." In *Angèle de Foligno: Le Dossier*, edited by Giulia Barone and Jacques Dalarun, 7–27. Rome: École Française de Rome, 1999.

Beatus vir. In "Anonymi spiritualis responsio 'Beatus vir,'" by Albanus Heysse. *Archivum franciscanum historicum* 42 (1949): 213–16.

Becker, Marvin. "Florentine Politics and the Diffusion of Heresy in the Trecento." *Speculum* 24 (1959): 60–75.

Benvenuti Papi, Anna. "L'impianto mendicante in Firenze, un problema aperto." In *Les Ordres mendiants et la ville en Italie central*. Rome: École Française de Rome, 1977.

————. *In castro poenitentiae*. Rome: Herder, 1990.

Berg, Dieter. *Armut und Wissenschaft*. Dusseldorf: Pädagogischer Verlag Schwann, 1977.

Bernardus Guidonis. *Practica inquisitionis heretice pravitatis*. Paris: Alphonse Picard, 1886.

Bettoni, Efrem. *Le dottrine filosofiche di Pier di Giovanni Olivi*. Milan: Società Editrice "Vita e Pensiero," 1959.

Biget, Jean-Louis. "Autour de Bernard Délicieux." In *Mouvements franciscains et société française, XIIIe–XXe siècles*, edited by André Vauchez, 75–93. Paris: Beauchesne, 1984.

————. "Culte et rayonnement de Pierre Déjean Olieu en Languedoc au début du XIVe siècle." In *Pierre de Jean Olivi (1248–1298): Pensée scolastique, dissidence spirituelle et société*, edited by Alain Boureau and Sylvain Piron, 277–308. Paris: J. Vrin, 1999.

Bihl, Michael. "Aventures du messager envoyé par les spirituels de Narbonne et de Béziers au chapitre général de Naples en mai 1316." *Archivum franciscanum historicum* 5 (1912): 777–79.

————. "Formulae et documenta e cancellaria Fr. Michaelis de Cesena, O.F.M." *Archivum franciscanum historicum* 23 (1930): 106–71.

————. "Statuta generalia ordinis edita in capitulis generalibus celebratis Narbonae an. 1260, Assisii an. 1279 atque Parisiis an. 1292." *Archivum franciscanum historicum* 34 (1941): 13–94, 284–358.

Biscaro, Gerolamo. "Eretici ed inquisitori nella marca trevisana (1280–1308)." *Archivio veneto* 62 (1932): 148–72.

Boase, T. S. R. *Boniface VIII*. London: Constable, 1933.

Bock, F. "I processi di Giovanni XXII contro i ghibellini delle Marche." *Bulletino dell'Istituto Storico Italiano per il Medio Evo e Archivio Muratoriano* 57 (1941): 19–70.

Bonagratia de Bergamo. *Nuper controversia*. In *Archiv für Literatur- und Kirchengeschichte des Mittelalters*, by Heinrich Denifle and Franz Ehrle, 3:36. Berlin: Weidmannsche Buchhandlung, 1885–1900.

Bonaventura da Bagnoreggio. *Opera*. Quaracchi: College of Saint Bonaventure, 1882–1902.

Botineau, Pierre. "Les Tribulations de R. Barrau O.P. (1295–1338)." *Mélanges d'archéologie et d'histoire publiés par l'École Française de Rome* 77 (1965): 476–528.

Boureau, Alain, and Sylvain Piron, eds. *Pierre de Jean Olivi (1248–1298): Pensée scolastique, dissidence spirituelle et société*. Paris: J. Vrin, 1999.

Brentano, Robert. *A New World in a Small Place*. Berkeley and Los Angeles: University of California Press, 1994.

Brooke, Rosalind. *Early Franciscan Government*. Cambridge: Cambridge University Press, 1959.

———. *Scripta Leonis, Rufini et Angeli Sociorum S. Francisci*. Oxford: Clarendon Press, 1970.

Brufani, Stefano. "Angela da Foligno e gli spirituali." In *Angela da Foligno, terziaria francescana*, edited by Enrico Menestò, 83–104. Spoleto: Centro Italiano di Studi sull'Alto Medioevo, 1992.

———. *Eresia di un ribelle al tempo di Giovanni XXII*. Florence: La Nuova Italia, 1989.

Bullarium franciscanum. 5 vols. Rome: Vatican, 1759–1904.

Burkitt, F. C. "Ubertino da Casale and a Variant Reading." *Journal of Theological Studies* 23 (1922): 186–88.

Burnham, Louisa. "The Visionary Authority of Na Prous Boneta." In *Pierre de Jean Olivi (1248–1298): Pensée scolastique, dissidence spirituelle et société*, edited by Alain Boureau and Sylvain Piron, 319–39. Paris: J. Vrin, 1999.

Burr, David. "Did the Béguins Understand Olivi?" In *Pierre de Jean Olivi (1248–1298): Pensée scolastique, dissidence spirituelle et société*, edited by Alain Boureau and Sylvain Piron, 309–18. Paris: J. Vrin, 1999.

———. "Exegetical Theory and Ecclesiastical Condemnation: The Case of Olivi's Apocalypse Commentary." In *Neue Richtungen in der Hoch- und Spätmittelalterlichen Bibelexegese*, edited by Robert Lerner and Elisabeth Müller-Luckner, 149–62. Munich: R. Oldenbourg Verlag, 1996.

———. "Na Prous Boneta and Olivi." *Collectanea franciscana* 67 (1997): 277–300.

———. "Olivi, Apocalyptic Expectation, and Visionary Experience." *Traditio* 41 (1985): 273–88.

———. "Olivi, Prous, and the Separation of Apocalypse from Eschatology." In *That Others May Know and Love*, edited by Michael Cusato and F. Edward Coughlin, 285–304. St. Bonaventure, N.Y.: Franciscan Institute, 1997.

———. *Olivi and Franciscan Poverty*. Philadelphia: University of Pennsylvania Press, 1989.

———. "Olivi on Marriage: The Conservative as Prophet." *Journal of Medieval and Renaissance Studies* 2 (1972): 183–204.

———. "Olivi on Prophecy." *Cristianesimo nella storia* 17 (1996): 369–91.

———. *Olivi's Peaceable Kingdom*. Philadelphia: University of Pennsylvania Press, 1993.

———. *The Persecution of Peter Olivi*. Philadelphia: American Philosophical Society, 1976.

———. "Petrus Ioannis Olivi and the Philosophers." *Franciscan Studies* 34 (1971): 41–71.

———. "Raymond Déjean, Franciscan Renegade." *Franciscan Studies* 57 (1999): 57–78.

Burr, David, and David Flood. "Peter Olivi: On Poverty and Revenue." *Franciscan Studies* 40 (1980): 18–58.

Caliendo, Philip. "Ubertino da Casale: A Re-evaluation of the Eschatology in the Fifth Book of his *Arbor vite crucifixe Jesu.*" Ph.D. diss., Rutgers University, 1979.

Callaey, Frédégand. *L'Idéalisme franciscaine spirituel au XIVe siècle.* Louvain: Bureau de Recueil, 1911.

Cannon, Joanna, and André Vauchez. *Margherita of Cortona and the Lorenzetti.* University Park: The Pennsylvania State University Press, 1999.

Cardini, F. "Una signoria citadina 'minore' in Toscana: I Casali di Cortona." *Archivio storico italiano* 181 (1971): 241–55.

Cargnoni, Costanzo. "La povertà nella spiritualità di Angela." In *Vita e spiritualità della Beata Angela da Foligno,* edited by Clement Schmitt, 341–54. Atti del Convegno di Studi per il VII Centenario della Conversione della Beata Angela da Foligno (1285–1985). Perugia: Serafica Provincia di San Francesco O.F.M. Conv., 1987.

Carlini, Armandus. "Constitutiones generales ordinis fratrum minorum anno 1316 Assisii conditae." *Archivum franciscanum historicum* 4 (1911): 269–302, 508–36.

Casagrande, Giovanna. "Forme di vita religiosa femminile nell'Area di Città di Castello nel secolo XIII." In *Il movimento religioso femminile in Umbria nei secoli XIII–XIV,* edited by Roberto Rusconi. Florence: La Nuova Italia, 1984.

———. "Un ordine per i laici: Penitenza e penitenti nel duecento." In *Francesco d'Assisi e il primo secolo di storia francescana,* edited by Maria Pia Alberzoni, et al., 237–55. Turin: Einaudi, 1997.

———. *Religiosità penitenziale e città al tempo dei communi.* Rome: Istituto Storico dei Cappuccini, 1995.

———. "Il terz'ordine e la beata Angela." In *Angela da Foligno, terziaria francescana,* edited by Enrico Menestò, 17–38. Spoleto: Centro Italiano di Studi sull'Alto Medioevo, 1992.

Cenci, Cesare. "Ordinazioni dei capitoli provinciali umbri dal 1300 al 1305." *Collectanea franciscana* 55 (1985): 5–31.

Chiappini, Anicetus. "Communitatis responsio 'Religiosi viri' ad rotulum Fr. Ubertini de Casali." *Archivum franciscanum historicum* 7 (1914): 654–75; 8 (1915): 56–81.

Chronica XXIV generalium. In *Analecta franciscana.* Vol. 3. Quaracchi: College of Saint Bonaventure, 1885–1941.

Cipolla, Carlo. *Moneta e civiltà mediterranea.* Venice: Neri Pozza, 1957.

Compagni, Dino. *Cronica.* Florence: Successori Le Monnier, 1917.

———. *Dino Compagni's Chronicle of Florence.* Translated by Daniel Bornstein. Philadelphia: University of Pennsylvania Press, 1986.

Corpus iuris canonici. Graz: Akademische Druck- u. Verlagsanstalt, 1959.

Correctorium corruptorii "quare." Kain: Le Saulchoir, 1927.

Courtenay, William. "Between Pope and King: The Parisian Letters of Adhesion of 1303." *Speculum* 71 (1996): 577–605.

———. "The Parisian Franciscan Community in 1303." *Franciscan Studies* 53 (1993): 155–73.

Dalarun, Jacques. "Angèle de Foligno a-t-elle existé?" In *Alla signorina: Mélanges offerts à Noëlle de La Blanchardière,* 59–97. Rome: École Française de Rome, 1995.

———. *La malavventura di Francesco d'Assisi.* Milan: Edizioni Biblioteca Francescana, 1996.

Damiata, Marino. *Pietà e storia nell'Arbor Vitae di Ubertino da Casale.* Florence: Edizioni "Studi Francescani," 1988.

Dante: Enciclopedia dantesca. 6 vols. Rome: Istituto della Enciclopedia Italiana, 1996.

Dante Alighieri. *La divina commedia*. Edited by Natalino Sapegno. 2d ed. 3 vols. Florence: La Nuova Italia, 1968.

Davis, Charles. *Ubertino da Casale and His Conception of "Altissima Paupertas."* Spoleto: Centro Italiano di Studi sull'Alto Medioevo, 1984.

Declarata. In "Ubertini de Casali opusculum 'Super tribus sceleribus,'" by Albanus Heysse. *Archivum franciscanum historicum* 10 (1917): 116–22.

Delorme, Ferdinand. "La Confessio Fidei du Frère Matthieu de Bouzigues." *Études franciscaines* 49 (1937): 224–39.

———. "Notice et extraits d'un manuscrit franciscain." *Collectanea franciscana* 15 (1945): 5–91.

Denifle, Heinrich. "Die Denkschriften der Colonna gegen Bonifaz VIII und die Cardinäle gegen die Colonna." In *Archiv für Literatur- und Kirchengeschichte des Mittelalters*, by Heinrich Denifle and Franz Ehrle, 5:493–524. Berlin: Weidmannsche Buchhandlung, 1885–1900.

Denifle, Heinrich, and Emile Châtelain. *Chartularium universitatis parisiensis*. Paris: Delalain, 1891.

Denifle, Heinrich, and Franz Ehrle. *Archiv für Literatur- und Kirchengeschichte des Mittelalters*. 7 vols. Berlin: Weidmannsche Buchhandlung, 1885–1900.

Desbonnets, Théophile. *De l'intuition à l'institution*. Paris: Editions Franciscaines, 1983.

Digard, Georges. *Philippe le Bel et le Saint-Siège*. Paris: Librairie du Recueil Sirey, 1936.

Dmitrewski, Michel de. "Fr. Bernard Délicieux, O.F.M.: Sa lutte contre l'inquisition de Carcassonne et d'Albi, son procès, 1297–1319." *Archivum franciscanum historicum* 17 (1924): 183–214, 313–37; 18 (1925): 3–32.

Döllinger, Ignaz von. *Beiträge zur Sektengeschichte des Mittelalters*. Munich: Beck, 1890.

Douais, Celestin. *L'Inquisition*. Paris: Librairie Plon, 1906.

Doucet, Ferdinand. "De operibus mss. Petri Io. Olivi Patavii." *Archivum franciscanum historicum* 28 (1935): 428–41.

Doucet, Victorin. "P. J. Olivi et l'Immaculée Conception." *Archivum franciscanum historicum* 26 (1933): 560–63.

Douie, Decima. *Archbishop Pecham*. Oxford: Clarendon Press, 1952.

———. *The Nature and the Effect of the Heresy of the Fraticelli*. Manchester: University of Manchester Press, 1932.

———. "Three Treatises on Evangelical Poverty." *Archivum franciscanum historicum* 24 (1931): 341–69.

Durieux, François-Régis. "Approches de l'histoire franciscaine du Languedoc au XIII siècle." In *Les Mendiants en pays d'Oc au XIIIe siècle*. Cahiers de Fanjeaux, no. 8, 79–100. Toulouse: Editions Privat, 1973.

Ehrle, Franz. "Die altesten Redactionen der Generalconstitutionen des Franziskanerordens." In *Archiv für Literatur- und Kirchengeschichte des Mittelalters*, by Heinrich Denifle and Franz Ehrle, 6:1–138. Berlin: Weidmannsche Buchhandlung, 1885–1900.

———. "Die Spiritualen, ihr Verhaltniss zum Franziskanerorden und zu den Fraticellen." In *Archiv für Literatur- und Kirchengeschichte des Mittelalters*, by Henrich Denifle and Franz Ehrle, 1:509–69; 2:106–64; 3:553–623; 4:1–200. Berlin: Weidmannsche Buchhandlung, 1885–1900.

———. "Petrus Johannis Olivi." In *Archiv für Literatur- und Kirchengeschichte des Mittelalters*, by Henrich Denifle and Franz Ehrle, 3:438. Berlin: Weidmannsche Buchhandlung, 1885–1900.

Emery, Richard. *Heresy and Inquisition in Narbonne*. New York: AMS Press, 1967.

Ferré, M. J. "Les Principales Dates de la vie d'Angèle de Foligno." *Revue d'histoire franciscaine* 2 (1925): 31–34.

Finke, Heinrich. *Acta aragonensia*. Berlin: Rothschild, 1908.

Fioretti di San Francesco da un codice quattrocentesco. Rome: Paoline, 1992.

Firmamenta trium ordinum. Paris: Johannis Petit, Francisci Regnault et Johannis Frelon, 1512.

Fournié, Michèle. "Deux femmes dans l'erreur: Rixende de Narbonne et Prous Boneta de Montpellier." *Perspectives médiévales* 21 (1995): 7–17.

Fournier, Jacques. *Le Registre d'inquisition de Jacques Fournier, eveque de Pamiers (1318–1325)*. Toulouse: Editions Privat, 1965.

Francescanesimo e vita religiosa dei laici nel '200. Rimini: Maggioli, 1981.

Franciscains d'Oc: Les Spirituels ca. 1280–1324. Cahiers de Fanjeaux, no. 10. Toulouse: Editions Privat, 1975.

Francis of Assisi. *Opuscula*. Edited by Kajetan Esser. Grottaferrata: College of Saint Bonaventure, 1978.

Friedlander, Alan. *The Hammer of the Inquisitors: Brother Bernard Délicieux and the Struggle Against the Inquisition in Fourteenth-Century France*. Leiden: Brill, 2000.

―――. "Jean XXII et les Spirituels: Le Cas de Bernard Délicieux." In *La Papauté d'Avignon et le Languedoc*, 221–36. Toulouse: Editions Privat, 1991.

―――. *Processus Bernardi Delitiosi: The Trial of Fr. Bernard Délicieux, 3 September–8 December 1319*. Philadelphia: American Philosophical Society, 1996.

Frugoni, Arsenio. *Celestiniana*. Rome: Istituto Storico Italiano per il Medio Evo, 1954.

Frugoni, Chiara. *Francesco e l'invenzione delle stimmate*. Turin: Einaudi, 1993.

Fumi, L. "Eretici e ribelli nell'Umbria dal 1320 al 1330 studiati su documenti inediti dell'Archivio segreto Vaticano." *Bollettino della R. Deputazione di storia patria per l'Umbria* 3 (1897): 205–425.

Fussenegger, Geroldus. "Relatio commissionis in concilio Viennensi institutae ad decretalem 'Exivi de paradiso' praeparandam." *Archivum franciscanum historicum* 50 (1957): 145–77.

Galletti, Anna Imelde. "Insediamento e primo sviluppo dei frati minori a Perugia." In *Francescanesimo e società cittadina*, edited by Ugolino Nicolini. Perugia: Centro per il Collegamento degli Studi Medievali e Umanistici nell'Università di Perugia, 1979.

Germain, A. "Une Consultation inquisitoriale au XIVe siècle." *Publications de la Société Archéologique de Montpelier* 25 (1857): 334–38.

Giunta da Bevegna. *Iunctae Bevegnatis Legenda de vita et miraculis Beatae Margaritae de Cortona*. Edited by Fortunato Iozzelli. Bibliotheca Franciscana Ascetica Medii Aevi, no. 13. Grottaferrata: College of Saint Bonaventure, 1997.

Given, James. *Inquisition and Medieval Society*. Ithaca: Cornell University Press, 1997.

Glassberger, Nicholas. *Chronica*. In *Analecta franciscana*. Vol. 2. Quaracchi: College of Saint Bonaventure, 1885–1941.

Glorieux, Palemon. "Quodlibets I & II." Paris: J. Vrin, 1958.

Golubovich, Girolamo. *Biblioteca bio-bibliografica della Terra Santa e dell'oriente francescano*. Quaracchi: College of Saint Bonaventure, 1906–48.

Guarnieri, Romana. "Il movimento del libero spirito." *Archivio italiano per la storia della pietà* 4 (1965): 351–708.

―――. "Santa Angela? Angela, Ubertino e lo spiritualismo francescano: Prime ipotesi sulla 'Peroratio.'" In *Angèle de Foligno: Le Dossier*, edited by Giulia Barone and Jacques Dalarun, 203–65. Rome: École Française de Rome, 1999.

Henricus Gandaviensis. *Summa quaestionum*. Paris: Iodicus Badius Ascensius, 1520.

Herde, Peter. *Cölestin V*. Stuttgart: Hiersemann, 1981.

Heysse, Albanus. "Anonymi spiritualis responsio 'Beatus vir.'" *Archivum franciscanum historicum* 42 (1949): 213–16.

———. "Fr. Richardi de Conington, O.F.M., tractatus de paupertate fratrum minorum." *Archivum franciscanum historicum* 23 (1930): 57–105, 340–60.

Hugh of Digne (Hugo de Digna). *De finibus paupertatis. Archivum franciscanum historicum* 5 (1912): 277–90.

———. *Disputatio inter zelatorem paupertatis et inimicum domesticum eius*. In *Figure del primo francescanesimo in Provenza*, by Alessandra Sisto. Florence: Leo S. Olschki, 1971.

———. *Rule Commentary*. Grottaferrata: College of Saint Bonaventure, 1979.

Ini, Anna Maria. "Nuovi documenti sugli spirituali di Toscana." *Archivum franciscanum historicum* 66 (1973): 305–77.

In nomine domini. In *Archiv für Literatur- und Kirchengeschichte des Mittelalters*, by Heinrich Denifle and Franz Ehrle, 2:372. Berlin: Weidmannsche Buchhandlung, 1885–1900.

Ioachim de Fiore. *Liber concordiae novi ac veteris testamenti*. Venice, 1519. Reproduction, Frankfurt am Main: Minerva, 1983.

———. *Liber de concordia novi ac veteris testamenti*. Edited by E. R. Daniel. Philadelphia: American Philosophical Society, 1983.

Jacobelli, Maria Caterina. *Una donna senza volto*. Rome: Edizioni Borla, 1992.

Jacopone da Todi. *Laude*. Bari: Laterza & Figli, 1974.

Jacques de Vitry. *Lettres de Jacques de Vitry*. Leiden: Brill, 1960.

Jean de Joinville. *Histoire de Saint Louis*. Paris: Hachette, 1874.

Johannes XXII. *Extravagantes Iohannis XXII*. Vatican City: Biblioteca Apostolica Vaticana, 1983.

Johannes de Rupescissa. *Liber secretorum eventuum*. Fribourg: Editions Universitaires, 1994.

Jordan, William. *Louis IX and the Challenge of the Crusade*. Princeton: Princeton University Press, 1979.

Kelly, Samantha. "King Robert of Naples (1309–1343) and the Spiritual Franciscans." *Cristianesimo nella storia* 20 (1999): 41–80.

Koch, Joseph. "Der Prozess gegen die Postille Olivis zur Apokalypse." *Recherches de théologie ancienne et médiévale* 5 (1933): 302–15.

Krey, Philip. "Nicholas of Lyra: Apocalypse Commentary as Historiography." Ph.D. diss., University of Chicago, 1990.

Ladurie, Emmanuel Le Roy. *Montaillou, village occitan de 1294 à 1324*. Paris: Gallimard, 1982.

Lambert, Malcolm. *The Cathars*. Oxford: Basil Blackwell, 1998.

———. "The Franciscan Crisis Under John XXII." *Franciscan Studies* 32 (1972): 123–43.

———. *Franciscan Poverty*. St. Bonaventure, N.Y.: Franciscan Institute, 1998.

Landini, Lawrence. *The Causes of the Clericalization of the Order of the Friars Minor*. Chicago: Pontifica Universitas Gregoriana, 1968.

Lea, Henry Charles. *History of the Inquisition of the Middle Ages*. New York: Harbor Press, 1955.

Lee, Harold, Marjorie Reeves, and Giulio Silano. *Western Mediterranean Prophecy*. Toronto: Pontifical Institute of Mediaeval Studies, 1989.

Leff, Gordon. *Heresy in the Later Middle Ages*. New York: Barnes and Noble, 1967.

Legenda trium sociorum. Archivum franciscanum historicum 67 (1974): 89–144.

Lempp, Edouard. *Frère Elie de Cortone*. Paris: Fischbacher, 1901.

Leonardi, Claudio, and Enrico Menestò, eds. *S. Chiara da Montefalco e il suo tempo*. Florence: La Nuova Italia, 1981.

Lerner, Robert. *The Heresy of the Free Spirit in the Later Middle Ages.* Berkeley and Los Angeles: University of California Press, 1972.

———. "Peter Olivi on the Conversion of the Jews." In *Pierre de Jean Olivi (1248–1298): Pensée scolastique, dissidence spirituelle et société,* edited by Alain Boureau and Sylvain Piron, 207–16. Paris: J. Vrin, 1999.

———. "Writing and Resistance Among Beguins of Languedoc and Catalonia." In *Heresy and Literacy, 1000–1530,* edited by Peter Biller and Anne Hudson, 186–204. Cambridge: Cambridge University Press, 1994.

Lewis, Warren. "Peter John Olivi: Prophet of the Year 2000." Ph.D. diss., Tübingen University, 1972.

Limborch, Philippus a. *Historia inquisitionis cui subjungitur Liber sententiarum inquisitionis tholosanae.* Amsterdam: Henricus Wetstenius, 1692.

Little, A. G. "Statuta provincialia provinciarum Aquitainiae et Franciae (saec. XIII–XIV)." *Archivum franciscanum historicum* 7 (1914): 466–501.

Longpré, Ephrem. "Le B. Jean Duns Scot. Pour le Saint Siège et contre le gallicanisme (25–28 juin 1303)." *La France franciscaine* 11 (1928): 137–62.

———. "Le Quodlibet de Nicolas de Lyre, O.F.M." *Archivum franciscanum historicum* 23 (1930): 42–56.

Madigan, Kevin. "Peter Olivi's *Lectura super Matthaeum* in Medieval Exegetical Context." Ph.D. diss., University of Chicago, 1992.

Maier, Annaliese. "Annotazioni autografe di Giovanni XXII in Codici Vaticani." *Rivista di storia della chiesa in Italia* 6 (1952): 317–31.

Manselli, Raoul. *La "Lectura super Apocalypsim" di Pietro di Giovanni Olivi.* Rome: Istituto Storico Italiano per il Medio Evo, 1955.

———. *Spirituali e beghini in Provenza.* Rome: Istituto Storico Italiano per il Medio Evo, 1959.

———. *Spirituels et béguins du Midi.* Translated by Jean Duvernoy. Toulouse: Editions Privat, 1989.

Mansi, Johannes. *Sacrorum consiliorum nova et amplissima collectio.* Florence: A. Zatta, 1759–98.

———. *Stephani Baluzii Tutelensis Miscellanea.* Paris: Riccomini, 1761–64.

Marini, Alfonso. "Ubertino e Angela: 'L'Arbor vitae' e il 'Liber.'" In *Angèle de Foligno: Le Dossier,* edited by Giulia Barone and Jacques Dalarun, 319–44. Rome: École Française de Rome, 1999.

May, William. "The Confession of Prous Boneta, Heretic and Heresiarch." In *Essays in Medieval Life and Thought,* edited by John H. Mundy, et al., 4–30. New York: Biblo and Tannen, 1965.

Les Mendiants en pays d'Oc au XIIIe siècle. Cahiers de Fanjeaux, no. 8. Toulouse: Editions Privat, 1973.

Menestò, Enrico. "Angela da Foligno: Da donna del popolo a maestra dei teologi." In *Umbria: Sacra e civile,* by Enrico Menestò and Roberto Rusconi, 107–122. Turin: Nuova Eri Edizioni Rai, 1989.

———. "Chiara da Montefalco." In *Umbria: Sacra e civile,* by Enrico Menestò and Roberto Rusconi, 137–64. Turin: Nuova Eri Edizioni Rai, 1989.

———. "La 'Legenda' di Margherita di Città di Castello." In *Il movimento religioso femminile in Umbria nei secoli XIII–XIV,* edited by Roberto Rusconi. Florence: La Nuova Italia, 1984.

———. "Il processo apostolico per la canonizzazione di Chiara da Montefalco (1318–1319)." In *S. Chiara da Montefalco e il suo tempo,* edited by Claudio Leonardi and Enrico Menestò, 269–301. Florence: La Nuova Italia, 1981.

————, ed. *Angela da Foligno, terziaria francescana*. Spoleto: Centro Italiano di Studi sull'Alto Medioevo, 1992.

————. *Niccolò IV: Un pontificato tra oriente ed occidente*. Spoleto: Centro Italiano di Studi sull'Alto Medioevo, 1991.

Menestò, Enrico, and Roberto Rusconi. *Umbria: Sacra e civile*. Turin: Nuova Eri Edizioni Rai, 1989.

Mercati, Angelo. "Frate Francesco Bartoli d'Assisi Michelista e la sua ritrattazione." *Archivum franciscanum historicum* 20 (1927): 260–304.

Merlo, Grado. "Controllo ed emarginazione della dissidenza religiosa." In *Francescanesimo e vita religiosa dei laici nel '200*, 365–88. Rimini: Maggioli, 1981.

————. *Tra eremo e città*. Assisi: Edizioni Porziuncola, 1991.

Moorman, John. *Sources for the Life of S. Francis of Assisi*. Manchester: Manchester University Press, 1940.

Mosti, Renzo. "L'eresia dei 'fraticelli' nel territorio di Tivoli." *Atti e memorie della Società Tiburtina di Storia e d'Arte* 38 (1965): 103–10.

Moynihan, Robert. "Development of the 'Pseudo-Joachim' Commentary 'super Hieremiam,'" *Mélanges de l'École Française de Rome: Moyen Âge, temps modernes* 98 (1986): 109–42.

Müller, Daniela. "Les Béguines." *Heresis* 13–14 (1989): 351–89.

————. "Der Prozess gegen Prous Boneta." In *Ius et Historia: Festgabe für Rudolf Weigand zu seinem 60. Geburtstag*, edited by Norbert Hühl, 199–221. Würzburg: Echter, 1989.

Musto, Ronald. "Franciscan Joachimism at the Court of Naples, 1309–1345: A New Appraisal." *Archivum franciscanum historicum* 90 (1997): 419–86.

————. "Queen Sancia of Naples (1286–1345) and the Spiritual Franciscans." In *Women of the Medieval World*, edited by Julius Kirshner and Suzanne Wemple, 179–214. Oxford: Basil Blackwell, 1985.

Nessi, Silvestro. "Chiara da Montefalco, Angela da Foligno e Iacopone da Todi." In *S. Chiara da Montefalco e il suo tempo*, edited by Claudio Leonardi and Enrico Menestò, 14–25. Florence: La Nuova Italia, 1981.

Newman, Barbara. *From Virile Woman to WomanChrist*. Philadelphia: University of Pennsylvania Press, 1995.

Nicholas Eymerich. *Directorium inquisitorum*. Rome: In Aedibus Populi Romani, 1585.

————. *Directorium inquisitorum*. Venice: Marcus Antinius Zalterius, 1595.

Nicolaus Minorita. *Nicolaus Minorita: Chronica*. St. Bonaventure, N.Y.: Franciscan Institute, 1996.

Nimmo, Duncan. *Reform and Division in the Franciscan Order*. Rome: Capuchin Historical Institute, 1987.

Oliger, Livarius. *De secta spiritus libertatis in Umbria saec. XIV*. Rome: Edizioni di Storia e Letteratura, 1943.

————. "De sigillo fr. Angeli Clareni." *Antonianum* 12 (1937): 61–64.

————. "Documenta inedita ad historiam fraticellorum spectantia." *Archivum franciscanum historicum* 3 (1910): 253–79, 505–29, 680–99; 4 (1911): 688–712; 5 (1912): 74–84; 6 (1913): 267–90, 515–30, 710–49.

————. "Fr. Bertrandi de Turre processus contra spirituales Aquitaniae (1315) et Card. Jacobus de Columna littera defensoria spiritualium provinciae (1316)." *Archivum franciscanum historicum* 16 (1923): 323–55.

Orcibal, Jean. "Le 'Miroir des simples âmes' et la 'secte' du Libre Esprit." *Revue de l'histoire des religions* 176 (1969): 35–60.

Orioli, Raniero. *Venit perfidus heresiarcha*. Rome: Istituto Storico Italiano per il Medio Evo, 1988.

Orwell, George. *1984*. New York: Harcourt, Brace and Company, 1949.

Papini, Niccola. *Notizie sicure della morte, sepoltura, canonizzazione e traslazione di S. Francesco d'Assisi.* 2d ed. Foligno: Presso la Tipografia del Tomassini, 1824.

Papka, Claudia Rattazzi. "Fictions of Judgment: The Apocalyptic 'I' in the Fourteenth Century." Ph.D. diss., Columbia University, 1996.

Passio sanctorum martyrum. In *Analecta franciscana.* Vol. 3. Quaracchi: College of Saint Bonaventure, 1885–1941.

Pásztor, Edith. "Chiara da Montefalco nella religiosità femminile del suo tempo." In *S. Chiara da Montefalco e il suo tempo,* edited by Claudio Leonardi and Enrico Menestò, 183–267. Florence: La Nuova Italia, 1981.

———. "Girolamo d'Ascoli e Pietro di Giovanni Olivi." In *Niccolò IV: Un pontificato tra oriente ed occidente,* ed. Enrico Menestò, 53–72. Spoleto: Centro Italiano di Studi sull'Alto Medioevo, 1991.

———. "Gli scritti leonine." In *La "questione francescana" dal Sabatier ad oggi,* 198–212. Assisi: Edizioni Porziuncula, 1974.

———. "I papi del duecento e trecento di fronte alla vita religiosa femminile." In *Il movimento religioso femminile in Umbria nei secoli XIII–XIV,* edited by Roberto Rusconi, 29–65. Florence: La Nuova Italia, 1984.

———. "S. Francesco e l'espansione del francescanesimo: Coscienza storica e problemi emergenti." In *Il francescanesimo in Lombardia. Storia e arte,* 9–16. Milan: Silvana, 1983.

Paul, Jacques. "Le Joachimisme et les joachimites au milieu du XIIIe siècle d'après le témoignage de Fra Salimbene." In *1274: Année charnière: Mutations et continuités.* Colloques internationaux du Centre National de la Recherche Scientifique, no. 558. Paris: CNRS, 1977.

Pazzelli, Raffaele. "Movimenti e congregazioni con la regola di Niccolò IV." In *La "Supra montem" di Niccolò IV,* edited by Raffaele Pazzelli and Lino Temperini, 249–88. Rome: Analecta TOR, 1988.

Pazzelli, Raffaele, and Lino Temperini, eds. *La "Supra montem" di Niccolò IV.* Rome: Analecta TOR, 1988.

Péano, Pierre. "Les Ministres provinciaux de la primitive province de Provence (1217–1517)." *Archivum franciscanum historicum* 79 (1986): 3–77.

———. "Ministres provinciaux de Provence et spirituels." In *Franciscains d'Oc: Les Spirituels, 1280–1324.* Cahiers de Fanjeaux, no. 10. Toulouse: Editions Privat, 1975.

———. "Raymond Geoffroi ministre général et défenseur des spirituels." *Picenum Seraphicum* 11 (1974): 190–203.

Peck, George. *Fool of God.* Tuscaloosa: University of Alabama Press, 1980.

Peckham (Pecham), John. *Tractatus tres de paupertate.* Aberdeen: Typis Academicis, 1910.

Pelegrino da Bologna. *Chronicon abbreviatum de successione ministrorum.* In *De adventu fratrum minorum in Angliam,* by Thomas of Eccleston, Appendix II. Paris: Librairie Fischbacher, 1909.

Pelster, Franz. "Nikolaus von Lyra und seine Quaestio de usu paupere." *Archivum franciscanum historicum* 46 (1953): 211–50.

Perarnau, Josep. *Alia informatio beguinorum d'Arnau de Vilanova.* Barcelona: Facultat de Teologia de Barcelona, Seccio de Sant Pacia, 1978.

———. "Una altra carta de Guiu Terrena sobre el procés inquisitorial contra el franciscà Fra Bernat Fuster." *Estudios franciscanos* 82 (1981): 383–92.

———. "El bisbe de Barcelona Fra Bernat Oliver (1345–1346) i els framenors de Vilafranca del Penedès: Un episodi de la 'Qüestió Franciscana' a Catalunya." *Estudios franciscanos* 83 (1982): 277–306.

———. "La butlla desconeguda de Joan XXII 'Ut vester religionis ager' (Avinyó, 19 de febrer de 1322) sobre l'examen dels aspirants al Terç Orde de St. Francesc." *Estudios franciscanos* 83 (1982): 307–10.

———. "Noves dades sobre beguins de Girona." *Annals de l'institut d'estudis gironins* 25/1 (1979–80): 237–46.

———. "Opere di Fr. Petrus Johannis in processi catalane d'inquisizione della prima metà del XIV secolo." *Archivum franciscanum historicum* 91 (1998): 505–16.

Petrus Iohannis Olivi. *Epistola ad Conradum de Offida*. In "Petri Iohannis Olivi de renuntiatione papae Coelestini V quaestio et epistola." Text established by Cynthia Kilmer and Eliza Marmursztein; revised, introduced, and annotated by Sylvain Piron. *Archivum franciscanum historicum* 91 (1998): 33–64.

———. *Epistola ad R.* In "Petrus Ioannis Olivi, epistola ad fratrem R." *Archivum franciscanum historicum* 91 (1998): 133–71.

———. *Epistola ad R.* In *Quodlibeta*. Venice: Lazarus de Soardis, 1509.

———. *Lectura super Apocalypsim*. Edited by Warren Lewis in "Peter John Olivi: Prophet of the Year 2000." Ph.D. diss., Tübingen University, 1972.

———. *Lectura super Genesim*. In *Sancti Thomae Aquinatis Opera Omnia*. Vol. 23. Parma: Typis Petri Fiaccadori, 1868.

———. *Lectura super Ioannem*. MS Florence, Bib. Laur. Plut. 10 dext. 8.

———. *Lectura super Isaiam*. In *Peter of John Olivi on the Bible*, edited by David Flood, O.F.M., and Gedeon Gál, O.F.M. St. Bonaventure, N.Y.: Franciscan Institute Publications, 1997.

———. *Lectura super Mattheum*. MS Vat. lat. 10900.

———. *Peter Olivi's Rule Commentary*. Wiesbaden: Franz Steiner Verlag, 1972.

———. *Quaestiones de perfectione evangelica*, q. 8. In *Das Heil der Armen und das Verderben der Reichen*, by Johannes Schlageter. Werl/Westfalen: Dietrich-Coelde-Verlag, 1989.

———. *Quaestiones de perfectione evangelica*, q. 9. In *De usu paupere: The Quaestio and the Tractatus*. Florence: Leo S. Olschki, 1992.

———. *Quaestiones de perfectione evangelica*, q. 11. In MS Florence, Bibl. Laur. 448.

———. *Quaestiones de perfectione evangelica*, q. 12. In "Una questione inedita dell'Olivi sull'infallibilità del Papa," by Michaele Maccarone. *Rivista di storia della chiesa in Italia* 3 (1949): 309–43.

———. *Quaestiones de perfectione evangelica*, q. 13. In "Petri Iohannis Olivi de renuntiatione papae Coelestini V quaestio et epistola," by Livarius Oliger. *Archivum franciscanum historicum* 11 (1918): 309–73.

———. *Quaestiones de perfectione evangelica*, q. 14. In MS Florence, Bibl. Laur. 448.

———. *Quaestiones de perfectione evangelica*, q. 15. In MS Florence, Bibl. Laur. 448.

———. *Quaestiones de perfectione evangelica*, q. 16. In "Peter Olivi: On Poverty and Revenue," by David Burr and David Flood. *Franciscan Studies* 40 (1980): 18–58.

———. *Quaestiones de perfectione evangelica*, q. 17. In "Fr. P. J. Olivi quaestio de voto regulam aliquam profitentis." *Antonianum* 16 (1941): 131–64.

———. *Quaestiones in secundum librum sententiarum*. Quaracchi: College of Saint Bonaventure, 1921–26.

———. *Responsio quam fecit P. Ioannis ad litteram magistrorum praesentatam sibi in Avinione*. In "Fr. Petri Ioannis Olivi, O.F.M., tria scripta sui ipsius apologetica annorum 1283 et 1285," by Damasus Laberge. *Archivum franciscanum historicum* 28 (1935–36): 115–55, 374–407.

————. *Tractatus de usu paupere*. In *De usu paupere: The Quaestio and the Tractatus*. Florence: Leo S. Olschki, 1992.

Piron, Sylvain. "Marchands et confesseurs." In *L'Argent au Moyen Âge*, 289–308. Paris: Publications de la Sorbonne, 1998.

————. "Voeu et contrat chez Pierre de Jean Olivi." *Cahiers du Centre de Recherches Historiques* 16 (1996): 43–56.

Potestà, Gian Luca. *Angelo Clareno*. Rome: Istituto Storico Italiano per il Medio Evo, 1990.

————. "Dall'annuncio dell'Anticristo all'attesa del pastore angelico: Gli scritti di Arnaldo di Villanova nel codice dell'archivio generale dei Carmelitani." *Arxiu de Textos Catalans Antics* 13 (1994): 287–344.

————. *Storia ed escatologia in Ubertino da Casale*. Milan: Università Cattolica del Sacro Cuore, 1980.

Poulenc, Jerome. "Hughes de Digne." In *Dictionnaire de spiritualité*, edited by Marcel Viller, 7.1:876–79. Paris: G. Beauchesne, 1932–69.

Pou y Marti, José. *Visionarios, beguinos y fraticelos catalanes (siglos XIII–XV)*. Vich: Editorial Seráfica, 1930.

Il processo di canonizzazione di Chiara da Montefalco. Florence: La Nuova Italia, 1984.

Pryds, Darleen. "Clarisses, Franciscans, and the House of Anjou." In *Clarefest*, edited by Ingrid Peterson. St. Bonaventure, N.Y.: Franciscan Institute, 1995.

————. *The King Embodies the Word: Robert d'Anjou and the Politics of Preaching*. Leiden: Brill, 2000.

Pseudo-Joachim of Fiore. *Super Jeremiam*. Venice: Bernardinus Benalius, 1525.

Quidam casus. In "Notice et extraits d'un manuscrit franciscain," by Ferdinand Delorme. *Collectanea franciscana* 15 (1945): 53–58.

Ratzinger, Joseph. *The Theology of History in St. Bonaventure*. Translated by Zachary Hayes. Chicago: Franciscan Herald Press, 1971. Originally published as *Die Geschichtestheologie des heiligen Bonaventura* (Munich: Schnell and Steiner, 1959).

Raymundus de Fronciacho. *Sapientia aedificavit*. In *Archiv für Literatur- und Kirchengeschichte des Mittelalters*, by Heinrich Denifle and Franz Ehrle, 3:95–137. Berlin: Weidmannsche Buchhandlung, 1885–1900.

————. *Sol ortus*. In *Archiv für Literatur- und Kirchengeschichte des Mittelalters*, by Heinrich Denifle and Franz Ehrle, 3:7–32. Berlin: Weidmannsche Buchhandlung, 1885–1900.

Raymundus de Fronciacho and Bonagratia de Bergamo. *Infrascripta dant*. In *Archiv für Literatur- und Kirchengeschichte des Mittelalters*, by Heinrich Denifle and Franz Ehrle, 3:141–60. Berlin: Weidmannsche Buchhandlung, 1885–1900.

Raymundus Gaufridi. *Ad primum articulum*. In *Archiv für Literatur- und Kirchengeschichte des Mittelalters*, by Heinrich Denifle and Franz Ehrle, 3:142–44. Berlin: Weidmannsche Buchhandlung, 1885–1900.

Reeves, Marjorie. *The Influence of Prophecy in the Later Middle Ages*. Oxford: Clarendon Press, 1969.

Regestum Clementis Papae V. Rome: Typographia Vaticana, 1885.

Religiosi viri. In "Communitatis responsio 'Religiosi viri' ad rotulum Fr. Ubertini de Casali," by Anicetus Chiappini. *Archivum franciscanum historicum* 7 (1914): 654–75; 8 (1915): 56–81.

Responsiones ad obiectiones. In "Notice et extraits d'un manuscrit franciscain," by Ferdinand Delorme. *Collectanea franciscana* 15 (1945): 67–72.

Rigon, Antonio. "Frati minori e società locali." In *Francesco d'Assisi e il primo secolo di storia francescana*, edited by Maria Pia Alberzoni, et al., 259–81. Turin: Einaudi, 1997.

Rotelli, Elena. *Fra Dolcino e gli Apostolici nella storia e nella tradizione*. Turin: Claudiana Editrice, 1979.

Rubio Vela, Agustín, and Mateu Rodrigo Lizondo. "Els beguins de València en el segle XIV: La seua casa-hospital i els seus llibres." In *Miscel·lània Sanchis Guarner,* edited by Antoni Ferrando, 185–277. Barcelona: Publicacions de l'Abadia de Montserrat, 1992.

Rusconi, Roberto, ed. *Il movimento religioso femminile in Umbria nei secoli XIII–XIV.* Florence: La Nuova Italia, 1984.

Saint Francis of Assisi: Writings and Early Biographies. With an introduction by Théophile Desbonnets. Chicago: Franciscan Herald Press, 1972.

Salimbene da Parma. *Cronica.* Bari: Laterza, 1966.

Schiff, Otto. *Studien zur Geschichte Papst Nikolaus IV.* 1897. Reprint, Vaduz: Kraus Reprint, 1965.

Schmitt, Clement. *Une Pape réformateur et un défenseur de l'unité de l'Eglise: Bénoit XII et l'ordre des frères mineurs.* Quaracchi: College of Saint Bonaventure, 1959.

———, ed. *Vita e spiritualità della Beata Angela da Foligno.* Atti del Convegno di Studi per il VII Centenario della Conversione della Beata Angela da Foligno (1285–1985). Perugia: Serafica Provincia di San Francesco O.F.M. Conv., 1987.

Schwartz, Orit, and Robert Lerner. "Illuminated Propaganda: The Origins of the 'Ascende Calve' Pope Prophecies." *Journal of Medieval History* 20 (1994): 157–91.

Sensi, Mario. "Angela nel contesto religioso folignate." In *Vita e spiritualità della Beata Angela da Foligno,* edited by Clement Schmitt, 39–96. Atti del Convegno di Studi per il VII Centenario della Conversione della Beata Angela da Foligno (1285–1985). Perugia: Serafica Provincia di San Francesco O.F.M. Conv., 1987.

———. "Foligno all'incrocio delle strade." In *Angèle de Foligno: Le Dossier,* edited by Giulia Barone and Jacques Dalarun, 267–92. Rome: École Française de Rome, 1999.

———. "Incarcerate e recluse nei secoli XIII e XIV: Un bizzocaggio centro-italiano." In *Il movimento religioso femminile in Umbria nei secoli XIII–XIV,* edited by Roberto Rusconi, 85–121. Florence: La Nuova Italia, 1984.

———. "Margherita da Cortona nel contesto storico-sociale cortonese." *Collectanea franciscana* 69 (1999): 223–62.

———. *Le osservanze francescane nell'Italia centrale.* Rome: Istituto Storico dei Cappuccini, 1985.

———. "La regola di Niccolò IV dopo la costituzione 'Periculoso.'" In *La "Supra montem" di Niccolò IV,* edited by Raffaele Pazzelli and Lino Temperini, 147–98. Rome: Analecta TOR, 1988.

———. *Storie di bizzoche tra Umbria e Marche.* Rome: Edizioni di Storia e Letteratura, 1995.

Sisto, Alessandra. *Figure del primo francescanesimo in Provenza.* Florence: Leo S. Olschki, 1971.

Stanislao da Campagnola. *Francesco e francescanesimo nella società dei secoli XIII–XIV.* Assisi: Edizioni Porziuncula, 1999.

Stephens, John. "Heresy in Medieval and Renaissance Florence." *Past and Present* 54 (1972): 25–60.

Tabarroni, Andrea. *Paupertas Christi et apostolorum.* Rome: Istituto Storico Italiano per il Medio Evo, 1990.

Thomas Aquinas. *Opera.* Parma: Fiaccadori, 1853–73.

———. *Opera omnia.* Paris: Vivès, 1890–95.

Thomas of Celano. *Vita prima s. Francisci.* In *Legendae s. Francisci Assisiensis saeculis XIII et XIV conscriptae.* In *Analecta franciscana.* Vol. 10. Quaracchi: College of Saint Bonaventure, 1927.

———. *Vita secunda s. Francisci Assisiensis.* In *Legendae s. Francisci Assisiensis saeculis XIII et XIV conscriptae.* In *Analecta franciscana.* Vol. 10. Quaracchi: College of Saint Bonaventure, 1927.

Thomas of Eccleston. *De adventu fratrum minorum in Angliam.* In Vol. 1 of *Monumenta franciscana.* Rerum britannicarum medii aevi scriptores, no. 4. London: Longmans, 1852–82.

————. *De adventu fratrum minorum in Angliam*. Paris: Librairie Fischbacher, 1909.

Thomson, Williell. *Friars in the Cathedral*. Toronto: Pontifical Institute of Mediaeval Studies, 1975.

Tierney, Brian. *The Origins of Papal Infallibility*. Leiden: Brill, 1972.

Todeschini, Giacomo. "Olivi e il *mercator* cristiano." In *Pierre de Jean Olivi (1248–1298): Pensée scolastique, dissidence spirituelle et société*, edited by Alain Boureau and Sylvain Piron, 217–37. Paris: J. Vrin, 1999.

————. *Il prezzo della salvezza*. Rome: La Nuova Italia Scientifica, 1994.

Tognetti, Giampaolo. "I fraticelli, il principio di povertà e i secolari." *Bulletino dell'Istituto Storico Italiano per il Medio Evo e Archivio Muratoriano* 90 (1982–83): 77–145.

Torrell, Jean-Pierre. *Recherches sur la théorie de la prophétie au Moyen Âge*. Fribourg: Editions Universitaires, 1992.

————. *Théorie de la prophétie et philosophie de la connaissance aux environs de 1230*. Louvain: Spicilegium sacrum Lovaniense, 1977.

Ubertino da Casale. *Arbor vitae crucifixae Jesu*. 1485. Reprint, Turin: Bottega d'Erasmo, 1961.

————. *Contra quasdam responsiones*. In "Notice et extraits d'un manuscrit franciscain," by Ferdinand Delorme. *Collectanea franciscana* 15 (1945): 72–82.

————. *Declaratio*. In *Archiv für Literatur- und Kirchengeschichte des Mittelalters*, by Heinrich Denifle and Franz Ehrle, 3:162–96. Berlin: Weidmannsche Buchhandlung, 1885–1900.

————. *Rotulus*. In *Archiv für Literatur- und Kirchengeschichte des Mittelalters*, by Heinrich Denifle and Franz Ehrle, 3:93–137. Berlin: Weidmannsche Buchhandlung, 1885–1900.

————. *Sanctitas vestra*. In *Archiv für Literatur- und Kirchengeschichte des Mittelalters*, by Heinrich Denifle and Franz Ehrle, 3:51–89. Berlin: Weidmannsche Buchhandlung, 1885–1900.

————. *Sanctitati apostolicae*. In *Archiv für Literatur- und Kirchengeschichte des Mittelalters*, by Heinrich Denifle and Franz Ehrle, 2:377–406. Berlin: Weidmannsche Buchhandlung, 1885–1900.

————. *Super tribus sceleribus*. In "Ubertini de Casali opusculum 'Super tribus sceleribus,'" by Albanus Heysse. *Archivum franciscanum historicum* 10 (1917): 103–74.

d'Urso, Giacinto. "La B. Angela e Ubertino da Casale." In *Vita e spiritualità della Beata Angela da Foligno*, edited by Clement Schmitt, 157–70. Atti del Convegno di Studi per il VII Centenario della Conversione della Beata Angela da Foligno (1285–1985). Perugia: Serafica Provincia di San Francesco O.F.M. Conv., 1987.

Vicaire, M.-H. Introduction to *Franciscains d'Oc: Les Spirituels ca. 1280–1324*. Cahiers de Fanjeaux, no. 10. Toulouse: Editions Privat, 1975.

Vidal, J.-M. "Un Ascète de sang royal, Philippe de Majorque." *Revue des questiones historiques* 45 (1910): 361–403.

————. *Bullaire de l'inquisition française*. Paris: Librairie Letouzey et Ané, 1913.

————. "Procès d'inquisition contre Adhémar de Mosset." *Revue d'histoire de l'église de France* 1 (1910): 555–89, 682–89, 711–25.

Villani, Giovanni. *Cronica*. 2 vols. Florence: Sansone, 1844.

Wessley, Stephen. *Joachim of Fiore and Monastic Reform*. New York: P. Lang, 1990.

————. "The Thirteenth-Century Guglielmites: Salvation Through Women." In *Medieval Women*, edited by Derek Baker, 289–30. Oxford: Basil Blackwell, 1978.

Zorzi, D. "Testi inediti francescani in lingua provenzale." *Miscellanea del Centro di Studi Medievali*. Ser. 1. Milan: Vita e Pensiero, 1956.

INDEX